KU-428-203

Universal

HISTORY OF THE WORLD

VOLUME EIGHT

UNIVERSAL HISTORY OF THE WORLD

Written by One Hundred and Fifty of our Foremost Living Authorities in all Branches of Historical Knowledge

Edited by
J. A. Hammerton

VOLUME EIGHT
pages 4553–5212

From the Late Victorian Age to the Present Day

London
THE AMALGAMATED PRESS LTD.

Printed in Great Britain by
The Amalgamated Press Ltd., London

VOLUME EIGHT

TABLE OF CONTENTS

Chronicle XXXI. THE WORLD DRIFT TO WAR : 1878–1914

CHAPTER 172
THE BRITISH EMPIRE : AN HISTORICAL STUDY

By Reginald Coupland

Beit Professor of Colonial History in the University of Oxford

CHAPTER 173
CHINA UNDER THE MANCHUS

By J. O. P. Bland

CHAPTER 174
TRADE UNIONISM : ITS ORIGIN AND GROWTH

By E. Lipson

Reader in Economic History in the University of Oxford

CHAPTER 175

ECONOMICS AND THE MENACE OF WAR

By Sir L. Chiozza Money

CHAPTER 176

SCIENCE AND INVENTION

By J. W. N. Sullivan

CHAPTER 177

THE U.S.A. ON THE EVE OF THE GREAT WAR

By Robert McElroy, Ph.D., LL.D.
Harmsworth Professor of American History, Oxford

Chronicle XXXII. THE GREAT WAR: 1914–1918

CHAPTER 178

SCIENCE AND WAR

By Maj.-Gen. Sir George Aston, K.C.B.
Lecturer on Naval History, University College, London

CHAPTER 179
THE NEW ELEMENTS IN WARFARE
By Colonel J. F. C. Fuller, D.S.O.

CHAPTER 180
THE ROLE OF SEA POWER IN THE WAR
By H. W. Wilson

CHAPTER 181
EFFECT OF THE WAR ON FAITH AND PHILOSOPHY
By C. E. M. Joad

Chronicle XXXIII. AFTERWARDS: 1918–1929

CHAPTER 182
THE ECONOMIC CHAOS OF EUROPE
By John Maynard Keynes, C.B.
Fellow of King's College, Cambridge

CHAPTER 183

THE NEW EUROPE AND THE LEAGUE

By Wickham Steed

Lecturer on Central European History, King's College, London

CHAPTER 184

THE RUSSIA OF THE BOLSHEVIKS

By F. A. Mackenzie

CHAPTER 185

SOCIALISM, COMMUNISM AND WORLD REVOLUTION

By Arthur Shadwell, M.D., LL.D.

CHAPTER 186

THE ECONOMICS OF CAPITALISM

By J. A. Hobson

CHAPTER 187

THE NEW PHILOSOPHY OF SCIENCE

By Hugh Elliot

CHAPTER 188

MODERNISM IN LITERATURE AND ART

By Osbert Burdett

CHAPTER 188—*continued* PAGE

CHAPTER 189

PUBLIC HEALTH : A RECORD OF MEDICAL PROGRESS

By Sir George Newman, K.C.B., M.D.

Chief Medical Officer to the Ministry of Health

CHAPTER 190

SOCIAL SURVEY OF THE WORLD TO-DAY

By Ian D. Colvin

CHAPTER 191

THE PHILOSOPHY OF HISTORY

By L. P. Jacks

Professor of Philosophy and Principal of Manchester College, Oxford

---

LIST OF SPECIAL PLATES

PLATES IN FULL COLOURS

PLATES IN DUOTONE

SELECT BIBLIOGRAPHY

CHRONICLE XXXI

BOURGEOIS, EMILE, Modern France, 2 vols., 1919
FAY, SIDNEY BRADSHAW, The Origins of the World War, 2 vols., 1929
HALÉVY, ELIE, History of the English People in the 19th Century, Vol. IV, 1926
PHILLIPS, ALISON, Modern Europe, 1908
ROSE, J. Holland, Development of the European Nations, 1915
STEED, H. WICKHAM, Through Thirty Years (1892–1922), 2 vols., 1924
TIMES HISTORY OF THE WAR IN S. AFRICA, 7 vols., 1900–9
WARD, A. W., Germany, 3 vols., 1916–18
WAR OFFICE, LONDON, The Russo-Japanese War, 4 vols., 1908

CHRONICLES XXXII–III

ASPINALL-OGLANDER, Brig.-Gen. C. F., Military Operations, Gallipoli, 1929
BRIDGE, F. M., A Short History of the Great World War, 1920
BUCHAN, JOHN, A History of the Great War, 4 vols., 1921
BURNS, C. DE LISLE, A Short History of the World (1918–1928), 1929
CHURCHILL, WINSTON S., The World Crisis, 1927
HISTORY OF THE GREAT WAR based on Official Documents, 1920, etc.
HURD, A. S., The Merchant Navy, 1921
MASEFIELD, J., Gallipoli, 1923
POLLARD, A. F., A Short History of the Great War, 1920
RALEIGH, Sir W. A., The War in the Air, 1921
RAWLINSON, A., The Defence of London, 1923
WAVELL, A. P., The Palestine Campaign, 1928

CHAPTER CLXXII

THE BRITISH EMPIRE

CAMBRIDGE HISTORY OF THE BRITISH EMPIRE, Vol. I, 1929
COUPLAND, REGINALD. Raffles, 1926
  Wilberforce, 1923
EGERTON, H. E., Short History of British Colonial Policy, 7th Ed., 1928
EVANS, I. L., The British in Tropical Africa, 1929
LUCAS, C. P., The British Empire, 1915
  Lord Durham's Report on the Affairs of British N. America, ed. C. P. Lucas, 1912
MUIR, RAMSAY, Short History of the British Commonwealth, Vol. II, 1924
NEWTON, A. P., and EWING, J., The British Empire since 1783, 1929
SEELEY, J. R., Expansion of England, 1883
ZIMMERN, A. E., The Third British Empire, 1926

CHAPTER CLXXIII

CHINA UNDER THE MANCHUS

BLAND, J. O. P., Li Hung-Chang, 1917
BLAND, J. O. P., and BACKHOUSE, E., China Under the Empress Dowager, 1910
  Annals and Memoirs of the Court of Peking (c. 1620), 1914
CANTLIE, J., and JONES, C. S., Sun Yat-Sen and the Awakening of China, 1912
KENT, P. H., The Passing of the Manchus, 1912
SUN YAT-SEN, International Development of China, 1920

CHAPTER CLXXIV

TRADE UNIONISM

COLE, G. D. H., Short History of the British Working Class Movement, 3 vols., 1925–27
  The World of Labour, 1913
COLE, G. D. H., and ARNOT, R. PAGE, Trade Unionism on the Railways, 1917
CREECH-JONES, A., Trade Unionism To-day, 1928
LIPSON, E., The History of the Woollen and Worsted Industries, 1921
  The Economic History of England, Vol. I (5th ed.), 1929, Vols. II & III, 1929
LLOYD, C. M., Trade Unionism, 1919
SLESSER, H. H., and BAKER, C., Trade Union Law, 2nd ed., 1926
WEBB, S. and B., The History of Trade Unionism, rev. ed., 1920
  Industrial Democracy, 1920

CHAPTER CLXXV

ECONOMICS AND THE MENACE OF WAR

COLVIN, I. D., Safety of the Nation, 1919
EDGEWORTH, F. T., Relations of Political Economy to War, 1915
MONEY, Sir LEO CHIOZZA, The Triumph of Nationalization, 1920

CHAPTER CLXXVI

SCIENCE AND INVENTION

CRESSY, E., Discoveries and Inventions of the 20th Century, 1914
GLAZEBROOK, R. T., Science and Industry, 1917
SCHUSTER, ARTHUR, and SHIPLEY, Sir ARTHUR E., Britain's Heritage of Science, 1917
THOMSON, J. A., Progress of Science in the Century, 1908

CHAPTER CLXXVII

THE U.S.A. ON THE EVE OF THE GREAT WAR

BASSETT, J. S., Expansion and Reform (1889–1926), 1926
KEMMERER, E. W., The A B C of the Federal Reserve System, 1920
OGG, F. A., National Progress (The American Nation Series), 1918
ROGERS, LINDSAY, The American Senate, 1926
ROOSEVELT, THEODORE, An Autobiography, 1914
  New Nationalism, 1911
SEYMOUR, CHARLES, Woodrow Wilson and the World War, 1921
SHIPPEE, L. B., Recent American History, 1924
WILSON, T. WOODROW, The New Freedom, 1913

Chapters CLXXVIII and CLXXIX

SCIENCE AND WAR, AND NEW ELEMENTS IN WARFARE

Aston, Maj.-Gen. Sir G. G., War Lessons, New and Old, 1919
Austin, F. Britten, The War God Walks Again, 1926
Fries, Brig.-Gen. Amos A., and West, C. J., Chemical Warfare, 1921
Fuller, Col. J. F. C., The Reformation of War, 1923
Tanks in the Great War, 1920
On Future Warfare, 1928
Haldane, J. B. S., Callinicus, A Defence of Chemical Warfare, 2nd ed., 1925
Hart, Capt. B. H. Liddell, The Remaking of Modern Armies, 1927
Paris, or the Future of War, 1925

Chapter CLXXX

THE ROLE OF SEA POWER IN THE WAR

Bacon, Adm. Sir R. H. S., The Dover Patrol, 2 vols., 1919
Carpenter, Capt. A. F. B., The Blocking of Zeebrugge, 1922
Churchill, W. S., The World Crisis, 4 vols., 1923–27
Corbett, Sir J. S., and Newbolt, Sir H., History of the Great War: Naval Operations, 1920
Fayle, C. E., History of the Great War: Seaborne Trade, 3 vols., 1920–24
Frothingham, Capt. T. G., Naval History of the World War, 3 vols., 1924
Garner, J. W., International Law and the World War, 2 vols., 1920
Jellicoe, Viscount, The Crisis of the Naval War, 1920
The Grand Fleet, 1919
Mantey, Rear.-Adm. E. von., Der Krieg zur See, 1920
Scheer, Adm. Reinhard, Germany's High Sea Fleet in the World War, 1920
Sims, Adm. W. S., The Victory at Sea, reprinted 1921
Wester Wemyss, Adm. Lord, The Navy in the Dardanelles Campaign, 1924
Wilson, H. W., Battleships in Action, Vol. II, 1926

Chapter CLXXXI

EFFECT OF THE WAR ON FAITH AND PHILOSOPHY

Contemporary British Philosophy, ed. J. H. Muirhead, 2 vols., 1925
Harris, W. S., Christian Science and the Ordinary Man, 1917
Joad, C. E. M., Towards a New Religion, 1929
Lambeth Conference, 1920. Encyclical letter from the Bishops with the Resolutions and Reports, 1920
Lodge, Sir Oliver, Raymond, 3rd ed., 1916
Towards Reunion, by Church of England and Free Church Writers, 1919

Chapter CLXXXII

THE ECONOMIC CHAOS OF EUROPE

Bergmann, Carl, The History of Reparations, 1927
Dobb, M., Russian Economic Development since the Revolution, 1927
Fry, A. Ruth, A Quaker Adventure (nine years' relief and reconstruction), 1926
Jack, D. T., The Restoration of European Currencies, 1927
Keynes, J. M., The Economic Consequences of the Peace, 2nd ed., 1920
A Revision of the Treaty, 1922
A Tract on Monetary Reform, 1923
Manchester Guardian, Reconstruction Supplements, 1923
Schacht, Hjalmar, The Stabilisation of the Mark, trs. R. Butler, 1927

Chapter CLXXXIII

NEW EUROPE AND THE LEAGUE

Baker, Phillip Noel, The League of Nations at Work, 1926
Economic Consequences of the League (World Economic Conference), intr. Sir A. Salter, 1927
Harris, H. Wilson, What the League of Nations Is, 1925
International Labour Office, Unemployment; Report of London Conference, 1924
League of Nations, The Covenant Explained, introd. G. Murray, 1920
See also various official publications of the League

Chapter CLXXXIV

THE RUSSIA OF THE BOLSHEVIKS

Baring, Hon. Maurice, The Russian People, 2nd ed., 1914
Brailsford, H. N., The Russian Workers' Republic, 1921
Buchanan, Sir George W., My Missions to Russia, 2 vols, 1923
Denikin, Gen. A. I., La Décomposition de l'armée et du pouvoir, février-septembre, 1917, 1922
Farbman, M. S., After Lenin, 1924
Gilliard, P., Thirteen Years at the Russian Court, trs. F. A. Holt, 1921
Gorky, Maxim, Ecrits de Révolution, trs. André Pierre, 1922
Guest, L. Haden, The New Russia, 1926
Kerensky, A. F., The Prelude to Bolshevism: the Kornilov Rebellion, 1919
Kropotkin, P., The Terror in Russia, 5th ed., 1909
Lenin, N., The Great Initiative, trs. P. Lavin, 1920
Mackenzie, F. A., Russia before Dawn, 1923
Mavor, James, The Russian Revolution, 1928
Popov, G., The Tcheka and Red Inquisition, 1925
Stalin, I., The Theory and Practice of Leninism, 1925
Trotsky, Lev., The Real Situation in Russia, 1929

Chapter CLXXXV

SOCIALISM, COMMUNISM AND WORLD REVOLUTION

Beer, M., History of British Socialism, 1929
Kautsky, K., The Labour Revolution, 1925
Lenin, N., The State and Revolution, 1917
Lorwin, L. L., Labor and Internationalism, 1929
See, H., Modern Capitalism, 1928
Shadwell, A., The Socialist Movement, 1824–1924, 1925
Sombart, W., Der Moderne Kapitalismus, 1927

Chapter CLXXXVI

ECONOMICS OF CAPITALISM

Ashley, W. J., The Economic Organization of England, 1914
Cressy, Edward, Outline of Industrial History, 1925
Hobson, J. A., The Evolution of Modern Capitalism, 1917
The Industrial System, 2nd ed., 1910
Marshall, Alfred, Elements of the Economics of Industry, 3rd ed., 1899
Marx, Karl, Capitalism, 1887
Meakin, W., The New Industrial Revolution, 1928
Webb, S. & B., The Decay of Capitalist Organization, 1923

Chapter CLXXXVII

NEW PHILOSOPHY OF SCIENCE

Bragg, Sir William H., X-rays and Crystal Structure, 1924
Eddington, A. S., Space, Time and Gravitation, 2nd ed., 1921
Theory of Relativity and its Influence on Scientific Thought, 1922
Einstein, Albert, Theory of Relativity, trs. R. W. Lawson, 1920
Elliot, Hugh, Modern Science and Materialism, 1919
Planck, Max, Origin and Development of the Quantum Theory, trs. H. T. Clarke and L. Silberstein, 1922
Russell, Bertrand, A B C of Relativity, 1925
Sullivan, J. W. N., Aspects of Science, 1923–6
Atoms and Electrons, 1924

Chapter CLXXXVIII

MODERNISM IN LITERATURE AND ART

Bell, Clive, Art, 3rd ed., 1916
Proust, 1928
Muir, Edwin, Transition, 1926
Quennell, Peter, Mr. T. S. Eliot, Life and Letters, 1929
Rutter, Frank, Evolution in Modern Art, 1926
Sitwell, Edith, Poetry and Criticism, 1925
Wilenski, R. H., The Modern Movement in Art, 1927

Chapter CLXXXIX

PUBLIC HEALTH

Collis, E. L., and Greenwood, M., The Health of the Industrial Worker, 1921
Creighton, Charles, History of Epidemics in Britain, 2 vols., 1891–94
Foster, Sir M., Lectures on the History of Physiology, 1901
Garrison, F. H., Introduction to the History of Medicine, 3rd ed., 1922
Hewlett, R. T., and Nankivell, A. T., The Principles of Preventive Medicine, 1921
Keith, Sir A., The Engines of the Human Body, 1919
Newman, Sir G., Interpreters of Nature, 1927
Outline of the Practice of Preventive Medicine, new ed., 1926
Osler, Sir W., The Evolution of Modern Medicine, 1921
Simon, Sir John, English Sanitary Institutions, 2nd ed., 1897
Vallery-Radot, René, Life of Pasteur, 2 vols, trs. Mrs. R. L. Devonshire, 1902

Chapter CXC

SOCIAL SURVEY OF THE WORLD TO-DAY

Austin, Bertram, and Lloyd, W. F., The Secret of High Wages, 1926
Brasol, Boris, The Elements of Crime, 1927
Dawson, Sir Philip, Germany's Industrial Revival, 1926
Kidd, Benjamin, Principles of Western Civilization, 1908
Science of Power, 2nd ed., 1918
Social Evolution, 1894
O'Dwyer, Sir M., India as I knew it, 1925
Spengler, Oswald, The Decline of the West, trs. C. F. Atkinson, 1926
Stamp, Sir Josiah, British Incomes and Property, 1920
Studies in Current Problems in Finance and Government, 1924
Wallas, Graham, The Great Society, 1920
Human Nature in Politics, 2nd ed., 1910
Yerkes, R. M., Psychological Examining in the United States Army, 1921

Chapter CXCI

PHILOSOPHY OF HISTORY

Fiske, John, The Destiny of Man viewed in the Light of Human Origin, 1912
Grote, John, Examination of Utilitarian Philosophy, ed. J. B. Mayor, 1870
Inge, W. R., The Idea of Progress, 1920
Jacks, L. P., The Alchemy of Thought, 1910
Progress and History, ed. F. S. Marvin, 1921
Russell, Bertrand, Principles of Social Reconstruction, 1917
Problems of Philosophy, new ed., 1919
Scientific Method in Philosophy, 1914
See, Henri, Science et philosophie de l'histoire, 1928
Spencer, Herbert, Social Statics, 1868
Study of Sociology, 9th ed., 1880

See also bibliography to Chapter CXC

Chronicle XXXI

THE WORLD DRIFT TO WAR: 1878–1914

THE ostensible effect of the Turco-Russian War, followed by the San Stefano treaty and the Berlin Congress, was the establishment or the strengthening of sundry independent principalities in the Balkan peninsula, and the reassertion of the principle that the 'Concert of Europe,' not the particular interests of a successful military power, must have the deciding voice in material redistributions of European territory, which necessarily have their repercussions upon Europe generally. For thirty years to come the Concert of Europe was the background of international politics.

Rift in the 'Dreikaiserbund'

BUT in actual fact the episode had another effect quite as far-reaching though not so superficially obvious. It had brought about the thing which the most powerful statesman in Europe was most anxious to avert, a rupture in the relations subsisting between Germany, Austria and Russia. For in Bismarck's view there were three European powers which counted for Germany, since England's non-intervention could generally be ensured, though definitely to alienate her would be inadvisable: Russia, Austria and France. French hostility to Germany was a matter of course. Austrian hostility had melted away under tactful management; Austrian and Prussian interests no longer clashed, since Germany had identified itself with Prussia; Austrian friendship was the best security available for Germany. But Russia remained.

Germany had a hostile France, which might again become powerful, on one flank. A hostile Russia on the other flank would be a serious menace, especially in conjunction with a recovered France. It was therefore essential for Germany to preserve friendly relations with Russia, only in less degree than with Austria. If Germany should ever be forced to choose between Russia and Austria, she must choose Austria. Since the French war it had been a main object with Bismarck to maintain the friendliness of the three powers—the 'Dreikaiserbund'—and to avert any complications which would drive Germany into siding with one against the other. But the antagonistic interests of Russia and Austria in the Balkans had been too much even for Bismarck. However skilfully he might pose as the 'honest broker,' the fundamental fact remained that by the Berlin Congress the ambitions of Russia in the Balkans suffered a set-back, those of Austria were advanced, and Germany had done nothing to forward Russian interests, though it was at the hands of England that Russia had most conspicuously suffered diplomatic defeat.

There was no open breach between Germany and Russia; but the rift was there. Bismarck suffered from no illusions on that point. It became of the utmost importance to prevent the rift from developing into a breach, but also to find a means of strengthening the two Central powers, in case of accidents; of drawing still closer the bond between those two powers; of keeping France and Russia apart, and of discouraging any rapprochement between either of them and England.

Franco-Russian Rapprochement

NEVERTHELESS, the trouble that Bismarck had been so anxious to guard against developed by degrees. The rift between Russia and the Central empires widened. France, already convalescent, grew stronger as the years passed. The gulf between the despotic tsardom in the east and the democratic republic in the west proved not to be an insuperable barrier. The perpetual sources of friction between England and France on the one hand and Russia on the other proved capable of accommodation. So that at last all Germany convinced itself that those three powers were joint conspirators whose common aim was her own destruction.

And the outcome of that conviction was—Armageddon. These developments, however, were not immediate. For a quarter of a century the British Empire remained in 'splendid isolation,' and France hardly less than Great Britain, though after a long interval the beginnings of amity sprang up between her and Russia; while the effect of the Berlin treaties was at first to intensify the established antagonism between Russia and Great Britain.

Russia's intention had been to create what may be called a Greater Bulgaria, which would be very much the largest of the Balkan states, would dominate Constantinople and control the Aegean coast, and would be Russia's henchman. The revised partition under the Berlin treaties reduced Bulgaria to about one third of the size proposed by Russia; another third, as Eastern Rumelia, was to be autonomous but under Turkish suzerainty, while Macedonia and the Aegean coast were to be left in Turkish hands but under joint supervision by the powers. The independence of the new Bulgaria, and of Serbia and Montenegro, was to be complete. Austria was to occupy and administer Bosnia. Rumania had to be content with Dobruja instead of Bessarabia, which was annexed to Russia.

Each of the Balkan states was left sorely aggrieved, because each held that it was itself entitled to territories awarded to another; Serbia, Greece and Bulgaria were each convinced that Macedonia belonged of right to her; both Bulgaria and Serbia were denied effective access to the sea; while Rumania was particularly sore because Russia had rewarded her extremely valuable services by appropriating Bessarabia herself.

Great Britain had made a private bargain with the Porte guaranteeing the Asiatic possessions of the Turks—other than those ceded to Russia under the treaties—conditionally upon the carrying out of reforms, and upon the British occupation and administration of the island of Cyprus; which would provide her with a naval station of considerable value in the eastern Mediterranean.

Nor was Russian policy in Bulgaria successful in furthering her own projects. The prince nominated for Bulgaria was the tsar's nephew, Alexander of Battenberg. At the outset, Russian influences predominated, arousing patriotic antagonism to foreign control. But the prince established his own despotic authority by a coup d'état setting aside the theoretically admirable but practically paralytic constitu-

SATIRE ON THE CYPRUS CONVENTION

While the Berlin Congress was in session in June, 1878, Britain and Turkey came to a separate agreement by which the former guaranteed the latter's Asiatic dominions and was allowed, in return, to occupy Cyprus. The Punch cartoon, A Blaze of Triumph, represents Lord Beaconsfield carrying a smiling Turk.

By permission of the proprietors of 'Punch'

FIRST KING OF BULGARIA

Nephew of the Russian tsar, Alexander of Battenberg was elected first prince of Bulgaria in 1879. His acceptance of the sovereignty of Eastern Rumelia in 1885 aroused Russian indignation and he was forced to abdicate in 1886.

tion which had been bestowed on the principality. Russia applauded, but when he turned his powers to account, assumed the championship of Bulgarian independence, and dismissed the Russian counsellors, Russia was wroth. He could and did gain popularity by restoring the constitution (1883), without loss of authority.

In 1885 Eastern Rumelia ejected its Turkish governors and proclaimed its own union with Bulgaria. Alexander hastened to assume the proffered sovereignty. Serbia took alarm—she must be compensated for this Bulgarian expansion. Compensation was not forthcoming, so she declared war, and was badly beaten at Slivnitza. Austria intervened and stopped the fighting. The Porte saved its face by appointing Alexander governor of Rumelia, a practical acceptance of the fact that he had got it and meant to keep it. Only a threatened blockade by a British squadron restrained Greece from attempting to snatch 'compensation' for herself.

But Alexander's triumph wrought his fall. The tsar's indignation was high; Russian conspirators kidnapped the Bulgarian king, forced him to sign his abdication and carried him over the border. But the national government carried on under his indomitable minister Stambulov; Alexander, less indomitable, threw up the struggle in the face of the tsar's implacable hostility, and resigned the crown which the Bulgarians would have restored. Stambulov, fervidly anti-Russian, remained dictator until in 1887 a new prince was found—ready to take the risks and play a waiting game—in Ferdinand of Saxe-Coburg. Meantime, Stambulov remained at the helm in Bulgaria, while the Balkan states continued to seethe.

As concerned the Balkans, then, the actual outcome was that Russia lost ground, since she succeeded in alienating both Rumania and Bulgaria without definitely attracting Serbia or Greece under her influence. Austria had gained by establishing herself in Bosnia and giving to that region an administration infinitely better than it had ever known before. England had acquired a dominating influence at the Porte, though she was too unsympathetic to Turkish methods

'THE BISMARCK OF THE BALKANS'

Stepan Nikolov Stambulov (1854–95), the strong-minded Bulgarian minister of Alexander, headed a council of regency upon that prince's abdication. In 1887 he became premier and dominated Balkan politics for eight years.

for the satisfaction of the Turkish government; which continued in its old ways, but with a much smaller Christian population under its rule than of yore. And between the several Balkan states there was no love to lose, while none of them was gratefully conscious of a deep debt to any European power for disinterested services rendered.

France's Colonial Ambitions

BISMARCK'S position as the dominating factor in international politics was unchanged. From France in isolation there could be nothing to fear for a long time to come, and to keep her isolated was no very difficult task. A republic which could set up no administration of tolerably convincing stability could hardly be attracted by or attractive to the iron despotism of Russia. Between her and Great Britain Egypt provided a constant source of friction; and an opportunity occurred for providing another source of friction between her and Italy, incidentally attracting the latter to the Central powers.

THE PRINCE IMPERIAL

Eugène Louis Jean Joseph Napoléon (1856-79), the only son of Napoleon III and the Empress Eugénie, was known as the Prince Imperial. Until his death in a British expedition to Zululand, he was the centre of Bonapartist hopes.

France had effected an amazing economic recovery since the war, but in 1878 it was still uncertain whether monarchism might yet take the place of the republic. The resignation of Macmahon marked the turning point; Bonapartism disappeared with the death of the Prince Imperial in Zululand, in 1879; the legitimism which clung to the house of Bourbon was paralysed in the country by the firmness or obstinacy with which the Bourbon princes, like the exiled Stuarts, clung to their religious and political convictions or prejudices; no glamour attached to the house of Orléans. From that time monarchism was merely a pious opinion, and the continuity of the republic grew continuously more secure.

It was at this time that France found herself encouraged to develop her aspirations in Africa by taking possession of Tunis, for which she found a pretext in 1881. England had no objection, as it might make her less irritable on the subject of Egypt. Germany had no objection, having no African interests and a perception that Tunis might bring to France more trouble than profit; for Italy, with her own eyes on Tunis, would certainly regard the annexation of Tunis by France as an unfriendly act towards herself. She did; and her annoyance made it comparatively easy for Bismarck to draw her into a somewhat non-committal alliance in 1882 with Germany and her former bête noire, Austria. If trouble with France should arise, Italy would be on Germany's side.

France's acquisition of Tunis did nothing to mitigate her jealousy of British influence in Egypt, which she had never ceased to covet since the days of the first Napoleon. In the successive complications of the Eastern Question, she had kept that objective before her throughout the Bourbon and Orleanist monarchies; while Palmerston, with preservation of the 'integrity of the Turkish Empire' as a fundamental aim of his policy, had been a constant obstacle. But the maintenance of French influence there had remained a constant aim, furthered by the construction of the Suez Canal, a

AN INTERESTING STAGE IN THE HISTORY OF THE SUEZ CANAL

Disraeli's politic purchase of Suez Canal shares from the impoverished khedive of Egypt, in 1875, ensured British control of this important waterway. In 1869 the future King Edward VII was conducted over the canal's then unfinished works by the French engineer de Lesseps, as seen in this contemporary wood engraving. The royal visitor performed the ceremony of opening the sluices of the dam that admitted Mediterranean waters into the first section of the canal.

French project in which Palmerston had no share, though Disraeli had more than made up for the oversight by his dramatic purchase from Khedive Ismail of the bulk of the company's shares in 1875, virtually placing control of the canal in the hands of the British government.

At the same time the khedive's extravagance, and his huge debts to British and French financiers, had forced him to

FOUNDER OF THE 'DUAL CONTROL' AND ITS OPPONENT

The extravagance of Ismail Pasha (1830–95), who became khedive of Egypt in 1867, led to his appeal for financial assistance to France and Britain, which occasioned the 'dual control' of his country by these two powers. Under Ismail's feeble successor, Tewfik, the discontent felt by Egyptians with their government and with European interference manifested itself in an agitation nominally headed by Arabi Pasha (right), whose revolt was crushed, and who was himself deported.

Left, photo, Elliott & Fry

place the Egyptian finances in the hands of a dual board of control, British and French, with the inevitable result—illustrated in Indian history by the British assumption of the Diwani in Bengal—that the board became in effect, though not in form, largely responsible for the government; a state of things by no means to the liking of the officials, drawn for the most part from other parts of the Turkish empire, who had hitherto battened according to custom upon the khedive's helpless subjects and the revenues, of which only a fraction reached the treasury.

British Occupation of Egypt

It was not difficult, in the circumstances, to raise the cry of 'Egypt for the Egyptians,' or to draw an army colonel, Arabi Pasha, into the rôle of patriot leader and champion of the anti-foreign sentiment. Ismail's successor, Tewfik, found himself powerless; the anti-foreign agitation became a grave danger to the very considerable European population in Alexandria and elsewhere. The Porte (the suzerain) would not and the khedive could not do anything. The French and British governments offered Tewfik their support at the beginning of 1882, and sent naval squadrons; the only effect was to produce riots. A European conference was called to deal judicially with the problem; but the position at Alexandria and the menace to the Europeans there from Arabi's troops were too critical for delay. The British admiral took the responsibility, which the French admiral declined to share, of sending an ultimatum to Arabi and, when it was ignored, of opening a bombardment and occupying Alexandria, while the French retired.

The force at the admiral's disposal was obviously inadequate for the restoration of order and security. With due notification to the sultan, troops were dispatched to Egypt from England and India. Arabi's army was shattered in a brief and decisive campaign, and he himself was deported. But the whole situation had been changed. The khedive's government—anything that could be called a government—could be restored only by the British. In the public interest the British on their own sole responsibility had taken upon themselves to do the thing that was admittedly necessary but which no one else had been ready or willing to undertake either alone or in conjunction with them; the French had had the opportunity but had deliberately rejected it. The British had therefore done the thing single-handed, and it was recognized that they were entitled to a perfectly free hand in the necessary reconstruction on their own terms.

But just as in India they had repeatedly refrained from annexation or had restricted annexation to the lowest practical limit, so now they did not annex Egypt, though it would have been more than difficult to deny their right to do so. Reconstruction required at the least an army of occupation to maintain order during the process, and effective control of the entire administration. They 'occupied' Egypt as the Austrians occupied Bosnia, on the theory that they would evacuate it as soon as a government had been established which could stand securely upon its own feet. And in the meanwhile the government continued to be the khedive's, the Egyptian government, not the British; though the army of occupation was British, the reorganization of an Egyptian army was in the hands of British officers, and the administration was in the hands of British officials in the service of the khedive. There was no room for French ambitions in Egypt, and though France was thoroughly conscious that she had no one but herself to thank for the fact, that made her none the less resentful.

Unrest in Italy, Spain and Russia

Italy had attained her unity under Victor Emmanuel, but half the country had not yet been accustomed to the idea that governments exist for some other purpose than the oppression of the people. Economic stability was still distant, and, if she ranked as a great power, it was still only by courtesy, eager though she was to assert herself. The almost simultaneous deaths of Victor Emmanuel and Pius IX did not heal the breach between the crown and the Papacy.

Spain on the other hand was entering upon an era of recuperation after her prolonged sufferings. The king, Amadeo of Savoy, who had accepted her crown when it was refused by Leopold of Hohenzollern, resigned it again in disgust in 1873; but after a year of dictatorship in the guise of a republic she recalled Alfonso XII, the son of the formerly expelled queen Isabella. There was a brief struggle before the old Carlist party was finally broken up; the young king set himself seriously to the task of government; and when he died prematurely in 1885 his widow, Maria Christina, discharged with tact and discretion the duties of regent on behalf of the infant Alfonso XIII, until he reached man's estate.

Russia as we saw lost ground in Europe. Within the tsardom, Alexander II had striven or rather groped after ideals, while lacking the resolution and the insight without which it was impossible to bring them to realization. He had liberated the serfs without restoring to them what they regarded as their own rights in the soil. He had encouraged Western education, but it had fallen upon ground in which it was only the seed of passionate revolt, and government terrorism was faced by the black spectre of Nihilism. The tsar himself was no enemy of reform; but even at the moment when an effort was being made in that direction the world was shocked by his murder at the hands of the nihilists (1882). All thought of reforms vanished, and under the dead tsar's son, Alexander III, the tyranny became if possible more rigid and more merciless than before.

Foiled in the Balkans, Russia as usual became more active in Asia, pushing constantly and in British eyes alarmingly in the direction of India. But the collision, in 1885, between Russian and Afghan troops known as the 'Penjdeh incident,' which threatened to be the beginning of an Anglo-Russian war, actually prepared the way for an adjustment—thanks in no small measure to the hard-headed shrewdness of the Afghan amir Abd er-Rahman—and an agreed delimitation of frontiers in 1887. For Russia was changing her Asiatic objective, aiming at the Farthest East and the Pacific; as yet no more conscious than the rest of the world that a power had arisen, and was consolidating itself in that quarter, with which she would have to try conclusions before her aims could be accomplished.

A WISE AFGHAN AMIR

Abd er-Rahman (1830–1901), proclaimed amir of Afghanistan by the British in 1880, proved himself a strong ruler. His shrewd handling of the situation at the time of the Penjdeh incident prevented imminent Anglo-Russian hostilities.

Photo, E.N.A.

Colonial Expansion in Africa

There was at this period a general European movement towards expansion. France had turned her eyes once more to the East; if India was unattainable, there were still lands beyond India where a footing might be established; though it was not without many troubles that she acquired from China the protectorate of Annam by the Treaty of Tientsin in 1885. Her activities in Indo-China were probably the real though not the ostensible warrant for the British annexation of Upper Burma in 1887. European interests in the Farthest East were developing. But it was the scramble for Africa that set in most vigorously in the years immediately following the Berlin Congress.

Expansion manifestly could take place only in lands—whether densely or sparsely populated—where the civilization in general and the community organization in particular were on a lower plane than those of Europe. America was already occupied by Europeans; so was most of

SCENE OF A BOER VICTORY OVER THE BRITISH

On the night of February 26, 1881, Sir George Colley, governor of Natal and commander-in-chief of the British forces in South Africa, seized and occupied Majuba Hill. Driven from this position early next morning, the British forces suffered heavy losses, to the great detriment of British prestige, Colley himself being among the fallen.
Photo, E.N.A.

Australasia and the islands of the Pacific. Western Asia was not an open field; northern and central Asia were out of reach except for Russia. In the farthest east of Asia there were perhaps possibilities, but there was the Chinese empire to be reckoned with. But the whole African interior was an almost unknown region, scarcely penetrated except by an occasional adventurous missionary, peopled by negro races whose culture was primitive and barbaric. The coastal districts on the Mediterranean were provinces in which such governments as existed might fairly be classed as barbaric. The Atlantic sea-board was dotted with European 'colonies' which were little more than very unhealthy trading depots. The south was occupied by the British, the Boers and the Portuguese. Farther north, on the east, Zanzibar and Abyssinia, like Morocco on the north-west coast, and to some extent the island of Madagascar, claimed a doubtful recognition as independent states. But the rest of Africa was open to any Europeans who could take effective possession.

The British then, as we have seen, established a 'temporary' protectorate in Egypt, to which other powers could hardly refuse assent; France established her own protectorate in Tunis, not only with assent but with positive encouragement from Great Britain and Germany, though very much to the annoyance of Italy, who could only hope to find compensation on the north of Abyssinia and ultimately in Tripoli. France without European intervention set up (1885) a protectorate in Madagascar which was later transformed into annexation. But all the European powers, including Germany, who had hitherto felt no call to colonial expansion, had suddenly realized that Africa was the only division of the earth's surface still open to appropriation, and that the British, with a northern base in Egypt, a southern base in Cape Colony and sundry starting points on the western and eastern coasts, would by mere force of circumstances absorb the interior and leave nothing for anyone else to appropriate unless they made haste to anticipate her.

The precedents of the eighteenth century, when France and Great Britain had fought each other to a finish for America and India on the hypothesis that there was not room there for both, were not promising. In Africa after all there was room for everyone; and so between 1880 and 1890 a series of treaties or compacts was entered upon, partitioning the Dark Continent into protectorates or 'spheres of influence' appropriated to one or another of the European states, though not without leaving occasions for acute controversy in the future.

AT the same time events were taking place which were of moment to the future expansion of the British in Africa. First in the south, in 1879, they came into collision with the military power of the Zulus, which led to the annexation of Zululand. Immediately preceding this, they had resumed the control which they had abrogated in 1852 over the Boers in the Transvaal, who without British protection were in danger of being wiped out by the Zulus. Freed from that menace by the Zulu war, the Transvaalers demanded the retrocession of their virtual independence, rose in arms, and at Majuba Hill (1881) cut up the British regiments which had been sent out to restore the British authority, though the British government had already resolved to concede the demand of the Boers. On the hypothesis that the justice of that demand was not affected by Majuba, the government stopped the hostilities and carried out the retrocession, practically claiming to retain control over the foreign relations of the Boers; who, on the other hand, were firmly convinced that they had extorted their rights by force of arms from a government which had neither the power nor the energy to maintain its own claims—whereof the consequences were manifested in the South African War, which broke out before twenty years had passed.

Meanwhile in Egypt trouble was brewing. The effective rule of Egypt had

EMPEROR FREDERICK I

Prince Frederick William succeeded to the German imperial throne as Emperor Frederick I in March, 1888. His tragic death in June of the same year from cancer of the throat crushed the hopes of the Liberal party whose views he shared.

Engraving by D. J. Pound

GENERAL GORDON

The heroic endeavour of Charles George Gordon (1833–85), renowned for his almost uncanny influence over half-civilized peoples, to 'smash the Mahdi' in the Sudan ended in tragedy. The expedition to his relief in Khartum was too late.

never extended above the lower cataracts of the Nile, though she had habitually claimed lordship over the Upper Nile and the desert tribes of the Sudan; among whom there arose at this time a 'Mahdi' claiming to be the successor of the Prophet of Islam who was to overthrow the Khalifate and establish the supremacy of the Faith. Before long he was exercising a despotic authority over the Sudanese; the Egyptian garrisons in the Sudan were powerless, and Egypt herself was threatened by his fanatical hordes. The British government had taken up the task of providing Egypt with a healthy government; it was not prepared to take upon itself also the business of restoring the Egyptian authority in the Sudan; the abandonment of which was the only alternative, involving the withdrawal of the garrisons.

It appointed for the execution of that task General Gordon, soldier and mystic, with virtually a free hand; subject to the instruction that withdrawal and nothing more was to be attempted, and the warning that no great military expedition would be sanctioned, though it was known to be Gordon's own conviction that the 'smashing' of the Mahdi was imperative; while he was a man who would certainly

'DROPPING THE PILOT'
Dissension soon arose between the Emperor William II, who ascended the German imperial throne in 1888, and Bismarck. Sir John Tenniel's well known cartoon affords a poignant illustration of the latter's dismissal on March 20, 1890.
By permission of the proprietors of 'Punch'

not allow his own conviction of a sacred duty to be overridden by the expediencies of politicians. Tragedy followed. Gordon, in the Sudan, found himself shut up in Khartum by the Mahdist hordes, and when at last a long-delayed expedition was dispatched up the Nile to rescue him it reached Khartum only to find that the place had been stormed two days before its arrival, and Gordon had fallen in the defence. There was nothing more to be done, and the Sudan was abandoned till the time should be ripe for its conquest after the lapse of thirteen years.

In 1888 the emperor William I died at the age of ninety; three months later his son Frederick I followed him, and his grandson William II became the German kaiser. The German Empire had been achieved through the never-failing loyalty of the old man and his great chancellor to each other. What might have befallen if Frederick had not been already a dying man when he succeeded to the imperial crown none can say, for it was notorious that there were many points on which emperor and chancellor did not see eye to eye; but during those months there was no breach between them. On Frederick's death it seemed at first that Bismarck's ascendancy would be unimpaired, but the new kaiser believed implicitly in himself; he had ideas of his own which were not Bismarck's, and in 1890 William 'dropped the pilot' and took the management of affairs into his own hands. The world did not know what to make of Germany's new master and his passion for unexpected activities and startling pronouncements, which were occasionally somewhat nerve-racking; but it was, on the whole, inclined to regard them as temperamental eccentricities which must not be taken too seriously. How far the chancellor's fall had actually changed the European situation was a matter of much uncertainty.

Alliance between France and Russia

One thing, however, was clear. Bismarck had striven to the last to placate Russia and prevent any rapprochement between her and France. That a rapprochement was taking place became more apparent every day. In 1891 the French channel fleet visited Kronstadt, where it received an ovation; two years later a Russian squadron paid a return visit to Toulon, where its reception was even more enthusiastic. Alexander III died in 1894, when he was succeeded by the third of the tsar-idealists, Nicholas II; next year an alliance between France and Russia became an accomplished though not a published fact, the existence of which was acknowledged and even emphasised by somewhat ostentatious displays of mutual good will in the two following years. Germany can hardly be reproached if the conviction was implanted, and grew ever stronger, that hostility to her was the bond between the two powers, otherwise so inappropriately yoked together, which lay on her western and eastern marches.

There could be no question about the solidarity of the interests of the two Central powers. If they broke with each other, neither would be secure against attack by one or, more probably, two hostile powers ; while they stood together, holding strategetically the 'interior lines,' the risk of attacking them would be too great to be undertaken lightly. And at the same time they had no clashing interests, and no material divergences of political sentiment such as those which made a firmly rooted friendship so difficult between a typically despotic and a typically democratic state. By attaching Italy to themselves they had gained an additional security in relation at least to France. On the other hand, concord between Russia and France gave to each security against aggression by the Central powers. An equilibrium was established simply because the issue of an armed conflict would be too doubtful—the more because no one was able to gauge the real efficiency of Russia's strength.

Britain's 'Splendid Isolation'

At the same time the isolation of Great Britain was complete, nor had she any desire that it should be otherwise. She was in possession or occupation of the greater and better part of so much of the world as had not been occupied by Europeans before the middle of the eighteenth century, a position from which no one could hope to oust her while her fleets commanded the ocean highways ; those fleets were an impassable bulwark except where their place was taken by the all but impassable mountains of the Indian frontier, or where her only neighbour was the American republic. She was hardly conscious of a challenge to her commercial and manufacturing supremacy, which she had learnt to regard as a matter of course. So long as she kept her navy up to standard she had nothing to fear from powers whose resources were under the perpetual strain of maintaining huge armies, while she could content herself with one comparatively insignificant in size.

She could see no cause of quarrel with any of her neighbours save Russia, except what she felt to be their rather unreasonable jealousy ; she had no sense of hostility to any of them—with the same exception, Russia. Consequently she had no desire for alliances which might prove embarrassing, but if she should incline to one scale or other in the European balances it would fairly certainly not be the Russian scale. Though French and English had fought each other often enough in the past, they had also occasionally fought side by side, and towards France England had no sort of ill will ; France might persist in her annoyance about Egypt, but common sense would forbid her to manufacture a casus belli ; while if at times the British relations with Austria and Prussia had not been over cordial, they had not fought each other for more than a century, nor was there any apparent reason why they should wish to fight each other now. If the other powers chose to quarrel with each other, the less the British Empire allowed itself to be implicated in their differences the better, though it would be always in her interest that peace should be preserved.

NICHOLAS II OF RUSSIA

Nicholas II succeeded his father as tsar of Russia in 1894 and shortly afterwards married Princess Alix of Hesse, this photograph being taken in the same year. He was assassinated in 1918.

THE MARQUESS OF SALISBURY
The British public had great confidence in the conservative and pacific Lord Salisbury (1830–1903) both as premier and foreign secretary. His cession of Heligoland to Germany in 1890, however, was not universally approved.

She was hardly alive, however, to the fact that jealousy was growing in Germany, who had embarked on an active career of trade expansion, was pushing her way into markets which the British had hitherto monopolised, and was very ill satisfied with the bargains struck over the partitions of Africa—though the British expansionists were no less displeased by the 'graceful concessions' of Lord Salisbury's diplomacy. The German commercial community felt more and more that British rivalry and British intrigues were barricading her out of her rightful 'place in the sun.' On the other hand, the kaiser had realized the fundamental fact that 'peaceful penetration' was the only useful weapon that could be employed until there was a German navy which could hold its own against the British navy.

But an equilibrium depending simply on equality of armament between two groups of powers filled with suspicion and mistrust of each other could only mean that each group would strive ceaselessly to raise its own standard of armament above that of the other group; and so the exhausting race went on year by year—touching Great Britain less than anyone else, because as concerned armies she saw no need to enter the race, and as concerned navies she already held a lead which kept her above immediate competition. None of the powers wanted a conflagration, however, and so long as that was the case it was to the interest of all that the status quo should be maintained at least within Europe.

No one then was disposed to interfere in the troubles of minor states or nationalities. No one was concerned if Norway wanted the separation from Sweden which she achieved, by strictly constitutional methods, at the opening of the twentieth century. The depression of the Poles by Russia might demand sympathy, but certainly not intervention. The absorption of Finland into the Russian system disturbed no one but the Swedes. The subordination of the Slavs within the Austrian Empire to Austrian or Magyar domination made Slavs everywhere look to Slavonic Russia, developing the race hostility between Slav and Teuton; but

ABDUL HAMID, SULTAN OF TURKEY
Considerable diplomatic talent was shown by Abdul Hamid II in his dealings with the European powers, and German influence in Turkey throve under his encouragement. He was sultan from 1876 until 1909, when he was deposed.
Photo, W. & D. Downey

the time was not ripe for a duel—and the astute sultan was very well aware that all the powers would fight shy of active interference with his doings, lest they should thereby be brought into active collision with each other. The inflammability of the Balkan peninsula was the standing menace to that general peace which the 'Concert of Europe' was most anxious to preserve, while that same desire paralysed the Concert itself for drastic action. Incidentally, since Germany had no territorial interests of her own in the Turkish Empire, Abdul Hamid, having nothing to fear from her 'friendship' and possibly much to gain, was ready enough to cultivate it, while the kaiser was thoroughly alive to the advantages that might accrue therefrom.

Friction between the Balkans and Turkey

In the Balkan storm centre, Serbia was too much torn by domestic troubles to endanger the peace of her neighbours, though a period of reconstruction was promised by the fall of the Obrenovitch dynasty and the accession of a prince of the former rival house of Karageorgevitch in 1903; though the consequent development of pan-Slav doctrines was ominous from the Austrian point of view.

In Bulgaria, Ferdinand watched and waited while Stambulov ruled, till the chance came in 1894 for accepting the minister's resignation—much to the surprise of Stambulov himself, who was assassinated not long afterwards. Ferdinand was far too wary to commit himself to provocative action in any direction, while he was especially careful to cultivate the good will of the Porte on one side and Germany on the other. With a Hohenzollern reigning in Rumania and a Coburg in Bulgaria—both states which declined to regard themselves as Slavonic, and both having very definite grudges against Russia—the gravitation of both towards the Central empires was inevitable.

When definite trouble arose, it was within the Turkish dominions. It appeared in 1894 that there was a revolutionary movement in Armenia which needed repressing. The Turk repressed it, finding himself under the unhappy necessity of massacring some fifty thousand of the population before the European Concert was in tune for intervention, though, as a matter of course, he then accepted the paper scheme of reforms submitted by the powers, which as usual failed to materialise. Next came the revolt of Crete, bent on escaping from the Moslem sovereignty and on joining herself to the Greek kingdom. Greece answered the call of Crete and sent a force to the island. The Concert intervened; when a joint squadron arrived at Canea, bringing peremptory orders that the fighting was to stop, that the Greeks were to withdraw and no more Turkish troops were to be landed, the orders were perforce obeyed. But the Greeks lost their heads and invaded Thessaly, whence they were decisively ejected by the Turkish troops.

To deny the right of the Turks, in the circumstances, to demand rectifications of the Thessaly frontier was impossible; but the powers—without Germany and Austria, who refused to co-operate—required from Turkey autonomy for Crete under their joint supervision, with the second of the Greek princes as governor. In Crete, Greek patriotism centred in the future minister, Venizelos. But with Abdul Hamid German influence was supreme, though a 'Young Turk' party, a Turkish nationalist party, was now coming into being with a programme of its own which was not favourable to the khalif, who in the last twenty years had lost for Islam effective sovereignty in Cyprus, Egypt, Rumelia, Bosnia and finally Crete. Its existence, however, was as yet unsuspected. The accord of Germany and the Porte bore significant fruit in 1902, in the authorisation of a German railway to Basra and Bagdad, which would give the Germans their first foothold in the Middle East. For in the Far East the scramble for penetration bases in China had already begun.

Development and Expansion of Japan

The nature and characteristics of the Japanese Revolution are the subject of study in Chapter 165. Japan had remodelled herself upon Western lines, somewhat as, long ago, Peter the Great had sought to remodel Russia. But her aim was not to Westernise herself, but to hold her own among the Westerns by learning and adapting scientifically to her own use all that a critical study of Western methods could teach her. She reorganized her government, her army, her navy and her policy. She turned her eyes to the continent of Asia, as she had done long ago in the days of Hideyoshi. Organization, not aggression, was her immediate object; but the king of Korea forced war upon her, rather as Burmese monarchs had forced war upon the British in India; and the position which she then took up in Korea displeased China, who claimed there a shadowy suzerainty. In 1894 China proposed to submerge her, with the result that after a few months' fighting China was very thoroughly ejected from Korea, and Japan proposed to reap the natural fruits of her victory by the treaty of Shimonoseki.

Great Britain was the only European power which had recognized the status of Japan as a civilized, not a merely semi-civilized, nation. Europe intervened and forbade her to reap the fruits, and the powers were duly rewarded by China for their intervention; Russia in concessions for the railway she was carrying across Siberia to Vladivostok, France in the neighbourhood of Tonkin, Germany at Tientsin—arrangements which made an ultimate collision between Russia and Japan certain, unless Japan should give way to Russia. Germany, whatever her ultimate aim may have been, ranged herself along with Russia and France, and England could not encourage Japan to defy that combination. Japan submitted with dignity, and bided her time.

China, however, did not love the 'foreign devils.' A year later (1897) two German missionaries were murdered. Germany demanded compensation, and got it in Kiao-chau. France and Russia demanded equivalents for the concessions to Germany, and got them; on the same principle, Weihaiwei was leased to Great Britain. The concessions intensified the popular Chinese hostility to the foreigners, and to the emperor Kuang Hsü, who was deposed next year by the dowager-empress, Tzu Hsi, the incarnation of the anti-foreign reaction; while North China was seething with the 'Boxer' rebellion.

All the foreign powers had 'legations' at Peking, and in 1900 came the news that the legations were either in the hands of the Peking mob or were on the point of falling into them. All the powers, Japan and the United States included, took joint action, and dispatched to China contingents which marched on Peking, where they found that the legations had, after all, held out successfully. The Chinese government submitted, with professions that it had done its best but had been unable to control the rebels. The allies refrained from demanding

FORMER BRITISH NAVAL AND COALING STATION AT WEIHAIWEI, CHINA

The British leased Weihaiwei, a Chinese naval station on the north-east coast of the Shantung peninsula, from China in 1898, and retained possession of it until, at the Washington Conference of 1921, it was agreed that it should be restored to China. The territory consists of all the islands in Weihaiwei bay, the island of Liukung and a strip, ten miles wide, along the coast, in all 285 square miles.

Photo, B. R. Muddett

further concessions, though insisting on effective guarantees for security in the future; and in the following years it appeared that the progressive or Westernising element predominated in the Chinese government, though Tzu Hsi continued to reign.

The conduct of Japan throughout had more than established her right to recognition on an equal footing with the Western powers, which was sealed by a treaty of alliance with Great Britain in 1902. The treaty meant that, if and when Russia and Japan should come into armed collision, Great Britain would not join Japan against Russia by herself, but would intervene if anyone else joined Russia against Japan.

The collision was not long postponed. Russia wanted both Manchuria, where she had established herself, and Korea, where Japan had established herself. Japan proposed mutual accommodations; Russia claimed that the compromises should not be reciprocal. Japan proposed control for Russia in Manchuria and for Japan in Korea. Russia returned no answer, and in February, 1904, Japan declared war. She had only the resources of her own islands to draw upon, while Russia's resources in men at least were incalculably greater. But she could bring her whole force to bear at once; of Russia's naval squadrons one was ice-bound at Vladivostok, while she could reinforce her armies in Manchuria only by way of the single-line trans-Siberian railway, which was still far short of completion.

On February 9 Japan broke up the second Russian fleet from Port Arthur,

KUROPATKIN AT MUKDEN

In March, 1905, after much strenuous fighting, the Japanese under Oyama defeated the Russians at Mukden, in China. Kuropatkin, the Russian commander, is here seen in Mukden imperial cemetery with the Chinese authorities.

JAPAN'S GREAT ADMIRAL

The destruction of the Russian fleet at Port Arthur in February, 1904, was one of the most celebrated exploits performed by the Japanese naval commander-in-chief, Heihachiro Togo, here seen heading a procession in Vyeno Park, Tokyo.
Photo, E.N.A.

PART OF THE SUNKEN RUSSIAN FLEET IN PORT ARTHUR HARBOUR BEFORE THE SURRENDER TO THE JAPANESE

Leased by Russia from China in 1898, the fortified seaport of Port Arthur, in Manchuria, became the chief base for the Russian eastern fleet. Its harbour was blockaded by the Japanese from the beginning of the Russo-Japanese war, and after a siege of eleven months General Stoessel surrendered to the besiegers on January 1, 1905. This view of the harbour shows the submerged Russian battleship, Retvizan, sunk by gunfire on December 8.

From a photograph by General A. M. Stoessel

whither she drove it back and which she proceeded to blockade. A little later she was able to invest it on the land side also, while the Russian commander Kuropatkin was endeavouring not to overwhelm but to hold back her main army on the Yalu till he should be adequately reinforced. Port Arthur held out stubbornly, and in spite of heavy fighting the Japanese commander could make no impression until a desperate effort was put forth at the end of the year in order to anticipate the expected arrival of a new Russian fleet, the Port Arthur squadron having sallied forth in August, only to be annihilated by Admiral Togo.

Progress of the Russo-Japanese War

KUROPATKIN had been pushed back from the Yalu in May; he was again pushed back upon Mukden in August, as the result of the nine days' battle of Liao-yang, in which the Japanese actually suffered more heavily than the Russians. Being at last reinforced in October, he resumed the offensive, but was again compelled to retire upon Mukden after a fifteen days' battle on the Sha-ho, which left both armies so exhausted that neither could take the offensive. Port Arthur, however, was so hard pressed by Nogi's final onslaught that it was forced to surrender on January 1, 1905.

Nogi was thus released to reinforce the main army, after which another prolonged and exhausting struggle drove Kuropatkin from Mukden at the end of February back to the lines which he was able to hold for the remainder of the war, since there was no more heavy fighting on land. The sea, however, provided one more episode. Rhozhdestvenski's fleet arrived in May, only to be obliterated by Togo in the battle of Tsushima. Japan could not hope to add to her gains; Russia could not hope to recover ground; both had suffered enormous losses, and both were thoroughly exhausted. The war was ended by the treaty of Portsmouth, U.S.A., in August, 1905; Russia evacuating Manchuria, while Japan retained Korea with the Liau-tung peninsula.

The Russo-Japanese war had upon Russia's position among the powers the same sort of effect that the defeat of the Armada had upon Spain at the end of the sixteenth century. She ceased to be a bogy credited with incalculable power. Her navy had shown itself almost grotesquely inefficient, and her armies, without being outnumbered, had left the Japanese masters of the field after each of the prolonged and stubbornly contested engagements. To strike effectively at Russia would always be as desperately difficult as Napoleon had found it, but holding her at bay would present no insuperable difficulties.

GENERAL COUNT NOGI

Count Maresuke Nogi (1849–1912), the victorious Japanese commander at Port Arthur in the Russo-Japanese War, showed his devotion to an old tradition of his country by committing harakiri on the death of his emperor Mutsuhito.

Photo, Swaine

As concerned Europe, no change in the isolation of Great Britain had taken place when the twentieth century opened. It was a moment when every country on the Continent was sympathising not with her but with her stubborn antagonists in the South African War, under the curious conviction that all the dominions of the British Empire were craving to be free from a bondage which had no existence. As late as the middle of the nineteenth century it had been the commonly accepted doctrine that colonies break away from the mother country as soon as their own security is not endangered by doing so; the cleavage of the British Empire in the

A DAMP JOURNEY: JAPANESE INFANTRY ADVANCING ON LIAO-YANG

Furious fighting took place in the nine days' battle of Liao-yang, whence the Japanese drove the Russians in 1904. Although the result of the battle was favourable to the Japanese, they were not successful in cutting off the retreat of the Russians, under their commander, Kuropatkin, on Mukden, and the value of the victory was modified by the terrible losses suffered by the Japanese troops.

Photo, F. A. Mackenzie

THE PORTSMOUTH PEACEMAKERS
President Roosevelt stands in the centre of this group of statesmen who arranged the Treaty of Portsmouth (U.S.A.), which ended the Russo-Japanese war in 1905, by excluding Russia from Manchuria and giving Korea to Japan. On his right are Witte and Rosen; on his left. Komura and Takahira.
Photo, Underwood and Underwood

last quarter of the eighteenth century being regarded as a typical instance of a general law.

In actual fact, for fifty years past Great Britain had consistently fostered autonomy in her colonies, which were aware of no bondage except when the exigencies of international relations made the imperial government actually or apparently neglectful of the interests of particular colonies. Regarding themselves and being regarded as partners in the Empire, not subordinates, they had no desire for separation, however jealous they might be in regard to their own rights and privileges; and the sense of imperial solidarity was growing, not diminishing. South Africa was on a different footing from the rest, for the simple reason that the Dutch element there declined to regard itself as British, looked upon the British as interlopers, and resented the British claim to sovereignty in territories which the Dutch, who had been there long before them, regarded as being rightfully their own. And that sentiment among the Boers had been intensified by the retrocession of the Transvaal's independence in 1881.

KITCHENER OF KHARTUM
In 1892 Sir Herbert Kitchener (1850–1916) was appointed Sirdar or commander-in-chief of the Egyptian army. He avenged Gordon's death by his crushing victory at Omdurman in 1898, and his capture of Khartum.

When this antagonism issued in the South African War in 1899, the popularity of Great Britain .in Europe had not been increasing. Her prospective evacuation of Egypt seemed to grow more remote; it could not come till the Egyptians could be trusted to govern themselves, and she was not teaching them the art of self-government. She was teaching them how the thing ought to be done, giving them stable rule, developing their resources, bringing to the fellaheen an unprecedented prosperity; but the men who were doing it all, holding all the responsible posts, were not Egyptians but Britons—after the Indian precedent, and for the same reasons.

In 1896 she made the first open move towards the reconquest of the Sudan by pushing the Egyptian frontier defences up to Dongola. The business was done in the single campaign of 1898. The fanatical hordes of the Khalifa, the Mahdi's successor, were completely shattered at the battle of Omdurman. The Sudan became what it had been before in theory, but never in fact, a province of Egypt, and virtually a British protectorate. But the concentration of the Khalifa's forces against the British advance had enabled a small expeditionary party from the French Congo to reach Fashoda unharmed and hoist the French flag there; and French susceptibilities were painfully irritated when Sir Herbert Kitchener, the conqueror of the Khalifa, declined to recognize the validity of the French occupation. The French government acknowledged the British claim, but French sentiment cherished yet another grievance against what it regarded as British aggression.

Two years after the reconquest of the Sudan, the antagonism of the Dutch to the British in South Africa issued in the outbreak of the South African War. The antecedents of the quarrel, as well as its repercussions in the British Empire, are analysed in Chapter 172. In the first months the British troops met with a series of reverses, but by the following midsummer they were in occupation of the two capitals, Bloemfontein and Pretoria. In September the annexation of the Boer states was proclaimed. Nevertheless they refused to submit, maintaining a persistent guerilla warfare until so many of them had been rounded up that the remnant could no longer keep the field; and in May, 1902, the peace of Vereeniging terminated the war. The republics were annexed, to be administered temporarily as 'crown colonies,' but instead of exacting indemnities the victors provided large sums for the reinstatement of the farms which had suffered in the war.

All told, the casualties—mainly incurred not in the field but from enteric—in the two and a half years' fighting were to be repeatedly outnumbered in a single week, sometimes in a single day, in the Great War, of which it was in no sense a foretaste. There had certainly been on the Continent a strong inclination to intervene, but though the Kaiser's attitude in the preceding years had caused some resentment in England, during the war his influence was certainly exerted to discourage intervention. It may be that he realized the practical futility of attempting, as matters stood, to challenge the British fleet; for it was while the war was in progress that he developed an unprecedented naval programme for

TOMB OF THE MAHDI AFTER BRITISH BOMBARDMENT

At Omdurman, chosen by the fanatical Mahdi as his capital in place of Khartum in 1885, this gigantic tomb was built upon his death in the same year. It was constructed by order of the Khalifa, the Mahdi's successor. After Kitchener's capture of Omdurman in 1898 the British destroyed the tomb, and only its ruins now remain.

Photo, Captain E. A. Stanton

BRITISH TROOPS RETURN TO LADYSMITH AFTER THE DISASTER OF NICHOLSON'S NEK

In the early stages of the South African War of 1899–1902, the superior artillery of the Boers forced Sir George White's troops to retreat on Ladysmith from the advance position which they held at Glencoe near Dundee. Battles were fought on the way at Talana Hill, Elandslaagte and Nicholson's Nek, where a stampede of mules carrying ammunition and guns rendered the British artillery useless. The troops in action being compelled to surrender on October 30 1899, Sir George White withdrew the main body, whose entry into Ladysmith, thereafter invested for four months, is the subject of this photograph.

Photo, Horace W. Nicholls

Germany which was difficult to dissociate from the idea of rivalry with the leading maritime power.

THE South African War had not long been ended when new factors began to influence European relations. In Great Britain, where for half a century free trade had been the accepted theory and practice on all hands, a new propaganda was vigorously pushed and in some quarters enthusiastically adopted, of which the economic merits or demerits cannot here be discussed (see Chap. 168); but it had a political effect which could hardly have been anticipated; it was interpreted in Germany as being malevolently directed against German commerce and German prosperity. That conception was unaffected by the defeat of the tariff reformers at the ensuing general election of 1906, and the conviction was thoroughly established in the popular mind that the British were saturated with jealousy of her commercial progress.

It befell, moreover, that at the moment when the propaganda was in full swing Great Britain and France discovered that their outstanding differences were capable of reasonable adjustment and that living on terms of mutual good will was much more satisfactory than the perpetuation of needless friction. The long reign of Queen Victoria had just ended; the new king, Edward VII, had the gift of popularity, and a visit to France facilitated the development of the new spirit of friendliness. The position of the monarch in England is not readily grasped in other countries, and it was not difficult to imagine that a Machiavellian diplomacy was at work. Coupled with the supposed anti-German tariff agitation, the new accord between Great Britain and France was doubly ominous and the belief in England's sinister designs gained ground.

Nor was this all. France had already established friendly relations with Russia, and the accommodation of interests between France and Great Britain was soon followed by a similar accommodation between Great Britain and Russia, made possible as it had never been before by the effects upon Russia of the disastrous Japanese war. It had been a fundamental part of Bismarck's policy to keep those three powers at arm's length from each other. There had been plenty of motives holding them apart; there could be only one for their reconciliation—their common desire for the destruction of Germany. The development of this idea was at least a fundamental factor in the complicated

KING EDWARD VII IN 1910

Unfailing industry and an acute understanding of men characterised Edward VII (1841–1910), who succeeded Queen Victoria on the British throne in 1901. Throughout his reign he exerted his very great diplomatic gifts to maintain that world peace which was shattered so soon after his death.

Photo, E. H. Mills

AN INTERNATIONAL CONFERENCE AT THE HAGUE DISCUSSING THE PROMOTION OF WORLD PEACE

At the suggestion of Nicholas II, tsar of Russia and a man with humanitarian ideals, the first international peace conference was convoked at The Hague in 1899. It was attended by representatives from European countries and the United States. The conference achieved the establishment of an international court known as the Hague Tribunal, but was unsuccessful in its endeavours to reach an agreement on the question of disarmament. The assembly, which held its meetings at the Huis ten Bosch (House in the Wood), is shown in a drawing from sketches by an artist who was present.

story of the ensuing years, and its catastrophic climax in August, 1914.

It is curious to observe that the most idealistic if not the most successful efforts to design an organ for the preservation of the world's peace have emanated from Russian tsars, Alexander I and Nicholas II. Long ago, the first of these two dreamers had designed the Holy Alliance of Christian Princes, which under Metternich's manipulation was converted—so far as it operated at all—into an instrument for the suppression of popular liberties. But he had also dreamed the dream of Nicholas, the dream which held in it the germ of the League of Nations.

In the last thirty years of the nineteenth century international disputes had with increasing frequency been referred for decision to a neutral arbitrator, Great Britain and the United States having practically led the way by referring their own dispute over the Alabama claim to a neutral court of arbitration. The same course had been followed by the same nations in relation to Alaska, to Vancouver and to Venezuela (though in the last case the United States arbitrated in a dispute between Great Britain and Venezuela). Similarly the Penjdeh incident had been referred to arbitration.

In 1898 Nicholas invited the powers to send delegates to a conference to be held at The Hague to discuss ways and means for the reduction of armaments by consent, the common adoption of what may be called humanitarian regulations in warfare, and the establishment of a permanent court of international arbitration to which nations might, if so minded, refer their disputes. As a result the Hague Tribunal was actually set up. No agreements could be reached as to reduction of armaments, because no scheme was in the German view compatible with Germany's security. Regulations were generally though not universally accepted later for the humanising of warfare which were loyally observed by the belligerents both in the South African and the Russo-Japanese wars; but in them there was the grave defect that no sanction existed for their enforcement if any belligerent chose to ignore them; just as it was open to any nation to refuse the appeal to arbitration.

Here, however, we must revert to the progress of events in the western hemisphere. The South American states in general had at last attained a stability which was more than a temporary equilibrium with intervals of revolution. Brazil had turned itself into a republic, a change which had been carried through without violence and accepted with cheerfulness by the deposed emperor, Pedro II. In Mexico Diaz still ruled with a masterful hand. Great Britain had a boundary dispute with Venezuela in 1895, and when the United States threatened to intervene satisfied them by submitting

SALVAGE MEN AT WORK ON THE MAINE

The short war which took place in 1898 between Spain and America resulted from the latter's belief that the former was responsible for blowing up the American warship Maine in Havana harbour. The men employed in the salvage boats shown in this photograph found it an extremely difficult task to work upon the shattered vessel.

CHAMPION OF THE MOSLEM

A cartoon by Bernard Partridge which appeared in Punch in May, 1905, represents Kaiser William II theatrically posed in Moslem robes, thus satirising his attitude as the friend and protector of the Moslem peoples.

By permission of the proprietors of 'Punch'

the British case to investigation by an American commission, which confirmed the British claims on every point; a diplomatic concession which went far towards setting the relations between the two great English-speaking nations on a more harmonious footing.

The improved sentiment was confirmed by a quarrel between the United States and Spain—the first armed collision between the western republic and a European state since the Anglo-American war of 1812–14. The island of Cuba was under the Spanish crown, and Spaniards governed or misgoverned it, though only a fraction of the population was Spanish. The Americans had considerable commercial interests in Cuba, where trade and production were brought almost to a standstill by repeated insurrections and attempts to suppress them by drastic but very unsuccessful methods. Should the United States intervene—by the same warrant that the Concert periodically claimed to intervene in Turkey?

American public opinion was divided as to the expediency of going beyond vigorous protest; non-intervention seemed to have definitely carried the day in January, 1898; and then in February the American warship Maine, lying in the harbour of Havana, was blown up. The Spanish government inquired, and satisfied itself that the thing was a pure accident in which no Spaniard was concerned; the American public was entirely convinced to the contrary.

The Spanish-American War

On April 22 war was declared. On August 12 peace was signed. At the outset an American squadron annihilated the Spanish squadron in the Philippines, where the Filipinos were in revolt. The Spanish West India squadron was annihilated in July a fortnight before the capture of Santiago. Porto Rico was practically, though not completely, conquered, and Manilla was on the eve of surrender when the peace terms were signed—it fell the next day, the news of the peace arriving later. Any disposition on the part of European powers to intervene was effectually damped by the certainty that such action would bring the British fleet into the picture.

The United States annexed Porto Rico and the Philippines—where, however, the Filipinos, who had risen against the Spaniards for their own independence, maintained a prolonged resistance to an equally alien if more enlightened domination. Cuba was made an independent republic, and, failing in the task of self-government, lost its independence a few years later. Europe and America were already in contact on the east of Asia. To be involved in the political complications of the Old World was still the last thing that America desired; whether she would be able to preserve her isolation was already becoming doubtful.

A question was soon to arise in regard to which she could not wholly maintain her aloofness.

Great Britain and France reached their mutual understanding, their 'entente,' in

1904. Both powers had interests in Morocco, both had interests in Egypt; each recognized in effect that the other should have a free hand in the country where her interests were paramount. Their agreement, which was not an alliance, was laid before the Triple Alliance, and no objections to it were raised. But the kaiser had for some time been posing as the friend of Moslem peoples in general —both Russia and Great Britain had a vast number of Mahomedan subjects. In 1905 it became apparent to Germany that the interests of the sultan of Morocco as well as those of Germany in Morocco required protection from France's peaceful penetration. Incidentally, Russia was having a bad time in her struggle with Japan, and France could not count upon effective support from that quarter. Unless Great Britain supported her she would have to give way.

When it became apparent that Great Britain would stand loyal, Germany proposed that the question should be dealt with by a conference. The proposal was accepted, though it involved the resignation of the French foreign minister, Delcassé. The Conference of Algeciras was held in 1906, all the powers, including the United States, participating. Germany's demands were supported by Austria alone. It appeared, however, that she was satisfied with the result, while no one suggested that she had met with a rebuff, though for practical purposes the position of the French in Morocco was confirmed.

The conference was preluded by the sanctioning in Germany of a huge programme of naval construction; on the other hand, only a year later, the entente between Great Britain and France was supplemented by the entente between Great Britain and Russia, already the ally of France; while at the conference Italy had rather significantly affirmed the identity of her interests with those of England. It was not clear how far Italy regarded herself as committed to support the policy of her imperial allies.

Thus the grouping of the powers and their attitudes towards each other had

REPRESENTATIVES OF THE POWERS MEET AT THE CONFERENCE OF ALGECIRAS
Germany's objection to French action in Morocco secured the convocation of an international conference at Algeciras to discuss the regulation of Moroccan affairs. Lasting from January 16 to April 7, 1906, the conference, under the presidency of Spain, resulted in an agreement being signed that accorded France her privileged position in the country and provided for the sultan of Morocco's acceptance of France's proposed administrative reforms.
Photo, Topical Press Agency

KING GEORGE V
Born June 3, 1865, King George V succeeded to the throne of Great Britain, May 6, 1910, and was crowned June 22, 1911. This portrait of his Majesty as admiral of the Fleet was taken shortly before his coronation.
Photo, Thomson & Co.

changed materially in the four years 1903–7. At the beginning (as also at the end) Germany and Austria were balanced against France and Russia; while the security of the central alliance against Franco-Russian aggression was guaranteed by the actual adherence of Italy and by the constant friction between the Dual Alliance and Great Britain. At the end Russian prestige and self-confidence had suffered a shattering blow, in itself a sufficient guarantee against aggressive action on her part; but the friction with Great Britain had passed, while between Great Britain and Germany friction had undoubtedly set in. The expectation, little short of certainty, that the maritime power would operate against Franco-Russian aggression had given place to the still more confident expectation that it would operate against Teutonic aggression, while little but neutrality could be looked for from Italy if the Central powers should be the aggressors. That was the lesson of the Algeciras episode.

If, then, each group suspected the other of aggressive intent, the one security against a general conflagration was the consciousness on both sides of the doubtfulness of the issue; whereof the corollary was that one side at least was resolved to ensure beforehand that the issue should not be doubtful. At the same time, there were in the Balkans uncontrollable factors which might at any moment upset the calculations of the most acute statesmen.

Declaration of Bulgarian Independence

EUROPE, then, in 1908 was staging for a new drama, in which the first act was unexpectedly opened by the Young Turks. Their organization had secured the support of the army at Salonica; in July they suddenly demanded the long-promised constitution which had never materialised. The sultan promptly acceded. The powers hopefully withdrew their supervisors from Macedonia, to give the reformers free play. Consequently, in October, Ferdinand of Bulgaria judged that his time had come; he proclaimed the complete independence of Bulgaria, and assumed the ancient title of tsar. Two days later Austria announced the annexation of her protectorate in Bosnia, in defiance of the undertakings under which the protectorate had been established. This was very definitely the concern of Russia. But beside Austria, in the kaiser's significant phrase, stood Germany 'in shining armour'; after brief hesitation, Russia acquiesced.

If the Central powers had been checked at Algeciras, they recovered now more than they had lost then. But the price was the intensification of Slavonic hostility to the German-Magyar domination over the Slavs in the Austrian empire. It was generally believed that the Austrian heir-presumptive favoured a constitutional reconstruction which would have placed the three races on an equal footing; but the ascendancy party was too strong to allow such a solution to be attempted; the racial antipathy was fostered by pan-Slavism within and without the Empire, and the fruit thereof was bitter.

For two years there was no further move. Each of the Entente powers had its own domestic troubles. England was in the thick of a prolonged constitutional crisis, in the course of which Edward VII died, and was succeeded by George V; conflict raged round the powers of the House of Lords, arising from the unexpected exercise of their technical right to reject the financial proposals of the Liberal government, which were carried in the Commons by the support of the Irish parliamentary party. The strife was marked by exceptional bitterness, which increased in virulence when, after two general elections within twelve months, which proved the parties within Great Britain to be of all but equal strength, the Irish group obviously held the scale; and the Liberals held that their pledge in 1905 to suspend their avowed Home Rule policy was no longer valid.

At the same time one section of the British press was crying aloud that the British navy was no match for the German navy, while another section was proclaiming with equal fervour that expenditure on naval construction was blatant folly. Also in India (see Chap. 167) the Morley-Minto scheme was introduced, admitting Indians to the enlarged provincial councils, exciting lively opposition among British officials and residents in India; while it was accompanied by a highly seditious agitation in the vernacular press, which was treated by the Indian government with what was zealously denounced as pusillanimous leniency or intolerable tyranny according to the predilections of the critic.

Between factions at home and Indian unrest, it did not appear that any formidable intervention in European affairs on England's part was to be looked for, whatever her commitments to the other Entente powers might be. Russia's weakness had been manifested by the Bosnian affair. In 1911 Germany made the real testing move. France's paramount interest in Morocco had been recognized at Algeciras and later by separate agreements both with Spain and with Germany. But the sultan of Morocco was totally incapable of controlling his turbulent subjects; anarchy in Morocco had its repercussions upon the tribesmen of Algeria; and in the spring of that year France marched troops to the capital for the defence of the sultan and the restoration of order. On the assumption that this was merely a preliminary to the partition of Morocco between France and Spain, Germany dispatched the corvette Panther to Agadir (July), an unmistakable threat of war.

GERMAN CRUISER AT AGADIR

The dispatch of the German gunboat Panther to Agadir, Morocco, in 1911 was a minatory gesture that came near to evoking war. The Panther was shortly replaced by the German cruiser Berlin, which this photograph from a contemporary journal shows at anchor beneath the walls of the old fortress.

Photo. André Morizet

It appeared, however, very shortly that this was by no means what Germany intended. In the interval the minister in England, Lloyd George, who was at that time credited with being the most zealous of pacifists, made a speech which in the view of pacifists was almost truculent. Thereupon the Agadir incident was explained away. Germany was only anxious lest her commercial interests in Morocco should be prejudiced by the French domination, for which fears a portion of the French Congo territory would be adequate compensation. The agreement was duly signed in November, and harmony was officially restored.

MEANWHILE, however, war had broken out in another quarter—war with which neither the Central powers nor the Entente could claim to be directly concerned. When France occupied Tunis, Italy had been in some degree placated by the recognition of her own paramount interests in Tripoli. This, however, did not prevent peaceful penetration by German commerce and the development of German influence, which threatened to supersede that of Italy, which could only be saved by the declaration of a formal protectorate. The Young Turks, moreover, were doing their best to undermine all infidel influences. Italy demanded from the Porte, the nominal suzerain of Tripoli, the recognition of her own protectorate; acquiescence was not immediately following, and she declared war on Turkey (September, 1911).

Twelve months of desultory maritime warfare followed. Italy occupied the Tripolitan coast towns, and seized islands in the Aegean whereby she annoyed the Greeks, in whose eyes Aegean islands were 'Hellas irredenta.' Austria would not allow her to seize territory on the Balkan mainland, the war was expensive and unprofitable, and in October, 1912, peace was made which left her in possession of

A MOMENTOUS OCCASION IN THE BRITISH HOUSE OF COMMONS

General uneasiness was caused throughout Europe by Germany's action in the matter of the Agadir incident. On November 27, 1911, Sir Edward Grey, who was foreign secretary at the time, made a speech which demonstrated that the pacifist intentions of the government must not be misinterpreted as indicating invertebracy in regard to matters of principle. Occupants of the front bench, from left to right, are Winston Churchill, Lloyd George, Sir Edward Grey, H. H. Asquith and Sydney Buxton.

Drawing by Cyrus Cuneo in 'Illustrated London News'

TERRITORIAL CHANGES EFFECTED IN THE BALKANS BETWEEN 1878 AND 1914
The map on the left shows the distribution of the various Balkan States after the San Stefano treaty of 1878, when the independence of Rumania, Serbia and Montenegro was recognized and an autonomous Bulgaria, tributary to Turkey, was established. The map on the right gives the reconstruction after the Balkan Wars of 1912–13, wherein Greece received Macedonia, Albania became independent, Serbia was enlarged and part of Thrace went to Bulgaria, who ceded much of Dobruja to Rumania.

Tripoli and her captures in the Aegean, while the doubtful bonds which held her to the Triple Alliance had been loosened.

ALMOST at the moment when Turkey and Italy were signing the peace, four Balkan states were declaring war on Turkey, where the Young Turks had thoroughly established their ascendancy, exiled Abdul Hamid and set in his place his feeble-minded brother Mohammed V, but had by no means dissolved the amity with Germany. Their rule in Macedonia was no more to the liking of the independent Balkan states than that of Abdul Hamid. The Cretan leader, Venizelos, had now become the trusted minister of the king of the Hellenes. Mainly through his diplomacy, Greece, Bulgaria, Serbia and Montenegro reconciled their differences and united in the Balkan League with a view to the liberation and absorption of Macedonia upon agreed lines, as an alternative to its erection into an independent state; the various negotiations between state and state having been conducted separately without any of the powers being privy thereto. This point was reached before midsummer in 1912.

At that moment the Albanians, whom no one, Mahomedan or Christian, had ever been able to rule except by sheer force of a dominating personality like Skanderbeg, revolted against the Turkish governors, whose troops mutinied and either joined the rebels or broke before them, and the Albanians began to invade Macedonia. At Constantinople the Young Turks, who were held responsible, were turned out of office. In September the new League appealed to the powers to intervene; the powers remonstrated, but forbade the League to move; but by the middle of October war had been declared between Turkey and all the states of the League.

There followed, before the Concert could recover from its astonishment, an amazing débâcle. The old Turkish army had been broken up, and a new one was in course of organization under German officers—but it was not yet organized. Each of the League states had its allotted task. The Greek fleet swept the seas; in the western area the Serbs routed the

Turks in one battle after another ; in the eastern the Bulgars were threatening Constantinople and investing Adrianople. Before the end of November the Greeks only just anticipated the Bulgars in capturing and occupying Salonica. Then the powers stepped in ; there was a brief armistice ; a conference in London was apparently on the point of achieving a settlement, when the Young Turks suddenly recovered control at Constantinople and rejected the peace terms. The fighting started again (February) ; Janina, Adrianople, Scutari fell in

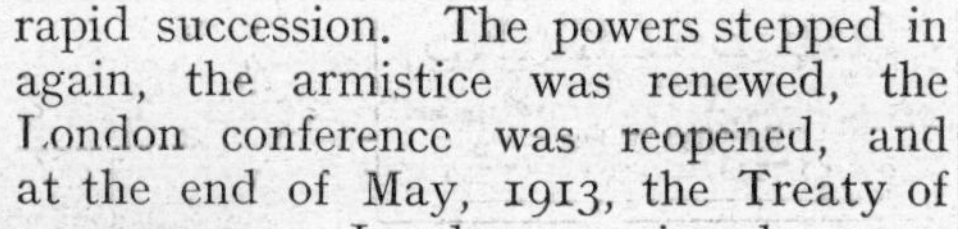

rapid succession. The powers stepped in again, the armistice was renewed, the London conference was reopened, and at the end of May, 1913, the Treaty of London was signed.

Much as after Japan's triumphant victory over China, the powers which had merely looked on and written notes arranged matters according to their own ideas, to the unmitigated dissatisfaction of every one of the states which had shared the triumphs of the war. But the most—and most justly—dissatisfied was Bulgaria, which had been allotted

Eleutherios Venizelos

Mohammed V of Turkey

George of Greece

Ferdinand of Bulgaria

Peter of Serbia

Nicholas of Montenegro

Carol of Rumania

RULERS OF THE RESTLESS STATES INVOLVED IN THE BALKAN WARS

Liberation of Macedonia from Turkish rule was the primary object of the Balkan League formed in the summer of 1912. Bulgaria and Serbia first entered into a military convention against Turkey ; Montenegro adhered to Serbia and Greece joined the League later. After the victorious conclusion of the first Balkan War disagreements arose, and in January, 1913, the second Balkan War broke out, Bulgaria pitted against Serbia and Greece ; in July Rumania also intervened against Bulgaria.

Photos, Boucas and Exclusive News Agency

TURKISH SOLDIERS ON THE MARCH NEAR ADRIANOPLE

Adrianople, on the Sofia-Constantinople railway near the Bulgarian frontier, was Turkey's chief fortress in Europe and, barring as it did the road to Constantinople, was the first objective of Bulgarian attack in the Balkan war. It was held by a force of 60,000 Turks, and in October, 1912, was completely invested by the Bulgarians. The investment was maintained during the armistice, and siege operations were renewed in February, 1913. On March 26 the fortress succumbed to a combined assault by 100,000 Bulgarians and Serbians.

Photo, T. J. Damon, Constantinople

the hardest task, achieved the most striking victories and got next to nothing for her pains. In an evil hour Bulgaria resolved to remedy the injustice by a sudden attack (June 29) on Serbia, to which had been allotted portions of Macedonia that she regarded as rightfully her own. The Serbs defeated the Bulgars, the Greeks came in to the support of the Serbs, Rumania joined in on her own account, and the last state of Bulgaria was worse than the first.

In August she was compelled to accept the Treaty of Bukarest, whereby she lost territory to Rumania, to Serbia, to Greece and finally to Turkey. Before, if she had not the spoils she had at least the honours. Her tragic blunder had lost her the honours, and subjected her to actual spoliation ; but it

KING GEORGE OF GREECE IN SALONICA

Hostilities between Greece and Bulgaria nearly broke out over the possession of Salonica. The Greeks occupied the town on the morning of November 9, 1912, and refused admission to the Bulgarians, who arrived in the afternoon. But, giving way to a threat of force, they yielded it to the Bulgarians next day.

Photo, Illustrations Bureau

Notwithstanding the veto of the great powers who had constituted Albania an autonomous state, King Nicholas of Montenegro ordered the investment of Scutari, which was defended by Essad Pasha with some 30,000 Turks and Albanians. On April 22, 1913, Essad Pasha capitulated and surrendered the key to Prince Danilo, who, a few days later, carried it to his father at Cettinje,

Janina in Epirus, near the Albanian frontier, was famous from 1788 to 1818 as the stronghold of Ali Pasha, the tyrannical 'Lion of Janina.' It remained a Turkish stronghold, and in the first Balkan War was held by a large garrison. A Greek division arrived before the place in November, 1912, and, reinforced by troops released by the capture of Salonica, invested the fortress, delivered a general assault on March 5, 1913, and captured the town the following day.

SCUTARI AND JANINA FALL TO THE BALKAN LEAGUE

Photos, Illustrations Bureau

had done more. It had shattered the new accord among the Balkan states, and brought back the old atmosphere of brooding and vindictive suspicion.

The Central powers would have profited by Bulgaria's victory over the other members of the now shattered league, of which, on the other hand, the consolidation would have been particularly inconvenient for Austria. As matters stood, the state which gained most by the war was the one whose depression she most desired—Serbia. But Serbia had failed to gain access either to the Adriatic or the Aegean sea ; her want of a sea-board made it the easier to bring a strangling economic pressure to bear on her ; and she had been deprived of Monastir, which she had captured, and on the acquisition of which she and Greece and Bulgaria were all set. Monastir would be a bone of contention calculated to keep alive the mutual jealousies and suspicions of the Balkan states, which were all to Austria's advantage, since it had been her purpose to open for herself the way to the Aegean, which would be blocked to her as long as they remained even superficially united. And while Bulgaria, and possibly Greece, might be won over, Serbia was at once the main obstacle to

COLONEL ENVER BEY

Enver Bey (1882–1922) was a foremost leader of the Young Turks. In July, 1913, he recovered Adrianople from the Bulgarians, to whom it had been ceded by the Treaty of London.

CROWD OUTSIDE THE SUBLIME PORTE DURING THE YOUNG TURK COUP D'ETAT

Reconstruction of the Turkish Empire and complete Turkification of its peoples were the objects of the political organization known as the Young Turks. Their secret Committee of Union and Progress was formed in 1905, Colonel Enver Bey holding the foremost place in it. In February, 1913, by a sudden coup d'état they overthrew the Kiamil cabinet nominally over the question of the surrender of Adrianople, and with but little unrest set up a Young Turk government in its place.

GUN RUNNING IN IRELAND JUST BEFORE THE GREAT WAR

Civil war in Ireland was imminent in the summer of 1914, and gun runners were boldly supplying the nationalists with arms and ammunition. One specially notable incident occurred on July 26, when some three thousand rifles were landed at the Hill of Howth, about eighty miles from Dublin. The National Volunteers of Ireland, marching with their newly landed rifles to Dublin, were intercepted by a battalion of the King's Own Scottish Borderers, but resisted an attempt to disarm them.

Photo, Sport & General Press Agency

the Austrian expansion, and the external focus of Slavonic sentiment which was the most disintegrating influence within the heterogeneous Austrian empire.

THE motives which actuate governments and those which actuate their peoples at moments of crisis are not necessarily the same, though the peoples may be unconscious of the difference—the more in those countries where the governments do not derive their authority directly from the people. It is not difficult to believe in the genuine conviction of the German people that the Entente was a grand conspiracy, born of political vindictiveness and begotten of commercial jealousy, for the overthrow of Germany; that the organization of the nation for war was nothing more than necessary preparation for self-defence, and that when the Central powers flung down the challenge it was only because no other course was open to them. But it is not possible to credit the German government with the same belief, or to doubt that it chose its own moment under the impression that it would have only France and Russia to fight and would be able to wipe France off the board before Russia could come into action effectively. Nor is it easy to doubt that the kaiser and his entourage, like Napoleon a century before, were deliberately aiming at a world domination, that Algeciras, Bosnia and Agadir were all moves intended to test the strength of the opposing combination, and that the mastery of the Near East was regarded as the key to the situation.

In the affairs of Algeciras and Agadir the British attitude had been disturbing; England, without acknowledging the existence of any formal alliance, had manifested a determination to stand by France if she were made the definite object of aggression. England had indeed professed her own warm desire for such a mutual understanding with Germany as she had already reached with France and Russia, her readiness to do her best to facilitate a similar understanding between the two empires and the other Entente powers, and even to pledge herself to neutrality should the latter take aggressive action against the Central powers; but she had firmly declined to pledge herself to neutrality should the Central powers be the aggressors.

But in 1914 a change had apparently befallen. England was paralysed. The Irish question had reached such a pitch of intensity that Ulster was proclaiming her right to resist in arms her subordination to an Irish national parliament and executive, half England was declaring that Ulster was in the right, and officers of high standing in the army were openly asserting that they would refuse to act against Ulster. Civil war was in the air. A Liberal government was in office, and it was the established belief of European chancelleries that Liberal governments were peace-at-any-price governments. All the circumstances being taken into consideration, the risk of England being drawn into a European war was small, and if she did come in, her army was small and apparently mutinous, her fleet, according to her own vociferous publicists, was inefficient, either Nationalist Ireland or Ulster would seize the opportunity to revolt—England was probably off the board altogether; if she were not, she might give some trouble, but the risk was worth taking.

The hour, then, had come for striking. The Bismarck tradition required that an occasion should be manufactured, and that the occasion should have at least the appearance of being an unwarrantable aggression by the party that was in fact being attacked.

The occasion arose in June, 1914. The archduke Francis Ferdinand, heir presumptive to the Austrian imperial crown, the

EMPEROR WILLIAM II

From his accession as German emperor in 1888 until his abdication, November 9, 1918, William II was a restless and disturbing figure in Europe owing to his military preoccupations and ambitions. This photograph was taken in 1913.

Photo, Voigt

VICTIMS OF THE TRAGEDY THAT PRECIPITATED THE GREAT WAR

Archduke Francis Ferdinand, heir to the Austrian imperial throne, accompanied by his wife, paid a visit to Serajevo, the chief town of Bosnia, on June 28, 1914. On their way to the Town Hall a bomb was thrown into their car; this the archduke himself threw away on to the road, where it exploded. When they had left the Town Hall, only two or three minutes after this photograph was taken, a Bosnian high-school student fired two shots at the royal pair, instantly killing them both.

Photo, Walter Tausch

prince who was generally believed to be Slavophil, was assassinated in the streets of the Bosnian city of Serajevo. The assassins were Austrian subjects but they were Serbs. The murder, then, must be a Serbian plot fostered by the Serbian government. It was indeed not difficult to suggest an entirely different origin for the crime, since it could in no conceivable manner further Serbian or Slavonic interests; but the Austrian government had no doubts about the matter. Even at the best, the intolerable Slavonic propaganda emanating from Serbia must be at the bottom of the outrage. After a brief interval, on July 23, Austria sent to the Serbian government a series of demands acceptance of which would be a complete abrogation of Serbia's sovereignty. Austria was to be at once the accuser, the investigator and the judge, exacting such penalties as she thought fit. Serbia pleaded for appeal to the Hague Tribunal; Austria would have none of it.

Serbia, by herself, lay at Austria's mercy. But Austria's action was a direct challenge to Russia. If Russia failed to defend Serbia, that would be an end to the particular matter, but it would also be the end of Russian influence in the Balkans, and an intolerable humiliation in the sight of all the world. If she took up the challenge France could not withhold her support; Germany would uphold Austria as the aggrieved party. England, which was under no pledge, urged reference of the whole question to a European conference; Germany explained that in her view this was Austria's private affair. England offered mediation; Austria declined it. No one had a doubt that at a word from Germany Austria would waive her claim to be the sole arbiter, but the word was not forthcoming.

LICHNOWSKY'S LAST DAYS IN LONDON
Prince Charles Max Lichnowsky, appointed German Ambassador to the Court of St. James's in 1912, was consistently actuated by desire to improve Anglo-German relations. His dejection is reflected in this photograph of him leaving the Foreign Office the day before the ultimatum.

Outbreak of the Great War

On July 28 Austria declared war on Serbia. Russia, if she left Serbia to her doom, would cease to count as a European power. During the next two days Germany suggested that Britain should remain neutral if the outbreak of war should compel her to attack France via Belgium—whose neutrality all the powers were bound under the most solemn obligation to respect, as Bismarck had respected it in 1870. In the British view, however, those obligations were binding. On July 31 mobilisation orders were issued both in Austria and Russia. If, as it is possible to believe, there was still, as concerned Austria and Russia, some shadow of a chance of peace, it was obliterated by an ultimatum—on the same day—from Germany to Russia and to France. On the next day, August 1, she declared war on Russia. France, bound to take her stand by Russia, renewed her pledge to respect Belgium's neutrality, which Belgium declared her determination to maintain; Germany evaded the question—on which the British government resolved to stake its own action. On August 2 German troops entered Luxemburg and Germany declared war on France. On August 3 her troops entered Belgian territory. On that night the British ultimatum was sent to Germany. The violation of Belgium had welded the whole country into solid support of the government. On August 4 Great Britain declared war on Germany.

TABLE OF DATES FOR CHRONICLE XXXI

1878 Victor Emmanuel d.; acc. Humbert I.
Pius IX d.; acc. Leo XIII.
Berlin Congress and treaties. Complete independence of Serbia, Montenegro and Rumania; Bulgaria much reduced from the Russian plan; Bosnia a temporary Austrian protectorate; Russia takes Bessarabia, giving Rumania Dobruja; British protectorate in Cyprus.

1879 Macmahon resigns French Presidency; Bonapartism perishes with the death of the Prince Imperial in the British Zulu war; permanence of the French Republic gradually assured.
Alexander of Battenberg accepts principality of Bulgaria as the tsar's protégé.
Afghanistan: British legation at Kabul cut to pieces, beginning Afghan war.

1880 Afghan campaigns. After decisive victories the British retire, leaving Abd er-Rahman to establish himself as amir.
Gladstone ministry; Lord Ripon Indian viceroy.
U.S.A.: President Garfield assassinated.

1881 France, encouraged by Bismarck, occupies Tunis, causing friction with Italy.
Transvaal war; Transvaal retroceded to Boers.
Bulgaria: Prince Alexander's coup d'état.
Alexander II murdered by nihilists; acc. Alexander III.

1882 Italy joins in Triple Alliance with Germany and Austria.
Bombardment of Alexandria and overthrow of Arabi Pasha. Tewfik's government restored under British protectorate and control. Mahdi appears in Sudan.

1883 Alexander restores Bulgarian constitution and dismisses Russian advisers.

1884 India: Racial feeling aroused by Ilbert Bill. Lord Dufferin succeeds Ripon as viceroy.
General Gordon sent to the Sudan.
U.S.A.: Grover Cleveland elected president (1).

1885 Union of Rumelia with Bulgaria under Prince Alexander; Serbia declares war on Bulgaria, and is heavily defeated at Slivnitza.
Alfonso XII of Spain d.; acc. Alfonso XIII; regency of Maria Christina.
Penjdeh incident (collision of Russian and Afghan troops) smoothed over.
France acquires protectorate in Annam and Madagascar.
Fall of Gordon at Khartum; temporary abandonment of Sudan.

1886 Alexander of Bulgaria is kidnapped, and resigns. Bulgar government maintained under Stambulov.

1887 Agreed delimitation of Afghan, Indian and Russian frontiers. Annexation of Burma. First meeting of Indian 'National Congress.'
Bulgaria: Acc. Ferdinand of Saxe-Coburg.

1888 William I d.; acc. Frederick I, then William II.
U.S.A.: Benjamin Harrison president.
India: Lord Lansdowne viceroy.

1889 William II pays first state visit to the Sultan.

1890 William II dismisses Bismarck.
Anglo-German treaty delimiting spheres of influence in Africa.

1892 U.S.A.: Cleveland president (2).

1893 Serbia: Fall of Obrenovitch dynasty; acc. Peter Karageorgevitch.

1894 Alexander III d.; acc. Nicholas II.
France: Murder of President Sadi Carnot.
Bulgaria: Fall of Stambulov; Ferdinand takes control into his own hands.
India: Lord Elgin viceroy.
Chino-Japanese war; defeat of China. Treaty of Shimonoseki. The powers intervene to scramble for Chinese concessions.

1894-6 Turkey: Armenian massacres and insurrections.

1895 Franco-Russian agreement, developing into Dual Alliance, balancing central Triple Alliance.
S. Africa: the Jameson Raid.

1896 Final Armenian massacres; the Kaiser compliments Abdul Hamid.
U.S.A.: Venezuelan-British boundary dispute submitted to American arbitration. McKinley elected president.

1897 First German naval programme.
Cretan revolt helped by Greeks; stopped by the powers (Germany and Austria abstaining) who guarantee Cretan autonomy. Greek invasion of Thessaly totally defeated by Turks.
The European powers demand and obtain concessions in China, where hostility to foreigners raises the Boxer rebellion.

1898 China: Empress-dowager usurps power, deposing the emperor.
The tsar assembles first Hague Conference.
American-Spanish war; complete defeat of Spain; U.S.A. annex Philippines.
Re-conquest of Sudan. The Fashoda incident; irritation in France against England.
India: Lord Curzon viceroy.

1899 S. Africa: Boers invade Natal; beginning of South African war (Oct.).

1900 China: European legations in Peking besieged by Chinese 'rebels.'
Germany: Great development of naval programme.

1901 Commonwealth of Australia established.
Queen Victoria d.; acc. Edward VII.
China: International forces march on Peking and relieve the legations; submission of the Chinese government.
U.S.A.: Murder of President McKinley; Theodore Roosevelt succeeds to the presidency.

1902 Germany obtains Bagdad railway concession from Turkey.
Anglo-Japanese treaty of alliance.
End of South African war.

1903 Tariff reform agitation in England intensifies German suspicions of British hostility.

1904 Japan declares war on Russia (Feb.); Yalu battle and siege of Port Arthur (Ap.); Russians driven back on Mukden; Russian fleet destroyed (Aug.); Russian defeat on Sha-ho (Nov.).
Anglo-French entente adjusting outstanding causes of friction.
U.S.A.: Roosevelt president (2).
India: Lord Minto viceroy.

1905 Japan: Port Arthur surrenders (Jan.); Russians driven from Mukden (Feb.); new Russian squadron annihilated (May); war ended by treaty of Portsmouth (Aug.).

1906 Responsible government restored in Transvaal and Orange River Colony.
Germany submits a dispute with France supported by England (Morocco) to Algeciras conference.

1907 Anglo-Russian adjustment; the Triple Entente.

1908 The 'Young Turks' compel Abdul Hamid to concede a constitution. Ferdinand proclaims independence of Bulgaria and assumes title of tsar. Austria, supported by Germany, announces annexation of Bosnia; Russia has to acquiesce.
U.S.A.: Election of President Taft.

1909 Indian Councils Act.
Abdul Hamid deposed by Young Turks; acc. Mohammed V (Mehmed Reshed).

1910 Union of South Africa established.
Edward VII d.; acc. George V.
India: Lord Hardinge viceroy.

1911 The king-emperor George V visits India; Delhi reinstated as capital of the Indian Empire.
Italy demands protectorate of Tripoli; Turco-Italian war. Italy annexes Tripoli.
Agadir incident; immediate threat of war averted.

1912 Venizelos organizes the Balkan League. Albanian revolt. War declared between League states and Turkey (Sept.); Turkish débâcle; armistice (Nov.).
Chinese imperial dynasty ends; Chinese republic.
U.S.A.: Woodrow Wilson elected president.

1913 Balkan war renewed; stopped by powers. Treaty of London (May); Bulgaria attacks Serbia (June) and is totally defeated. Treaty of Bukarest (Aug.).

1914 Irish crisis.
June 28: Francis Ferdinand murdered at Serajevo.
July 23: Austrian ultimatum to Serbia; 28: War declared on Serbia; 31: Austria and Russia mobilise.
Aug. 1: Germany declares war on Russia; 3: Germany declares war on France; 4: Great Britain declares war on Germany.

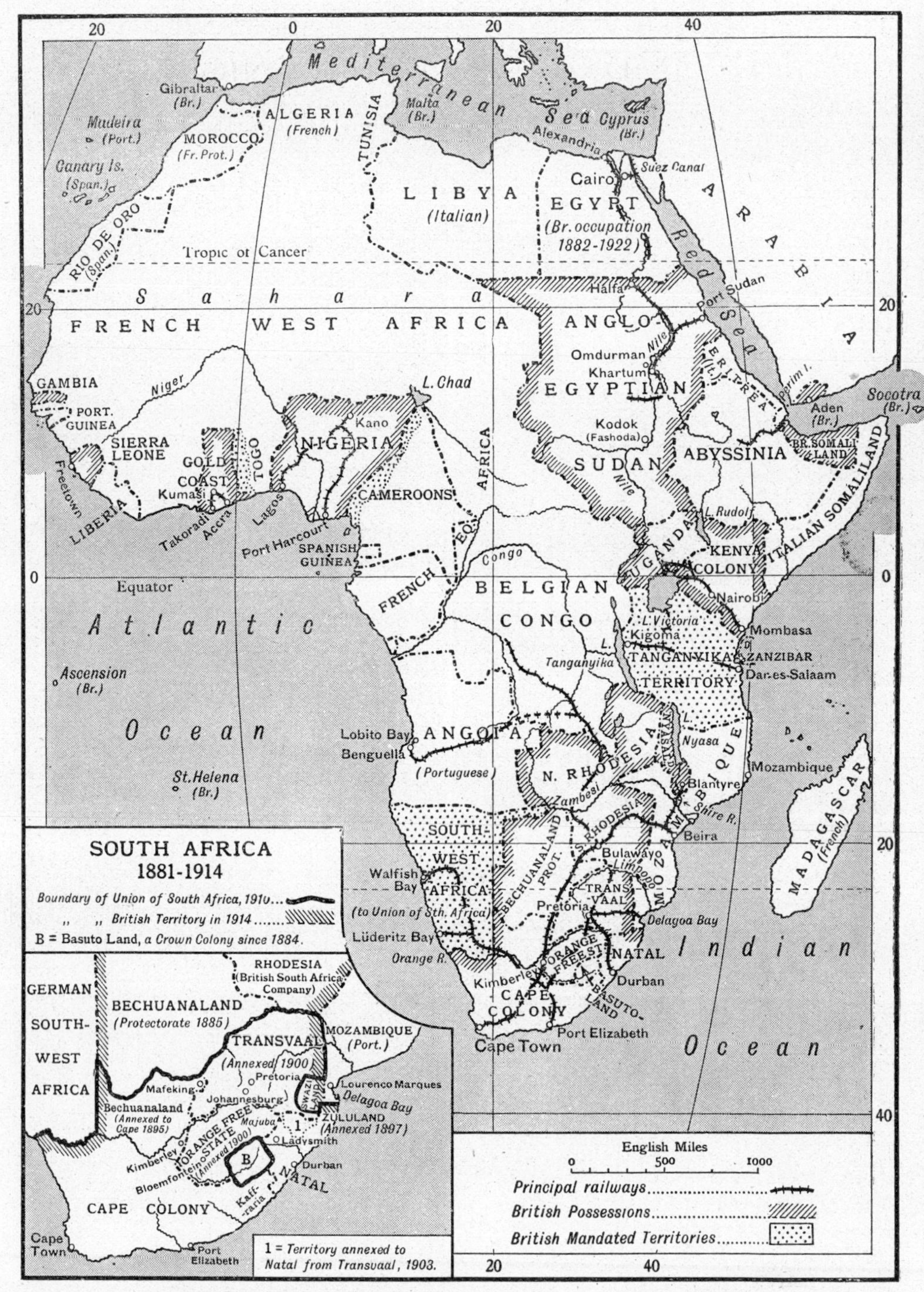

BRITISH EXPANSION IN AFRICA DURING FORTY YEARS

Long friction between the British and Dutch culminated in the annexation of the Orange Free State and the Transvaal Republic in 1900 and the constitution of the Union of South Africa in 1910. German South-West Africa was entrusted to the Union under mandate after the Great War. Southern Rhodesia was given responsible government in 1923, and, with Tanganyika, ceded to Britain under mandate, British control in Africa extended from the Cape to Cairo. In West Africa the Gold Coast and Nigeria were also expanded by mandated territory.

CHAPTER 172

THE BRITISH EMPIRE: AN HISTORICAL STUDY

How the Lessons learnt in a tragic Colonial Failure were used for building up a Commonwealth of Nations

By REGINALD COUPLAND

Beit Professor of Colonial History in the University of Oxford and Fellow of All Souls College; Author of Wilberforce, Raffles, etc.

IN 1763 the territories under British rule outside the British Isles consisted of four groups of colonies or dependencies. Of these, by far the most important was the North American group. It comprised, first, Newfoundland, the oldest colony, founded in 1583; secondly, the thirteen colonies along the Atlantic coast, containing an almost wholly British population of about two million; and thirdly, a vast and largely unexplored domain to the north, ceded to Britain by France in 1763 as the result of the Seven Years' War, including Acadia (now Nova Scotia), the islands of Ile Royal and St. Jean (now Cape Breton and Prince Edward Islands), and the large province of Quebec, stretching from the outlet of the St. Lawrence to the Great Lakes and inhabited by some 70,000 French colonists, to which may be added the little fur-trade settlements established on the west of Hudson Bay by the Hudson's Bay Company. The North American group also included, for a time, the Spanish colonies of East and West Florida, ceded to Britain in 1763.

The second group was the West Indian group—the Bahamas and the British Caribbean islands, of which the largest was Jamaica, together with the Bermudas out in the ocean northwards and two strips of the Central American sea-board known as Honduras and the Mosquito Coast. In this group may be included at that time the handful of British trading posts on the west coast of Africa, since, as will presently appear, they formed one economic system with the West Indies.

The third group lay in Asia. Since its foundation in 1600 the East India Company, which enjoyed a monopoly of the Indian trade, had built up a highly successful commercial system in India. But about the middle of the eighteenth century it was forced, almost despite itself, from commerce into politics (see Chronicle XXVII and Chapter 166), and by 1765 was virtually master of eastern India from Bengal to Travancore. Though these huge territories were not yet de jure British territories, they were part of the British Empire. Outside continental India the company's activities were confined to one small trading post at Bencoolen on the west coast of Sumatra.

Fourth and last, there was a little group of strategic naval stations, occupied to safeguard the maintenance of British sea power over the main trade routes. It included Gibraltar and Minorca in the Mediterranean, and in the Atlantic St. Helena, and a post in the Falkland Islands.

The First British Empire

The ground plan of the first British Empire was thus far smaller than that of the second British Empire as it stands to-day. But, relatively limited as it was, the first British Empire was still an immense structure, sprawling far across the world, its component parts separated by thousands of miles of sea. If distance, indeed, be judged by the time spent in transit, the gaps were much wider than they are now; and the modern student, looking back to those days of sailing ships, may well wonder how that straggling fabric could possibly be held together in any single frame. And certainly the men of 1763 were confronted with a very difficult task—so difficult that it proved, if not perhaps too much for their strength, at any rate too much for their minds.

On what principles, with what purpose in view, did they try to hold it together? The answer to that question is simple. They regarded the overseas Empire as a field of trade and virtually nothing else. The outcome was not unnatural. Chained to the economic standpoint, unable to think about the Empire except in the familiar commercial terms, British statesmen failed to envisage, and still more to deal with, the other aspects of the imperial question. Yet, deeply rooted in that unwieldy structure lay political and moral problems no less vital to its life and welfare than the problems of profit and loss.

Except in the fourth area, that little group of strategic posts which, being maintained for purely naval purposes, lay apart from the other groups under military government, the result of this failure of vision was disastrous throughout the Empire. But it was a different result in accordance with the different character of each of the three other groups—the North American, the West Indian and West African, and the East Indian. The American colonies stood in a class by themselves, and the political blunders that led to the War of Independence (Chronicle XXVII) are accordingly dealt with in Chapter 152. In the upshot the greater part of the first British Empire—the really 'colonial' part, the British part, with all its possibilities of development and expansion across the wide, rich, untouched spaces of the North American continent—broke away. The attempt to maintain communities of Englishmen separated by the Atlantic in one political society had ended in utter failure.

In the other two sections of the Empire, in the British West Indies and West Africa, and in British India, the disaster was moral rather than political. It did not involve

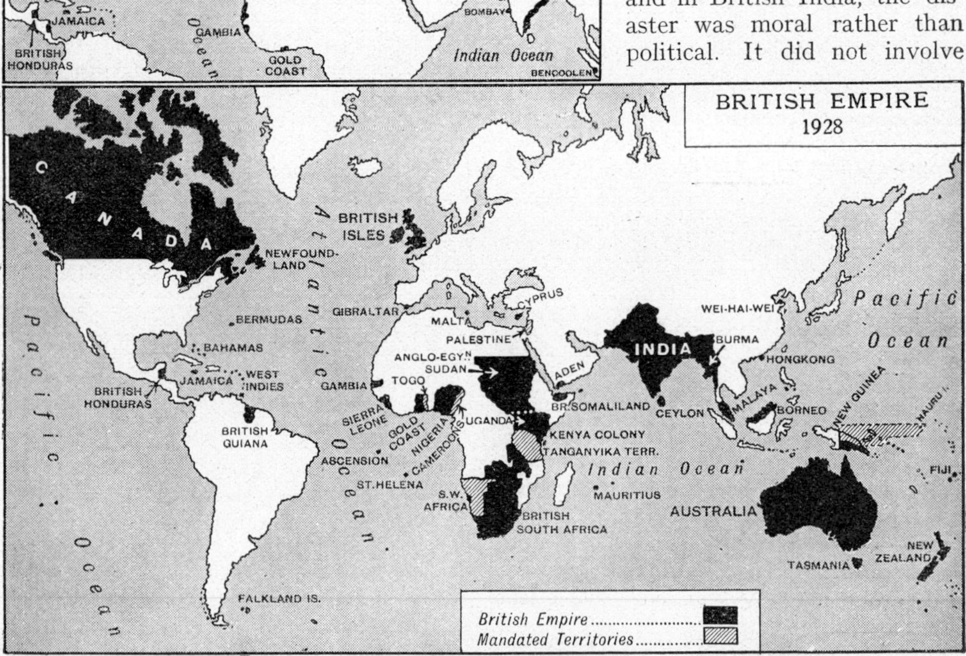

GROUND PLAN OF THE FIRST AND SECOND BRITISH EMPIRES

With the wresting of Canada from the French in 1763 the first British Empire reached its fullest extension; with the separation of the North American colonies in 1783 it virtually ceased to exist. The lower map, drawn to the same scale, shows the astonishing recovery effected by wiser statesmanship. In less than 150 years the second British Empire absorbed Australia and the upper portion of North America, and, with its possessions in India and Africa, covered more than one fifth of the globe.

rebellion and separation but degradation, not loss of territory but loss of honour.

The English plantations in the West Indies, like those in the more southerly American colonies, had been faced from the outset with a labour problem. Under a tropical or sub-tropical sun continuous hard work out-of-doors is impossible for white men, and the economic exploitation of such areas has always depended on a supply of labour by coloured races. Neither in the West Indies nor in the southern American colonies was an adequate supply obtainable on the spot. The Red Indians were wholly unsuited for the purpose. The Caribs and South American natives were too few and feeble. The cultivation of sugar and tobacco for European consumption would indeed have proved impracticable if the Portuguese, when exploring the west coast of Africa in the fifteenth century, had not discovered that this hitherto unknown continent was peopled in parts by a strong, healthy, prolific but primitive race of black men who could, with little risk or cost, be kidnapped or purchased from local chiefs or traders and sold as slaves overseas.

The other maritime nations of Europe were soon following where the Portuguese had led. And since the West African negroes were exactly the sort of labourers required on the trans-Atlantic plantations, their growth coincided with—was indeed only made possible by—the growth of a great trans-Atlantic slave trade. And Britain, though slow to join in the trade, soon acquired, once in it, the lion's share. At the period of the American Revolution about fifty per cent. of the slaves were carried in British ships. Nothing could better illustrate the basic defect of the old-fashioned mercantile imperialism. Men accepted this establishment of British colonies on a foundation of labour obtained by force or fraud from Africa because it seemed economically sound and even necessary. Beyond the economic issue they scarcely thought of looking. That a gigantic moral issue had also been raised they were, for the most part, quite unaware.

Growth of the Slave Trade

What was the outcome of this West Indian system ? In the first place, slavery became an accepted institution in the British Empire. The number of slaves on British soil across the Atlantic steadily increased—creating, it may be mentioned in passing, a problem in the southern American colonies of which they could not rid themselves when they broke away from Britain and which still haunts the United States to-day. At one time there was even a danger of slavery taking root in England ; for a custom grew up among the planters of bringing their domestic slaves with them when they came home for a holiday or on retirement. There were actually more than 10,000 slaves in England when at length public opinion roused itself to combat it. As the result of the activities of Granville Sharp, the pioneer of a new humanitarian movement, the issue was raised in the courts in 1772, and Chief Justice Mansfield delivered the historic judgement that slavery could not legally exist on English soil. A similar judgement was shortly obtained in the Scottish courts ; and so, in Britain at least, every slave was freed and there could never be another. But slavery could still legally exist on British soil overseas. At the beginning of the nineteenth century there were nearly 800,000 slaves in the British West Indies.

Slavery illegal in England

The second result of the old West Indian system was still more evil. Slavery implied the slave trade. The total number of Africans transported oversea ran into several millions ; and almost as many must have died or been killed in the process. The slave trade, in fact, from its first operation to its last, was sheer cruelty. On the march in chained gangs to the coast many died of exhaustion or brutal treatment. On the slave ships they were packed so tight, on shelves between decks, that sometimes they could not lie flat on their backs ; and the conditions of their six weeks' voyage across the tropical Atlantic—known as the ' middle passage —were so indescribably bad that sometimes as many as a quarter of them died. Finally, arrived in port, they were doctored up and exposed for sale in the open market —some of them fetching high prices, others bundled together in ' parcels ' and sold cheap as ' refuse.'

The modern student of these eighteenth-century days cannot help asking how the slave trade could have been tolerated so long. It is easy to answer him. Economics smothered ethics. The slave trade was accepted even by humane and thoughtful Englishmen as an economic necessity. The West Indian colonies were a purely economic proposition. They existed to supply sugar and tobacco. For this supply slaves were necessary. And a second 'necessity' grew out of the first. British capital became deeply involved in the trade, the profits of which were so safe and large, being often as high as 30 per cent., that it was regarded as the most lucrative of all trades; and the ports of Liverpool especially, but also of Bristol and London, owed much of their prosperity to their share in it. Thus its continuance seemed a 'necessity' for British commerce. And out of these again grew a third 'necessity'—political necessity this time. To stop the trade, it was argued, would simply mean that the British share therein would be at once appropriated by Britain's ancient rival and enemy, France, and by other foreign states, and that Britain's mercantile marine, the nursery of her naval strength, would be proportionately diminished and the French increased.

Scarcely less grave, though happily far briefer in duration, were the evils resulting from the old conception of empire in British India. By 1765, as has been seen, the East India Company had become the virtual master of Bengal and other wide tracts of India. To statesmen of insight it should at once have been clear that this situation involved Britain in political responsibilities. To evade those responsibilities by pretending that the British government on the one hand was not concerned with the affairs of a private commercial company in India, and that the company on the other hand was still concerned with trade alone, was bound to lead to trouble. But so potent was the traditional theory of empire that even Clive and Chatham, with all their grasp of practical politics, succumbed to it.

Failing annexation to the British crown, the dangerous divorce of power from responsibility continued. And power without responsibility sets too hard a strain on the virtue of ordinary men. When Clive returned to England in 1760 the Company's officials, with the exception of the few men of honour and humanity among them, seized their chance. They did not merely accept 'presents' from native potentates, they extorted them. They interfered in the administration of the puppet nawab of

DISEMBARKATION OF A BATCH OF SLAVES

The enormous profits yielded by the slave trade to its controllers ensured its rapid growth in the eighteenth century. Under appalling conditions African negroes were shipped off to the West Indies, where their labour on the sugar and tobacco plantations was regarded by the British as an economic necessity.

From Stedman, 'Surinam.' 1776

Bengal and distributed offices in his government at a price. They insisted further on obtaining for their own private trading operations exemption from all transit dues, with the result that they soon began to monopolise the internal trade of the country and to ruin the native merchants. Under such conditions any approach to good government was quite impossible, and Bengal drifted fast into general licence and anarchy.

At last, the Company's directors, alarmed at the diminution of their revenues and of their shareholders' dividends, intervened. In 1765 Clive was sent out again as governor of Bengal. 'I shall only say,' he reported, 'that such a scene of anarchy, confusion, bribery, corruption, and extortion was never seen or heard of in any country but Bengal; nor such and so many fortunes acquired in so unjust and rapacious a manner.' Besides obtaining the Diwani (see page 4443) and establishing the so-called 'dual system,' he compelled every official to sign a pledge against accepting 'presents.' He enforced the payment of the transit dues on all their private trade. But these measures could only be effective as long as Clive was on the spot; and in 1767 he finally retired. At once the tide of oppression flowed back over Bengal. The dual system in dishonest hands made extortion even easier than before. It was not till 1772, when Warren Hastings was promoted to the governorship, that once more the tide was checked and the process of reform resumed.

Age of Misrule in India

For ten years—from 1760 to 1765 and from 1767 to 1772—British rule in India had been gross misrule. Nobody can whitewash that black decade. It can only be pleaded that it was the inevitable result of the old, unenlightened imperialism, that the British were no worse than other Europeans, and that, when their consciences had been awakened to the realities of the scandal, when the new imperialism replaced the old, they made the British government of India a better, purer and more efficient government than the Indian people had ever known.

In each of these fields, then, the first British Empire had proved a political or moral failure. It had failed politically in North America. It had failed morally in the West Indies, West Africa, and India. And the reason was quite plain. Trade is an essential factor in human relations and in the organization of any society; trade in itself is a good thing. But to make trade the sole or the dominating factor in human relationship, to regard its profits as the only motive of a society, is to seek to live by bread alone; trade by itself is a bad thing.

The Second British Empire

To nations, as to men, second chances are rarely offered; but such was the development of the world's history that the British people, having signally failed to construct the first British Empire on good and lasting foundations, were enabled to construct a second British Empire, and, profiting by the lessons of their failure, to make it far better and far more durable than the first. To-day, after nearly 150 years, it still exists.

In the course of a speech in which he recommended the House of Commons to accept the humiliating treaty that closed the American War of Independence, the son of Chatham called on his countrymen to face their losses bravely and make the most of what remained. 'Let us examine what is left,' said the younger Pitt, 'with a manly and determined courage . . . The misfortunes of individuals and of kingdoms that are laid open and examined with true wisdom are more than half redressed.' What, then, was there left? To begin with, besides Newfoundland, a great continental territory in North America was still subject to the British crown. When the thirteen colonies rose in revolt, they naturally aspired to win the whole continent to independence; but all their efforts failed to bring over the part which then included the islands off the St. Lawrence estuary, the peninsula of Nova Scotia and the great province of Quebec, and which now constitutes the eastern half of the Dominion of Canada.

They failed because in this one field of the Empire British ministers had shown a real understanding of the political situation and a real statesmanship in handling it. They recognized that the first need was to conciliate the French colonists, who formed the vast majority of the population, to British rule; but, in pursuit of this end, they were confronted by the problem of conflicting nationalities, which is all too familiar to our modern world. For on the heels of the conquering British army, into a country long populated by Catholic Frenchmen, who regarded their religion and their system of civil law as the hall-marks of their treasured nationality, had come a handful of British settlers, all Protestants, imbued with the hatred of Romanism which was traditional in New England, and mostly traders who found their prospects of commercial enterprise hampered by the lack of English law. Moreover, while the French Canadians, who had always been subject to the purely autocratic rule of the kings of France, had no knowledge or experience of self-government and no capacity or desire for it, the British newcomers maintained that at least such a measure of representative government as had long existed in the southward colonies was their inalienable birthright.

The problem in Canada

The British ministers wavered; but happily they were persuaded by the 'man on the spot,' Sir Guy Carleton, a great soldier and statesman, a friend of Wolfe and the second civil governor of Quebec, that to grant the British minority's demand, to replace the French law by English and to set up a representative assembly consisting of British Protestants alone, was not only a gross injustice to the French Canadians but an abandonment of the primary policy of conciliation. Accordingly, the same Lord North government which passed the unwise penal measures that precipitated the American Revolution passed, at the same moment, in 1774, the wise Quebec Act which confirmed the free exercise in Canada of the Roman Catholic religion, maintained the French-Canadian law, and continued the 'crown colony' system of government by a governor and nominated council. The British minority was bitterly disappointed; but the French Canadians, or at least the educated classes among them, recognized in the act a proof that the British government and Parliament were genuinely determined to tolerate and protect their nationality. Thus the keystone was preserved for a new imperial fabric, which was one day to bestride the North American continent and to point onwards over the Pacific.

It so happened that one of the results of the American Revolution was the

VIEW OF QUEBEC THE YEAR AFTER ITS CAPTURE FROM THE FRENCH

From 1663 until it was taken by the British in 1759 Quebec was the capital of French Canada. Its new rulers had therefore to decide their policy towards the French Canadians who composed the majority of its population. The wisdom of Sir Guy Carleton's conciliatory principles was recognized by the British government, and found expression in the Quebec Act of 1774, which confirmed the French colonists in their religion and law. This sketch of the intendant's palace is by Richard Shortt.

From Shortt & Doughty, 'Canada and its Provinces: Quebec.' Publishers' Assn. of Canada

provision of a kernel of British population for this vast and still mainly unoccupied territory. There had always been a minority in the thirteen colonies—'Tories' they were called—who clung to their old allegiance; and, at the close of the war, several thousands of them resolved to abandon their homes and begin a new life somewhere under the old flag. Some forty thousand of them crossed the border into Canada. Twenty-eight thousand settled in the western part of Nova Scotia, which was presently constituted a separate province called New Brunswick. Twelve thousand settled in Quebec, mostly in the wild upper country near Lake Ontario.

This latter immigration inevitably revived the question of nationality. The British settlers were now no longer a small and insignificant body; and they had a claim on the gratitude of the mother country. An official title of honour, United Empire Loyalists, was bestowed on them and they were compensated for the losses they had suffered. But was that enough? Could they be expected to accept the French regime of the Quebec Act? Were they to be deprived of the English law and those very forms of English liberty to which they had proved their devotion? It was a difficult problem, for clearly the French Canadians had also some claim on British good will; and Pitt's government decided to cut the knot. The Canada Act of 1791 divided the old Province of Quebec into two provinces, Upper and Lower Canada (corresponding to the present Ontario and Quebec). In the latter, where the bulk of the French Canadian population lived, the French system of law—the Quebec Act system—was retained. In the former, where the bulk of the loyalists had settled, English law was introduced.

Immigration of the Loyalists

In both, since it seemed impracticable to deny to one what was conceded to the other, representative institutions were set up. They were on the same limited scale as in the old, lost thirteen colonies; it was still 'representative' and not 'responsible' government; it was still purely local in its scope and provided no inter-provincial machinery nor any means of sharing in external or imperial affairs. If a clause had not been inserted in the act declaring that the Imperial Parliament would never again tax these colonies for revenue, it might almost have seemed as if the American Revolution had never happened. But it would be false to assume that the statesmen who framed the act had learned no lesson at all from the American disaster.

The real importance of the act was that its authors regarded it as only a beginning. Its object was, said Pitt in the House of Commons, 'to bring the government of the province as near as the nature and situation of it will admit to the British Constitution.' And his intimate political colleague, Dundas, was still more explicit. 'We will not pretend,' he said, 'to give Canada the same constitution as we ourselves live under. All we can do is to lay the foundation for the same constitution when increased population and time shall have made the Canadians ripe to receive it.' Those statements inaugurated a new epoch in British imperial history. For they tacitly admitted that British citizens in Canada had a right, in course of time, to the same political status as British citizens in Britain. In other words, the old mercantile principle of empire had been at least half abandoned.

Beginnings of Autonomy

Just at this time, moreover, the foundations were being laid of a new colonial structure in another continent. Though Britain had lost the command of the sea at one fatal crisis of the American War, she had recovered it by the Battle of the Saints (1782), so that when peace came the sea ways lay open to her and none could prevent the establishment of new British colonies in any unoccupied area in the world. The existence of such an area—vast, fertile and admirably suited for European settlement—in the Southern Seas at the other side of the earth had long been known to European explorers; and as recently as 1769–70 Captain Cook had made his famous voyage to New Zealand and Australia. The French were also sending expeditions thither at the same time with an eye to commercial or colonial expansion. Yet neither Britain nor France had ventured to attempt a settlement so far away; and Australasia might have remained yet longer unoccupied by white men if the American Revolution had not forced the question on the attention of the British government.

It had been customary to transport a large number of English convicts to work out their sentences on the plantations in the old American colonies; the Revolution had closed this area; a new one had somewhere to be found; and, after trying the west coast of Africa and discovering its climate to be fatal to the convicts' health, Pitt and his colleagues decided that, if Australia was not the best place for a loyalist colony, it might well be the best place for a penal settlement. If at first sight a penal settlement might seem a dubious foundation for a new colony, it must be remembered, first, that the old penal code was incredibly severe by modern standards and sentenced men to transportation for what would now be regarded as political or petty offences, and secondly that, very soon and in growing volume, free emigrants accompanied the convicts.

BOTANY BAY, NEW SOUTH WALES

Botany Bay was discovered by Captain Cook in 1770 and selected in 1787 as the site for a British penal settlement. Captain Phillip, who visited the place in 1788, considered it unsuitable for the purpose, and the scheme was carried out in the locality where Sydney now stands, five miles north of Botany Bay.

From Arthur Phillip, 'Voyage to Botany Bay'

From this first little foothold British colonisation was presently to spread over all Australia, across the ocean to New Zealand 1,200 miles away, and out among the myriad islands of the Pacific. Not only, therefore, was the character or the principles of the second British Empire in its colonial or strictly British field to be different from those of the old. The ground plan also was to be far wider.

A similar transformation was occurring at the same time in the other imperial fields. The growth of the humanitarian movement in England, led by the Quakers and high-minded men like Granville Sharp, was already beginning to threaten the mainstay of the West Indian and West African system—the slave trade—at the time of the American Revolution; and slavery itself was being condemned on moral grounds by religious philosophers like Paley and on material grounds by economists like Adam Smith. After the Revolution the attack took definite shape in the formation of an Abolition Society bent on the destruction of the trade. It was fortunate in enlisting the sympathies of two great men, William Wilberforce, an intimate friend of Pitt, who led the

A FAMOUS EXPLORER

The British owe their first foothold on the Australian continent to the voyages of Captain James Cook (1728–79), the daring commander who circumnavigated New Zealand and visited Australia. This portrait is by Nathaniel Dance.

Greenwich Hospital

campaign in Parliament, and Thomas Clarkson, who preached the cause throughout the country and collected evidence against the trade at the seaports.

Results were soon obtained. In 1788 a bill was carried through Parliament which struck at one of the worst cruelties of the trade by limiting the number of slaves carried in any ship in proportion to its size. In 1791 a resolution in favour of abolition secured a third of the votes of the House of Commons. And in 1792, after an organized movement throughout England and Scotland (the first such movement in British political history) had brought to Parliament a huge pile of abolitionist petitions, a resolution in favour of the gradual abolition of the trade was carried in the Commons by 238 to 85. Wilberforce and his friends had pressed for immediate abolition, and in support of them Pitt had made the finest speech of his career. But gradual abolition was far better than nothing, especially as it was agreed that the process should be completed by 1796. In principle, in fact, the root evil of the old Empire in its West Indian and West African field had been condemned. It was only a matter of time for the sentence to be carried out.

Anti-slavery agitation

The same new humanitarian ideas were mainly responsible for the transformation of British rule in India, which may be studied in Chapter 166. In its purpose and in its character the British Empire in India was so radically changed that after 1785, though it retained all its old territories, it can be called a second British Empire no less truly than the new imperial fields in other continents.

The student of these developments cannot fail to be impressed by the speed with which the advice Pitt gave at the close of the disastrous American War was adopted by his countrymen. In less than a decade the whole system of the old Empire was examined, and in each of its fields the old principles were condemned, and new principles affirmed and partly put into practice. Now, this great work might never have been done if it had not been so quickly done. For that decade, 1783–1793, was only a brief breathing-space between two wars. In 1793 the British Empire was involved in the conflict with the French Revolution which presently developed into the conflict with Napoleon. With one short break (1802–3), this great war lasted for over twenty years, and, as it grew into a desperate struggle to the death between the French military command of Europe and the British naval command of the sea, so the minds and energies of Englishmen became more and more concentrated on the immediate needs of self-defence. If they had not reviewed and reorganized their imperial policy before 1793, they would never have had the time or the will to do it till after 1815.

There was one exception. They did find the time, they did acquire the will, during the actual course of the war to complete the work begun for the abolition of the slave trade. And this was mainly due to the pertinacity of one man. In the earlier days of the war it seemed to most of the supporters of abolition that their cause must needs be shelved till peace returned. But Wilberforce would not wait. The continuance of the slave trade was, in his eyes, a great national crime, and a time when the nation was fighting for its existence seemed to him the very time for it to clear its conscience. And so, year after year, he continued to plead the cause of the negroes in Parliament and outside it.

Final triumph of Emancipation

For a long while nothing happened. The parliamentary inquiry into the facts of the trade petered out. Wilberforce's annual resolutions were voted down by large majorities. But, all the time, the conscience of the country was being kept awake. It only needed some shifting of political forces to enable it to ease itself. And when, broken by the war, Pitt died in 1806, and a coalition government was formed, which included Fox, at long last the old resolution was carried; and in 1807 a bill was enacted by which the slave trade was 'utterly abolished, prohibited, and declared to be unlawful.' In 1811 participation in the trade was made a felony. And so at length the British people ceased doing the worst thing they had ever done. They had taken the first step in humanising their relations with the people of Africa. And the second step—the abolition of slavery itself—could not now be long delayed.

Meanwhile, the ground plan of the British Empire had been expanding as the inevitable result of the operation of British sea power during the war. It is an instructive illustration of the manner in which a defensive strategy becomes offensive; for all, or almost all, the British conquests in the war were made with the purpose of counteracting Napoleon's aggressive designs. The acquisition of British Guiana, Trinidad, Tobago and St. Lucia in the West Indian area was partly due to the need of curtailing French attacks on the adjacent British colonies and on British trade. The acquisition of Malta and the Ionian Islands was wholly due to the need of preventing Napoleon from using the Mediterranean as the pathway to Egypt and the East. And it was the need of thwarting those designs of conquest in the East that led to still further and wider British annexations round the outskirts of the Indian Ocean, as well as in India itself.

Expansion during Napoleonic Wars

Napoleon's proposed encirclement of India from the sea was frustrated by a series of naval and military strokes. As soon as Holland had been forced into alliance with France, the Cape of Good Hope, the first link in the sea chain to India, and Ceylon, the most dangerous hostile base because the nearest, were attacked and occupied (1795); and by this prompt action the danger was averted for some years. But at a later phase of the war a combined Franco-Dutch movement from each side of the Indian Ocean was only prevented by the capture of Mauritius and Réunion in 1810, and in 1811 of Java, which carried with it the control of all the jealously-guarded preserve of the Dutch East Indies. The occupation of Java was made memorable by the determined efforts of the new British governor, Stamford Raffles, a young official of the East India Company, of whom more will be heard later on, to apply the new doctrine of responsibility for the welfare of native races by freeing the Javanese from the bonds of the semi-servile system in which their Dutch masters had confined them.

It is sometimes suggested that the history of the expansion of the British Empire is an unbroken record of 'insatiable grab.' If the suggestion needs any refutation, it can be refuted by the conduct of the British government at the close of the Napoleonic war. Of all the victorious powers that participated in the treaties of peace, Britain alone did not retain all the conquests she had fairly won. She restored Martinique, Guadeloupe, Réunion, Pondicherry and other lesser captures to France. She restored Surinam, Curaçao and the whole of the Dutch East Indies—an immeasurably wealthy area, the source of the spice trade with Europe—to the Dutch, and paid, moreover, a large indemnity for the retention of the Cape. The ground plan of the British Empire, with its vast possibilities of further peaceful expansion in empty and unknown lands oversea, was quite large enough in 1815, without any of these surrendered conquests, to employ all the energies of the British people in building up, in the coming nineteenth century, a far greater and better structure than that which had fallen into ruin or decay a generation earlier.

Building of the Second Empire

In the century that lies between 1815 and 1914 the British people were involved in no first-class European war—the Crimean War with Russia was a relatively minor conflict—and in that century of peace they achieved a development in prosperity and population, in science and literature, in commerce and industry, which dwarfed any similar development in any similar age. All the circumstances were thus propitious for another wave of oversea expansion, for the building of a new empire on new principles. And the opportunity was not neglected. There were hitches, delays, set-backs; but at the close of the century the new British Empire had been built.

In the true colonial field, that part of the building which had already been begun was naturally finished first. It was in Canada that the problems associated with each stage of the process first arose, and were first solved, the solutions being then almost automatically applied to the other colonial groups. The development of events in Canada, therefore, must be first described.

Soon after 1815 political opinion in Upper Canada began to range itself into two camps. The first, and for long the larger, camp was that of the Conservatives or Tories, who represented the original United Empire Loyalists, and from whom the executive council or provincial government was almost exclusively appointed. The second camp was that of the Reformers, who mainly represented the later immigrants and who felt themselves permanently shut out from political influence and power. Now, as long as the Tories maintained their majority in the Assembly, there might be constant friction with the opposition, but no serious deadlock. But the Reform party steadily grew in numbers. At last it obtained a slight, and in 1828 a decisive, majority at the elections. Yet nothing happened. The executive, not being under the Assembly's control, remained precisely as it was before. It was obvious at once that, unless the majority of the electorate was Tory, the measure of self-government enjoyed by the people of Upper Canada was scarcely self-government at all. The old story of the American colonies before the Revolution was being repeated. Nor was that the only repetition. In questions which required joint action by Upper and Lower Canada —in the control of the St. Lawrence waterway, the natural outlet of Upper Canadian trade, and in the sharing between the two provinces of the customs revenue collected at the Lower Canadian ports—the lack of an inter-provincial, pan-Canadian machine of government made itself acutely felt.

An uncontrolled Executive

Meantime, a similar but more serious political crisis was developing in Lower Canada. It was similar because it was also the result of a conflict between a majority in the popular chamber of the legislature and an irresponsible and irremovable executive. It was more serious because to this purely political issue was added the

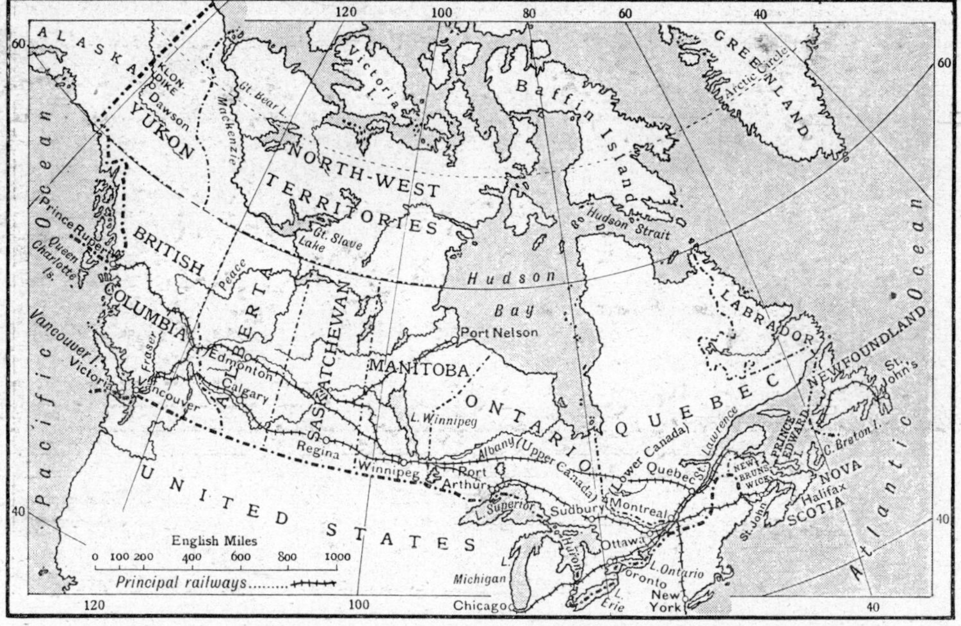

CANADA: FIRST OF THE BRITISH SELF-GOVERNING DOMINIONS

Great Britain's colonial empire began with the foundation of Newfoundland in 1583, and after the débâcle of 1783 it was in the region of the St. Lawrence that its reconstruction began. A new era of colonial autonomy was initiated by the grant of responsible government to the united Canadas in 1847, the Pacific district was organized as British Columbia in 1856, the Dominion of Canada was created in 1867, and in 1885 the Canadian Pacific Railway spanned the continent from sea to sea.

far more dangerous issue of race against race. For the vast majority of the electors in Lower Canada and of their representatives in the Assembly were French Canadians, whereas the executive council was almost wholly British. And unhappily some of the French Canadian leaders were quick to interpret the inevitable opposition between executive and legislature in terms of a race feud. The Quebec Act was forgotten. Any opposition to their policy was denounced as deliberate oppression of their nationality. The British minority, whose commercial energy was a valuable factor in the economic life of the province, were described as 'aliens and intruders.' Nor were the British on their side conciliatory or patient. They gave as good as they got. In the Assembly and in the newspapers a bitter race quarrel went on. In society, in business, in every field of their common life the two races drew apart and stood aloof.

Meantime, the French Canadian majority in the Assembly pressed their attack on the executive, in the sacred name of nationality, to more vigorous extremes than the Reformers of Upper Canada, and even attempted to bring the administration to a standstill by refusing to vote the budget. A deadlock was evidently

DOMESTIC SCENE IN A FRENCH CANADIAN FARMHOUSE

This lithograph of Krieghoff's painting of a French Canadian family was made in 1848. The earlier years of the century had been filled with friction between the French Canadians and the British settlers; Macnaughten's painting (top) represents a typical specimen of the sturdy 'habitant,' who would not readily part with his hardly won rights. A clash between the French and British races was inevitable, and the rebellion which broke out in 1837 was the chief reason for Lord Durham's mission.

From Shortt & Doughty, 'Canada and its Provinces: Quebec,' Publishers' Assn. of Canada

at hand. And how could it be resolved? Only by a fearless application of the doctrine of assimilation. But, since 1791, that doctrine had lain neglected and forgotten on the shelf; and, when it was now reconsidered, the policy to which it pointed seemed quite impracticable. It was an evolutionary doctrine, a doctrine of successive steps, and the next step was obviously the concession of responsible government. But to British statesmen, to Whigs as much as to Tories, responsible government seemed impossible. For, if the executive of a colony were responsible to its own legislature, if ministers were appointed almost automatically from the leaders of the elected majority in the Assembly, if the governor thus became merely a kind of constitutional sovereign like the king at home, the colony would no longer be a colony; it would be virtually an independent state.

Baffled by this dilemma, both political parties in Britain began to feel that the second colonial experiment was bound to break down like the first; and, since the independence of the colonies, their separation from the mother country, was apparently in the long run inevitable—for nobody, since the lesson of the American Revolution, supposed that they could be retained by force—the best hope was that the breach, when it came, might be friendly. But it soon seemed as if even this hope was not to be fulfilled, as if the story of the American Revolution was to be repeated right up to its tragic end. For when in Britain in 1830 the long Tory regime at last collapsed, when the Whigs had come in, carried the Reform Bill and opened a new era of political advance, when it became clear that there was to be no similar advance in Canada, when the Whigs refused as stubbornly as the Tories to concede responsible government, then at last, in 1837, despairing of any remedy but force, a small extremist section in both Upper and Lower Canada rose in armed rebellion.

Threatened revolt in Canada

The rebels were only a tiny minority of the population and they were easily suppressed. But the mere fact of rebellion had deeply stirred public opinion in Britain. Something, clearly, was very wrong in Canada; and if it were not put right, might not the next rebellion be a veritable revolution? The government, as has been seen, had no policy; but at least they were compelled to reconsider the whole question and they were happily inspired to send out to Canada a brilliant young statesman who had been one of the authors of the Reform Bill and a member of the Whig cabinet. In 1838 Lord Durham arrived in Canada as high commissioner. Within six months he was forced by political intrigues against him at home to resign. But from what he had learned in those months he was able on his return, with the assistance of his gifted lieutenants, Gibbon Wakefield and Charles Buller, to draft the immortal Durham Report. Soon afterwards, his frail physique undermined by disappointment at the apparent failure of his mission, he died. He was only forty-eight; but he had done more than any of his contemporaries to save the second British Empire. 'Canada,' he murmured as he lay dying, 'will one day do justice to my memory'; and he was right.

THE EARL OF DURHAM

Governor-General of Canada from May to October, 1838, Lord Durham (1792–1840) produced his influential report on British North America in 1839. The union of the two Canadas therein advocated was carried out in 1840.

From Dent, 'Canadian Portrait Gallery'

LORD ELGIN

James Bruce Elgin (1811–63) was governor-general of Canada from 1846 to 1854. He pursued Lord Durham's policy and became extremely popular with the colonists. He was made a baron of the United Kingdom in 1849.

From Dent, 'Canadian Portrait Gallery'

The cardinal sentence of the Durham Report was this:

> It needs no change in the principles of government, no invention of a new constitutional theory, to supply the remedy which would in my opinion completely remove the existing political disorders. It needs but to follow out consistently the principles of the British Constitution.

And after demonstrating the impossibility of harmoniously working a system which was representative only, he directly recommended that responsible government should be established in Canada on the same lines as it then existed in Britain. But what of the dilemma which had puzzled his colleagues at home? It was Durham's great achievement that he evaded this dilemma by the device of dividing up the field of government. In all local affairs, he said, the colonists must be as free as Englishmen at home. But in imperial affairs, of which the most important were the control of defence and foreign policy and of external trade, the imperial government and Parliament must still be supreme, and in these respects the governor would still act as their agent. With this division, he held, the colonists would be content.

Nor was Durham satisfied with an improvement in the quality of Canadian self-government; he recommended also an increase in its scope.

Recommendations of Lord Durham

It should no longer be provincial only, it should also be pan-Canadian. His first idea was to propose a federation of all the British North American colonies—and this idea, as will be seen, was right—but, owing to the aloofness of the Maritime Provinces and owing to the difficulty of leaving the French Canadians in their existing state of race antagonism to control a province of their own, he finally advised, not federation, but a legislative union, beginning with the reunion of Upper and Lower Canada into one big province. He hoped—and here, as will be seen, he was wrong—that in this union French Canadian nationalism would gradually fade away till the French Canadians had become virtually 'anglicised' and absorbed into one homogeneous British community.

Only half of the report, and the weaker half, was adopted at once. In 1840 the Union Act was passed, reuniting the Canadas. But the issue of responsible government was evaded until Earl Grey, a disciple of Durham, became colonial secretary, and instructed Sir John Harvey, the governor of Novia Scotia (1846), and Lord Elgin, the governor of Canada (1847), that their ministers must be chosen from the party which had a majority in the Assembly and that in local affairs the advice of those ministers must be accepted. In 1849 the genuineness of the new concession was sharply tested. The majority of the Canadian Assembly, largely composed of French Canadians, passed a Rebellion Losses Bill, providing compensation for damage suffered in the rebellion, which was regarded by the British minority as virtually condoning the rebellion and flouting the sentiments of the loyalists. So high did feeling run that there were riots at Montreal, Elgin's life was threatened, and the 'loyalists' talked of abandoning the Empire and joining the United States. But Elgin stood firm. Durham's admirer and son-in-law, he applied Durham's logic. The majority wanted the bill. He would not veto it. It therefore became law; and his action was endorsed, after full debate, by both Houses of Parliament at Westminster.

At that moment, in 1849, the second British Empire passed out of the experimental stage. It was not now going to fail, as the first British Empire had failed. There was not to be another American Revolution. For the saving principle of equality had been recognized and its adoption confirmed beyond dispute. Moreover, once this first difficult step had been taken, once it had been admitted that the will of the majority of the Canadian people was the decisive factor, there could be no retreat from it; so that the taking of each successive step in the further application of the doctrine of assimilation became practically certain as soon as the Canadian people desired to take it.

Of this last fact there was soon a convincing proof. Durham, it has been seen, maintained that the imperial government should continue to control colonial oversea trade by tariffs and otherwise. Earl Grey and everyone else in Britain agreed. And so, when Britain abandoned the old system of protection and adopted free trade, it was assumed that free trade would be automatically imposed on the colonies. Young countries, however, need protection, if only to enable their own infant industries to live and grow; and Canada particularly needed protection against the competition not only of the fast-developing manufactures of the United States, but also of the mature and potent industries of Britain herself. In 1858, therefore, the Canadian Assembly set up a small tariff wall against imports from both Britain and the United States; and, when this was retained and increased in 1859, strong protests were made by British manufacturers. The duke of Newcastle, now colonial secretary, brought pressure to bear on the Canadian government; but

MONTREAL, CANADA'S COMMERCIAL CAPITAL, IN 1860

Situated on an island in the St. Lawrence, Montreal was taken from the French by the British in 1760. The city was the capital of Canada from 1844 to 1849, in which year it was deprived of the honour because of an outbreak in which the Parliament buildings were destroyed by the mob. Its natural advantages and magnificent harbour furthered trade, and it became the chief centre for the export of western products. The sketch is from Mount Royal and shows the towers of Notre Dame.

THE FIRST DOMINION PARLIAMENT HOUSE, OTTAWA

In 1829 Ottawa, then known as Bytown, was founded as a residence for British engineers working in the district. Its wealth and importance developed as a centre of the lumber trade, and in 1858 it was selected by Queen Victoria to be the capital of Canada. The corner stone of its splendid Parliament House was laid in 1860 by the then Prince of Wales. This building was destroyed by fire in 1916, and replaced by a similar structure but with a different tower—the Tower of Peace.

Photo, Canadian Government

its finance minister, Galt, at once replied that 'self-government would be utterly annihilated if the views of the Imperial government were to be preferred to those of the people of Canada.' If British ministers, he added, insisted on having their way, then they must govern Canada. The logic was unanswerable, and Newcastle submitted. A big breach was thus made in Durham's system of division, only twenty years after the publication of his report.

Meanwhile, the inadequacy of the Union Act to solve the pan-Canadian problem was fast becoming clear. In the first place, the reunited Province of Canada had developed no real unity. French Canadian nationality, rooted in the St. Lawrence valley long before the British came to Canada, had shown no prospect whatever of becoming absorbed in British nationality; and since the French Canadian representatives remained a compact and distinct group in the Assembly, party government on the usual lines soon proved impossible. So stubborn was the deadlock that between 1861 and 1864 there were two elections and four ministries. Secondly, some pan-Canadian control of such common interests as inter-provincial tariffs, trunk roads and especially the new railways now beginning to be built, banking, currency and so forth was increasingly needed.

Thirdly, there was the necessity, which Durham had pointed out, of consolidating all British North America within one national framework, so as to maintain its strength and individuality against the powerful, progressive neighbour nation of the United States—a necessity now stressed by events. American pioneers were beginning to compete with Canadian pioneers for possession of the Far West; and Canada might have been cut off from the Pacific if the Oregon Treaty had not been successfully negotiated in 1846, under which the line of 49° N. was accepted as the frontier right across to Vancouver. In 1856 the Pacific district between this line and Alaska was organized as a British colony, called British Columbia; but until it was linked with eastern Canada, until, above all, a railway was built right across the continent, a task which obviously required pan-Canadian effort and control, it seemed as if the strip of British territory from ocean to ocean might somehow, some day, snap in the middle. Lastly, the American Civil War (1861–5), during which there was great tension at times between the British and United States governments, made Canadians feel how feebly they were organized, in separate provinces, for the common purpose of defence.

And so, in 1864, a conference assembled at Quebec, at which both the Conservatives under Macdonald and the Liberals under Brown, both British Canadians and French Canadians, jointly determined to establish a federal system. In 1866 Canadian delegates met in London and drafted a bill, with the sympathetic aid of Lord Carnarvon, the colonial secretary; and in 1867 the British North America Act was passed, creating the Dominion of Canada as a confederation of provinces. It consisted at the outset of Ontario and Quebec, into which the united province was dissolved, and Nova Scotia and New Brunswick. Manitoba, a new province westward of Ontario, joined in 1870; British Columbia in 1871; Prince Edward Island in 1873; and the new prairie provinces of Saskatchewan and Alberta in 1905. Newfoundland, though geographically so close to Canada, remained and still remains outside, a separate colony.

Thus, by the action of the Canadian people themselves—a further proof of their powers of self-government—another great stage in their political progress had been achieved. And two needs had been met at one stroke. The old problem of nationality had been solved by restoring to the French Canadians a province of their own, in their ancient home by the St. Lawrence, in which they could maintain their own provincial life and at the same time, combining two loyalties, take their proper place and pride in the life of the Canadian nation as a whole. Secondly, federation had settled the pan-Canadian question. Henceforward a Canadian citizen could share in the government not only of his province but of all Canada. And, that step once reached, the Canadian nation grew fast from adolescence into manhood.

In 1876 the Intercolonial Railway linked Ontario with the Maritime Provinces. In 1885 the Canadian Pacific spanned the continent from sea to sea. Agriculture and industry advanced side by side in eastern Canada. The vast prairies began to

THE SITE OF WINNIPEG AS IT APPEARED IN 1870

From its humble beginnings as a trading post for fur traders in the eighteenth century, Winnipeg became the capital of Manitoba. It forms an important centre for the marketing and distribution of the rich grain of the west. The Winnipeg river supplies electric power for its numerous industries, and the Lake of the Woods provides an adequate water supply. Winnipeg became a city in 1874—four years after this view was taken, in the year in which Manitoba joined the Union

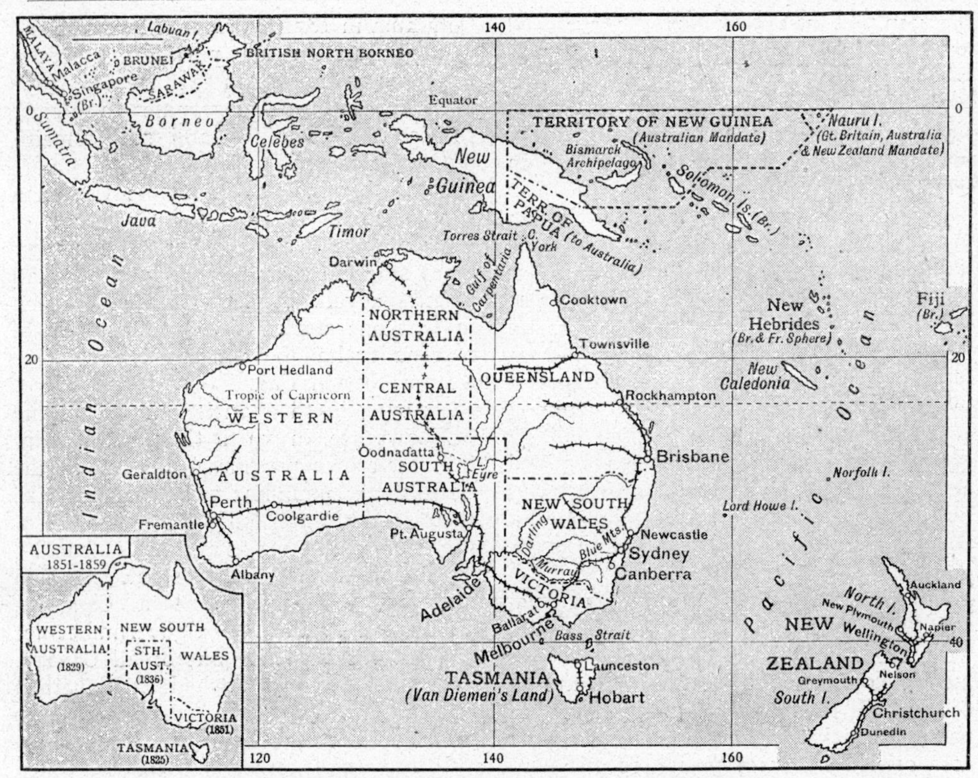

THE FEDERAL COMMONWEALTH OF AUSTRALIA

British occupation of Australia actually began with the establishment of a penal settlement at Port Jackson, in 1788. From 1793 onwards free settlers arrived in increasing numbers and formed the nucleus of the colony of New South Wales. Western Australia was established as a colony in 1829 and Victoria, South Australia and Queensland were carved out of New South Wales in 1851, 1836 and 1859 respectively. In 1901 the Commonwealth of Australia, Tasmania included, was proclaimed.

blossom into acres of wheat. Schools multiplied. Universities grew up and flourished. And all the while population steadily increased until, at the outset of the twentieth century, the Canadian people, seven million strong, could take their place among the younger nations of the world. Nor had Durham's prophecy been falsified. The stronger, the freer Canada grew, the more closely did she recognize and value the ties that bound her to the Empire. As soon as Britain ceased to interfere in her affairs, the one barrier was removed to the natural influence of kinship and sentiment, of common traditions and common ideals. The twentieth century was not yet old when, at one great crisis, the unity of the Empire was to be confirmed and at the same time the doctrine of assimilation was to reach its consummation of complete equality within that unity.

While Canada thus took the lead and set the example, other nations of the Empire were growing up in other continents. The British government, although, as has been seen, it regarded Australia at the outset as nothing more than a convenient convict station, was nevertheless reluctant to see it occupied by any other European power; and when the French continued to prospect the empty continent and actually described it in a French map as 'Terre Napoléon,' one or two more British posts were established along the coast of New South Wales and on the island of Van Diemen's Land, afterwards called Tasmania. Settlement, meanwhile, was expanding into the interior from Sydney. In 1813 a way was found through the Blue Mountains to the fertile inland plain whose rivers led the explorers down to the south coast; and in 1829, on the other side of the continent, the colony of Western Australia was founded at Perth. The frontier dividing Western Australia from New South Wales was fixed at the line 129° E., so that the whole continent was now definitely annexed; and, while the area of settlement in the remote west, cut off by the deserts of Central Australia, long remained small, the parent colony of New South Wales expanded rapidly inland and up and down the coasts. In 1836 the province of South Australia (with its capital at Adelaide) was carved out of it, in 1851 Victoria (Melbourne) and in 1859 Queensland (Brisbane).

In this work of expansion the British government had taken little part. Both Western and South Australia were founded by private companies with small encouragement from the Colonial Office; and it was only after an initial period of great economic and financial difficulty that they struggled to success. The admirable climate, the fertility of the huge coastal belt, the rapid development of sheep breeding and corn growing—all these attractions drew a steady stream of colonists from the mother country; and when gold was discovered in Victoria (1851) the volume of immigration was increased by a host of miners seeking

A LESSON IN PICTURES

Governor Davey's proclamation to the aborigines of Tasmania in 1816 gave the natives a pictorial statement of the policy of friendship that he intended to institute between blacks and whites, based on equal justice to both races.

From Dilke's Greater Britain 1868

A WIDE THOROUGHFARE IN MELBOURNE, CAPITAL OF VICTORIA

In July, 1851, Victoria was constituted a separate colony from New South Wales, and Melbourne, situated on the banks of the river Yarra, became its capital. This view of the town, which appeared in Victoria Illustrated in 1857, shows Collins Street, now famous for its fashionable shops. The discovery of gold at Ballarat in 1851 stimulated the already rapid growth of population, which increased from 30,000 to 100,000 in the course of two or three years. The town was named after Viscount Melbourne.

EAGER PARTICIPANTS IN THE SEARCH FOR GOLD AT PORT PHILLIP

The Australian gold discoveries of 1851 brought a host of immigrants to seek their fortunes in the colonies. The Illustrated London News on July 3, 1852, published this picture of men at work in the Forest Creek Diggings of Mount Alexander, Port Phillip. It shows operations being pursued with great energy. In the right-hand corner two native mounted police, members of a corps established not twelve months earlier, regard the animated scene with interest.

their fortunes at Bendigo and Ballarat. So industry was added to agriculture, and an urban population grew up in the chief towns which was presently to equal and surpass the rural population. Meantime, the only obstacle to the natural evolution of a normal social life had been removed. The transportation of convicts to Sydney was stopped in 1840, and confined thereafter to Tasmania until, in 1853, the whole antiquated system was finally abolished.

The rapid development of the Australian colonies into free and progressive British communities inevitably raised the political problem. Owing to the

NUCLEUS OF THE FINEST CITY IN THE AUSTRALIAN COMMONWEALTH——

Sydney, on the east coast of Australia, was founded by Captain Arthur Phillip in 1788, and was named after Viscount Sydney, who was British colonial secretary at the time. Sydney's advantageous situation on the south shore of Port Jackson, a magnificent natural harbour, favoured its rapid expansion along the coast and inland. Beautiful beaches and a mild climate attract many residents.

From Perou et Freycinet——

nature of its origin New South Wales had begun with a purely military government, and it was not till 1842 that representative government, which was conceded to Canada as early as 1791, was partially introduced. But the next stage was carried with a rush, mainly owing to the acceptance of Durham's Canadian policy. In 1850 New South Wales, Tasmania, South Australia and Victoria were invited practically to draft their own constitutions; and the result was the establishment of virtually the same system as existed in Canada, with responsible government as an essential part thereof. It was extended to Queensland, when it was cut off from New South Wales in 1859, and to Western Australia, where colonisation and development proceeded more slowly, in 1890.

But the advance to the next stage, the pan-Australian stage, was not so swift. Canada passed from responsible government to national government in twenty years (1846–1867). Australia took fifty years. The reason for this difference was partly that New South Wales, being much the largest of the states (as the colonies were called instead of 'provinces'), did not wish to share her functions of self-government with her smaller sisters in a federal system, while they on their part did not wish to be dwarfed by New South Wales, and partly that the unifying factor of a contiguous foreign power, so influential in Canada, was absent in Australia. Thus, although the other arguments for union—the need for common action as to tariffs, ports and communications, and the linking together of the continent, disjointed more seriously than Canada by the great arid central wastes—were obvious, the jealous aloofness of the individual states delayed the inevitable step.

Australia becomes a commonwealth

That, at last, the step was taken was mainly due to two factors: first, the fear that the teeming population of Eastern Asia might spill over into Australia, the determination to prevent this intrusion and to keep a 'white Australia' free from the well known difficulties, social, economic and political, which arise from the mingling of white and coloured races in one land, and the conviction that the task involved therein—to open up, to people, to consolidate a vast continent—demanded the united efforts of the whole nation; secondly, the appearance in the South Seas of rival colonising powers, and particularly of Germany, which in 1883 annexed a 'place in the sun' in the neighbouring island of New Guinea. Under these influences a pan-Australian convention met in 1891 and drafted a

——SYDNEY AS IT WAS SEVENTEEN YEARS AFTER ITS FOUNDATION
The panorama above gives a view of the southern portion of the town (left-hand page) and the mouth of the Parramatta river as the site appeared in 1805. As early as 1793 emigrant ships had been arriving with free settlers who were given free grants of land, and by the end of the eighteenth century the population numbered 5,000. In the census of 1921 it had risen to over 900,000.
——*'Voyages aux Terres Australes'*

BUILDERS OF EMPIRE IN NEW ZEALAND

A keen student of colonial problems, Edward Gibbon Wakefield (left), 1796–1862, became managing director of the New Zealand Company in 1837, and by his action in 1839 forestalled the French in annexing New Zealand. Sir George Grey (right) twice served New Zealand as governor, and from 1877–84 was premier.

National Portrait Gallery, London and (right) from Gudgeon, 'War in New Zealand'

federal bill; but even then the states, voting separately, rejected it.

In 1897, however, a convention met again, and this time the states accepted the bill, which was embodied by the Imperial Parliament in the Australian Commonwealth Act of 1900. It bore on its face the traces of its slow and difficult birth; for the states had insisted on retaining more independence than the provinces retained in Canada, and so weakening the power of the federal government. But such defects, which can and will be remedied in time, were of minor importance compared with the fact that the Commonwealth of Australia entered the twentieth century as a united nation, side by side with the Dominion of Canada. And, as in Canada, national development followed fast on union. A transcontinental railway began to span the gulf between east and west (it was completed in 1917), and another line was put in hand to link the south with the luxuriant semi-tropical northern territory. Plans for closer settlement were adopted, irrigation extended, immigration encouraged and organized. By 1914 Australia contained a big-built, virile, adventurous population of about five million, mainly of British and Irish stock.

Some 1,200 miles south-east from Sydney the two islands of New Zealand

A GREAT DAY IN MELBOURNE: THE AUSTRALIAN COMMONWEALTH PROCLAIMED

The union of Australia was finally achieved as the result of the conference held in 1899 between the premiers of the Australian states. A bill was submitted to the British Parliament, and on January 1, 1901, it was proclaimed that the people of New South Wales, Victoria, South Australia, Queensland, Tasmania and Western Australia were united into the Commonwealth of Australia. This drawing shows the duke of Cornwall and York opening the first Commonwealth parliament on May 9.

Courtesy of Australian Commonwealth Government

offered a second field of colonisation in the Southern Seas, no less fertile and salubrious than Australia. But its only colonists for many years after the foundation of New South Wales were migrant whalers and traders and fugitive convicts from Sydney. Unlike Australia, where the primitive aborigines were few and feeble and withdrew before the white man into the wilderness, New Zealand contained a vigorous native population of at least 100,000, mainly settled in the North Island. It was of good omen for the future of British colonisation in the country that the Maoris, though they retained some barbarous customs, were by no means barbarians, but in many respects a cultured and attractive people, capable of assimilating the white man's civilization. They were also a warlike people; and it was the inevitable friction and fighting between them and the earlier British settlers over the ownership of land that induced the government reluctantly to annex New Zealand in 1839.

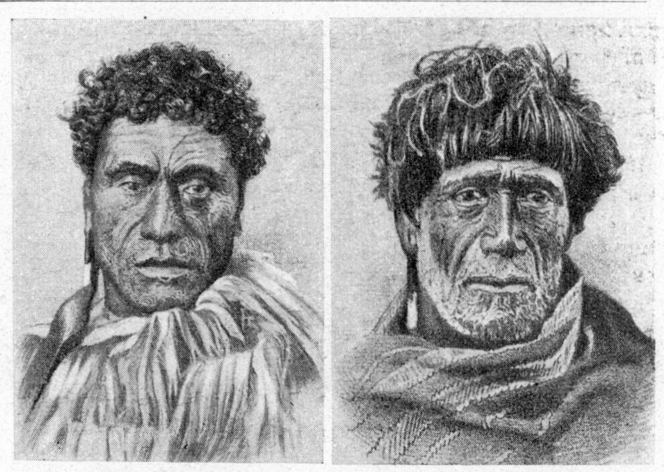

POWERFUL MEMBERS OF THE MAORI TRIBE

Colonisation of New Zealand was impeded by the opposition shown to the intrusive white man by Maori tribes already in occupation of the country. Two bitter wars ensued before the power of the stubborn native chiefs, of whom these two specimens are representative, was finally subdued.

From Gudgeon, 'Reminiscences of the War in New Zealand'

In the same year the New Zealand Company, the offspring of the enthusiasm and energy of Gibbon Wakefield, who had also taken the lead in the colonisation of South Australia, planted a colony at Wellington, destined to be the national capital. In 1840 the Treaty of Waitangi opened the way to a settlement with the Maoris. At first it was misinterpreted. Some of the colonists infringed Maori

WELLINGTON, CAPITAL OF NEW ZEALAND, IN 1843

The first settlement of New Zealand colonists was made at Wellington, founded in 1840. It is situated on the north-west shore of North Island and possesses a fine harbour. Wellington replaced Auckland as the seat of government in 1865 being selected by three Australian commissioners as occupying the best site on Cook Strait. This view shows Te Aro Flat in 1843.

From Shrimpton, 'Maori and Pakeha'

WHERE BRITISH EMPIRE IN SOUTH AFRICA BEGAN

The Cape of Good Hope was discovered and given its name by the Portuguese in 1488, and a Dutch settlement was first made there in 1651. In 1814 it was ceded to Britain, who regarded it primarily as a useful calling station on the sea route to India, and its earliest British settlers arrived there in 1820. Its possession proved finally to be the initial stage in Britain's colonisation and expansion in South Africa. This Dutch engraving shows the tiny town beneath the slopes of Table Mountain.

From 'Beschryving van de Kaap,' 1777

rights. Some of the Maori tribes revolted. But in 1845 Sir George Grey, one of the greatest 'proconsuls' of the nineteenth century, having fulfilled the task of saving South Australia from its early economic difficulties, was transferred to New Zealand, and, taking his stand on the treaty, he succeeded by mingled firmness and conciliation in restoring peace.

But the quarrel was not yet dead. The Maori chiefs of the old generation refused to acquiesce in the white man's occupation of their country. The colonists, on their part, became impatient of conciliatory methods. And when Grey had been called away to yet another imperial task in South Africa, war broke out afresh. In 1860 Grey returned; but this time the war smouldered on till in 1866 the power of the Maoris was broken, and in 1870 a permanent peace established. The old conflict thus at last abandoned, the Maoris settled down in that half of the North Island which remained to them. In course of time they were accorded equal political rights with the British; and, with their social adaptability and their gifts of speech and song, they contribute an interesting and harmonious element to New Zealand life.

Maori situation in New Zealand

The Maori trouble ended, social and political progress in New Zealand was as rapid as in Australia. From the seacoast towns of Wellington, Auckland, New Plymouth and Napier in the North Island, and Nelson, Dunedin and Christchurch in the South Island, the colonists spread out over the plains and upland valleys of the interior, breeding sheep and cattle, raising corn and fruit, exploiting minerals and developing industries. But the sense of provincial separatism never developed so strongly as in Australia. As early as 1852 a federal constitution was set up, and in 1875 even that measure of local differentiation and independence was supplanted by a unitary constitution such as that of Britain. Nothing could be stronger, on the other hand, than the feeling that this homogeneous New Zealand was different from and independent of Australia. Her white population, drawn more exclusively than in any other colonial group from Britain, her sentiment towards the motherland more deeply rooted, her people naturally similar to and yet easily distinguishable from Australians, New Zealand was determined to develop her own distinct nationality and shape her own destiny in the South Seas. The suggestion that she should enter into an Australasian Federation was therefore rejected; and in 1907 the Dominion of New Zealand became a separate nation of the Empire.

In Australia and New Zealand, with the exception of the Maori wars, the story of national construction is one of smooth and steady progress. The building of a nation in South Africa, on the other hand, was only accomplished after generations of schism and strife. When the Dutch colony at the Cape of Good Hope was annexed by Britain at the close of the Napoleonic wars it was still regarded as primarily a strategic post on the sea route to India.

Beginnings of South African history

The Dutch, it is true, had already begun to 'trek' away from Cape Town and settle with their flocks and herds in the outlying districts of Cape Colony; but the idea that the European race was destined to penetrate and occupy the great upland 'veldt' in the interior was in nobody's mind; and when, in 1820, a settlement of British colonists was planted in the eastern part of the colony, its purpose was not expansion but the need of peopling and defending territory already partly colonised.

This need of defence arose from the greater of the two questions that have dominated the history of South Africa—the native question. Less fortunate than the invaders of Australia and New Zealand, the South African colonists found the country occupied by three kinds of native races—the primitive bushmen, who faded away before them like the Australian aborigines; the Hottentots, a more advanced race, but also relatively feeble and non-resistant; and the Bantu (or Kaffirs, as the colonists called them), a very different people or group of peoples, prolific and powerful, yet quite uncivilized and, except, as with the Zulus, for purposes of war, undisciplined. Successive waves of these Bantu were rolling down the eastern side of South Africa at the very time that the Dutch colonists were moving upwards. A conflict was inevitable. The treatment of this conflict, the framing of a native policy, was the primary task of the government responsible for Cape Colony.

Unfortunately, it was the British government's native policy that created, or at least intensified and perpetuated, the second great question—the Anglo-Dutch question. Now, if the native question were to be rightly settled, there should have been no Anglo-Dutch question. In other words, it was essential that the two European peoples should assume a more or less similar attitude to the natives and pursue a common and consistent policy. But circumstances forbade it. Most of the Dutch colonists were farmers (Boers) who had gradually drifted

KAFFIR WARRIORS WHO IMPERILLED AFRICAN COLONIAL LIFE

The colonists who settled on the eastern side of South Africa soon came into conflict with natives of the savage Kaffir tribes. Farmers lived in perpetual dread of sudden raids, which destroyed their cattle and their crops and incurred famine and ruin. Throughout the greater part of the nineteenth century there was intermittent warfare between the black men and the colonists who sought a livelihood in the territory. The last Kaffir war ended in their defeat in 1878.

From Samuel Daniell, African Scenery,' 1804

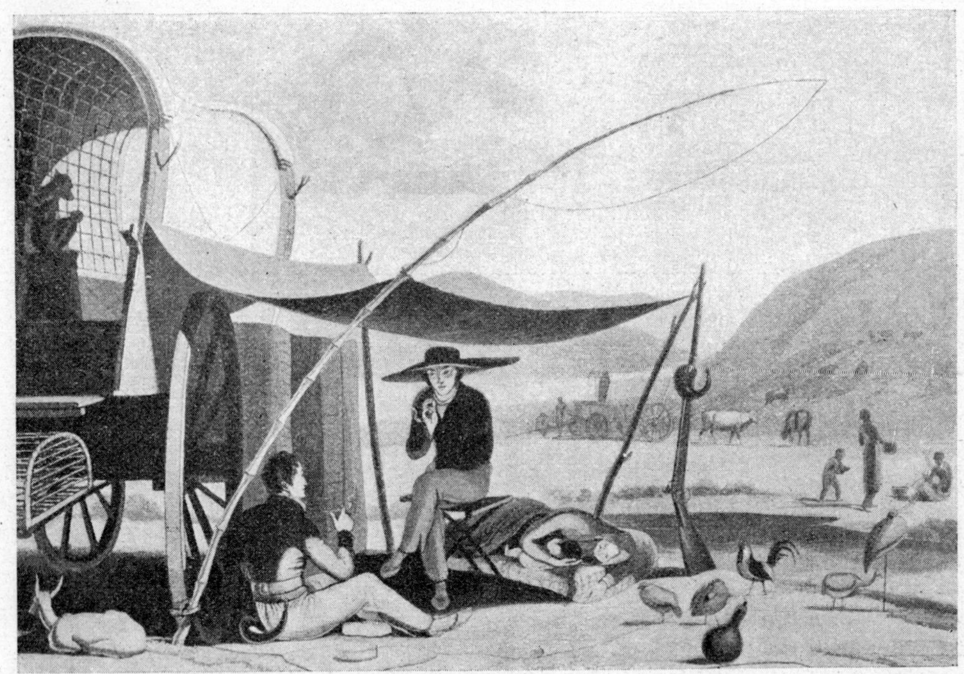

SCENES OF BOER LIFE IN SOUTH AFRICA

The tendency of South Africa's Dutch farmers (Boers) was to trek ever farther north from Cape Town, thus retaining the simple habits and outlook of their ancestors and differing widely from the colonists who penetrated the continent in later times. The aquatint after Samuel Daniell shows a Boer's wife drinking her coffee in homely surroundings, while a native servant fans her. Top (also by Daniell): A Boer's family halts for rest on one of the long journeys that their race so frequently undertook.

From Samuel Daniell, 'African Scenery,' 1804, and (bottom) Barrow, 'Travels,' 1806 away from Cape Town, their only link with Europe, and in their lonely, isolated life remained, so to speak, in the atmosphere of the seventeenth century. Simple, hardy, hospitable folk, clinging strongly to their Calvinistic faith, and to the Old Testament as much as to the New, they came to conceive themselves, as they penetrated farther and farther into the unknown, to be a chosen people entering their promised land. And almost inevitably they regarded its native inhabitants as ordained to be their 'hewers of wood and drawers of water.' Slavery, for example, seemed to them a right and natural dispensation, and though they did not treat their slaves or hired labourers with the brutality of British slave traders, they looked on them as unalterably their inferiors and subjects.

SIR BENJAMIN D'URBAN

Just administration of Cape Colony during his four years' governorship which he began in 1834 won for Sir Benjamin D'Urban (1777–1849) the approval of both British and Dutch.

From 'The Times History of the War in South Africa'

The British colonists, on the other hand, came straight from the European civilization of the nineteenth century, and from a country which had recently taken the lead in transforming the old ideas about the relations between the white and coloured races of mankind. The individual Briton in South Africa may not have been particularly enlightened in this matter, but the government at least was pledged to the new humanitarian ideals, and among the individual immigrants were some of the earliest and most zealous servants of the new missionary societies which, under the impulse of men like Wilberforce, had been formed to advance those humanitarian ideals in the religious field. Was not a conflict between Boer and Briton, then, almost as inevitable as the conflict between European and Bantu?

Before the native question came to a head friction had already developed between Dutch and British. Curiously enough, the British statesmen who dealt with the Dutch colony acquired in 1815 were far less successful than their predecessors who had dealt with the French colony in 1763, although the Dutch South Africans were far more nearly akin to the British in race and in their Protestant religion than the French Canadians. The old Roman Dutch law was retained, indeed; but the imposition of English forms of justice and local government, and of English as the official language, seemed to threaten the survival of Dutch nationality. The opening of any deep and lasting breach, however, might well have been avoided but for a succession of events in the field of native policy.

First came the missionaries, horrified at the degraded status of the natives, impulsively taking up their grievances, repeating their stories—sometimes false and often exaggerated—of cruel treatment at their masters' hands, and appealing to influential friends in London. Next, in 1828, came a government ordinance giving a greater measure of equality and freedom to the Hottentots than they had ever known. Next, in 1834, came a heavier blow; for in that year (as will be seen) the British Parliament abolished slavery throughout the British Colonies. Thus, at a stroke, the Boers were deprived of a substantial part of their property—nor, owing to a faulty system of payment, did they receive their due share of the money voted for their compensation—and of their available supply of agricultural labour.

The Boers and the native question

Last, and worst, came a decision by the British government that could only be interpreted as a sacrifice of the colonists on the north-east frontier to the Kaffirs. More than once there had been fighting and bloodshed along the line where advancing colonist and Kaffir met, and in 1834, after a Kaffir invasion in which many colonists had been killed and their farms destroyed, Sir Benjamin D'Urban, the governor, had determined that the most practical method of preventing future inroads was to annex a portion of Kaffraria and constitute it a kind of unoccupied buffer state between the races. In 1835 the colonial secretary, Lord Glenelg, an earnest disciple of the humanitarian school, reversed this decision. The Kaffirs, he believed, were right in the quarrel ; the colonists wrong. The annexed territory was retroceded. But to the colonists this policy seemed worse than futile, since the Kaffirs would regard it as a sign of weakness rather than of justice or generosity, and would thus be incited to renewed aggression ; and for many of them it was the last straw. In 1836 and the following years some ten thousand of the more adventurous Boers, taking their slaves with them, their big wagons loaded with household goods, trekked away over the colonial frontier into the no-man's-land of the interior.

What was the British government to do ? The Boer trekkers had thrown off their allegiance to the British crown and refused to submit to its authority. They were determined to maintain independent republics of their own, and to deal with the native tribes within and without their borders as they pleased, without considering the effects of their policy on the relations between the natives and Cape Colony.

Policy towards the Trekkers

But the only way of preventing this was to follow up the Boers with a large military force, to declare the territory they had occupied to be British territory, and to compel their submission to British rule. If, however, as was probable, the Boers retreated farther and farther into the interior, were they to be pursued into the tropical heart of Africa ? What limits could be set to the time and cost involved ? Confronted by this dilemma, successive British governments tried first one policy and then another. But vacillation was worse than useless ; the schism deepened.

At the outset, after some hesitation, a forward policy was adopted. Port Natal, afterwards called Durban, had been occupied by a few British traders : and since it was easy of access by sea, the port and its hinterland up to the Drakensberg Mountains were annexed in 1842 as the colony of Natal. The majority of the

AT PORT NATAL IN THE EARLY YEARS OF BRITISH RULE

The arrival of the first steamer, the Sir Robert Peel, at Port Natal, the harbour of Durban, in 1852 was greeted with wild excitement by the inhabitants, and is the scene represented in this drawing from a contemporary newspaper. English colonists had arrived at Port Natal in 1824 and laid out Durban in 1835 : it passed into Dutch hands for a few years, but a British military force under Sir Benjamin D'Urban occupied it in 1842, and British sovereignty was recognized by treaty.

DIGGING FOR DIAMONDS AT KIMBERLEY, SOUTH AFRICA

On a site then known as Colesberg Kopje in Griqualand West, between the Modder and Vaal rivers, diamonds were discovered in 1870. Possession of this valuable property was disputed between the British government and the Orange Free State, the former finally taking it under British protection in 1871. The mine and, later, the town were named Kimberley after the British colonial secretary. This view of mining operations in Kimberley is from a wood-engraving published in 1872.

trekkers who had settled there migrated, in high dudgeon, into the interior. Then in 1848, with the consent of some, but not all, of the trekkers therein, the area between the Orange and Vaal Rivers was annexed as the Orange River Sovereignty. But friction continued and the tide turned in favour of leaving the Boers alone. So in 1852 the Sand River Convention recognized the independence of the Boers in the Transvaal under the leadership of Pretorius, and in 1854 the Convention of Bloemfontein recognized the independence of the Orange Free State. There were thus four political units now established in South Africa—two British colonies, and two Boer republics—and the prospect of national unity seemed almost to have disappeared.

One chance, perhaps, was still open—a federation by mutual agreement; and, when Sir George Grey arrived from New Zealand, he determined to try it. He might have succeeded in 1858 in at least the first step by persuading the friendlier of the two republics, the Orange Free State, to federate with the two colonies; but government opinion in Britain was still on the backward path and the proposal was abandoned. So the separation continued, and the evils of it became more and more apparent. There was continual trouble with the natives, especially the Basutos. There was friction between the Transvaal Boers and British missionaries pushing up, with David Livingstone at their head, along the western frontier of the republic towards Central Africa. There was a dispute between the Orange Free State and the British government, rather dubiously settled in the latter's favour, as to the ownership of the border land at Kimberley in which diamonds had been found.

Finally, in 1874, Lord Carnarvon resumed the forward policy. Having assisted in Canadian federation, he drafted himself a measure for federating South Africa and sent over Sir Bartle Frere to work for its adoption at the Cape. Again, however, the proposal failed, partly, no doubt, because it had originated outside and not inside South Africa. But the forward policy was still in the ascendant; and when, as it happened, the Transvaal was threatened not only by a collapse of its finances but also by attack from the militant and powerful Zulus on its borders, a British mission was sent to Pretoria and the republic annexed to the British crown (1877).

The next event was an almost inevitable war between the British and the Zulus, in which, after a terrible British defeat at Isandhlwana, the Zulus were finally crushed (1879); whereupon the Transvaal Boers, relieved of their danger and resenting the annexation to which most of them had never assented, rose in revolt and defeated the small British force dispatched against them at Majuba (1881). At once British policy swung back again; and by the Conventions of Pretoria (1881) and London (1884) the Transvaal was recognized as the independent South African Republic, under the vague suzerainty of the British crown. So in 1884 the position was the same as it had been in 1854, except that it was now worsened by bitterness and bloodshed. Many of the Boers, moreover, had been convinced that, if ever they were forced to fight again, they would win again.

SIR BARTLE FRERE

Appointed high commissioner of South Africa in 1877, Sir Bartle Frere (1815–84) failed to bring Lord Carnarvon's scheme of confederation to fruition. His conduct of affairs evoked government censure and he was recalled in 1880.

Photo, Elliott & Fry

BOER MONUMENT OF INDEPENDENCE

This monument, the Paarde Kraal, was raised at Krugersdorp by the Boers as a commemoration of the independence of the Transvaal recognized in 1881. It is regarded, however, as the symbol of their victory at Majuba Hill.

The last chapter of the unhappy story now opened with the discovery of gold along the great reef at Johannesburg (1884–5). The result, as in Australia, was an invasion of European immigrants and the development in the heart of an old-fashioned, agricultural or pastoral community of a great modern industrial centre. To Paul Kruger, president of the Republic and a typical representative of the old trekker tradition, and to the more conservative of his Boer 'burghers,' this invasion was disturbing and distasteful; and, while the taxation of the Uitlanders (foreigners) soon provided a far bigger revenue than it had ever enjoyed before, the government refused to admit them to citizenship and the franchise, at least until they had resided in the country for many years. The Uitlanders protested. They were taxpayers. More, they were, for the most part, British subjects. And what did British 'suzerainty' mean if the interests of British subjects were not to be protected? It was a deadlock, and this time there seemed no escape.

Men began to talk of an impending conflict, the result of which was to be, according to the talker's nationality, a purely Dutch or a purely British rule over all South Africa. And, if on the one side Kruger's obstinacy was reprehensible, a terrible blunder was presently committed by the leading figure on the other side, Cecil Rhodes, who had made a great fortune in diamonds and gold and had become prime minister of Cape Colony. Convinced that his dream of a united South Africa could never be realized as long as the Kruger regime continued in the Transvaal, he allowed himself to be secretly associated with a plan for a rising in Johannesburg which aimed at the establishment by force of a more liberal government at Pretoria. Unfortunately for Rhodes and British honour, at the beginning of 1896 his lieutenant, Dr. Jameson, learning that the plot had miscarried, decided on his own initiative to make a dash for Johannesburg with the volunteer troops in his charge. The surprise failed; Jameson and his troops were surrounded and captured by the Boers; and, after an anxious interval, they were handed over to the British government, by whom they were leniently punished. Rhodes was forced into retirement.

And now the shadow of war drew nearer. While Kruger imported artillery from Europe by a railway which he had promoted from Pretoria to the Portuguese port at Lourenço Marques, the British government continued to urge him to concede the franchise to the Uitlanders as the only means of maintaining peace, and in 1898 sent out the able Sir Alfred Milner as high commissioner to try to secure a settlement.

In 1899 negotiations failed, and in the autumn the second Boer War broke out. The rights and wrongs of it will probably

REACTIONARY PRESIDENT OF THE TRANSVAAL
The Boer politician Paul Kruger (1825-1904) became president of the Transvaal in 1883 and was re-elected in 1888, 1893 and 1898. A strict conservative, he resisted reforms and his conduct of negotiations with Britain regarding the unenfranchised Uitlanders in the Transvaal led to the South African War.
From 'The Times History of the War in South Africa'

LEADER OF THE JAMESON RAID

A close friend of Cecil Rhodes, Dr. Leander Starr Jameson (1853-1917) was appointed administrator of Rhodesia in 1891. In 1895 he organized his disastrous invasion of the Transvaal that was 'severely censured' by the colonial office.

Photo, Elliott & Fry

be always a matter of dispute. Some will think that the British government, with an eye, perhaps, to its mineral wealth, was determined to bring the little republic within the frontiers of the Empire. Others will think that the conflict was justified by the grievances of the Uitlanders, by the notorious corruption and misgovernment of the Kruger regime and by the probability that, if the issue were not settled once and for all, the Dutch would have seized a favourable opportunity, say in 1914, to attack and dominate the British. Others, again, will think that there was right and wrong on both sides and that, in any case, the war was unavoidable. But all will agree, whatever their opinions as to its cause, that its chief effect was to make possible at last a united South Africa. And all will agree that, whatever the mistakes of earlier times, this final opportunity was quickly and wisely used.

So the last tragic chapter had a happy ending. After three years of war, which had proved a far longer and costlier struggle than anyone had expected, a peace treaty was signed at Vereeniging (1902) by which the republics accepted British sovereignty, but with a promise of self-government in the near future. In 1907 the British government boldly decided that the time was already ripe; and responsible government, which had been instituted in Cape Colony in 1872 and in Natal in 1893—the delay being mainly due to the native question—was conceded to the two ex-republics. Encouraged by this gesture of trust and friendship, the Boer leaders, Botha and Smuts, more liberal-minded men than their old chief, who had retired to Holland during the war, agreed with the British leader, Jameson, who had outlived the scandal of the raid and was now prime minister of Cape Colony, to work for union. In 1908 a conference of delegates from the four colonies met and in 1909 completed a draft of a constitution which, with slight amendments, was accepted by the four legislatures.

Because South Africa, though it had needed unity so much, had been so deeply divided, it was agreed that the unity now at last achieved should be as complete as possible. The constitution, therefore,

CECIL JOHN RHODES

In 1890 Cecil John Rhodes (1853-1902), whose dearest dream was of an 'Africa British from the Cape to Cairo,' became premier of Cape Colony. His connivance in the plot that gave rise to the Jameson Raid compelled his resignation in 1896

Photo, W. & D. Downey

was unitary and not federal, the sometime colonies and republics becoming provinces with minor powers. It also provided that the native protectorates of Basutoland, Bechuanaland and Swaziland should continue under the old direct administration of the imperial government until they could be handed over on certain conditions to South Africa. This constitution was quickly passed through the Imperial Parliament as the Union of South Africa Act; and in 1910 General Botha, so recently the ablest of Britain's enemies in the field, took the oath as first prime minister of united South Africa.

Thus, by 1914, the groups of British colonies in Canada, Australia, New Zealand and South Africa had grown into self-governing nations. It remains to answer certain questions as to their political status.

PROMINENT BOER LEADERS
Notable among those generals who commanded the Boers in the war of 1880–81 were (top left) General Joubert, the victor of Majuba; (right) General Cronje; (bottom left) Commandant Hans Botha and (right) General Nikolos Smit.
From 'The Times History of the War in South Africa'

GENERAL LOUIS BOTHA
In the South African War of 1899 Louis Botha attained chief command of the Transvaal Boers and influenced their acceptance of the peace of Vereeniging in 1902. In 1910 he became the first premier of united South Africa.
Photo, Langfier

For many years the process of political evolution seemed to have halted at 1867. The example of Canada in attaining responsible government and national government and in securing control of her own commercial and fiscal policy was followed in due course by each of the other Dominions. But there remained in the list of fields of government reserved by Durham for sole control by Britain the two most important fields of all—the fields in which the issues of freedom itself and of life and death might be raised—defence and foreign policy. As long as these vital matters were dealt with only by the British government over the heads of the Dominions, they were still in some degree 'dependencies.' Sooner or later this last inequality had to be adjusted if the Empire was to endure.

But the process was very gradual because the peoples of the Dominions were far more interested in the immediate task of developing their own new countries than in the course of events in old and far-off Europe with which British foreign policy was mainly concerned; and, conscious of their youth and their inexperience in the intricate business of diplomacy, they were quite content to leave their destiny in the hands of the British foreign office and under the shield of the British navy. Some forward steps, however, were taken. It was soon evident, for instance, that colonies could not be regarded as self-governing unless they undertook the primary duty of their own local defence. In 1870–1, therefore, the garrisons of British regulars were withdrawn from all the colonies except South Africa; colonial troops were organized to take their place; and, while Canada remained content with a mainly voluntary militia system, the other three Dominions, after achieving national unity, created national defence forces on a basis of compulsory military service. Canadian and Australian contingents volunteered for service in the Sudan campaign of 1884, and some 30,000 Canadians, Australians and New Zealanders took part in the Boer War of 1899.

Political Evolution in the Dominions

Meantime the colonies had begun to share also in the burden of naval defence. At first they contributed annual sums towards the cost of the British navy besides maintaining small local ships for police and training purposes. But during the 'navy scare' of 1909 New Zealand made an advance on this method by supplying a battleship of her own to the imperial fleet. Finally, by 1914, Australia and New Zealand had decided to provide and maintain first-class warships as local Dominion squadrons, and Australia already possessed one battle-cruiser, two cruisers and some smaller vessels.

Meanwhile the question of foreign policy, on which the use of these military and naval forces depended, was gradually coming to the front. As the colonies grew out of tutelage, as they became dominions, they were bound to enter into relations with foreign countries on their own account and not merely through British mediation. The results of this were first apparent in the commercial field; and Canada, the elder sister, leading the way, obtained first the right to share with British representatives in negotiating commercial treaties with foreign governments, and finally the right to negotiate and conclude such treaties by herself. Commercial relations may involve political relations; and it was but one step further for Canada to share in the negotiation of political treaties, though only, to begin with, in those that directly concerned her local interests, such as the Alaska boundary treaty with the United States (1903).

At that point the process of advance had halted by 1914. Outside these special treaties, in the general field of foreign affairs, the Dominions still played little part. On the organization of the defence of the Empire as a whole, they had, it is true, been consulted for many years past. Colonial representatives sat from time to time on the Committee of Imperial Defence; and it was primarily for the same purpose that the first Colonial Conference was held in London (1887). Similar conferences were held in 1894, 1897, 1902 and 1907, and on this last occasion it was decided that the Conference should meet at regular intervals of four years. It was also decided—and it marked an advance towards equality—that the conference, which was now to be called the Imperial Conference, should consist of the prime ministers of Britain and the Dominions on an equal footing, with the British prime minister (and not, as heretofore, the colonial secretary) as primus inter pares in the chair.

Dominions and Imperial Defence

It is somewhat remarkable that, while these conferences dealt with all other matters of common interest, they never dealt with foreign policy. It was not till 1911, the last conference before the Great War, when the clouds were already gathering over Europe, that the British foreign secretary informed the Dominion prime ministers as to the secret facts of the international situation. Even then they were only informed and not consulted; and when the prime minister of New Zealand suggested that an Imperial Council should be formed for the joint control of foreign policy, he received no support from his colleagues, who agreed with the British prime minister that the British government could not share its responsibility with other governments. And so, when the Great War came, the Dominions were involved in it without ever having had a voice in the shaping of the policy that had led up to it.

But if, in this last surviving point, they were still not equal in status with Britain, they willingly accepted their position and never asked for more. There was nothing, therefore, to mar the grand demonstration of imperial unity which followed the outbreak of war. In 1914 the success of the second attempt at maintaining a community of British peoples, divided by the seas, within one great political society was shown to all the world to be no less complete than the failure of the first attempt in 1783.

In the course of the Napoleonic wars (as has been seen) the British Empire in India had been extended and consolidated; and the security of the sea route from Britain was confirmed by the acquisition of Cape Colony, Mauritius and Ceylon. In the early years of the peace this ring of strategic posts was further strengthened by developments in the East Indies. The Dutch, back in Java, had quickly reasserted their monopoly over the Malay Archipelago; but they had not yet occupied the Malayan mainland, except at Malacca, when, in 1819, Sir Stamford Raffles was commissioned by Lord Hastings, governor-general of India, to find a suitable port in those waters as a base for British trade with Farther Asia. He found it at Singapore, at the extreme southern point of the Malay Peninsula, a perfect site for a commercial or naval base, dominating the route to China and Japan. By agreement with the local chiefs the British flag was hoisted, to the indignation of the Dutch; and in 1823 a settlement was made by which the British exchanged their posts in Sumatra for Malacca so that the Dutch possessions were now limited to the islands and the British to the Malayan mainland.

British Empire in the East

THE LAST IMPERIAL CONFERENCE HELD BEFORE THE GREAT WAR

Originating in a meeting of representatives of self-governing colonies in London in 1887, the Imperial Conference was established as a quadrennial meeting in 1907. In this photograph of the Conference held in 1911, the premiers seated are, from left to right, Sir Edward Morris, Newfoundland; Sir Joseph Ward, New Zealand; Sir Wilfrid Laurier, Canada; H. H. Asquith, Great Britain; Andrew Fisher, Australia; and Louis Botha, South Africa. Lewis Harcourt, colonial secretary, is in the centre.

Photo, Russell

VALUABLE BRITISH COLONY AND TRADING CENTRE: THE ISLAND OF HONG KONG, CHINA

At the mouth of the Canton river lies Hong Kong, an island some ten miles in length by four and a half in breadth. By the treaty of Nanking in 1842 it was ceded to the British, who had taken possession the previous year. This view, taken about 1875, shows the town of Victoria resting on the slope of the hill, with massed shipping round the promontory. On the left is Morrison's Hill.

From Singapore, which became in time one of the twelve greatest ports in the world, from Malacca and from the older post at Penang British trade and influence radiated over the peninsula; and in 1867 the three districts were united as one crown colony. In course of time, also, the native sultans accepted a British protectorate, with British advisers at their courts, under the general supervision of the governor of Singapore, so that the whole peninsula became part of the Empire as British Malaya. The subsequent development of the country has been wholly beneficial to its people. The old piracy and warfare have been put down, roads and railways built, schools established; and the material prosperity of the country has been enormously increased by the development of tin mining and rubber planting, largely with the aid of immigrant Chinese labourers.

Development of Malay Peninsula

Meanwhile British trade with China was developing. The Chinese government at first confined it to Canton; but in 1841, after a period of friction and conflict, they ceded to Britain the island of Hong Kong as a commercial base. Inhabited at that time by only a thousand natives, it grew as a British colony and a free port, which, like Singapore, was open to all nations, into a great city and a great centre of trade. Its population to-day is about 900,000. In 1860, at the close of the so-called Opium War, other Chinese ports were opened by treaty to British trade, known as the 'treaty ports,' including such important entrepôts as Shanghai and Hankow, and lands were leased for the erection of commercial buildings and residences by British merchants—a precedent soon followed by other European powers.

One further field of Empire in the Far East was opened up in the nineteenth century. In 1842 a private Englishman, James Brooke, acquired a grant of land in the northern part of the great island of Borneo, the rest of which was occupied by the Dutch; and, having aided the native government of Brunei in the suppression of a rebellion, he was rewarded with the gift of the province of Sarawak, of which he and his descendants to this

SINGAPORE, CHIEF OF THE STRAITS SETTLEMENTS

Its position midway between India and China renders Singapore, a town and island situated off the south extremity of the Malay Peninsula, of great value as a naval base and commercial centre. In 1824, five years after its foundation by Sir Stamford Raffles, it was formally recognized as a British settlement and developed into a port of vast importance. A coloured lithograph from the painting by J. T. Thomson gives a view of the town, about 1856, from Government Hill, now Fort Canning.

From Buckley, 'Anecdotal History of Singapore'

day became the legitimate and hereditary 'rajas.' In 1888, under the second Raja Brooke, Sarawak became a British protectorate, retaining its own internal independence, an example followed in the same year by the neighbouring sultan of Brunei. Meanwhile, in 1881, the old system of development by means of chartered companies was revived by the formation of the British North Borneo Company, which obtained the concession of the northern corner of the island. This territory was also placed under British protection in 1888. The only other

FOUNDERS OF EMPIRE IN THE FAR EAST

James Brooke (left, by Sir Francis Grant) visited Borneo in 1839, and, in return for crushing a rebellion that threatened the sultan of Sarawak, was created raja of Sarawak. The province later became a British protectorate. Sir Thomas Stamford Raffles (right, by Joseph) entered the service of the East India Company in 1795 He did distinguished governmental work in Java (1811–16) and in Bencoolen, Sumatra. In 1819 he accomplished the acquisition and founding of Singapore.

National Portrait Gallery, London

British foothold in the East Indies is the little island of Labuan, ceded in 1846 as a base for the suppression of piracy—the permanent curse of all the Malayan world until the British navy stamped it out.

Thus, as the century drew on, the British position in India was buttressed to the south-east by strategic and commercial posts in the area that lies between the Indian and Pacific Oceans and links Asia with Australia. But, when the Suez Canal was opened in 1869 and the course of shipping thus diverted from the Cape to the Red Sea and the Arabian coast, further safeguards were needed to protect the Anglo-Indian trade route, the most vital of the arteries by which the Empire lives. It was this need which led to the occupation of Cyprus in 1878—a foothold in the eastern Mediterranean, already guarded farther west by Malta and Gibraltar—and which was the chief cause of the occupation of Egypt in 1882. Between Egypt and India, Aden, a rocky little post at the eastern approach to the Red Sea, had already been ceded to Britain by the local Arab chiefs in 1838–9. In 1857 the island of Perim, in the very mouth of the Red Sea, was occupied. In 1884 Somaliland, on the opposite African coast, and in 1886 the island of Socotra, some 200 miles out in the Indian Ocean, became British protectorates. And when, finally, a British 'sphere of influence' was established at the mouth of the Persian Gulf, the protection of the route was complete.

Stations on the Indian route

Meantime, by the same almost inevitable process as before, the area of British rule in India had grown as far as it could grow. The purpose by which this rule was inspired, its methods, and the measure of success and failure attending them, may be studied in Chapter 166. The achievements of the period were more striking than those of any other period of the British Raj; but although when the war came Indian opinion as a whole rallied loyally to the defence of the British Empire, it was evident that the political problem had not yet been solved.

While, in the course of the century between 1815 and 1914, the British Empire in Asia was being extended, consolidated and organized in accordance with the principles of a new age, the British Empire in the great central area of Africa was undergoing a still more drastic transformation. In 1815 it consisted of one little settlement of freed slaves and a handful of derelict slave-trade depots on the west coast, while the east coast and the centre of the continent were practically unknown to Europeans except for the remnant of the old Portuguese Empire in the province of Mozambique. In 1914 the British Empire included a great group of colonies and protectorates, in both the eastern and western parts of the tropical belt, covering a wider area than India and containing a population of between thirty and forty millions.

The Empire in Africa

It was not till the latter half of the century that this remarkable expansion took place. At the outset it almost seemed as if the connexion of Britain with Africa had been severed for good and all by the abolition of the slave trade. There was one British foothold, however, on the west coast which was not concerned with the slave trade. In 1787 the group of philanthropists who were fighting the trade had obtained from the local chief the concession of some territory at Sierra Leone; and with the sympathy and assistance of the government they had established a colony there with the object, first, of providing a home for some of the negroes released from slavery by the Somerset judgement, and thrown on the world without any means of subsistence; and, secondly, of developing a legitimate trade in African produce as distinct from the nefarious slave trade.

When abolition had at last been carried (1807), Sierra Leone proved a useful base for the British cruisers engaged in suppressing the trade. It was converted into a regular crown colony and became the centre of British administration on the west coast. Mainly for the same reason the old depots along the Gold Coast and at the mouth of the River Gambia were maintained under government control. Before long British merchants were following the lead set by Sierra Leone and developing a growing trade along the coast and up the rivers; and meantime the interior was being explored partly by adventurous traders like MacGregor Laird and partly by scientific expeditions under the government. Before 1850 the course of the Niger had been followed from source to sea and the desert tracks of the Sahara traversed from Lake Chad to the Mediterranean.

But, apart from exploration, the government took no share in the development of West Africa. In 1861 the island of Lagos, off the Nigerian coast, was annexed, but only as a means of destroying the nest of slave smugglers lodged therein. So far, indeed, was public opinion in Britain from harbouring ideas of imperial expansion that in 1865 a committee of the House of Commons actually recommended an ultimate withdrawal from all West Africa except Sierra Leone.

British trade, however, had already taken root. On their own initiative British merchants were steadily extending their operations into the interior. In 1879 the chief of them united to form the National African Company, which became in 1886 the Royal Niger Company; and their agents kept pushing up the Niger, making treaties of amity and commerce with the native tribes on its banks.

Meantime, from 1870 onwards, the whole situation had begun to change. In the first place, the career of David Livingstone, his journeys across the heart of Africa, his discovery that the Arab slave trade was as great a curse to the Africans as the old European slave trade, and his appeal to the British public to destroy it by developing civilization, trade and mission work throughout the dark interior, had revived the idea that, in Africa as in Asia, Britain had not merely a commercial opportunity but also a duty towards the native peoples. Secondly, the French after 1871 began rapidly to occupy and annex territory in the north-west districts of Africa as compensation for the losses they had suffered in the Franco-Prussian War; and as they pressed southwards from Algeria across the Sahara they came into contact with the British merchants pushing inland from the west coast. Unless their further advance had been resisted, the whole of this section of Africa would soon have become French. Thirdly, it was becoming evident that a fuller development of African produce was needed to provide the raw materials and the markets for the growing industries of Britain and other European countries.

PREMPEH, KING OF ASHANTI

Wars with the barbarous Ashantis frequently menaced the British inhabitants of the Gold Coast. The terms of a treaty made in 1874 were ignored by Prempeh, who became king of the Ashantis in 1886, and he was taken captive by the British in 1896. This photograph shows him in native robes.

Photo, Deaville Walker

Finally, Germany, which had hitherto played no part in colonisation, determined to secure a foothold in Africa, and in 1884 annexed Togoland and the Cameroons.

All these factors combined to force the reluctant British government into a forward policy. The limits of the little Gambia Colony were defined and secured against French encroachment. The hinterland of the Gold Coast was occupied and pacified, and the power of the Ashantis, a barbarous fighting people, addicted to the practice of human sacrifice on a ghastly scale, was finally broken. On the Niger the operations of the Company were now encouraged and supported; in 1887 a British protectorate was declared over all the territory under its control; in 1890 the conflict with the French was terminated by the delimitation of British and French spheres of influence; and in 1900 the government took over from the Company the charge of all its territories, which in 1912 were united with Lagos to form the British Colony and Protectorate of Nigeria.

Forward policy on West Coast

The method of governing this group of territories which constitutes British West Africa has varied widely according to the character of the native peoples concerned; but it was everywhere inspired from the outset by two cardinal principles. The first was the principle of 'trusteeship'—that the primary object of government was the welfare of the governed. Thus, in West Africa as in India, the government set itself to maintain internal peace and order, to open paths for trade and civilization by building roads and railways, to suppress such barbarities as human sacrifice, to stamp out the Arab slave trade and eliminate slavery, and to assist the missionaries in the task of education. But in all these activities and in the actual forms of government adopted, a consistent attempt was made to preserve as far as possible the native methods and customs, and, where a reasonably just and efficient system of native administration already existed, to maintain and supervise it rather than destroy it in favour of direct British rule. Thus, while among the primitive pagan tribes of southern Nigeria and the Gold Coast hinterland direct rule is necessarily undertaken by British officials, in the Moslem states of northern Nigeria, with their ancient and relatively advanced system of Islamic law, the native emirs are left in charge of their own people, with their own councils, law-courts and police, the British officials merely acting as their advisers.

The second principle is that the economic resources of the country should be developed as effectively as possible for the

MOSLEM RULERS OF NORTHERN NIGERIA AT THE DURBAR OF 1913

In conformity with the British policy of preserving the existing laws and customs in their protectorates whenever expedient, the administrative system of northern Nigeria remains in the hands of native emirs with their own laws and law courts. At the great Durbar held on New Year's Day, 1913, in Kano, all the sultans and emirs of the north assembled on amicable terms, although feuds of long standing had existed between many of them. In the centre of the group is the Shehu of Bornu.

Photo, courtesy of H. S. Goldsmith, C.M.G.

LAKE NYASA FROM SPHINXHAVEN

Third largest of the great Central African lakes, Nyasa was discovered in 1859 by Livingstone from the south and by Albrecht Roscher, the German traveller, from the east. In its neighbourhood mission stations were established by the Universities' Mission to Central Africa, whose foundation was inspired by Livingstone.

Courtesy of the Universities' Mission to Central Africa

benefit of the world as a whole. That the world needs the produce of the tropics is obvious enough. But it is essential that the pursuit of the second object should not lead to the neglect or contravention of the first and major principle. Happily in British West Africa there has been no such conflict of interests between Europeans and Africans. Its climate is unsuitable for the permanent residence of European settlers; it cannot become a white man's colony like South Africa; the white residents are mainly officials, missionaries and traders, not settled landowners; the natives themselves own the land and cultivate it and sell its produce to the merchants, who convey it to the markets of Europe. Already, before 1914, the success of this economic system was apparent in the great increase of production, especially of cocoa and palm-oil, and in the rising standard of living among the native cultivators. As in India, the virtues of the second British Empire can be set against the vices of the first.

Meanwhile, the unknown heart of tropical Africa had been slowly penetrated and occupied. In the middle of the nineteenth century the whole of the east coast between Portuguese Mozambique and the approaches to the Red Sea were nominally under the control of the Arab sultan of Zanzibar. Throughout that area and beyond it, among the tribes that dwelt about the upper waters of the Zambesi, the Arab slave traffic left its trail of misery and bloodshed.

To Europe it was an unknown, mysterious land, until the greatest of British missionaries, David Livingstone, slowly pushing up from his first station to the north-west of Cape Colony, broke into 'darkest Africa,' and revealed its secrets to the world. In 1873, worn out by hardship and

DAVID LIVINGSTONE: MISSIONARY AND EXPLORER

David Livingstone (1813–73), here shown writing his journal, laboured among the natives of Bechuanaland for nine years before he undertook his exploratory expeditions into darkest Africa. He was a powerful advocate of the suppression of the slave trade, and his work inspired those who followed later.

From the sketch by H.M. Stanley

disease, he died. But his work lived after him; for his solemn call to his countrymen to continue the task he had begun had not gone unheeded. His message was quite simple. The Arab slave trade, that 'open sore of the world,' must be abolished as utterly as the European slave trade before it. And the way to abolish it was for Englishmen to go to Central Africa to settle there where the climate permitted, as it did in the Nyasa country he had himself explored, and, by the development of mission work and lawful commerce, to advance the frontiers of civilization until the forces of barbarism on which the slave trade fed were driven back into the sea.

The first result of this appeal was the foundation of the Universities' Mission to Central Africa, and the establishment of other mission posts in the neighbourhood of Lake Nyasa. Soon afterwards the African Lakes Company was founded to facilitate transport up the Shire River and on the lake; and British settlers began to occupy the fertile and healthy Shire Highlands. The fantastic claim of Portugal to the sovereignty over all Central Africa was rebutted; treaties were made with the native chiefs; and before the close of the century the country was definitely included in the British Empire as the Protectorate of Nyasaland.

Meantime, the pioneers of colonisation had been following Livingstone's work from the south. The Nyasa district was but part of a great belt of highland country, apparently suitable for European settlement, which stretched from Uganda through Kenya and Tanganyika to link up with the 'high veldt' of South Africa; and to the quick imagination of Cecil Rhodes it seemed as if another group of British colonies might be planted there, linking South Africa with the Sudan and Egypt. 'Give me the centre of the continent,' he said, 'and let who will have the swamps which skirt the coast.' His first step was to obtain, in 1888, a concession for the exploitation of minerals from

VICTORIA FALLS STATION ON THE CAPE TO CAIRO RAILWAY

An important part of Cecil Rhodes' imperial dream was a railway some six thousand miles in length which should connect Cape Town with Cairo. The southern section of this vast undertaking starts from Cape Town and runs by Kimberley to Vryburg, whence the Rhodesia Railway Company carries the line on to Mafeking, Bulawayo, the Victoria Falls on the Zambesi and the Belgian Congo frontier. From Cairo the line has been carried to Shillal in Egypt and from Wadi Halfa to Khartum.

Photo, E.N.A.

CATHEDRAL AT ZANZIBAR

Arab traders once bartered their human merchandise upon the site now occupied by this English cathedral at Zanzibar. It was due to the tact and personal influence with the sultan of Sir John Kirk, one of Livingstone's disciples, that the flourishing slave market there was destroyed.

Photo, Universities' Mission to Central Africa

Lobengula, king of the Matabele, a warrior tribe located north of the Transvaal between the Limpopo and the Zambesi; and in 1889 yet another chartered company, the British South Africa Company, was founded.

In 1890 the company occupied Mashonaland—a step which was bound to cause trouble with the Matabele, who regarded the weaker Mashonas as their natural prey. Hence, in 1893, a Matabele attack on the Mashonas precipitated a conflict in which the Matabele were crushed by the company's troops, Bulawayo, their capital, occupied, and their country annexed. But the martial tribesmen did not finally submit until, after a rebellion in 1896, a permanent peace was established through the personal intervention of Rhodes. Meanwhile, the new settlers had begun to develop the agricultural and mineral resources of the country, and a railway was rapidly constructed from the borders of Cape Colony up to the Zambesi and beyond—the first stage of the all-British Cape-to-Cairo line of which Rhodes had dreamed. Before his death in 1902 the company he controlled had pushed its operations beyond the Zambesi, and occupied the area between Matabeleland and Nyasaland; and in commemoration of their founder the new territories were named Northern and Southern Rhodesia.

Half of Rhodes' prayer had thus been answered. The British had occupied 'the centre of the continent,' between Portuguese Angola and the Belgian Congo on the west and Portuguese Mozambique on the east, as far north as Lake Nyasa. There remained the great block of country stretching from the string of inland seas that lie below the sources of the Nile eastwards to the Indian Ocean. The sovereignty over all this area was claimed by the Moslem sultan of Zanzibar, an island off the coast, which had long been a great centre of the Arab slave trade, and it was mainly the influence exerted over the sultan and his successor by one of Livingstone's younger companions and disciples, Dr. (afterwards Sir John) Kirk, that determined the fate

ENEMY OF SLAVE TRADERS

At Zanzibar, where he became consul general in 1873, Sir John Kirk (1832–1922) influenced the sultan to abolish the slave trade. He attended the Slave Trade Conference at Brussels in 1889–90.

Photo, Elliott & Fry

NATIVE MONARCH OF UGANDA

By the Anglo-German agreement of 1890 Uganda, between the Anglo-Egyptian Sudan and Kenya Colony, became British. Four years later it was declared a British protectorate. This warrior is Mtesa, one of Uganda's native kings.
From Speke, 'Journey to Discover the Source of the Nile'

of this last survival of the Arab empire in Africa.

Kirk was stationed at Zanzibar as the consular agent of the British government for twenty years (1867–1887); and it was primarily due to him that the sultan consented to abolish the slave trade in his dominions (1873). An English cathedral now stands on the site of the old slave-market at Zanzibar. So completely, moreover, did the sultan learn to trust Kirk and the nation he represented, that in 1878 he offered the lease of all his mainland territories to the British India Company. But the British government, now, as always, reluctant to extend its colonial responsibilities, refused to authorise the company to accept the offer; and, a few years later, the whole question was complicated by the entry of Germany into the African arena, bent on securing a footing in such districts as had not yet been occupied by other powers.

In 1884 a German protectorate was declared over Togoland and the Cameroons, as has been seen, and also over the unattached area between British South Africa and the Atlantic, which was named German South-West Africa. In 1885 the German East Africa Company was founded; and since the British government of the day was anxious not to quarrel with Bismarck over his colonial designs, Kirk was instructed to persuade the sultan, much against his will, to assent to a German occupation of the southern half of his territories. At the same time he conceded to the newly founded British East Africa Company similar rights in the northern half. After a period of latent conflict and intrigue, during which German agents attempted to outflank and narrow down the British sphere, a definite division was effected by the Anglo-German agreement of 1890. The larger and more populous southern area between Lake Tanganyika and the sea became German East Africa; the northern area, up to Somaliland and Abyssinia, became British East Africa; and with the sultan's full consent a British protectorate was also assumed over the island of Zanzibar.

Acquisitions on the East Coast

The agents of the British East Africa Company had penetrated, meanwhile, into Uganda, the country lying between the lakes and the Sudan, and thus the last link in the northward chain. But their German rivals were also on the scene, and it was only by the coolness and tact of Captain Frederick (afterwards Lord) Lugard, who had previously been involved in some dangerous fighting with Arab slave traders in Nyasaland, that the native king was persuaded to take the British side. Further difficulties arising from violent dissension between the Protestant and Catholic missions were also settled by Lugard. It seemed, however, as if Uganda would be abandoned to some other European power since the Company, convinced that its work in British East Africa was more than enough for its financial resources, decided to withdraw. But, after prolonged discussion, the British government consented to undertake the responsibility itself; and in 1894 it declared Uganda a protectorate.

In these new territories the aims and methods of British administration were the same in principle as in West Africa. In those districts of Uganda in which an elaborately organized quasi-feudal system had long been established under a native king the method of indirect rule was adopted. Among the more primitive tribes of Rhodesia, Nyasaland and British East Africa direct rule was assumed by British officials. And in East as in West Africa economic development proceeded side by side with the development of mission work, education and scientific research to combat the tropical diseases that preyed on men and beasts. The Cape-to-Cairo railway was advanced across Northern Rhodesia up to and beyond the frontier of the Belgian Congo; and another line was built from Mombasa through British East Africa into Uganda.

But in one dominant feature British East Africa differed from British West Africa. Apart from the lowlands on the coast it is a country in which white men can live. British settlers, few at first, but gradually increasing in numbers, began to lease or purchase land from the government and to develop farms of their own. The task of cultivating the natural resources of the country was thus directly undertaken by British colonists as well as natives, and not, as in West Africa, by natives only; and the fulfilment of the other and higher task to which British rule is dedicated, the maintenance of a 'trust' for the welfare of the natives, was rendered more difficult by the possibility of a conflict between their economic interests and those of the colonists.

There remain the northern links in the chain of British territory—Egypt and the

NATIVE RULERS OF BUNYORO

Bunyoro, lying between the Victoria Nile and Albert Nyanza, was annexed to the Uganda Protectorate in 1896. The people, of Wahima stock, have considerable civilization and are ruled immediately by their own king and the Sacred Guild of great chiefs under British control.

Photo, Rev. J. Roscoe, Mackie Ethnological Expedition

FREDERICK, LORD LUGARD

Very distinguished service was rendered to British colonial government by Lord Lugard. The offices he held include those of administrator of Uganda, commissioner of West Africa, and governor of Northern and Southern Nigeria.

Photo, Russell

Sudan—connecting Central Africa with the Mediterranean by way of the Nile valley. That Egypt should have been brought within the orbit of the British Empire was wholly due to its geographical position. It lies across the route from Britain to India; and when the Suez Canal was opened in 1869 it became an essential object of British policy to safeguard the passage of British shipping through this vital artery. The canal itself was and is managed by an international company, in which the British government, having purchased a large block of shares in 1875, is fully represented, and it is open to the use of all nations on payment of the same tolls.

But British opinion has always maintained that, owing to the extent and importance of the British Empire in Asia, British interests in the security and freedom of the Canal are greater than those of any other nation; and for that reason it has always objected to Egypt being brought under any other nation's control, since in that case, in the event of a European war, Britain might find herself cut off from India.

LORD CROMER

Evelyn Baring, the first Lord Cromer (1841–1917) held office as British consul-general in Egypt from 1883 to 1907. During most of this period he was virtually ruler and carried out various legal and financial reforms.

Photo Elliott & Fry

This need not, however, have led to any direct British interference in Egyptian affairs if Egypt had possessed an orderly and efficient government of its own. But it was part of the old Turkish Empire and it was grievously misgoverned by an Albanian dynasty of khedives or viceroys and a body of corrupt and tyrannical Turkish officials. The Egyptians were taxed to the bone, and millions were recklessly borrowed from Europe and recklessly squandered. At last, in 1879, Britain and France, the two countries most concerned in those loans, interfered to prevent a complete financial collapse and established a system of control over revenue and expenditure. But this, in turn, provoked in 1882 a nationalist rebellion under Arabi Bey, an Egyptian officer, and the British government, with manifest reluctance and after vainly trying to secure the co-operation of France, landed a force in Egypt to put a stop to rioting and bloodshed and protect the lives of European residents.

Interference in Egypt

It was intended that the troops should be withdrawn as soon as order had been restored; but, once in Egypt, it was almost impossible to get out, until at least some stable system of government and finance had been constructed out of the chaos of misrule and rebellion. Sir Evelyn Baring, afterwards Lord Cromer, was therefore appointed British agent and consul-general to advise the khedive, assisted as time went on by a corps of British officials. Egypt remained a province of the Turkish Empire; the sultan's suzerainty was still recognized and a form of tribute paid to him; but, since it was understood that the khedive was bound to accept Cromer's advice if it were pressed, Egypt became in fact something like a British protectorate under the system of indirect rule.

Withdrawal, meantime, was made more difficult than ever by the development of grave trouble in the south. A Moslem prophet, known as the Mahdi, appeared in the Sudan, the great subtropical province on the upper waters of the Nile which had been annexed by Egypt early in the nineteenth century, and, summoning the warlike and fanatical tribesmen to a holy war, he easily defeated the feeble Egyptian troops and threatened to let loose a tide of conquest and destruction right down the Nile valley. The British and Egyptian governments decided to evacuate the Sudan; but unfortunately the British officer, Gordon, sent to carry out this difficult task, allowed himself to be cut off and besieged in Khartum. Public opinion in England demanded that an effort should be made to rescue him; but it was only after many months' delay that the relief expedition started up the Nile, and it reached Khartum just too late. Two days earlier the town had fallen and Gordon had been killed (January, 1885).

A MOSLEM FANATIC

Believing that it was his mission to deliver Egypt from foreign domination, the Mahdi raised an army and overran the Sudan. He died in 1885, and his successor was crushed at Omdurman.

The expedition returned to Cairo; but it was recognized that the problem of the Sudan had not by any means been settled and that, quite apart from questions of prestige or retribution, the peace of Egypt would never be secure while the power of the Mahdi, menacing the southern frontier and controlling the Nile waters on which Egypt lives, remained unbroken. In 1896, therefore, a combined British and Egyptian army under General Kitchener ascended the Nile and after several minor battles completely crushed the forces of the Khalifa, the Mahdi's successor, at Omdurman (1898). The Sudan was thus reconquered and reoccupied under the joint administration of Britain and Egypt. Under British and Egyptian officials a new regime of peace, order and justice was established. Irrigation works were undertaken and the productivity of the country, especially in cotton, was immensely increased.

Meanwhile, under Cromer's patient and firm control, the whole political and economic life of Egypt was being transformed. When he came to Cairo in 1883 he found Egypt burdened almost to bankruptcy by a huge public debt, its administration incompetent and dishonest, its army in disorder, its peasant people oppressed and exhausted. He left it in 1907 a prosperous and progressive country, with its finances restored and soundly organized, with an efficient and trustworthy administration, with a well trained army under British leadership, with an elaborate system of modern irrigation which had vastly increased the yield of the soil, and with its eleven million people more lightly taxed, better protected from injustice, more prosperous and more contented than they had ever been in all the long history of their race.

None the less, in Egypt as in India, alien control, however benevolent and beneficent, could not satisfy the younger generation of educated Egyptians; and already before the Great War a nationalist movement had developed whose leaders declared that Britain's work in Egypt was now finished and that the time was ripe for the fulfilment of her old promise to withdraw. To the British, on the other hand, it seemed that a hasty relaxation of control, a premature abandonment of Egypt to Egyptian self-government, might mean the undoing of all the good work done. Political concessions were made, however, between 1907 and 1914.

Steps to Egyptian independence

Wider powers of local government were given to provincial councils, and the bicameral legislature was replaced by a single chamber, mainly elective, and with increased authority over the executive. But in vital matters the advice of the British consul-general was supreme.

No survey of the British Empire as it exists to-day would be complete without some account of its two groups of island colonies, one in the Atlantic, one in the Pacific, which, though some of the units which compose them are separated by many leagues of sea, can be conveniently discussed together. The first group, the West Indies, was, as has been seen, economically united with West Africa under the first British Empire. But the old link was broken by the abolition of the slave

WEST INDIAN SLAVERY

In 1833 the duke of Wellington, among others, signed a protest against Lord Stanley's West India Slavery Bill; and this satire shows a negro, with the features of the duke, 'protesting' against entering the waters of emancipation.

trade (1807); and soon after the close of the Napoleonic wars the same humanitarian movement which had abolished the slave trade brought the whole slave system to an end by the abolition of slavery itself. A measure which deprived them of their human property and transformed the economic basis of their industry was not unnaturally opposed by the majority of the British planters and their agents in Britain. But the planters refused to accept the British government's advice to take in hand themselves the task of ameliorating the conditions of the slave system and preparing the way for emancipation. Led by Buxton and cheered on by the veteran Wilberforce from his retirement, the attack was opened in Parliament in 1823; but for ten years the government maintained its policy of patient but fruitless

OPTIMISM ON 'THE FIRST OF AUGUST'

At midnight of the last day of July, 1834, Lord Stanley's bill came into force, and this extravagant drawing of the period reflects the jubilation of the anti-slavery agitators. Actually, however, emancipation was not an unmixed blessing at first, the negroes taking time to learn what freedom meant.

From Madden, 'West Indies,' 1835

exhortation, till at last in 1833, when it was clear beyond question that the colonial legislatures would never do their duty by themselves, the first Reform Parliament passed an Abolition Act. At midnight on July 31, 1834, over 800,000 slaves in the British Empire became free men, their masters being compensated by a grant of £20,000,000. The act prescribed that the ex-slaves should continue to work for their masters as apprentices for a period of years; but this system operated so badly that in 1838 complete freedom was enacted.

Stagnation in the West Indies

Inevitably the planters suffered from the subsequent dearth of labour, for the freed slaves were none too ready to hire themselves to their old masters; and the economic welfare of Jamaica and her sister islands was further injured by the introduction of free trade in Britain and the development of beet sugar in Europe. The West Indies, once regarded as so vital to the Empire, became a neglected backwater. The European population diminished. Many of their estates passed into the possession of half-castes and negroes. A class of negro peasant proprietors developed, growing their own food. As a final symptom of social and political decay the old colonial representative assemblies were abolished and the islands were administered as crown colonies.

Latterly there has been some recovery. The fruit trade, especially in bananas, and the British preferential duties on sugar have restored in some degree the prosperity of Jamaica; and demands have been made for the restitution of the old political status and even for the grant of responsible government. Of the other islands Trinidad has prospered most, owing to its fruit and oil and asphalt; and, out in the ocean to the north, the Bermudas and Bahamas have benefited by their close commercial relations with the United States. There are special economic links, moreover, between the islands as a whole and Canada; and a commercial agreement between them has been made.

The West Indies are one of the oldest parts of the British Empire; the British islands in the Pacific are one of the newest. It was not till the nineteenth century, after colonisation had begun in Australia and New Zealand, that British traders and missionaries began to penetrate in any numbers into the beautiful, romantic world of the South Seas. They found its myriad islands populated by primitive peoples, who were addicted to savage customs but amenable to European control, and productive of such marketable goods as sandalwood and copra. Side by side with the British intruders came the French; and the story of West Africa was repeated. Rival spheres of influence were marked out; protectorates established; and finally annexations made, until in the end the French had occupied most of the eastern group together with New Caledonia and its satellites in the west, and the British had occupied the Polynesian and Melanesian groups, while the New Hebrides were assigned to a cumbrous Franco-British 'condominium.' Towards the end of the century the United States annexed the Hawaii or Sandwich Islands and Germany the Bismarck Archipelago and part of northern New Guinea.

Protection for the Pacific Islanders

This partition of the South Seas among the European powers was, no doubt, inevitable; but inevitably also the islanders suffered in the process. The earlier traders were none too scrupulous; and when sugar plantations were developed in Queensland a traffic grew up for supplying labourers from the islands which rapidly degenerated into something not unlike the slave trade. Few of the natives could understand the terms of their contracts and many of them were actually kidnapped. This 'blackbirding,' as it was called, might have long continued in those remote unpoliced seas if public opinion had not been awakened to the scandal by the tragic fate of Bishop Patteson, Bishop Selwyn's lieutenant and successor in the Melanesian mission field, who was murdered in 1871 by some islanders determined to take vengeance for their kinsmen on the first white man they could catch. In 1872 a Pacific Islanders Protection Act was passed by the Imperial Parliament, and in 1875, under another act, the governor of Fiji, the largest of the British islands and the centre of administration, was appointed high commissioner of the Western Pacific with the duty of enforcing the law and safeguarding the natives from injury.

In 1914 the second British Empire had existed for 130 years. It had grown far beyond the limits of the first, until it covered about a quarter of the earth. Its political, economic and social conditions varied widely in its different parts. And, while its development had been guided in the main by two great principles—by the principle of equality in the European or self-governing field and by the principle of trusteeship in the non-European or dependent field—another no less vital principle, that of unity, seemed to have been neglected. What was it, men asked, which really kept the Empire together?

Two movements therefore developed in British political circles with the object of attaining a closer imperial unity. The first was political and aimed at imperial federation, that is, the application to the self-governing Empire of the system already adopted in Canada and Australia, under which the common affairs of Britain and the Dominions, such as foreign policy and defence, would be controlled by an imperial body directly representative of all the national units concerned. The second movement, led by Joseph Chamberlain, was economic and aimed at a system of inter-imperial preferential duties which might ultimately become a 'Zollverein' or customs-union, prescribing free trade within the Empire as a whole and protection against the rest of the world (see further in page 4477).

Unity of the British Empire

Both movements failed—the first because the Dominions, who were proudly conscious of their new national individuality, were unwilling to contemplate any increased measure of control over their destiny by a body sitting in far-off London in which, though they would themselves be represented, the representatives of Britain would constitute a decisive majority; the second because the British electorate resented the increase in the cost of raw materials, especially food stuffs, which any system of imperial preference would involve. And so, in 1914, the framework of the Empire was as loosely knit as ever.

Despite this, or rather, perhaps, because of it, the unity of the Empire, when the Great War came, was such as to astonish the world. Instantly, spontaneously, unanimously the Dominion peoples determined to take their part in meeting the German challenge. The decision was formally registered by their respective parliaments; and at the earliest possible moment a stream of virile soldiers began to cross the oceans from each of the Dominions to fight in Europe or other areas of the war. Of their fine military record this is not the place to speak. It is enough to say that, at the end of the war, nearly a million men had been recruited in the Dominions for service at the front, and that more than a tenth of them had been killed in action. And in the production of munitions and food supplies and in every field of war effort the Dominions took their full share.

Nor was it only the self-governing part of the Empire which thus rallied to the common cause. The Indian Army, drawn mainly from the martial races of North

VICTIM OF A TRAGIC MISTAKE

After ten years' devoted missionary labour in Melanesia, John Coleridge Patteson (1827–71), consecrated bishop in 1861, was murdered at Nukapu by natives in misguided vengeance for wrongs that they had suffered from white traders.

Engraving from photograph

India, was shipped overseas and fought beside the British in France and Mesopotamia and Palestine, and its strength was maintained by a strong current of recruits. The general loyalty of the Indian people, moreover, was so manifest that it was possible to withdraw some thousands of the British regular troops in India. Generous financial contributions were also made by the native princes and other wealthy Indians. The African members of the Empire likewise played their part. Native regiments were engaged in the campaigns in the German colonies in East and West Africa; many thousands of Africans provided the essential transport service and suffered terribly, especially in East Africa, from exhaustion and disease; and among the South African natives labour corps were formed for work behind the lines in France.

Five empires entered the war—the British, Russian, German, Austrian and Turkish. Four of them collapsed under the strain. The British Empire alone emerged into a new age in which the old-fashioned imperialism of an earlier day, long discarded by the British peoples, is everywhere damned, if not yet everywhere dead. And, as after other wars, the British Empire had been enlarged by victory. It can honestly be said that the British people in 1919, as in 1815, were not eagerly bent on acquiring yet more territories and yet more responsibilities; but, once it had been decided that the German colonies and the Arab provinces of the Turkish Empire were not to be restored to their old masters, it was almost inevitable that the British should share with their allies in assuming the government of those territories under the new mandate system. Thus Britain accepted mandates for Irak, Palestine and Transjordania—a special type of mandate based on the idea of temporary trusteeship. In the case of Irak the mandate was dropped and the country recognized as an independent state associated by treaty with Britain. Mandates of a more permanent kind over more backward peoples were assumed by Britain in German East Africa, renamed Tanganyika, and in part of Togoland and the Cameroons; by South Africa in German South-West Africa which was incorporated in the Union; by Australia in German New Guinea; and by New Zealand in Samoa; while the rich islet of Nauru in the Pacific was entrusted to the joint mandate of Britain, Australia and New Zealand.

AN AFRICAN SOLDIER

Fine service has been rendered to Britain by native regiments in her international colonial struggles and in the Great War. This private, fully equipped, belongs to the King's African Rifles.

Photo, E.N.A.

The Empire was not only thus enlarged, it also underwent a change during the war and the first years of the peace—a change so important that the Empire is now sometimes described as the third British Empire. But this conveys a false idea. It suggests that the post-war Empire is as different in its character from the pre-war Empire as that in turn was different from the first Empire, whereas the change was not so much a transformation as an evolution. It confirmed, continued, carried to their logical climax the principles of life and growth on which the second British Empire had been built since 1783.

Thus, in the first place, the principle of the mandate system, which declares, in the words of the Covenant of the League of Nations, that the well being and development of backward peoples form 'a sacred trust of civilization,' is no new principle to the British Empire. It is the old principle of trusteeship; and in obeying the regulations of the mandates for the protection and advance of native interests, British administrations in Tanganyika or other ex-German colonies have had merely to carry on the rules and methods of government long established in British tropical Africa. The only real novelties in the mandate system are, first, that the principle of trusteeship has now been solemnly accepted by all the great colonial powers; and secondly, that the mandatory state has to render account of its execution of the trust to the Mandates Commission of the League.

More striking was the post-war development in India. Before 1914 educated Indians were not content with the measure of self-government conceded to them by the Morley-Minto reforms (see page 4474); and when the war came, when India proved her loyalty to the Empire, and when the leaders of the allied and associated powers declared that they were fighting for freedom and democracy,

ACCESSION OF KING FEISAL TO THE THRONE OF IRAK

On August 23, 1921, the emir Feisal, son of the king of Hejaz, was inaugurated as king of Irak under British auspices. On a dais in the Great Court of the Serai at Bagdad the new king is in this photograph seen seated in state between (left to right) the British high commissioner, Sir Percy Cox, and the general officer commanding-in-chief, Sir Aylmer Haldane.

Photo, Hana Studios

it seemed difficult to refuse to India a greater meed of freedom, a first instalment at any rate of democratic institutions. Yet to concede this boon seemed scarcely less difficult. The old arguments against attempting democracy in India had lost none of their validity. It was as clear as ever that the welfare of its multitudinous peoples—now grown to over 220 million in British India alone and to over 300 million if the native states were included—was bound to suffer if government were transferred from the hands of the experienced British bureaucracy to those of inexperienced Indian politicians, chosen by an electorate constructed somehow out of a population of which more than 90 per cent. were illiterate and unable to comprehend the meaning of a vote. On the other hand, how were the Indian people ever to achieve political progress, how were they ever to be fitted to govern themselves, unless some day they were given the opportunity of learning to do it? And how could they learn self-government except by practising it?

Post-War events in Indian affairs

These last considerations decided the issue in the minds of British statesmen. They determined to make one of the boldest experiments in history. Accordingly, in 1917, the British government declared its policy to be 'the gradual development of self-governing institutions with a view to the progressive realization of responsible government in India as an integral part of the British Empire'; and in 1919 this policy was incorporated in the Government of India Act. The Act was based on the Montagu-Chelmsford Report, the fruit of a joint inquiry by the secretary of state and the viceroy, which had been subjected to careful examination by a committee of both Houses of Parliament. As regards the All-India government, it replaced the old Legislative Council by a national bicameral parliament, composed of an Assembly and a Council of State, the former consisting of elected representatives from all parts of British India. To this body representative, but not responsible, government was conceded. Thus the Assembly can debate and carry or reject legislation, including the budget, like the House of Commons; but it cannot, like the House of Commons, control the executive, the members of the government of India being still responsible to the Imperial Parliament.

It was in the provinces—each of them great states with many millions of people—that the first step in real responsible government was taken. By a system known as 'dyarchy' the field of government was divided into 'reserved' and 'transferred' subjects. Over the reserved subjects, such as the maintenance of justice and order and the collection of revenue, the governor and his executive council remained as before responsible only to the Imperial Parliament and not to the elected Legislative Council of the province. But the transferred subjects, such as education, agriculture, public works and public health, were handed over to the full control of Indian 'ministers,' responsible, like ministers in Britain, to the Legislative Council. Thus, in this wide field, real self-government was initiated; and the act suggested the possibility of further development by prescribing the appointment of a commission in 1929 to examine the operation of the system during its first decade and to advise Parliament as to its continuance. In 1927, two years before it was due, this commission was appointed with Sir John Simon as chairman. Finally as a guarant ee, so to speak, of the future, a promise of the distant day when India will have learned to govern and guard herself like the Dominions, she was admitted as a separate member to the League of Nations.

Initiation of Self-government

The war also brought about a change in the political status of Egypt. When the Turkish Empire allied itself with Germany, the old formal subjection of Egypt to Turkey was abolished, and Egypt was proclaimed a British protectorate. After the war, however, the nationalists continued their agitation for complete independence; there was a short and easily suppressed revolt; and in 1923 the British government, influenced in the case of Egypt as in that of India by the reactions of the war, declared Egypt to be an independent state under its own hereditary monarchy and a representative legislature. Many of the British officials in the country were retired and replaced by Egyptians; but a British high commissioner remained in Cairo and a garrison of British troops was retained there pending the settlement of certain outstanding questions, such as the security of the Suez Canal, the government of the Sudan and the protection of European residents.

Lastly, the war brought to its conclusion the long process of political assimilation in the Dominions. By 1914, it was noted, they had attained equality with Britain in all fields of government except the last dominant field of foreign affairs. After 1914 it was manifestly impossible for them to continue to take no share in deciding issues which, as they now realized, were issues of life and death. Never again could they permit themselves to be involved in war as members of the British Empire through a foreign policy shaped by Britain only. Nor were British statesmen slow to accept the claim that in foreign affairs, as in all else, the Dominions must be the equals of Great Britain, at least in status if not yet in stature.

SIR ROBERT BORDEN
Elected to the Canadian House of Commons in 1896, Sir Robert Borden became leader of the Conservative party in 1901 and premier in 1911. In 1919 he represented Canada at the meetings of the Peace Conference in Paris.

Photo, Lafayette

In 1917, on the invitation of the British government, the prime ministers of the dominions came to London, not merely to participate in an imperial war conference of the old deliberative and advisory type, but also to sit with the British war cabinet to constitute an imperial war cabinet with executive authority over the conduct of the war. This system was maintained for the rest of the war; and it was continued at the peace conference, at which the British Empire was represented not by British statesmen only, but by a British Empire delegation wherein each Dominion had its representatives. The principle of 'equal nationhood' was finally confirmed, on the initiative of the Canadian prime minister, Sir Robert Borden, when the Treaty of Versailles was separately signed by the Dominion plenipotentiaries and separately ratified by the Dominion parliaments. Similarly, the Dominions became separate members of the League.

A commonwealth of equal nations

Thus, the long process of political assimilation was completed. The self-governing portion of the British Empire had developed into a commonwealth of nations, including the Irish Free State, which was given 'Dominion status' by the treaty of 1922, each free and equal yet all united. At the Imperial Conference of 1926 a statement was drawn up and confirmed by all the prime ministers which summarised this great achievement and made its meaning clear:

> The tendency towards equality of status was both right and inevitable. Geographical and other conditions made this impossible of attainment by the way of federation. The only alternative was by the way of autonomy; and along this road it has been steadily sought. Every self-governing member of the Empire is now the master of its destiny.

And the mutual relations of Great Britain and the Dominions were thus defined:

> They are all autonomous communities within the British Empire, equal in status, in no way subordinate one to another in any aspect of their domestic or external affairs, though united by a common allegiance to the Crown, and freely associated as members of the British Commonwealth of Nations.

CHAPTER 173

CHINA UNDER THE MANCHUS

How the last Days of Imperial Rule epitomise the recurrent Alternations of Chinese History

By J. O. P. BLAND

Author of Recent Events and Present Policies in China, etc., and Part Author of Annals and Memoirs of the Court of Peking

THE history of China has been fittingly described as a series of paroxysms. It is the history of a race whose social system has made frequent famines, rebellions and civil wars inevitable, but which, at the same time, has given to Chinese civilization its unparalleled cohesion and duration. It is impossible to form a correct estimate of the significance of any period or event, such as the fall of the native Ming dynasty and the establishment of the Manchus as rulers in their place, unless we bear in mind the nature of this social system and the fact, arising out of it, that in China the forms of government are of less importance than the men who administer it.

The social structure of the race, based on ancestor worship, the institution of the family and the 'three relations' of the Confucianist philosophy, is something wholly independent of the acts or omissions of the nation's rulers, something which, amidst ever-recurring cataclysms of disorder and distress, has triumphantly stood the test of time; also it has given to the world's oldest civilization a philosophic serenity and to its members and citizens certain qualities which dignify their lives and command our instinctive admiration.

For more than two thousand years the Chinese people have accepted without questioning and acted upon the belief that 'the first duty which man owes to Heaven and to his ancestors is to have posterity.' The result of this deep-rooted belief is that, for the masses of the people, the eternal question, outweighing every other, has always been the problem of daily bread; the peace and prosperity of the Empire have depended far less upon wisdom or wickedness of Mongol, Ming or Manchu rulers than upon the pressure of population on the means of subsistence. The cause of unrest, throughout the ages, has been the acute economic pressure necessarily resulting from an excessively high birth rate. The Chinese have observed the fifth commandment more thoroughly than any other Oriental race, and their days have been long in the land.

But they have not been days of fatness. The author of a modern scientific inquiry into the causes of chronic famine in China puts the facts accurately when he observes that the social system based on ancestor worship 'has produced a race of human beings who are willing to make sacrifices, even to the point of starvation, in order to honour not only their parents but their remote forebears.' To understand the permanence of certain features of China's national life this fact must be borne in mind; also, that no exterior influences can easily displace this religion of the dead in the deep affection of the race which has evolved it. Let the government call itself what it will, this religion retains its hold upon the soul of the people, and continues to exercise a paramount influence both upon the material existence of the masses and upon their outlook on life and death.

Consequences of Ancestor Worship

Studying Chinese history on a large scale, we perceive that paroxysms, such as that which ended in the collapse of the Ming dynasty and those which first shook and then overthrew the Manchus, can generally be traced to a gradually increasing pressure of over-population on the national food supply, which is the immediate and inevitable result of any considerable period of peace and prosperity. We perceive also that these prosperous intervals usually followed upon periods, such as the

Taiping and Mahomedan rebellions, in which uncounted millions 'went to their graves like beds,' leaving vast tracts of country destroyed and depopulated. Thus, according to the figures compiled by the Jesuit missionaries at the court of the emperor Ch'ien Lung, the first census taken by the Manchus after they had definitely established their authority in 1651 showed a population diminished by civil strife to about 55 millions. The first census of the Han dynasty (A.D.1) and that compiled by Kublai Khan at the beginning of his reign in 1280 gave slightly higher figures. In both instances, as the result of the slaughter that marked the violent end of a dynasty or the suppression of a rebellion, the new ruler took over an empire unafflicted by overcrowding.

For forty years after the accession of the Manchu dynasty its rulers were engaged in continual campaigns against the adherents of the Mings in the southern provinces; peace was not completely restored throughout the empire until 1681. The official census of that year showed a total of about 75 millions. From that time forward, under the firm and enlightened rule of the emperors K'ang Hsi and Ch'ien Lung, the nation enjoyed a prolonged period of peace, law and order, which resulted in a rapid increase of the population. In 1720, three years before the death of K'ang Hsi, the total had reached 125 millions. Sixty years later the official estimate was 283; in 1812, under Chia Ch'ing, it had increased to 360, and in 1842, before the outbreak of the Taiping rebellion, it had risen to the saturation point, that is to say, about 400 millions. After the terrible slaughter of that protracted rebellion, in 1862, the Chinese government census estimated the number of survivors at 261 millions. Moreover, the dynastic annals record that during the period of extreme pressure from 1810 to 1830, before battle, murder and sudden death had decimated the population and devastated whole provinces, four great famines had carried off some 45 millions.

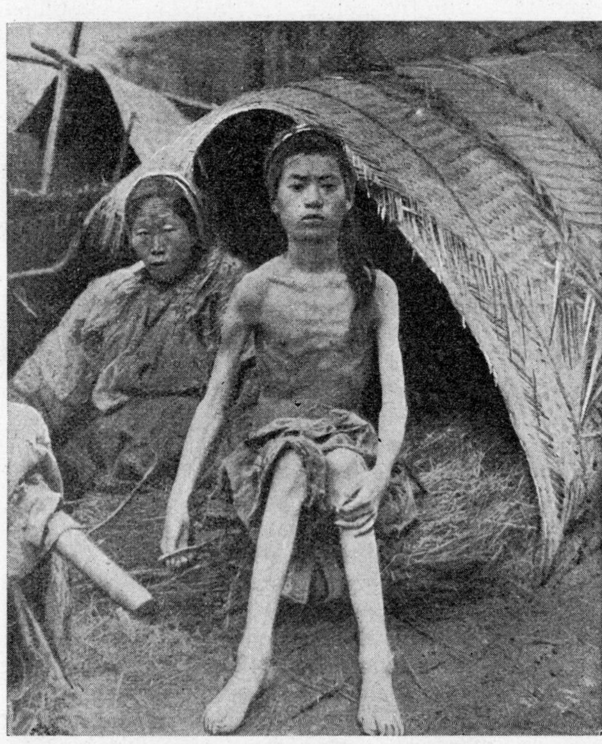

VICTIMS OF FAMINE IN HONAN

With a food supply wholly inadequate for the teeming population, China is subject to constant famine, no year passing in which the death rate is not swollen by sheer starvation. These unhappy creatures are examples of the distress caused by one such visitation in the Lu Shan region of Honan Province.

Photo, E.N.A.

The regular recurrence of famine, as a necessary corrective of over-population, alternative to the swift slaughter of civil strife, is a constant feature of China's national life, a phenomenon which deserves to be seriously studied, not only in interpreting the past but in estimating the future. According to figures published in 1926 in a study by the Agricultural Society of the University of Nanking, no fewer than 1,828 famines were recorded in Chinese history between the years 108 B.C. and A.D. 1911. In other words, for the last 2,000 years—and probably long before that—the normal death rate in China has contained a constant starvation factor, and must inevitably continue to do so unless the natural increase of the population can be kept in check by other and less painful means. Given sufficiency of food, China's 400 millions might easily become 800 in 20 years, and exceed the present population of the planet in half a century. But the actual food supply being wholly inadequate even for 400 millions, and emigration only possible on a limited scale, the fact stands out, undeniable, that the problem of China, past, present and future, is essentially one of social economics, insoluble either by political revolutions or by pious resolutions.

Constant menace of starvation

Under strong rulers, such as the emperors K'ang Hsi and Ch'ien Lung, and later the empress-dowager Tzu Hsi, or under a system of government which, by virtue of precedent and prestige, exercises effective authority, an unstable equilibrium may be maintained, despite the acute pressure of over-population. But whenever the strong hand of recognized authority becomes ever so slightly relaxed, as that of the Manchus became during and after the reign of Chia Ch'ing (1796–1821), the starving multitudes, to whom revolution means food and opportunities of loot, have swiftly joined the company of the nearest freebooter or rebel chief and proceeded to the sacking of cities. The history of China under the Manchus emphasises a truth repeatedly demonstrated under earlier dynasties, namely, that vast masses of human beings, howsoever fatalistic and pacific, will not abide quietly under the constant menace of starvation unless held in check by the strong hand of despotic authority.

Thus the Taiping rebellion, which nearly succeeded in overthrowing the Manchu dynasty, grew swiftly to a devastating force out of the local forays of a handful of Kwangsi bandits. The motive power behind it was the increased severity of economic pressure due to over-population; its rapid successes were chiefly due to the fact that the military organization and race cohesion of the Manchus had degenerated; in fact, the Imperial Clans no longer represented a ruling race. Had it not been for the assistance rendered to them at a critical juncture by General Gordon and his 'ever victorious army' (1862–64), the Taipings would probably have ejected them and established a new native dynasty at Peking, thus following the precedent of the Ming and Han dynasties, founded by 'captains of troops of vagabonds.'

As it was, the Manchus received a new lease of precarious life and gradually succeeded in restoring something of the prestige and authority of the Dragon Throne. Their success in so doing was entirely due to the courage and statecraft of the empress-dowager Tzu Hsi; but the comparative tranquillity which the country enjoyed for a quarter of a century after the collapse of the rebellion must also be ascribed to the fact that throughout large areas the land had gone out of cultivation for lack of inhabitants. Thus the chief incentive to large predatory movements of lawless men had, for the time being, been eliminated.

Rise of the Manchu House

Broadly considered, in the light of many centuries, the Manchus play no very important or impressive part in the long pageant of Chinese history, nor has their rule left many traces upon the structure of the Chinese race. They rose to power and eventually established their authority at Peking, partly as the result of their superior military efficiency and statecraft, but also because the misrule of the eunuch-ridden and incompetent Ming sovereign had left the empire disorganized by internal strife. The actual overthrow of the Mings was effected by the successful rebellion of Li Tzu-cheng, who had actually taken his seat upon the Dragon Throne and might have remained there if another ambitious military commander, Wu San-kuei, had not joined forces with the Manchus to eject him. The fate of China at this juncture depended upon the successful rebels maintaining a united front against the growing power of the forces on their northern frontiers. The country passed under alien rule because, as usual, they quarrelled over the spoils; the immediate cause of Wu San-kuei's defection lay in his chagrin at Li's seizure of his favourite concubine. Wu, having thrown in his lot with the Manchus, was rewarded with the congenial mission of pursuing

Li Tzu-cheng; the latter, after thoroughly plundering the capital, had started southwards with his loot-laden forces. When, having relieved Li of his booty and driven him into the wilderness, Wu returned to Peking, he found the Manchus firmly in the saddle; he then became, and remained for thirty years, a pillar of their state.

The Manchus found the country, decimated by years of civil war and banditry, generally ready to recognize the 'mandate of heaven' in any rulership which promised surcease of strife; their authority was therefore consolidated without much difficulty in the northern and central provinces. Within a year of the proclamation of the Ta Ching dynasty, Nanking had fallen to their forces, and the shaved head and pigtail, imposed by Tatar sovereignty, were generally adopted by all classes. But the separatist tendencies, for which the southern maritime provinces (Kwangtung, Kwangsi and Fukhien) have always been noted, continued to be manifested for several decades in resistance to the Manchus, ostensibly inspired by loyalty to the Mings. It is to be observed—because the facts have a direct bearing on modern events—that even after all organized opposition had been subdued by the armed forces of the emperor K'ang Hsi, the activities of the White Lily, Triad and other secret societies, representing the irreconcilable spirit of the Cantonese, were still in evidence, manifested in piracy, banditry and armed smuggling; and, so soon as the 'moral' of the central government began to show signs of weakening, they speedily assumed the complexion of an anti-dynastic and national movement. The watchword of the Triad society in the earliest days of the Taiping rebellion was 'destroy the Manchus; restore the Mings.' Though that rebellion was eventually suppressed with the aid of General Gordon, it clearly foreshadowed the impending doom of the Manchu dynasty and opened up wider fields of activity for the next generation of Cantonese conspirators and agitators.

The comparative ease with which the Manchu warrior kings established their authority over the greater part of China, and the success with which they subsequently governed it for over a century, may be primarily ascribed to the wise statesmanship and military efficiency of Nurhachi, the founder of the dynasty, by whom war had been declared against the Mings as early as 1618. It was carried on in a number of campaigns until his death in 1626, and thereafter by his son, canonised in Chinese history as Tai Tsung, the Great Ancestor. Before 1618, as the

MAUSOLEUM OF THE MANCHU RULER, TAI TSUNG

Mukden, officially named Fengtien, is one of the oldest towns in Manchuria, and was made the capital of the Manchu line in 1625. In its neighbourhood are three imperial mausolea, the one shown here being the Chao-ling, or Pei-ling, the 'Northern Tomb' in which the emperor Tai Tsung was buried in 1644. A wall 1,800 yards in perimeter encloses the tomb, and rows of granite figures of horses, camels, lions and tigers represent the departed spirits of the emperor's ministers.

Photo, E.N.A.

result of desultory frontier and tribal warfare, Nurhachi had conquered all the region lying between the mouth of the Amur and the Tumen rivers and was in receipt of an annual 'subsidy' from the Chinese court. Tai Tsung, after consolidating his empire over Mongolia and Korea, made several successful raids into China as far south as the capital of Shantung, so that, when eventually they came to ascend the throne of China, the ruler and his kinsmen, the Princes of the Imperial Clans, were well equipped, by experience and study of Chinese affairs, to deal with the problem of administering the country. From the outset, the Manchu sovereigns wisely adapted their rule to the institutions that they found in China, and recognized the necessity of preserving the Confucian philosophy and principles of government.

LACQUER THRONE OF CH'IEN LUNG

Lacquer work, a very early Chinese industrial art, is divided into two classes—painted and carved, the latter made principally at Peking. Ch'ien Lung particularly favoured carved lacquer and had many articles made for the palace. His throne, carved of solid red lacquer, is a fine specimen of the period.

Victoria and Albert Museum

It has been the custom of the revolutionary Cantonese to describe the Manchus as alien rulers, but as a matter of fact, at the period when they succeeded the Ming dynasty, they were probably more nearly akin in temperament and culture to the people of northern and central China than the inhabitants of the southern maritime provinces have ever been. The dispatches addressed by the Manchu sovereign, Tai Tsung, to the last of the Mings in 1642 afford conclusive evidence that, to the Chinese, the Manchus were a little more than kin, if less than kind. They made good their hold on the government of China by virtue of a remarkably efficient military organization, war-seasoned troops and a martial spirit, in all of which the Chinese were lacking. They established and maintained their authority by force of arms, placing Tatar garrisons at strategic points and imposing the tonsure and queue on the conquered nation; but, for the rest, they recognized the superiority of Chinese culture, philosophy and literature. Once again the Canons of the Sages led captivity captive.

Manchu Kinship to the Chinese

The Manchu dynasty reached its zenith of power and prestige under the emperors K'ang Hsi, Yung Chêng and Ch'ien Lung. Under K'ang Hsi the frontiers of the empire were extended from Siberia to Cochin-China, and from the Yellow Sea to Turkistan and Tibet; Ch'ien Lung's campaigns added Ili, eastern Turkistan and Nepal to the imperial dominions. But the enduring fame of these great monarchs rests not so much upon their military conquests as upon their achievements as Chinese scholars, historians and writers. They retained the Manchu language at court, and used it, side by side with Chinese, on their coinage and monuments; but in the domain of literature and philosophy they followed the classical Chinese tradition and achieved their distinction as scholars in conformity with the principles of literary orthodoxy.

The seventeen years' reign of the first Manchu ruler of China, Shun Chih, was so fully occupied with campaigns for the subjection of the Ming dynasty's adherents

A GREAT EMPEROR

Patron of literature, science and art, and himself a distinguished author of an ethical code, K'ang-Hsi was China's most enlightened emperor. During his sixty years' reign (1662–1722) China's native civilization was permanently consolidated.

From Bouvet, 'Histoire de l'Empereur de la Chine'

in the south, that the administration of the provinces, their fiscal relations with the capital and the organization of the public service throughout the country remained more or less in the confused condition to which they had been reduced during the years of chaos preceding the fall of the Mings. The system of competitive examinations for the civil service had ceased to operate ; the southern provinces were administered by three semi-independent satraps, upon whom princedoms and wide powers had been conferred in return for services rendered to the Manchus in their conquest of the empire. It was not until 1681, after defeating a rebellious coalition of these three princes, that the emperor K'ang Hsi was able to consolidate the full authority of the central government and to restore the civil service, composed of classical scholars, to the position which it had held, with occasional periods of disruption, for centuries.

K'ang Hsi was not only a great military commander and a wise ruler ; the fame which he conferred upon his dynasty, probably higher in the eyes of the Chinese than that of any sovereign since the legendary age, rests chiefly on his literary achievements (notably the monumental K'ang Hsi dictionary) and on his encouragement of classical scholarship and the arts. More important than his enlargement of the empire's boundaries,

ODE OF THE EMPEROR CH'IEN LUNG ON A CLOISONNE PICTURE

Ch'ien Lung reigned from 1736 to 1795, and throughout his reign maintained the high literary and artistic reputation established for the dynasty by K'ang Hsi. Ch'ien Lung was an industrious poet, and his odes were often inscribed in facsimile on porcelain and jade. Above is one of his odes carved on the wooden back of a cloisonné enamel plaque mounted as a screen picture. The poem, which interprets the picture, is in the handwriting of the emperor's grand secretary, Liang Kuo-chih.

Victoria and Albert Museum

in its effect upon the social structure and mind of the race, is the 'Sacred Edict,' wherein, as a teacher of morality for the masses, K'ang Hsi expounded the fundamental principles upon which the peace and prosperity of the nation should be established. As monarch, he subscribed unreservedly to the time-tested wisdom of China's ancient worthies and to their philosophy of government by moral agency in preference to physical force. To the preservation and purification of the classical system of education, as prescribed by the Four Books, he devoted years of energetic effort. In re-establishing and reforming the classical system of examinations in the classics for the public service he restored that which, in the opinion of many competent observers, has constituted the chief cause of the time-defying cohesion and longevity of China's civilization.

Classical system of education

Thus, the rule of the Manchus did not produce any influential movement of national life in China reflected either in literature or in art; its achievements, under the best of its sovereigns, lay rather in restoring and consolidating the state in accordance with the great native traditions of the past and in proving, once more, that when the orthodox principles of wise government are applied by rulers who not only prescribe but practise these principles, the nation is likely to enjoy peace and prosperity and unity.

Modern events in China, and the chaotic conditions which have prevailed since the Revolution, have made it more than ever essential for the student of Chinese affairs to appreciate the importance of the old system of competitive examinations for the public service as a permanent factor in preserving the unity of the nation. By this system the collective intelligence of the Chinese has been bound together for ages by the ties of a common language, literature, philosophy and public polity; and it is this which has repeatedly enabled the nation to recover stability after cataclysmic upheavals. It has constantly proved itself stronger than the disruptive and separatist tendencies of the southern maritime provinces and served to restore the authority of the central government, when shaken or overthrown by internal rebellions or foreign invasions. It is a system which gratified the democratic instincts of the masses, because it enabled the studious son of the humblest parents to aspire to the highest honours in the land. Above all, it served to preserve the unbroken continuity of ancient traditions and to enlist all the best brains of the nation on the side of any government which ruled in accordance therewith.

Seen in their right perspective, against the background of the centuries, none of the acts or policies of the Manchu sovereigns, whether wise or foolish, virtuous or wicked, can compare, in its importance for the future of the Chinese race, with the new forces and new influences which were brought to bear upon it from Europe, as the result of the

EXAMINATION CELLS AT CANTON

Until the reforms of 1904 admission to the Chinese civil service had for centuries been exclusively by examination in the Chinese classics. Throughout the examination period candidates were kept in solitary seclusion, day and night, in cells like these in the Grand Examination Hall at Canton.

Photo, Will F. Taylor

traffics and discoveries of the Dutch, Portuguese and English navigators who first invaded the profound seclusion of Asia. Regarded in the light of modern events in China, the arrival of the first Portuguese ship at Canton in 1516 (see page 3525), and the appointment of the Jesuit missionary, Matteo Rixi, as scientific adviser to the court of the Ming emperor Wan Li (1604), appear to be matters of far greater moment than the decadence and downfall of either Mings or Manchus. The history of China, stretching back to the dim ages, shows that the passive, contemplative philosophy which underlies and preserves China's civilization and social system has survived all unperturbed the rise and fall of many dynasties, the crafts and assaults of many invasions. The soul of the people has learned to regard such things as visitations of heaven, to be endured with silent fortitude, like plague, flood and famine. But the coming of the first merchant adventurers and missionaries from Europe, by way of the newly discovered sea routes of the sixteenth century, was as the 'little cloud out of the sea, like a man's hand,' the portent of a new kind of peril which, by undermining the spiritual foundations of the Confucianist system, seems destined to threaten all those things to which Chinese civilization owes its cohesion and recuperative force.

During the first 150 years of the Manchus' rule, that is to say, until the end of the reign of the emperor Ch'ien Lung, there were Jesuits at the court of Peking. The emperor K'ang Hsi, in particular, showed them great favour and devoted much time to literary and scientific studies under their guidance, notably that of Verbiest, famous throughout the empire for his skill in casting cannon and his knowledge of astronomy. As early as the year 1716, however, a viceroy of Canton had become alarmed at the spreading influence of the new doctrines from the West and had petitioned the throne, urging the repeal of the edict of toleration which the emperor had issued in 1692, and that foreigners should be forbidden to preach doctrines contrary to the Canons of the Sages. Later, K'ang Hsi, irritated by the magisterial attitude adopted by the pope with regard to ancestor worship and other matters, issued a decree expelling all missionaries from China, except a few to whom special permits were granted.

THE EMPEROR CH'IEN LUNG

Notwithstanding the enlightened form of government he maintained, and his own intellectual attainments, Ch'ien Lung consistently adhered to the traditional policy of excluding foreigners and foreign influence from China. This drawing portrays him about the date of Lord Macartney's arrival in China.

From Staunton, 'Lord Macartney's Embassy to China'

Henceforward the Roman Catholic missionaries, like the Portuguese, British and Dutch traders, resided in China upon sufferance, and frequently at their peril. Nevertheless, despite the increasing fear and distrust which prompted the mandarinate to keep the foreign merchants at a distance

ROBERT MORRISON TRANSLATING THE BIBLE

Robert Morrison (1782–1834) was sent by the London Missionary Society to Canton in 1807 and became translator to the East India Company's factory. His three great achievements were his Chinese Dictionary, the Anglo-Chinese College at Malacca and his translation of the Scriptures into Chinese.

Engraving after a painting by G. Chinnery

and to limit their activities, their numbers gradually increased, until, at the end of the reign of Ch'ien Lung (1795), they had become a constant source of anxiety to the throne. Incidentally they had also become a constant and profitable source of 'squeezes,' regularly levied by the provincial authorities at Canton and the high officers of the Manchu court.

During the eighteenth century, despite the dictatorial attitude and insatiable exactions of the mandarins, the traders' business steadily grew. In 1807 the first Protestant missionary, the Rev. Robert Morrison, landed at Canton; the 'little cloud' was already beginning to darken the horizon of Cathay. The representatives of the East India Company at Canton, holding a monopoly of the China trade, were becoming more and more restive under a policy of exclusion which compelled them to submit to conditions that were always humiliating and often intolerable. Towards the end of Ch'ien Lung's reign the question had become of sufficient importance to induce the British government to send Lord Macartney as special envoy to Peking, for the purpose of obtaining redress and relief from the exactions and restrictions to which British traders had long been exposed. The venerable emperor received with courtesy the strangers from afar; but the mission produced no improvement in the attitude of the mandarins; on the contrary, the indignities which the traders at Canton had to suffer at their hands gradually increased to a point where they became intolerable, and a resort to force inevitable.

It has been said so repeatedly that Great Britain's first war with China was fought to compel the Chinese to allow the importation of opium that, by sheer force of reiteration, the statement has become very widely accepted. The easily verifiable truth of the matter, admitted by all competent historians, is that, after two centuries of intercourse between Europeans and Chinese at Canton, the only possible alternatives to war were either complete abandonment of the position or abject submission to the petty tyranny of the mandarins. The secretary of state for foreign affairs put the matter quite clearly, four years before

LORD MACARTNEY

George Macartney (1737–1806) had proved his ability in diplomacy and governorship in Russia, Ireland and India before going to China in 1792 as first British ambassador to Peking. He was created Earl Macartney on that appointment.

From Staunton, 'Lord Macartney's Embassy to China'

the dispatch of Lord Macartney's mission, when he wrote:

> Great Britain has long been obliged to pursue this trade under circumstances the most discouraging, hazardous to its agents, and precarious to the various interests involved in it. At Canton . . . our supercargoes are kept altogether in a most arbitrary and cruel state of depression, incompatible with the very important concerns entrusted to them, and such as one hardly supposes could be exercised in any country that pretends to civilization.

The opium dispute was merely one of several burning questions; the cause of the trouble which led inevitably to war lay far deeper than in any question of trade or treaties. It lay in the opposition between two different race minds and philosophies, between the dynamic mobility of the West and the static equilibrium of the East. In so far as the attitude of the Chinese represented their instinctive perception of these differences and of their own weakness, it was justifiable; for them, the prudent path of wisdom undoubtedly lay in keeping the foreigner at arm's length and discouraging by all possible means his endeavours to invade the serene seclusion of the Middle Kingdom. It was the natural attitude of a race fully convinced of its intellectual and moral superiority, and at the same time aware of its inability to face the ordeal by battle.

It is worthy of note that the arrival of the first British envoy to the court of Peking should have synchronised with the end of the reign of the last of the warrior-emperors of the Manchu dynasty. Ch'ien Lung, like his father and grandfather before him, had maintained the military efficiency and martial spirit of the Imperial Clans during the sixty years of his reign and had given peace and prosperity to the nation. By keeping the palace eunuchs severely in their place he had preserved the court from the abuses and demoralisation which their ascendancy had produced under the Mings, and was destined to produce again under his successors. His son, the emperor Chia Ch'ing, inherited an empire of wide frontiers and great prestige; but it was an empire whose population had increased during a cycle of peace and plenty to the saturation point at which, failing the strong hand of authority, the ubiquitous elements of unrest were bound to assert themselves.

With the death of Ch'ien Lung, the Dragon Throne passed into the keeping of one who, in his dissolute person, typified the decline of the Manchu house, and the

CHINA'S EMPEROR ON HIS WAY TO RECEIVE BRITAIN'S AMBASSADOR

Official hostility on the part of the mandarins was unable to stop the influx of foreign merchants, but it imposed restrictions and exactions upon them that became intolerable. It was with the object of improving these conditions that Lord Macartney was dispatched to China in 1793. The emperor Ch'ien Lung received the embassy at Jehol with every courtesy, but he was inflexible in his refusal of the concessions asked for, and Lord Macartney returned home in the following year.

From Staunton, 'Lord Macartney's Embassy to China'

A TAIPING SUCCESS : NAVAL ENGAGEMENT WITH IMPERIALISTS

The Taiping rebellion, ostensibly an attempt to set up a new southern dynasty in the person of Hung Siu-tsüan, was in fact one of the periodically recurrent symptoms of over-population. It was finally suppressed in 1864 by General Gordon, lent to the government by Great Britain. This drawing of the capture of imperialist gunboats by a rebel steamer is from sketches by Augustus F. Lindley, who organized the Taiping naval forces and bitterly denounced British policy and Manchu corruption.

From Lin-Le (Lindley), 'Ti-ping Tien-Kwoh: History of the Ti-ping Revolution,' 1866

degeneracy produced by the enervating influences of their tribute-fed ease. No sooner had Chia Ch'ing mounted the throne than all the symptoms of disintegration began to appear. Corruption and disorganization were manifested in the mandarinate; piracy and lawlessness became endemic throughout the land, while in the south the activities of the secret societies broke out into organized rebellion against the government. Six provinces were laid waste by the White Lily insurrection between 1797 and 1806. The process of demoralisation was rapid and widespread. Some idea of its rapidity may be formed by comparing the descriptions of the court and provincial administration contained in the records of Lord Macartney's mission with those of Lord Amherst's mission twenty-one years later.

The symptoms of disorder, first manifested in the White Lily insurrection, though temporarily repressed, continued to spread and to increase in strength as the moral of the central government weakened, until, forty-four years later, they took definite shape and direction against the Manchu dynasty in the Taiping rebellion. In the eyes of Chinese historians, the course of events after the death of Ch'ien Lung signified that the Manchus had 'exhausted the mandate of Heaven,' and that before long the kingdom must be taken from them. By the aid of General Gordon's 'ever-victorious army,' and by the statecraft of the empress-dowager Tzu Hsi, the dynasty survived the Taiping rebellion, and for half a century contrived to retain its hold on the Empire exhausted by that vast upheaval; but even before the Boxer rising it was clear that it no longer possessed the fibre of resolution and other moral qualities which the Chinese people require of their rulers.

By sheer strength of will power, courage and intelligence, and with the loyal aid of one famous soldier and three great viceroys, the empress-dowager succeeded in restoring something of the prestige and authority of the Dragon Throne. Under her firm rule, for forty years after the final collapse of the Taiping rebellion (1864), the nation enjoyed comparative freedom from internal disorders and insurrections, its recuperative energies being fully engaged in repairing the devastation wrought by the rebel hordes in the central provinces. The Mahomedan rebellion, which broke out in Yünnan and Kansuh in

1868, followed by a revolt of the central Asian tribes, was ruthlessly suppressed by the soldier-viceroy Tso-tsung T'ang. After a ten years' campaign he succeeded in recovering for the Dragon Throne all the territory that had ever come under the imperial sway, from the Yellow Sea to Kashgar and Yarkand. The prestige of the government was temporarily restored by this manifestation of energy, and by the unswerving devotion to her Majesty of such great viceroys as Tseng Kuo-fan, Liu K'un-yi, Chang Chih-tung and Li Hung-chang.

The genius of this remarkable woman, loyally supported by these provincial satraps and by the great majority of the literati, was sufficient to cope effectively with the nation's domestic problems and to carry on the business of government in accordance with the principles to which the masses were accustomed. But neither her genius as a ruler nor the mental equipment of China's viceroys could permanently avert the consequences of the pressure of the West, steadily increasing on all her borders, as the result of the introduction of steam navigation and the outside world's increasing perception of China's commercial possibilities and military inefficiency. Tzu Hsi understood the art of government à l'orientale, but neither she nor her Manchu kinsmen had any real conception of the dangers which henceforth threatened their empire at many points, defenceless alike against the man-killing devices and disruptive influences of Western civilization.

THE DOWAGER EMPRESS OF CHINA

One of the world's greatest women, Tzu Hsi (1835-1908) entered the seraglio of the emperor Hsien Fêng at the age of fifteen. On his death in 1861 her son came to the throne, but Tzu Hsi seized the imperial power and thenceforth remained the wise and all powerful mistress of China until her death.

Photo. E.N.A.

The generation which knew the empress, first as the masterful consort and then as widow of the dissolute emperor Hsien Fêng, had heard the military forces of Great Britain and France knocking at the gates of Peking. Before their pressure was released, China had signed a treaty permitting Europeans to travel in the interior and missionaries to preach Christianity. In the same year Russia, seizing her opportunity, persuaded the helpless Chinese government to cede to her all the territory north of the Amur and between the Ussuri and the Pacific. Fifteen years later China's suzerainty over Korea was challenged by Japan; in 1884 Annam and Tongking passed under the protectorate of France; in 1886 China recognized British sovereignty over Burma. In 1894 the Empire's utterly defenceless condition was clearly manifested by the ease with which her military

K'un-ming Hu, the lotus lake beneath the slopes of Wan Shou Shan, is dotted with islets to which access is given by marble bridges of strange shapes and perfect symmetry. This one with its seventeen arches was built by Ch'ien Lung in 1755 and leads to the 'Temple of Broad Fertility.'

The lovely grounds of the imperial summer palace, or Yuan-ming Yuan, near Peking are a museum of Chinese architecture; they were first laid out by the emperor K'ang Hsi. The palace itself remains in ruins since the sack during the allied expedition of 1860, but many other buildings, like this pavilion on a bridge beside the lake of K'un-ming Hu, were restored by the dowager empress Tzu Hsi.

BRIDGES IN THE PLEASURE GROUNDS OF THE MANCHU EMPERORS

Photo, E.N.A.

Chinese architecture has a uniformity of plan that extends even to the temples of different faiths; only the three miniature stupas on the roof of this example in the grounds of the Yuan-ming Yuan show that it is Buddhist. A handsome 'pailou' or memorial gateway fronts the entrance.

Wood is the basis of Chinese architecture—wooden beams and columns supporting a curvilinear roof which, with its antefixes and coloured tiles (see plate facing page 3519) is the chief feature. The wall spaces may be filled in with stone, as in the temple (top), but in dwelling houses, like this sleeping apartment of Tzu Hsi in the summer palace, its place is often taken by lattice work.

WHERE THE DOWAGER EMPRESS SPENT HER SUMMER LEISURE

Photos, E.N.A.

In the days of imperial rule the Forbidden City, enclosing the palaces, was sacrosanct and unapproachable, but four 'arches of peace,' of which this is one, gave access to the Imperial City. Below are the great towers of the Ch'ien Men leading from the Chinese City through the Tatar Wall.

The names of three rulers are associated with Peking as it stands to-day: Kublai Khan the Mongol, who laid it out; Yung Lo the Ming, who largely rebuilt it on Kublai's ground plan; and Ch'ien Lung the Manchu, who embellished it afresh. It is really four cities in one: the Chinese City on the south, and the Tatar City enclosing the Imperial and Forbidden Cities like a Chinese box.

THE CHINESE GATEWAY: SCENES IN THE NORTHERN CAPITAL

Photos, E.N.A.

Right: Yung Chêng period. Hexagonal lantern; pierced 'famille rose' panels

K'ang Hsi. Plum-blossom tea jar; white on marbled blue

Chi'en Lung 'imperial.' Egg-shell saucer

'Famille verte' vase

Translucent egg-shell lantern

Flowers on black ground.

The Manchu period represents the high-water mark of Chinese porcelain. Of all the many combinations of coloured glaze, under-glaze painting and over-glaze painting, in two or more colours, those in which green predominates (famille verte) characterise the reign of K'ang Hsi; those in which pale reds (famille rose), that of Yung Chêng. The bottom row are all K'ang Hsi, five-colour style.

CHINESE PORCELAIN IN ITS PERFECTION UNDER THE MANCHUS

Victoria and Albert Museum

and naval forces were defeated in the disastrous war with Japan; four years later, Germany's seizure of Kiao-chau was followed by a scramble on the part of the great powers for concessions and spheres of influence.

The tide of China's humiliation ran full flood. The Boxer rising of 1900 in Shantung was not only a danger signal and an indication of severe economic pressure in that region; it was, on the part of the empress-dowager and of the Imperial Clansmen who supported it, a gesture of desperation and of pride stung beyond endurance, a last passionate attempt, using the first weapon at hand, to 'drive the hated foreigner into the sea.' The triumphal march of the military forces of the allied powers through the sacred precincts of the Forbidden City foreshadowed not only the doom of the Manchu dynasty, but the invasion of the Middle Kingdom by new forces, new influences, new ideas, perilous to the very foundations of China's civilization, a menace to the philosophy which for ages had kept the race mind of the nation unperturbed even when divided by internal strife or harassed by invasions.

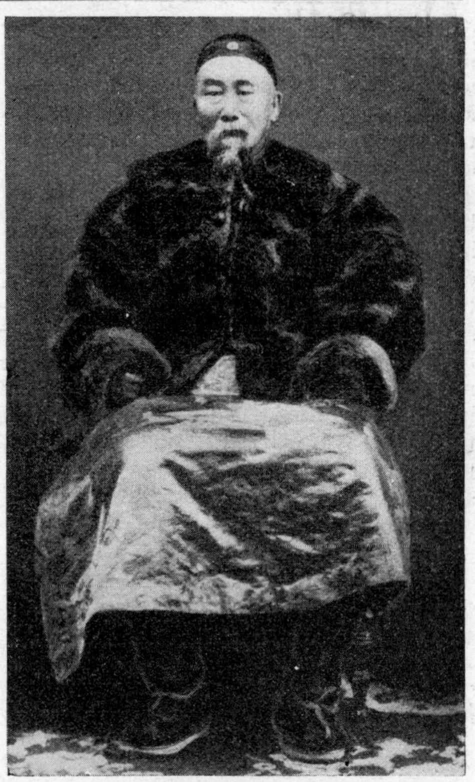

LI HUNG-CHANG

After winning distinction in the suppression of the Taiping rebellion and in various provincial governorships Li Hung-chang (1823–1901) became in 1875 the right hand man of the empress-dowager and a figure of international importance.

Photo, E.N.A.

Western menace to China's civilization

Until the nineteenth century the Chinese were justified, by all the teachings of their long history, in accepting with comparative equanimity the recurrence of cataclysms and calamities inseparable from their social system. The race had heard too often the thunder of the legions, had seen too often the sacking of great cities, to be greatly perturbed by any armed invasion. Its philosophy of history is succinctly summarised in the classical couplet which says: 'Divided long, unites; united long, divides.' Wanderers there might be from the national fold, rebels against the Son of Heaven, but sooner or later they would surely return to their spiritual home, and the nation be once more united from the Great Wall to the Pearl River. For ages the doctrines of the Sages, and the system of public service examinations based thereon, had sufficed to restore the immemorial order.

From this point of view, and having regard to the future of the race, the most important event of the present century in China was the issue by the empress-dowager in 1904 of the edict whereby the ancient classical system of examinations for the public service was abolished, to be replaced by a new curriculum of national education based principally on Western learning and science. Chastened by the capture of her capital by the allies' armies and by the painful experiences of her exile in the provinces, she allowed herself to be persuaded into the belief that China could acquire the secret of the foreigner's material strength, as Japan had done, by encouraging the rising generation of aspirant officials to study in foreign universities, factories, dockyards and workshops. But her decree was not the outcome of a co-ordinated policy, deliberately adapted to the needs of China's national life; it was rather a politic gesture on the part of a tired and disillusioned ruler, fully conscious of the ignorance and helplessness of her Manchu kinsmen and of the growing strength of the insurrectionary movement against the dynasty in the south.

The remarkable series of edicts issued between her return to power in 1901 and her death in 1908 clearly reflect her conviction that the only hope of maintaining the rule of her house, and preserving China as an independent state, lay in a gradual introduction of new methods of education and radical reforms in administration. Also she perceived that her avowed conversion to liberal principles and readiness to grant a constitution, after due preparation, was calculated to impress public opinion abroad and to conciliate the disaffected elements in the south, thus giving the dynasty a breathing space and a last chance of setting its house in order. Had she lived and had her proposed measures for political and administrative reform been carried out under the wise guidance of her faithful 'elder statesmen'—Yung Lu, Yuan Shih-k'ai and Chang Chih-tung—the national system of education and the civil service might possibly have been reformed by the cautious introduction of new methods, skilfully adapted to the raw material with which China's rulers have to deal.

She and they were fully aware that no constitution could be of any real benefit to the nation until the electorate had been educated up to it and the administration organized to apply it—an elementary truth which the Cantonese 'constitutionalists' persistently ignored. Moreover, she realized, and in her edicts proclaimed, the still more important truth, that in introducing reforms care must be taken not violently to uproot the fundamental institutions, but to graft the new on to the old, 'so that officials and people may be led to understand what executive government means as a foundation and preparation for the granting of a constitution.' But Tzu Hsi died a few months after the issue of the decree in

MAIN STREET OF TSINGTAU AFTER THE GERMAN OCCUPATION

In November, 1897, Germany seized the territory of Kiao-chau in the province of Shantung, a high-handed proceeding subsequently regularised by the concession of a lease of the territory for ninety-nine years, during which Germany was to enjoy full sovereign rights. Melton Prior's sketch, made shortly after the occupation, shows the Germans in the main street of Tsingtau, the chief town. In German hands, Tsingtau was developed into a good harbour, strongly fortified.

ENTRY OF THE VICTORIOUS ALLIES INTO CHINA'S CAPITAL

In 1900, China's immemorial hostility to foreign intrusion culminated in the nationalist Boxer rising. Following the siege of the foreign legations in Peking actual war broke out in June, terminated by the occupation of the capital by a combined force of the Allied powers. This sketch by John Schönberg shows General Count von Waldersee, generalissimo of the Allied forces, attended by the American, Austrian, British, German and Russian generals, entering Peking on October 17, 1900.

which she had outlined the programme for constitutional reform, and, so far as the government of China was concerned, wisdom died with her.

The immediate effect of the abolition of the classical curriculum as the highway to official employment was to throw the whole business of national education into confusion and to send large numbers of students in search of Western learning to Japan, America and Europe. Secondary results were speedily manifested in the well meant but frequently misguided educational activities of American and English missionary societies, rapidly followed by the ascendancy of the new undisciplined student class, organized by the Cantonese radicals, as the dominant political force in China. In its ultimate effect, the empress-dowager's momentous break with the past has served to diminish the moral authority and restraints of the Confucianist principles, upon which China's self-contained civilization is based. It has also produced a new class of aspirant rulers who are obviously incapable of ruling, inasmuch as they profess no respect for the fundamental beliefs which constitute the inner life of the people—ancestor worship, and the basic philosophy of the Book of Changes.

Everything in the record of the 'Western-learning' intelligentsia since 1885 goes to prove—if proof be needed—that their social and political ideas can never appeal to the soul of the race, wherein reverence for the patriarchal philosophy of its ancestors has attained to the force of instinct. Throughout the centuries the Chinese people has frequently displayed its willingness to accept the government of alien rulers, if administered upon the principles to which it is accustomed; it has never manifested any disposition to allow an alien culture to modify its

THE LAST MANCHU EMPEROR

Born in 1906, Hsüan T'ung succeeded Kuang Hsü in 1908. He was deprived of his throne in 1912 after the revolution; in 1924 his title of emperor was abolished and he became an ordinary citizen under his personal name, Pu Yi.

From Backhouse and Bland, 'China Under the Dowager Empress'

ethical ideals, its outlook upon life, or social structure. Herein, then, lies the central factor which differentiates the chaos prevalent in China since the overthrow of the Manchus from that produced by the violent ends of earlier dynasties. As the result of the infectious influence of the West, China stands threatened to-day with the loss of that great inheritance of philosophy which in the past has successfully carried her through many perils of change.

Factors making for disintegration

The revolution which overthrew the Dragon Throne in 1911 means therefore something more than the customary crisis in the Chinese organism; it may even mean, in the course of one or two generations, a collapse of the whole venerable structure of Chinese civilization. The history of the race would appear to justify the hope that the deep-rooted qualities which have hitherto enabled it to survive the consequences of its own defects and of alien invasions will in the end triumph over the dangers that now encompass it. If it should not be so, then with the old order must perish all that which has made China worthy of admiration and reverence—the inspiration of that conscious, cohesive national life which is a direct expression of the wisdom of the Sages, and of a political morality closely identified with the laws of nature which, with all its faults, has stood the test of time. The glory that was China, a system of civilization whose external manifestations are deep-rooted in permanent realities, the type of human being who in his daily life, howsoever humble, demonstrates the eternal truth that contentment comes from within—all these are the result of education in the principles of Confucianism, and must stand or perish with those principles.

Another new factor, making for national disintegration, was created when, after the introduction of steam navigation, the inhabitants of the south-eastern maritime provinces began to seek relief from economic pressure by migrating to the Malay States, the Dutch Indies, the South Seas and the Pacific Coast of America. For some time before the downfall of the Manchu dynasty the growing influence of large and prosperous communities of Chinese overseas—practically all southerners—had proved itself to be a disruptive force, possessed of new material resources and imbued with new ideas, which made it something far more significant than the old traditional antagonism between north and south. Throughout Chinese history the inhabitants of the Kwang provinces and Fukhien have been distinguished from the more rigidly localised and passive population of central and northern China by their restless and rebellious tendencies; but sooner or later, after the paroxysms of civil war and rebellions, they had always resumed their place as members of the great celestial family, impelled and held thereto by the cohesive force of the doctrines of Confucianism and the civil service. Even after prolonged insurrectionary movements, such as those against the first Manchu sovereigns and the Taiping rebellion, the southerners' tendencies to political separation had eventually yielded to the inherent force of common traditions, language and beliefs. They, like the northerners, were bound to their ancestral homes by the cult of their dead, and generally impelled by ambition and self-interest to accept Peking as the centre of the Chinese system.

DR. SUN YAT-SEN

Sun Yat-sen (1866–1925), a westernised Cantonese, was an organizer of the revolutionary party which overthrew the Manchu dynasty in 1911. After Yuan Shih-k'ai's acceptance of the Presidency he became the leader of the Southern party.

Photo, Elliott & Fry

But the nineteenth century brought to the knowledge of the inhabitants of these densely crowded maritime provinces new outlets for their restless activities and a new prospect of relief from intolerable economic pressure. It was a natural result of Canton's long monopoly of trade and direct relations with foreigners, and of the cumulative effect of the southern provinces' experience with them in trade and war, that the teeming millions of Kwangtung and Fukhien should be the first to perceive and grasp the opportunities created by the new means of communication with the outside world. The practical monopoly which they rapidly established in the control of emigration to the United States and the Philippines, Malaya, Siam and the South Seas represented not only a quick-witted perception of the value of the opportunities created by the 'open door' overseas, but their readiness to adapt themselves to radically new conditions as an alternative to collective starvation. Between 1870 and 1910 about ten millions of southern Chinese workers found new homes overseas, and gradually, as their economic superiority asserted itself, a new outlook.

Emigration and its consequences

In 1868 the United States, unaware of the real nature of the Yellow Peril, placed on record in the Burlingame Treaty its belief in 'the inherent and inalienable right of man to change his home and allegiance and the mutual advantage of free immigration.' By the time, twelve years later, when this sentimental delusion had been dispelled and the first Asiatic Exclusion Act applied, the large Chinese communities overseas had not only acquired sources of wealth, which have since played a very important part in Chinese politics, but had absorbed new ideas, chiefly of American origin, concerning the rights of nations and individuals, and had begun to apply them by means of effective organization. The republican programme proclaimed by Sun Yat-sen in 1911 meant little or nothing to the vast majority of the Chinese people; but it undoubtedly represented the sentiments of the Cantonese communities overseas, who saw in it the prospect of Cantonese supremacy in China and of a profitable movement for the recovery of the financial control and extra-territorial privileges exercised by foreigners.

In the years which have elapsed since the Revolution the disruptive effect of 'Western learning' in China, combined with the influence of the Cantonese residents abroad, has produced in the new generation of southerners a spirit of reckless iconoclasm, a tendency to break away from the Confucianist traditions and social system, even in matters of fundamental principle. Whether this tendency represents wide-spread and genuine convictions, or merely political opportunism deliberately invoked with a view to enlisting the support of Liberalism in Europe and America, time will show. In any event, however, as the result of the abolition of the ancient system of education for the public service, and the influence of the Chinese colonies overseas, the lines of cleavage between the Cantonese party and the political factions of central and northern China are bound to become wider and deeper, and the prospect of a wholly united China therefore more remote.

While it is true that the inhabitants of southern China are no more capable than their northern fellow countrymen of organizing effective self-government based on democratic institutions, it may well be that the new conditions created by the impact of the West will lead them to reject the moral restraints and social ethics to which the nation as a whole adheres. In that event the natural recuperative processes which have always restored national unity in the past are likely henceforth to be impeded by difficulties of a kind for which the experience of the race provides no immediate remedy.

FIRST PRESIDENT OF THE REPUBLIC OF CHINA

China was proclaimed a republic on February 12, 1912, and Yuan Shih-k'ai (1859-1916) was appointed its first president. He had proved his statesmanship as imperial resident in Korea, and later as viceroy of Chihli his progressive ideas had great influence on the empress-dowager's reform policy after her return to Peking in 1902. In spite of his dismissal by the regent in 1909, he was always a believer in the monarchical form of government for China and opposed to the republican movement.

CHAPTER 174

TRADE UNIONISM: ITS ORIGIN AND GROWTH

How the Movement has fought its Way to Social Recognition in the Country that saw its Birth

By E. LIPSON

Reader in Economic History in the University of Oxford; Author of The Economic History of England: Vol. I, The Middle Ages, Vols. II & III, The Age of Mercantilism

Among the forces that shape and mould modern economic life trade unionism occupies a unique position, exerting as it does an immeasurable influence on the industrial system. England was its birthplace and its growth can best be studied in its original setting. Elsewhere the history of trade unionism covers a much shorter period, and its organization is still imperfect in many countries: in England it has had a continuous existence of over two centuries and has attained its highest development.

In tracing the history of English trade unionism we may glance first at its antecedents. Trade unions are sometimes regarded as descended from the medieval craft guilds; but there are several important differences between them. The craft guilds comprised not only wage earners (journeymen) but masters, and their functions were very much wider. They were intended to protect the interests of consumer as well as producer, and to ensure good quality, sound workmanship and a just price reasonable alike to buyer and seller. A trade union resembles more closely the yeomen or journeymen guilds, embryonic labour organizations formed as early as the fourteenth and fifteenth centuries, and confined to wage earners united together in opposition to their employers. These journeymen guilds failed, however, to establish a stable and permanent organization, partly on account of the hostility of the authorities, and partly because they were always liable to lose their most intelligent and enterprising members owing to the latter becoming themselves masters.

The rise of a continuous trade-union movement dates from the beginning of the eighteenth century, and the reason why trade unionism emerges at this particular period merits attention. Trade unionism in its origin was not in any way connected, as we might suppose, with the introduction of machinery and the growth of the factory system near the end of the eighteenth century. We must connect the beginnings of trade unionism with the constitutional changes in the latter part of the seventeenth century. The policy of the state in economic affairs changed after the Revolution of 1688. Capital and labour, formerly controlled by the state, were now left free, in a large measure, to work out their economic problems; and the workers began to find that they must depend upon their own efforts for the maintenance and improvement of the standard of life. It is, at any rate, significant that the Revolution of 1688, which brought to a final close the era of benevolent autocracy, should have been followed within a few years by an outburst of trade-union activity. The conclusion seems irresistible that we must associate the rise of trade unionism in England with the movement in the eighteenth century towards 'laisser faire.'

Beginnings of Trade Unionism

We should naturally expect to find evidence of trade unionism in those industries in which capitalist influences were strongest: it is in those industries where a permanent class of wage earners had developed that the consciousness of class interests would first be quickened. Now before the Industrial Revolution capitalism was most developed in the woollen industry, particularly in the west of England,

and it is here that we find the most notable examples of trade-union activity.

Admittedly, however, the Industrial Revolution gave an enormous impetus to trade unionism. Machinery reduced the wage earners to a complete dependence upon their employers, while the concentration of the workers under one roof made it easier for them to combine together. But the growth of trade unionism did not commend itself to the governing classes, and in 1799 was passed the famous Combination Act, which provided that any workman who combined with any other workman to increase his wages, or decrease his hours, was liable to be brought before a single magistrate, perchance one of his own employers, and, if convicted, sent to prison for three months. The same penalty was imposed if he attempted to persuade any other worker to leave his work, or if he refused to work with any other person, and even if he simply attended any meeting for the purpose of reducing hours and raising wages. He was also compelled to give evidence against himself—a violation of one of the fundamental principles of English jurisprudence. This law was modified the following year in two or three respects: thus two magistrates were to act instead of one; and they must not be engaged in the same trade as the defendant. It was also provided that wage disputes could be referred to arbitration; but this provision seems to have remained a dead letter.

In connexion with these famous combination laws, which occupy so large a place in the history of the trade-union movement, two things must be noticed. In the first place the principle of forbidding combinations of wage earners was not new. It was stated, indeed, by a member of Parliament that there were at the end of the eighteenth century no fewer than forty laws directed against combinations in particular trades. The novelty of the act of 1799 lay in the fact that it was a general act —it penalised all combinations in all industries. Moreover, earlier statutes had been framed on the principle that the regulation of wages and apprenticeship was the function of the state, and that trade unions could not be allowed to override and supersede the proper legal machinery. But the act of 1799 was not framed on this understanding, for Parliament was now definitely opposed to the legal regulation of wages or apprenticeship. And further, the act was largely political. The French Revolution had created a panic in the minds of the governing classes in England. It put back the reform of Parliament a generation, and it was also responsible for a crop of repressive legislation that has given to the period a sinister aspect. Thus the govern-

MARTYRS IN THE CAUSE OF LABOUR

By common law, and under the Combination Act of 1799, any combined action by workmen was illegal and punishable with imprisonment. In 1763 there was a tailors' strike, commemorated in this contemporary print of tailors in prison, but with their distress relieved by gifts from sympathisers.

FRANCIS PLACE
Francis Place (1771–1854), a leather breeches maker, organized a union of his trade in 1793 and devoted himself to reform, becoming an able and practical politician. His greatest triumph was the repeal of the Combination Acts.
Drawing by Daniel Maclise in Frazer's Magazine, 1836

ment, dreading a revolution, prohibited associations of working men, partly at any rate from the fear that these associations would be directed to political objects.

In the second place, the workers themselves put forward demands which in the altered circumstances of the time were clearly impracticable. They demanded, for example, the prohibition of machinery, and the revival of obsolete laws restricting the number of apprentices and requiring seven years' apprenticeship. Prohibition of machinery would have meant economic stagnation. The insistence on a long apprenticeship took no account of the ease with which many technical operations could now be learnt. And, finally, it was impossible, in view of large-scale production, to restrict the number of employees that a master might employ. Thus, by associating itself with impracticable demands, trade unionism seemed to be incompatible with industrial progress.

The history of trade unionism in the nineteenth century may be divided into four periods. The first (1800–1825) was the period of legal repression when trade unions were banned by the law of the land. The second (the 'twenties and 'thirties) was the period of militancy and revolutionary tendencies, largely inspired by the doctrines of the early Socialists. The third was the period of construction and organization, and it culminated in the legislative achievements of the 'seventies. The fourth was the period of the 'eighties when unskilled labour was brought within the scope of the trade-union movement. Trade unionism thus followed natural lines of development. Emerging from obscurity and oppression, it rioted at first in its newly found liberty, but finally settled down to the work of building up a stable and permanent labour edifice, gaining its reward in full legislative and social recognition.

The outstanding figure in the first phase of trade union history was Francis Place,

JOSEPH HUME, REFORMER
Beginning life in the service of the East India Company, Joseph Hume (1777–1855) started his political career at home in 1812, and for thirty years was a leading radical reformer. C. B. Leighton made this chalk drawing of him.
National Portrait Gallery, London

a master tailor of Charing Cross, to whose devoted efforts, aided by Joseph Hume, a member of Parliament, the repeal of the combination laws was mainly due. For several years Place worked to procure the repeal, but he worked almost single-handed. The workmen did not believe that repeal was possible, and they fastened their hopes for the improvement of their condition upon an extension of the franchise. But in 1824 Parliament agreed to the appointment of a committee to inquire into the working of the combination laws, and this provided an opportunity for stating the case against them.

The strongest argument was their oppressive character. The mere act of striking was construed as an infringement of the law. The Scottish weavers, for example, struck work in 1812: the justices found the rates which were demanded reasonable: nevertheless the men were sentenced to imprisonment. If workmen went in a body to lay their grievances before a master they could be prosecuted for combination; if they agreed to leave his service in consequence of a reduction in wages they were liable to imprisonment; if they held a meeting—even at the employer's request—or if one man merely asked another to attend a meeting, they had broken the law and were subject to its penalties. Another criticism was that, while the combination laws nominally applied to masters as well as men, it was notorious (as Adam Smith pointed out) that the masters combined with impunity for the purpose of regulating wages. A prosecution was bound to be ineffectual since the law did not compel the masters, as it did the men, to give evidence against each other. On one occasion, indeed, the masters at Nottingham held a public meeting at the police office at which the town clerk acted as secretary, and passed resolutions for joint action against their men; yet no prosecution ensued for breach of the law.

Iniquities of the Combination Laws

And, lastly, the combination laws had a pernicious influence because they embittered the relations of capital and labour. They created an atmosphere of irritation and ill will. The men smarted under a sense of grievance. They felt that they were not at liberty to dispose of their labour to the best advantage, and they looked upon their employers as oppressors. The settlement of disputes was also made more difficult. The men were afraid to lay their grievances before an employer for fear of prosecution, and instead met in private and decided on a strike, or resorted to acts of violence. Trade unions being unlawful, the best men kept themselves in the background and refused to hold office. The extremists, therefore, took the lead, and so there was greater danger of outrage and acts of violence. On their side, the masters were tempted to take their stand on the high ground of the law and to show less inclination for compromise.

Convinced by the evidence placed before it, the committee recommended the repeal of the combination laws, and a bill was hurried through both Houses, 'almost,' says Place, 'without the notice of members within or newspapers without.' As a result, trade unions sprang up everywhere, accompanied by an epidemic of strikes, due partly to an unwonted sense of freedom, partly to a rise in the cost of living. This aroused the employers, who had been taken by surprise, and pressure was brought to bear upon the government to re-enact the combination laws. Another committee was appointed; but the workers, though they had done little to win the repeal, now exerted themselves to retain it. So successfully was the case of the men presented before the committee that it dared not propose the re-enactment of the combination laws. Instead, it recommended that the common law, which had also been abrogated in favour of trade unions by the act of 1824, should be restored. This would have had the effect of making all associations illegal; but an exception was to be made in favour of meetings held to settle wages and hours of labour. These recommendations were embodied in the act of 1825, which legalised trade unions, but only for the purpose of settling wages and hours. Their other activities were still illegal: for example, efforts to limit the number of apprentices, to intervene in the master's conduct of his

Partial recognition of trade unions

business, or to induce any man to leave his work 'by threat, intimidation, or insults.' This remained the legal position for the next half century.

The repeal of the combination laws inaugurated the militant phase of trade unionism. This phase was due to a combination of circumstances. Attempts on the part of employers to suppress trade unions exposed the weakness of isolated unions, and discredited the ordinary methods of collective bargaining. Moreover, in 1832 Parliament had been reformed, but power was given only to the middle classes, and the restricted scope of the Reform Act seemed to show the futility of political agitation. The result was that organized labour became, for a time, enamoured of socialistic aspirations. It is at this stage in the history of the labour movement that the two streams of socialism and trade unionism commingled. For one brief moment, indeed, it appeared as if the trade-union movement would be captured by Robert Owen and completely diverted from its traditional and normal lines of development. The beginnings of this new departure may be traced to a proposal put forward by Doherty in 1829 for one 'grand general union' of all spinners in the United Kingdom. Four years later the formation of a Grand National Guild of Builders seemed to foreshadow an even more ambitious scheme, by which all the workers of the country would be combined in one national society.

The Scheme of Robert Owen

Owen announced that the time was now ripe to suggest to working men 'a plan of organization by which they might in a short time emancipate themselves from the thraldom of their present condition.' The 'plan,' which anticipated what is now called Guild Socialism, was set forth by Owen in one of his addresses: 'I now give you a short outline of the great changes which are in contemplation and which shall come suddenly upon society like a thief in the night,' but without violence or injustice. 'It is intended . . . to include all the working classes in (one) great organization. . . . All individual competition is to cease; all manufactures are to be carried on by national companies. . . . All individuals of the specific craft shall become members, and these shall include all producers of wealth or whatever contributes to knowledge or happiness.' Henceforth, Owen proclaimed, 'there shall be no more masters, no more servants.' According to the ambitious scheme with which Owen now dazzled the vision of the trade-union world, associations of producers were to supersede the capitalist organization of society, and the workers in each industry were to own and control that industry.

Failure of the National Union

To give effect to these ideas there was formed in 1834 the Grand National Consolidated Trades Union, which was attended at first with remarkable success. It was rapidly joined by over half a million members, including many thousands of agricultural labourers and women. The exact policy of the union is obscure. The executive apparently contemplated the gradual transformation of trade unions into co-operative associations, for it recommended the unions to employ their own members and to open shops for the mutual exchange of their products; presumably it was intended for each union in this way to get the whole industry into its hands. But a general strike was also contemplated, and modern events give added interest to the views expressed by one of its earliest advocates, Benbow, a disciple of Owen's:

> There will not be insurrection; it will simply be passive resistance. The men may remain at leisure: there is, and can be, no law to compel them to work against their will. They may walk the streets or fields with their arms folded, they will wear no swords, carry no muskets; they will present no multitude for the Riot Act to disperse. They merely abstain, while their funds are sufficient, from going to work for one week or one month; and what happens in consequence? Bills are dishonoured, the Gazette teems with bankruptcies, capital is destroyed, the revenue fails, the system of government falls into confusion, and every link in the chain which binds society together is broken in a moment by this inert conspiracy of the poor against the rich.

However, the general strike never materialised. Instead, the union found itself involved in sectional disputes over wages and hours, and in these disputes its energies were largely frittered away. In March, 1834, occurred the famous incident of the trial and transportation of the six Dorchester labourers for administering an oath. This created a great sensation in the country and dealt a fatal blow at the National Union. The employers set to work to destroy it by refusing to employ men who would not sign the 'document,' as it was called, in which they were required to dissociate themselves from the trade-union movement. The National Union thus disappeared, its members deserting it in thousands.

Although the trade unions had been brought within the pale of the law they still remained outside the social pale. Public opinion was almost unreservedly hostile. The lord chancellor openly declared in 1834 that 'of all the most pernicious devices that could be imagined for the interests of the working classes as well as the interests of the country at large, nothing was half so bad as the existence of those trades unions.' The question then arises: What were the causes of the unpopularity of trade unions?

Hostility of public opinion

The first ground of complaint against the trade unions was their secrecy. The privacy in which they shrouded their proceedings and the oaths they imposed were inspired originally, no doubt, by motives of safety at a time when it was illegal to hold meetings; but critics of the unions declared that secrecy was favoured because it influenced the minds of the ignorant. The ceremony of initiation into the society was designed to impress the superstitious fears of uneducated members. A pamphlet published in 1834 describes the reception of members into the Wool Combers' Union. The scene, we are told, is usually the first floor of a tavern, and the time eight or nine in the evening. On one side of the apartment is a skeleton, above which is a drawn sword and a battle axe, and in front stands a table upon which lies a Bible. The principal officers of the union are clothed in surplices. The proceedings open with a prayer, then the workmen who are about to be made members are admitted with their eyes bandaged. After various preliminaries the bandages are removed from the eyes of the strangers, and they are placed opposite the skeleton. An oath is taken upon the Bible, in which they bind themselves never to 'act in opposition to the brotherhood in any of their attempts to support wages,' nor to disclose the proceedings of the lodge. The oath ends with an imprecation on the violator: 'May what is now before me plunge my soul into the everlasting pit of misery.'

The commonest charge against the trade unions was their alleged tyranny. They were believed in some cases even to have instigated the murder of recalcitrant employers and workmen. Apart from violence and outrage the unions were accused of adopting a dictatorial manner towards the employers. One example is the Builders' Union. A contemporary writer says:

> The lofty and imperious tone assumed in their communications with the masters brings to mind the grandiloquent edicts of Chinese dignitaries. . . . 'We consider,' says one of these dispatches, 'that as you have not treated our rules with that deference you ought to have done, we consider you highly culpable and deserve to be highly chastised.'

They actually required one master in a strike to pay the sum of four shillings per day to each of his men for every day the strike lasted. A Yorkshire union, we are told, ordered the woollen manufacturers to pay time wages instead of piece rates. One of the manufacturers complained that his men did less work when paid on a time basis, upon which he was instructed to keep no books.

Yet another criticism of the unions was that they did no good even to their own members. It was argued that high wages attracted new hands, whom the union must support to prevent the beating down of wages; and the contributions for this purpose must come out of the pockets of those in work. The members must also bear the cost of officials and meeting-rooms, and suffer restriction of employment due to a rise in prices and a fall in demand. Again, those who arrogated to themselves, not always with justice, the right to speak

Criticisms of the movement

in the name of political economy also declared the impossibility of a general rise in wages as a result of trade-union pressure. The theory of the wages-fund was at this period the orthodox explanation of wages. It was thought that at any given moment a fixed portion of the wealth of the country was set apart to pay wages, so that if any section of the workers increased their wages by trade-union action they did so at the expense of their fellow workers.

Lastly, trade unions were condemned on the ground that it was disastrous to put any restrictions on capital. A rise in wages, ran the contention, meant a rise in prices; this would endanger the whole fabric of foreign trade, and workmen would be the first to suffer for their misguided efforts to improve their position. 'Were we asked,' said a writer on trade unionism, 'to give a definition of a trades union we should say that it was a society whose constitution is the worst of democracies, whose power is based on outrage, whose practice is tyranny, and whose end is self-destruction.'

Triumph over opposition

It is a testimony to the solidity of the trade-union movement that, in the face of powerful hostile criticism and an antagonistic public opinion, it was able to win for itself a great place among the constructive forces of the nineteenth century. In the 'thirties barely tolerated by the law of the land and bearing the stigma of a social ban, trade unionism within half a century had achieved full legal recognition and even a distinct measure of social prestige. Trade-union officials were no longer contemned as paid agitators, but were now accorded seats in the legislature and on royal commissions, and the changed attitude of employers was reflected in a growing willingness to meet union representatives around a common board. The causes and consequences of this transformation we have now to examine.

After the failure of the Grand National Union, the fever of militancy burned itself out. The glowing projects of Owenism were discarded, and trade unionism entered on an era of constructive activity and sober practical administration. One reason for this change was the prosperity of the country during the 'fifties and 'sixties, but another was the growth of a new spirit among trade unionists. The desire for knowledge, the anxiety to comprehend the realities of the industrial situation, became more general. The new spirit manifested itself in the institution of classes for the discussion of economic problems, and in the publication of trade journals dealing with the interests of particular industries. In one of these trade journals remarkable stress was laid upon the value of education: 'If you do not wish to stand as you are and suffer more oppression, we say to you get knowledge, and in getting knowledge you get power. . . Let us earnestly advise you to educate: get intelligence instead of alcohol—it is sweeter and more lasting.'

Moral effect of the Unions

Moreover, trade unionism in itself exercised a sobering influence upon the workers, for it gave them a training in self-government; and Ludlow, writing in 1867, thought this 'the most important result produced by the trade society, and one which no other form of government as yet evolved among the working classes can develop on so large a scale. No greater mistake,' he added, 'can be made than, as journalists and politicians are apt to do, to treat the mass of members of a trade society as dupes, idlers, drunkards, or incapables, their leaders as knaves, strikes for higher wages as their common object. . . They represent almost invariably the bulk of the able, industrious and provident workmen in each trade: they are habitually well governed by men fairly elected by the members as the most trustworthy, respectable and intelligent amongst them.'

The effect of trade unionism upon the character of the workmen was warmly disputed. Hostile critics asserted that the better class of workmen were losing their character of self-reliance and independence, their desire to excel and rise in the world being damped by the thraldom in which they were held by the rules of their union. But it is more probable, as the trade unions maintained, that the real tendency was to raise the character of the worker by making him feel that he was not the helpless victim of oppression, but the member of a strong, united body, capable of defending his rights and ensuring him a resource in case of temporary need.

The spread of education, coupled with the experience gained in trade-union administration, produced a great reaction against the militant ideas of the 'thirties, which showed itself in a strenuous denunciation of strikes. One union warned its members against what it called the dangerous practice of striking. 'Keep from it,' they were urged, 'as you would from a ferocious animal that you know would destroy you. . . . We implore you, brethren, as you value your own existence, to avoid in every way possible those useless strikes.' The Smiths' Union prided itself on being the original 'anti-strike' society. The preface to their rules states that at first they had indulged freely in strikes, but in 1845 a meeting of delegates decided that strikes were an unmitigated evil: they were 'battles between the employers and the employed . . . too often unwisely got up by one or both parties and continued more for the purpose of trying which shall gain the mastery over the other than otherwise.' In many cases the local branches were deprived of the power of calling a strike, for it was recognized that the authority of a branch committee was more liable to be overborne by the clamours of the rank and file. As a result the leaders of the trade-union movement were able to claim before the royal commission of 1867 that the effect of trade unionism was to diminish the frequency of strikes, and certainly the disorder of strikes.

Reaction against militant methods

The growing moderation of trade unionism, alike in its aims and methods, did not mean that the leaders were prepared to acquiesce in economic oppression, but they believed that their ends could be best attained by other methods. Accepting the view, which was then almost universally prevalent, that wages depend upon supply and demand, and that when the demand for labour exceeds the supply wages rise, they drew the conclusion that the best line of policy, in order to raise wages, was to limit the supply of labour in any given trade and to restrict the amount of work which any individual might do. One method of carrying out this policy was to reduce the number of apprentices; another was to get rid of surplus labour by emigration; a third was to discourage overtime in order to make the work last longer or go round a larger number of men. The same end was indirectly secured by the prohibition of piece work, although this prohibition was defended on other grounds.

It was during the 'forties and 'fifties and 'sixties that the structure of trade unionism in its modern form was built up on sound lines. The keynote of the period is organization, and the three features of this organization were: first, the creation of a body of trade-union officials; secondly, continuity of membership; and thirdly, increased financial strength as a result of combining industrial with friendly benefit activities. Take the first point: the creation of a body of trade-union officials. As the unions grew in membership, it was necessary to have whole-time secretaries, and so there developed a body of trained officials expressly chosen for their business capacity, and uniting a sense of responsibility with a more intimate knowledge of the industrial situation. There can be no question that the growth of a class of trained officials was a most important factor in laying the foundations of modern trade unionism.

Three planks of Organization

Another significant development was the evolution of a 'new model' of trade unionism, as it was then called. Instead of the trade union being purely a trade society, concerned mainly with protecting the trade interests of its members, a type of union was evolved which, in addition to its trade functions, was also a benefit society serving the purpose of an insurance society. This had the twofold result of securing for the unions additional members and larger funds. It also strengthened the hold of a union over its members, since any member who was expelled for disobedience might forfeit the superannuation and other benefits. The outstanding example of the 'new model' of trade unionism was the Amalgamated Society of Engineers, established in 1851 out of a number of independent societies. The subscription was one shilling per week, in addition to special levies, and the accumulated funds amounted in 1867 to £140,000.

In process of time the defects of the 'new model'—that is, the combination of trade functions with insurance benefits—were revealed in the unwillingness of trade union officials to hazard the funds of their union by aggressive action. The aim of the 'new model,' in fact, appears to have been to establish uniformity of wages and hours throughout the country rather than to engage in constant endeavours to improve them. It was this combination of financial solidity and moderation of purpose which effected a revolution in the public attitude towards trade unions, and so made it possible for them, in the 'seventies, to win a greatly improved legal status.

The trade-union movement must now be studied in another aspect. It is a mistake to consider trade unionism exclusively from one standpoint: as an industrial society for regulating wages and hours, and as a friendly society for providing benefits. It has played an important part in raising the whole level of working-class life, and takes rank as one of the great social forces of the nineteenth century. This aspect has not received the attention which it deserves. The history of the Miners' Union, in particular, furnishes a remarkable record of trade-union achievements. Macdonald, the president of the Miners' National Association, claimed before the royal commission of 1867 that the act of 1842, which forbade the employment of women and children in the mines, was due solely to the representations of the workers. Among other reforms the union pressed for more stringent laws to ensure the safety of the miners, more efficient inspection of the mines, uniform methods of weighing the coal and the right to have a check-weigher at every pit, the prohibition of truck, the punctual payment of wages and the education of the children. Fifty thousand

The movement as a social force

A CHRISTIAN SOCIALIST

Joseph Malcolm Forbes Ludlow (1821–1911) was one of the first promoters of Christian Socialism, the co-operative movement and, in 1854, of the Working Men's College. From 1875–1900 he was chief registrar of friendly societies.

Photo, Braconnier

miners signed a petition in 1854 for a compulsory assessment on their wages to provide money for educational purposes. In short, the Miners' Union placed foremost among its objects 'legislation for the better management of mines to protect the miners' lives, promote their health, and to increase among them a higher moral status in society.' Critics of trade unionism, who fastened entirely upon the efforts of trade unions to regulate wages, ignored their other activities in promoting legislative changes which otherwise might have been indefinitely retarded.

Side by side with the growing moderation and enlarged vision of organized labour proceeded another change. Ludlow, in his book on the Progress of the Working Class, published in 1867, remarked that

> the offensive spirit of mastership, which sought to carry everything with a high hand and settle all matters without considering the wishes or interests of the workers, has also greatly softened within the last few years. The capitalist is beginning to acknowledge the propriety of considering the welfare of the workers whose help he needs. He has almost ceased to insist upon his right to do all things in his own way simply because the capital is his.

The changing attitude of employers manifested itself in two directions—in the willingness to meet their men around a common board, and in the willingness in some instances to foster community of interests between capital and labour by admitting labour to a share in profits.

Nevertheless, the old type of employer who refused to recognize the trade-union movement, or to admit the principle of collective bargaining, yielded ground slowly. He was represented at the royal commission of 1867 by Nasmyth, the great engineer, a relentless opponent of trade unionism, who refused to deal with men except 'one at a time.' Yet Nasmyth's own career furnished an instructive commentary upon the results which his attitude towards organized labour provoked:

> I was so annoyed with walking on the surface of this continually threatening trade union volcano that was likely to burst out at every moment that I was glad to give it up and retire from the business at a period of life at least ten years before the age at which I otherwise would have retired. . . And I am the envy of some engineers. They say: 'You are a lucky fellow, Nasmyth; you took down your sign-board at the right time.'

AN ENLIGHTENED EMPLOYER

Anthony John Mundella (1825–97), a Nottingham hosiery manufacturer, established the first conciliation board for the settlement of trade disputes in 1866. As president of the Board of Trade in 1886 he created the labour department.

The new type of employer, on the other hand, sought to solve the labour problem in other ways than by taking down his sign-board. Mundella, an example of the enlightened employer who had moved with the times, endeavoured to develop new relations between capital and labour on the lines of arbitration and conciliation, while the principle of profit sharing was also attracting attention as a means of attaining industrial harmony. Thus the pressure of trade unionism was gradually winning for the worker a new status as an equal partner to the industrial contract; and, in the face of this momentous development, employers were constrained to recognize that their business was no longer their business alone. This was the starting point of a new order of things.

We now enter the period of the 'seventies when trade unionism reached its climax in the attainment of a new legal status.

Some legal insecurities

The legal insecurity of the trade unions was brought home to them by an event which happened in 1867. The unions had begun to accumulate large funds, and at this time they had over a quarter of a million. It was suddenly discovered that these funds had no legal protection. In 1867 the Boilermakers' Society summoned the treasurer of a Bradford branch for embezzlement. The magistrates ruled that, as unions did not come under the Friendly Societies Act, their funds could not be protected. The decision in the case of the Boilermakers was confirmed upon appeal, when the judges also declared that the union was illegal on the ground that its objects were in restraint of trade. To understand this legal pronouncement it must be remembered that the law of 1825 had legalised trade unions expressly for two purposes, and two purposes only: the regulation of wages and hours. Now nearly all trade unions had rules relating to piece work, overtime, the number of apprentices, etc., rules which, according to the law of the land, were 'in restraint of trade.' Hence trade unions were unlawful associations according to the act of 1825, and their funds therefore were not protected by law.

The same year which witnessed this legal bombshell also saw the political emancipation of the working classes when the Reform Act of 1867 gave the vote to working men in towns, and the unions were not slow to use the political power they had acquired. The Liberal government in 1871 recognized their power by bringing in a bill under which no trade union was to be considered illegal on the ground that it was in restraint of trade. Further, every union could be registered as a friendly society and so receive protection for its funds; and finally no trade union could be sued in a court of law. It seemed as though trade unionism had secured everything which it desired, but the bill was found to contain a serious flaw. While trade unions now obtained full legal recognition and protection for their funds, their action was restrained by the prohibition of peaceful picketing. This prohibition largely nullified the advantages which the trade unions had gained in other clauses of the bill.

The question of Picketing

The question of picketing plays a large part in trade-union history. It involves the fundamental problem whether a trade union may bring pressure of any kind to bear upon a workman who remains outside its ranks and claims the right of 'freedom of labour.' The act of 1825 had made it penal to induce any man to leave his work by threat or intimidation or insult. A subsequent law (1859) enacted that it was not illegal to persuade others to cease work, provided it was done in a peaceable and reasonable manner, without threat or intimidation. This was considered unsatisfactory since it left the judges to interpret what was reasonable. The method of persuasion adopted in the event of a strike was to post members of the union at all the approaches to the works where the strike was in operation, and it was the task of these pickets to influence men from accepting work there. A writer in the 'thirties gives a graphic description:

> When a strike has taken place in any factory men are always stationed to keep watch on the building, and also on every avenue leading to it, whose business it is to prevent fresh workmen being engaged in the place of those who have turned out. Every labouring man who appears to be seeking employment in the direction of the factory, or—having accepted employment in it—is returning from it, is stopped and interrogated, and should he prove refractory is threatened or maltreated. This system of picketing mills has been carried to the greatest extent in Manchester, where the obnoxious factory is always watched by five or six men, unknown in the immediate neighbourhood, and who—on a given signal—can be reinforced to the extent of three hundred. These pickets are regularly relieved by night and by day . . . so that an establishment is not infrequently kept in a state of literal siege: no one can enter it or leave it without danger of molestation, and if fresh workmen have by any means been introduced, beds and provisions are prepared for them within the walls of the factory.

The case in favour of picketing was presented by Applegarth, secretary of the Carpenters and Joiners Society, who addressed the commissioners as follows:

> It is perfectly justifiable for men to appoint other men to wait at a shop door and say to those who come: 'The men were dissatisfied with the terms upon which they were working at that place, and if you go in you will go and undersell us: now we beg that you will not do that.' That is as far as I would justify the men in going. If they use threats and coerce or intimidate, that is beyond the instructions, and which the laws of the society gives them. . . . If they did not do what I have justified, it would be absolute folly to strike in many instances . . . If you gentlemen imagine that all those men who come to fill other men's places when they are on strike are models of excellence you are quite mistaken . . . There are a class of men in all trades who make it a business to find where strikes are pending. The men are obliged to support them to keep them from filling their places. They come for the strike pay and the beer attending it.

Others, again, expressed the opinion that in a strike threats and persuasion were convertible terms, and they recommended that, just as violence and threats were penal, so persuasion should be made penal. The government came to the conclusion that picketing implies in principle an interference with the right of non-unionists to dispose of their labour as they think fit, and it inserted a clause in the bill which prohibited peaceful picketing. The trade unions raised a great outcry, but the only concession which the government would make was to divide the bill into two, and embody the clause relating to picketing in a separate bill, which was known as the Criminal Law Amendment Act. The general election of 1874 gave the trade unionists their opportunity. The Liberal party was defeated and a Conservative government came into power. At this election, for the first time, two Labour members entered the House of Commons, Alexander Macdonald and Thomas Burt. The Conservative government recognized the power of the trade unionists by repealing the Criminal Law Amendment Act of 1871. This legalised a limited degree of picketing.

PARLIAMENT'S FIRST LABOUR MEMBERS

Both Alexander Macdonald (left) and Thomas Burt (right) started working life in the coal mines, and in 1874 they shared the distinction of being the first labour men to be elected members of parliament. Burt became parliamentary secretary to the Board of Trade in 1892, and in 1906 a privy councillor.

Photo (right), Russell & Sons

The 'seventies also saw an attempt, associated with Joseph Arch, to spread trade unionism among agricultural labourers. Trade unionism has always been backward among farm labourers. In other industries the advent of the Industrial Revolution has done away with the isolation of the worker. The factory system serves to concentrate great masses of men under one roof, and the result has been not only to render possible concerted action among them, but to imbue them with a consciousness of economic power. But the changes brought about by the Agricultural Revolution during the same period produced the opposite result. The open-field system of cultivation has vanished from the face of England, and with it has gone the system of intermixed holdings and joint husbandry. The inhabitants of a village no longer work side by side in the fields, associated together in a general partnership, and carrying on in common all the chief farming operations. The English countryside is now covered with hawthorn hedges and ring-fenced farms, and the labourer stands alone, like the tiller of the soil in Millet's famous picture. The scattered condition of the rural population appeared to oppose an insuperable obstacle to the development of a vigorous trade-union movement. The individual farm worker lacked the confidence which is instilled into a crowd by the security of numbers. Moreover, his exiguous resources did not easily stand the strain of a weekly contribution to the trade-union funds. The difficulty of carrying

THE FARM LABOURERS' FRIEND

Joseph Arch (1826–1919), a Warwickshire labourer, devoted his life to the interests of his class. In 1872 he founded the National Union of Agricultural Labourers, and in 1885–1900 represented West Norfolk in three parliaments.

on propaganda work in these discouraging circumstances was extreme.

In the 'thirties many thousands of farm labourers had joined Robert Owen's movement, but this soon collapsed. After an interval of forty years a new movement started in Warwickshire, in 1872, under the inspiration of Joseph Arch. The movement attracted the attention of the press, and public sympathy was aroused. The National Agricultural Labourers' Union was formed, and by the end of the year counted nearly 100,000 members. Other trade unions came to its support, recognizing that underpaid labour in agriculture is a menace to organized labour in towns. The farmers retorted with a lock-out. They were unwilling to concede to the labourers the right to combine and the right to strike. The movement which had commenced auspiciously was not maintained. Agriculture now began to enter upon a period of acute depression, owing to the influx of American corn. Under the altered circumstances the labourers found it useless to strike for higher wages, since arable land was everywhere being laid down to grass with a consequent reduction in the number of men employed. In 1881 the numbers of the National Union were reduced to 15,000, and thirteen years later they had fallen to 1,100.

Trade Unionism & Agriculture

We now reach the period of the 'eighties and 'nineties. The outstanding event of this period was the emergence of unskilled labour. The great mass of unskilled workmen were outside the trade-union movement. It is true that at various periods in the nineteenth century unskilled labourers had been brought within the trade-union movement: for example, in Owen's union (the Grand National Consolidated Trades Union), but this was a temporary phenomenon. The reasons for their exclusion from the movement were the high weekly contributions and, in some unions, the fact that admission was only through apprenticeship. 'The great bulk of our labourers,' wrote John Burns, 'are ignored by the skilled workers. It is this selfish snobbish desertion by the higher grades of the lower that makes success in many disputes impossible.' There was thus a real danger that the trade unions would be confined to superior workers, the aristocracy of labour, and isolated from unskilled labour—with a consequent cleavage in the labour world.

'THOSE IN FAVOUR'—STRIKERS AT THE INDIA DOCK

Organization of workers employed at the docks was a matter of exceptional difficulty owing to the vast numbers of unskilled and unemployed men always competing for casual employment. But the condition of these casual labourers aroused compassion and in the dock strike that began in August, 1889, public opinion helped them to obtain most of their demands. The strike was led by Benjamin Tillett, who organized the Dockers' Union, now associated with the Transport Workers' Federation.

The situation was transformed by the great dock strike in 1889, a famous landmark in the history of the trade-union movement. The success of a strike by the women employed in making lucifer matches, in spite of their lack of funds and organization, followed by the success of the gas workers, who won a reduction of hours from twelve to eight, stimulated the efforts to organize the dock labourers. The dockers were unorganized and had no funds, but public opinion rallied to their support and the result was that they gained their demand of sixpence an hour. In all these instances victory had been achieved in spite of weakness and the absence of organization. New unions thus came into existence, among dockers, railway workers and others, which at first were intended to be fighting unions unencumbered with sick or accident funds. Their object was to be purely the improvement of the conditions of labour, and the funds were to be used only for purposes of strike pay. In other words they were trade societies only. This was known as the new trade unionism—the 'new model' of the 'eighties. But the fact is that there were always unions which had only trade objects, just as there were always unions which combined trade objects with friendly benefits.

The great Dock Strike of 1889

The reasons why unskilled labour favoured the purely trade society were partly that a union which was not burdened with friendly benefits was believed to be a better fighting instrument, less cautious and more aggressive, and partly that for poorly paid workers it was necessary to have a low contribution. Thus a union which had no friendly benefits would be recommended to the poorest workers by its greater cheapness. The refusal to combine friendly benefits with trade functions was short-lived, but the permanent effect of these years remained in the increased solidarity of the labour world. The older unions modified their exclusiveness, and greater sympathy was shown with the unskilled labourers.

Early in the twentieth century trade unionism found its legal position once more assailed. In 1900 a strike, at first unauthorised, occurred among the employees of the Taff Vale Railway Company in South Wales. The strikers committed certain unlawful acts, and the railway company, against the advice of its own lawyers, sued for damages, not the workmen, but their union—the Amalgamated Society of Railway Servants. The case was taken to the House of Lords, and the law lords decided that a trade union could be sued for damages alleged to have been caused by the action of its officers. This meant that the trade unions were now liable for any injury or damage done by any person deemed to be acting as an agent of the union. The Amalgamated Society had not authorised the strike, nor the unlawful acts, but it was compelled to pay £23,000 in damages. The decision implied that a union was responsible for unlawful acts, even when committed by an agent contrary to its express instructions. In 1906 the Trade Disputes Act gave a trade union immunity from civil action on account of any unlawful act 'committed by or on behalf of the union.'

Shortly afterwards followed the Osborne judgement. In 1908 a member of the Amalgamated Society of Railway Servants took legal proceedings to prevent the union using its funds for political purposes, and the House of Lords gave a decision in his favour. The law lords determined, first, that trade unions were to be considered corporate bodies; secondly, that as corporate bodies they existed for certain defined purposes; thirdly, that these defined purposes were laid down in the act of 1876; and fourthly, that since political action was not expressly referred to in the act, it must be considered outside the scope of the trade-union movement. It is necessary to observe that it was not a matter of protecting the interests of a minority, because even if all the members of a union favoured political action they were prohibited by the Osborne judgement from undertaking it. The result of the judgement was to stultify all trade-union activities not included in the act of 1876; for example, even educational work. In 1913 the Trade

Osborne judgement and its results

Union Act allowed a trade union 'to include in its constitution any lawful purpose,' so long as its chief objects were those of a trade union as defined in the act of 1876, but in the case of political objects expenses were to be met out of a political fund, from which any member was at liberty to claim exemption. The act of 1927 substituted the system of 'contracting in' for 'contracting out.'

In other directions the trade-union movement has made notable advances since the early years of the century. In the first place, there has been a great extension of membership. The number of trade unionists now exceeds five millions, and it is believed that about sixty per cent. of the adult male manual wage earners of the kingdom are organized, while the financial strength of the unions is shown by the fact that their accumulated funds in 1920 exceeded fifteen millions. The unskilled workers, organized as we have seen at the end of the 'eighties, account for thirty per cent. of the trade-union membership. Women unionists were estimated in 1920 to number three-quarters of a million, though this was less than thirty per cent. of the adult women wage earners. The organization of women workers has been, indeed, one of the features of the present century. It was stimulated in particular by the Great War. Although some unions are organized exclusively for women, the majority—about nine-tenths—are members of trade unions admitting both men and women.

Organization of Women Workers

In the case of agricultural labourers the movement of Joseph Arch has revived, and it is estimated that the number of agricultural labourers in trade unions is about one third of the number of men employed in agriculture. Another noteworthy feature of trade-union development has been its extension to what is sometimes called the black-coated proletariat. Shop assistants have been organized, clerks (particularly those in the service of the railway companies), teachers, civil servants, actors, journalists, bank officers and law court officials.

An important development in trade unionism during the present century has been the progress made by the unions of railwaymen. The National Union of Railwaymen affords a striking example of a 'new model' of trade unionism (this is the third use of the term we have noticed)—what is usually called to-day 'industrial unionism.' The structure of a trade union may assume various forms: a craft union embraces men engaged on the same kind of work, for example, cutlers or bricklayers; occupational unionism brings together people working on processes which are kindred, for example, engineers; and industrial unionism exists when the structure of the union follows the employers and brings together everybody connected with the employer. Thus the National Union of Railwaymen seeks to include even employees at railway hotels and railway printing works, and so forth. In short, instead of the workers being organized on the basis of their occupation, they are organized on the basis of the industry to which they belong.

National Union of Railwaymen

While railwaymen have thus given a notable example of the 'new model' of trade unionism, there has grown up among the engineers a movement known as the Shop Stewards' Movement. The shop steward at first was responsible for the payment of trade-union contributions in the workshops. During the Great War he became the spokesman of the men to voice their grievances, and committees of stewards from different shops assumed control in matters relating to workshop conditions.

In these latter years organized labour has not only won a unique legal status, but it also enjoys an official status in all matters which concern manual workers. This measures the remarkable advance made by trade unionism since a century ago, when the movement was proscribed by law. This development had already begun before the Great War; for example, when the trade unions were made agents of the state in the administration of the Insurance Act. But it was during the war that organized labour secured especial recognition in all matters which affect labour. Trade unions have now gained the right to be consulted by the government, and in this way their position has been fortified by state recognition and their dignity, prestige and strength proportionately enhanced.

Two other developments in the trade-union movement must be briefly recorded. The first is the organization of trade unionism as a definite political movement. The second is the claim of organized labour to participate in the control of industry. Organized labour no longer seeks to confine its activities to maintaining the standard of life of the workers in respect of hours and wages. Its horizon has widened, and it now seeks a share in management. Thus the National Union of Railwaymen in 1914 declared that 'no system of state ownership of the railways will be acceptable to organized railwaymen which does . . . not allow them a due measure of control and responsibility in the safe and efficient working of the railway system.' Again, the miners demand not merely nationalisation, but joint control and administration by the workmen and the state, and the institution of national and district councils and pit committees, half their members to be nominated by the Miners' Federation.

One feature of trade-union history is the change in the attitude of economists towards trade unionism. We have seen how the economists, with some conspicuous exceptions like Adam Smith and M'Culloch, were on the whole opposed to trade unionism. But it is now generally considered that, while there may be defects in the organization of labour, the benefits predominate.

New attitude of economists

In the first place, trade unionism has been one of the most important factors in raising the standard of life of the workers during the nineteenth century. It has not been the only factor, for other causes have operated to give the working community a higher standard of life at the end of the century than it enjoyed at the beginning: mass production resulting from the invention of machinery; improved methods of transport; free trade, which has cheapened the price of imported food and so left a wider margin to the wage earner for the purchase of other commodities. Thus machinery, transport and free trade have all helped to raise real wages, that is, wages as interpreted in terms of purchasing power. Still, these factors would not have exerted their full influence but for the strength of trade unionism, which has enabled workers to reap direct personal benefit from the improved economic situation.

In the second place, it is now almost universally recognized that collective bargaining is necessary to place employers and employees on a footing of equality. Labour is a perishable commodity, and the workman who is not supported by a powerful union must take whatever wages are offered to him. Without combination it is impossible for workmen to make their voices effectively heard.

Political and moral effects

In the third place, trade unionism protects a good employer from unscrupulous rivals who seek to capture the market not by superior efficiency of management but by reduction of wages.

Fourthly, trade unionism leads on the whole to stability in industry. It prevents, as a rule, spasmodic strikes, for where the workers are well organized they tend to have a sense of greater responsibility and also a greater sense of security in the feeling that their interests are safeguarded by their own officials with an intimate knowledge of industrial conditions. Most employers, in fact, now recognize that it is preferable to deal with representatives of organized labour, since this makes for less friction in running the industrial machine.

The moral effects of trade unionism in inducing a feeling of confidence, and increasing the self respect and dignity of the workmen, must also be taken into account. And, finally, trade unionism, in so far as the members of the union are alive to their responsibility, gives a training in democracy. These moral and political effects of trade unionism have an economic reaction, because they make for greater intelligence, and so help to produce the type of artisan that modern economic conditions necessitate; for the modern machine demands of the worker intelligence, high character and regularity of conduct.

CHAPTER 175

ECONOMICS AND THE MENACE OF WAR

How human Thought and Action in the Years before and after 1914 were affected by Economic Necessities

By Sir L. CHIOZZA MONEY

Parliamentary Secretary to the Ministry of Shipping, 1917–18 ; Author of Riches and Poverty, The Nation's Wealth, etc.

IN the century which elapsed between Waterloo and the outbreak of the Great War of 1914–18 the modern industrial system had its growth, and mechanical means of transport at last made possible the effective distribution and employment of the world's natural wealth. The factory system had its origin at the end of the eighteenth century (see Chap. 163) ; but it was not until the nineteenth century that machine production made enormous progress, and when it got well under way the population of the industrial nations grew by leaps and bounds. If we are to understand the increasing pressure of economic forces during the nineteenth century and those first fourteen years of the twentieth century that preceded the greatest war of history, we must realize that the populations of Europe made comparatively small progress until means were found to produce wealth in great quantities.

It had always been a problem, not of producing new births, but of finding means of keeping children alive. Thus, during the first half of the eighteenth century, the population of England and Wales was almost stagnant ; in 1700 it was roundly 5,800,000 and in 1750 it had grown to about 6,300,000. Yet, as we know, large families of ten, twelve or fourteen children were the rule ; the majority of the children born failed to survive because of a condition of natural poverty. Then came the turning point, the year 1750, in which iron was first successfully smelted with coal fuel, and in which also James Watt first had his attention directed to Newcomen's atmospheric steam engine (see page 4351), which led to his own wonderful series of engineering devices. With the getting of coal on a comparatively large scale, with the production of considerable quantities of iron, and with the consequent inventions of machinery made of iron, the population began to grow apace. The stagnant conditions of 1700–50 passed, and in 1750–1800 the population of England and Wales grew by about 50 per cent. The figure for 1801 was 8,900,000, which, added to 1,600,000 for Scotland and 5,000,000 for Ireland, gave the United Kingdom an aggregate population of 15,500,000. Thereafter the pace accelerated, and in 1901 the United Kingdom, despite a fall in the population of Ireland, numbered 41,500,000 people, which again increased by 1914 to 46,000,000 people. We have to notice, also, that the major growth occurred after the invention of the locomotive and the steamship.

The New Wealth and big armies

Mechanical transport was to transform the world in all its activities. There is no more remarkable fact in history than that the armies which fought at Waterloo could move no more quickly than the legions of Rome 2,000 years before. The transport of the world had not altered for thousands of years ; the horse in 1815 could pull no more weight and move no more quickly than on the Roman roads of A.D. 15. Indeed, the magnificent organization of the Roman roads makes it possible to say with truth that the armies of Caesar could move on land more swiftly than the armies of Napoleon. But the railway and steamship changed alike the conditions of peace and war.

They carried fuel and raw materials to factories, they carried exports of manufactured goods to pay for raw materials, and in war they were to make it possible to conduct operations on a scale hitherto undreamed of. In multiplying wealth they multiplied populations, and in multiplying populations they multiplied the masses of soldiery which could be wielded by the dictators of warlike operations.

The rapidity of the British rise to affluence, from a condition of stagnation in which British industries were unimportant in Europe, may be illustrated by reference to what became the nation's chief industries. Whereas in 1740 Great Britain produced only 17,000 tons of pig iron, in 1806 she produced 258,000 tons, in 1835 a million tons, in 1870 six million tons and in 1913 nine million tons. If we turn to the British consumption of raw cotton, we find that whereas in 1785 it was 18 million lb., in 1811 it was 90 million lb. The figures relating to wool are equally eloquent of progress; in 1775 the wool used in the British woollen and worsted industries amounted to 82 million lb., in 1875 to 351 million lb., and in 1913 to 633 million lb. Or, if we turn to the export trade and to the first available figures for the United Kingdom, those of 1805, we find that in that year the British exports of British goods were valued at £38,000,000, whereas by 1870 they had risen to £199,000,000 and in 1913 to £525,000,000.

Tremendous growth of populations

It was by virtue of the activities expressed in such figures as these that the British population made the enormous advance that we have already noted. Between the end of the eighteenth century and the opening of the twentieth white men had learned how to preserve life as it had never been before preserved in the history of mankind; the result was an unparalleled expansion of population—an expansion which had been deemed impossible by economic writers who could not foresee the invention of means to produce wealth on a gigantic scale. In passing, we may note that the years preceding the Great War were notable for a marked decrease in the birth rate consequent upon the rise in the standard of comfort and the desire to restrict families within a compass which would make their up-bringing less onerous to their parents and leave more time for pleasure and recreation.

The conditions of wealth changed and populations grew, but the ancient conceptions of international fear and hostility remained. The growth of populations meant the growth of armies—the growth of what has been so expressively termed 'man power.' Each expansion of wealth and population, instead of being considered a proof of the power to live and grow in peace, was too often regarded as creating a new necessity for defence against possible aggression. So Europe, which had been for so many centuries impoverished and desolated by war, used the new economic conditions provided by modern science to prepare big battalions for war on a larger scale.

By her exploitation of splendid coal resources, made possible by the ingenuity of her inventors, Britain secured an astonishing lead in industrial development and became, in a well known phrase, the workshop of the world. Where before the British people had been backward in economic development, they became exporters instead of importers of manufactures, and importers instead of exporters of raw material. Before this striking period of British inventiveness the nation had had to rely upon foreign engineers and foreign devices in many departments of work. The textile trades, pottery manufacture, paper making and other trades had been imported from abroad, and in the eighteenth century the best goods in use were gained by importation, paid for by the export of crude products.

Economic growth and rivalry

No one has put the great change into clearer terms than Professor Stanley Jevons, who, in his work The Coal Question, wrote:

> The history of British industry and trade may be divided into two periods, the first reaching backward from about the middle of the eighteenth century to the earliest

times, and the latter reaching forward to the present and the future. These two periods are contrary in character. In the earlier period Britain was a rude, half-cultivated country, abounding in corn, and wool, and meat, and timber, and exporting the rough but valuable materials of manufacture. Our people, though with no small share of poetic and philosophic genius, were unskilful and unhandy, better in the arts of war than those of peace; on the whole, learners rather than teachers.

But as the second period grew upon us many things changed. Instead of learners, we became teachers; instead of exporters of raw materials, we became importers; instead of importers of manufactured articles, we became exporters. What we had exported we began by degrees to import, and what we had imported we began to export.

While this great development proceeded, and Britain grew apace in wealth and population, her possible and potential rivals were out of the running. The other great European coal country, Germany, was still no more than a geographical expression, divided into many states differing in politics and in economics, with high tariffs against each other. Germany, destined to become the chief industrial country of Europe, was, in an economic sense, in embryo. There was no possibility of considerable economic development until the establishment of the German Zollverein in the nineteenth century. It was not until 1833 that the German Zollverein began to cover the larger part of North and South Germany, and it was not until the formation of the German Empire at the conclusion of the Franco-German war that German industry may be said to have obtained its full opportunity. From that time onwards German progress was remarkably rapid, and Britain experienced serious German competition in home, colonial and foreign markets.

Competition from Germany

It was with Germany as with Britain. The possession of coal and iron furnished a firm foundation for modern industry, and although she had not the long coast line that was such an asset to Great Britain, she made splendid use of her central position in Europe by establishing a fine national railway system. Even on the sea, despite her natural disadvantages, she became a serious competitor. As for the United States, that modern giant of industry, for different reasons her development of great industrial resources came late in history. The smelting of iron with coal in America did not begin until long after it had become a commonplace in Britain. The country that possessed the greatest coal resources in the world, enormously greater than those of any other country, made such late use of them that even in 1880 the quantity of pig iron produced by her was less than half that produced in the British Isles. It is difficult to realize how small was the population of America in times quite recent. When the Franco-German war was fought the population of the United States was about as large as that of France, and the great majority of her less than forty million people was engaged in primary pursuits.

Late development of United States

It was between 1880 and 1890 that America and Germany began to work their great resources upon a large scale, and from that time forward the industrial supremacy of Great Britain began to wane. As recently as 1885, Britain produced as much iron as America and Germany put together. Then came the great change. Five years later, in 1890, the United States produced 9,200,000 tons of pig iron against 7,900,000 tons produced in the United Kingdom, and from then onwards the disparity increased, the American population and the American industrial production alike increasing by leaps and bounds.

To give one more illustration of economic change, it may be recalled that in 1867 the whole world produced 7,500,000 tons of iron, and that Britain produced nearly 4,000,000 tons of this world output. Two generations later, when the Great War broke out, the world was producing about 75,000,000 tons of pig iron, and the contribution of the United Kingdom was 10,260,000 tons. The last half of the nineteenth century was a period of rapid economic mutation in the world at large, and the changes increased in rapidity as time went on. New industries quickly sprang into existence and old industries were eager to change their methods. A world which for centuries had seen trades carried on by old traditional methods arrived at conditions in which it became a commonplace for a great industry to change its processes fundamentally in a decade or less.

Amidst these changes Britain contrived to raise the standard of living of an ever increasing population; for, although there was industrial development in the world at large, markets grew as well as competitors. There proved to be room for all, and, indeed, the opening years of the twentieth century down to the beginning of the Great War saw a remarkable increase in the exports of the chief exporting nations.

Just as the rapid growth of populations in the nineteenth century meant, in the survival of international hostility, the growth of armies, so the growth of scientific industry meant the growth of armaments, the invention of weapons of precision, the building of bigger war vessels, the perfecting of the means of destroying human life. Science, which taught men how to keep their children alive, also taught them how to kill on the principle of mass production. The Industrial Revolution meant a revolution in methods of warfare, and the Europe of the century after Waterloo employed its best talents and its greatest discoveries to make possible a scale of human destruction undreamed of by Napoleon.

Acquisition of Colonies

While world trade and industry, as we have seen, were expanding, the world's colonial development was also proceeding. The colonisation of the American continent, of Africa and of Australasia by the European nations was conditioned partly by human enterprise and partly by geographical conditions. It was natural for those countries which faced the Atlantic to breed seamen, and for those seamen to explore the high seas. That is how it came about that the great new communities of European blood came to be chiefly derived from the nations bordering the Atlantic sea-board, and of these Britain, France, Spain, Portugal and Holland became the chief colonisers. This pegging out of colonies virtually ceased long ago. The new worlds came to be divided up among a few nations, while those who through their geographical situation had taken no part in discovery and annexation were left out in the cold. So, in 1913, Germany and Italy, two of the great powers of Europe, were almost without colonies of any particular value. In 1921 there were 12,300,000 Germans and 11,100,000 Italians living outside Europe, and for the most part living under foreign flags.

Advantages of a Colonial Empire

Here, too, as in commerce, there is plenty of room for misapprehension of the true meaning of things. The old conception of a colony was of a thing owned, a thing ruled, a thing tributary, and it was this conception that led to colonial resentment and colonial rebellion. But it was learned, if slowly, that people were not content to be ruled from afar by a home government necessarily ignorant of colonial needs and conditions. The great British colonies have become British Dominions as independent of home control as if they were foreign states. However, it should not be overlooked that in questions of raw material and emigration the 'possession' of independent colonies in the modern sense may still be of special importance to a mother country. The ties that exist, free as they are of obligation, do make it possible to consider economic problems in the best possible spirit, and do assist in the solution of problems of emigration. It is a continuous cause of ill feeling in some countries that there are few or no parts of the world to which their people can migrate to places under their own flag; that they are denied as foreigners the means of taking a share in the development of new lands. These are considerations which the world has seriously to face.

We have said that the experience of long years of trade proved that, while competition increased in modern times, there was room enough in the world's markets for all competitors. The point is of such great importance that we give the facts. The commercial expansion of the years 1900–1913, measured by export trade in millions of pounds sterling, was as follows for the chief countries:

	1900	1910	1913
United Kingdom ..	291	430	525
United States ..	286	356	510
Germany	231	367	496
France	164	249	275
Italy	54	83	100
Austria-Hungary ..	81	101	115
Holland	141	218	258
Belgium	77	136	143
Switzerland	35	49	55
Spain	32	39	42
Russia	76	153	150
Norway	10	15	21
Sweden	22	33	46
Denmark	16	27	43
Argentina	35	75	97

This very remarkable account of progress begins, we should note, with the year 1900, which was justly accounted one of 'booming' trade. In that year the United Kingdom exported £291,000,000 worth of goods, and every commentator rejoiced in the fact as being exceedingly creditable to an old-established commercial people. The figures of 1910 and 1913 compare with what was a good year, and we see that in 1913 British exports reached the remarkable total of £525,000,000, or £234,000,000 greater than in 1900. And this was done, we may observe, while America, Germany, France, Italy and indeed every other nation in the list made advances to which the adjective enormous can justly be applied. There was a certain rise in prices which affected the figures, but for the most part the growth was in actual quantity of trade. The world of commerce was increasing its dimensions at an unparalleled rate.

Relation of Trade to War

This must be regarded as vital to the argument. The conception that the common development of the whole world is necessarily hostile to the interests of any particular country is thereby shown to be contrary to recorded facts, just as it is entirely contrary to economic theory. The economist properly looks upon trade as a matter of mutually satisfactory exchanges, knowing that the exports of one country are the imports of another, and that buying and selling are profitable alike for buyer and seller.

Country A does not discharge a hostile broadside by furnishing exports to country B. On the contrary, it furnishes B with goods which are bought by persons who need them for their own economic purposes. Moreover, the purpose of exports, the function of exports, is to gain imports. Great Britain does not send products abroad, either to a foreign country or to a British dominion, to get rid of them, but to pay for the all essential imports without which she cannot maintain her great population. She exports textiles to Canada to gain in exchange corn and apples, and sends locomotives to South America to gain in exchange meat and hides.

The conception that trade can be greatly affected by the possession of armaments is an inheritance from ancient days when the capture of territory and the enslavement of its population were commonly practised. For so many centuries did it remain true that the conqueror gained by his conquest not territory alone, but riches, that the ancient conception of the meaning and consequences of conquest survive, if vaguely, in the thought and in the arguments of our own day and generation. In the years preceding the Great War never a week passed without the printing of some article in which one could trace the conception of warring for trade, of warring for wealth. But a nation can no longer enslave a rival or destroy by conquest its people and its industries. While modern warfare is deadly enough, by comparison with a large population the life losses are small. In ancient times the loss of a war often meant the destruction of a people; in modern times such destruction is impossible.

Foreign Conquest and Commerce

It is not to deny the horror of modern warfare, nor to minimise the terrible loss of life which it entails, to declare with truth that in modern conditions it is childish to think of warfare as destroying a people. In 1928 the populations of the nations which engaged in the great contest of 1914–18 were larger than when they entered it in 1914, save perhaps for France, whose stagnation in population is due not to the effects of warfare, but to the deliberate restriction of births.

From the fact that modern warfare cannot destroy a population, it follows that it cannot destroy the trade of that population, although it may seriously affect it. If country A conquers country B and destroys a certain proportion of its manhood, we may be quite sure that in the process country A will lose approximately as many men as she herself contrives to kill. Further, if country A succeeds by warfare in crippling the trade of country B, we may be quite sure that in the process she will greatly cripple her own trade. In our time, the conqueror may be little or no better off than the conquered when it comes to making peace. The greatest economic sufferer by the Great War was undoubtedly Great Britain, and the indemnity payments she has been able to obtain from Germany, even if we leave out of account the repayment of British war debt to the United States, are a mere trifle compared with the losses incurred through the dislocation of commerce caused by the process of conquest. Emerging from the war as a conqueror, Britain found herself with an enormous army of unemployed workpeople and a crushing burden of debt.

Repercussions on the victor

Writing some years before the Great War began, in his book entitled Europe's Optical Illusion, Norman Angell very well summarised the fallacy of all modern conquest in the following words :

> As the only possible policy in our day for a conqueror to pursue is to leave the wealth of a territory in the complete possession of the individuals inhabiting that territory, it is a logical fallacy and an optical illusion in Europe to regard a nation as increasing its wealth when it increases its territory, because when a province or state is annexed the population, who are the real and only owners of the wealth therein, are also annexed, and the conqueror gets nothing. The facts of modern history abundantly demonstrate this. When Germany annexed Schleswig-Holstein and Alsatia not a single ordinary German citizen was one pfennig the richer. Although England 'owns' Canada, the English merchant is driven out of the Canadian markets by the merchant of Switzerland, who does not 'own' Canada. . . Conversely, armies and navies cannot destroy the trade of rivals, nor can they capture it. The great nations of Europe do not destroy the trade of the small nations to their benefit, because they cannot ; and the Dutch citizen, whose government possesses no military power, is just as well off as the German citizen, whose government possesses an army of two million men, and a great deal better off than the Russian, whose government possesses an army of something like four millions.

Nevertheless, we must remember certain things which do not seem to have been always present to the mind of the writer of the words quoted. While it is true that Britain endured a great economic loss through the Great War, although a conqueror, it is also true that she would have lost economically more heavily still if she had been a loser. For, while her trade was dislocated in a thousand places by the exigencies of war, she was still able to maintain her sea connexions and a large part of her shipping, and was in a position at the close of the war to resume business, even if admittedly on a smaller scale and in circumstances of the greatest difficulty.

Let us imagine for a moment that the Central empires had succeeded. Success would have meant the destruction of the British navy, the capture of British shipping and the surrender of the British government through the consequent failure of supplies. With so large a part of the food supply and of the materials of industry derived from beyond the seas, the United Kingdom's 46,000,000 people would have been quickly reduced by starvation, and surrender would have been forced upon them. The economic position of the British Isles is peculiar. All civilizations are artificial, but the British organization is based to such a large degree upon commerce that there must remain very great doubt whether, in the event of such a calamity as the destruction of its economic basis, the trade of Britain would return in such measure as to enable her to resume her old standard of life and to support so great a population. The imagination boggles at the idea of so tremendous a catastrophe.

Effects of defeat on Great Britain

Even here, however, the conqueror would find his difficulties. In possession of the ports of Britain, Germany would have found it necessary herself to make provision for the conquered population. She herself would have had to organize supplies, or to allow trade to continue, to save herself from the troublesome task of maintaining a conquered people. Some compromise would have been necessary to prevent a disaster which would have shocked the world.

Whatever the arrangements made, it is idle to ignore the fact that Britain after the conquest might have found the very greatest difficulty in recovering her old position. As emigration would have been impossible for her people, she would have had to endure an extraordinary degree of deprivation and discomfort, probably accompanied by a great increase in the death rate for a considerable period. It is impossible to escape the general conclusion that Britain would have sunk in the scale of nations and would have had to endure a very much lower scale of living. A large part of her shipping might have been taken from her and much of her carrying trade might never have returned. Productive industry no doubt would have been gradually restored, for no conquest could alter the fact that Britain possesses great coal resources and iron and limestone beds. Much of British wealth, however, is not founded on production, and it is precisely because this is true that the defeat of Britain would assuredly have had the gravest economic consequences. These are the facts which were not faced by Norman Angell in his writings, great as was the truth underlying many parts of them.

War destructive of intangible assets

And Britain is something more than an island state. She is the head and front of a great federation of free self-governing dominions, and she exercises imperial rule in India and the crown colonies. The conquest of Britain, therefore, would have meant the disruption of the Empire, and that disruption would have had far-reaching economic consequences. And economic issues are largely bound up with others not less important. The shock to British prestige and the profound discouragement which would have ensued upon the destruction of so proud an edifice would undoubtedly have had a profound effect upon every department of British endeavour. It is idle to meet these considerations merely with the argument that conquest of a thickly populated European territory is not worth while.

Five years before the Great War broke out, Professor Hans Delbruck wrote:

> What Germany has set herself to do is to enforce such a position that German influence, German capital, German engineering and German intelligence can compete on equal terms with those of other nations.

That is a very fair expression by a German of what has been called the struggle for 'a place in the sun.'

Struggle for a Place in the Sun

We have already observed how the world outside the old established civilizations of Europe and Asia came to be colonised by seafaring nations bordering the Atlantic. That process left important nations without any share in the development of new lands, and we must not wonder if at last a united Germany, rising to wealth and influence by virtue of great natural gifts, came to regard with some degree of bitterness a world in which she could take no reasonable share as a colonising power. We must not forget that German organizing ability, applied to a favourable territory, would undoubtedly produce good results. Those who know German cities and German industries, and who have been witness of the genius which informs their activities, could have no reasonable doubt that if the Germans had had a coast facing the Atlantic, and had bred seamen, they would have taken a great and worthy part in world development. In large part the same observations are true of Italy, which remained a geographical expression until quite recent years, and became a great nation too late to find a place in the sun.

The control of raw materials also came to present itself as of supreme importance. The old nations of Europe are necessarily largely dependent upon supplies of raw products from undeveloped territories. The liberal economic policy of the British Empire, however, never denied its natural wealth to the world at large, and when the Great War broke out it was even discovered that German interests had monopolised the zinc of Australia, which British capital had neglected. There is no doubt, however, that the feeling that the world's resources were unequally divided amongst its governing powers played its part in the production of ill feeling and the growth of armaments. Traditional misconceptions about the economics of war mingled with real and practical modern issues in creating a war spirit in Europe. Political and economic prestige were counted one, and each nation saw itself as defending or enlarging its economic dominion.

So the Europe of the nineteenth and early twentieth centuries, growing in industrial power, made preparation for war not the least of its industries. Millions of men were divorced from production and made a burden upon working populations to secure nations from feared aggression. Conscription was everywhere the rule save in the United Kingdom, and most of the finest working men of Europe became parts of a great war machine. Germany, with her long land frontiers, built up the largest and best equipped army the world had ever known. Britain, maintaining a small voluntary army which could at best do no more than place a small expeditionary force upon the Continent of Europe, rested her defences upon the maintenance of a supreme navy. In the opening years of the twentieth century it became evident that Germany was aiming at the possession of both a supreme army and a supreme navy. German fleet laws were enacted, the effects of which, failing adequate building by Britain, would have been to give Germany supremacy at sea. The German fleet law, thrice amended, ran thus in 1913:

Huge preparation of armaments

We, William, by the Grace of God, German Emperor . . . decree . . . there shall be:

(1) The Battle Fleet, consisting of:
- 1 fleet flagship*
- 5 squadrons of 8 battleships each*
- 12 large cruisers* } as scouts
- 30 small cruisers }

(2) The Foreign Service Fleet, consisting of:
- 8 large cruisers*
- 10 small cruisers.

This meant the eventual building of 61 capital ships of the first class (i.e. the items marked with an asterisk in the above list), and therefore an aim to possess the world's greatest navy in addition to the world's greatest army. The British government, faced with this issue, found it necessary to build capital ships in reply, and, as events showed, if she had not done so the war of 1914–18 would have ended differently. Those who had a proper respect for German industry and German ingenuity entertained no doubt that German capital ships in action would be able to give a good account of themselves. And so it proved to be. When we consider the results of the Battle of Jutland, we may indeed wonder what would have been the issue if the British government had neglected to reply to the German fleet laws.

The organization of Europe as an armed camp not only placed an enormous burden upon the shoulders of European working citizens, but, we must remember, was a draft upon the productive powers of Europe. It is easy to forget that a soldier represents a double economic loss—that producing nothing himself he has to be supported by those who produce. The standing armies of Europe thus represent a tremendous deduction from economic power. Preparation for war is an industry destructive of wealth, save in so far as it calls out ingenuity resulting in inventions which may be useful in peace (see Chapter 178); for the most part, however, science works for peaceful purposes, and finds its productions turned to destructive employments.

Economic loss of big armies

The growth of modern wealth, the growth of great populations—and the correlative growth of great armies—were unaccompanied by any enlargement of the ability of individual statesmen. It is unfortunate for mankind that as the factors of peace and war increase in magnitude men do not gain any corresponding power of organization or leadership. Thus the formation of enormous armies gave men the power to launch movements on an unprecedented scale, with no more ability than was possessed by statesmen and commanders in days when armies were comparatively insignificant in size.

During most of the nineteenth century military commanders disposed of men by the hundred thousand ; in the twentieth century soldiers are employed by the million. The millions have to find leaders in men whose powers of disposition are not one wit greater than, if as great as, those possessed by bygone generals who wielded forces which would have been considered negligible in the Great War.

Thus also it is with economic powers. Men of necessarily limited experience and ability find themselves charged with the conduct of gigantic economic operations whose ramifications affect the lives and happiness of millions. No doubt to some extent men rise to the occasion, but it is questionable whether the ability to deal with work and its products in great masses is possessed by more than a few distinguished men, and the chances of finding them when they are wanted must be extremely rare. The deficiencies of men, their limitations and proneness to error, their failures of judgement, their inevitable spells of fatigue in moments of severe strain and stress, matter little when small affairs are in progress ; we have to remember that when the scale of affairs is magnified enormously men are no less subject to the weaknesses to which all flesh is heir.

The control of increased powers

The Great War of 1914–18 witnessed the conscription of fighting men, the conscription of industrial power and the conscription of wealth upon a scale unknown before, but it produced few if any men capable of handling the tremendous forces which were set going. At any given moment the direction of the lives of tens of millions of soldiers and war workers was in the hands of overworked and physically weakened committees who could at best see only partially the forces under their command. Thus, errors came necessarily to be large-scale errors, and when lives were wasted it was not by the thousand but by the ten thousand. It is with war as with vehicles. A man driving a small cart can by error at worst kill one or two people. The same man at the levers of an express railway train can, with an error of judgement no greater, cause the death of hundreds of people. When war, as in the twentieth century, comes to mean the enlistment of all the forces of a nation and their concentration upon one purpose, there are bound to be human mistakes on a scale which it is terrible to contemplate.

The economics of the Great War came to mean the enlistment of the entire working powers of the nations. This was not foreseen. No one at the beginning of hostilities dreamed that before the contest was ended the three British government departments which controlled ships, munitions and food would, in effect, take charge of the greater part of the national supplies. In 1918 the imports of the United Kingdom were almost entirely chosen, controlled and directed by the government in the interests of the nation. When the Armistice was signed in 1918 nearly 95 per cent. of British imports were under control. The economics of modern war cannot be understood unless we realize this. In the year 1918 British imports were roundly 35,200,000 tons, and they were thus controlled :

Commerce controlled by the government

	Tons
Ministry of Food	12,700,000
Ministry of Munitions : munitions, metals, ores, nitrate, lubricating oil, machinery	12,000,000
War Office and Admiralty : wool, flax, hemp, jute, hides, leather, oil, steel plates, guns, etc. ..	5,000,000
Timber Controller	2,500,000
Board of Trade : cotton, oil, paper, pulp, tobacco	3,000,000
Total	35,200,000

This table refers solely to imports. Of home operations, the mines, the railways, agriculture, food distribution, alcohol—all these and many more were under government control or supervision. Without previous experience of such far-reaching operations, men had to adapt themselves to unwonted tasks. There were generals in the field and generals in civilian operations, and all of them necessarily made mistakes on a large scale in dealing with affairs of such magnitude.

The Europe of 1914 had attained to a condition of economic interdependence between its component nations, and between those nations and the world outside Europe, upon which depended the welfare and livelihood of its nearly 500 million people. The interchanges between the European nations were enormous, and the imports into Europe in exchange for the exports of Europe were vital to her civilized existence. The three chief commercial nations of Europe—Britain, Germany and France—had great foreign investments in the Old and New Worlds. It is estimated that Germany in 1914 had some £1,200,000,000 invested abroad, nearly one half of which was invested in Austria-Hungary, Russia, the Balkans and other parts of Europe. Britain's foreign and colonial investments probably amounted to £4,000,000,000, of which, however, only some £200,000,000 were invested in Europe. France had very considerable sums invested in Russia and elsewhere.

War & national interdependence

In particular, Germany's economic connexions with her European neighbours were very close. She utilised her central position to great advantage, and became the largest trader with many European countries. With her foreign trade, her foreign investments and her organizing ability Germany took a great and systematic part in the economic development of pre-war Europe. Hence the term 'peaceful penetration,' which was so frequently heard, and expressed the truth that a nation can by peaceful means do more to spread its influence and culture than by any process of conquest.

While internally the nations of Europe became increasingly interdependent from economic causes, the dependence of Europe upon extra-European supplies was always increasing with its growth of population. The demand in Europe for a higher standard of life meant, in economic terms, a demand by Europe upon the rest of the world for more food and raw materials. With the population approaching 500,000,000 (in 1921 the number was closely estimated at 453,000,000) Europe was making an enormous call upon Asia, Africa, America and Australasia for products with which to supplement her own limited resources. This dependence of Europe upon supplies from without was by no means equal throughout the Continent, and it was most marked in the places where the standard of life was highest.

The world outside Europe, and particularly Africa, America and Australasia, owed its economic development to European enterprise and exportation of capital. In effect, Europe for many years exported to the New World railways, docks, harbours, factories and all the working apparatus of modern trade and industry. Britain played the chief part in this development. Hence the extraordinary figure of £4,000,000,000 for British overseas investments which we have already noted as existing when the Great War broke out. Other nations played a much smaller part in this economic process, but they gained much by it. The economic development of Australia, for example, mainly accomplished by British capital, enabled all Europe to gain by the resultant products. The enormous British investments in North and South America produced for the world at large supplies of food and material which were an especial gain to Europe. It is generally true that one cannot improve any part of the world without favourably influencing the world as a whole, and the more we come to realize the economic interdependence of nations, the more we realize the real interest they have in each other's progress and welfare.

Nations benefit by mutual prosperity

An enterprising trader seeking a sphere of activity would not think of setting up business in a poor neighbourhood with no prospects; his aim is to find well-to-do customers in a rich area. It is not a little strange that this consideration is so often neglected when international trade is discussed. A nation existing in a world of poor nations must necessarily be poor itself unless it has within its own borders supplies of everything it needs. A trading population like that of Britain, Germany, France or Italy, inhabiting a territory of definitely limited resources, must, if it is to advance economically, trade freely with the world at large and, if it has a true economic outlook, rejoice that it exists in a world of progressive and well-to-do nations and not in one in which universal poverty reigns. Britain, a nation naturally poor, grew wealthy by trading freely with all the world and by bringing to her ports the wealth which nature denied her.

If we regard Europe as an economic unit, we see it a well endowed area and yet one which has great need to go outside its borders to supplement its own natural provisions. This important economic fact led to the great exchanges between Europe and the world outside Europe which were so marked a feature of world commerce when the Great War broke out. And what the war did was not only to break the economic links which existed within Europe, but to violate the fruitful exchanges between Europe and the New World which had done so much to raise the standard of civilization in Europe.

In such economic circumstances, war in Europe was a menace alike to the worker and to the capitalist. All the real interests of both capital and labour are opposed to war.

To the worker, selling the products of his hand or brain for wage or salary, war, by destroying or limiting the power of international exchange, lowers the value of real earnings. Real wages are counted in the commodities which one can obtain in exchange for one's work. The count by money received means little or nothing; the real test is what money will buy, and the intrinsic value of what money buys is determined by the facilities for free exchange. The ideal position for the earner of wage or salary is that he shall be able to exchange his earnings for any product produced in any part of the world; only by that means can he, as a citizen of the world, make the best use of its products. What war does is to destroy the means by which a worker exchanges his work for what the world has to offer.

War lowers real wages

So in the Great War there was the spectacle of men unable to command with their wages the first necessities of life. Things were bad enough in the Allied countries which had access to the sea, but in the Central empires the sufferings during and after the war were indeed terrible. Hundreds of thousands perished from malnutrition. Diseases such as consumption had fell sway, and millions of European citizens carried and will carry to their graves the marks of deprivation which they and their parents endured (see page 4907).

The sufferings of the peoples through war and the economic consequences of war are, however, well known, and it is unnecessary here to dwell at length upon them. It is sometimes said that while the masses suffer through war, the capitalists and financiers make gains. We have even heard the assertion made that capitalists promote war to enrich themselves. What we have said, however, of the economic interdependence of nations, and of the mutuality of interest which exists and is growing among the world's economic governing powers, forbids the conception that capitalists and financiers have any interest in war. The successful operations of modern capital can only be pursued in conditions of settled peace. It was the large measure of peace in Europe that reigned between 1871 and 1914 that enabled the continent as a whole to make such unparalleled progress in wealth and population. As we have seen, the trade of the great nations increased enormously in the opening years of the twentieth century, and there is no doubt whatever that, if the war of 1914–18 could have been avoided, the economic progress of the years 1914–29 would have eclipsed all previous records. The capitalists and financiers of Europe, in that half generation of advance, would have made further great progress in national and international economic organization, and from their point of view nothing could have been more disastrous than the actual course of events.

Financiers do not gain by war

It is perfectly true that when war breaks out a great demand is set up for the products of certain industries, and that great immediate gains may be made by government contractors. Even for these, however, there is no prospect of permanent gain, and indeed not a few of the British firms who took a large part in furnishing the main munitions of war suffered most severely from the economic reactions after the war. Generally, the gains accruing from war contracting are most unevenly divided; one business firm may win a fortune; another may as easily lose all that it possesses. There can be no question that economically the Great War was a terrible disaster for British mining, British shipping and British industry; and that war profiteers were an accompaniment of war operations does not in the least invalidate the conclusion that all the real and substantial financial, industrial and commercial interests of Great Britain were put to hazard and suffered disastrously. The great staple trades of Britain, cotton and wool, coal and iron, shipping and ship-building, had not even in 1929, eleven years after the conclusion of the war, recovered from the blows dealt them in a world-wide economic disaster, which necessarily affected most of all the nation that relied upon world trade and world peace for its prosperity.

Terrible losses to British trade

It proved to be the finest and most characteristic of British industries that suffered most severely by the economic upheaval. The very trades upon which British greatness was built went to pieces, and indeed had to be deliberately torn to pieces to satisfy the greed of war. Measures were framed for safety in shipping which amounted in effect to the suppression of old trade routes and the diversion of ships from one sea to another. This strategy, while it helped to secure the safety of the nation, was nevertheless fraught with far-reaching consequences to British shipping in peace. Britain was compelled to risk her dearest and most arduously won economic possessions to secure her war position. Because ships were short in supply, she had to cut off materials from great trades. As for coal, the first factor in British prosperity, the war was merciless to British interests, and it remains questionable, after the lapse of more than a decade, whether British coal will ever recover its pre-war position. These are considerations which affect industry as a whole, and they have as much significance for master as for man, for capital as for labour.

Nor must the human element be forgotten. Whether a man be employed or employer, his personal relations to his country and his kind are the same; he has to suffer in his own person the evils and the sorrows of war. If he has sons to give, they are given. The economic operations of war are directed by business men and officials many of whom lose their sons. How idle it is, therefore, to speak of war as affecting classes unequally; the truth is that all alike have to share the common consequences of a conflict which does not pass until the flower of a nation's manhood, drawn from all classes, has been sacrificed for uncertain ends.

The economics of war here discussed, although a matter which embraces the fortunes of the entire world and of all its inhabitants, is of peculiar importance to the white races, and especially to Europe, which is still the fountain of white civilization. The world is led by the white races, and it is to be remarked that the whites, at the most liberal estimate, amount to no more than one in three of the whole population of the world. The Great War thus appears as an internecine conflict among that minority of the world's people which is responsible for the leadership of civilization.

War as it affects the white races

Such a conflict was bound to have profound reactions in the world at large. In India, in China, indeed in all Asia, in Egypt and elsewhere, the white races suffered a loss of prestige and of power which may have far-reaching consequences for the world at large, in all its activities, whether political or economic. If the white leadership of the world is to remain, the economic and political disasters which accompanied the greatest war in history must not occur again. White civilization could not sustain the repetition of such a conflict, enforced by the new implements and methods of destruction which science is still busily adding to the fighting powers of the world's governments.

What the world needs is an economic synthesis which will enable it to make the most of its limited resources. The best of the world's organizers perceive this, and despite the grave difficulties which are presented by political boundaries and customs barriers do their best to co-operate in the interests of a general economic advance. We see increasingly the formation of international associations for the improvement of industry and for the conservation of resources. These have to function in a world in which political boundary lines cut clean through natural economic fields, and in which customs barriers sever both natural and artificial links of economic communication. Nothing is more remarkable than the manner in which men, seeking to do the best for the development of industries, struggle to overcome the unfortunate political divisions and differences which are so utterly opposed to economic considerations.

There can be no possible doubt that if the resources of Europe could be used as an economic unit, just as the resources of the United States are used, there would be an enormous increment of wealth to the European peoples. Conversely, if the United States, instead of being established as an economic unit, was broken up into many political states, each with a customs tariff hostile to the other, every part of America would suffer disastrously. The progress of divided Europe, in face of constant war and preparation for war, can only be considered wonderful.

Need for an economic union

It is not that a self-contained Europe is possible, or that self-containment is in itself ideal. The world as a whole is necessarily self-contained, for it can have access to the resources of no other planet; who can doubt, however, that it would gain immeasurably if the rich resources of a larger and superior planet were open to its people? The United States, rich as it is in coal and iron, field and forest, oil and copper, lead and silver, is nevertheless dependent upon other nations for a large variety of products. A Europe united economically, or bound together by liberal commercial treaties, would not be self-contained, and would still have to seek without its borders products which nature has denied it or given it inadequately. But there is no doubt whatever that peaceful and liberal economic intercourse within its fine area, continued for a generation, would add enormously to its economic powers and to that yearly flow of consumable wealth which we term income.

In Chapter 182 the economic chaos in Europe resulting from the War is described in detail. It is for the gravest consideration that the menace of renewed European war still remains, and that while it remains white civilization is in danger. Civilization is an inheritance, and it has no necessary permanence. It is a thing that each generation has to learn from its predecessor, and which it may or may not continue or develop. Life is a succession of lives, a unity which may be either linked or broken by generations of decay. Human history is full of examples of the discontinuity of human progress; civilizations have developed and died again and again. If there could have been continuous development, the world of the twentieth century would be much better worth living in. The preservation of white civilization is a trust which we inherit, and which it is our duty to safeguard and uphold.

Menace of a second World War

Civilization connotes much more than the development of economic powers; nevertheless, a sound economy lies at the basis of the lives of men, since they must be fed and housed and provided for. The struggle with economic forces does not end; its continuance is forced upon mankind. That is the true and worthy warfare, the real battle of life. If it is to be waged successfully, if men are to obtain more than poor results from arduous labour, they must put away the ancient conception that wealth is to be gained or sustained by war and preparation for war. The Europe of 1914 was an armed camp; post-war Europe remains an armed camp, with great additions to aerial fighting forces which menace mankind with new and swifter methods of destruction. In these circumstances, the white leadership of the world remains in peril, and a large part of the work of mankind is frustrated.

James Clerk-Maxwell (1831–79), left, working upon the concepts of Faraday, published his electro-magnetic theory of light in 1864. A development of Maxwell's theories by the German physicist Heinrich Hertz (1857–94), right, produced results upon which wireless communication was afterwards based. In 1888 he demonstrated the analogy between electro-magnetic waves and light waves.

Left, National Portrait Gallery, London

His investigation into the electro-magnetic waves discovered by Hertz led the distinguished scientist Sir Oliver Lodge (left), born in 1851, to pursue his great pioneer work of demonstrating the possibility of wireless communication. The first working system was demonstrated in 1896 by Guglielmo Marconi, born in 1874 and here seen at the age of twenty-five, whose genius lay in his immediate perception of the practical possibilities inherent in a theoretical discovery.

SCIENTISTS AND INVENTORS TO WHOSE WORK WIRELESS IS DUE

Left, photo, Elliott & Fry; right, Marconi's Wireless Telegraph Co.

CHAPTER 176

SCIENCE AND INVENTION

How the Scientific Discoveries of the Nineteenth Century reacted on the World of Practical Affairs

By J. W. N. SULLIVAN

Author of History of Mathematics in Europe, Aspects of Science, etc.

During the nineteenth century the external characteristics of civilization underwent a greater change than had occurred in them during any preceding century. Indeed, it would hardly be too much to say that during this one century civilization changed more than it had done hitherto since the decline of the Roman Empire. This change has been so great and so rapid that it has created a new mental outlook.

The modern mind expects change; it takes change for granted. New technical discoveries of all kinds are taken as a matter of course. Nobody doubts that motor-cars, aeroplanes, wireless sets will be continually improved. Further, nobody doubts that radically new things, such as television, will speedily become practical and commercial propositions. The modern man lives in a world whose progress has become, as it were, automatic. Now it must be remembered that the whole of this outlook is new; this habit of mind is completely modern. Up to the beginning of the nineteenth century the vast majority of mankind lived in a static world. The horse and the sailing ship were, as they had been for centuries, virtually the sole means of transport, and—a very important point—communication depended on transport.

On a rapid survey of the technical progress made during the nineteenth century our attention is naturally arrested by two characteristics—the revolution in means of transport, and the revolution in means of communication. And we further notice the interesting fact that, for the first time, communication has become largely independent of transport. Much of our communication still depends upon transport, it is true. It is the motor-car, the train, the steamship, the aeroplane that carry our letters. But the land telegraph, the submarine cable, the telephone, wireless telegraphy and telephony are means of communication pure and simple.

In a discussion of the scientific inventions of the nineteenth century, therefore, it is inevitable that our attention should be concentrated chiefly upon the development of means of communication and means of transport, implying by 'means of communication' those that exist for communication only. And we shall see that the histories of these two great advances are entirely different.

Communications and transport

The one owes comparatively little to pure science, while the other is the direct outcome of the most abstract researches of the greatest scientific intellects of the time. Indeed, nowhere is the influence of science on invention more marked than in the history of our present means of communication. They are the offspring of electromagnetism, which to-day includes almost the whole of physics, the science which holds pride of place amongst all the sciences. No amount of practical knowledge and experience would have led to the invention of wireless telegraphy. That invention only became a concrete fact on the basis of certain recondite and highly theoretical speculations, supported by the profoundest mathematical analysis. The invention of the steam engine was an entirely different matter. For that only a comparatively rudimentary scientific knowledge was required, in addition to the skill and ingenuity of the experienced practical man. The one was born, the result of the severest analysis, in the dreaming mind of a mathematician; the other was born, the result of trial and error, in the sweat and grime of the workshop.

There is evidence that the idea of the electric telegraph occurred to Samuel Morse in 1832. The first telegraph line, however, was not installed until May, 1844, when it was laid between Washington and Baltimore in the United States. At that period knowledge of electrical science was in a comparatively rudimentary state. Certain simple phenomena of the electric current had long been known, and its generation by chemical processes had become fairly familiar. But certain characteristics of the transmission of electrical currents, which were to lead to practical difficulties later, were not even suspected. Morse's achievement was by no means an accident, but he was dealing, in the land telegraph, with particularly simple electric phenomena. This became apparent, later, when the submarine cable was invented.

The first submarine cable was laid, between Dover and Calais, in 1850. It was certainly not ideal, judged by modern standards, but it was sufficiently successful to inspire the grandiose project of laying a cable across the Atlantic. The history of this enterprise is one of the most romantic in the history of invention. Again and again did the pioneers of this great undertaking suffer defeat. Indeed, had it not been for the imagination and public spirit of the American financier, Cyrus Field, they would have had to retire from the contest. After many disappointments and a huge expenditure of money, material and labour, the satisfactory and permanent communication of England with America was achieved in 1866. To the success of this great invention there contributed, as is usual, very many small inventions. The manufacture, winding, storing and paying out of so great a length of cable required special apparatus of various kinds. The ingenuity of many practical men and small inventors was fully requisitioned for the service of the great cable. But one essential contribution to the success of the whole enterprise was that of the mathematician—in this case, Lord Kelvin.

The importance of this fact for us is that it is characteristic of the nineteenth century advances in communication.

EARLY ELECTRIC TELEGRAPH

Charles Wheatstone (1802–75), professor of experimental physics at King's College, London, promoted, with W. F. Cook, the progress of telegraphy in England. This is the five-needle telegraph which they patented in 1837.

Science Museum, South Kensington

INVENTOR OF THE MORSE CODE

His experiments with electricity led Samuel Finley Breese Morse (1791–1872), the American artist and scientist, to invent a system of communication by electric telegraph. The code he introduced perpetuates his name.

Those advances were achieved only by a stricter association between science and industry than had ever occurred before. An interesting aspect of this association is that the science involved was, apparently, the most remote from practical affairs of all the sciences—the science, namely, of mathematical physics. Kelvin's services were invoked because it was found that the electric current in a long submarine cable seemed to behave quite differently from a current in an ordinary land wire. Kelvin, to begin with, knew no more of the reason for this state of affairs than did anybody else. But, with the instinct of genius, the idea occurred to him that the diffusion of electricity through a submarine cable was analogous to a certain problem in the diffusion of heat through a conductor. This problem had already been worked out by the great French mathematician, Fourier. All that Kelvin had to do was to interchange, in his mind, certain characteristics of heat conductors for corresponding characteristics

A GREAT MATHEMATICIAN

The mathematical genius of Lord Kelvin (1824–1907), whose name is borne by many valuable inventions, played an important part in the laying of the first Atlantic cable. He was thereafter consulted on many similar enterprises.

Photo, Russell

AN EVENTFUL MOMENT IN THE HISTORY OF THE ATLANTIC CABLE

After a series of failures to establish permanent connexion between the Old and New Worlds by means of a cable across the Atlantic, success was finally achieved in 1866. In the same year the cable laid by the Great Eastern in 1865, which broke two thirds of the way across, was picked up and completed. A painting by Robert Dudley represents the recovery of the lost cable.

Courtesy of Sir Daniel F. Gooch, Bart.

of electrical conductors. Once this was done, the form of the two problems was the same. He could then use the solution given by Fourier and interpret it in electrical terms.

The moral of this story is obvious, and it is one that subsequent progress in the nineteenth century was to confirm over and over again. Fourier's researches were undertaken for their mathematical interest. It did not seem that they would ever have any practical applications. His book on The Theory of Heat was not designed for heat engineers. It was intended for mathematicians, and by them it was described as a 'mathematical poem'—as beautiful and as useless as a poem. Yet it has turned out to be of the first importance to electrical engineers, of whom Fourier never dreamt. Telephone engineers to-day, besides telegraph engineers, would find it impossible to design their circuits were it not for a purely mathematical discovery called Fourier's Theorem, a discovery which was made without either the hope or the expectation that it would ever prove useful. Indeed, as we shall see still more clearly when we come to consider wireless telegraphy, the history of the communication inventions of the nineteenth century may be described as the discovery of uses for mental achievements that everybody considered useless.

MICHAEL FARADAY

Great service was done to the foundation of electrical science by the investigations of Michael Faraday (1791–1867), the brilliant experimenter whose discoveries include magneto-electrical induction, whence proceeded the modern dynamo.

National Portrait Gallery, London

JEAN BAPTISTE FOURIER

Experiments on the theory of heat early absorbed the attention of the great French scientist, Jean Baptiste Fourier (1768–1830), famed for his mathematical series. His striking researches are embodied in his Théorie analytique de la chaleur.

Engraving by F. Boilly

In order to see the advances in communication during the nineteenth century as one connected whole, we must begin with Michael Faraday's discovery of electro-magnetic induction in 1831. This is, from the purely scientific point of view, the central scientific discovery of the century. The biological theory of evolution is usually regarded as the century's outstanding scientific achievement, but it is very questionable whether even that theory will affect our views of the universe as profoundly as the scientific outlook that Faraday's discovery has made possible; for Clerk-Maxwell derives from Faraday, and Einstein from Clerk-Maxwell. However that may be, there is no question about the greater practical importance of Faraday's discovery.

He discovered that if the electric current in a wire is varying in strength, it can create a current in a neighbouring, separate wire. The current in the second wire is strongest when the current in the first wire is being made or broken, for then the variation of current in the first wire is greatest. On this one fact rest practically all the applications of electricity to industry. The dynamo, for instance, is nothing but an embodiment of this principle. Scientifically considered, the phenomenon of electromagnetic induction is the intimate link between the phenomena of electricity and those of magnetism. For it can be shown that an electric current is surrounded by a magnetic field, and that it is the increase and decrease of this field that creates the 'induced' current in the second wire. If a wire be made to move across a magnetic field a current is created in the wire. This is the simple principle employed in an electric generator, where a coil of wire is made to revolve between the pole pieces of a magnet. But before Faraday's discovery could be fully utilised its mathematical laws had to be investigated.

Prime importance of Faraday's discovery

Now Faraday was not a technical mathematician. His way of thinking shows very great mathematical insight, but he had had no technical mathematical training. For this reason, although his discoveries were welcomed by the scientific world, his theories about them were considered quite unintelligible. Highly trained mathematicians, used to the very precise vocabulary of their own science, stared helplessly at Faraday's descriptions of 'lines of force' and 'axes of power.' Faraday could not translate these conceptions into the conventional language of science, and many mathematicians, after fruitless efforts, found themselves quite unable to understand him.

Besides this difficulty, however, there was a deeper reason for their lack of comprehension. Nowadays, everybody with a wireless set can talk glibly about electro-magnetic waves in the aether, but in the early nineteenth century nobody referred electric occurrences to outer space at all. Electricity was vaguely thought of as some kind of fluid which resided on the surface of bodies or else flowed along conducting wires. The fact that two electrified bodies could act upon one another at a distance was well known, but this action was regarded as immediate and inexplicable. It was inexplicable in the same sense as gravitation was inexplicable. The mutual gravitation of bodies had to be accepted as an ultimate fact about matter; matter simply happened to be that kind of thing. Similarly, the attraction or repulsion of electrified bodies was regarded as an ultimate fact. It was further supposed that electrical attraction, like gravitation, took place instantaneously. An electrified body was

THE EARLIEST DYNAMO

One practical demonstration of Faraday's theories was the electro-magnet which he constructed in 1831. When the copper disk was rotated a current was generated in it and the apparatus acted as a rudimentary dynamo.

Model in Science Museum of original in the Royal Institution

supposed to act on another at a distance without any time whatever being required for the transmission of this action.

It is not surprising that, with such ideas current, no particular importance was attached to the space separating electrified bodies. Whatever went on in that space happened instantaneously. Attention was directed wholly to the electrified bodies and away from the intervening space. We can see that the mathematical mind, in this instance, actually had a bad effect on science. It is the defect of that mind that it is too easily satisfied with purely formal explanations, provided they are of a kind that enables results to be correctly calculated. The aether was, at that time, a perfectly well known concept. It had been invented to explain the phenomena of light—in particular, the fact that light takes time to travel. It was invented to answer the question: 'If light takes eight minutes to reach the earth from the sun, where is it after it has left the sun and before it has reached the earth?' It could be shown that light did not consist of little pellets shot out by the sun. It could only be a wave motion in some universal medium. But although scientific men were quite familiar with the aether, they made no attempt to apply it to electrical phenomena.

Limitations of the mathematical mind

Faraday's whole conception of electric phenomena was radically different. In his mind's eye he saw the electrical influence spreading out in all directions from the conductor in straight or curved lines—his 'lines of force.' These lines repelled one another and also other lines coming from a similarly charged body. They reached across space in huge curves to terminate on some other body. Along these lines existed a state of tension. They were trying to contract, as stretched elastic tries to contract. Hence the 'attraction' between an electrified body and some other body. The whole field of operations, in Faraday's view, existed in the intervening space between electrified bodies. If his view was correct the interesting and vital part of an electric current was to be found outside the wire, and not inside it, or on its surface. This notion seemed to his contemporaries extremely paradoxical. But it was this inspiration of Faraday's, as we now know, that made wireless telegraphy and telephony possible.

Faraday's actual discoveries were speedily utilised but, as we have seen, his theories were neglected. It required a very rare type of genius to see the inner meaning of Faraday's remarks, and to give this meaning precise mathematical expression. The genius appeared in the person of James Clerk-Maxwell, to whom the whole of the great and expanding world of wireless is primarily due. Other researches of Clerk-Maxwell would have to be discussed in any account of the pure science of the nineteenth century, but here our attention must be confined to his electrical researches. He agreed with Faraday that the space around any electrified or magnetised body was the scene of stresses and strains in the aether. Variations in the electrification or magnetisation of a body were attended by variations in the electric and magnetic forces in the surrounding space.

Clerk-Maxwell gave these connexions precise mathematical expression, and he made the astonishing discovery, on examining his equations, that these variations of electro-magnetic force were propagated through the surrounding space, not instantaneously, but with a certain definite velocity. He was able to calculate this velocity, and reached the extraordinarily interesting result that it was equal to the velocity of light.

Electrical researches of Clerk-Maxwell

The scientific importance of this discovery is overwhelming. It united the two separate sciences of electro-magnetism and optics. The phenomena of light became, in fact, a branch of electromagnetism. Light is an electro-magnetic phenomenon; light waves are merely short electro-magnetic waves. This discovery was published in 1864. But Clerk-Maxwell's ideas were too original to be appreciated immediately. Scientific men, in order to follow him, had to adopt an outlook entirely different from that to which they were accustomed. Most of them were unable to make the effort. Even

Kelvin, to the end of his long life, never accepted Clerk-Maxwell's theory.

Amongst those who did was Heinrich Hertz, the brilliant young German physicist. But he saw that, if the theory was to be accepted, it must be experimentally confirmed. Clerk-Maxwell had mathematically prophesied the existence of electro-magnetic waves travelling through the aether with the velocity of light. How were they to be produced experimentally? This is the problem Hertz set himself, and which he magnificently solved. It was in 1888 that he artificially produced electro-magnetic waves in his laboratory, and, by various experiments, such as reflecting and refracting them, showed their analogy to light waves. Thus a great scientific theory, a product of the rarest insight, was proved beyond all doubt. Hertz was probably quite satisfied at having made a contribution to pure knowledge; but it very soon dawned on more than one mind that in this discovery were the seeds of a mighty revolution in our means of communication.

WIRELESS CONQUERS THE ATLANTIC

On December 12, 1901, the first wireless message was received on this lonely aerial at Signal Hill, Newfoundland, from Poldhu, Cornwall, thus eclipsing all Marconi's previous experiments in long-distance transmission, and announcing a revolutionary change in the means of trans-Atlantic communication.

Courtesy of Marconi's Wireless Telegraph Co. Ltd.

As early as 1894, Sir Oliver Lodge made successful experiments in transmitting messages by wireless waves.

The advent of Wireless

With the advent of Marconi the practical side of the discovery progressed rapidly. In June, 1897, Marconi sent a message over a distance of nine miles. A year later he was able to send a wireless message across the English Channel, and in 1901 he successfully telegraphed over a distance of three thousand miles. We may say, therefore, that by the end of the nineteenth century the new means of communication was a practical success.

A full account of the practical difficulties that had been overcome and which yet remained to be overcome would be irrelevant to our present purpose. The important aspect of the discovery, from our point of view, is that it was the direct outcome of the most abstract scientific speculations. It is natural for the outside world to pay more attention to the man who makes a scientific discovery a practical success than to the man who makes the discovery. That is why Marconi's name is a household word while Clerk-Maxwell's name is known by comparatively few. Yet there can be no question as to the relative importance of the two men.

The point is important, because the governing classes have hitherto shared the ignorance of the ordinary public. Nothing is stranger than that the whole complexion of civilization was changed by science during the nineteenth century, and yet that this dominant power received no state support. The burden of the public speeches of the scientific men of that time is their complaint at the lack of government recognition and support. Clerk-Maxwell, as it happened, was a Scottish landowner, and so was free to devote all his time to his scientific speculations. Had he been less fortunately placed we should probably still be without wireless telegraphy.

In reviewing the history of telegraphy we see that pure theory has played the dominant part. The further developments of wireless telegraphy, and telephony also, are connected with the further developments of theory. It was in 1879 that Sir William Crookes published his researches on the electric discharges in vacuum tubes, researches which were to lead to the electron theory and to the discovery of X-rays. Certain modern processes in wireless depend directly on the theory of electrons, which again is an outcome purely of the passion for scientific knowledge. But although the consequences of the electron theory, should it ever lead to the artificial disruption of the atom, will dwarf all the scientific applications of the past, these applications are not yet practical, and do not concern us.

A MASTER SCIENTIST

Albert Einstein, a German Jew born at Ulm in 1879, owed his early scientific reputation to the special or restricted theory of relativity which he formulated in 1905. For the implications of his later general theory see Chapter 187.

Photo, E.N.A.

SIR WILLIAM CROOKES

The researches of Sir William Crookes (1832–1919), inventor of the Crookes tube, form an important progressive step towards the electronic theory developed from them by Sir J. J. Thomson (see page 5004). Crookes was knighted in 1897.

Photo, Elliott & Fry

Another great scientific discovery which falls within our period, Einstein's Restricted Principle of Relativity, published in 1905, is even more innocent of practical results. It would be unwise to say that it always will be, for even the history of telegraphy is enough to show us that we cannot regard any scientific discovery as practically useless merely because it is highly abstract.

Amongst scientific discoveries whose practical application became immediately obvious we must rank X-rays, discovered by Röntgen in 1895. The use of their marvellous penetrative properties was immediately realized. It was through these properties that they were discovered, by what we might term an accident. They were not, like Clerk-Maxwell's electromagnetic waves, foreseen theoretically. Indeed, for a long time their nature was not understood. We know now that they enter into Clerk-Maxwell's general scheme; they are, in fact, extremely short electromagnetic waves and it is to their shortness that their penetrative properties are due.

Their use in medicine and surgery is well known and this is, indeed, the most obvious of their applications. A less known use of them, at present of small practical but of great scientific interest, is their application to the analysis of crystals. This branch of research is of growing practical importance because of the light it throws on the intimate constitution of certain substances, but the origin of this analysis is worth describing as one of the prettiest ideas in modern science.

X-Rays and Crystal analysis

The problem to be solved was the apparently quite useless problem of determining the exact length of X-rays. Now the length of ordinary light waves is usually determined by what is called a diffraction grating, a sheet of glass on which lines are ruled very close together. It is essential that the distance between adjacent lines should be of the same order of magnitude as the length of the waves to be measured. That such instruments can be constructed for visible light is sufficiently marvellous. Gratings having more than 1,700 lines to the millimetre have been made. But it was suspected that X-rays were one or two thousand times shorter than light waves. It was obviously hopeless to rule a grating to measure them. Nobody could hope to rule a million lines to a millimetre.

The brilliant idea occurred to Professor von Laue that nature had already provided such diffraction gratings. It was known that the atoms in a crystal are arranged in an orderly manner, and von Laue saw that a crystal, regarded as made up of equally spaced layers of atoms, was exactly the diffraction grating required. The distance between the layers of atoms is just the distance required to diffract the X-rays. This idea proved perfectly successful in practice, and it was found that the method could be, as it were, inverted. Not only could the crystals be used to analyse the X-rays, but the X-rays could be used to analyse the crystals. A good deal of work has been done along this line, and the intimate structure of many crystalline bodies is now understood. The further extension of this branch of knowledge will enable us to control the formation of many substances, with results of which the artificial manufacture of diamonds would be one of the most insignificant.

We have spoken so far of those inventions which were the outcome of the theoretical developments of Faraday's discovery of electro-magnetic induction. That discovery, however, was capable of immediate application without waiting for the long train of theoretical consequences worked out by Clerk-Maxwell. In the dynamo, as we have said, the principle is applied directly. Dynamo designers have, of course, their own technical problems, but the only important discovery in pure science that they utilise is Faraday's. And with the invention of the dynamo a whole host of industries came into being. Its

FIRST PRACTICAL DYNAMO

The progress of electric lighting by arc lamps was greatly accelerated by the introduction of the dynamo of Zenobe Theophile Gramme, a Belgian electrician, in 1870. This photograph shows one of his earlier models, an advance incorporating the ring armature invented by Pacinotti in 1860.

Science Museum, South Kensington

EDISON AND ONE OF HIS INVENTIONS

Almost every branch of science has been affected by the prolific inventive genius of the American Thomas Alva Edison, here seen seated in his study before the phonograph that he devised. The introduction of vast improvements on former methods of telegraphy was due to his investigations.

Photo, Underwood & Underwood

importance in transport is obvious. Apart from electrically propelled vehicles the whole motoring industry, since dynamo or magneto is an essential part of any motor-car, rests upon Faraday's discovery. And there are other industries which, although not directly dependent on the dynamo, would not exist in their present form without it. A very good example of this is offered by electric lighting.

The first form of electric lighting was by the use of the arc lamp. It was in 1801 that Sir Humphry Davy first observed that if an electric current be made to flow through two pieces of carbon, whose ends are in contact, an electric arc can be created by slightly separating the ends. In this experiment, of course, the electric current was generated chemically, by 'cells.' A large arc required a very large number of cells. In a repetition of this experiment in 1808, Sir Humphry Davy used a battery of no fewer than 2,000 cells. This system of lighting, although interesting scientifically, was not a commercial proposition. It could not become one until means of producing suitable carbons for arc lamps were discovered, and, more important still, until electric current could be generated cheaply.

Even when the first problem was solved there was no large demand for carbons until after the Gramme dynamo was invented in 1870. This was the first really practical and economical dynamo. With its invention electric lighting by arc lamps made rapid progress, and its application to commercial purposes is therefore dependent on the dynamo. Besides Faraday's theories, then, the great factor in the development of electric lighting was Davy's discovery of the arc. Any other scientific principles involved are of comparatively minor importance. Photometric investigations, for instance, as to how the light from an arc is distributed in surrounding space are of importance to designers, but are not essential to the production of electric light.

The invention of incandescent electric lamps was equally dependent on the dynamo and is, even more than the arc, a record of trial and error. Experiments began as early as 1841, when De Moleyns constructed a very imperfect lamp. They were continued by King and Starr in 1845, by Staite in 1848 and by Watson in 1853. None of these attempts was successful, partly because an efficient dynamo had not yet been invented. Even when the dynamo was invented the construction of a satisfactory filament continued to present great difficulties. Edison, in 1878, employed a filament composed of platinum covered with carbon for trial purposes, but abandoned it. Many other attempts were made along these lines. Metals such as platinum and iridium were mixed with refractory oxides such as magnesia and zirconia, but in no case was the result satisfactory. Finally, it began to dawn upon a large number of people, of whom Edison was one, that the incandescent electric lamp must fulfil certain conditions. These were as follows: The filament must be of carbon; it must be in a vacuum; the containing vessel must be of glass; the filament must be led in by platinum wires hermetically sealed in the glass. With the construction of a lamp fulfilling all these conditions the problem was solved.

Subsequent researches were concerned chiefly with the nature of the filament. In 1897, Nernst produced a lamp where the filament was of magnesia. In the latter part of the nineteenth century and the first decade of the twentieth several metallic filament lamps were invented. Osmium, tantalum, tungsten were the chief materials used. Welsbach suggested the osmium lamp, and the tantalum lamp was produced by von Bolton in 1904. These variations are interesting, but, in essentials, electric lighting has not changed much since the time when it first became efficient. An attempt to strike out a new path was made with the invention of the mercury vapour lamp by Cooper-Hewitt, Bastian and others. But the high hopes at one time entertained of it have not been fulfilled. It is certainly a very economical form of lighting, but the fact that it does not reveal objects in their natural colours weighs against it.

The manifold advantages of electric lighting are obvious, and it must be regarded as one of the great inventions of the nineteenth century. But it is by no means an ideal solution of the problem of providing artificial light. In all the systems of lighting hitherto invented a very considerable proportion of the total energy consumed is radiated as heat. This heat is useless, or even worse, and greatly diminishes the efficiency of the system. In this respect nature is far ahead of man. The glow-worm, which gives a cold light, is much nearer the ideal illuminant than is the electric arc or metallic filament lamp.

As we have said, the other great branch of our subject, the invention of means of transport, owes comparatively little to the development of pure science. All the earlier inventive work described in Chapter 163 had been done in almost

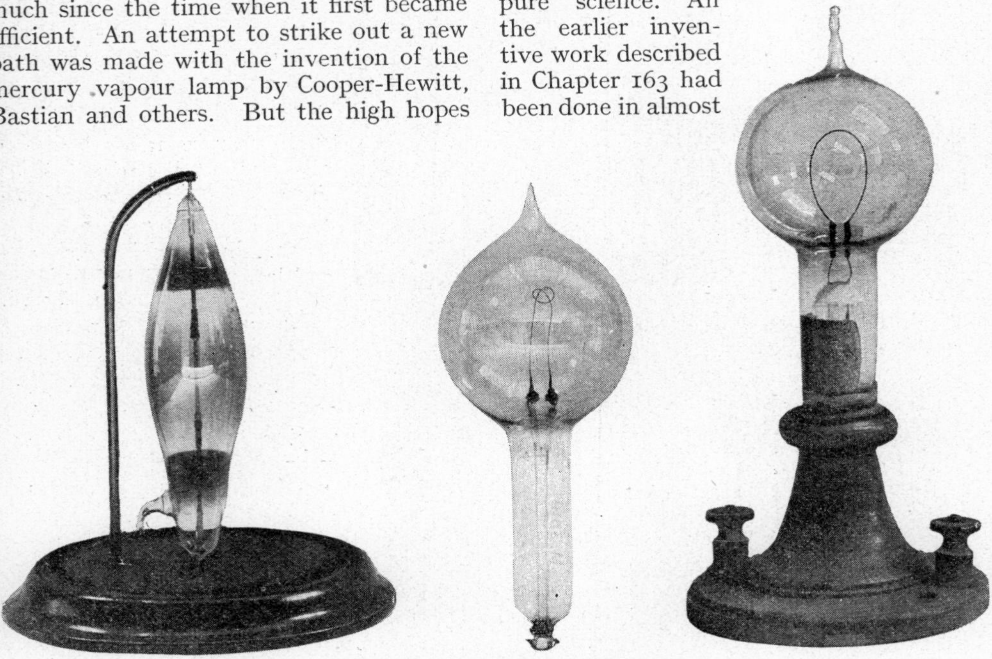

EARLY TYPES OF INCANDESCENT ELECTRIC LAMP

About 1841 experiments were begun in the construction of the incandescent electric lamp, now an article of almost universal and indispensable household use. Its creation was made possible by the invention of the dynamo and of the carbon filament. These examples are, left, a Swan experimental carbon pencil lamp, 1878–9; centre, a Swan early commercial type, c. 1880; and, right, an early experimental Edison lamp, 1880. The last two have a filament produced by the carbonisation of a vegetable substance.

Science Museum, South Kensington

complete ignorance of the true science of heat. The various improvements that had been thought of from the time of Watt to that of Stephenson were suggested almost wholly by empirical considerations. Watt, it is true, acknowledged his indebtedness to Joseph Black's doctrine of latent heat, but that doctrine, by itself, could have had little influence on the design of the steam engine.

The relation between heat and work, the essential part of the science of heat from the point of view of the steam-engine designer, was quite unknown in the time of Watt. It was only long afterwards that Sadi Carnot showed that heat only does work by being let down, as it were, from a higher to a lower temperature. Thi discovery was remarkable for its time, bu it was incomplete. The actual quantitativ relations between heat and work wer still unknown. Those relations were dis covered by Joule, in 1843, as part of th great scientific generalisation called th 'conservation of energy.' A quantitativ basis being provided, the science coul develop.

From 1849 onwards the branch o science known as thermodynamics was de veloped by Clausius, Rankine and Kelvin The practical advantages for the design o steam engines were considerable, but the were not as great as might have been expected. Thermodynamics is an exact science, but it chiefly contemplates relatively simple processes and idealised substances. The phenomena presented by a steam engine cannot be so satisfactorily brought within the abstractions of science as can, for instance, the phenomena presented by a dynamo. It is for this reason that Rankine's applications of the new science to steam engines were faulty. A complete scientific description of the steam engine cannot even yet be given. Our knowledge of certain actual processes is still largely empirical.

A great practical advance resulted from the Hon. C. A. Parsons' invention of the turbine. In this machine jets of steam or water are made to impinge on rotating blades, or, in another form of the machine, it is the reaction exerted by the issuing jets that causes rotation. The compound steam turbine was introduced by Parsons in 1884. It was fitted with a condenser in 1891, and then began to be used in electric supply stations. It has achieved its greatest triumphs in transport in its application to the steamboat. Two of the largest ships in the world, the Lusitania and the Mauretania,

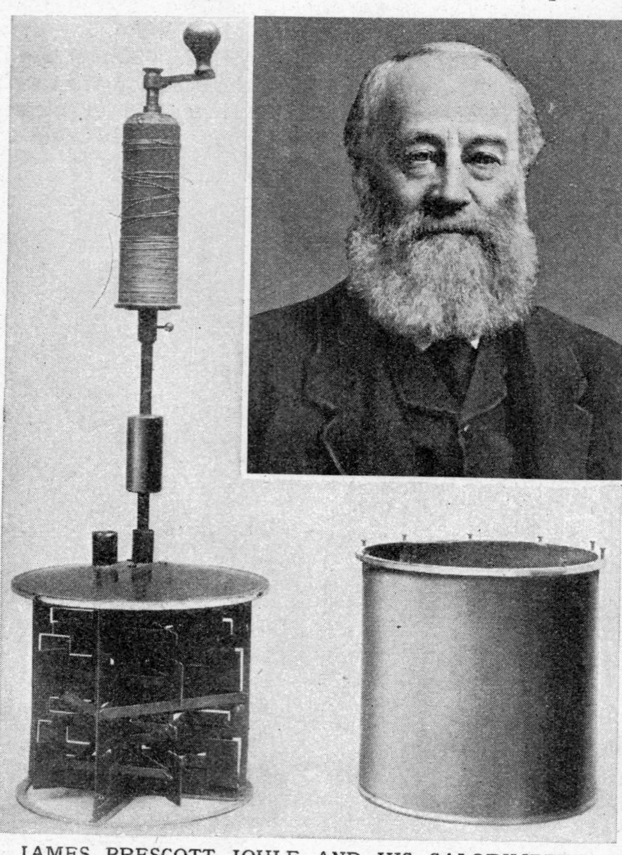

JAMES PRESCOTT JOULE AND HIS CALORIMETER

For more than forty years James Prescott Joule (1818–89) pursued his experiments with electricity and magnetism. He is chiefly remembered for his discovery of the 'mechanical equivalent of heat.' This calorimeter is the one originally employed by Joule in 1849 during the course of the investigation.

Above, painting by Hon. John Collier, Royal Society; below, Science Museum, South Kensington

INVENTION THAT MARKS AN IMPORTANT ADVANCE IN STEAM ENGINEERING

Sir Charles Algernon Parsons, born in 1854, founded the Newcastle engineering firm of C. A. Parsons & Co. In 1884 he first introduced his parallel-flow steam turbine, the original model of which is shown in this photograph coupled to a dynamo (right). In 1891 it was fitted with a condenser, and in 1897 an experiment in its utility for marine propulsion carried out with S.S. Turbinia made clear its advantages. Further experiments with larger and faster ships produced successful results.

Science Museum, South Kensington, by permission of Sir Charles Parsons

were provided with turbine engines developing as much as 70,000 horse-power.

The main transport invention of this period is unquestionably the steam engine. A great auxiliary is the motor-car. But the discovery of the aeroplane, both on account of its dramatic interest and of its future possibilities, is probably of even greater importance. Here again we have an invention which is almost wholly empirical. We may fairly date the history of the aeroplane from 1904, when the Wright brothers made two flights of three miles each round a circular course. This triumph was the result of long and laborious experiments. It was most emphatically the outcome of trial-and-error methods. There is, of course, a science of aeroplanes. Many good mathematicians are working at the problems of aerodynamics, but it is safe to say that even now the development of aeroplaning

THE FIRST FLIGHT OF THE FIRST MAN-CARRYING AEROPLANE

The gliding experiments laboriously made by two American brothers, Orville and Wilbur Wright, at Kitty Hawk, North Carolina, led to their discovery of a solution to the problems of aeroplane control. They enjoy the distinction of being the first constructors of a practical power-driven flying machine to carry a man from the ground. The Wright aeroplane first flew on December 17, 1903, and the original machine was presented to the Science Museum by Wilbur Wright in 1928.

Science Museum, South Kensington

owes more to step by step experiments than to pure science.

We cannot conclude our survey without a reference to the gramophone. Edison's phonograph was invented in 1887, and exhibited at Paris in 1889. Since then, as all the world knows, the gramophone has been greatly improved. It can be regarded as a means of communication, not in the ordinary sense, but as books are a means of communication. Its nearest analogy is the invention of the art of printing. Just as that invention brought the thoughts of great writers into the home, making the student no longer dependent on infrequent perusals of rare copies, so the gramophone makes possible a knowledge of that other great medium of expression, music, which is not confined to what may be obtained by infrequent attendances at rare performances. The invention of the gramophone must, on the whole, be ranked amongst the empirical inventions. The science of sound has, unfortunately, always proved itself singularly useless in practical applications. Even a bell presents almost insuperable theoretical difficulties, and improvements effected in the gramophone have been chiefly the result of trial and error.

PROTOTYPE OF THE MODERN GRAMOPHONE
Although sound vibrations had been graphically recorded on moving surfaces before 1877, no successful method of reproducing them was available until, in January of that year, Edison took out a patent for his tin-foil phonograph. He later effected many improvements upon this early model.
Science Museum, South Kensington

We have seen that our survey falls naturally into two divisions: those inventions that are the outcome chiefly of pure theory, and those that are the outcome chiefly of empirical observation. To the first division belongs, on the whole, the development of our modern means of communication, and to the second division belongs principally the development of means of transport. So far as the influence of science on invention is concerned, we have been occupied almost wholly with the science of mathematical physics. It is the mathematician who has played the leading rôle in making our present means of communication possible. Even in the problems of transport his services have been by no means negligible, although here the chief honour must be awarded to the so-called 'practical' man. But though it is true that the services of physics to industry have been of enormous importance, we should have to mention other sciences in any extended survey.

The World's debt to mathematical physics

There are hundreds of processes, for instance, which depend upon chemistry, a science that also underwent great developments during the nineteenth century. The biological sciences, on the other hand, except by helping us to conserve forests and sea fisheries, have had very little influence on practical life. We cannot suppose that this will always be so. It is no part of our present task to prophesy future inventions; but nobody who is familiar with the effect of the ductless glands in altering personality, or with the experiments in rejuvenation, can help wondering whether the great biological inventions of the future will not prove to be the most important of all. In the meantime, we may say that our modern world differs from the old chiefly because of the insight and reasoning of a few mathematicians, and the exhaustless ingenuity and patience of a vast host of practical men.

CHAPTER 177

THE U.S.A. ON THE EVE OF THE GREAT WAR

The Country and the President under whom it had to face the greatest crisis of its foreign Policy

By ROBERT McELROY Ph.D. LL.D.

Harmsworth Professor of American History, Oxford; Sometime Edwards Professor of American History, Princeton; Author of Grover Cleveland, the Man and the Statesman, etc.

EVERY presidential election in the United States is a critical election, for the president wields power that the most ambitious monarch may envy but in the twentieth century dares not emulate. In domestic affairs his voice is potent, for he has the ear of the people as no one else has; he can command the ear of the people's representatives as no one else can; and, when their decision runs counter to his desires or his convictions regarding legislation, he can exercise the veto which no British sovereign has ventured to exercise since the days of Queen Anne. In theory, the initiation of legislation belongs to Congress, financial bills originating only in the House of Representatives; but in practice the hand of the executive is often as strong in the initiation as in the execution of laws, and a skilful president may easily break down the middle wall of partition that separates the executive from the legislative branch of the government, and initiate even financial measures.

But while of potential authority in domestic affairs, especially when his party happens to control both branches of the legislature, in foreign affairs his is the controlling voice, until his agreements with foreign governments are ready to be submitted to the Senate for the 'advice and consent' which alone can make them binding agreements. The Constitution declares simply: 'He shall have power, by and with the advice and consent of the Senate, to make treaties, provided two thirds of the Senate present concur' (Art. 2, Sect. 2); and the debates in the Federal Convention which 'formulated' the Constitution—it was 'formed' in essence by a process of evolution which covers centuries of Anglo-Saxon history—make it quite clear that the president was expected to avail himself of the advice of the Senate during the period of negotiation, and to ask its consent not for a new proposition, but for one every stage of which had been followed by the Senate.

The Department of Foreign Affairs

In 1782, under the Articles of Confederation, the newly appointed secretary of the Department of Foreign Affairs was required to submit in advance to Congress all letters to ministers of foreign powers relating to treaties, all letters of credence and plans of treaties, and it was under this clumsy machinery that the treaty of peace of 1783 was negotiated; and in this, as in most respects, established custom at first determined the procedure of the new and more powerful executive under the new constitution of 1789. Thus, during the earlier years of President Washington's administration, when methods were taking shape, it was customary for the president to appear in the Senate, with such of his cabinet advisers as he deemed necessary, and explain the general plans which he intended to follow in pending negotiations with foreign governments.

This practice, if continued, might easily have developed that close connexion between the executive and the legislative branches of the government which gives coherence to the British system of a responsible cabinet, a system which has been copied, and with varying degrees of success, in so many parliamentary governments of later development. But President Washington on one memorable

PRESIDENT WILSON

Thomas Woodrow Wilson was elected president of the United States in 1912. At first an advocate of peace, he finally countenanced America's entry into the Great War. This photograph was taken during the electoral campaign.

Photo, E.N.A.

occasion experienced opposition from his Senate that was not to his liking, and the practice of personally seeking the Senate's advice in advance of negotiation was soon abandoned. Until the accession of President Thomas Jefferson in 1801, however, presidents continued the practice of delivering their messages to Congress in person; but, long before the abandonment of this practice by President Jefferson, it became the custom for the executive to conduct treaty negotiations with foreign governments without asking the guidance of the Senate, and to present for their 'advice and consent' only the finished product, to be debated, accepted, rejected or amended according to the Senate's pleasure, and at times according to its temper.

Such was the long established practice when the presidential campaign of 1912 opened, to usher in a president destined to face greater international complications than any other in history, and to fail of the consent of the Senate in matters of world moment largely because he failed to seek their advice while planning his methods of settlement. And yet, as an academic writer, this leader, Woodrow Wilson, had called attention to the wise course, in a series of lectures at Columbia University in 1908, using the words:

> He [the President] may . . . establish intimate relations of confidence with the Senate on his own initiative, not carrying his plans to completion and then laying them in final form before the Senate to be accepted or rejected, but keeping himself in communication with the leaders of the Senate while his plans are in course . . . in order that there may be veritable counsel, and a real accommodation of view instead of a final challenge and contest.

For over a century and a decade before 1914 successive presidents had followed the custom of conducting foreign negotiations without formal consultation with the Senate, and of sending their messages to Congress by messenger, there to be read for them by officials of the two houses. As the two major parties, the Republican and the Democratic, manoeuvred for advantage, pending the presidential nominations of 1912, none contemplated the future that awaited the successful presidential aspirant; none could foresee the restoration of the long abandoned practice of delivering presidential messages in person; and none dreamed of the complications that would follow from the practice of complete executive control of treaty negotiations. Indeed, even the most far-sighted of American politicians reckoned little of foreign affairs. All had their minds fixed almost exclusively upon domestic problems, although Mexico was furnishing more than normal food for thought regarding a somewhat wider horizon, and the problems of Panamá were obtrusively forcing themselves into the foreground.

Executive control of Treaty negotiations

So far as Europe was concerned, its pressing problems seemed to Americans little related to the issues of their pending problem of selecting a president. His major tasks, as they firmly believed, were to be concerned with disputes between capital and labour; monetary reform;

ballot reform; the enlargement of the franchise to include women; the popular election of United States senators; preferential primaries (a device for enabling the voters of the several parties to express their preference respecting the nomination of party candidates); the initiative (to give to the ordinary voter a means whereby he may propose laws without the intermediary agency of his regular representative); the referendum (to enable him to express his personal opinion respecting proposed laws); the recall (to enable him to join with his fellow voters in removing officials whom they have ceased to trust); the regulation of transportation, and the control of trusts. To no one did it seem necessary that the candidates should be sounded upon questions that proved to be more vital than all of these combined: military preparedness, and the meaning of 'entangling alliances'; the ideals of Germany as compared with those of Great Britain, France or Italy; the implications of membership in the family of nations; the right of the executive, by virtue of its established right to direct pending negotiations, to make promises or implied promises to foreign governments or associations of foreign governments; the power of the government to carry the nation into a world court or a world League of Nations without amendment to the Constitution.

New problems pending in 1912

Yet these last were the questions awaiting the leadership which the presidential election of 1912 was to determine, questions which soon placed the successful candidate in the centre of the largest stage ever occupied by mortal man, and gave him a power which might well have dazed even Napoleon.

When the political waters of America began to be troubled in 1912 by the spirit which always appears towards the end of each administration, both the great parties were torn by factions, factions born wholly of domestic issues. In each party there existed a faction, how great no man could tell, which believed that America had been sold into bondage; and these, in each party, awaited a heaven-sent Moses to lead them back into liberty. In the Democratic party William Jennings Bryan, a spent comet, still held the public attention, still represented, though in lessened degree, the leadership of the Democratic 'new-eraists,' whose vision of duty lay in the task of breaking the chains which they believed predatory capital to have placed upon their nation. Three defeats for the Presidency had lessened Bryan's personal availability; but they had by no means destroyed his leadership. This leadership, however, was disputed by the latest of the long line of defeated Democratic candidates, a line unbroken since Grover Cleveland's victory of 1892. Judge Alton B. Parker, whom Theodore Roosevelt had beaten in the presidential contest of 1904, was still the centre of Conservative Democracy, a not inconsiderable body of voters with less faith

LEADERS OF DEMOCRATIC FACTIONS

The leadership which William Jennings Bryan (right) maintained over a section of the Democratic party was disputed by Judge Alton Brooks Parker, with whom he is shown in the grounds of the latter's home at Esopus in September, 1912. In 1913 Bryan took office as secretary of state under Wilson, for whose nomination he had been largely responsible.

Photo, E.N.A.

THEODORE ROOSEVELT
Republican president in 1901 and re-elected in 1904, Theodore Roosevelt (1858–1919) fought political corruption at home and upheld prestige abroad. He is seen speaking during his unsuccessful campaign for the Presidency in 1912.
Photo, E.N.A.

than that of the Bryanites in the theory that the nation was in bondage, and therefore with less enthusiasm for the methods proposed by Bryan and his 'progressive' followers for her release.

In view of this division within the party, however, the selection of a candidate was obviously a task involving grave difficulties, especially as a two-thirds vote of the party convention would be necessary to nomination.

The year 1912 found the Republican party even more rent by faction, even more divided between a conservative and a radical wing. The former Republican president, Theodore Roosevelt, dynamic centre of the party, had won the title of militant reformer as a member of the New York legislature, civil service commissioner, police commissioner for New York City, assistant secretary of War, and pre-eminently as governor of the State of New York at a time when the 'big boss,' Thomas C. Platt, had held the Republican party of the state in the hollow of his hand. During his two years as governor, Roosevelt had fought the 'invisible government' so effectively that his administration marks the beginning of the end of a system that had menaced not only local but national government. The 'big boss' system survives in certain cities, but as a menace to national power it is a scourge that has passed, and no man did more to speed its passing than Theodore Roosevelt.

In 1900 'Boss' Platt had shown an interesting eagerness for the nomination of Governor Roosevelt as Republican candidate for the Vice-Presidency. On February 3 of that year Roosevelt had written this explanation to Senator Lodge: 'I have found out one reason why Senator Platt wants me nominated for the Vice-Presidency. The big moneyed men with whom he is in close touch, and whose campaign contributions have certainly been no inconsiderable factor in his strength, have been pressing him very strongly to get me put in the Vice-Presidency, so as to get me out of the State.' Reluctantly Roosevelt had consented to the plan, and had been elected vice-president, with William McKinley as president, only to succeed to the Presidency upon McKinley's death, in September, 1901.

JOHN PIERPONT MORGAN
The United States Steel Corporation was the creation of the American financier John Pierpont Morgan (1837–1913), whose firm, J. P. Morgan & Co. of New York, financed many great enterprises.
Photo, Topical Press Agency

As president, Roosevelt had found the movement for unified control of industry and of transportation alarmingly powerful. In 1900 J. Pierpont Morgan had effected the greatest corporation ever organized, the United States Steel Company, with stocks and bonds aggregating $1,100,000,000 (about £220,000,000), and with untold power over mines, transportation and subsidiary manufactures. So vast was its power that for several years it dominated the price of steel products. Upon a similar scale had come the consolidation of minor railways into vast systems. E. H. Harriman had secured control of a huge area of transportation extending from Chicago to Portland, San Diego and New Orleans. The Gould System, the Morgan combination, the vast sphere of railway influence dominated by the genius of James J. Hill, culminating in the formation of the Northern Securities Company, which attempted to bring under one directing head the Great Northern, the Northern Pacific and the Chicago, Burlington and Quincy, had clearly heralded the approaching end of railway competition.

At the Northern Securities Company, however, President Roosevelt had aimed a blow that had checked the tendency. In 1904, by a suit under the Sherman Anti-Trust Law, he had obtained from the Federal Supreme Court an order dissolving it as an illegal combination; and in 1912 the court had divorced the illegal union between the Union Pacific and the Southern Pacific.

INDUSTRIAL PALACES OF BROADWAY

In this photograph of Broadway, New York City, as viewed from Battery Park, may be seen the giant buildings of the Standard Oil Company (right) and of the International Mercantile Marine (left)—'interests' such as Roosevelt fought.

Photo, E.N.A.

WILLIAM HOWARD TAFT

Born in 1857, William Howard Taft was elected president of the U.S.A. in 1908. His tariff acts of 1910 diminished his popularity, and he was defeated at the presidential election of 1912. He was appointed chief justice in 1921.

Photo, Keystone View Co.

By such measures, and by virtue of a genius of personality not approached by any president since Lincoln, Roosevelt, president by reason of President McKinley's death, had stood forth by 1904 as the champion of progressive doctrines; and so complete was his control that his nomination for a second term of the high office to which he had succeeded was unanimous. Elated by success, and unmindful of the latent possibilities of the future, he had declared that he would follow the tradition started by Washington and, considering that he had served two terms as president, retire to private life at the end of his new term.

Roosevelt's progressive activities had continued during the years 1905–1909, with schemes for corporation control, suits against great trusts suspected of violating the Sherman Anti-Trust Law, arrangements for conserving public interests in minerals, water power, forest areas, schemes for irrigation, pure food laws and laws for the proper protection of labour. At the end of what he considered a second term as president he had planned and effected the election of William H. Taft as his successor, and retired to hunt, explore and study nature in the wilds of Africa.

During his absence President Taft had made clear his sympathy with the Conservative wing of the Republican party; and, when Roosevelt returned in June, 1910, he found his party showing alarming signs of splitting up into two factions, the Progressives and the Conservatives. The insurgent movement had shattered party unity, and the 'lunatic fringe' led by Senator Robert M. La Follette, of Wisconsin, was teaching the public that Roosevelt was no progressive, and that his two terms of service as president had demonstrated the fact. Openly denouncing trusts and combinations, Roosevelt, says La Follette's autobiography, 'made concessions and compromises which tremendously strengthened these special interests.' 'Taft,' he adds, 'co-operated with Cannon and Aldrich in legislation. Roosevelt co-operated with Aldrich and Cannon in legislation. Neither President took issue with the reactionary bosses of the Senate upon any legislation of national importance. Taft's talk was generally in line with his legislative policy. Roosevelt's talk was generally at right angles to his legislative policy.'

There are to-day few Americans who will agree to that statement. On the contrary, public opinion, regardless of party, has accepted rather the view that Roosevelt was a broad-minded, far-seeing and inherently progressive leader, but one too wise in the wisdom of the ages to accept trite phrases as solutions for great public evils. It is doubtless possible, as Lincoln declared, to 'fool all of the people some of the time and some of the people all of the time,' but the politicians found it difficult to fool Theodore Roosevelt any of the time.

SENATOR LA FOLLETTE

Robert Marion La Follette, governor of Wisconsin from 1901–7, became U.S.A. senator in 1905. He led the progressive faction of the Republican and denounced Roosevelt's 'conservatism.'

Photo, Keystone View Co.

In January, 1911, a National Progressive Republican League was organized, apparently in the interest of the candidacy of Robert M. La Follette, now leader of the senatorial revolt from the policies of President Taft. Its specified demands were:

1. Election of United States senators by popular vote.

2. Direct primaries for the nomination of elective officials.

3. Preference primaries through which the people might directly register their choice of candidates for president and vice-president; and the direct election of delegates to national party conventions.

4. Amendments to state constitutions which would establish the initiative, the referendum and the recall.

5. A stringent corrupt practices act.

Roosevelt, soon after his return from Africa, declined an invitation to join this Progressive League, a course which increased the existing suspicion among certain Progressive Republicans that he was not really progressive at heart. News of this refusal was followed by the publication by Colonel Roosevelt of a letter that President Taft had written to him soon after the latter's inauguration, declaring: 'I cannot forget that the power I now exercise was voluntarily transferred from you to me.' The Rooseveltian comment, made at Worcester, Mass., on April 26, 1912, was 'It is a bad trait to bite the hand that feeds you.' Clearly, on the eve of the National Republican Convention, Roosevelt was out of sympathy with important elements in both sides of his badly divided party. There were of course many Republicans of both wings who wished to see Colonel Roosevelt himself nominated, but even among them there was the memory of the fact that he had served as president for almost two terms, that tradition had fixed the limit of two terms for any president, and that Roosevelt had himself declared himself ineligible for re-election.

On February 10, 1912, however, seven Progressive governors, with seventy other Progressives representing twenty-four states, had met and urged Roosevelt to become a candidate for the Republican nomination. On February 11, at Columbus, Ohio, he had announced his personal platform, which included some, though not all, of the principles previously proclaimed by the Progressive Republican League. He endorsed the initiative, the referendum, the short ballot, the popular election of senators and presidential primaries. The recall he applied, much to the consternation of the more conservative of his friends, to the recall of judicial decisions, asserting that the courts should not be allowed to make law (see page 4519). Although not declaring himself, in the Columbus address, a candidate against Taft and La Follette, he had tossed off to the newspaper reporters after it was over the characteristic phrase: 'My hat is in the ring.'

Theodore Roosevelt's personal platform

As Taft had the support of the regular party machinery and was therefore likely to be the choice of the party convention if it were left free to choose, Roosevelt demanded that the nomination be made by means of 'direct primaries,' which would enable the voters within the Republican party to choose the party nominees without the intervention of a nominating convention. The Taft organization resisted the demand, and was met by the accusation of championing the system of boss rule. The fact that the Barnes machine in New York, the Lorimer machine in Illinois, the Penrose machine in Pennsylvania and similar organizations of less reputation were ranged upon the side of Taft gave colour to the accusation; but most Americans to-day are willing to absolve Taft from the suspicion of deliberate, unworthy methods. Like most men elected to power through the machinery of an organized party, he was compelled to accept the organization or the alternative of certain defeat.

In the end the states took their own courses respecting the choice of delegates to the Republican National Convention. Thirteen states made use of primaries to select their delegates, and of these Roosevelt carried nine, Taft two and La Follette two. Most of the states without primaries selected Taft delegates; but in many states which returned Taft delegations, the Progressive element named contesting delegations which claimed to be the lawful representatives and therefore entitled to cast the votes of those states. The states which had held primaries sent a total of 278 delegates for Roosevelt, 68 for Taft, and 36 for La Follette.

William Taft and La Follette

Although manifestly the weakest of the three candidates, as the choice of delegates showed, La Follette by no means despaired of victory in the Convention. 'Both Taft and Roosevelt,' says his autobiography, 'claimed a majority of the delegates elected to the Convention. I felt confident that neither had a majority, and believed that if the contest were settled with anything like fairness, it would leave them with their strength so nearly even that the twenty-six delegates from Wisconsin and the ten from North Dakota instructed for me would constitute the balance of power in the Convention.' This prophecy of a deadlock proved true—but the hope that a deadlock would mean the nomination of La Follette proved utterly groundless.

For about a week before the Convention opened, the Republican National Committee was in session, deciding contests and preparing the lists of delegates entitled to seats as voting members of the convention. Of the 254 disputed seats which came before the committee, which had power to make up the temporary roll of the Convention, 235 were given to Taft delegates. The temporary roll gave Taft a majority of about 20; the election of Elihu Root as temporary chairman proved Taft's control effective; and the approval of the report of the credentials committee proved that neither Roosevelt nor La Follette had any chance of the nomination by the Convention as now constituted. Roosevelt therefore advised his followers to take no further part in the proceedings, and his name was not formally presented. On the first ballot Taft received the nomination, with 561 votes, to 107 for Roosevelt and 41 for La Follette. There were, however, 344 members who refused to vote, and they were the potential nucleus of a new party.

The Republican party had been thus split, and a new party was in train, which was actually convened in national convention two weeks later, at Chicago.

Three days after the adjournment of Taft's convention, and twelve days before the seceding delegates nominated Roosevelt as the Progressive candidate, the Democrats met in national convention at Baltimore (June 25), conscious of the fact that the Presidency might be captured if only they could unite upon a candidate. The problem of agreement was, however, a difficult one, for the Democratic party too was menaced by faction. The Conservative wing, for lack of a more magnetic leader, gathered about Alton B. Parker; but, when a movement was started to make Parker temporary chairman of the Convention, Bryan denounced it as an effort to 'sell the Democratic party into bondage to the predatory interests of the country.' With the aid of some of the followers of Champ Clark, speaker of the House of Representatives and a candidate for the presidential nomination, however, Parker was elected temporary chairman. The Conservatives then organized the Convention, just as Republican Conservatives had organized the Republican Convention; and the Conservative press calmly declared Bryan eliminated from the list of possible nominees.

CHAMP CLARK

Born in Kentucky in 1850, Champ Clark became a member of Congress in 1893, leader of the Democratic party in Congress in 1909–10, and its speaker in 1911. In the Democratic Convention of 1912 he was Woodrow Wilson's rival.
Photo, E.N.A.

Elimination of William Bryan

But Bryan had no idea of accepting elimination. On June 29 he electrified the Convention by presenting a resolution that pledged the Convention to nominate no man who either represented or was under obligation to the great financial interests of the country; and with the forensic skill for which he was justly famous he carried it by an overwhelming majority. Thus the Democratic party, before the actual balloting for candidates began, had committed itself to the choice of a progressive candidate. With Bryan himself out of the race for nomination—for three previous nominations each followed by defeat had eliminated him as a candidate—the candidate with the most progressive record was clearly Governor Woodrow Wilson, of New Jersey.

Two years before, at the call of the Irish-led Democratic machine of New Jersey, he had suddenly stepped out of the academic into the political world. Ex-Senator 'Jim' Smith, master of those that knew in New Jersey's Democratic circles, had 'consulted the entrails' and issued this augury: 'Dr. Wilson will have 800 delegates on the first ballot [for Governor], and in November [1910] will sweep the State.' When the votes of the first ballot had been laid before the

Convention, Dr. Wilson had actually counted 747 and a half, forty more than a majority, and the nomination.

During the campaign that followed, to the consternation of the machine that had called him into political being, Wilson had calmly hitched his soaring kite to progressive principles, and uncompromisingly promised to fight boss rule with 'pitiless publicity,' and to introduce not machine made men but independent men into public office.

In the state elections of 1910 Wilson had amply fulfilled 'Jim' Smith's second prophecy: 'Doctor Wilson . . . will sweep the State.' He had been elected governor by 49,000 in a state that in recent years had been consistently Republican. At once he had declared against 'Jim' Smith's plan to have himself chosen United States senator by the newly-elected New Jersey legislature, and had secured the choice of Smith's opponent, James E. Martine.

As governor of New Jersey Wilson had shown his ability to 'sweep the state' in a way other than that which 'Jim' Smith had had in mind; for he had put aside the machine men's demands for 'their share,' had pushed through the legislature his Electoral Reform Bill, his Corrupt Practices Act, his Employers' Liability Act and his bill for creating a public service commission, practising himself what he called 'lobbying for the public.' The Smith-Nugent machine that had called into being this new Frankenstein publicly branded him as 'an ingrate and a liar,' and even gained a majority of the legislature at the ensuing election; but the governor of New Jersey was already setting the stage for his next advance, the Democratic presidential nomination of 1912. He had capitalised a defeat at Princeton to win the governorship of New Jersey. He now capitalised a defeat in New Jersey to win the high office of president of the United States.

Wilson's reforms in New Jersey

With a gift for formulating popular ideals in glowing sentences, never surpassed in American history, Wilson had toured the country preaching progressive sermons from the text of his own progressive programme that his legislature had enacted into laws. So frequent were his expeditions from the state capital at Trenton that an enterprising cartoonist had pictured him, standing alone on a railway platform, travelling-bag in hand, with the train from which he had descended fast disappearing, and out of his mouth rolling the words: 'So this is Trenton!'

These wider contacts had convinced him that the support of his first great journalistic sponsor, Colonel George Harvey, editor of Harper's Weekly, was a source of weakness, as tending to connect him with the 'interests.' He had therefore requested Colonel Harvey to withdraw from his journal the standing motto calling for Wilson's nomination as president. Colonel Harvey's friends had expressed indignation, Colonel Henry Watterson in particular treating the incident with vitriolic fury. At a famous dinner, soon after Colonel Watterson's attack, Wilson had been mentioned, in racing language, as a competitor 'sired by "Jim" Smith, dammed by Henry Watterson'; but the incident was interpreted by the more progressive as proof that Wilson dared to spurn Wall Street, for it was understood that Harper's Weekly was controlled by J. P. Morgan & Co. He had also incensed another powerful group by expressing the wish that something at once dignified and effective 'might be done to knock Mr. Bryan into a cocked hat.'

Friction with the big 'Interests'

But, while making enemies, he had made friends during his flying trips from his capital city of Trenton. In October, 1911, he had visited the state fair at Dallas, Texas, where he had met for the first time Colonel Edward M. House, a Bryan democrat, and the master politician (in the best sense of that much abused term) of the Lone Star State. The friendship there formed became a vital factor in the aftermath, not alone of the election of 1912, but of the eight years of Wilson's Presidency.

Recent events in Washington had cleared the stage for a man with Wilson's conception of the presidential office. For years the speakers of the House had practised the direction and promotion of legislation which, in Wilson's theory, properly belonged to the president. But on March 19, 1910, had come a revolution in the House of Representatives that had stripped the speaker of this power, and thus left vacant exactly the kind of leadership that Wilson believed to belong of right to the presidential office.

Thus when the Democratic National Convention assembled at Baltimore on June 25, 1912, to choose a candidate for the Presidency, Woodrow Wilson was a factor that caused anxiety to seasoned political aspirants such as Oscar Underwood, of Alabama, Governor Judson Harmon, of Ohio, and the speaker of the House of Representatives, Champ Clark, whose followers' chief joy was centred in the song: 'You gotta quit kicking my dog around.' Even La Follette admitted that Wilson 'had made a progressive record as governor of New Jersey,' and it was the belief of the general public that he could be relied upon to make a similar record as president.

Democratic National Convention assembles

The first ballot of the Democratic National Convention showed 440½ votes for Clark, 324 for Wilson, 148 for Harmon, 117½ for Underwood and 56 for unimportant candidates. As the Democratic rule, unlike the Republican rule, required a two-thirds majority to nominate, this was prophetic of a prolonged deadlock. As ballot succeeded ballot, Clark gained consistently, Wilson less consistently.

While the fourteenth ballot was being taken, Bryan skilfully checked the trend toward Clark by declaring that he would no longer support Clark, who was evidently New York's candidate, or any other man who was under obligations to Morgan, Ryan, Belmont 'or any other member of the privilege-seeking, favour-hunting class.' At once Wilson's chances began to improve, for the favour of Bryan was evidently tending in his direction. The knowledge that Bryan was to be the arbiter of his fate was, of course, unpalatable to Wilson; but candidates should not be choosers, and Wilson gratefully accepted Bryan's advances.

The twenty-fourth ballot showed that Clark had dropped below 500 votes and Wilson had mounted to over 400. The landslide that most conventions are doomed to await with heart-breaking intensity at one stage or another was apparently close at hand. It was to be Clark or Wilson; and McCombs, Wilson's campaign manager, was inclined to withdraw Wilson's name, while Bryan gave similar advice. In view of the contest to follow, Democracy against Republicanism, party unity was vital. But Wilson was not convinced, and his name remained before the Convention.

The fortieth ballot passed with no decision in sight; but Wilson was now past the 500 line; Clark and Underwood still trailed behind; while Harmon had ceased to breathe, politically. After the forty-second ballot an adjournment was taken, and when the Convention resumed balloting, on Tuesday, July 3, Wilson showed 602 votes and Clark 329. On the forty-fourth ballot Wilson showed 625. On the forty-fifth it was Wilson 633, Clark 306.

After that came the deluge. When the forty-sixth ballot was announced Underwood's name was formally withdrawn. Champ Clark released his delegates from their pledge to support him. Senator Harmon's name was then formally withdrawn, and the ballot proceeded, Wilson against Clark, with delegates released. The Convention waited breathless as the teller's report was received on the stand. Clark received 84 votes, Wilson 990. The two-thirds had been secured and Woodrow Wilson was the leader of the Democratic party, and almost certainly the next president; for the Roosevelt secession had split the Republican party into two, the Taft Republicans and the Roosevelt Progressives.

Wilson chosen by the Democrats

On August 5 Roosevelt's Progressive followers met at Chicago in national convention, listened to the analysis of their party principles by Roosevelt—to give the government back to the people, destroy machine rule, enfranchise women, give to labour shorter hours and better wages, and safeguard social justice; and on August 7 it formally announced a third party ticket with Theodore Roosevelt, of New York, and Hiram Johnson, of California, as the Progressive candidates for president and vice-president.

ROOSEVELT'S SUPPORTERS ASSEMBLED IN NATIONAL CONVENTION AT CHICAGO

ʌfter the Republican party had split into the two factions of Taft Republicans and Roosevelt Proɪressives, the latter met in national convention at the Coliseum, Chicago, on August 5, 1912. Rooseelt here enunciated the principles of his party, including the enfranchisement of women and the estruction of machine rule. He lost in the three-cornered fight for the Presidency that followed, and he onus of determining America's attitude in the Great War fell on the victor, Woodrow Wilson.

Photo, E.N.A.

The presidential election of 1912 that ɔllowed was a bitter, boisterous and not ɔo illuminating three-cornered fight, 'aft's Conservatives, Roosevelt's New Jationalism, and the latter's near relative, Voodrow Wilson's New Freedom, conɜnding for what most unexpectedly roved to be the right to lead America ı the greatest crisis of history, the Great Var. But in neither party was there the ıintest suspicion of that fact. All signs ɜemed still to point to an administration ıat would expend its chief energies upon omestic problems, with the customary addition of Mexican troubles to give a wider horizon.

The constitution of the United States provides for the election of the president and the vice-president, not by the direct vote of the people, but by presidential electors (the Electoral College) especially chosen for that purpose alone. The popular vote, while an index of public opinion, does not decide the election. In November, 1912, electors pledged to vote for Wilson were chosen in overwhelming numbers, 435 in all, as compared with 88 for Roosevelt and eight for Taft. The popular vote was less overwhelming, but it too was convincing: Wilson 6,293,019; Roosevelt 4,119,507; Taft 3,484,956; Debs (Socialist) 901,873; Chafin (Prohibitionist) 207,828; and Reimer (Socialist Labour) 29,259.

It was easy to point out that the popular vote thus cast against Wilson was vastly greater than that cast in his favour; but the fact remained that he was overwhelmingly victorious in the Electoral College, the only matter of practical importance. It is also true, as La Follette later expressed it, that 'it was Bryan's superb leadership and courage at Baltimore' which had nominated him.

Woodrow Wilson elected President

On March 4, 1913, at the age of fifty-six, Wilson entered the White House for the first time in his life; but he entered it as master. For the first time since 1861 his party had been given effective control of the government, the executive and both houses being Democratic. Under Cleveland's second administration, from 1893 to 1895, they had held the Presidency and a majority in both Houses of Congress, but the so-called majority was so rent by faction that effective action along clear party lines had been impossible. Wilson, however, had small cause to fear a similar nullification of victory. As a new-comer in national politics, he was unembarrassed by the host of enemies within the party which had confronted the restored Cleveland, and there seemed every likelihood of that continued party cohesion which is indispensable to effective control. Even the 2,500 Federal posts to be filled did not destroy it, although the president-elect refused to allow his peace of mind to be upset by the appalling political 'bread-line,' and left most of the more important officials, except diplomats, to fill out the terms for which they had been appointed by the previous president and confirmed by the Senate. The diplomats found their inevitable resignations accepted, and their places made ready for what Bryan later termed 'deserving Democrats.'

President Wilson's inaugural address was an interesting combination of the progressive ideals that had secured his election, with a long cherished desire to see the nation return to the original principles upon which it had been first operated: 'to square every process of our national life again with the standard we so proudly set up in the beginning and have always carried in our hearts.' 'Our work,' he added, 'is a work of restoration.' The subjects that formed the centre of his programme of restoration were a revision of the tariff downward; the reform of currency and banking; the curbing of the control which the trusts had secured over the industrial life of the country; and laws for the promotion of social justice.

The first restoration, however, was naturally the restoration of the South to something like the position of influence which it had held in that 'beginning' to which he desired to return. The overwhelming victory of the Democratic party had indeed made this, in some degree, necessary; the rule of seniority of service inevitably gave the chairmanship of many committees to Southern men whose constituencies had kept them in office despite all changes, for the South had never ceased to be Democratic, and her representatives held seats never rendered precarious by the Republican victories that had kept the Democrats in opposition for sixteen years.

President Wilson's first Congress

President Wilson's first Congress had 291 Democrats in the Lower House, and a combined opposition of only 143, of whom 124 were Republicans, 6 were Progressive Republicans and 13 were Progressives. The Senate was more evenly divided, with 51 Democrats, 44 Republicans and one Progressive. Since the end of Reconstruction the Southern states had enjoyed their full share of leadership in Congress, but under this new Democratic regime they became dominant. Of the 58 committees of the House of Representatives, Southern men held the chairmanships of 40, and among these were nine of the ten most important. The Senate showed a smaller percentage of Southern leaders in important chairmanships; but 30 of the 73 Senate committees were under Southern chairmen. Of the ten cabinet ministers, four were from Southern states.

Thus it came about that the world crisis found the machinery of America's Federal government directed by men habituated to opposition, and, in many cases, by men wont to think of their own states as hardly in full partnership with those of the long dominant North.

The nation gets its first clear vision of a new president not from his inaugural address, but rather by the prosaic announcement of his cabinet. Wilson's inaugural address breathed a lofty note of dedication. 'This is not a day of triumph,' he said, 'it is a day of dedication.' But his cabinet, when announced, bore the names of men largely responsible for his political triumph: William J. Bryan, secretary of State; William G. McAdoo, secretary of the Treasury; Albert S. Burleson, of Texas, postmaster-general; Josephus Daniels, of North Carolina, secretary of the Navy: appointments which conformed to the best traditions of party reward for party service. Of his entire cabinet, only three appeared to the public to have been fitted by previous training or experience for the work of their departments: McReynolds, of New York, the new attorney general, had been concerned in prosecutions of trusts; Franklin K. Lane, of California, secretary of the Interior, had served on the Civil Service Commission; and William B. Wilson, secretary of Labour, had held high office in the United Mine Workers of America.

Criticism of the Cabinet

No student of politics will be likely to quarrel with a president-elect for allowing politics to direct his choice of cabinet advisers. It is the road that every president, save perhaps John Quincy Adams, has frankly travelled; and all will travel it so long as party government endures, or pay the heavy price of failure. But the public, while ready to pardon action or to applaud ideals, insists that ideals and actions shall run a common course, and the announcement of such a cabinet after such an inaugural address caused adverse comment in all parties and in all circles. The nation could not avoid the opinion that it was politics and not lofty idealism that had selected Bryan as secretary of State, a post for which, by training, by habits, by the very character of his mind, he was ideally unfitted. But Bryan's appointment was essential to any effective Democratic government; his associates brought with them a combined political influence over all sections of the party; and all offered one quality not unpleasing to a president frankly desirous of power: they were men likely to accept his leadership if not his domination in the programme that he was mapping out for himself and for them.

'A One-Man Democracy'

These appointments therefore were less rewards for party services than a bid for party unity, a unity which ultimately became so great as to give rise to the phrase 'a one-man democracy.' It was grossly unfair to insinuate, as many did insinuate at the time, that Wilson had sold himself to the long-detested faith of Bryanism, or bowed to the yoke to win a personal triumph. He had opposed Bryanism for years, but the issues that had brought Bryan into the white light of national leadership sixteen years before, and the issues that later emerging had kept him there, were no longer the issues of prime importance. The free silver heresy (see page 4512) was gone from the arena of national conflict. Imperialism was no longer the cloud that menaced traditional Americanism. In both parties the fight now centred about the basic question of control of government, and of the vast material development which those sixteen years had so enormously accentuated. Bryan's chief fear was the same as Wilson's, the same indeed as Roosevelt's and La Follette's—Wall Street control of the government of America; and Bryan's chief demand was the same as theirs, a larger share of the common blessings of life and the rewards of labour for the toiling masses of the republic.

There was thus nothing dishonourable, nothing even of doubtful morality, in Wilson's acceptance of Bryan's aid, and in Wilson's assignment of the post which alone could secure that aid. Had he known the character of the problems soon to be hourly confronting his secretary of State, and still made the selection, he would have merited all the abuse that Bryan's appointment brought upon him. But such knowledge was denied not alone to him, but to all mankind. The selection of Bryan as secretary of State proved an unwise selection; but his rejection might quite as well have proved an unwise rejection.

Roosevelt had accustomed the American people to expect Napoleonic surprises from their chief executive, an expectation which his judicial successor, William H. Taft, had made no attempt to fulfil. Wilson was constitutionally unable to flash in the limelight as Roosevelt had done; but his historical-mindedness served to furnish the surprise that was needed, at the very beginning of his term of office. Discarding the established practice of the executives of over a century and a decade, he announced that his messages would be delivered to Congress in person, instead of in writing and by the hand of an executive messenger. Jefferson had abandoned the practice knowing himself more effective in written than in spoken words; and each succeeding president had followed his example, impelled for the most part by no stronger motive than a natural tendency to follow precedent. Wilson, however, prided himself, and with ample justification, upon the command of the arts of a trained and experienced rhetorician, and wisely extended his policy of restoration to this field also.

It is a statement not likely to be disputed that much of Wilson's power came from his ability as a public speaker. Indeed, while not in the strict sense an orator, he possessed beyond any of his predecessors in the White House the power to sound the note of idealism in politics. Whether in the vague promises which of necessity make up the inaugural address, in the discussion of the normally cold propositions of finance and tariff or in the illimitable field of international affairs, his speeches and state papers abound in phrases which quicken the pulse. But eloquence and statesmanship have surprisingly little in common; and in general the world's constructive statesmen have not ranked among the world's

WOODROW WILSON DELIVERS HIS FIRST PRESIDENTIAL MESSAGE TO CONGRESS

For 112 years no president of the United States had addressed Congress in person when on April 7, 1913, President Wilson spoke personally on the subject of tariff reform to Congress assembled in special session in the House of Representatives. The new president is seen at the reading desk, with Speaker Clark (left) and Vice-President Marshall (blurred) seated on the rostrum behind him.

Photo, Topical Press Agency

greatest orators. The aim of the orator is to arouse emotion : the aim of the statesman is to solve knotty problems, problems that yield only to patient labour, calm, reasoned processes and balanced judgement ; and in the end it is deeds, not words, that qualify statesmen for the hall of fame.

In an attempt to assess Wilson's achievements, and weigh them against his failures, it is only fair to remember that his so-called fellow leaders were for the most part experienced only in the work of opposition. Before the products of the restored South had become accustomed to the rôle of national leadership, they were called upon to face foreign problems greater than had confronted American leaders in any previous period, even that of the Civil War when their states had been 'the enemy.'

Wilson's political philosophy made him necessarily the leader, the man to assume the powers which had so lately been wrested from the speaker of the House of Representatives ; and accordingly, on April 7, 1913, he summoned Congress into special session, and delivered in person his first presidential message. It devoted itself to the topic of tariff reform. 'The object of the tariff duties, henceforth laid,' he said, 'must be effective competition.' Already the Democratic leader, Underwood, chairman of the Ways and Means Committee of the House, had framed a tariff bill on the lines which the president indicated, a gradual reduction. It lowered the rates by about eleven per cent., and provided an income tax to overcome the deficit expected to result. Despite the combined opposition of 120 Republicans, 14 Progressives and 5 Louisiana Democrats, who wanted more protection for sugar, the Underwood tariff passed both houses, but only after the president, on May 26, 1913, had warned the country that an insidious lobby of 'the interests' had invaded Washington and was seeking by stealth to defeat the measure, a warning which a later Congressional investigation convincingly justified. On October 3, 1913, President Wilson signed the Underwood tariff bill, not as a perfect measure, but as an earnest of good faith on the part of the party that the people had placed in control.

Wilson's first presidential message

Long before that date, however, the administration was deep in the problem of banking and currency reform. Senator Owen, chairman of the Senate Committee on Banking and Currency, and Congressman Glass, chairman of the Corresponding House Committee, in consultation with the president, had prepared a bill to that end, which, on June 23, the president commended to Congress. On June 26 the bill was introduced into the House of Representatives ; after prolonged debate it passed both houses without material alteration, and on December 23, 1913, it received the president's signature. Its aim, and its result, was the creation of an elastic currency, with the consequent lessening of the danger of panics such as had so often devastated American business. As the bill borrowed not a little from previous Republican proposals for currency reform, and was sustained by thirty-four Republican and eleven Progressive congressmen, and by one Progressive and three Republican senators, it takes rank above mere partisan measures.

Banking and Currency reform

Under its provisions the nation is divided into twelve districts, in each of which the national banks are required to form a district reserve bank with a capital of not less than $4,000,000. In this district or regional bank, member banks, which include national banks, and such state banks and trust companies as have joined, deposit reserve funds, and from it they can borrow on approved collateral. These regional banks are under the control of the Federal Reserve Board composed of the secretary of the Treasury and the comptroller of the Currency, ex officio, and five members appointed by the president, with the consent of the Senate. This central board restrains the regional banks in general policies and supervises the conduct of their business, to the ends first of security and secondly of the circulation of a currency that may be safely expanded or contracted as the needs of business demand. This Federal Reserve Bank, opening for business on

November 16, 1914, steadied the finances of the nation during the trying days of world war that had already begun, and was a powerful instrument for financial soundness during the critical years that followed.

So far the Bryan connexion had undoubtedly proved a source of strength; and it was not less so in carrying out the third element of the president's programme, the control of trusts, whose increasing dominance had been one of the outstanding features of American history for about three decades or more (see page 4515)

The centralising of the control of industry had greatly increased production.

Centralisation of Industry

The steel industry, barometer of business in the modern world, had produced 4,277,071 tons in 1900; by 1914 its output was approximately 32,000,000 tons. And many other manufacturing industries, during that same period, showed gains as great; but in all alike the gains were made by methods of centralised control which tended to submerge the individual into the group, and to make highly organized groups, employers or employees, the units of human society.

With a racial diversity such as no other nation has ever known, America had been standardised beyond all precedent. The story is told of Lord Northcliffe that on a visit to America he was asked the question: 'Will America ever have a revolution?' Calling his interlocutor to the window of the great office building, Northcliffe pointed to the polyglot multitude that crowded the street, and remarked: 'Do you see those people? Every one is wearing exactly the same hat. Every one looks the same. Every one is the same. There will be no revolution.' So far as material existence was concerned all races had been levelled to a pattern; and the conviction was growing that this process extended to the minds and souls of men as well as to their outward appearance. Disregarding the fact that for every able machine keeper there was an ever-open way of escape upward, the cry was being raised that centralised industrial control and intense specialisation were turning human souls into mere automatons. 'The machine,' the critic cried, 'has become the master, and to man has been assigned only the unindividualistic task of its keeper.'

In his volume, The New Freedom, President Wilson had already written down his interpretation of what had happened, and his prophecy of what would happen unless present tendencies toward absolute control by corporations could be altered. His election to the Presidency had placed him in a position where he might properly hope to alter them; and early in 1914 he announced his preliminary plan of attack. It contained five specific elements:

1. A Federal commission to supervise all persons, whether individuals or corporations, engaged in interstate trade.

2. The prevention of interlocking directorates among great banks, railways, mining corporations and trust companies.

3. The clarification of the Sherman Anti-Trust Act of 1890, by specifying a number of actions that should be considered unlawful under its provisions.

4. The definite prohibition of rebates, price discrimination, and other acts of unfair competition.

5. The conferring upon the Interstate Commerce Commission of power to regulate the issue of railway stocks and bonds, and the expenditure of funds accruing from such issues.

State control of Corporations

As his laws against corporation abuses in the state of New Jersey, the final successes of his term as governor, had been called the 'Seven Sisters,' so this new presidential programme became known as the 'Five Brothers'; but in process of enactment the five were telescoped into two, the first creating a Federal trade commission, to check the rising power of trusts, and the second, called the Clayton Anti-Trust Act, designed to afford suitable punishments for such corporations as ventured to exercise undue powers. The latter law made it unlawful, for example, for one corporation to acquire control of another by securing possession of its stock, and prohibited interlocking directorates, save under specified conditions. Under it the Interstate Commerce Commission, the Federal Reserve Board and the Federal Trade Commission were given power to execute the law under court supervision. Another important feature of the Clayton Anti-Trust Act provided that labour organizations should not be deemed 'combinations or conspiracies in restraint of trade' in the sense contemplated by anti-trust legislation; but a Federal Supreme Court decision of January, 1921, considerably restricted the immunity thus accorded labour unions by declaring secondary boycott not legalised by the Clayton Act.

Thus the first nineteen months of Wilson's administration in large measure justified the praise of William Allen White, who declared the first term 'the fastest-moving four years in our economic and social history.' So far the Bryan connexion had apparently been a source of strength, and had the problems remained chiefly domestic, as the outlook at the time of Bryan's appointment seemed to prophesy, it might on the whole have produced more strength than weakness.

In the field of foreign affairs, however, perils soon proved more fast-moving than solutions; and Bryanism soon ceased to be reckonable, even by the administration, as an asset. Having packed the diplomatic service with his own partisans, whom he euphemistically called 'deserving Democrats,' he faced his problems with child-like faith in the efficacy of phrases, and child-like ignorance regarding the ways of diplomats. Important questions of foreign policy had, of course, been waiting for this as for every new administration; but they had fortunately moved slowly to the point of dominance.

Problems of Foreign Policy

Since the outcome of American intervention in the affairs of Cuba had become apparent, a new idealism had tended more and more to appear in America's relations with the West Indies and with Central America. Under Presidents Roosevelt and Taft the spirit of the Cuban policy had been cautiously applied to avert the financial ruin that from time to time had menaced one or another of the states of the Caribbean. President Roosevelt, in 1903–4, had taken Panamá under American protection by specific treaty agreements. In 1907 he had convened at Washington, with the aid of President Diaz, of Mexico, a conference representing Guatemala, Honduras, Salvador, Nicaragua and Costa Rica, and there treaties and conventions were signed by the delegates of the latter states pledging their respective governments to ten years of peace. In 1907 Santo Domingo's request to be taken under the financial control of the United States had been accepted by the Senate at President Roosevelt's suggestion, and a formal treaty had been made defining that relationship. By the date of Wilson's inauguration it was evident that the old policy of leaving American neighbours to their fate, provided that fate did not mean the extension of European control over them, had given place to a new policy of keeping them from falling into financial or political conditions that might tempt aggression from European powers.

New relations with Latin America

This new American policy had met with grave suspicion in Mexico, and Americans had been securing concessions and initiating developments which aroused the fear, perhaps not wholly groundless, that Mexico was in a fair way to become a sort of industrial dependency of the United States. In 1911 Francisco Madero had succeeded, by a combination of arms and promises to the peons, in driving out President Diaz, securing an election that made himself president and winning the recognition of the United States and other leading powers. But his promises had remained unfulfilled; he had lost his dominant following, and in 1913 had been captured and imprisoned by a new rebel leader, General Victoriano Huerta. Five days after his capture Madero and his vice-president had been shot at night, February 23, 1913, while in the hands of Huerta's officers; and on March 3, 1913, the day before Wilson's inauguration, Huerta had taken the oath of office that made him president of Mexico.

Following long established custom, the European nations had recognized Huerta, as they had recognized his predecessors, asking no questions regarding the origin of the power which was his. But President Wilson sternly refused to follow such

VICTORIANO HUERTA

His desertion of Madero in 1913 resulted in General Victoriano Huerta's accession to short-lived governmental power in Mexico. Popular antagonism brought about his resignation in 1914, and in 1916 he died in exile.

Photo, Associated Press

precedent. Toward the end of March, 191 he formulated his general policy, to cove Mexico and all Central and South Americ in the words that pledged co-operatio 'only when supported at every turn b the orderly processes of just governmen based upon law.' But it soon became un mistakably evident that a 'just govern ment based upon law' did not exist nor was likely to arise, in Mexico; an President Wilson expressed his realiza tion of that fact in the words: 'We ca have no sympathy with those who see to seize the power of government t advance their own personal interests o ambition. . . . We dare not turn fro the principle that morality, not ex pediency, is the thing that is to guide us.

These statements made no change i Huerta's plans, nor did they appeal to th Mexican people, suspicious as they wer of America's attitude toward their in dependence. But the refusal of recogni tion made it difficult for Huerta to borro money, and encouraged other ambitiou rebel leaders, Venustiano Carranza an Francisco Villa, to rebel against him.

REBEL MEXICAN LEADERS WHO CHALLENGED HUERTA'S POWER

The murder of Madero in 1913 drove Venustiano Carranza (left) into strong opposition to the pro-visional president Huerta, and he proclaimed himself general in chief in the revolution that h initiated. Recognized by Wilson as Mexico's de facto president in 1916, Carranza was himself kille by revolutionaries in 1920. Francisco Villa (right), famous as a leader of guerilla warfare, supporte Carranza against Huerta in 1914, but later opposed the former and attacked the government he set up.

Photo, Keystone View Co. and (right) E.N.A.

PRESIDENT WILSON AND HIS CABINET IN 1914

Upon Huerta's refusal to agree to President Wilson's demands in April, 1914, the latter asked Congress to pass a resolution justifying armed intervention in Mexico. By 337 votes to 37 the House of Representatives passed the resolution, declaring that their action was directed, not against Mexico as a country, but against General Huerta. Preparations for war went forward, but it was averted by the mediation of Argentina, Brazil and Chile. Huerta resigned on July 15.

Photo, American Press Association

President Wilson's policy was by this time bitterly denounced by many of his own party leaders, by the leaders of the opposition party and by the American ambassador in Mexico, Henry Lane Wilson, a Taft appointee who had been left undisturbed by the new administration. To recall the offending ambassador was easy, but to supply the deficiency thus created at a time of crisis required recourse to the expediency of sending a personal representative, since the sending of a new ambassador would have been in effect the recognition of Huerta. Accordingly John Lind, of Minnesota, was selected to bear to Mexico the demands of the American chief executive, which included a cessation of warfare, a general amnesty, a general election free from control by the existing Mexican authority, and one in which Huerta himself should not be a candidate. These demands Huerta scornfully rejected, thus chancing the 'big stick' that had been so often referred to in the strenuous days of Roosevelt.

But the 'big stick' failed to appear. Instead there emerged a new species of foreign policy, one that puzzled the Mexican usurper, enraged the American opposition and the party of the president alike, and called from Europe unbounded scorn. Its first tenet declared: 'Everything that we do must be rooted in patience and with calm, disinterested deliberation. We can afford to exercise the self-restraint of a really great nation which realizes its own strength and scorns to misuse it.' In essence, these words describe the policy that Britain adopted towards China in 1927, but in 1913 they were novelties.

In October, 1913, came the additional Wilsonian announcements, heartening to Mexico and her neighbours, distant and close at hand, in exact proportion as they believed it: 'The United States will never again seek one additional foot of territory by conquest.' Mexico was certainly excusable if she received these statements as the convenient phrases of a subtly aggressive neighbour; for no American can say, unless possessed of the gift of prophecy, what America will never seek.

These declarations once made, President Wilson settled down to what he called 'watchful waiting,' a phrase susceptible of being understood as waiting for an opportunity. In the face of not inconsiderable provocation from Huerta, he exercised admirable self-restraint; but left Huerta unrecognized. At last one action, interpreted by Huerta, and perhaps with justice, as inconsistent with America's verbal creed, precipitated a crisis. On April 10, 1914, some American bluejackets who had landed at Tampico for oil and gasoline were arrested by Huerta's officers. Although Huerta promptly released the prisoners and expressed regret for their arrest, Admiral Mayo, commander of the American forces in the harbour, without express authority from President Wilson, demanded additional reparation in the form of a specific, formal apology, the punishment of the officers responsible for the arrests and a salute of the American flag before six o'clock p.m. on April 19. These things Huerta refused, and on April 20 President Wilson appeared before a joint session of Congress and asked for the passage of a resolution that would justify the employment of force against Huerta. The House promptly adopted the resolution, 337 to 37, but in ignorance of the fact that on April 21, compelled by the arrival of a German ship loaded with munitions for Huerta, the American forces had occupied Vera Cruz. War with Mexico now seemed inevitable; but the mediation of Argentina, Brazil and Chile managed to avert it, 'though 126 Mexicans had been killed and 195 wounded, and 8 American marines had perished, during the capture of Vera Cruz in preparation for the salute that never came.

But the odds were too strong for Huerta, who retired to Europe on July 15; and within about a month the new dictator, 'First Chief' Carranza, marched triumphant into the capital city. About his present power there was no doubt, and on September 15 President Wilson ordered the removal of American troops from Vera Cruz, leaving Carranza to face, not peace, but his embittered ally, Francisco Villa, now bent upon revolution. Soon his efficient devastation of the northern provinces had brought them to starvation; and on March 6, 1916, Villa ventured to invade American territory, killing eighteen American citizens on the soil of New Mexico.

At once 6,000 American troops under Pershing were

HOISTING THE AMERICAN FLAG AT VERA CRUZ

A salute to the American flag was part of the reparation demanded for the arrest of some American sailors by Huerta's officers in April, 1914. A captain of marines and an ensign are here shown hoisting the stars and stripes over the Terminal Hotel, headquarters of the U.S. force that occupied Vera Cruz.

Photo, W. F. Taylor

detailed to pursue him into Mexican territory, there to aid Carranza and capture his rebellious antagonist, Villa. But Carranza at once declared foreign invasion, even though it professed to be in the interest of the existing government, an outrage on Mexican sovereignty; and while the two nations disputed over this fine point of procedure Villa again crossed the American border and invaded Texas. Again General Pershing pursued him into Mexico; but when the year 1917 dawned Villa was still at large, Carranza was still unreconciled to America's method of aiding his government, and the world was wondering what difference the president of the United States could see between the banished Huerta and the victorious Carranza, and why international morality had dictated the banishment of the one and the success of the other.

In January, 1917, the American troops were withdrawn from Mexico, and the American nation was conscious of the fact that neither 'watchful waiting' nor military invasion had served to lessen the Mexican problem.

Meanwhile Colombia had raised the issue of damages due to President Roosevelt's Panamá Canal policy, and on June 16, 1914, a treaty had been signed giving Colombia $25,000,000 and preferential privileges on the canal in return for her recognition of the independence of Panamá, a treaty not to be ratified until 1919, after the Senate had eliminated the first article expressing the regret of the United States for events that had interrupted the course of friendly relations between the two nations, Colombia and the United States of America.

Friction over the Panamá Canal

In one other respect, also, the canal had led to friction and foreign adjustment. In 1912 Congress had exempted American coastwise trade from a toll of $1.25 per ton imposed upon vessels passing through the canal. Great Britain had protested, declaring that the Hay-Pauncefote Treaty guaranteed uniform charges upon all vessels using the canal. On March 4, 1914, President Wilson boldly declared in favour of the British contention, and succeeded in bringing a reluctant Congress to his point of view, greatly to the credit of the nation over which he presided.

GENERAL PERSHING

This photograph of the well-tried American general, John Joseph Pershing, was taken during his Mexican expedition against Francisco Villa in 1916. In 1917 Pershing commanded the American Expeditionary Force in the Great War.

Photo, E.N.A.

On the whole it is fair to say that, in foreign affairs, despite inevitable errors of judgement, the Wilson administration had so far merited the sympathy of self-governing nations by making it abundantly clear that it approached its international problems in a spirit of generous, if at times quixotic, idealism. Despite the suspicions that the Mexican policy had accentuated, President Wilson had demonstrated a sincere desire to promote justice, to discourage despotism and to respect not alone the letter but the spirit of every international obligation.

But mere idealism solves few international tangles in this stage of strife between nations, whatever fate may be reserved for it in future; and the contest with Mexico had measurably lowered the prestige of the Democratic regime, not alone in America, but in Europe as well. The Great War, now in progress, had already demonstrated the fact that the world was facing problems little connected with the desire for 'just government based upon law,' and each successive act of Germany in defiance of international law had forced the United States nearer and nearer to the ultimate resort to force.

Despite this fact, the pacifist philosophy, so ardently advocated by Bryan and so fruitlessly followed by the administration in the hope that participation in the war might be avoided, was still in the ascendancy, and no preparation for effective action had been taken by the government. In vain did far-sighted leaders of both parties urge preparation for the defence of the nation's basic rights. In vain did the leaders of the Plattsburg movement, initiated by Major-General Leonard Wood and a group of representative civilians, and aiming to train a body of officers against the hour of need, plead for one word of sympathy with their work. In vain did great civilian organizations, conscious of the danger of America's defenceless condition, and of the difficulty of creating an army out of a non-military civilian population, pour into the mail bags of the Federal government petitions in favour of preparedness. Secretary of State Bryan believed that, at a word from the president, an army of a million soldiers could be assembled between sunrise and sunset; and the president, while too wise to see safety in such a foolish vision, persisted in the assertion that the nation was already adequately prepared for any likely contingency. The advocates of preparedness he contemptuously dismissed as 'nervous and excitable,' men whose debates were merely 'good mental exercises.' But all the time the war cloud was drawing nearer, and those who believed in the inevitability of American participation increased.

MAJOR-GENERAL LEONARD WOOD AND STAFF

From 1910–14 the American army was reorganized by its chief of staff, Leonard Wood, who was created major-general in 1903. He strongly advocated a policy of preparation for war and served in France when America eventually intervened. In 1921 he became governor-general of the Philippine islands.

Photo, Keystone View Co

On May 7, 1915, the Lusitania was lawlessly sunk by a German submarine, with a loss of 1,200 lives, including more than a hundred Americans. In view of the president's consistent assertion from the first that America's neutral rights must be respected by all belligerents, the nation impatiently awaited action; but it waited in vain. His first public utterance after the outrage dismayed all preparedness men, disgusted all Allied sympathisers and brought the flush of triumph to those whose sympathies were with the Central powers. On May 10, 1915, he said to an audience of newly naturalised citizens in Philadelphia: 'There is such a thing as a man being too proud to fight; there is such a thing as a nation being so right that it does not need to convince others by force that it is right.'

Thus Bryanism in war appeared ensconced, impregnable; but on May 13, 1915, the president's Lusitania note

GERMAN COMMEMORATION OF THE SINKING OF THE LUSITANIA

The German justification for their action in sinking the Cunard liner Lusitania in May, 1915, is allegorised on a satirical medal struck at Munich by Karl Goetz to commemorate the event. On the obverse, ignoring the warning finger of Count Bernstorff, crowds buy tickets from Death at the Cunard office, which bears the motto 'Business above everything.' On the reverse (right) the sinking ship is seen to carry aeroplanes and munitions in defiance of the 'No contraband' declaration.

British Museum; photo, Oxford University Press

appeared, with a dash of menace that dismayed Bryan, and gave pause to all who had read full meaning into the unfortunate phrase, 'too proud to fight.' The president's formal position seemed irreconcilable with his Philadelphia speech, for he calmly warned the German government that America would not 'omit any word or act' needed to defend the rights of her citizens; and on June 8, 1915, Bryan resigned his post as secretary of State, with the declaration that the maintenance of peace rather than the maintenance of rights was the only policy that he could consent to execute.

Thereafter the president's attitude toward the preparedness movement seemed to alter. In his message to Congress in December, 1915, he denounced 'hyphenates' and urged national preparedness; but Congress was still facing in the direction in which the president had so long led, and the country was uncertain about the real meaning of his apparent 'about face.' Indeed, Secretary of War Garrison was himself sceptical, and now emphasised his doubts by resigning his post on the ground that the president was not supporting him and that Congress was not willing to make any adequate preparations for the nation's defence.

It is hard for a camel to go through the eye of a needle; it is hard for a rich man to enter into the kingdom of Heaven; but for an ambitious president, approaching the end of his first term, to hold his face like flint in one direction, with multitudes surging in every direction, is a task analogous to both. When Wilson was re-elected president for his second term in 1916 the chief argument of his supporters was compressed into one telling phrase: 'He kept us out of war.'

But one month less two days after his second inauguration, on April 2, 1917, he delivered to Congress, assembled in extraordinary session, a war message whose glowing phrases and lofty idealism thrilled all civilization. America, he said, had been thrust into belligerency, but she must meet her unwelcome responsibilities with clear vision, with purposes clearly defined:

> We must put excited feeling away. Our motives will not be revenge or victorious assertion of the physical might of the nation, but only the vindication of right, of human right, of which we are only a single champion. . . . The wrongs against which we now array ourselves are no common wrongs; they cut to the very roots of human life. . . . We are glad, now that we see the facts with no veil of false pretence about them, to fight thus for the ultimate peace of the world and for the liberation of its peoples, the German people included:

for the rights of nations great and small and the privilege of men everywhere to choose their ways of life and obedience. The world must be made safe for democracy. Its peace must be planted upon the tested foundations of political liberty.

It is easy to scorn the rhetorician when no crisis calls for his art. Tyrtaeus the poet was but an insignificant figure in peaceful Greece; but when the crisis came the Spartans, facing battle, thanked their gods for a voice that could still all petty passions and give unity of soul. No generation bent upon the gains of peace can understand the response that followed the clarion note from the presidential trumpet which so often had given but uncertain sounds. On April 4 the Senate, with but four dissenting votes, accepted his definition of the nation's aims, and on April 6 the House followed with only fifty votes in the negative.

As Austria had taken no part in the submarine warfare that had proved the deciding factor in bringing about this declaration, she was not included in the declaration of war; but later, on December 7, 1917, the declaration was extended to her also. Turkey and Bulgaria, the other allies in the group known as the Central powers, were never included in America's formal declarations of war; but their cause was, of course, inextricably linked with that of Germany and Austria.

The Standard of Living

America faced her world war—hers from the first if the president's interpretation of its meaning be accepted, as Congress had accepted it—with a standard of living the highest in the world, if not the highest in any land, in any age. With a population approaching 120,000,000 and the largest entirely free market in the world, stretching over 3,000,000 square miles, she had not yet discovered any very active interest in foreign markets, but was content to prosper apart, behind her high tariff walls, and to thank God that the strife of nations was not her strife. England she gladly accepted as her middleman, trusted to bring to her shores the tea, furs, rubber, raw silk and other foreign material needed for her comfort and industrial prosperity.

Her educational machinery, decentralised and locally controlled, while far from perfect, was available for all classes, and her vast system of public libraries brought the elements of culture within easy reach of virtually everyone who cared to make the slight exertion necessary to enjoy them. The development of railways, so rapid since the Civil War, had opened even the most distant corners of the country to communication with the outside world. In 1860 there had been only 36,626 miles of railway in the country. By 1900 there were 194,262 miles, and the next decade showed an increase of 22·6 per cent., while the total railway mileage in 1914 was 263,547.

This extension, with accompanying improvements in roads and waterways, had wrought a marvellous change, in both urban and rural life.

The Life that has passed

The farmer or ranchman of a few generations earlier had produced on his own grounds almost everything that his life demanded. His heat came wholly from wood, cut with an axe wielded by his own hand. He killed and cured his own meat and produced his own wool, which was cleaned and carded on his own premises and worked on domestic looms or spinning-wheels which were part of the normal household furniture. A tiny village within not too easy reach was resorted to for a few articles such as pepper, salt, sugar and spices, and served as an exchange for such surplus products as he could readily carry with him on horseback or pack-mule. His shoes had been generally made by the village shoemaker, who used the leather that his customer's own cattle had supplied; and his own grain was ground for 'toll' by the local mill. In the village, if not too small, there was likely to be a factory that made the small agricultural implements with which he laboured. But in general he had owed astonishingly little to 'the settlements.'

By the opening of the decade before the Great War rural conditions were completely altered. Centralised manufacturing and shipping facilities beyond all precedent in history connected him with the hitherto distant world. A free market throughout the entire nation offered unparalleled opportunity for the development of organized, nation-wide economic service, and the most secluded rancher of 1914 was within easy reach of the latest Paris models, the newest styles of manufactured goods, the most recent patents in prepared foodstuffs, the latest editions of metropolitan papers and magazines that brought him the world's news of the hour.

This transition from the period of the farmer's self-sufficiency to that of rural dependence upon cities had been so gradual that the new generation, born to new privileges of world contact, scarcely realized how amazing was the difference between its position and that of its fathers and grandfathers.

These changes had, of course, been accompanied by enormous growth in the size of factories, a standardisation of products, and the inevitable congestion of population into great industrial centres. In 1890 only about 36 per cent. of America's population had dwelt in towns of over 2,500 inhabitants. By 1910 the urban population had grown to over 46 per cent., and by 1914 probably one half of the nation's population lived in urban centres; while the increasingly industrial character of immigrants, who numbered 1,285,549 during the high-water mark of 1907, tended always toward the cities.

Among new manufacturing industries that had most strikingly altered American life during the decade before 1914 the automobile held first place. In 1899 there had been only 600 automobiles built and sold in the United States; by 1909 there were 114,891 sent out of American factories, and with the increase had come a sudden era of road building. By 1914 the automobile industry promised to become in the near future the leading manufacturing industry in America. Under its influence suburban life had taken on a new aspect, as it had ceased to mean social isolation; and the great motor-truck industry had emancipated the horse as a beast of burden. The predictions of increased automobile production uttered in 1914 have been amply realized by

PRESIDENT WILSON HEADS THE WAR PROCESSION AT WASHINGTON

America had held aloof from the Great War throughout Woodrow Wilson's first presidential term, and his supporters urged his re-election in 1916 on the grounds of his pacifism. In 1917 American feeling, earlier aroused by the Lusitania episode, was outraged by the sinking of further American ships, and Wilson decided upon American intervention. He is here seen, flag on shoulder, marching up Pennsylvania Avenue, Washington, when the first recruits were called to the colours.

Photo, E.N.A.

subsequent development. In 1925 America had 19,954,000 automobiles, or 81 per cent. of the world's supply. It has been estimated that there was an average of one automobile for each $5\frac{6}{10}$ inhabitants of the United States in 1925. In California the ratio was one to each $3\frac{3}{10}$ persons.

The changes wrought by the automobile were amplified by the vast progress that electrical invention and manufacture had made during the same period. By 1914 Alexander Graham Bell's 'latest American humbug,' as a critic had called the electric telephone in 1876, had reached the ten-million mark within the United States, and the figure was increasing at an astonishing rate. So rapid has been that increase since 1914 that the American Telegraph and Telephone Company's report of 1925 declared that 61 per cent. of the world's telephones were in the United States, and that they carried 49,000,000 conversations daily. This meant, of course, to urban populations an incalculable saving of time; and for rural populations it meant, in addition, easy social contacts and a knowledge of market conditions that helped to defend them against exploitation by middlemen.

The electric light, made possible in 1878 by the genius of Edison in America and Swan and Stearns in England, had by the year 1914 practically supplanted all other methods of illumination; the electric motor and the insulated copper wire had displaced the flying belt in hundreds of manufacturing plants, and there was not an important factory of any kind in the country that did not depend upon electric current for light or power. In many industries electric motors fed by currents from a central power plant constructed to supply many customers had completely displaced the once dominant steam engine; and there was scarcely a community which could not readily be served from convenient hydro-electric plants. New York was drawing 262,300 horse power from Niagara and 48,000 from the St. Lawrence, with another 48,000 clearly available. All told, New York was producing about 713,371 horse power, Washington 300,510, Maine 233,698, Indiana 151,400; and a Federal survey had estimated that the water power available for the nation was good for over $61\frac{1}{2}$ million horse power.

The domesticated duties of the housewife had also been greatly lightened by the near-by source of power. Electric washing machines, vacuum cleaners, sewing machines, cooking stoves, refrigerators and minor household implements were 'stocked' by furnishing houses exactly as were beds

MASS PRODUCTS OF THE DODGE AUTOMOBILE FACTORY

One of the most striking American industrial features of the ten years preceding 1914 was the rapid progress made in motor manufacture. With each year the volume of production increased and America is now the leading car producing nation in the world. A photograph of the Dodge Automobile Factory at Detroit, Michigan, shows a 'sixty-minutes output.'

Photo, E.N.A.

VIEW OF THE MILLING DISTRICT AT NIAGARA FALLS CITY

A considerable proportion of New York's electrical power supply is derived from the Niagara Falls. The buildings seen in this view of Niagara Falls City belong to the Niagara Falls Hydraulic Power and Manufacturing Company, while the Cliff Paper Company's pulp mill at the water's edge is worked by the water which has already been used for power purposes higher up the cliff.

Photo, E.N.A.

and dining-room tables; and the farmer drew from distant electric power stations a silent helper that sawed his wood, milked his cows, separated and churned his cream and lighted, with little risk of fire, his barns and outhouses.

Indeed, the uses of applied science had become so common by 1914 that the farmer who stopped his Ford in the road to gaze at the comparatively rare spectacle of an aeroplane thought little of the wonders of recent achievement in his interest in this new, potential method of transportation. Only a decade before, in 1903, Wilbur and Orville Wright, with the machine made possible by electricity and the petroleum condensed fuel, had flown for 59 seconds in a heavier-than-air machine. The next year, Santos Dumont flew 220 metres in 21 seconds; and in 1908 Wilbur Wright flew 56 miles in one hour 31 minutes and 25⅕ seconds, convincing even the most sceptical that the dream of Icarus had at last come true. But the achievements that waited for the 'ace' in the years soon to come were then beyond the faith even of the credulous; and the prediction that within nineteen years a young American, Captain Charles A. Lindbergh, would mount his plane, with five sandwiches and a bottle of water as his only supplies, and fly alone to Paris without a stop, in 33½ hours, would then have been dismissed as fanciful.

The modern industrial chemist had come also with a skill more valuable than the transmutation dreams of the medieval alchemist, if realized, could have been. Artificial synthetic dyes, coal-tar medicines and a myriad inventions in aid of manufacturing processes had made the chemist a factor in economic life; while another branch, the development of explosives, had already made him a terrible factor in international contests. Since about 1876 the work of creating chemical explosives had been in progress. Just before the Great War derivatives of cresol had been developed and heavy artillery had been remodelled, the world over, to make use of this most destructive of explosives.

The physicist, with experiments on new elements, uranium, radium and polonium, and the electro-physicist with the mysterious X-ray, had given a new practical meaning to his ancient science. And photography, once a static art, had transmigrated and presented itself to the world in a new form, the motion picture, which before the Great War began had already demonstrated to the world its potential twin functions of public entertainer and public instructor.

Thus by 1914 the once isolated American farmer's wife, so long the victim of desperate loneliness, could mount her Ford, or her Buick, when her mechanical aids had enabled her speedily to discharge her once never-ending domestic duties, and repair to a neighbouring cinema, to enjoy a few hours of diversion with Charlie Chaplin, Douglas Fairbanks or Bill Hart, and then enjoy the luxury of dinner in an automatic restaurant, or return home to 'pick up' New York or Philadelphia and listen to a lecture on Japan, or an orchestral concert, on the radio, over half a million of which were installed in American farm houses within ten years after the Great War began.

Not every American rural household enjoyed the equipment just described; but all were to be found in almost every region of America; for the communities which, isolated by natural barriers, had been left outside the stream of progress were few, and were steadily growing fewer.

And the luxury of life for wage workers dwelling in towns and cities was multiplied in proportion; yet the American savings banks reports for 1914 showed that not all the earnings were dissipated upon cars, telephones, radios and moving pictures. The average deposit in savings banks for that year was $89 per capita; while the total savings bank deposit was $8,729,000,000. In addition, the American savings deposited in the form of life insurance amounted to over $500,000,000.

It was a bewildering array of proofs of progress; and it is difficult to believe that the world will ever see its like again. But for the possibilities of the future of applied science no wise man will venture to draw the line. What has been done to draw together the ends of the American nation may yet be done to bring together the ends of all the earth.

LINDBERGH AND THE AEROPLANE IN WHICH HE FLEW THE ATLANTIC

On May 20–21, 1927, Captain Charles A. Lindbergh, a young American air-mail pilot, accomplished his magnificent non-stop flight from New York to Paris in 33½ hours, an achievement which forms a landmark in the history of aviation. This photograph shows his machine, the Spirit of St. Louis, a 220 h.p. monoplane, at Croydon Aerodrome after his arrival there. America accorded her hero a tremendous ovation when he returned to Washington on June 11.

Photos, Keystone View Co.

Tenth Era

THE GREAT WAR AND AFTER

1914–1929

Chronicle XXXII—THE GREAT WAR, 1914–1918

Chronicle XXXIII—AFTERWARDS, 1918–1929

The Tenth Era of our record is that wherein we are still living, the era inaugurated by the greatest convulsion known in the history of mankind. The Great War raged for four years and a hundred days. It devastated a vast area of Europe beyond recognition; it cost millions of lives on the battlefield; it paralysed productive industry and destroyed sources of production; it shattered political systems; and it wrecked the entire nineteenth-century outlook upon life. It gave to old problems a new aspect, and created new problems for solution, involving complete reconstruction. The grand inclusive problem of reconstruction was that with which the world found itself faced, the problem with which it has been struggling, not we believe without some success, in the ensuing decade. But we can no longer feel even that degree of finality in our judgements with which we pronounce upon the past; there can be no considered consensus. Consequently there can be no uniformity in the pronouncements upon the various aspects of the story of the years since 1914 such as we have been able to maintain heretofore in this work, no 'judgements of history'; the views expressed, often divergent and sometimes it may be even contradictory, are individual views and must be so regarded. The tale is the tale of the beginnings of the grand attempt to lay the foundations of permanent world peace not only between nations but also between classes; to substitute co-operation for rivalry, to dissipate jealousies and distrust. And as yet we are only at the beginning.

TABLE OF DATES FOR CHRONICLE XXXII

1914 Aug. 3: Germans invade Belgium.
„ 7: Fall of Liége.
„ 22: British at Mons.
„ 23: Japan declares war. Battle of Mons. Fall of Namur. Retreat of British, and French left.
Russian invasion of East Prussia; successes, followed by disaster of Tannenberg. Russian invasion of Galicia.
Aug. 26: British stand at Le Cateau.
„ 28: Fall of Longwy; retreat continues.
Serbians repulse Austrians and invade Bosnia.
Sept. 5: Retreat ends, still covering Paris.
„ 6: French counter-offensive begins; battle of Marne forcing German retirement, and developing (13) into battle of the Aisne. German line stabilised; both lines extend north till the coast is reached.
Russians capture Lemberg; drive through Galicia.
Oct. First German invasion of Poland held up on the Vistula.
„ 10: Fall of Antwerp and (16) of Ostend.
„ 19: Belgians at Nieuport. The opposing lines extend from Belfort to the sea.
„ 20: Battles of Arras and Ypres begin.
Nov. 1: Battle of Coronel.
Britain declares war on Turkey.
„ 18: Last German attack at Ypres broken.
Second German thrust in Poland held up on the Vistula.
British force lands at head of Persian Gulf.
Dec. 8: Battle of Falkland Islands.
S. African revolts of De Wet and Maritz ended.
Russo-Turkish campaign begins in Caucasus.

1915 Jan.: Third German thrust in Poland held up.
Russian victories in the Caucasus.
Feb.: Fourth German thrust narrowly escapes disaster at Prasnytz.
Turkish attack on Suez Canal shattered.
British naval attack on Dardanelles opens.
Germany announces submarine war on commerce.
March: Russian advance in Galicia; Przemysl taken.
Failure of naval attack in Dardanelles.
Battle of Neuve Chapelle.
British declare naval blockade of Germany.
April: Russians partly penetrate Carpathian passes.
British victory at Shaiba (Mesopotamia).
Second battle of Ypres. First use of poison gas.
British troops force landing on Gallipoli.
May: Mackensen opens German offensive in Galicia. Russian line driven back to Przemysl by the end of the month.
Sinking of the Lusitania.
French advance in front of Arras.
Italy declares war on Austria.
June: Conquest of German South-West Africa.
Fall of Przemysl and Lemberg (Galicia).
July: German advance in Poland, on Warsaw.
Aug.: Russians abandon Warsaw.
British landing at Suvla Bay; surprise fails.
Mesopotamia: British occupy Kut el-Amara.
Germans take Kovno and Brest Litovsk.
Sept.: Battle of Loos.
German invasion of Russia checked on Vilna-Rovno line.
Oct.: Bulgaria declares war on Serbia and attacks.
French and British troops occupy Salonica.
Nov.: Serbia overrun by Bulgars, Austrians and Germans.
British advance on Bagdad abandoned.
Dec.: British force isolated at Kut.
British evacuate Gallipoli.

1916 Jan.: Russian advance in Caucasus.
Feb.: Russians take Erzerum
„ 21: First German blow at Verdun; French lines driven in; thrust stopped on 26th.
March 2–14: Second drive at Verdun.
Great Britain adopts general conscription.
April 9–12: Third drive at Verdun.
Relieving force fails to reach Kut; surrender.
Rebellion in Ireland fails.
May 3–June 6: Fourth battle of Verdun front.
May: Austrian thrust in the Trentino.
„ Battle of Jutland.
June: Last German effort before Verdun fails.
Russians open great offensive in Galicia; Austria abandons Trentino adventure; German and Austrian reinforcements called east.
Arab revolt under Sherif of Hejaz declares Arabian independence.

1916 July: Allied offensive opens in the west; British begin battle of the Somme. Russian successes in Galicia.
Aug.: Rumania enters the war and drives through Carpathian passes into Transylvania. Russian progress in Galicia checked.
Italians take Gorizia.
Constant fighting and gradual gain of ground by Allies on the Somme.
Sept.: Rumanians pushed back by German counter-offensive. Mackensen invades the Dobruja.
First appearance of 'tanks'; considerable advance of Allies on the Somme front.
Venizelists set up provisional Salonica government.
Oct.: Allied push continues, very gradual advance on western front. German invasion of Rumania advances, but is stoutly resisted.
Nov.: Western push suspended by weather conditions; Mackensen forces Danube, compelling Rumanian retreat.
Serbians and French capture Monastir.
Dec.: Fall of Bukarest; Rumanians confined to Moldavia.

1917 Jan.: Allies reject German peace overtures.
Feb.: Turks cleared from Kut.
Renewal of the Allied push in the west.
March: British in Bagdad. Advance on Palestine from Egypt held up at Gaza.
Western front approaches St. Quentin.
Constitutional revolution in Russia; Nicholas II abdicates (15); provisional government.
April: United States declare war on Germany.
Vimy Ridge stormed; French gain footing on Chemin des Dames, but fail to master it.
May: Continuous development of submarine campaign.
Russian army undermined by Bolshevik teaching.
June: Messines ridge blown up; partial British advance.
Constantine abd.; Venizelist government.
July: Brussilov with loyal troops opens desperate offensive in Galicia; which is wrecked by disloyal troops. Russia ceases to count.
Aug.: Desperate Rumanian stand against Mackensen.
Obstinate but futile campaign in the mud of Flanders.
French recover ground before Verdun.
Sept.: German advance in Baltic provinces.
Oct.: French master Chemin des Dames.
Germans shatter Italian centre at Caporetto Italian retreat, pursued by Austrians, turns to bay on the Piave.
British push to Passchendaele.
Nov.: Lenin overthrows Kerensky government Bolshevik domination in Russia.
Surprise British spring at Cambrai; countered by heavy German reinforcements.
Allenby captures Gaza.
Dec.: Allenby occupies Jerusalem.

1918 Jan.–Feb.: Preparations for decisive struggle.
March: Russo-German treaty of Brest Litovsk.
German drive against British right on Somme British stand on the Ancre, 'back to the wall.'
Foch appointed commander of Allied armies.
April: German thrust towards coast held up.
American troops arriving.
Zeebrugge wholly and Ostend partially sealed.
May: German drive against French left, to Marne
American troops in fighting line.
June: Failure of last Austrian offensive on Piave
July 15: Final German thrust across the Marne.
„ 18: Foch opens victory offensive.
German withdrawal begins.
Aug. 9: British join offensive on French left Additional offensives develop continuously t[o] left and right.
Sept. British penetrate Hindenburg line; Germans evacuate St. Mihiel, taken by Americans.
„ 15: Allied offensive against Bulgars.
30: Armistice dictated to Bulgars.
„ 19–21: Battle of Megiddo; Syria invaded.
Oct.: Cambrai taken; Lille and Douai evacuated
„ 23: Rout of Austrians on Italian front.
Decisive defeat and surrender of Turkish arm[y] in Mesopotamia. 30: Armistice dictated.
Nov. 3: Austrians sue for armistice. Battle o[f] Sambre. 7: Americans enter Sedan. 9: fligh[t] of Kaiser; German provisional governmen[t]
„ 11: Mons entered; Armistice.

Chronicle XXXII

THE GREAT WAR: 1914–1918

THE Central powers entered upon the Great War with a confident expectation of rapid and decisive victory, for which there was no small warrant apart from certain miscalculations. In the first place, the presumption was that at least in the initial stages they would have to deal with only two powers that counted, France and Russia, one on the west and the other on the east, while on the north and on the south they were secure. Holding the interior lines, and provided with a network of strategic railways, they could mass troops on either front and transfer them from one to the other in overwhelming force as circumstances might demand; whereas the French and the Russians were each of them pinned to a single front.

In the second place their own military machine—or that of the Germans, at least—was in perfect working order; those of France and Russia were not. It was barely ten years since the weakness of the Russian system had been revealed in the Japanese war, and there had been very recent revelations of defects in the French military administration. It was almost certain that Russia would not be able to bring her full power into play for some months, which would give Germany time to clear France off the board.

It would give time because one section of her frontier, where it marched with Belgium, was very nearly defenceless, so that it could be swiftly penetrated by a march through Belgium, whose neutrality, guaranteed by treaty, had been faithfully observed in the war of 1870 by both sides—but while several powers, including Prussia, were then pledged to observe that neutrality, none were pledged to oppose its violation in arms. The invasion of France through Belgium was an integral though unavowed part of the German plan.

The German staff, however, had taken into consideration the possibility that Great Britain might, sooner or later, join with France and Russia. It was in itself improbable, since in the first place there was no treaty obligation binding her to give armed support (as there was between Russia and France) to the other members of the Entente; secondly, there was a Liberal government in power, and Liberal governments were notoriously averse from war; thirdly, the critical position in Ireland would greatly strengthen the peace party. And if, after all, the war party should predominate, England's military power was all but negligible; the German navy believed itself able to neutralise the naval power which a vociferous section of the British press had long been declaring to be totally inadequate for its task; and rebellion in Ireland, in South Africa and in India would tie her hands.

Finally, the German government was assured that in the east the Central powers would be supported by Turkey, while it was extremely unlikely that any of the other Balkan states would come to the aid of Serbia; and it was highly improbable that Italy would desert the Triple Alliance, though she might deny any obligation to give it armed support. It was not unreasonable, therefore, to anticipate that the war would be won for Germany before Christmas, possibly in the early autumn.

Opposed Views on War Guilt

THE German government had a solid Germany behind it; a Germany convinced that she was embarking on a war imposed upon herself in self-defence by the machinations of enemies who were awaiting their opportunity to crush her. It is not easy to credit the imperial government itself with a similar belief, or that of Austria. To the Entente powers it appeared quite simply that German militarism had been consistently planning for years to force on them at the moment of its own selection a war that should lay Europe prostrate before it, and should

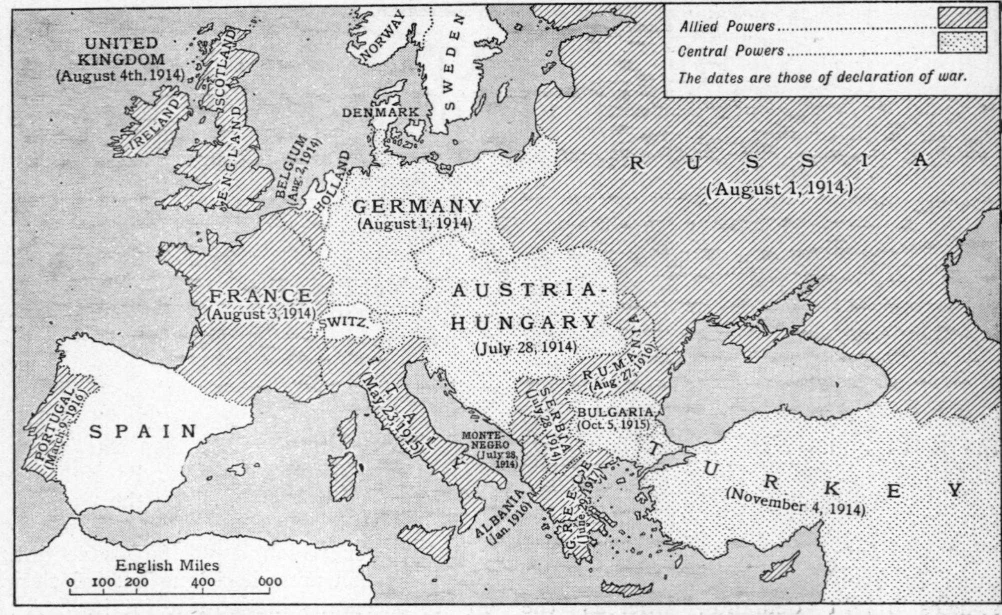

HOW EUROPE WAS DIVIDED AGAINST ITSELF IN THE GREAT WAR

This map of the belligerent European countries in the Great War of 1914–18 shows that, in spite of the imposing numerical array of nations actually or nominally at war with the Central powers, the territorial discrepancy, especially at the beginning, was inconsiderable. Furthermore, Germany held what are known as the 'interior lines,' and could transfer forces from front to front by a system of strategic railways. Hence she was not unjustified in counting on a speedy victory.

achieve for Germany what Napoleon I had attempted to achieve for himself.

The flaw in the German plan lay in its miscalculation of factors which were not obvious. It was reckoned that the French would fight brilliantly to win but would go to pieces in the face of defeat; whereas when they were defeated they fought on as tenaciously as ever. It was reckoned that Russia would only come slowly into action, and would be fully engaged in meeting the Austrian offensive; whereas before a month was over she was delivering an offensive on the east German front which, disastrously though it ended for her, was an invaluable diversion for her allies in the west. It was reckoned that Belgium, seeing the hopelessness of resistance, would give the German troops a free passage; resistance was hopeless, but the free passage was not given and, though Belgium paid the penalty for her heroic sacrifice, she impeded the rush while the Allies were reinforcing that front. Most fatal, however, was the miscalculation of the part to be played by the British.

Down to the last moment the British cabinet was divided, one section of it being convinced that if the European war could not be averted, honour and interest alike demanded British intervention; the other that there was no obligation of honour and that British interests would be best served by present neutrality. At the last moment the ranks were closed, not only in the cabinet but from end to end of the country, by the German invasion of Belgium. It was a breach of faith of a kind which, if it were tolerated, would render all treaties futile. Without that, Great Britain might and probably would have entered the war, but only in the face of a strong opposition at home from the Liberal and Labour benches and from the Irish; by it Great Britain was rendered practically solid, and Ireland swung into line with Great Britain. Nor was it long before it was abundantly manifest that the Dominions of the Empire would play their part no less zealously, that in South Africa there remained only a fractional body of Boer intransigents, and that Indian loyalty was assured.

Nor was this all; for the 'decadent' fleet, providentially concentrated in home waters, had already been quietly stationed precisely where it was most wanted, so that from the first day of the war no German squadron or surface ship was able to appear upon the North Sea for any purpose except a hasty raid on the British coast, or an engagement with a British squadron from which it had to extricate itself and seek security in its own mine-defended ports before it should be annihilated by the arrival of an overwhelming naval force. Moreover, from the first week of the war this control of the seas outside the Dardanelles and the Baltic enabled the British to carry across the Channel, not indeed without risk but without appreciable loss, troops, munitions and other accessories to military operations, to the full extent of the country's capacity for providing them; while it established at headquarters a complete confidence that dreams of a German invasion were chimerical, so that practically all the fully trained fighting force was available to take its place in the French fighting line.

That force was numerically insignificant and was grievously lacking in the heavy-gun equipment required for the campaigning methods developed by the Germans; but in other respects it was astonishingly efficient, as was the organization which placed it in the field on the other side of the Channel within three weeks of the declaration of war. Great Britain even now for a time persistently declined to envisage the compulsory training and service which the experts had warned her would be needed in a

ARRIVAL OF SIR JOHN FRENCH AND HIS STAFF AT BOULOGNE

The moment it became evident that British intervention in the war was inevitable Field Marshal Sir John French was selected for the command of the British Expeditionary Force to be despatched. On August 14, 1914, he landed with his staff at Boulogne—he can be identified behind the officer in the centre of this photograph of the occasion—and went to the French army headquarters. Next day he visited Paris, and on Monday, August 17, reached his own headquarters at Le Cateau.

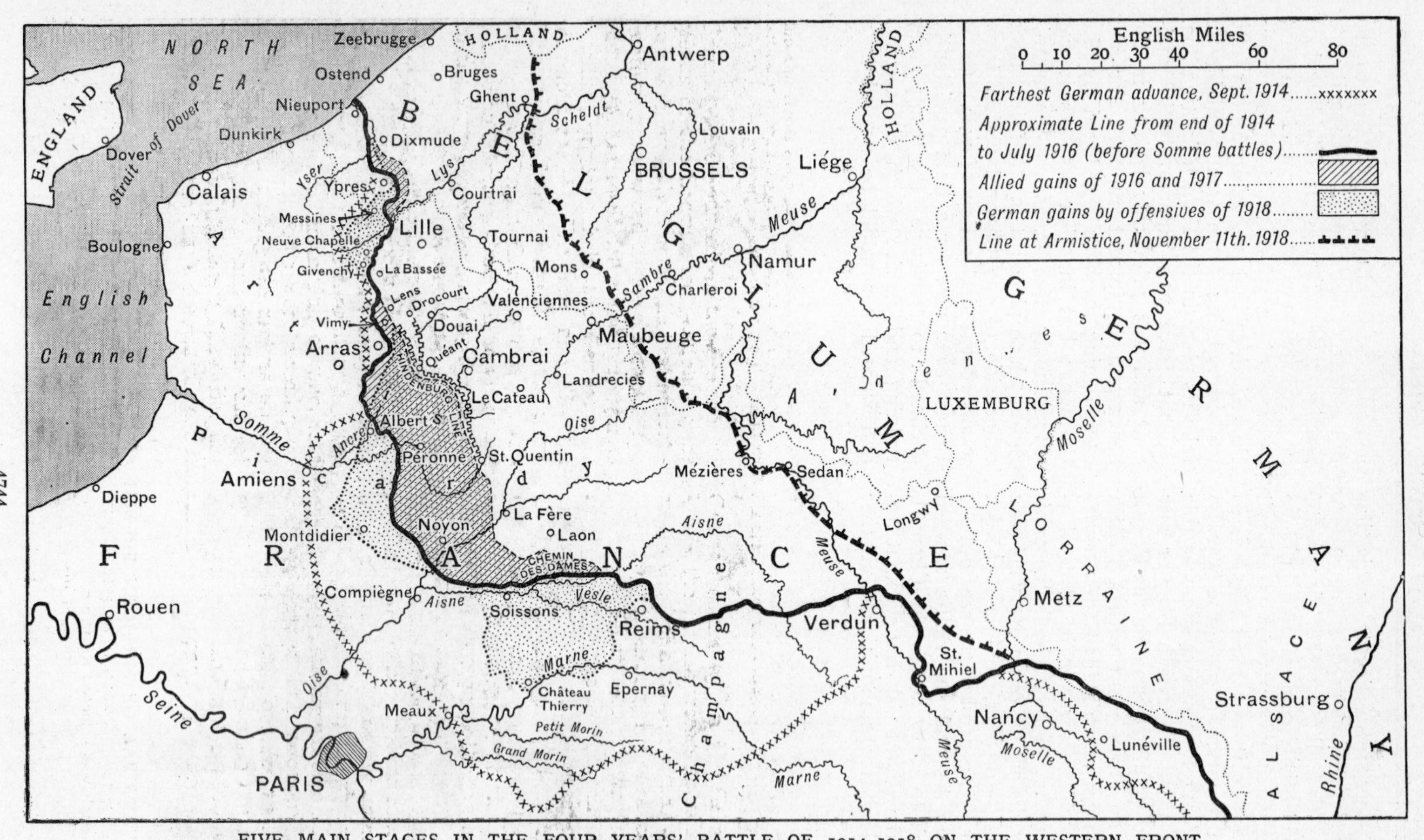

FIVE MAIN STAGES IN THE FOUR YEARS' BATTLE OF 1914–1918 ON THE WESTERN FRONT

From 1914 to 1918 most of the so-called ' battles ' on the western front—really the whole campaign was a prolonged battle—resulted in gains and losses of territory, entirely disproportionate to the loss of life involved, that appear insignificant on a large-scale map. Hence the operations can be simplified into five broad phases. First there was the German maximum advance. This the battles of the Marne and the Aisne, followed by the outflanking race northwards, converted into the stabilised trench line from sea to Switzerland that remained substantially unaltered for more than a year. Next, there

European conflict. But even as matters stood the 'expeditionary force' was twice the size of any British force which had taken part in any previous war; and the call to arms was answered by multitudes of volunteers, who were ready and fit to take the field in less than half the time that had been looked upon by the most optimistic as the minimum for producing even a moderate efficiency. Among these must be reckoned the recently organized and partly trained Territorial forces, whose terms of enrolment had exempted them from the service oversea for which almost without exception they now volunteered.

The neutrality of the small state of Luxemburg, as well as that of Belgium, was guaranteed, and was ignored to maintain the continuity of the German line. The Franco-German frontier was protected by a powerful line of fortresses, from Belfort at the gap between the Vosges and Switzerland (whose neutrality was not to be challenged) to Longwy on the Belgium-Luxemburg frontier, by way of Nancy and Verdun. It was on this line that the attack was anticipated, and the French were in strength. North of this in Belgium lay the Ardennes, not a good country through which to deliver an attack in force, though the French line was of course tenuous. The real German attack (see page 4798) therefore was to be delivered across the Meuse on the weak line between Lille and Maubeuge, turning the French left and clearing the way for a march on Paris, and taking the French army in rear; the Allies being quite unconscious of the concentration upon this line.

The plan would almost certainly have been carried out successfully but for the unexpected resistance of Belgium, which compelled the Germans to account for Liége and Namur before they could cross the French border. No one outside

FORT LONCIN, LIEGE, SHATTERED BY GERMAN SIEGE GUNS

Brialmont designed and superintended the Belgian defences of the valley of the Meuse, completing the fortification of Antwerp, Liége and Namur in 1884–86. The principal feature was the cupola fort, carrying guns in domed turrets. The method is open to criticism on the grounds that it cannot be concealed, provides a fixed target, and is liable to have its machinery put out of gear; a lesson enforced by this view of a fort after the German heavy guns had dealt with it on August 15, 1914.

Photo, Imperial War Museum

GENERAL SHAW AND HIS STAFF AFTER THE BATTLE OF MONS

The first encounter between the British and German infantry occurred when the latter made their sudden attack on the British position at Mons ; after heavy fighting, evacuation and retreat proved for the British the only alternative to envelopment. A photograph, taken while the Germans were actually firing into and over the barricade at the top of this street at Frameries, shows General Shaw discussing operations with his staff after the battle.

Germany had counted on the destructive effects of the German long-distance guns and high explosives upon the best of fortifications constructed on the old lines ; yet, though Liége itself fell on August 7, its satellite fortresses held the Germans up for another week. While the main Belgian forces were being pushed north upon Antwerp the main German column advanced on Namur ; though it was checked on the way, the bombardment opened on the 20th ; Namur fell on the 23rd, though satellite forts held out for three days more. All the defences had been blown to pieces, and of the Belgian southern army nothing was left. But by this time it was three weeks since the declaration of war, and the British army corps were already, on the 22nd, entrenching themselves on the French left, west and north-west of Charleroi through Mons. The Belgian resistance to the rush for turning the French flank had been crushed ; but it had been maintained just long enough to enable a new obstacle, the British expeditionary force, to take its place.

To overwhelm or envelop that force was now the immediate objective of the German command on the German right. While the British were entrenching themselves the Germans were uncovering their right by thrusting the French on the Ardennes front back over the Meuse and forcing the retirement of their extreme flank on the Somme, so that on the 23rd Von Kluck, with four army corps, was able to make a frontal attack on the whole British line, at the same time threatening to turn both its flanks. The frontal attack was actually held up, though Mons had to be evacuated, and it had become clear that retreat was the only alternative to envelopment. Next day (24th), therefore, the whole line fell back to a line running west from Maubeuge, fighting heavy but effective rearguard actions both on its right and left, and again on the 25th to Le Cateau ; where a desperate stand was made on the 26th which gave pause to the German onslaught, so that on the 28th the British were on a line from La Fère to Noyon. But for a second week the retreat was continued in conformity with the French retirement on the right, past the Marne, till the British force lay behind the Grand

Morin, with its left extended by a new French force covering Paris.

For the armies on the Belgian front from Longwy to Charleroi, though not definitely pierced, had been swung back, hingeing on Longwy; and when Longwy fell on the 28th, Verdun became the hinge, the line falling back behind the Aisne and then the Marne until it lay from Paris on the west to the salient including Verdun on the east, from which point it remained unshaken south-eastward through Nancy to Belfort. The failure of the Germans either to outflank the left or to pierce the centre—though they had come very near to doing both—had saved the situation. The momentum of the attack was exhausted, and that fact was very possibly due to the strain on the eastern front imposed by the unexpected Russian diversion in East Prussia.

Now, however, at the end of the first month the French line was being reinforced by reserves. At the moment when Von Kluck was almost at the gates of Paris, the immediate fall of which was anticipated in some quarters, the French opened the counter-offensive (September 6) on the Marne. The result was that now it was the Germans who had to swing back on their hinge before Verdun, the envelopment of their right flank being threatened by the Anglo-French left, as well as the penetration of their centre. (See further in pages 4797–98.)

On the 9th began the retreat of the German right, while Foch was delivering a smashing attack on the weakened right centre. On the 10th the whole line was in retreat, but it was an organized retreat covered by stubbornly fought rearguard actions. On the 13th the retirement from the Marne developed into the battle of the Aisne, which resulted immediately in the stabilising of the German line westward from the Verdun salient across the front of Reims and Soissons, leaving them still in occupation of two-thirds of the French territory over which they had advanced. This was followed by a continuous

MEN OF THE BRITISH NAVAL EXPEDITION SENT TO RELIEVE ANTWERP

The German thrust southward towards Paris had left the Belgian forces isolated in the north of their country, where they gradually concentrated on Antwerp. The condition of the town was already precarious—the outer fortifications and an inner fort having fallen—when, on October 4, the British Naval Division and a brigade of Marines were sent in by Winston Churchill for strategical reasons that have been questioned. This photograph shows a trench being dug at Vieux Dieu.

Photo, Imperial War Museum

GENERAL VON KLUCK

Alexander von Kluck, who commanded the German forces at the battle of the Marne, was born in 1846, and entered the Prussian army in 1865. He served in the Austro-Prussian and Franco-Prussian wars and retired in 1916.
Photo, Record Press

struggle for the extension of both lines northward, past the front of Amiens and Arras, primarily for the envelopment of the opposing flank—an end attained by neither—till both reached the North Sea, so that from Ostend and Dunkirk to Belfort each presented an unbroken front with no flank to be turned, while the occupation of Ostend by the Germans gave them the whole Belgian coast line.

The hope of the Allies that they would carry their line up to Antwerp was foiled. The Belgian forces, penned in the north, had continued to hamper the German invasion of France by raids for which they were mercilessly penalised, and the doom of Antwerp was sealed. With the help of a gallant but half-trained British force and British ships the Belgian troops were enabled to evacuate Antwerp before its fall on October 10, and to take up their position on the extreme left of the Allies, their front soon protected by ground submerged by the old device of opening the dykes, while the British held the famous Ypres salient.

In the course of the extending movement there was much hard fighting. Antwerp had already fallen before the British left was in front of La Bassée, from which it failed to expel the Germans, who occupied Lille next day. On October 16 the Germans were in Ostend, and on the 19th the Allied line had been extended by French and Belgians up to Nieuport, covered from the sea by the guns of British monitors.

The last phase of this struggle was the first battle of Ypres and the battle of Arras. The German object in the latter was to snap the connexion between the French at Arras and the British to the

GERMAN ARTILLERY IN THE COASTWISE PURSUIT OF THE BELGIAN ARMY

On October 9 Antwerp was evacuated, and, apart from 18,000 who escaped into Holland, the Belgian army retreated down the coast, eventually to form the left wing of the Allied forces which had by now worked their way almost to the sea in an attempt to outflank the German right. The final move by which the Germans countered this attempt was their pursuit of the Belgians over the dunes, which by the 19th had given them the whole of the Belgian coast to the Yser.

north of them. It began on the 20th, but though Arras was smashed by the German bombardment the French line held, while at the end of a week's fighting the Germans still held their position on the almost impregnable Vimy ridge. The battle for Ypres began on the 20th; its crisis came on the 31st when the Germans, making their greatest effort, were nevertheless repulsed at the end of a day during which the fray had rocked furiously backwards and forwards. In the next three weeks the assaults were thrice renewed and thrice repulsed, in spite of greatly superior numbers and artillery, and the stabilising of the two opposing lines from the North Sea to the Swiss frontier was completed. Until 1918 there was no advance of either line for more than a few miles upon a small sector.

On the western front, then, the first round of the great conflict was over before the end of November. The Central powers had delivered a very heavy blow, and remained in possession of a very substantial area of enemy territory, while their own soil was intact; but their attempt to make that blow decisive had definitely failed. On the eastern front they had been less successful.

Russian Advance in East Prussia

According to plan, Germany was to concentrate upon her own great offensive in the west, while holding in the east her own strongly protected frontier with its elaborate support of strategic railways. Russia, it was assumed, would not be ready to move for some time to come.

Russian Poland formed a great salient with East Prussia on the north, Prussian Poland on the west and Austrian Poland or Galicia on the south. The whole was practically without frontier defence. Austria then was to invade Poland from Galicia, and at the same time to put Serbia out of action. But, as it happened, Russia had much stronger forces ready than was supposed, and some commanders of high ability; whereas, at the moment, the German commander in East Prussia was incompetent and the Austrian command was extremely defective.

Consequently, while the Germans were trampling through Belgium the Russian northern army poured over the eastern borders of East Prussia, flinging the Germans back in rout to Königsberg, and creating something like a panic in Berlin. The German command was promptly transferred to Hindenburg, an old general, then of no great reputation, but one who knew the country thoroughly. The Russian left pushed forward into the Masurian lakes, losing touch with the centre, and there, in the last days of August, when the Anglo-French line was being rolled back towards Paris, was all but annihilated by Hindenburg, in the tremendous disaster of Tannenberg. East Prussia was saved, and the Russian main army had to fall back. It can hardly be doubted, however, that the critical moment in the east reacted upon the force of the German advance in the west.

Serbians in Bosnia and Russians in Galicia

Meanwhile the Serbians had dealt faithfully with the Austrian punitory expedition, ejecting it from Serbia before the end of August, and proceeding to the invasion of Bosnia; here, however, they made no material advance, though there was some heavy fighting in September. But the Austrians had to be content with holding them up, since their own offensive in southern Poland was being more than cancelled by an unexpected Russian offensive in Galicia. Before the end of August the Russian armies were threatening its capital, Lemberg; at the beginning of September they inflicted on the Austrians a rout only less overwhelming than the rout of Tannenberg, occupied Lemberg, almost cleared Poland of the invading Austrian force by the middle of the month, and were soon investing the powerful fortress of Przemysl, on the way to Cracow.

Hindenburg, on the other hand, after Tannenberg, which had established his reputation, attempted a counter-invasion not of Poland but of Russia from East Prussia, but was completely held up on the Niemen, and forced to retire across the Prussian frontier before the end of September. Apart from the actual check

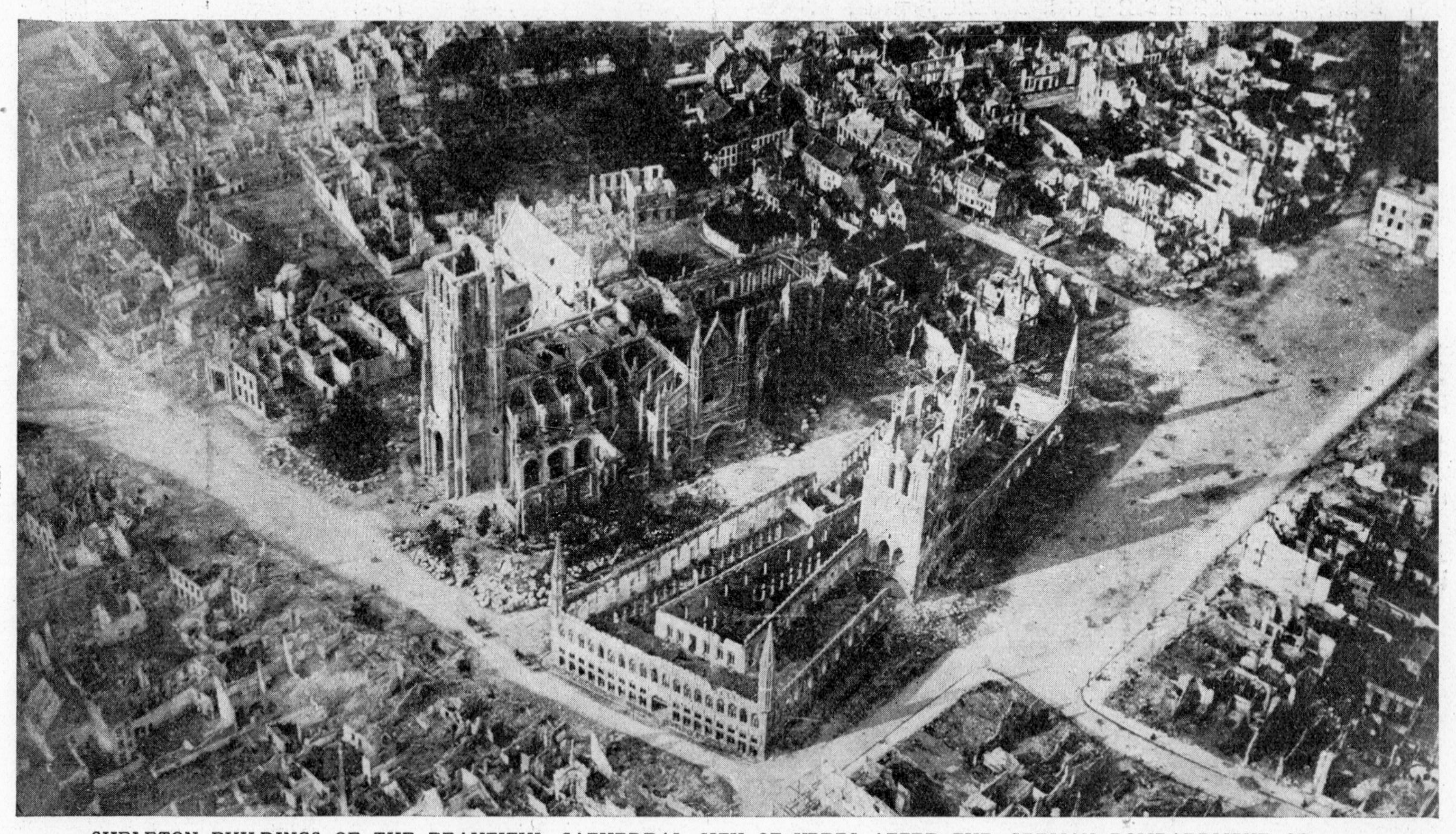

SKELETON BUILDINGS OF THE BEAUTIFUL CATHEDRAL CITY OF YPRES AFTER THE GERMAN BOMBARDMENT OF 1915

While the Belgians, with the aid of British monitors, were holding up the German advance in the flooded region of the Yser, the British on their right were engaged in a fierce conflict, centred round Ypres but stretching south to La Bassée, whose result was to stabilise the line in Flanders. The town itself was not seriously affected until the second battle of Ypres, in April, 1915; the civil population were then evacuated and the town virtually destroyed. The ruins of the famous Cloth Hall appear almost in the centre of this photograph with the Cathedral of S. Martin beyond. Compare page 3080.

he had received, it had become imperative to relieve the pressure in the south. The fall of Cracow would be an incitement to all the northern Slavs to revolt against their Austrian masters, would threaten to turn the flank of Hungary whose Galician front was protected by the Carpathians, and might have on the Balkan states effects which it was not possible to calculate; and already Russian troops were penetrating the Carpathian passes.

VON HINDENBURG ON THE EASTERN FRONT

His outstanding military abilities and victories over the Russians early raised Paul von Hindenburg to the rank of German generalissimo on the eastern front, where he is here seen at headquarters with his staff. In 1916 he received the appointment of chief of the general staff of the field army.

Photo, Central News

Early in October, then, Hindenburg had organized the invasion of West Poland, with Warsaw as his objective, expecting a Russian retirement. But the Russians prepared their stand along the line of the Vistula, and the Germans, when they tried to cross it, were not only held up in the centre, but found both their flanks threatened and were rolled back all along the line. In the first week of November Poland had been practically evacuated, and the fall of Cracow seemed imminent. But by this time the German command was satisfied that its own line in the west was established impregnably for defence from the North Sea to Switzerland, and had learnt in front of Ypres that the prospect of creating a flank in the Allied line was remote; therefore an intensive onslaught on the eastern front was in preparation. Cracow did not fall.

About the same time the finishing touches were given to the British command of the sea. The Central powers had no battle fleet in the Mediterranean, where the French were in charge; their main fleet was shut up in the North Sea ports, sheltered by their mine fields, whence only an occasional cruiser could emerge to make a dash for the English east coast, shell one or two watering places and race back to its own port before it could be overtaken by pursuers; though loose mines and submarines made the movement of ships in the North Sea somewhat precarious. At the beginning of the war, however, there was a German squadron in Chinese waters, as well as some cruisers in the Mediterranean. The last escaped to the nominally neutral port of Constantinople, to help the Turks in their preparation for dropping the mask.

On the other hand, Japan took her place with the Allies and declared war on Germany in August, so that Von Spee's squadron, which could not hope to engage the Japanese fleet successfully, after detaching the Königsberg and the Emden retired from Tsingtau (the port of the leased territory of Kiao-chau) across the Pacific, to experience the success and final disaster narrated in pages 4838–40. The Japanese intervention was followed by the fall of Tsingtau, and the Japanese fleet rendered further service in patrolling

ABOARD THE GOEBEN

At the beginning of the war French command of the Mediterranean drove the few German cruisers into Turkish waters; among them the Goeben, aboard which the Kaiser and Enver Pasha are shown at Constantinople in 1918.

Photo, Abrahams, Devonport

the Pacific and convoying Australian and Indian troops to the West, the latter taking their place temporarily in the fighting line immediately on their arrival.

The Porte, while proclaiming its neutrality, had made its secret treaty with the Central powers at the moment of the war's outbreak. The alliance was an integral part of the scheme; it was designed to place western Asia under German control, to turn the Russian flank and to eject the British from Egypt and the Suez Canal. Turkey openly entered the war at the beginning of November.

THE last heavy attack before Ypres was repulsed on November 11. A week later Hindenburg was renewing the assault on the Russian front in West Poland, and Mackensen was driving its centre back, only to find that his drive forward promised to result in his own envelopment; and it was only with great difficulty and heavy loss that he extricated himself from his perilous position. The Russian wings, however, fell back on a more secure line; the threat to Cracow was relieved by the threat to Warsaw. Another German drive on the centre in January (1915) was held up, renewed in February and again held up, while the Russians were once more threatening East Prussia. The Germans concentrated on the northern flank; the experiences of November were almost repeated at the end of February; the thrusting columns were first stayed and then almost encircled at Prasnytz, only escaping after a desperate struggle. The onslaughts on the Russian centre and right had both failed.

Meanwhile the Austrians were endeavouring to thrust the Russians back from the Carpathian passes and to recover the lost ground in Galicia. Though they met with some successes, Przemysl fell before the end of March. Its fall enabled the Russians to renew the attack on the Carpathian passes; by the middle of April they had made considerable progress. But by this time a fresh drain on their resources and an additional field of operations in the Caucasian region had been forced upon them by Turkey's entry into the war; and the Germans had resolved to take the saving of the situation on the Carpathian front into their own hands. The attacks in Poland had indeed saved Cracow, but had accomplished little or nothing more. Now they were concentrating—though the design was not understood elsewhere—on the Russian flank in Galicia. Mackensen, not the unsuccessful Austrian general, was to be in charge.

Fighting in the Colonial Area

SINCE the beginning of the lull on the western front neither side had down to this point made definite progress in spite of the heavy fighting in the east. In the colonial areas, the British and Japanese command of the seas made it an easy matter to eject the Germans not only, as we have seen, from China, but from the islands they had occupied in the South Seas, and from their colonies on the northerly coast lands of West Africa. Except where such conquests were a preventive against the stirring up of native hostility, they were of no serious importance, as had been repeatedly demonstrate[d] in the Anglo-French and Spanish maritime wars for over two centuries past.

German West Africa in the south and German East Africa were another matter, because of their bearing upon the Anglo-Dutch Union of South Africa. Here the eviction of the Germans was postponed owing to the trouble caused by the remnant of Boer intransigents within the Union. The revolts, however, headed by Maritz and De Wet, were put down before the end of 1914 by Botha and Smuts—who with De Wet himself had been the most distinguished and indomitable of the Boer leaders in their war with the British; while in East Africa the small balance of gains was rather in favour of the Germans. In the spring, however, Botha and Smuts were conducting a skilful campaign which cleared German South-West Africa in the course of the summer.

ON the other hand, the entry of the Turks was about to have momentous results. To begin with, it inaugurated a winter campaign against Russia in the Caucasus region where the Turkish frontier marched with that of Russia and with a corner of Persia which had already been for some time occupied by both Russian and Turkish troops. The Turks in Asia, not having as in Europe the benefits of German military directorship, were defeated in their offensive; but the Russians, though they secured Tabriz, failed to reach Erzerum, while the diversion reacted upon their strength in Poland and Galicia. At the same time, however, the Turks were directly challenging the British by attacking the Suez Canal from Palestine. The attacks were repulsed; but there was a further effect. Great Britain, with the assent of France and Russia, converted the occupation of Cyprus into annexation, and the occupation of Egypt—where the khedive threw in his lot with his Turkish suzerain—into a formal protectorate.

Moreover, it gave the British warrant for a counter-attack upon the Turkish flank in Mesopotamia, which offered a field of action for the Indian army better than the Belgian front, and for the bold design of seizing the Dardanelles. Granting the possibility of success, the advantages of this scheme were obvious. The capture of the Dardanelles and the fall of Constantinople would inevitably have placed the whole of the Balkan peoples at the disposal of the Allies, bringing Italy also in on their side, and Russia would no longer have been isolated. Even in her isolation it appeared in the winter and the early spring that she was at least able to hold her own against the utmost efforts of the Central powers—though the appearance was illusory. If she were reinforced from

HEADQUARTERS OF SECOND AUSTRALIAN DIVISION GUARDING THE SUEZ CANAL

Turkey's entry into the war on the side of Germany was the result of a scheme to divert the attention of the Allies to fresh frontiers and to lessen their concentration in Europe. Defence of the Egyptian frontier and the Suez Canal necessitated the speedy despatch of troops to the East. Among the contingents sent to this area of the war were Australian troops, who built the floating bridge over the canal that this photograph shows being opened to allow a vessel to pass.

Photo, Australian Commonwealth

ALLIED NAVAL ATTACK ON THE DARDANELLES

This sketch, made by a naval officer during operations in the Dardanelles in March, 1915, shows the British battleships Queen Elizabeth, Lord Nelson, Agamemnon and Inflexible opening up a long-range bombardment in the general attack on the Narrows on the 18th. This attempt to force the Narrows ended in failure and heavy losses for the Allies; the Inflexible suffering serious damage from collision with a floating mine. See also the panoramic plan in page 4845.

the Balkans, there would be little chance for Hungary and Austria, and Germany would be involved in a desperate struggle for life on both fronts.

The Allies, under a mistaken impression of the German strength on the western front, had designed a great offensive there in the spring. Concentration upon this object forbade the diversion of troops to the eastern front. In February the navy, with no army in support, though aid from Greece was in contemplation, began its attack on the Dardanelles, cleared the entrance, and was then, in March, brought up short by the Narrows, which were under the concentrated fire of land batteries in every direction, as well as torpedoes from the shore, while the waters were sown with floating mines. French and British battleships were sunk, nothing was achieved, and in the coming weeks the Turks, under German leadership, were busily engaged in making their land defences impregnable.

The Mesopotamian expedition from India reached the head of the Persian Gulf in November, captured Basra and Kurna, inflicted a heavy defeat on the Turks at Shaiba in April, and did not continue its advance until June.

And, in the meanwhile, the Germans, who had learnt the futility of attempting, for the time at least, to challenge battles with British naval squadrons, inaugurated the submarine campaign described in page 4853; while the British replied by declaring a blockade of all German ports, affirming the largest rights of search and detaining all goods destined for Germany, whether contraband or not. As in the case of Napoleon's Berlin Decrees and the British Orders in Council, the Americans for the time resented the British more than the German action, because the one interfered immediately and effectively with their commerce, while the other did not take unmistakable effect until a later stage, in spite of the terrible object lesson given by the sinking of the passenger liner Lusitania in May, with more than a thousand non-combatants on board.

Allied Offensives of 1915

During the winter and spring fighting was continuous from end to end of the western front—murderous, costly, futile. Multitudes of volunteers from home or from overseas were training in England to pile up new armies, and to take their place in the fighting line as soon as they were trained and equipped; while the Germans were perfecting the trench system which was to hold up any possible onslaught. Then at the end of March the Allies began what was proclaimed as their grand offensive.

But the grand offensive was local and inadequately co-ordinated. The British began in the north with a thrust towards Lille at Neuve Chapelle, preceded by an intensive bombardment; it carried some three miles of front about a mile forward, with casualties on both sides—probably about equal—estimated as exceeding 25,000. The French made some progress in the south on both sides of the German salient at St. Mihiel between Verdun and Nancy; but, in fact, they hardly shook the German line, and in April the Germans retorted with an attack on Ypres, where they effected a temporary breach in the Franco-British line by the use of poison gas, which had been unanimously repudiated as a permissible instrument of war at the Hague Conference. The breach, however, was made good, before the Germans could thrust through, by the newly arrived Canadians, and Ypres was held, though the defensive line was shortened. In May the French a little farther south hurled themselves against the Vimy ridge, and made an advance more considerable than that of the British at Neuve Chapelle; but the ridge proved impregnable.

The Dardanelles Campaign

The futility of a purely naval attack on the Dardanelles had been demonstrated in March; at the end of April England began her military effort, though by this time the land defences had been scientifically strengthened. The real marvel of that glorious disaster was not that it failed, but that it so very nearly succeeded. The forces sent to Gallipoli were outnumbered by the defence, which was very thoroughly equipped, held all the commanding positions and was under very able conduct. The British troops detailed for the task were very largely the battalions of volunteers from Australia and New Zealand that had been detained in Egypt until it was clear that the Turkish menace to the Suez Canal was not likely to prove serious. Like the Canadians on the western front, the 'Anzacs,' as they were called, displayed magnificent qualities of dash and endurance, and it was precisely the quality of the troops which brought them within an ace of achieving the miracle.

THE VILLAGE OF NEUVE CHAPELLE AFTER THE BATTLE

The 'grand offensive' planned by the Allies in March, 1915, began with Sir John French's determined attack on Neuve Chapelle, a village north of La Bassée, which had been in German hands since 1914. The British bombardment began on March 10, and, although the casualties were heavy, Neuve Chapelle was captured the same day. The battle wore on, without further ground being gained, until March 12. This photograph conveys some idea of the effect of the British artillery.

Photo, Central News

SUVLA BAY, GALLIPOLI: SCENE OF A GREAT ALLIED ATTACK THAT FAILED

During the Gallipoli operations, in August, 1915, a British force landed unexpectedly at Suvla Bay, with the object of gaining control of the central heights of the peninsula. The advantage gained by the surprise element of the attack was lost by ensuing delay in advance and the Turks had time to consolidate before an assault in force was made on their positions. Substantially the project was a failure for the Allied arms.

Photo, Imperial War Museum

A landing successfully effected at fiv different points, and four days of har fighting, put the British in possessio of a very precarious foothold on th extreme tip of the Gallipoli peninsula. Fo six weeks bombardment of the Turkis trenches, impetuous assaults that wo positions impossible to retain, and counter bombardments of the much more expose positions actually held, continued; whil submarines took their toll among th covering battleships and, in effect, impose their withdrawal. The assaults wer repeated at intervals until the end o July, still without substantial progres towards the objective.

But a bigger effort was at hand reinforcements were at last arriving On August 7, while three attacks on th usual points were engaging the attentio of the Turks, a force had been landed at new and wholly unexpected point farthe north, Suvla Bay, on the comparativel unguarded side of the Turkish defences But the attack did not develop until th 9th, when it had lost the invaluabl element of surprise, and it was held up Fresh and more experienced troops wer added, and the attack was renewed on th 21st. It was too late; the defences ha been thoroughly organized, and, though substantial amount of ground was secured the last chance of carrying the peninsul had gone for good and all.

Entry of Italy into the Wa

Both sides had been doing their best t draw Italy, Bulgaria, Rumania an Greece into the struggle. Italy was th first to depart from her neutrality. Th temptations offered by Austria were no sufficiently strong; there was a chance o getting the whole of 'Italia irredenta by alliance with the Allies, none by allianc with the Central powers, who were makin to Bulgaria offers incompatible with Italia ambitions. The Entente was more sym pathetic to the historical claims of Ital on the east of the Adriatic. At the end o April Italy made her treaty with th Allies, and in May declared war upo Austria. But it was to war with Austri on the Italian front that the whole of he attention was devoted; which mattere

THE COLLIER RIVER CLYDE BEACHED AT GALLIPOLI

he naval attempt to force the Dardanelles having failed, the Allies sought to effect their object by ıpturing the Gallipoli peninsula, which forms the northern shore of the strait. The British steamer iver Clyde, converted into a troop ship, was used in the famous landing at Beach V on April 25, ›15. Disembarkation was effected after nightfall and the Turkish positions stormed the next day. In the centre of the photograph may be seen the explosion of a Turkish shell.

Photo, Imperial War Museum

ıe less to Austria, because the Russian .enace to her in the east was being dissipated by her German ally, and her Italian ontier was virtually impregnable, though ɛr most advanced lines were driven in.

Neither Bulgaria nor Rumania intended › move till they saw something like a ɛrtainty of profit to themselves from their tervention; while as yet they could be sure of nothing more than that Bulgaria would not get much out of the success of the Allies or Rumania from the success of the Central powers. The mind of Greece was painfully divided, since her leading statesman, Venizelos, was quite definitely on the side of the Allies, while her king, Constantine, primarily anxious to keep outside the quarrel, was alternatively

A QUIET MOMENT AT ANZAC COVE, GALLIPOLI

ıe term ' Anzac ' popularly applied to troops from Australia and New Zealand was adopted for ficial use by the War Office in 1916. It is derived from the initial letters of the words Australian nd) New Zealand Army Corps. This cove north of Gaba Tepe, Gallipoli, was christened ' Anzac ' y the troops who landed in April, 1915—the first occasion on which the use of the name is recorded.

Photo, Imperial War Museum

disposed in favour of the Central powers, all the more because Venizelos was endeavouring to coerce him. The Bulgarian and Greek crises arrived in October.

Success then had not attended the Allied offensive in any quarter except the head of the Persian Gulf, where its initial aims were not ambitious but were intended mainly to give security to the Persian Gulf itself and to worry the Turks by a threat to Bagdad. In June it had pushed up the Tigris to Amara. In August its advance troops occupied Kut. Without heavy reinforcement it was insufficient to undertake more than the holding of what had been won, but it was tempted to an effort to rush Bagdad. But the forces covering Bagdad at Ctesiphon made the odds so heavy that the attack had to be abandoned, and the troops were back at the beginning of December in Kut, where they were presently isolated by floods.

It was far otherwise, however, with the concentration of the German offensive upon the Russian left flank. At the end of April, when a Russian offensive throug the Carpathians was generally expecte Mackensen's hurricane burst upon Galic with an artillery storm such that t Russians were wholly unable to meet i They were rolled back staggering, b fighting hard, from the Dunajetz, over t San, out of Przemysl, out of Lember which fell on June 22. That was far enoug for the time. Meanwhile another army h been thrusting on the northern flank a the Russian line covering Warsaw h become an extended salient again. Macke sen turned his attack against its southe side, the second German army attack the northern, and the Austrians in t centre pressed on the salient's apex.

The Russians were forced to fall ba upon Warsaw, only holding the line un the city could be evacuated (August 4 then, behind it, fighting desperately the shortened line straightened up. T weakened right, however, was now mo seriously menaced than it had been by ev the heaviest of Hindenburg's onslaught The fall of Kovno in the middle of Augu

KUT PERILOUSLY ENVELOPED IN A BEND OF THE TREACHEROUS TIGRIS

The geographical position of Kut, situated in a U-shaped bend of the Tigris, renders it liable flooding and consequent isolation. This fate befell the British troops under Townshend in Decembe 1915, when the Turks invested the town. After a valiant defence, Townshend surrendered K in April, 1916, but operations were begun for its recapture in December of the same year. In Fe ruary, 1917, Kut came again into the possession of the British, who reconstructed it after the w

Photo, Royal Air Force, Crown copyright

After the Russian evacuation of Warsaw in August, 1915, the German troops, commanded by Prince Leopold of Bavaria, entered the Polish capital in triumph. This spectacular view represents the prince outside Warsaw's Russian church watching his regiments march past. The retreating Russians blew up the three bridges over the Vistula as they went.

The Russians laid siege to Przemysl, a Galician fortress city, in September, 1914, and in December of the same year Hindenburg began operations for its relief. The city surrendered to the Russians in March, 1915, but they were unable to hold it long, for a successful Austro-German campaign in Galicia enabled Mackensen to advance on Przemysl in May and to accomplish its recapture in June. The Austro-German troops are here seen entering the town.

REVERSES OF RUSSIAN FORTUNE IN POLAND AND GALICIA

FLUCTUATING FORTUNES OF WAR UPON THE EASTERN FRONT

It should be noted that the lines on this map of the operations in the eastern area do not in mo instances represent continuous battle fronts. For one thing, the trench system was never so high developed as in the west; for another, they are intended to show limits of advance or retreat th were not necessarily contemporaneous. For instance, the advance of the Russians in East Pruss in 1914 had been broken at Tannenberg before their maximum advance in Galicia was attaine was followed by that of Brest Litovsk at the centre before the end of the month, and touch between the northern and southern Russian lines was severed by the Pripet marshes. By this time, however, the fury of the storm was abating, partly owing to the distance of the advance from the base, and the Russians in September were able to keep their hold on Vilna and the railway to Petrograd, and partly though not wholly on the rail from Vilna south to Rovno.

LAST ACT OF THE DARDANELLES TRAGEDY

The terrible if magnificent blunder of the Gallipoli campaign ended with a brilliant military operation when the peninsula was evacuated gradually throughout December, 1915, without the knowledge of the Turks. This photograph shows preparations for firing stores with straw and petrol, which were set off by time fuses after the last man had embarked on January 9.

Photo, Imperial War Museum

The defeat of the Russians cleared the way for the Central powers to carry out their programme in the Balkan peninsula. They had satisfied Ferdinand of Bulgaria that they were the winning side, and in October he mobilised against Serbia. A few French and British troops occupied Salonica at the invitation of Venizelos, who was determined to carry out Greece's treaty obligation to go to the help of Serbia if she were attacked by Bulgaria. But King Constantine dismissed the minister and repudiated the obligation. The Allied force at Salonica was too small to render effective aid, and Serbia, attacked on all sides, suffered her martyrdom, her people fleeing, while her armies fought a series of desperate rearguard actions to cover the retreat, to the coast and across the Adriatic; and Bulgars, Austrians and Germans overwhelmed them. And before the year was over the British accepted their defeat on the Dardanelles, and effected without loss the evacuation of the Gallipoli peninsula—a feat of skill difficult if not impossible to parallel.

The Battles round Verdun

The Allied offensive, if it should still be so called, on the western front continued in the autumn and early winter on the same unproductive lines on the British front and in Artois and Champagne. That is to say, there were fierce local attacks by which a few square miles distinguishable only on large-scale maps were left in occupation of the Allies instead of the Germans, and minor local attacks in which the losses and gains were balanced; while the casualties, also probably balanced, were very heavy on both sides. But the Germans had concentrated on their eastern offensive, which had carried them to the limits of their possible advance against Russia, having ever in mind the warning of Napoleon's disastrous advance to Moscow; they had established their own and their allies' predominance in the Balkan peninsula, though they had not yet won over Greece and Rumania, which were both still sitting on the fence; and they could afford to concentrate again on the west. The feature of the first half of 1916 was the western offensive of the Central powers; that of the second half was the Allies' counter-offensive.

While on the defensive, the Germans had virtually limited their expenditure of men and munitions to holding their

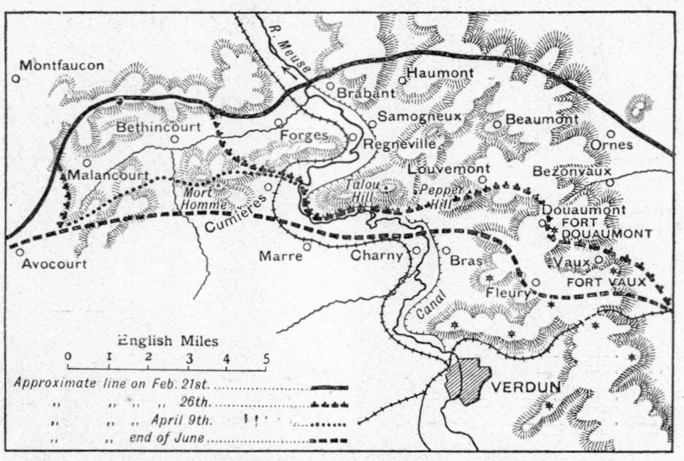

THE GERMAN ATTACK ON VERDUN

The German assault on Verdun during the first half of 1916 was divided into three main attacks, beginning on February 21, March 2 (with a subsidiary one on April 9) and May 3; all resulted in German advances, as shown in this simplified map, all failed in their ultimate object, and the last ended in a French recovery of ground.

lines, so that in spite of the enormous demands on the Russian front they were able to accumulate both for the coming onslaught in the west. On the other hand, the Allies had greatly increased their own production of war materials, and the small British army had grown into a comparatively large one, able to take over a longer section of the line than before, though it was only now that voluntary enlistment was superseded in Great Britain itself, though still not in the Dominions, by conscription.

The German grand attack was on Verdun, the salient thrusting out into the German line in the south; threatening movements against the French at other points and against the British were also made, but these were primarily to prevent reinforcement at Verdun, since it was imperative for the Allies to prevent a German thrust to the coast, to Calais and Boulogne. The object of the northern demonstration was to mask the main attack, which burst on February 21.

Verdun, with its own fortifications, stood at the centre of a defensive arc having a

FORT VAUX TWO YEARS AFTER THE CESSATION OF HOSTILITIES

What Ypres is to British sentiment Verdun is to French; at few points on the western front was the fighting more bitter, the combined French and German losses there in 1916 being estimated at nearly 700,000. Most of the German advance was achieved in the first attack, which drove in the outer French defences to a line running from Vaux fort on the east to the Mort Homme ridge on the west. On the extreme French left the line in front of Béthincourt and Malancourt still held.

Photo, Imperial War Museum

radius of nine or ten miles—about one-third of a circle—facing north, the line continuing southward at each end. Between the outer circle and Verdun were two more lines of defence. If those lines were carried, so that the siege guns could be brought within effective range, Verdun would become untenable, and the moral effect of its fall would be tremendous, though it might not sever the French eastern and western forces.

The German attack drove in the centre of the outermost and weakest line on the first day, and the rest of the line had to fall back in conformity. On the centre and right the French continued to be pushed back until they lay on the line from Vaux and Douaumont on the east, through Pepper Hill and Talou Hill in the centre, to Malancourt and Béthincourt on the west, as the result of four days' desperate fighting. Then Talou Hill had to be abandoned, and on February 25 the Germans launched the assault that was to shatter the defence. At nightfall they believed themselves to have achieved their object; next day they discovered their mistake. They had attacked the centre and right. In the centre they had carried Louvemont, but failed at Pepper Hill. On the French right they had concentrated great forces that carried them to the top of the Douaumont ridge and gave them the actual fort of Douaumont, of which they remained for the most part in possession, but not, as they had imagined, the command of the ridge, which remained perpetually contested; while they had only flattened the centre without bulging it, and the shortened line was rather stronger than the longer one. Also, French reinforcements were more than filling the gaps.

The first great thrust had failed, after all. On March 2 began the second great thrust, this time against the French left, in the direction of Mort Homme. For a week the Germans were gaining ground; then the battle on the left was supplemented by an attempt to turn Douaumont ridge on the right; which failed, however, though they were getting nearer to Mort Homme, on which they gained a footing on March 14. By the end of the month they had almost, but not quite, turned its left. Another heavy attack along the left and left centre began on April 9, and developed into a three days' battle, at the end of which Mort Homme and Pepper Hill and the line between them still held, though here again the fray had rocked furiously forwards and backwards.

MEMORIAL TO FRENCH HEROISM ON THE SUMMIT OF MORT HOMME RIDGE

After the first attack on the Verdun sector the Germans only made material progress on the two flanks of the flattened Verdun salient; Vaux fort fell on June 6, and the Mort Homme ridge, after changing hands several times in May, was left with the attackers established precariously on it. Here was the most desperate fighting of the whole engagement, and in 1919 the memorial seen above was erected; but the terrain, as at Vaux fort, was left otherwise untouched.

Photo, Imperial War Museum

The struggle had been frightfully exhausting and costly for both sides, and there was a lull for three weeks. The storm burst again on the left on May 3,

AUSTRIANS ON THE ITALIAN FRONT

The early fighting on the Italian front saw slight Italian successes; but in May, 1916, the Austrians developed a successful offensive. These are troops of the Austrian Alpine Corps scaling a hill during the first Italian offensive on the Isonzo.

Photo, Photo Press

accompanied by another attempt upon Douaumont ridge. The Germans were bent on achieving their object this time, whatever the cost. By the end of the month they forced the French back to a straight line from Avocourt to the left bank of the Meuse, while on the right they had carried Douaumont, lost it, and carried it again, threatening Vaux, which held out till June 6. But they could get no farther. There was a pause for nearly a week, and then, though it was the Germans who renewed the attack, it was the French who recovered ground. And at the moment when the attack on Verdun was exhausted the British, on July 1, opened their offensive on the Somme.

It was at the end of May that the German fleet broke its inaction and put to sea to meet the British fleet in what was the only serious naval engagement of the war—the battle of Jutland, described in pages 4845-53. Though it was a strategical defeat for the Germans, it may not unfairly be described as a tactical victory; for the German battle fleet escaped, having inflicted more damage than it had suffered. But no portion of it issued from its ports again till the war was over. From the day of the battle of Jutland it was out of action—action, for the German navy, was confined to the submarine campaign.

While the Germans were carrying out their offensive against French and British the Austrians were conducting their own counter-offensive against Italy, which was not as yet technically at war with Germany; practically the entry of Italy into the war was a resuscitation of her immemorial feud with the Hapsburg power. Austria might well have contented herself with holding her own frontier, which was of immense strategic strength; but the temptation to penalise Italy was too strong for her, and the threat might induce some dispersion of French and British forces for the defence of their Italian ally, which would be convenient for her own German ally. So in May she developed an attack through the Trentino, directed towards Venice.

The advance began successfully enough, turning the flank of the Italian offensive on the Isonzo line, which was directed against Trieste. But at the end of a month the advance was checked by Italian reinforcements, and by a sudden advance of the Russians in the east. The defence of Galicia was much more important than a spectacular advance in Italy, and by the end of June the Austrians were falling back. That offensive, too, had failed.

Renewed Activity of the Russians

ELSEWHERE the British had met with a reverse in Mesopotamia, where the Turks had been under German command since Ctesiphon. The advance force at Kut had been isolated, the attempts to relieve it were baulked by the Tigris floods, and it was forced to surrender at the end of April. On the other hand the Russians, though reduced to inaction in Europe, had conducted a very successful winter campaign in the Caucasus, whither the grand-duke Nicholas had been transferred from the chief command of the armies in Europe. Erzerum was captured in February, though it was not till April that the same fate befell Trebizond.

It was not the fault of the Russian troops or the Russian generals that they had been driven back to the last defensive lines in 1915. For that the ineptitude—or worse—of the Russian bureaucracy was responsible; and the great Allied offensive of 1916 was opened not by the British on the Somme, but by the Russians in Galicia.

The Russians, after being swept back to the line running north and south from Vilna to Rovno, had held up the further attacks aimed at Riga in the north, while Mackensen had been withdrawn in the south to deal with Serbia. Later they had made tentative attacks at various points; but it was at the beginning of June, when the Austrians were dissipating their forces in the Trentino adventure, that they opened a powerful offensive along their whole left front between the extremity of Galicia and the Pripet marshes; the forces opposed to them being mainly Austrian, though in their right centre they were under a German commander, Bothmer.

For a fortnight from its beginning on June 3 the attack drove forward successfully, crumpling up the Austrian resistance, held up before Tarnopol by Bothmer, but turning his right and thrusting into Bukovina, the province marching with Rumania. In the next three weeks the Austrians were out of Bukovina, Bothmer was finding it very difficult to cover Lemberg and Stanislau, and it appeared possible that from the north as well as the south of the Pripet marshes Russian armies might converge upon Brest Litovsk, while their left was sweeping through Galicia again. On the other hand, German troops—and commanders—had arrived and were still arriving at top speed from Verdun, and Austrians from the Trentino (where the Italians were rapidly recovering the ground previously lost).

The pressure was checked, not stopped. Concentrating on the Galician wing, the Russian advance on Bothmer's left and right in July compelled him to fall back, and early in August Stanislau was taken; but by the end of the month Bothmer was able to hold his ground, though in the two following months the Russians seemed about to penetrate the Carpathians.

The Russian successes ended Rumania's hesitation and brought her into the war in August—quite obviously for the purpose of joining to herself Transylvania, where the Magyars ruled over a mainly Rumanian population. As a matter of course, the Rumanian armies made Transylvania their objective, and swept triumphantly through the Carpathian passes on their frontier. But the result was unfortunate for the Allies and disastrous to

SOLDIERS OF THE ITALIAN ARMY ADVANCING THROUGH ALPINE SNOWS

The Austrian advance in Italy was a short-lived success; for under a vigorous counter-stroke by General Cadorna, in June, 1916, and alarmed by the renewed Russian activity in Galicia, they retreated, not without loss, to the old frontier lines. Italy's entry into the war on the side of the Allies (May 23, 1915) had been strongly influenced by the consideration that only from their victory did she have a chance of obtaining the 'Italia irredenta' under Austrian rule.

Photo Imperial War Museum

themselves. Russia, not without excuse, failed to give the support expected from her; and the Rumanians as they swung forward found themselves exposed to a German counter-offensive, the Germans having promptly taken the matter into their own hands on the top of the battle of the Somme and the defence of Galicia. In September Mackensen was invading the Dobruja and Falkenhayn was driving back through the Carpathian passes without any movement on his flank from the Russians. Even so it was not till November that the Rumanian resistance in Wallachia was broken and Bukarest fell on December 5. All that was left to her was the northern province of Moldavia.

The First Battle of the Somme

It was well for the Germans that the long struggle before Verdun had so exhausted the French for the time that their share in the Allied offensive in the west was less than it would otherwise have been; since masses of German troops and munitions were perforce withdrawn from the west to counter the Russian and then the Rumanian offensives in the east. The result showed what warrant there had been for their confidence in the strength of their own lines in the west.

The growing British armies had been able to take over from the French a great part of the line on their own right, which now extended almost to the north bank of the Somme between Amiens and Péronne, considerably to the south of the previous offensive of 1915. It was here on a front running some dozen miles north of the river (British) and a like distance south of it (French) that the battle of the Somme opened on July 1, carrying that line forward during the following months to a depth of about seven miles. The German trenches were constructed in series far away to their rear, running deep underground, so that even when a trench line had been shelled and carried, it had itself been rendered almost untenable for the victors while the line behind was intact.

Without very large maps it is impossible to follow the details of the prolonged struggle at one point or another, the captures and recaptures, advances, retreats and recoveries; there was never anything like a break through, though that was what

FIELD-MARSHAL VON MACKENSEN ENTERS BUKAREST IN TRIUMPH

The Rumanian decision to espouse the Allied cause was based on hostility to the Hungarians who ruled over a large Rumanian population in Transylvania; while the temporary Russian successes of June–August, 1916, seemed to indicate the moment for intervention. After successfully piercing the Carpathians, however, the Rumanian army found itself fronted by Germans under Mackensen; and the autumn saw a complete débâcle that only ended with the fall of Bukarest in December.

Photo, Imperial War Museum

A feature of the Somme offensive was the tremendous artillery bombardment that preceded it, lasting for seven days. Yet it is acknowledged that the artillery preparations were insufficient; shells began to run short before three weeks, and there was a lack of heavy guns for counter-battery work. This is the 39th siege battery of 8-in. howitzers between Fricourt and Mametz in August.

The German Verdun offensive had forestalled a great Allied push designed for the summer of 1916, in order to relieve the French the latter was started early (July 1) before preparations were quite complete. The front stretched from Gommecourt in the north to Soyecourt, the French under Fayolle being responsible for the sector from Hardecourt southwards; the whole operation is known as the first battle of the Somme. Supports are here moving up near Ginchy, September 25.

SCENES NEAR THE FRONT DURING THE BATTLE OF THE SOMME

Photos, Imperial War Museum

WHAT AN ATTACK DURING THE GREAT ARTILLERY BATTLES LOOKED LIKE: THE ADVANCE ON MAMETZ

The real innovation of the Somme battle was not the long preliminary bombardment, for that had been employed in 1915, but the creeping barrage, first introduced on a small scale by the French at Verdun. The infantry went forward behind an advancing wall of shells; and under these conditions it is not in the initial stages that the heaviest losses occur, the attack offering the unspectacular sight of a line of men proceeding over torn ground at a slow pace owing to weight of equipment. This photograph of the assault on Mametz on July 1 was taken just after the barrage lifted.

Photo, Imperial War Museum

CONSTANTINE, KING OF GREECE

In 1913 Constantine (1868–1923) became king of the Hellenes. His policy of maintaining Grecian neutrality in the Great War finally caused his deposition in 1917. Restored to the throne in 1920, he abdicated in 1922.
Photo, Russell & Sons

the uninstructed public across the Channel were looking for, whatever the actual anticipations of the commanders on the spot may have been. The most marked successes attended the fighting in September, when the British first brought 'tanks' into play (see Chapter 179). It is probable, however, that the line that had been reached by the British and the French on their right by the end of November was short of what it had been hoped to attain in the first week of the Somme battle. Whether it had cost the Allies or the Germans the more in serious casualties is a highly disputable question.

Meanwhile the Italians were making progress on the Isonzo front, having captured Gorizia in August; but Rumania was being broken, and her conquered territories gave the Germans control of invaluable oil fields. The Russians had latterly made little advance in Galicia, gave no help to Rumania, though they were progressing in Asia Minor, and made no diversion for the benefit of the Allied offensive in the Balkans from the Salonica base; for which things the responsibility lay not with the generals but with the political system. Austria was disintegrating, and the disintegration was hastened by the death of the aged emperor, Francis Joseph. Arabia was in revolt against Turkey and had declared its independence. In the Balkans the French, with the valiant remnant of the Serbian army, captured Monastir, but real progress was postponed for a long time, because Greece was divided against herself; and if the war party was the more popular, King Constantine retained control of the government and was apparently doing his best to play into the hands of the Central powers, while at Salonica the Venizelists set up a provisional government for themselves. And the German submarine campaign was developing steadily.

FRANCIS JOSEPH I, EMPEROR OF AUSTRIA

After a long and tragic reign Francis Joseph I, who ascended the Austrian imperial throne in 1848, died on November 21, 1916. His very real endeavour to rule his heterogeneous empire had done much to retard its disintegration. He was succeeded by his grand-nephew Archduke Charles.
After the painting by L. Horowitz

PERONNE WRECKED BY THE RETIRING GERMANS IN 1917

Throughout 1917 the initiative on the western front lay mainly with the Allies, who in the opening of the year began offensive operations with the old Somme front as the centre. Before them the Germans retreated methodically to the Hindenburg lines; Péronne beneath Mont St. Quentin fell to the British on March 18, but before evacuation the Germans wrecked it by fire and explosive.

ENTRY OF THE U.S.A.: BRITISH AND AMERICANS FRATERNISE

The deciding factor in the war was the entry of the Americans (April, 1917); for without them, whichever side eventually won, the final issue must have been delayed for many bitter months, perhaps years. Their first troops arrived in France under General Pershing in June of the same year and started an intensive training behind the lines. This photograph shows American and British officers meeting for the first time. By July of the following year a million troops had arrived.

Photos, Imperial War Museum

On the face of things, then, at the close of 1916, the presumptions pointed to a stale-mate, though it was easy for each side to persuade itself that the presumptions were in its own favour, since neither could fully gauge its own capacity for endurance, still less that of the other. If either side won, it would be the one which could hold out longest. Each wished to end the war, but only on its own terms, which meant that the other side must definitely acknowledge itself the defeated party and original aggressor. The Germans invited the friendly interposition of the United States to negotiate a peace; the Allies responded to the first overtures with a definite declaration of their own minimum requirements; the German government implicitly repudiated the American president's own demands in respect of the submarine campaign; the president finally came to the conclusion that Germany's ambitions were an intolerable menace to world progress, and that the cause of world progress demanded the armed intervention of America. In April the United States declared war on Germany (see pages 4733-34).

The American declaration of war and the Russian revolution were the two events of the spring of 1917 which wrought fundamental changes in the situation. The one meant that the Germans, if they were not to be beaten, must have the Allies decisively beaten before the American armies were ready to take the field in strength. The other, not at first so obviously, meant that Russia would cease to count. When Russia was off the board, Germany made her supreme effort in the spring of 1918, and when that effort reached its culmination the new armies from America were already taking their place in the fighting line.

Allied Offensives of 1917

When 1917 opened, however, the Allies were confident that they could win, and the Germans were confident that they could at any rate hold what they had already won, though on a slightly modified line more impregnable than that of which they were still in occupation. The British and French pressure began again in January along a front constantly extending both northwards and southwards, the Germans retreating gradually before it to the newly prepared line, since they had no intention of renewing a struggle for the devastated Somme battlefields; but it

VIMY RIDGE: PRIZE OF THE SECOND BATTLE OF ARRAS

When the Hindenburg lines proved impregnable the Allies endeavoured to outflank them by simultaneous attacks north and south. Both attempts failed in their ultimate object; but while the French under Nivelle were repulsed before the Chemin des Dames, the British made substantial advances in the second battle of Arras (April), capturing the immensely important Vimy Ridge and entrenching in the plain beneath. These Canadians are digging reserve trenches on the ridge itself.

Photo, Imperial War Museum

GENERAL MAUDE

Sir Frederick Stanley Maude (1864–1917) was in command of the 13th Division in Gallipoli, Egypt and Mesopotamia in 1915. In 1916 he was appointed to the chief command in the Kut area, and entered Bagdad in March, 1917.

Photo, Swaine

was an organized, if reluctant, retreat in which they fought for every inch of ground, but no longer than was necessary to prevent the retirement from being inconveniently hustled. The stolid repetition of the announcement after each withdrawal that it had been successfully executed 'according to plan' had more than an element of truth in it, though it excited the sarcastic comments of the Allied press. And the mangled territory they left behind them was itself a protection to that section of their front; which enabled them to concentrate forces upon the wings where the main struggle was bound to take place.

In March, then, the Somme advance at the centre, where the French and British armies joined, was pushed almost up to St. Quentin, running north to the southern point of the old 1915 sector in front of Arras and facing the Vimy ridge, and southward to the north-east of Soissons. On April 9, four days after the American declaration of war, the British began the second battle of Arras. In two days the Vimy ridge had been captured, and within the week the line south of it had been carried forward four or five miles so as to threaten the flank of the new 'Hindenburg' lines. But Nivelle's attack at the southern extremity on the Chemin des Dames was not equally successful; ground was won, but the Germans were not driven out, and the general effect of the second battle of the Aisne on the French was as depressing as that of Arras was encouraging to the British.

In the 'side-shows,' however, in Africa and Asia, which were mainly the concern of the British Empire on the one side and of Germany and Turkey on the other, the British were winning in every quarter. The South African Union and troops from India had at last cleared the Germans out of German East Africa, and their forces were now being added to the other Dominion troops in Europe. In the Mesopotamian area the new commander, General Maude, by a series of skilful operations, cleared the Turks from Kut in February and occupied Bagdad in March. The Turkish troops escaped from the trap in which they had almost been caught, but by the end of April, when climatic conditions suspended campaigning, Bagdad was eighty miles behind the British front. An offensive from Egypt had been hitherto prevented by the disturbances among the desert tribes; but these had now been quelled, and an advance on Palestine had opened.

Final Collapse of Russia

BUT the collapse of Russia was the factor for which the change of front in America was the much-needed compensation. In its initial stage the revolution looked as if it was likely to prove very much to the advantage of the Allies, since it seemed to be only the victory of the Russian constitutionalists over the poisonously corrupt bureaucracy, which was more than suspected of treason to the Allied cause. But the control of it rapidly slipped out of the hands of the constitutionalists into those of the socialist moderates, and from them to a fanatic of genius, Lenin, and his colleagues, the champions of a movement begotten and

Many official paintings serve to remind posterity that the Great War was a war of peoples and not of armies alone. The Phoenix steel works here portrayed by Sir Charles John Holmes were erected in Sheffield for Messrs. Steel, Peech and Tozer, solely to make munitions of war, and were no more than two years old at the date of the painting (1918).

Every great conflict has provided inspiration for artists, but never before the Great War has the artist received such recognition on the spot. The purpose of most paintings in official collections is documentary, but 'modernists' (see Chapter 188) were also employed. Thus, while few familiar with a trench will find photographic realism in John Nash's impression of the 1st Artists' Rifles at Marcoing (December 30, 1917), something of the atmosphere has been captured.

AS ARTISTS SAW THE WAR: HOME FRONT AND 'OVER THE TOP'

Crown copyright; photos, Imperial War Museum

Beauty was not absent from the battlefields of France for those who had eyes to see it. Many will remember the cornflowers and poppies of the Vimy Ridge; and Sir D. Y. Cameron, R.A., in the painting above shows that winter could cast an unearthly loveliness over the dreadful desolation of the Ypres Salient, pockmarked with the water-filled craters of the shells.

One of the most thankless tasks of the Great War was patrol work in the North Sea: a task which kept nerves strained to the utmost, was carried out under trying physical conditions and was relieved by little excitement. Much of it was performed by the destroyers of the Harwich flotillas, here seen putting to sea in a painting by Philip Connard, R.A. Its geographical position and its good harbour made Harwich an excellent base for the purpose.

THE SETTING OF MODERN WARFARE ON LAND AND SEA

Crown copyright; photos, Imperial War Museum

born of anti-Semite pogroms and the 'nihilism' that had first been created and then apparently crushed by the unspeakable tyrannies of the bureaucratic regime, having as its aim the total subversion of the existing social and political order, not only in Russia, but everywhere; something much more destructive than had been dreamed of by the most reckless of the French revolutionaries at the end of the eighteenth century.

At the beginning of March there were disturbances in the capital; troops there mutinied, and some of them shot their officers. The Duma—what passed for a parliament—set up a provisional government, of which the socialist moderate Kerensky became the leader, and on March 15 the tsar abdicated. But the effective power was in the hands of the council of delegates called the Soviet, in which the extremists, who were known first as Maximalists and then as Bolsheviks, very soon predominated. In May the provisional government, still led by Kerensky, was reconstructed on a more extreme basis. The subsequent internal developments are narrated in Chapter 184; in the meantime Kerensky strove hard to revive patriotic zeal in the conduct of the war, but the multiplying soviets organized by the extremists were zealous only for the social revolution which they had been preaching among the soldiery, whose discipline had gone to pieces.

With the most trustworthy of the troops Brussilov, at the beginning of July, opened a desperate offensive towards Lemberg, winning at first astonishing successes, reminiscent of the French revolutionary armies at the end of 1792. But he had no reserves; when the Germans delivered the inevitable counter-offensive on the 19th half the Russian troops refused to fight and fled in complete rout.

The last chance of a successful stand was gone. Lenin in Petrograd had raised an insurrection and the government was tottering. In August the Rumanians, deserted by the Russian government and the Russian troops, made a heroic stand against the onslaught of Mackensen which gave the shattered south Russian armies breathing space but did not prevent the Germans in the north from advancing upon Riga, though they were as anxious as Lenin himself to end the war on the eastern front and leave the Russian revolution to pursue its disintegrating and destructive career. In November Kerensky's government collapsed altogether, and the only government left was that of the Bolsheviks headed by Lenin and Trotsky, whose first aim was to negotiate the withdrawal of Russia from the war.

British Offensives in Flanders

In the west, the scheme of the great Allied 'push' all along the line broke down with Nivelle's failure to carry and hold the Chemin des Dames in April. The further efforts of the French and British were not concerted. Progress

NICHOLAS II AND BRUSSILOV

The Russian tsar Nicholas II (left) was compelled by the revolution to abdicate on March 15, 1917. Under General Brussilov, here seen beside the tsar, the Russian troops met first with some success, but finally with failure.

Photo, Central News

MARSHAL PETAIN

Born at Cauchy-à-la-Tour in 1856, Henry Philippe Pétain held a succession of distinguished commands in the French army, 1914–18. In March, 1918, he became commander-in-chief of all the French armies.

Photo, E.N.A.

at the centre against the Hindenburg line offered less promise than a northward extension of the British advance before Arras, with a view to diminishing the German control of the Belgian coast—the base of that submarine campaign which was the one effective offensive weapon of the Germans against Great Britain, the islands being so greatly dependent upon food supplies from overseas. For the air raids, though exasperating, did no great amount of military damage.

Hence the month of June witnessed the most resounding and nearly the most spectacular stroke of the war. On the way towards Ypres lay the Messines ridge; it had been the stage of much hard fighting which, as at Vimy until the Canadians stormed it, had failed to dislodge the Germans. Subterranean engineering operations had been in progress undetected for some time past. The whole of the surface defences were subjected to a terrific bombardment during the first week of the month, and on the 7th the simultaneous explosion of nineteen mines blew what was left to pieces in one vast eruption. The practical effect was to force on the Germans a retirement which left Ypres a salient no longer. But the success was not followed up for some weeks, during which the new German line was consolidated, with the advantages accruing from the shortening of it. No more effective advance was attempted

SPOIL OF WAR ON THE CAPTURED WYTSCHAETE RIDGE

The operations known as the battle of Messines were a continuation of the British 1917 offensives, but directed rather to the coast than to the outflanking of the Hindenburg line. They involved the Messines ridge itself, where the attack was opened by the explosion of nineteen enormous mines (June 7; see page 4810), and the Wytschaete ridge, its extension dominating the Ypres salient. Both were captured; and this is a German field gun being hauled off near Wytschaete on June 10.

Photo, Imperial War Museum

till the end of July, when, simultaneously, the weather broke and the Flanders flats were converted into an ocean of mud on which movement was almost impossible.

The British armies got no nearer to the Belgian coast. Still, however, they hammered on in Flanders, despite the adverse conditions, checked here and gaining some ground there, with little enough to show. In November there were some brilliant days when, without the warning of artillery preparation, an attack was launched by their right against Cambrai, where the Germans were taken by surprise. If the British success had been complete another withdrawal would have been imposed on them ; but just in time masses of reinforcements were rushed up from elsewhere, the attack was held up, being inadequately supported, before its objective was reached, and in the end the ground that had to be abandoned was more than what was won.

DRAMATIC SURRENDER OF JERUSALEM

General Allenby entered Jerusalem on December 11, 1917, an event that resounded throughout the Christian and Mahomedan worlds. The town had surrendered two days earlier to a small British advanced post in command of a sergeant, the mayor (seen with walking stick) coming out under the white flag.

Photo, Imperial War Museum

The French autumn campaign, Nivelle's place having been taken by Pétain, was not ruined like that in Flanders by climatic conditions, was less ambitious in its scope, less critical from the German point of view, and proportionately more successful in its achievement, and it did much to restore French confidence. Most of the ground won by the Germans in the attack on Verdun was recovered during August, and in October they were at last forced definitely to abandon the Chemin des Dames.

In the east, King Constantine's pretence of neutrality became so meagre that his authority could no longer be tolerated and the arrival of Allied warships in June forced him to abdicate in favour of his second son, who was a minor ; for practical purposes the government became a regency under Venizelos. But the collapse of Russia paralysed the advance projected on the Salonica front, besides releasing masses of German and Austrian troops for recuperation or for reinforcement of the west, and of Turkish troops for resistance to the British advance in Mesopotamia and on Palestine.

In this last quarter, however, was achieved a triumph of military skill which also made an intense appeal to all western sentiment. The advance on Palestine from Egypt had begun prematurely and with insufficient forces in the spring, when it was held up before Gaza. It was not till the end of October that Allenby suddenly opened his offensive. In the first week of November he had turned both flanks of the fortress and entered it. On

December 11 he was in Jerusalem, over which the flag of Islam had flown since the day when it was captured by Saladin. Nor was the triumph any shock to the orthodox Moslems of Arabia, who had already repudiated both the spiritual and temporal supremacy of the unorthodox Ottoman.

Victories in Asia, however, could exercise little immediate influence on the war in the west, where the German high command was well aware that if Germany was to win the war the thing must be done before the arrival in force of the Americans, and Ludendorff was preparing to win it. Probably it was with the primary purpose of compelling the diversion of French and British troops to Italy that in October the Germans struck hard on the Italian front, where hitherto they had not shown themselves.

GENERAL LUDENDORFF

Erich von Ludendorff, born in 1865, shared supreme command of the German army with Hindenburg in 1916, and organized the extensive use of surprise attack and gas in 1917. He was dismissed in October, 1918.

Photo, E.N.A.

SINCE the summer of 1916 the Austrians, absorbed at first by the great Russian offensive, and then in part by threatening disintegration within the empire, had contented themselves with maintaining their own frontiers, while the Italians had concentrated all their energies on a single objective, the capture of Trieste. They had captured Gorizia and bitten their way a little closer, but still the impregnable bastions stood between them and the prize on which their hearts were set. They had accomplished brilliant feats of daring and skill, but the odds of position even more than of numbers were overwhelmingly against them. Also parts of the population—and, more ominously, of the army—were seething with disaffection, the fruits of the new Russian propaganda, and were ready to follow the example of the Bolshevised Russian soldiery which had wrought such havoc with Brussilov's last desperate offensive. Some of those disaffected troops were stationed about Caporetto at the centre of the Italian line—and the Germans had found it out.

GENERAL ALLENBY

Edmund Henry Hynman, first Viscount Allenby, born in 1861, commanded the Egyptian expeditionary force in 1917–18 and directed the operations in Palestine that defeated the Turks. He became a field marshal in 1919.

Photo, H. Walter Barnett

It was at this point that they launched their surprise attack on October 24. The Italian centre was pulverised; only swift retreat screened by the most stubborn rearguard actions could save the wings from annihilation. They got across the Tagliamento, which rose behind them in a torrent, swollen by a fortunate break in the weather, and gave them some breathing space to reach the Piave, where they made their stand, covering the way to Venice. The German blow had done its work. Without extraneous support the Italians could not hope to hold out long against the Austrians, and British troops, which were soon to be badly wanted on the British front itself, as well as French, were dispatched to the Piave. They might hold out as long as they chose; from the German point of view the important thing was that they should be bottled up in Italy, not fighting in France or Flanders. The Germans left the rest of the Italian campaign to the Austrians.

Russia was already off the board; though her peace negotiations did not finally issue in the ignominious treaty of Brest Litovsk until the beginning of March, there was no need for the Central powers to retain large armies on the eastern front when Russian loyalist generals were struggling in vain to make head against the Bolshevik domination, and the main desire of the Bolsheviks themselves was to be free from the German imbroglio.

As the winter advanced to the spring of 1918 it became quite certain that Germany was preparing for the decisive effort. France believed with entire conviction that the storm would burst upon the French armies, and that the imperative necessity was the strengthening of the lines south of the Somme. The fact was palpable that all the Allied offensives had been robbed of effectiveness by the lack of that co-ordination of effort which characterised all the German movements, because all the German operations were directed as parts of a single plan controlled by a single command—just as in the wars between Napoleon and the coalitions. To counteract that disadvantage was an urgent need; France had for some time been calling for a unified command under a French generalissimo. But it was even more essential that the generalissimo should be the right man, a man equal to the enormous task, a man in whom the British chiefs would have confidence—and that man had not yet been found.

When Ludendorff struck, the French and British views of the military situation were not in complete accord, and the British, though calling for reinforcements which did not come, were reluctantly lengthening southward and weakening

GUARDS BRIGADE RUSHED TO THE DEFENCE OF ARRAS, MARCH 26, 1918

Ludendorff's whole scheme of attack in 1918 is known as the second battle of the Somme, or as the battle of St. Quentin, from the sector where the first smashing blow was delivered on March 21. But the Arras-Vimy area was also involved in the assault, and here the defence held firm, largely owing to the heroism of the Guards in the third defence system before Arras. The Second Brigade is here seen moving up the Arras road by motor lorry.

Photo, Imperial War Museum

their line, in order to shorten and strengthen that of the French. Both the French and British commands were more anxious about the strength of their defences southward and northward respectively than about the centre on the Somme. This, however, was precisely the point chosen by Ludendorff for the blow which was to sever the French and British armies.

On March 21, taking example by Byng's spring at Cambrai in November, with no warning preparation by the customary bombardment, the picked

FRENCH DEFENDERS OF AMIENS

Montdidier, a key position protecting Amiens on the south, is here being defended by French and British troops near Nesle, on March 25 occupying hastily dug pits more like the defences of 1914 than of 1918. The town fell on the 28th but further advance was stayed.

Photo, Imperial War Museum

MARSHAL FOCH

Ferdinand Foch (1851–1929) magnificently justified his appointment to the belated post of generalissimo of the Allied forces on the western front in the great crisis of March, 1918. On August 6 he became marshal of France.

Photo, Imperial War Museum

German troops sprang upon the extreme British right. The Germans had saved Cambrai by whirling up huge reinforcements, but there were no reserves, British or French, to whirl up to the British line. The surprise—aided by fog which concealed the German movement—was complete. The British were flung back reeling, fighting desperately, wherever a stand could be made, for a week across the old battlefields, French or British, while the force on their left was compelled to swing back to keep in touch, and the French also, on their right, succeeded in keeping touch ; back to the Ancre line running just in front of Arras and Albert and Amiens.

At more than one point there had been a rift, at still more points the line had been so strung out that it could scarcely have checked a rush ; but the drive was impeded by the devastated country ; it never thrust clean through ; and when the halt in the retreat was called before Amiens, the German attack was vigorously repulsed, though there was another week's hard fighting before it was certain that ıe attempted penetration was held up. he Germans had achieved a striking ıccess—but they had not attained their ɔjective, though the effort was the ggest that had yet been made. Also, ɛfore the fighting was finished, the uch needed generalissimo had been found -on March 25 Foch was appointed to the ıpreme command.

If the British right had been saved after ıe first shattering blow, it was by a rious weakening of the extreme left. A erman thrust to Calais would in fact be ss serious than a break through elsewhere, ıt it was in that quarter that Ludendorff rected his next effort, though on a much naller scale, when the British resistance the centre had been abilised. The attack was ɛlivered in accustomed yle north of La Bassée; ıt though it drove heavily rward the British right ɛld at Givenchy. A great ılge was made in the line, ıt more troops were now ossing the Channel, some rench reinforcements also rived, the Belgians fought anfully, and practically ɔthing more was gained.

By the end of April the ɔspect of another heavy fensive against the British ont had faded; and ıring that month the first eat contingent arrived om America to finish its aining in France. Twelve onths had passed since ıe American declaration war; when the stream ɛgan to flow it was soon velling into a flood; but ıe creation of an army ve times the size of the ritish army at the be-nning of the war, out of civilian population which ıd never been concerned ith so much as the pros-ɛct of a big war except in ıe fratricidal conflict, had ɛen a gigantic task.

Germany then must either acknowledge defeat or attempt to achieve a decisive triumph before that stream became a flood; the crash forward in the last week of March, the recovery in a few days of so much ground which the Allies had only won by months of furious fighting at enormous cost, appealed to the popular imagination—not only in Germany—far more than the fact of its actual failure; and Ludendorff staked everything on a last throw.

It was perhaps almost as much for the reassurance of English public opinion as for its effects upon the German submarine campaign that a British squadron at the end of April achieved the spectacular but

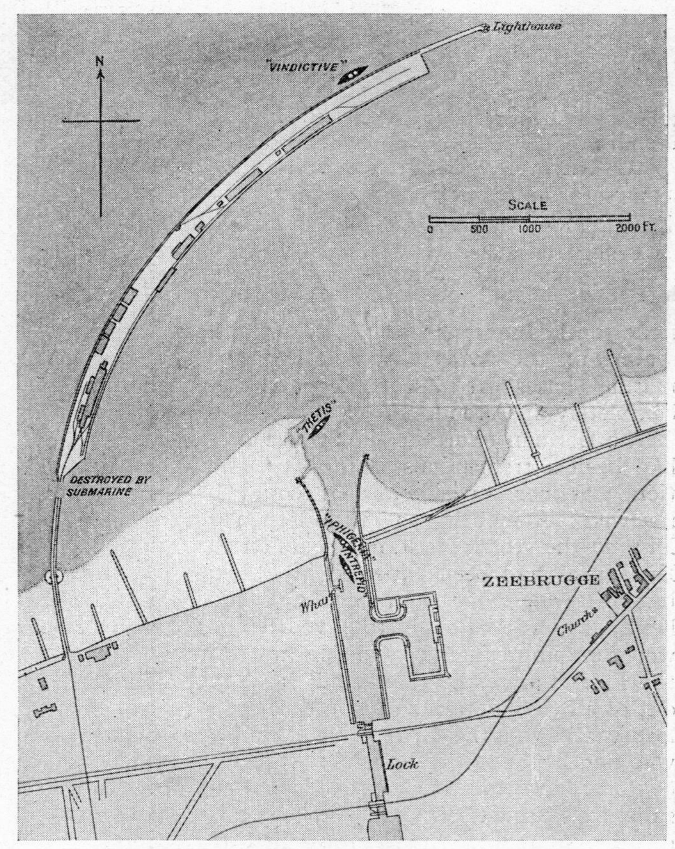

PLAN OF ZEEBRUGGE AFTER THE RAID

Zebrugge had been left intact when evacuated by the British navy in 1914, and formed a submarine base for the Germans. On April 23, 1918, an expedition under Vice-Admiral R. Keyes sealed up the harbour with block ships (see photograph in following page). The light-shaded portion of this plan represents foreshore.

Imperial War Museum

AIR VIEW OF THE BLOCK-SHIPS SUNK ACROSS ZEEBRUGGE HARBOUR

Spectacular in its heroism, the Zeebrugge raid was also successful, both in practical results and i its effect on public 'moral.' While Vindictive, with the ferry boats Daffodil and Iris, covere by Warwick and destroyers, created a diversion by landing a party on the mole (which the explosio of a submarine under a viaduct had isolated from the land), Thetis, Iphigenia and Intrepid crept i The first grounded prematurely, but the two last (seen above) were neatly sunk sealing the harbou

Photo, Imperial War Museum

none the less magnificently heroic feat of sealing up the powerfully defended submarine bases at Zeebrugge and less completely at Ostend.

The German effort in March and April had been a tremendous strain; preparation was necessary before it could be renewed. A month passed, and then on May 27 the storm burst, not again on the British, as had been expected in France, but on the left of the French line, which held positions that ought to have been but were not impregnable. On the first day the French were driven behind the Aisne out of all that Pétain had won during the last year; and the British on their left, who had held their ground, were forced to conform and fall back lest their flank should be turned. On the 30th the head of the German thrust had reached the Marne. Then they set about widening the thrust to right and left. On their left they were held up before Reims; on their right they were successful for a considerable distance to a point where they were again held up—this time by the first section of the American contingent brought into th fighting line.

The Marne 'pocket' between the Ves and the Marne was the way to Paris— to destruction. The weeks passed. Min attacks, which may have been intende only to draw troops elsewhere, came nothing, while they drained Ludendorff resources; and still the Marne flowe between the Germans and Paris. Foch well concealed preparations were comple when the last German onslaught wa launched on July 15 not only in th pocket but on the line to the east Reims. There it failed completely. I the pocket it crossed the Marne; but Foch hour had come. On the 17th Frenc counter-attacks began; on the 18th th German troops in the pocket found them selves fighting to cover retreat.

From that day all the German fightin was in the nature of rearguard actions the line swung back and back until th final catastrophe in November. For the

ere half a million Americans in France
ow with thrice the number to follow,
nd unlimited reserves to swing up to any
oint where they might be wanted; and
e German reserves were exhausted. The
oming of the Americans was the arrival
f Blücher's Prussians on the field of
Vaterloo. They won the war precisely
the sense that Blücher, not Wellington,
as the conqueror of Napoleon.

At this turning-point of the war the
talian campaign had already degenerated
to a merely subsidiary operation for which
itself there was no prospect of Austrian
uccess. The last Austrian offensive on
e Piave in June had failed disastrously;
e 'ramshackle empire' itself was on the
erge of dissolution; and Italian troops
ould even be spared to play a part in
och's operations—a sounder course than
ndeavouring to hasten the Austrian
ollapse by a precarious offensive. On the
talian front, in the Balkans and in Asia
atters continued to be quiescent—that is,
o conspicuous military movement took
lace—until September.

WHEN Foch opened his victory offensive on July 18, its import was guessed by few and its full import was known perhaps only to himself. There was no indication at the moment that he was doing more than successfully repelling an attack that had once more exhausted itself before reaching its objective; as the old drive on Verdun, the two drives into Italy and the recent drive on the centre towards Amiens had been arrested. On that day Mangin delivered an attack west of the Marne pocket that threatened to turn the pocket itself into a trap from which it required no little skill on the part of the Germans to extricate themselves. They did so; in the course of a fortnight the whole salient had been flattened out again, not without heavy losses but without anything verging on a rout at any point. Men were asking not 'What will be Foch's next stroke?' but 'Where will Ludendorff launch the next drive?'

There was no next drive. The French left continued to press the Germans back little by little for a few days; then

GERMANY'S FINAL EFFORT: TROOPS ON THE CAPTURED CHEMIN DES DAMES

hemin des Dames, the road that gives its name to the summit of the Craonne plateau in the heights
the Aisne, for the conquest of which the French shed so much blood throughout the summer of
917, was recaptured by the Germans in their last great 'push' of May, 1918. Here a column of
erman reinforcements is seen moving up the famous road in the early days of June, to their advanced
trenches which by then were over the Aisne and up to the Marne.

Photo, Imperial War Museum

suddenly on August 9 the British right before Amiens sprang forward, towards St. Quentin, its southern flank covered by French troops, against what was perhaps the strongest section of the German line. In a week they had made a material advance, capturing many prisoners and guns. On the 21st the British section on the left of the advance, north of the Ancre, swung forward, while there was no relaxation of the pressure by the British right and the whole French left. Thus the movement continued without pause, the pressure never ceasing along the whole line which had once come into action, but constantly extending to a new sector either on the right or the left. The Germans could never concentrate at any point for a counter-offensive, because to do so would involve weakening at the risk of snapping the line at some other point. By the middle of September the Germans were back on the lines they had held in March, and at points these had been penetrated.

The Americans in action had hither been brigaded with French or Briti troops; now they entered the line as third national army on the right of t French, compelling the retirement of t Germans on the line south of Verd which no French attacks had shak throughout the war. The American capture of the St. Mihiel salient was fo lowed by peace overtures from the oth side, but only of a kind that had possible chance of acceptance from t Allies. The German retreat was no longe as before, a planned withdrawal to stronger defensive line; it was a reti ment all along the line imposed by t enemy, which would not end until they we expelled from French and Belgian soil surrendered.

DURING the two concluding months of t war, while the Germans were bei forced back mile by mile across the deva tated lands, stubbornly contesting eve

AMERICAN TROOPS MARCH BACK AFTER CRUSHING THE ST. MIHIEL SALIENT

Long before the Americans were in the line they had helped to solve the pressing problem of reserve next they fought brigaded with other Allied troops; and finally they took the field independent in the St. Mihiel sector, where they succeeded in capturing the salient on September 12–13, 191 as part of Foch's general scheme of advance. Here a body of them is seen passing through t French village of Nonsard, flags flying, on return from the victory.

Photo, Imperial War Museum

FOUR YEARS AFTERWARDS: MONS RECAPTURED BY THE CANADIANS

The Belgian town where the British troops first saw action in 1914 was also the farthest advanced point occupied by them in the pursuit of 1918 when the Armistice came into force at 11 o'clock on the eleventh day of the eleventh month. On the 10th the Canadian Division had reached Mons, which was fairly strongly held, but an enveloping movement followed by an attack from two sides ensured its fall, and on the following morning they entered behind the pipes of the Canadian Scottish.

Photo, Imperial War Museum

step, their allies in every quarter were crumpling up. Even the Bolsheviks found a new enemy in the host of Czecho-Slovaks who had fought reluctantly in the Austrian ranks, had become Russian prisoners of war by thousands in the numerous Austrian defeats, and had then enthusiastically taken up arms on the side of their captors for the overthrow of the Austrian tyrant. They had held fast to their new loyalty (rooted in their immemorial hostility to the Teuton) when the Bolshevised Russian troops mutinied and fled, and now they attached themselves to the independent loyalist government which was seeking to establish itself in Siberia. They did not in fact crumple up the Bolsheviks—who were a useful bulwark to the Germans but not their official allies—but did add to their difficulties.

The Balkans went first. Since the abdication of King Constantine Greece had been unequivocally Venizelist. Nevertheless, no effective moves had been made until on September 15 the Serbs and the French, supported on their right by the British, launched their attack on the Bulgars. No effective help

LILLE AT LAST RESTORED TO FRANCE

It was a blow to France when Lille, the manufacturing centre, fell in the early days of the war. The town was recaptured on October 18 (this photograph shows the arrival of President Poincaré, welcomed by General Birdwood), but its prosperity had been temporarily ruined by destruction of factory plant.

Photo, Imperial War Museum

came from the Austrians. The Bulgar defences were pierced, their whole front collapsed, and on the 30th the French commander was able to dictate an armistice on his own terms. Bulgaria being lost, the Austrian hold on the Balkans was lost. The Turks were left alone.

The Turks were not yet gone, but they were going ; Allenby in southern Palestine had bided his time to deal an absolutely decisive blow. By a surprise attack consummately planned and consummately carried out he practically annihilated the entire Turkish force in Palestine in the three days' fighting (September 19 to 21) comprehensively known as the battle of Megiddo, and proceeded to the conquest of Syria. Damascus fell on the 30th, then Beirut, and then Aleppo (October 26). Meanwhile the Mesopotamian army had been pushed up the Tigris ; and after a battle which lasted for a week the Turkish army on the Tigris surrendered and an armistice was signed (October 30) which put the Allies in possession of the Dardanelles and the Bosporus.

Austria remained. She had been hustled out of the Balkan peninsula, the South Slavs were joining Serbia, the Czecho-Slavs were threatening her, Hungary was exhausted ; but through September and for three weeks of October the Italian front was stationary. If Italy was to reap, across the Adriatic, any of the coveted fruits of the imminent Austrian collapse she must precipitate it by her own action. Italians and British opened the attack on October 23, Italians and French almost simultaneously, and on the 27th the Austrians were in flight. On November 3 they signed an armistice dictated by the Italian commander. Germany stood absolutely alone, and she was fast in the toils.

WHERE THE ARMISTICE WAS SIGNED

The clearing in the forest of Compiègne where the trains bearing Marshal Foch and the German plenipotentiaries met to sign the Armistice was long marked by this simple notice, only replaced by permanent memorials in 1922.

Final Operations of the War

THE advance of the Allied line had been continuous. The Germans had exhausted their reserves in the last offensive at the moment when the available forces of the Allies were doubled. The British had penetrated the Drocourt-Quéant line early in September ; at the end of the month they were through the Hindenburg line, the Belgians were in Dixmude, and the French were on the point of entering St Quentin. By the middle of October the whole German line farther south had been pushed back on the Meuse by the northward thrust of the Americans and over the Aisne by the French, and Cambrai had fallen to the British with American support. In the northernmost sector the attack of Belgians, French and British compelled the abandonment of the Belgian coast, and the evacuation of Lille and Douai on the 17th.

Ludendorff's resignation on October 26 was significant. In the first week of November the American push northward down the Meuse was greatly accelerated ; on the 7th they were in Sedan. The French were pressing hard on the centre ; on the left the British captured Valenciennes on the 2nd and then drove forward in the decisive battle of the Sambre. On the 9th they were over the Scheldt. The fleet at Kiel was in mutiny, revolution was breaking out in Berlin, the Kaiser was safe on neutral territory, and a socialist provisional government was set up. In the early morning of November 11 the Canadians broke into Mons as the Germans were submitting to the crushing armistice terms dictated by the Allies. The last shot had been fired. In the military sense, the Great War was ended.

CHAPTER 178

SCIENCE AND WAR

Has War advanced Scientific Progress and will Science increase or lessen the Horrors of War?

By Maj.-Gen. SIR GEORGE ASTON K.C.B.

Lecturer on Naval History, University College, London; Author of Sea, Land and Air Strategy, War Lessons New and Old, etc.

THE mutual reaction between science and war is of considerable importance to the human race, but before such a subject can be approached it is necessary first to decide whether war itself is a 'science' or an 'art,' because these terms have both been applied almost indiscriminately by writers on warfare. Clausewitz, in trying to solve this problem of nomenclature, maintained that it was impossible to classify war either amongst the arts or amongst the sciences. He held that it belonged rather to the province of social life, being a conflict of great interests settled by bloodshed, and differing only in that respect from other forms of human activity that come within the social province.

'It would be better,' he wrote, 'instead of comparing war with any art, to liken it to business competition, which is also a conflict between human interests and activities; and it is still more like state policy, which again, on its part, may be looked upon as a kind of business competition on a great scale. Besides, state policy is the womb in which war is developed, in which its outlines lie hidden in a rudimentary state, as the qualities of living creatures do in their germs.' We cannot do better than to accept these views, which carry conviction, as our starting point in approaching the subject. Let us therefore treat the relationship between science and war on the assumption that war is a form of activity, in social life, that harnesses all sciences, and all the arts, to its chariot.

The general question of the effect of war upon the progress of the human race was dealt with from the historical point of view by Lord Bryce, who furnished a reply to Bernhardi and other German 'militarist' writers in his War and Human Progress, published in his collection of Essays and Addresses in War Time. Its connexion with what is generally known amongst us as 'art,' and the question whether art has been stimulated during periods of warfare, is dealt with in Ruskin's writings, to which no adequate rejoinder has hitherto been forthcoming. There remains, however, the question whether an impetus has been given by war, especially in modern times, to the progress of scientific discovery and to industries which are thereby affected. It would also be well for us to determine whether warfare of the future is likely to acquire more menacing aspects with the aid of applied science. A wealth of evidence, derived from modern experience, enables us to base certain conclusions upon lessons taught by history.

General effect of War on Progress

The progress of scientific discovery has been influenced, in one direction or the other, by several factors that result from warfare. It can, for instance, be said that brilliant scientists, while engaged in important research work, have been killed in action or have died of wounds or disease as the result of war; and that this cause has retarded scientific progress. On the other hand, we are told that such losses have been few in number, and that those who have thus been lost to science have soon been replaced by others. Then, again, it is a constant complaint among scientists that research work lacks a sufficiency of financial support in time of peace, while in time of war it is financed lavishly by governments of belligerent countries. In France especially — the example having been set by Napoleon—the point has been grasped that better use can be found for scientists in time of war than to employ them as food for powder, and the same can be said of other countries.

One of the most important incentives to scientific progress, especially in connexion with industries, has been the isolation of certain nations from their neighbours during war periods. This isolation has sometimes compelled scientists to devise expedients to enable them to dispense with the raw materials generally in use for productive processes; as, for instance, those needed to produce chemicals on a commercial basis. The alkali industry of France (see page 4136) is an outstanding example. Others that are germane to the point could be quoted from the experiences in 1914–18 of the Continental powers that were cut off, by sea blockade, from their usual access to foreign materials, and compelled to discover 'substitutes' for certain normal products that are looked upon as necessaries under present-day conditions of industry and agriculture. Several products of nitrogen come within this category, and rapid progress in the extraction of nitrogen from the air resulted from war conditions. In earlier periods we can take note of the impetus given by the discovery of various explosives, having their origin in war, to many great industries; and in more modern times, if we consider industries in general, we can cite Japan to prove the influence of war upon the spread of science, and upon the rate of progress in industries and in manufactures dependent thereon.

Incentive force of isolation

Here, referring for guidance to the publications brought out under the auspices of the Carnegie Endowment for International Peace, we come across various volumes, by learned Japanese in responsible positions, demonstrating in detail the extent to which industrial progress in Japan has resulted almost entirely from participation in warfare. One of these authorities (Uspisaburo) tells us that 'industries in Japan are mostly either the direct or the indirect product of military industry,' and 'that is not all. The advancement of science and arts, the diffusion of education . . . in these matters also the military industry in Japan has been an important factor.' It should, however, be remarked that, according to the same Japanese authority, military industries have now ceased to advance industrial progress in Japan. The writer based the opinions just quoted principally upon events up to the year 1905, which marked the conclusion of the Japanese war with tsarist Russia, and not to the same extent upon later events like the Great War of 1914–18, to which we will now revert.

In 1914 the science of human flight or aeronautics was in its infancy, and progress therein had been very slow during the preceding years. The rapid progress that followed was the direct result of war experience. War requirements produced machines specially adapted to such purposes, but since those days there have been rapid developments in civil aviation. Progress in such machines and in the achievements of their pilots is constantly being reported, and it may be said, without fear of exaggeration, that aviation, as we know it, had its origin in warfare. This is the most spectacular, though possibly not the most important example of the impetus that has been given by war to scientific discovery. When studying the figures that follow, it is necessary to bear in mind that individual types of aircraft, like classes of warships and merchant vessels, represent compromises in design, varying with the functions that they are to perform. The qualities described have not all been combined in any individual type of machine. Abnormal development of one attribute entails the sacrifice of others.

Development of Aviation

Taking lighter-than-air machines first, we find that dirigible airships, which in 1914 could lift weights of about 8,000 lb. in addition to their crews, in 1926 could lift 40 tons net (80 tons gross) into the air. The cruising period spent in the air rose from 30 to 78 hours; the speed from 3[illegible] to 76 miles an hour; the distance travelled in the air without alighting from 960 to considerably over 5,000 miles; and so on. Owing to their vulnerability it may be said

War stimulus brought about the development of airships shown in this page. Top: Non-rigid dirigibles, popularly termed 'blimps,' were used by the British Admiralty for scouting from the beginning of the Great War; the S.S. Zero class, evolved in 1917, weighed 4,500 lb. with crew and equipment. By the end of the war the rigid airship (centre, the R33, with loaded weight of about 59 tons and length of about 640 feet) had been evolved from the German Zeppelin type, of which two specimens surrendered to the British are seen in a hangar at the bottom.

PROGRESS IN AIRSHIP CONSTRUCTION SINCE THE BEGINNING OF THE WAR

Photos: Top, Royal Air Force, Crown copyright reserved; others, courtesy of 'Flight'

The B.E.2C was designed at the Royal Aircraft Establishment, Farnborough, and built in large numbers by private firms during the war. These machines carried pilot and observer, and later were used for offensive purposes, when they carried small bombs.

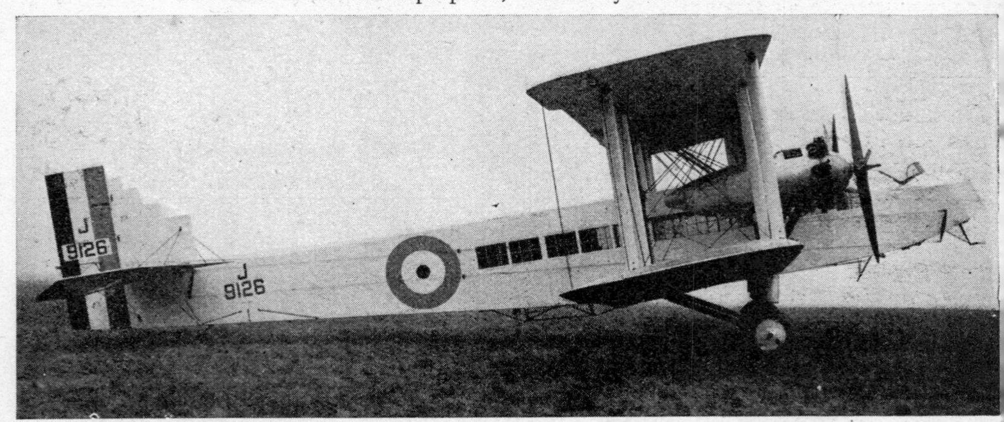

The post-war Handley Page Clive, with two Bristol Jupiter engines, is a troop carrier capable of transporting twenty-three men with full equipment. The total loaded weight is 14,500 lb.

Possessing three Armstrong Siddeley Jaguar engines of 400 h.p. each, the Armstrong Whitworth Argosy air liner of Imperial Airways, Ltd., will seat 18 persons. Unlike the two examples which appear above it, the primary purpose of this model is to serve the needs of peace. The accelerated development of aircraft from the war models at the top of the page to the large passenger-carrying aeroplane of 1928, with its unfailing regularity of service, was mainly due to war-time experience.

BRITISH FLYING MACHINES OF WAR AND PEACE

Photos, courtesy of 'Flight'

that lighter-than-air developed less rapidly than heavier-than-air machines (aeroplanes, seaplanes and flying boats) as the result of war conditions. In 1914 aeroplanes lifted about 1,500 lb. in addition to the pilot; in 1926 they had lifted over 13,000 lb., and seaplanes about 4,400 lb. The time spent by an aeroplane in the air went up between the same dates from a maximum of 16 hours to over 48 hours, the corresponding figures for seaplanes being $4\frac{1}{2}$ hours and $28\frac{1}{2}$ hours. The maximum speed attained by aeroplanes rose from 112 miles an hour to 278 miles an hour, and by seaplanes from 80 to 246 miles an hour. The distance covered by aeroplanes without alighting rose from 1,050 miles to nearly 3,000 miles, and by seaplanes from 240 to nearly 1,000 miles. The vertical climbing speed of

As used in 1917, the F.5 type of flying boats had a loaded weight of 12,268 lb. The one here illustrated is a later model, with duralumin hull, but otherwise only differs in details.

Photo, Royal Air Force, Crown copyright reserved

The great progress made in seaplane construction is illustrated by a comparison of this British flying boat with the earlier one above it. A masterpiece of design and construction, the Blackburn Iris II class possesses three Rolls-Royce Condor engines of 650 h.p. each, and has a total loaded weight of 27,000 lb. Equally at home on sea or in the air, no limit can be set to the potential utility of this type of aircraft, whether for military or for peaceful and commercial purposes.

RAPID DEVELOPMENT OF THE FLYING BOAT SINCE 1917

Photo, courtesy of 'Flight'

TRIUMPH OVER DIFFICULTIES

At the Queen Mary Auxiliary Hospital at Roehampton, devoted exclusively to men who had lost a limb, artificial limbs of astonishing ingenuity were invented. This man is giving an exhibition of running with an artificial leg.

Photo, Record Press

heavier-than-air craft also rose in due proportion, and the maximum height attained above the earth's surface, which in 1914 was 19,600 feet for aeroplanes, had reached in 1926 nearly 41,000 feet for aeroplanes and nearly 30,000 for seaplanes.

These few statistics suffice to indicate the great advances, having their origin in war needs, that were made in the science of aeronautics up to 1926. Civil needs have since caused much further progress. Similar conditions apply to submarine navigation. There, too, we find scientific progress accelerated in response to the war stimulus; and we must also take account of the impetus thereby given indirectly to other branches of science, as, for instance, to acoustics. The need to detect the approach of aircraft and of submarines, and also to judge the direction and distance of hostile guns or submarine explosions by sound-ranging, led to great advances being made in that science. Professor A. O. Rankine has written that 'the increase in our knowledge of the subject of acoustics during recent years has been largely associated with war conditions which prevailed from 1914 to 1918. As a consequence of the war the development of this science has been abnormal.' He proceeds to indicate the effect of this development, and Vice-Admiral Sir John Parry, hydrographer to the navy in the Great War, further explores the subject and shows how, when the war was over, inventions that had been utilised during its progress were turned to purposes of peace, more especially to deep-sea sounding.

It is difficult to estimate the extent to which war conditions accelerated progress in wireless telegraphy and telephony, though there is little doubt that expenditure on research and practical experience in the field has been one influence, not to be ignored, upon discoveries in this as in other sciences. It is at least certain that during the war years vast experience was gained in the practical uses of wireless telegraphy that could not have been gained under such varied conditions in normal times (compare page 4836). We can also attribute much of the rapid progress in wireless telephony, and in direction-finding, to the stimulus of war needs; the effect of these upon broadcasting and upon the safety of air and ocean travel needs no further emphasis. During the Great War experiments were made with a sound-reflector for listening to different types of aeroplane and submarine by means of a microphone placed at the centre of a concave mirror.

Orthopaedics and Plastic Surgery

In the realm of surgery we have the authority of Sir Robert Jones, president of the Association of Surgeons of Great Britain, for an estimation of the influence of war experience upon orthopaedic methods. The treatment of fractures during the early part of the war was attended not only by unnecessary deformity, but also by a high mortality. In compound fractures of the femur an initial mortality of 80 per cent. was ultimately reduced to 25 per cent. Knowledge gained has formed the basis of efforts to place the tending of fractures upon a different basis with a view to minimising the disabilities of industrial accidents.

The war supplied exceptional opportunities of acquiring an improved technique in certain reconstructive operations that have an important bearing upon civil surgery. Among these stand prominently the treatment of injuries to certain nerves, the transplanting of tendons, bone grafting and the treatment of bone infections. Experience with a vast number of complete nerve lacerations enabled a finished operative technique to be built up, largely wanting before the war; and many misconceptions were corrected. A whole new science of plastic surgery was elaborated. In the treatment of cripples, again, a notable advance followed war experience; and a further instance can be given in the evolution, under war influence, of the artificial-light treatment for tuberculosis of bones and joints and for rickets. The thought naturally occurs that the correction of misconceptions in remedial treatment has been dearly bought at the cost of millions of dead and tens of millions of disabled, unless the assumption can be made that the older remedies tended rather to kill than to cure.

To our first question, whether an impetus has been given by warfare—especially in modern times—to the progress of scientific discovery, and to industries that are thereby affected, the reply is therefore clearly an affirmative. If we had delved more deeply into the records of the past we should have discovered the extent to which machinery and the use of metals for supplying so many of our needs can trace their origin to the days when men first learned the superiority of metals over other materials for the making of weapons and armour. In more recent times we have taken note of a few discoveries in chemistry and in physical science, selected from a large number, that have been hastened by war, even if they did not owe their initiation altogether to that incentive. Whether or not the human race would have been benefited if these discoveries had come about more peacefully, and had thus been somewhat delayed, is a different question. Experts hesitate to pronounce an opinion; but some leading scientists maintain that their own sympathies would have favoured a more peaceful, though slower, development of scientific discovery.

War stimulates inventiveness

War, we have found, has speeded up movement on the surface of the earth and sea, and progress in the sciences of flight and of submarine navigation has been accelerated in response to the war stimulus. Not only in movement, but in other matters—such as communication by wireless, chemistry, physics and industries dependent thereon, as well as in the art of the physician and surgeon—we find that war, through the stimulus of fear or of stern necessity, has speeded up the progress of human achievements. Skill in all such matters can become either a blessing or a curse to mankind, according to the purposes to which it is applied. All that the scientist with prophetic vision can tell us about the future has been summed up briefly: 'Leagues of peace will have more arguments, and generals will have more weapons.'

Post-war use of war-taught skill

Mention has already been made of the argument, employed by some scientists, that one reason why warfare stimulates scientific discovery is that it stimulates governments to provide resources for research, and that it thus promotes the material well-being of mankind. Here Lord Balfour's remarks, in his introduction to the report of a research sub-committee of the British Empire Conference of 1926, are significant:

> The material well-being of mankind may be diminished by many causes—e.g. international wars, domestic disorder, industrial disorder, industrial disputes—but . . . there are only two causes that can increase it, namely, better natural sources of supply and better methods of turning these sources to account.

He adds that we must rely in an increasing degree upon the second of these causes, and that we must turn for aid to applied science. If that advice is followed by 'leagues of peace,' it will mean better endowment of research without the war impulse, and therefore more rapid progress in scientific discovery in time of peace. The argument that the human race can benefit by war through the progress in the sciences derived therefrom would then lose all weight, and 'international wars, domestic disorders and industrial disputes' might be recognized as reducing, but never increasing, the material well-being of mankind.

Meanwhile, realizing how long it takes for reason to prevail in international politics, it will be well to turn to the other branch of our subject, to the question whether wars in the future, with the aid of applied science, are likely to acquire more menacing aspects.

The purely logical view of warfare is that maintained by Clausewitz. War being an act of violence, the surest road to victory is to place no bounds upon the violence employed. His doctrine was embodied in the war book that was in force in Germany in 1914, in the words:

> By the means of conducting war is to be understood all those measures which can be taken by one state against another in order to attain the object of the war, to compel one's opponent to submit to one's will; they may be summarised in the two ideas of violence and cunning.

The argument has been freely used that the greater the violence, and the more deadly the weapons employed, the shorter the war and, therefore, in the long run, the more merciful.

Little evidence in support of this theory can be derived from the war of 1914–1918, a struggle that caused a holocaust of protracted horror and widespread sacrifice, only brought to a conclusion by a process of exhaustion involving whole nations, both victors and vanquished, and causing an aftermath of suffering, distress and economic unsettlement. This leads us to the argument, now frequently advanced, that, while nations in the early stages of past wars have used their fighting forces to defeat those of their enemies, the ultimate object has always been to obtain advantageous terms by compelling a hostile nation to concede some point in dispute; and that scientists may devise methods of achieving this ultimate object by direct action against the non-combatant population, especially when concentrated in industrial areas.

Since we cannot foretell with any certainty the date of the 'next war,' or the trend, in the meanwhile, of scientific discovery, it is impossible to predict the nature of the weapons which nations will employ against each other. Speculation is rife on this subject, especially about the prospects of explosives and harmful gases being used by airmen, not only against combatant forces, but also against

EARLIEST RESPIRATOR USED AS PROTECTION AGAINST POISON GAS

As first devised after the German surprise use of chlorine at Ypres in May, 1915, the gas mask consisted of a flannel bag fitted with mica goggles, and large enough to envelop the head and be tucked in round the neck under the tunic. The flannel was treated with a solution of sodium carbonate, which combines with free chlorine and purifies the air passing through. This was the first photograph taken of British troops equipped with this form of respirator. Its life as a gas neutraliser was limited.

Photo, Central News

EARLY GAS ATTACK: A CLOUD WIND-BORNE TOWARDS 'PLUGSTREET' WOOD

Chlorine gas—the first poison gas used in the Great War—was stored under pressure in cylinders in the trenches and discharged as a cloud against the enemy, the wind carrying the cloud along. Later, phosgene was employed in the same way, and was also used as a shell charge. Chlorosulphuric acid was used to some extent in smoke pots, and was sometimes mistaken for a defensive smoke screen. Gas-cloud discharges largely depended for their efficiency on meteorological conditions.

Photo, Imperial War Museum

a non-combatant population, and we are at once faced with the question of the extent to which international covenants and agreements are likely to act as a deterrent. Here we are reminded that at The Hague in 1907 the leading belligerent powers of 1914 agreed not to employ projectiles of which the sole object was to diffuse asphyxiating or harmful gases, and also forbade the bombardment of defenceless towns by any means whatsoever.

The extent to which these covenants were looked upon as binding by the belligerents is now a matter of history. When war broke out no nation embarked upon the contest with the intention of breaking these engagements, and no nation had prepared for 'chemical warfare,' either in attack or in defence. It was not until the definite failure of the original German offensive of 1914, upon which such high hopes had been built, that a serious attempt was made to obtain a victory by using gas, projected from cylinders on the ground, although gas shell containing an irritant substance were used ineffectively (at Neuve Chapelle) as early as October, 1914. Chlorine gas, discharged from cylinders, was used on a large scale by the Germans at Ypres in April, 1915. In the spring of 1916 the French retaliated by using shell containing phosgene in the defence of Verdun. In April, 1917, the British used shell containing lachrymatory substances in an attack in the Arras area. In July of the same year the Germans introduced mustard gas, an insidious agent that remains in the form of a liquid at low temperatures. From 1917 onwards, owing to increased supplies, gas became a serious factor.

Mustard gas was responsible for most of the gas casualties in the war. It can remain on the ground as a liquid, giving off, for a long time, vapour with a slight smell producing no immediate effects to indicate its dangerous nature, while contact with the liquid itself produces painful and slow-healing burns. Experience proved that a persistent gas of this nature, in sufficient concentration, could compel troops to evacuate an area which they wished to occupy. The eyes and lungs can be protected by respirators, but these must be removed to eat or drink, and protection of the skin from such harmful substances as mustard gas in its liquid form offers a difficult problem. Protective clothing is less efficient than respirators, and forms a great handicap to movement.

The general situation affecting gas warfare is that, in spite of international covenants, it is a matter of common knowledge that the leading nations are conducting experiments both in chemical substances for use therein and in protective measures. A leading British expert (Brigadier-General Sir H. Hartley) tells us that it is difficult to compare the effect upon moral of gas with that of other weapons, but that it is unquestionable that the ill-understood danger, the constant strain of watchfulness, the fear of new gases with more painful properties

CASUALTIES FROM MUSTARD GAS ON THEIR WAY TO THE DRESSING STATION: A FAMOUS WAR PICTURE

Mustard gas was first used by the Germans in July, 1917, and caused terrible suffering among the British troops, for whom no protection had yet been devised against that particularly insidious and persistent danger. Sargent's picture, Gassed, represents the plank road between Doullens and Arras in August, 1918, with files of men temporarily blinded by mustard gas being led by a hospital orderly to the dressing station at Le Bac-du-Sud, outside which hundreds of their comrades, already attended to, are waiting in distress and exhaustion to be sent back from the front line.

Photo, Imperial War Museum

and the feeling of confinement when wearing a respirator must tend to weaken the spirit of a force, especially of one with little experience of gas.

Like all weapons gas has its limitations, and these are often not sufficiently realized. For every gas there is a minimum effective concentration. Lachrymatory (tear gas) vapours blind the eyes in a few seconds where present in the proportion of one part to from two to five million parts of air. Phosgene causes a gas casualty after exposure of from one to two minutes to a concentration of one part to fifty thousand. Mustard gas causes eye or lung casualties after exposure for an hour to a concentration in the proportion of one part to a million of air, and so on. Although this seems very deadly, an immense quantity of gas is needed to produce even these concentrations over a large area, even very temporarily. A rough calculation has been made that, with a non-persistent gas like phosgene, 800 tons would have to be dropped on Paris to produce a lethal atmosphere, and even then if a wind were blowing, the gas would be quickly dispersed. Another estimate with persistent gas, puts the amount to contaminate a square mile effectively at 25 tons weight of mustard gas.

The speed of the wind and the state of the atmosphere greatly affect the concentration obtained from a given amount of gas, and no other weapon is influenced to the same extent by weather conditions. With a wind blowing at over twelve miles an hour gas disperses so quickly that even with persistent types there would be a great decrease in efficiency. There must therefore be much uncertainty about its employment, and meteorological forecasts will play an important part. General Hartley thus summarises the situation :

MASKED MACHINE GUNNERS IN ACTION

To counteract the effects of phosgene gas the British troops were supplied with improved gas helmets impregnated with sodium thiosulphate and sodium phenate ; a valve through which the exhaled air escaped eased the discomfort of wearing them for long periods. This photograph was taken in July, 1916, near Ovillers.

Photo, Imperial War Museum

> There is no lack of prophets and on the whole the experts, who realize more clearly the difficulties and limitations involved, and from their familiarity perhaps pay too little heed to the influence of gas on moral, make more modest claims than other writers who contend that gas will be the most powerful weapon of the future. Used at the right place and at the right moment, and in adequate amount, it offers brilliant possibilities, but theoretical victories might well be won with other weapons on the same assumption.

We find here an important reference to the difference of mental attitude between the experts and the ignorant, and our investigation of the question whether the wars of the future will be more menacing than the wars of the past leads us into difficult problems of human psychology. Experts in chemical warfare are few, the ignorant are many, and it is upon the moral of vast masses of them that success in a great war must ultimately depend. Rumour has a more important influence than reality has upon war psychology. It will be realized that the experiences quoted above were all based upon the effect produced upon disciplined troops, with whom it was not difficult to ensure the adoption of defensive measures against the effect of gas ; also that, under the conditions attendant upon the trench warfare of 1915–18, the troops were occupying the same areas for long periods. Such conditions were ideal for effective gas warfare. It may be that, in future wars, the issues will be determined by armies rendered more mobile by mechanisation, but here again we must avoid speculation on insufficient evidence.

TYPE OF GAS HELMET USED IN 1918

In the box-type respirator the mask is connected by a flexible tube to a box suspended over the breast, and containing layers of absorbent charcoal and pumice impregnated with sodium carbonate and hexamethylenetetramine.

Photo, Imperial War Museum

Even mechanised armies will, however, depend for continuous movement, as ships do, upon supplies of fuel and upon facilities for maintenance and repair. Bases or depots containing these requirements will be stationary targets, open to gas attack from the air if considered more effective than similar attack by high explosives. Such depots are usually situated at railway centres, which are generally surrounded by densely populated industrial areas. It is clear that such military objectives as fuel dumps and repairing shops, upon which mechanised armies are dependent for movement, would be legitimate objects for attack from the air by bombs containing high explosives or incendiary compounds and, owing to the greater permanence that can be claimed for the effect of persistent forms of gas, there might be a strong temptation to employ them for the same purpose. If such a policy were to be adopted, the wars of the future would certainly assume a more menacing aspect for the population, including women and children, of such areas. Similar conditions apply to the neighbourhood of naval bases on the sea coast, and of aerodromes.

In such circumstances it is not possible to improvise hastily any adequate measures for gas defence. Education, as scientists maintain, is the best means of allaying panic and mystery, but it has been proved that education in itself does not suffice. Discipline is required, and also food and effective organization, before protective measures can achieve their purposes of avoiding casualties, allaying panic and preserving moral. The difficulties in organizing and applying disciplinary measures to a crowded industrial population are notorious, and they vary in degree with national and racial characteristics.

Wide distribution of munition works

So far our argument has touched only the fighting forces and the civilian population residing in the immediate neighbourhood of their bases and magazines. There remain the factories for producing the vast amount of technical equipment demanded by modern fleets, armies and air forces. In pre-war days an inquiry was conducted into the extent to which the destruction of various commercial establishments and factories, large and small, and devastation by fire or by enemy action in different industrial areas would affect the efficiency of the fighting forces. The results were startling. Nearly all industrial towns were found to be honeycombed with objectives of military importance, in that they produced some form of technical equipment, or parts thereof, that could fairly be classified as war material. Examples were discovered of the concentration in one locality of the manufacture of some particular and essential appliance; others of the distribution all over the country of plant for the construction of various parts of weapons, war machines, ships or engines before they could be assembled in the usual well known centres. The movement of much material from one place to another was involved, and communications between different localities assumed a dominating importance on account of their value to the fighting forces; in addition to their function of meeting the needs of the population.

Future menace to civilian population

It is not possible to generalise about the future of warfare, as affecting the civilian population, because each nation has its own problem, depending upon its geographical situation; upon the distribution of industrial areas and upon their distances from the frontiers of potentially hostile nations, varying widely in different countries. Where these areas, or the capital cities and centres of government are within reach of intensive air attack or of artillery bombardment, now greatly extended in range, it is clear that, for reasons given, the wars of the future are likely to assume more menacing aspects for the civilian population, be they men, women or children, residing in such areas.

For such nations the days have passed when the bulk of the people could pursue their normal avocations unmolested, while fleets or armies, or both, decided the issue at stake by what may be described as gladiatorial combats on behalf of the nations concerned; though these conditions do not apply to the same extent to countries that are more sparsely populated. Conditions of strategy and of combat between the fighting forces themselves will be strongly affected in future wars by the advance of scientific discovery which has placed at their disposal aircraft, wireless communications, mechanised movement and lethal gases, and other new features and weapons dealt with more fully in the following chapter.

CHAPTER 179

THE NEW ELEMENTS IN WARFARE

Evolution in Tactics Strategy and Weapons produced by the Experiences of the Great War

By COLONEL J. F. C. FULLER D.S.O.

Author of Tanks in the Great War, etc.

BETWEEN the years 1871 and 1914 warfare was to a great extent looked upon by soldier and politician as a condition separated from the normal activities of peace, as something apart from civil and industrial life, as a necessary evil or as a useful means of enforcing policy. During these forty-three years the weapons and equipment of armies were completely changed. The introduction of smokeless powder, the magazine rifle, the machine gun and quick-firing artillery radically modified tactics. Yet the soldier, in place of examining these modifications, put his trust in numbers. Wars were to be won by hordes of men, hordes which when once set in motion would sweep all before them.

It is realized to-day that this outlook was fallacious, and to it may be traced most of the blunders of the Great War, as well as much of its cost, its destructiveness and the embitterments it engendered. The soldier of 1913 considered that the next war would be mobile and rapid; yet M. Bloch, a Polish banker, had predicted in 1897 that everyone would be entrenched in the next war, and that the spade would be as indispensable as the rifle. The block-house lines of the South African War and the entrenched and wired battle fronts of the war in Manchuria supported M. Bloch's contentions; but soldiers took not the slightest notice of these warnings, and so it happened that they plunged into the Great War mentally blindfolded.

The opening campaigns of the war, notably those of the Marne and of Tannenberg, shattered all faith in the strategical and tactical shibboleths of forty-three years. The Germans, leaving only a small force on the Vistula, assembled an enormous horde of seven armies along the Rhine. The whole formation may be compared to the phalanx of ancient Greek and Oriental warfare, for there were no reserves behind it; the troops composing it, so it was considered, were sufficiently numerous to make good their own losses. Once this ponderous machine was set in motion, its right wing, working on a scheduled time-table, was to march through Belgium, circle round Paris, attack the French armies in rear and sweep them into the arms of the left wing, which was to advance over the Franco-German frontier. The main French forces were assembled between the Meuse and the Vosges; they also were to advance in mass, all armies, except one in reserve, attacking simultaneously. By this means it was hoped to blast a huge hole in the German fighting front.

Collapse of pre-war Tactics

Both plans broke down. The French at once discovered that the resistance which could be exerted by modern firearms in defence more than outbalanced their pressure in attack. They could not advance as they had expected, and, as the Germans were pushing rapidly through Belgium, General Joffre drew in his right wing and assembled a new army north of Paris. If all had been well with the German phalanx, this little army—General Maunoury's—must have been swept up by the encircling right wing like a shrimp in a net; but though outwardly all looked well, inwardly a dry rot had set in. Casualties had forced contraction towards the centre, as they normally do. This contraction pulled the German right wing inwards, and forced it to pass on the east instead of the west of Paris.

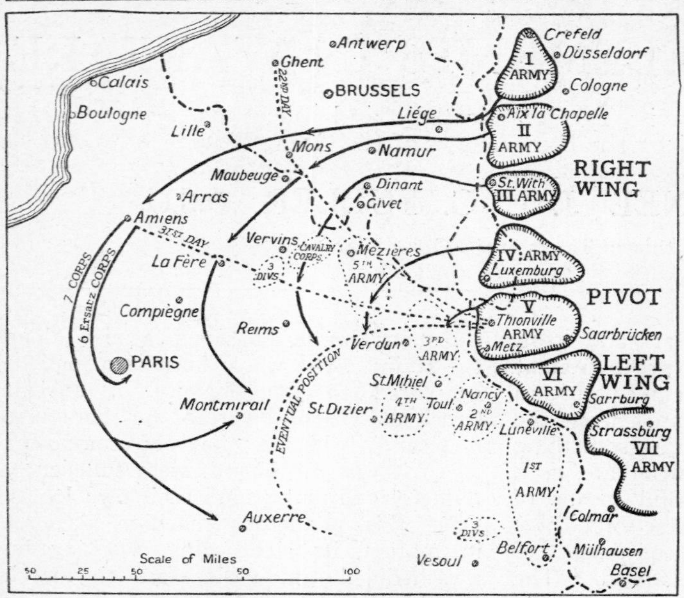

GERMAN STRATEGY THAT FAILED

The German campaign plan of 1914 is schematised in this map. Four armies were to wheel through Belgium and Luxemburg, lightly defended because of their guaranteed neutrality, encircle Paris, and drive the French armies (shown in dotted outline), massed on the Mezières-Belfort frontier, on to the front of the remaining three.

Meanwhile, thousands of men were being daily sent by rail to General Maunoury, who, from September 5 to 10, caught the German right in enfilade. To meet this blow required a reserve army, but the Germans possessed no reserves, and to stop the phalanx was most difficult—it was like attempting to stop an avalanche from rushing into the wrong valley. The German higher command now completely broke down; control was lost while the French and British advanced to the attack, and won a decisive strategical victory, but not a tactical one.

Simultaneously in the east another campaign was being fought. Two great hordes of Russians, under Generals Rennenkampf and Samsonov, were advancing in East Prussia, the first from the east and the second from the south-east. Before they could join hands the Germans concentrated their forces against Samsonov's army, and all but annihilated it on the field of Tannenberg. It was a great tactical victory, but not a strategical one, for Rennenkampf, though defeated when the Germans turned on him, slipped back, and winter anc lack of communications stopped a sustained pursuit.

To return to the westerı front. The battle of the Marne was followed by the battle of the Aisne in which trenches begaı freely to appear. Thougł hastily dug, these trenche generally defeated aı attack, and, if they were wired, to carry them by assault demanded no only an enormous sacri fice of life but the strongest possible artillery support. Then what ha been called the race for the coast began.

Tactically, it was no so much a race as th desire to seek an un entrenched flank, since to attack a trenched fron was an all but impossibl operation. Both sides began feeling rounc each other's exposed wing; directly they came into contact they dug trenches, and as both advanced at about the same pace trenches rapidly wriggled forward from the south towards the north until the last spadefuls of earth were cast into the North Sea. Then all movemen halted, and the 'rigor mortis' of pre war tactics set in; it was the death o a military epoch—the modern infantry cycle of war.

Old Tactic break dow

During the first four months of the war the tactical doctrines, largely derivec from the Napoleonic wars and the Franco Prussian War of 1870, were put to the test They broke down, and with them strategy hence the long duration of the struggle The main reasons for this may be tracec to two definitely ascertainable sources The first was the faulty appreciation o the human element in war, and the seconc the failure to grasp the nature of th changes that during the preceding century had taken place in the tactical elements.

During peace time, the period in whicl the soldier prepares for war, his one grea

.nd permanent difficulty is the lack of ·eality that surrounds his work. Danger ; absent, and it is almost impossible to ·ealize what fear means. Yet it is fear hat controls the battlefields, for whatever ·e the weapons of war they are, one and .ll, handled by men; and since on the ·attlefield, as when off it, men wish to live, heir first impulse is self-protection, and he more apparent the danger the stronger .oes this impulse grow. To prepare him o control this impulse the soldier is .isciplined to obey regardless of cost; .e is also imbued with what is called moral,' that is, endurance to face danger ombined with confidence in his skill, in is weapons, in his comrades and in his ·aders.

Thus far the problem is comparatively asy, but now comes the main difficulty –the discipline of mind. The private oldier may be a hero, but unless his ·aders and commanders are true artists f war, that is, unless they can paint, as were, a possible picture of the next war, a picture in which may be seen all that the soldier should and can do when surrounded by an atmosphere of danger, ıeir work of art will lack perspective. 'his lack of perspective was the one great oid that characterised military thought 'om 1870 onwards. The soldier was ·ained to become a wonderful fighting ıachine, but it was forgotten that in spite f this he was still human, and that on the attlefield the most powerful enemy he 'ould meet was not man, but the god f war—fear. This introduces the second oint.

A lack of erspective

For forty years the general staffs had ıought offensively. 'To advance is to onquer,' said Frederick the Great; ıerefore to hit out, and to continue itting, was the surest means of sustaining orward movement. So far as this goes ıey were right, for offensive power and ıovement are two of the three fundaıental elements of war: the third is otection, and this one they overlooked. very new, or improved, weapon was to .crease offensive power, but it was forotten that increase in ability to hit must e shared with a similarly equipped enemy, that the problem of increasing offensive power was incomplete unless simultaneously the soldier could be better protected.

The South African War had shown the high defensive power of the magazine rifle, and, though trenches were seldom dug, the war was largely defensive in nature, because in place of earthworks hundreds of miles of block-house lines were built and linked together by wire entanglements. To counterbalance the destructive power of the rifle, infantry extensions were increased, until at times fifty paces could be counted between the men of an infantry firing line. Yet after the war this fact (and many others) was lost sight of, minor tactics throwing back to their 1870 type.

In the Russo-Japanese war fire power became still more destructive; the machine gun could not be attacked frontally, and the field gun provided defensive action with so strong a backbone that time could be gained wherein to entrench and wire complete battle fronts. At Nanshan the Russian front was completely wired from flank to flank, and the Japanese lost 4,300 men in carrying the position. At Mukden the whole Russian front was entrenched, a continuous trench line of 50 miles being dug, and because of this the Japanese were compelled to outflank their enemy.

Defensive power of modern arms

Though the Russo-Japanese war was closely studied by the general staffs, it is an astonishing fact, and yet one which cannot now be controverted, that one and all misread, or could not see, the outstanding lesson taught by this war, and, more obscurely, by the South African war: that the offensive power of modern weapons was so great that, if these weapons were used defensively, the offensive power of the frontal attack could rapidly be reduced to zero; that is, it could be definitely halted from four to eight hundred yards in front of the defenders' position. Consequently the main problem was not so much to increase the offensive power of attacking troops as to protect them against the defender's fire.

Between the close of the Russo-Japanese war and the opening of the Great War a revolution took place in field artillery. The quick-firing gun was adopted by all armies, and indirect laying (ability to deliver aimed fire from behind a rise or hill) took the place of firing over the sights. Though these two tactical changes enormously increased the defenders' power of resistance, so hallucinated were the general staffs that they could see in them only a means of accelerating the attack. According to General Herr (a French artillery expert) this is how France saw the approaching Armageddon :

> The war will be short and one of rapid movements, when manoeuvre will play the predominating part ; it will be a war of movement. The battle will be primarily a struggle between two infantries, where victory will rest with the large battalions ; the army must be an army of personnel and not of material. The artillery will only be an accessory arm, and with only one task—to support the infantry attack. . . . . The obstacles which one will meet in the war of movement will be of little importance ; field artillery will have sufficient power to attack them. . . . The necessity for heavy artillery will seldom make itself felt.

Such was the outlook when, in August, 1914, the Great War flamed across Europe. It was going to be a stupendous infantry contest in which the side that possessed bulk numbers endowed with the highest offensive spirit must win. So misunderstood were the elements of war, and so overlooked was the element of protection, that four months later protection had completely monopolised tactics and all movement ceased. Infantry had ceased to exist as infantry, they had become indifferent field engineers encased in the earthy armour of their trenches ; for to attempt to attack above ground was to court immediate destruction. In four months of warfare the tactical theories of forty years were reduced to nothing.

The lessons of 1914

The war problem now became one of mobility, how to re-establish movement ; for unless armies could move, the war must end either in stale-mate or through the utter exhaustion of one side or the other. This, in fact, was what M. Bloch had predicted, for in 1897 he said : 'Soldiers may fight as they please ; the ultimate decision is in the hands of famine.' This problem was both strategical and tactical, and as it appeared at th time easier to shift battlefields, eve whole theatres of war, than to re-equi armies, both sides began to look for ne strategical objectives. For the German this was not difficult ; if they could n break through the French and Britis trenches in France, then they could tur on the Russian armies, which had a fa wider front to protect, which were badl equipped and most indifferently com manded. This change took place shortl after the battle of Tannenberg, but th lack of communications in Russia, th enormous depth of the empire, the lac of vulnerable points at which to strik and the severity of the Russian wint defeated all endeavours to bring Russi to her knees until internal revolutio had stabbed her in the back.

For the Allied powers it was mo difficult, and divided opinions result in the adoption of half-measures which are always the most dangerous in war. The 'western school' of thought said : 'Remain on t western front ; it is only there that t war can be won.' The eastern scho replied : 'Why continue to kick again the pricks ? Advance through the Balka and knock Turkey and then Austria c the head.' The former was in favour attacking strength, the latter of attackir supposed weakness. But the easte plan could only be carried out by se and when good railways exist the loc motive can always beat the ship as troop carrier, so it was overlooked th an initial success in the East was like to be followed by colossal failure.

Divided opinion among the Alli

Divided opinion resulted in the Dard nelles campaign, a grotesque failure whic in place of demonstrating the folly dispersion of force led to a still great dispersion. A third school of thoug now arose, the attrition school, which sai 'The Central powers cannot be defeat on any front ; they must be encircled b trenches and bayonets and starved in submission.' The circle was to run fro the Skagerak through France, Italy, t Balkans, Palestine and Mesopotamia, ar then link up with the Russian front. A far as the British Empire was concern he result was an extensive naval blockade of the Central powers, and the campaigns n Macedonia, Palestine and Mesopotamia. The answer to this stupendous siege was he blockade of the British Isles by German submarines. Such were the main strategical influences of the tactical breakdown—the strife of armies was to be replaced by the economic blockade of entire nations. The relationship of war to peace, that is, that war is a product of civilization, a part of it and not apart from it, was dimly beginning to be perceived.

Tactically, the influence of the stalemate was as far-reaching. Though infantry had completely failed in offensive action, during the whole of 1915 the railways pumped hundreds of thousands of riflemen on to the battlefields; there to stagnate in human puddles, to evaporate and to be replenished. To move these thousands resulted in enormous demands being made for shells, and then for guns of all calibres. To move these shells from the rail heads forward required thousands of extra lorries, and hundreds of miles of tramways and small-gauge railways. To 'spot' the fall of the shells when fired resulted in a demand for more and more aeroplanes, which in their turn had to be equipped with photographic appliances and wireless telegraphic apparatus. To supplement the aeroplane, electrical ranging instruments, such as 'flash-spotters' and 'sound-rangers,' were introduced.

One demand followed another in rapid succession; few could be met by the soldier himself or by his permanent arsenals. More and more were the civilian industries, trades, professions and sciences drawn into the war, until the old conception of 'a nation in arms,' which never meant more than conscription, was replaced by that of 'a nation of war workers.' More and more did it become apparent that not only could a nation be attacked economically, but that all the economic factors that in peace time produced its wealth could in war time be utilised to supply, reinforce and maintain

'A NATION OF WAR WORKERS': ACTIVITIES ON THE HOME FRONT
It was not long before the combatants in the Great War came to realize that the old conception of war as being the exclusive business of professional or conscript armies was outworn; and the still older conditions returned in which, as with the Greek city states, war affected every citizen. All civilian activities were viewed in their relation to war needs; this photograph shows girl workers, masked for protection against fumes, filling shells in a British munition factory at Chilwell.

Photo, Imperial War Museum

THE TRENCH SYSTEM IN EMBRYO

The earliest trenches of the war were very different from the elaborate defences of later years; shallow, and hastily dug where sudden need and infantry rather than artillery tactics demanded. The King's Liverpool Regiment is here holding a line of impromptu fire pits in the Ypres sector, 1914.

its war muscles. Thus was i learnt that the difference be tween war and peace is onl one of a change in policy and not one of a radical differ ence between working an fighting. Both require ex penditure of force, the one t create, the other to destroy and all this became apparen because an entrenched fron could not be broken by a infantry assault. The spade not the rifle, had become th controlling tactical implement

There was little essentiall new in the type of warfar that now set in. In the day of Caesar an entrenched cam was all but invulnerable t attack. In those of Vauba the increased use of fiel fortifications introduced th modern military enginee and tactical engineerin evolved into a science. I the Crimean War and the Civ

TRENCH ON A FORWARD SLOPE IN THE DAYS OF THE SINGLE LINE

Where the armies halted at the limit of German advance, or at the limit of German retreat in fro of Paris, there stagnation set in and the first trenches appeared—real trenches, as opposed to th shallow burrows seen at the top of the page. They were still designed, however, to afford a fiel of fire for infantry rather than protection from gunfire and were therefore built on forward slope as seen in this example elaborately equipped with fire recesses.

Photo, F. Kelly, Carlisle

War in America the assault of trenches proved most costly operations, as they again did in the Russo-Japanese war; but, because they were not extensively used in the Franco-Prussian War, in 1914 no European army was prepared to deal with entrenchments on the grand scale.

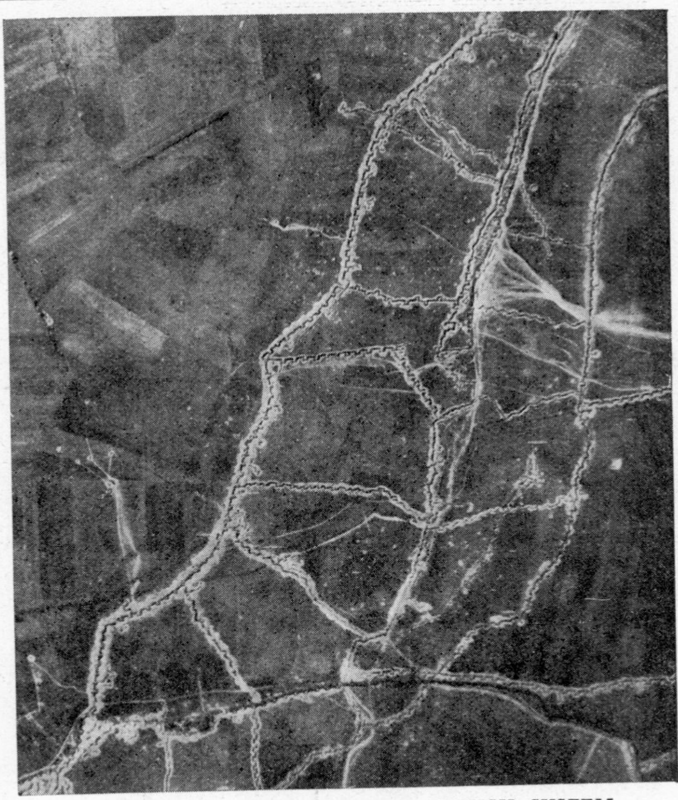

LAY-OUT OF THE MULTIPLE TRENCH SYSTEM

It was found that a single trench system offered very little guarantee against penetration, so in 1915 the multiple system appeared, linked by communication trenches. Note, also, in this air view of a typical section, how the fire recesses have given place to traverses, to restrict the effective range of shell bursts.

Photo, Royal Flying Corps

The first trenches that appeared in 1914 marked the high-water line of the attack and the defence; they were badly sited, and were generally developed along forward slopes so as to obtain a field of fire for infantry riflemen. While in 1914 defence consisted in holding a line of little depth, the time wherein to dig, and the continual increase in the range and weight of artillery, compelled each side to double, treble and quadruple its defences, until the line grew into a belt of lines some three to five miles deep. This evolution in trench warfare took place during 1915, a year which showed at the battles of Neuve Chapelle, the Dunajetz, Loos and Champagne that a single system of trenches afforded, at best, but an uncertain protection against massed artillery fire. The problem was now no longer one of breaking a line but of driving a substantial wedge of men through a broad belt of defences, the front of which could generally be shattered by artillery. This the battles of Verdun and the Somme proved in 1916.

In 1916 the majority of the German forces on the western front were placed in the forward defensive zone, and they suffered accordingly. In 1917 they changed their defensive policy; reducing their front line garrisons, they assembled in rear of them large reserves that could counter-attack the enemy when he broke through. They had not, however, grasped that as artillery formed the backbone of the defence it should be placed sufficiently far from the front to secure it from being over-run by the initial assault. This mistake on their part led to the loss of two hundred guns on the first and second days of the battle of Arras in 1917.

Immediately after this battle the Germans once again altered their defensive tactics, and the alterations made can best be shown diagrammatically. In the diagram in page 4805, suppose that AB is the German front line system, while CD, their second line, is so placed that the German guns at E can heavily shell the whole of CD, and yet be out of range of the enemy's guns at F. Suppose also that the area ABDC is strongly wired and well sprinkled

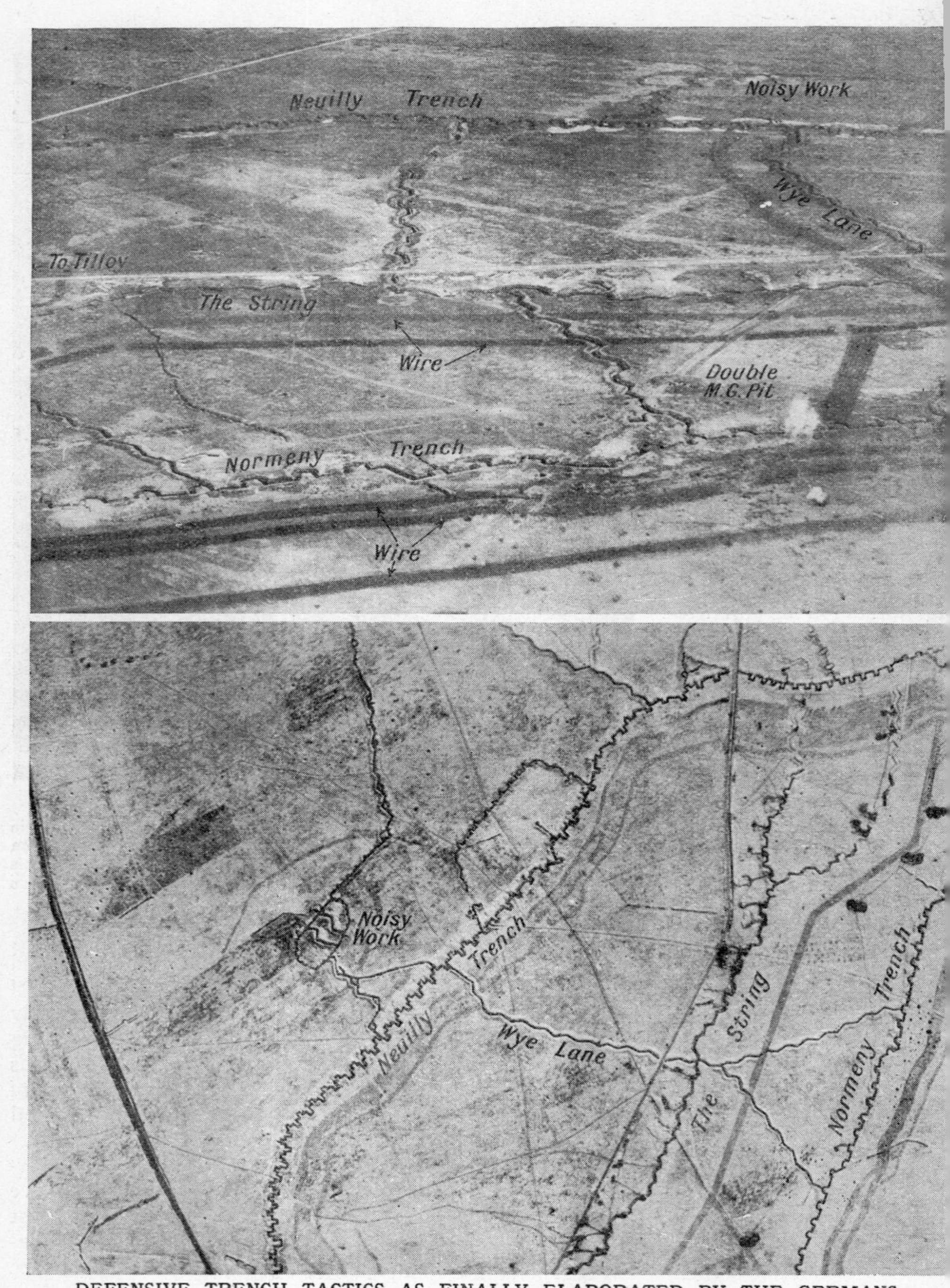

DEFENSIVE TRENCH TACTICS AS FINALLY ELABORATED BY THE GERMANS

By 1917 the Germans had fully developed defensive trench warfare. These air views, oblique and direct, both show the same system east of Arras. It will be seen that the front line, Normeny Trench, is sketchy compared with the reserve line, Neuilly Trench ; indeed, though heavily wired, it would be lightly held, while the area between the two is also wired and sprinkled with machine-gun posts (one marked). Thus the attacker, if he penetrates the first line (with little loss to the defender) will be caught by a counter-attack from Neuilly Trench while floundering in this difficult zone.

Photos, Royal Flying Corps

with machine guns, who will suffer most in an attack? There can be no question that it will be the attackers from LM, for they will not only be perpetually worried by machine gun and sharpshooter fire in ABDC, but as they advance towards CD they will come more and more under the enemy's gun fire. Suppose that the attackers capture CD, then at best they will only be able to remain there as impassive spectators of their own destruction, until such time as their guns at F can move forward to support them. To conclude these Fabian tactics, once the enemy's guns at E come under fire of those at F, they can retire, under cover of a machine-gun barrage, behind the line GH, and later on behind IJ, and by always keeping sufficiently far away from the front can avoid being over-run by the initial assault. Thus they can wear the attacker down until he is so weak that he is at the mercy of a counter-attack.

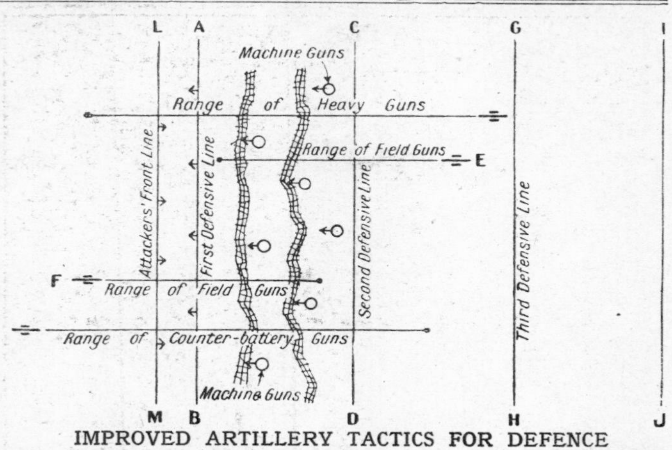

IMPROVED ARTILLERY TACTICS FOR DEFENCE

The only later modification of the German defensive methods illustrated opposite affected the disposition of artillery. Originally the guns were so far forward that an attack might overrun them; after the battle of Arras (1917) they were moved back, with the effect shown in diagram above, and explained in the text.

This system of artillery tactics began to be adopted about the time of the battle of Messines in June, 1917, and on the first day of this battle only fifty German guns were captured. At the third battle of Ypres they were fully developed by the Germans, and only eight guns were lost.

Let us now turn to the problem of the trench attack. The closing operations of 1914 showed that infantry were incapable of penetrating a trench line defended by wire and machine guns; that the attack must become more methodical; that strong forces must be concentrated at one point, not many; and that the infantry assault should be prepared by a heavy surprise bombardment carried out by as large a force of artillery as it was possible to assemble. These lessons were put into practice at the battle of Neuve Chapelle (March 10–12, 1915). Only two British divisions attacked on the first day, and the frontage of attack was about 3,500 yards; yet thanks to an intense and rapid bombardment which lasted only thirty-five minutes a definite penetration was effected. In spite of this valuable lesson in the power of surprise, method rather than originality of attack was rapidly gaining control over the mind of the higher commands, for in the conjoint Franco-British attack on May 9 we find the French replacing surprise by a preliminary bombardment lasting six days.

Surprise in the Trench Attack

All these assaults against one point ended in failure, so in the autumn a dual Franco-British attack was mounted and took place on September 25. The attack was launched against the Arras-Noyon-Reims salient, British and French forces attacking eastward from Loos and in Artois, and the main French force, under General Pétain, from Champagne northwards. The French objectives were unlimited; that is to say, the infantry attack was to push on until it had penetrated the entire German defensive system. This accomplished, seven French cavalry divisions were to carry out the pursuit. The result was a complete failure; first, because the two battlefields were too far apart to influence each other strategically; secondly, because infantry did not possess the tactical power to carry out an unlimited attack.

The increasing power of the defence induced increasing caution in the attack.

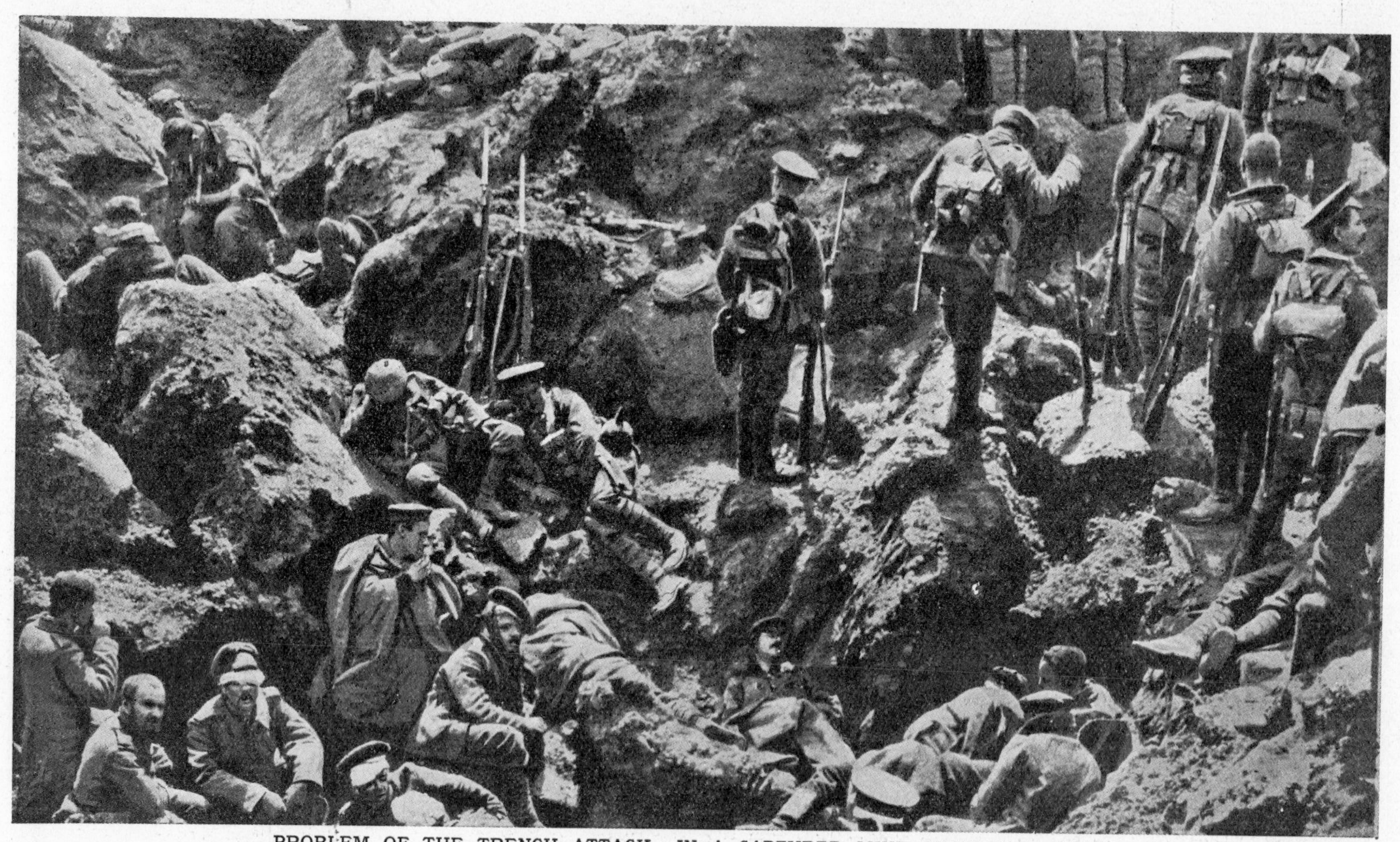

PROBLEM OF THE TRENCH ATTACK: IN A CAPTURED MINE CRATER AT LOOS

By 1915 it was realized that infantry alone was powerless against a properly defended trench line, and the great artillery phase of the war began. Neuve Chapelle in March and Loos in September (unexpectedly complete Allied successes that were not followed up) then demonstrated that with artillery preparation a single line could be pierced, and the multiple system, as we have seen, came into force. North of Loos on September 25 the attack was preceded by the explosion of a mine; this photograph shows the crater after its capture but before the dead and wounded were removed.

LOOS : EFFECT OF BOMBARDMENT ON BARBED WIRE, TRENCH AND VILLAGE

At the top is an example of what makes a trench impregnable unless it be first blasted to pieces by gunfire : wire, with machine guns behind it. Nor is it very vulnerable to any but the fiercest gunfire, for the section illustrated, in front of a German trench at Loos, is still uncut after a bombardment whose intensity can be measured from its effect on a captured trench (centre) and on the village of Loos (note the famous 'Tower Bridge,' a pit-head structure, in the background).

Photos, Imperial War Museum

DESOLATION OF WAR AFTER TWO MONTHS OF FIGHTING ON THE SOMME

Neuve Chapelle had been preceded by a surprise bombardment; Loos by a methodical one Similarly the tactical element, discernible in the dual attack with unlimited objectives of Loos Champagne, vanished and was followed in 1916 by vast single battles of attrition. The Somme offen sive is the classical example, and the desolation caused by such artillery battles is seen in this viev of the 8th Seaforth Highlanders holding a front-line trench in front of Martinpuich on August 25

Photo, Imperial War Museum

The French now began to realize that 'artillery conquers and infantry occupies.' Tactics were thus reduced to a matter of push of pikes, or rather push of shells. Drill took the place of manoeuvre, method of surprise, and shell fire replaced leadership. Tactics were, in fact, reduced to the level they occupied under the Spartans in the fifth century B.C.

The failure of the unlimited infantry attack, and the preponderating influence of artillery on tactics, introduced the period of the great artillery battles in which infantry moved at a slow pace behind hurricanes of shells, and merely collected prisoners, or occupied positions without fighting. Since 1914 the whole aspect of tactics had changed, and these changes reached their culminating point in 1916. During this year two stupendous battles of attrition were fought on the western front, namely the battles of Verdun (see pages 4762–3) and the Somme.

The first opened on February 21 with a surprise attack on the part of the Germans. The prolonged artillery bombardment was replaced by a violent cannonade lasting only a few hours. The infantry attack was then launched and succeeded in making considerable headway, not so much because the Germar guns had destroyed the French wire anc trenches, as because the garrisons o these trenches had been demoralised b the intensity of the bombardment.

At the battle of the Somme, whicl opened on July 1, preparations wer methodical in the extreme, the pre liminary bombardment lasting eight days during which 2,000,000 shells were fired The surprise of this battle was agai provided by the artillery, and was not bombardment of a new type but a rollin barrage under the cover of which it wa hoped that the infantry would be able t move forward from objective to objective Though this form of artillery suppor proved of the greatest assistance, th attack failed, the British losses on th first day totalling no fewer than 60,000.

The lessons learnt from these two grea battles were that the frontage of attacl must be as wide as possible; that th object of the attack was the zone of th enemy's guns; and that it was hopeles to expect success unless each wave o attack could pass through the one i front of it without delay.

The great single battles of penetratio having failed, in 1917 a return was made t the grand tactics of 1915, it being decided by the Allies to deliver a dual attack against the Arras-Noyon-Reims salient. The British were to attack from Arras towards Valenciennes, and the French from Soissons-Reims northwards. Most elaborate preparations were made for these battles. On the British front the chalk quarries under the city of Arras were prepared to accommodate two infantry divisions which were to cross no-man's-land by passing underground.

Then, in February, 1917, the whole of these arrangements were upset by the Germans retiring to a new line of entrenchments, popularly known as the Hindenburg line, which had been dug from south-east of Arras to Craonne. In spite of this withdrawal the attack was launched on April 9, after a fifteen days' preliminary bombardment in which 2,700,000 shells were fired. A penetration of some 7,000 yards was effected, after which the advance slowed down, and definitely halted on May 4. The French attack, however, which was launched on April 16, proved a complete fiasco.

The battle of Arras was followed on June 7 by the battle of Messines, which was opened by exploding no fewer than nineteen mines under the German front. The object of this attack was to capture the Messines ridge preparatory to delivering a more formidable blow east of Ypres. Round Ypres was assembled the largest force of artillery ever seen in British history, the gunner personnel numbering 120,000. Three hundred and twenty-one 400-ton train loads of ammunition were 'dumped' to supply a preliminary bombardment of nineteen days in which 4,283,000 shells, weighing 128,000 tons, were fired. The whole surface of the battlefield was torn up, all drains as well as roads were destroyed, and an all but uncrossable swamp was created, in which

A GERMAN ASSAULT IN THE DAYS OF THE ARTILLERY BATTLES

How artillery by 1916 dominated tactics was shown by the one great innovation on the Somme—the 'rolling' barrage (see page 4768). This German photograph is of unknown date and provenance, but it well epitomises the aspect now assumed by warfare. Leadership, tactics, manoeuvre are at their lowest ebb; men trudge through tangled wire behind a rain of shells to occupy positions that the artillery has or is supposed to have conquered; and a battle is 'won' if a few yards are gained.

Photo, Imperial War Museum

One variation from the normal artillery battle was provided at Messines by the explosion of nineteen huge mines beneath the German defences on the ridge immediately before the attack Twenty had been dug, but one was discovered and destroyed. Their moral effect was shattering; but the craters, which soon became tarns, did not add to the ease of advanced communications.

THE BATTLE OF MESSINES: PRELIMINARY BOMBARDMENT AND MINE CRATER

The last of the great Allied artillery offensives on the western front was the third battle of Ypre (July 31, 1917); but the Messines ridge had to be captured first since it dominated Ypres salient o the south. Accordingly the battle of Messines was staged on June 7, and as usual the attack wa preceded by an artillery bombardment whose effect can be judged from this air view of part of th ridge on June 5. Count the visible shell bursts, remembering that the exposure is instantaneous.

Photos, Royal Flying Corps

WHAT GUNFIRE DOES TO THE GROUND IN WHICH INFANTRY MUST ADVANCE

fter Messines ridge had been captured the British attacked east of Ypres, with a nineteen days' reliminary bombardment of unprecedented fury. The weather finally broke; and the total effect n the Flanders plain, low-lying and in normal times elaborately drained, is vividly brought home y these two photographs, from the ground and from the air. Tanks were almost useless in the orass. The ground photograph shows Clapham Junction with Sanctuary Wood in the background.

Photos, Royal Flying Corps and Imperial War Museum

the infantry wallowed for nearly four months. The ground gained was approximately forty-five square miles, and each square mile cost 8,222 casualties.

This third battle of Ypres was the last of the great artillery engagements. The spade had now definitely defeated the gun, and the defence the attack. The special reasons for this are worth inquiring into as they demonstrate clearly the influences of spade, wire and gun on the tactics of trench warfare.

How the Spade defeats the Gun

In slow, methodical attacks of penetration a battle salient, or pocket, is formed, and if the battle salients of the war are examined it will be found that their sides slope inwards at angles of about forty-five degrees. The reasons for this are: that artillery protection on the flanks is limited by the arc of fire of the guns; that hostile pressure on the flanks tends, as the attacker advances, to round off the flanks of the attack; that losses invariably tend to contraction towards the axis of the attack; and that, as the centre of the pocket is freer from the enemy's fire than the flanks, its supply is safer, and consequently more rapid.

Granted that the flanks of an attack will slope inwards at approximately forty-five degrees, then, if a penetration is to be effected, the width of the original frontage to be attacked will bear a close relationship to the depth of attack required. The controlling factor in this calculation is the final frontage after penetration, which must be sufficiently wide to permit of a large force passing through the centre c the gap unaffected by hostile fire on th flanks. In practice its width must b about fifteen miles, and the width of th initial frontage necessary to achieve may be arrived at by measuring th distance between these two frontage: multiplying it by two, and adding th distance to the fifteen miles in questio Thus in diagram 1 below: If the widt of the desired gap is AB, and the di tance between it and the original ba LM is CD, then EF (the initial frontag will equal AB + 2CD. In this case equals 15 miles + 2 × 5 miles, that is 2 miles, and the 'defiladed' cone JHCI will have a base of 15 miles and a truncate apex of 5 miles free from most projectile

The number of infantry divisions require to effect a penetration against a strong entrenched enemy, holding three defensi lines of a depth of five miles, may theoreti ally be worked out in the following manne

There are three lines of trenches to b penetrated, each of which will require separate line of divisions. The distan separating these lines in each case, we wi suppose, is two and a half miles. A infantry division had at this date (191 1917) a battle front of about 1,500 yar in the initial attack, 2,000 in the seconda attack, and 3,000 in the tertiary. Cons quently (see diagram 2) twenty-ni divisions will be required to penetrate t line EF, and eighteen and nine divisio to penetrate the lines NO and A

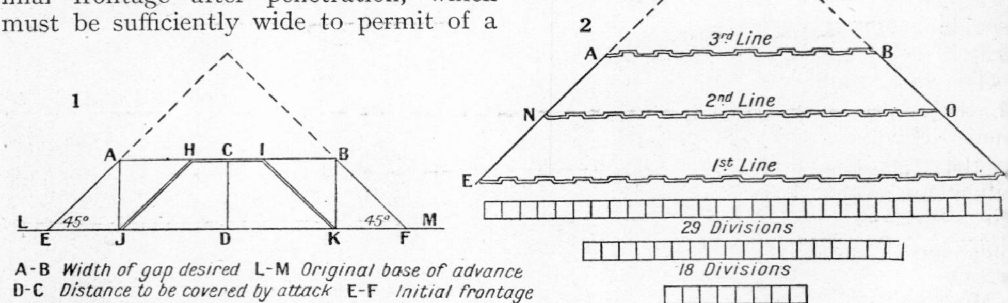

WHY SINGLE ATTACKS OF PENETRATION FAILED: DIAGRAMS 1 AND 2

For tactical reasons the flanks of a penetrating attack slope inwards at about 45° (diagram For the tip of the potential cone to reach the last defensive line is useless, since there must be a g broad enough to permit the attackers to pass through unshelled from the flanks: in practice, miles. The breadth of initial attack necessary to secure this is twice the depth of the defensi system + 15, for EF = 2CD + AB. Now if EF = 25 miles and the defence consists of three lir (diagram 2), fifty-six divisions will be necessary to carry them (see text).

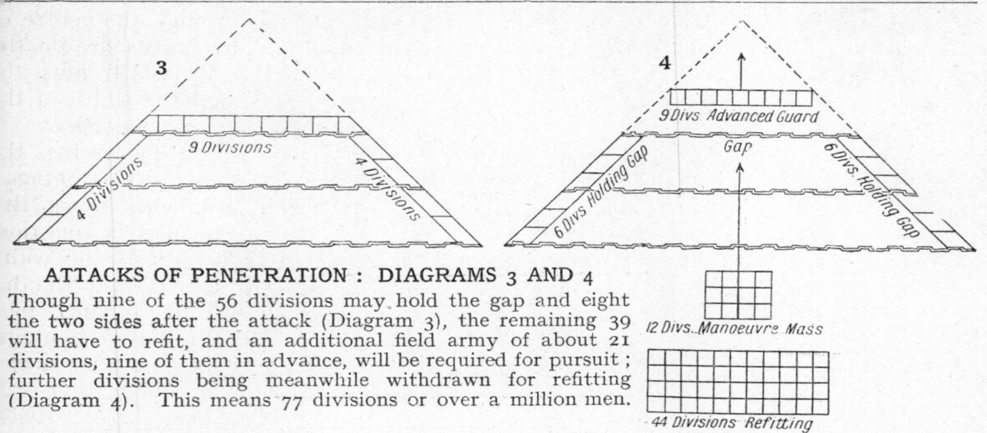

ATTACKS OF PENETRATION : DIAGRAMS 3 AND 4

Though nine of the 56 divisions may hold the gap and eight the two sides after the attack (Diagram 3), the remaining 39 will have to refit, and an additional field army of about 21 divisions, nine of them in advance, will be required for pursuit ; further divisions being meanwhile withdrawn for refitting (Diagram 4). This means 77 divisions or over a million men.

espectively. This amounts to a total of fty-six divisions. After the initial attack wenty-five divisions can be withdrawn to efit, and after the secondary fourteen. 'his means that, once the penetration has een effected, thirty-nine divisions will be ı potential reserve, and the remaining eventeen will be holding the sides and pex of the hollow truncated cone (see iagram 3 above). The area JHCIK diagram 1), with a base of fifteen miles, almost shell-free, and forms the ıanoeuvre ground for the forces which re to pass through the gap. As the hirty-nine divisions will take at least even days to refit, they cannot be em-loyed to pursue, therefore besides these ivisions a field army of at least twenty-ne divisions will be required, nine of hese to act as a general advanced guard o cover the approach of the remaining welve, which will act as a manoeuvre mass see diagram 4), supported by the with-rawn divisions once these have refitted.

The total number of divisions required , therefore, seventy-seven, or 1,200,000 ıen. The supply of this prodigious force ı the restricted area is manifestly most ifficult, if not impossible ; consequently, he result was that an attack of penetra-ion against a determined and well en-renched enemy was normally a failure.

We have here entered into considerable etail to show the immense difficulties of ttacks of penetration. The depth to be enetrated has been taken as being five ıiles, but already in 1916 many trench ystems were deeper than this, and every undred yards added to their depth meant thousands of men added to the penetrating forces. Operations of single penetration with artillery and infantry were not practicable against deep and well held entrenched zones, so tactics of the dual penetration, such as were attempted in 1915 and 1917 against the Arras-Noyon-Reims salient, were employed.

A dual attack is one delivered against two closely related sectors of the enemy's front, made with a view to break the section of trenches which connects them. In such an attack, as shown in the diagram below, it is advantageous if a salient be chosen. For an operation of this nature three separate forces are required. A attacks at D, not with a view to penetrate but to form a battle salient

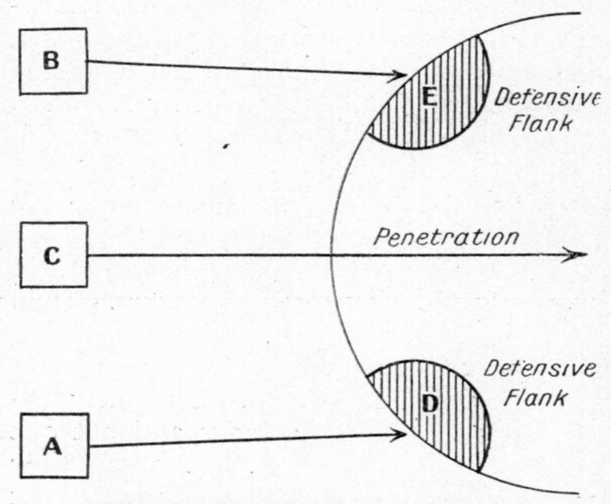

SCHEME OF THE DUAL ATTACK

More promising than the single attack of penetration was the dual attack against two related sectors of an enemy salient; the intention being to force evacuation of the sector between, followed by an unresisted penetration protected on the flanks by the two original attacks.

PONDEROUS INSTRUMENT OF THE TACTICS THAT RELIED ON ARTILLERY

This is an epitome of the tactics that reigned supreme up to the very end of 1917: a Royal Marir Artillery tractor hauling the 15-ton barrel of a 7.5-in. long-range gun from H.M.S. Swiftsure up t the forward area in July, in preparation for the third battle of Ypres, which proved the last b battle of the old tactical era. Even great pieces of this calibre, and millions upon millions of shell had been insufficient to force a decision in the wasteful artillery duels of the previous two years.

Photo, Imperial War Museum

which will draw in the enemy's reserves. B attacks at E, to do likewise. Meanwhile a tactical penetration is being automatically effected in the area between the salients D and E, not only by the exhaustion of the enemy's reserves which can reinforce this intermediary sector should it be attacked, but by a squeezing of the sector into so pronounced a salient that concentric fire will render it untenable. The enemy holding it will normally be forced to evacuate it, thereupon C, following up his withdrawal, will effect a penetration under the protection of the two tactical bastions formed by A and B at D and E, which prevent concentric fire being delivered against C's flanks.

This system of penetration, which in the conditions prevailing in 1916 and 1917 was in all probability the only practical one, was not properly understood. Dual attacks were attempted, but they were too far apart to influence the sector that connected them; they consequently became two separated attacks and not one co-operative engagement, and as such they were doomed to fail. The next great phase of the war opened a phase which was to disclose new tactics.

During 1917 not only had the entrenched zone grown deeper and the wire fields which covered them grown wider, but the fact that these trenches and wire field were being dug and constructed more an more on the reverse slopes of position made the task of their bombardmer increasingly difficult. Further, the newl dug Hindenburg system of trenches, whic ran across the most suitable sector fc offensive action on the Allied front, wa not a hastily sited battle line, but a extremely well chosen defensive belt, s much so that coupled with the new defer sive artillery tactics it would have bee exceedingly difficult to penetrate it b artillery fire. Outwardly the stale-mat was absolute, the spade had defeated th gun; but inwardly, and to a great exten unappreciated, subtler means of attac were being evolved.

Aeroplanes had now to a large exten ceased to occupy the purely auxiliar position they held during the earlie period. Their production was sufficientl great to permit of independent as we as co-operative action. Bombing raids o far distant points were daily and nightl being carried out, and the civilian popu lation two hundred miles in rear of th fighting front was beginning to taste th horrors of war, and on its will to endur aerial bombardment depended the 'moral of the soldiers and sailors who were prc tecting it against land and sea attack

As at sea the submarine was showing that it was possible to starve a nation into surrender, so in the air was the aeroplane making it clear to all that it was equally possible to frighten a nation into capitulation.

There was nothing new in either starvation or terror as weapons of war, but the methods of attaining these ends were novel and most difficult to meet. Before the outbreak of the war civilized nations had looked upon war almost entirely as a physical attack in which only soldiers and sailors were directly involved, because public opinion divorced war from the civil activities of every-day life. Now they were beginning to realize the all-embracing nature and influences of war, and to appreciate that besides the physical attack there were the moral and economic attacks, and that these forms of fighting could be employed not only against fleets and armies, but against entire nations.

Meanwhile another agent of destruction was being evolved, namely gas (see pages 4793-5). In this, also, there was nothing new, for in classical and medieval times sulphur, pitch and other asphyxiating and smoke-producing substances had been used to overcome an enemy. In 1812 gas had been suggested as a weapon, and again in 1854 by Lord Dundonald; but in war it was not used as such until April 22, 1915, when the Germans launched their first gas attack east of Ypres. Its object was to suffocate the garrison of an entire area, and

THE HOME FRONT FEELS THE TOUCH OF WAR: NEW METHODS OF ATTACK
While the artillery battles of the western front were achieving nothing beyond the proof of their own grim futility, war methods were insensibly becoming more subtle, involving the civilian populations. There were the Allied blockade and the German submarine war, designed to starve them; and the air raids, designed to break their nerve. Here is seen the damage done to the top floor of the G.P.O. by a 15-kilo bomb dropped in the aeroplane raid on London of July 7, 1917.
Photo. Imperial War Museum

A CASUALTY AMONG THE GREAT ENGINES DESIGNED TO DESTROY 'MORAL'

It is extremely hard to make accurate observations of bombing effects from a Zeppelin, but, in sp of the German official announcements of mythical destruction achieved, it is impossible not to belie that the real object of the air raids over England was to intimidate the civil population rather th to do military damage. This Zeppelin, the L33, is one that was forced down intact in a lonely pa of Essex, through engine trouble and loss of gas, on the night of September 23, 1916.

Photo, Air Ministry, Crown copyright

so permit of an unopposed advance. While gun fire mainly destroyed trenches, gas only destroyed their occupants, who were bombarded not by particles of steel but by chemical molecules. Gas, in fact, is but an extension of the shell, and its nature is such that it is not necessary to see a target or even know where it is, for as long as it is somewhere in the area inundated, the wind being favourable, it must be hit. As the aeroplane was nothing more than an extension of the howitzer, gas was nothing more than an extension of the shell, the 'fragmentation' of which is so minute that everything within its range can be hit.

Shortly before gas made its appearance as a weapon, yet another means of destruction was being considered, and this time in England. The heavy casualties, especially among the infantry, at once suggested the reintroduction of armour. Helmets and movable shields on wheels were first suggested. Helmets were rapidly adopted; but to move a bullet-proof steel shield by man power over trench and through wire was impossible; co sequently inventive minds turned mechanical power in the form of t petrol engine. As early as Septemb 1914, Colonel (later Major-General S Ernest) Swinton put forward this idea, a as wheels would be useless for trench a parapet crossing he advised that th should be replaced by caterpillar track The outcome was the tank, a self-propell armoured machine which could mo through wire entanglements and cro trenches up to ten feet wide. Again t idea was not a new one; in fact it was very old one dating back to the knight armour and beyond. Its novelty in co struction lay in its means of propulsio for it replaced human and animal musc power by mechanical energy.

To understand the astonishing influen of the tank on the tactics of this period, must not be forgotten that the predon nant problem since the autumn of 19 was how to move.

Shell warfare and gas warfare had both ailed, the first because, though wire and renches could be destroyed by shell fire, heir destruction carried with it the estruction of all forward communications. In fact the shelled areas were so blasted y fire that in many cases it was extremely ifficult for a man on foot to cross them, et alone a wheeled vehicle. If vehicles ould not follow up the attackers, the inantry and gunners could not be supplied, o it happened that the utmost mobility which could be gained in a great artilery battle was but a few miles at most, ometimes only a few hundred yards. Gas warfare had also failed, for lethal ases, such as chlorine and phosgene, were asily countered by the respirator, and esicant gases could not be produced in ufficient quantities for decisive results; urther, these chemicals could not be sed where an advance was contemplated.

The tank did not, however, destroy he ground; it could cross wire and renches, and it was little affected by mall-arm fire; its only enemy was the un. Its armour protected its mobility, nd simultaneously from this mobility was developed its high offensive power. Here we are confronted by a startling and adical change in tactics. Hitherto inantry, under cover of artillery, had used fire power in order to stimulate movement. The rifleman fired to move, and made use of the ground as a shield. Metaphorically the tank lifted the shield, in the form of bullet-proof armour, off the ground. The trench and its garrison now began to walk, or crawl, forward, and this enabled the tank to move in order to fire, and not merely to fire in order to move. The change was radical; never before in the history of war had it been possible so closely to combine the three fundamental tactical elements of protection, movement and offensive power.

An equally startling change was that the tank did not supersede the growing influence of artillery, but extended it. Even as early as the days of Napoleon artillery was becoming a rival to infantry as the superior arm. Between 1815 and 1870 this fact was lost sight of, then it once again appeared out of the mist of military history. In 1870 the German field gun more than outbalanced the inequality between the indifferent German rifle, the needle gun, and the superior French rifle, the chassepot. In 1904 Major S. M. Home, a British officer attached to the Japanese army in Manchuria, wrote: 'The greatest possible advantage should be taken of the tremendous fire-action of artillery . . . bearing

THE RETURN TO ARMOUR: NATIONAL VARIATIONS OF THE 'TIN HAT'

Armour had long been obsolete in European warfare, attention being concentrated on attack rather than defence. The appalling casualties of the Great War, however, caused the reintroduction of helmets, of which nine types are here shown. On stands, from left to right: Portuguese (1917 pattern), American, British, Belgian (1917), French ('Adrian' pattern with visor, 1916), French (without visor) In front: German with reinforcing piece, German sniper's helmet, Austrian.

Photo, Imperial War Museum

MACHINES THAT RESTORED MOBILITY TO MODERN WARFARE : A COMPANY OF 'TANKS'

It was armour that finally ended the stale-mate of the western front and revolutionised modern infantry tactics—not inert armour of the helmet type but mobile armour propelled by its own power : the land battleship, the 'tank.' This is a train of tanks, each with its bundle of fascines for crossing deep trenches, on the rail in readiness for the Cambrai offensive on November 20, 1917.

Photo, Imperial War Museum

in mind that artillery is nowadays the d cisive arm.' The years 1914–17 prov that he was right ; but the gun could on defend ; it could not attack, because must fire from a stationary position.

The tank provided the gun with a mob platform, or mounting, and during t war the only true adversary the tank h to encounter was the stationary field gu when the tank attacked it the resulti combat may be compared to one betwe a battleship and a coastal fortress. Mou the field gun in a tank, then mobile g will meet mobile gun, and landship w meet landship. In place of land warfa we have naval warfare on land ; so co pletely does the tank influence tacti However, all this was but dimly seen the time, and by very few. Tank tacti had to struggle on through trial and err opposition and prejudice.

Tanks firs used in bat

On September 15, 1916, tanks we first used in battle. It was a remarkal event, and this September 15 will o day be looked upon as one of those gre turning points that once every five six hundred years occur in the history war and change its course. On this d forty-nine tanks were assembled, of whi only thirty-two reached their starting points, and of these thirty-two only nine were able to push ahead of the infantry, and only one event of intere took place. Near the village of Flers t attacking infantry were held up by wi and machine-gun fire, when a tank, comi to their assistance, crossed wire a trench, and travelling along in rear of t defenders forced three hundred Germa to surrender. It was an amazing feat, n because it was so difficult, but because was so easy ; one officer and seven m succeeded in paralysing nearly forty tim their numerical strength—and why ? B cause these eight men were armoure The lesson was not seen at the time, b it was this : that the static trench cou be conquered by mobile iron. On Se tember 25 a somewhat similar operati took place near the village of Gueud court, one tank followed by two co panies of infantry killing a large numb of Germans and capturing three hundr and seventy, at the cost of five casualtie

These two operations, small though hey were, were sufficient to establish ntirely new tactics. Infantry could not ace the tank, since their weapons could o it no harm. Infantry could not cross ncut wire or face machine-gun fire, xcept at great cost. The tank could face nfantry, it could cross wire, and it had ittle to fear from the machine gun. At his period its speed was low, and it offered a good target to the gunner; urther, the number of tanks was small, consequently they could not be spared to hold a captured position. They required artillery to protect them, and infantry to hold the positions they overran. The first lesson was that the tank could replace the rolling barrage, and consequently should precede the infantry attackers, and that the artillery should cover the tanks. The next lesson was still more startling.

Offensive instead of defensive flanks

Hitherto, as has been explained, the depth of an attack of penetration depended upon the establishment of secure defensive flanks. These normally sloped inwards at an angle of forty-five degrees; and, if the initial base of attack was not sufficiently wide, they met within the enemy's defensive zone and formed a battle salient or pocket. With tanks two offensive flanks could be established; consequently from a comparatively narrow base two forces of these machines, one on each flank of the attackers, could work outwards, and so enlarge the base as the centre of the attack advanced, and consequently protect this centre. This was a revolution in tactics, but unfortunately it was not appreciated, and the result was that at the next great battle, the battle of Arras, in the spring of 1917, the few tanks used, sixty in all, were scattered along a wide front, were drawn up behind the infantry, and were not used for offensive work on the flanks.

Nevertheless, during this battle an interesting operation was carried out near the village of Bullecourt. Eleven tanks were used to replace the now normal rolling barrage, and to lead the attacking infantry through the enemy's wire and across his trenches. Though this operation proved a failure, two tanks accomplished their task, and showed that wire need no longer be cut by shell fire; it could be so completely crushed down by the tank tracks as to permit of infantry rapidly passing through the entanglements.

Tanks in the 3rd Battle of Ypres

This lesson was a priceless one, for wire now lost much of its terror and power; yet in the next two great battles, the battle of Messines in June and that of Ypres in July, the tanks again advanced to the attack behind the infantry. In the second of these two battles the condition of the ground can only be described as appalling; shell fire had reduced it to a porridge of mud, and deep mud is to the tank what uncut wire is to the infantryman. Yet out of this battle one interesting tactical change developed.

Before the war the infantry attack was based, in theory, on a firing line, the men of which were extended at from three to ten paces interval; this line was followed by supports in close or open order. When the artillery barrage was introduced the firing line followed, in the same extended order, the wall of bursting shells, but as the ground was covered with shell craters men were apt to bunch together to avoid them, or to occupy them in groups for the sake of the cover they afforded. As early as the autumn of 1916 an experimental system of platoon and section groups was tried. Later on, when tanks co-operated with infantry, again men would bunch behind the tanks for sake of cover, and when tanks crushed lanes through entanglements it was imperative that infantry should follow in single file. Though the whole development was slow it tended more and more to replace long extended lines by a series of small sections which could advance in file, and deploy in line to fire, and then ploy back into single file to advance again.

The third battle of Ypres brings us to the point at which the great artillery period of the war came to an end. From September 1916 to September 1917 tanks had not been given the opportunity of replacing the barrage, because they had been used on shelled ground, and, except for

WHAT TANKS COULD NOT CROSS : THE FLAW IN THE BATTLE OF CAMBRAI

Armoured machines moving on caterpillar tracks instead of wheels, first suggested in 1914, were n used before the Somme battles in September, 1916; and only at the battle of Cambrai was t Tank Corps allowed to show that tanks could replace bombardment and moving barrage with t added element of surprise. The attack, a wonderful success, was rendered local by the impassab barriers of the Canal du Nord and St. Quentin Canal, of which the former is here seen a week afterward

Photo, Imperial War Museum

the Bullecourt operation, in rear of the attacking infantry. The British Tank Corps firmly believed that on suitable ground tanks were capable of carrying out a surprise assault against the most formidable of entrenched systems, and ear in August, 1917, a suggestion was mad to deliver an attack south of Cambrai.

The area selected was between the Can du Nord and the St. Quentin Cana because the operation visua ised was of a limited natur and these two canals woul automatically confine its ma gins. On October 20 it w decided, however, to carr out a decisive operation in th area, in spite of the fact th the area itself rendered suc an action most difficult, f the two canals precluded t creation of offensive flank Not only did the flankin canals prohibit an extensi outwards, but, as the S Quentin Canal took a shar bend westwards at the villag of Crêvecoeur, unless tan could cross the canal at Ma nières the battle front woul be narrowed down to 8,00 yards, that is from Marcoi to the Canal du Nord. Th actually happened.

The attack took place o November 20. It was a r

HOW THE GERMANS OPPOSED THE TANK

Tanks gave protection against all but gun fire, and, becoming faster, were poor targets for guns. But so great was the alarm of the German command that they issued a special armour-piercing rifle, of which a captured specimen is here seen in the hands of two gunner officers (Bapaume, August, 1918).

Photo, Col. Fuller

markable local success, for a penetration of 10,000 yards was effected without any preliminary bombardment. At Ypres 120,000 gunners entirely failed to accomplish what in this battle was done by 4,000 tank soldiers; 8,000 prisoners and 100 guns were captured, while the British casualties were about 5,000, and not 60,000 as on the first day of the battle of the Somme. Though a German counter-attack on November 30 rendered this success abortive, the tank had definitely shown that at last the spade and wire were conquered, and that because of this mobility could be reinstated.

While a tactical solution to three years of stale-mate on the Western front was being worked out, German diplomacy exploited the Russian Revolution with dire results to the Allied powers. The outcome of the Russian collapse was that in the spring of 1918 Germany was once again in a position to concentrate all her might against the western front, where she hoped to win a decisive victory before America could land her millions. In the eyes of her general staff the tank had found no favour, but the astonishing success gained by a short and intensive gas bombardment against the Russians at Riga, on September 3, 1917, had opened their eyes to the possibilities of such an attack on the grand scale.

The last of the German offensive campaigns was launched on March 21, 1918. The front selected was seventy-four miles in extent, running from near Lens to La Fère. An enormous mass of guns was assembled, north of St. Quentin, one to every eight yards of front, and the British trenches were inundated with gas shells, and over-run. The attack was continued until April 4, when a penetration of thirty-eight miles had been effected, then it was closed down only to be followed by similar attacks west of Lille, south of Laon and north of Compiègne on April 9, May 27 and June 9.

All ultimately broke down, for though tactical mobility was now possible the problem of administrative movement had not been solved. From November, 1915, to November, 1917, the movement of supplies was comparatively easy, but

GERMAN ACKNOWLEDGMENT OF THE TANK'S SUPREME UTILITY

Armour-piercing bullets from ordinary rifles, effective against the earliest tanks, were countered by thicker armour, and the specially heavy rifle in the opposite page (·530 calibre) was too cumbrous to be of much use. Mines were too uncertain in their action; and imitation was a very sincere form of flattery when the Germans introduced tanks of their own towards the end of the war as the only possible counterstroke. This one was taken by Australians near Vaux on August 4, 1918.

Photo, Australian Corps

THE CAVALRY OF FUTURE WARS

The tank did not displace the ordinary armoured car, whose greater speed makes it useful for reconnaissance work, in which this pair was engaged when photographed on August 25, 1918, or for rapid pursuit and attack in unshattered country when once complete mobility has been restored.

Photo, Royal Tank Corps

tactical mobility all but impossible. Now the position was reversed ; the attackers could move forward under tank or gas protection, but the badness of the roads in the battle areas and the destruction of the railways prohibited sufficiency of supply. Though by the summer of 1918 the frontages of attack had greatly increased, insufficiency of supply slowed the attacker down, and the defender thus gained time to press in on the flanks of the attack, which normally ceased when the depth of penetration had equalled half the width of the original base of operations.

The great battles that followed the German offensive were pre-eminently tank battles and not gas battles. On July 18 a French attack preceded by 235 small tanks was launched against the Germans in the Soissons-Château-Thierry area, and on August 8 one of the most decisive battles of the war was won by combined British and French forces against the Germans in the salient east of Amiens. This battle was undoubtedly the greatest tank battle of the war ; 415 British tanks being engaged in it. Ludendorff has christened this day ' the black day of the German army,' and in very fact it was so. Not only was it a great tactical victory but also a great strategical one, for its repercussion was felt in every theatre of war. In Germany this disastrous defeat, though at first hidden from the masses of the people, soon became apparent as blow after blow followed it on the western front, in Palestine, in Macedonia and in Italy.

The secret of penetration was now common property ; nearly any sector of any front could be surprised and over-run, not up to the limit of gun fire but up to the limit of the system of supply. In Palestine the Turks were so thoroughly routed and demoralised that an old-style pursuit by cavalry was possible, but on the western front, though a war of movement had replaced trench warfare, it was in nature very different from the field battles visualised before the outbreak of the war. On the whole the Germans fell back in good order, and whenever they halted and deployed their machine guns the pursuit was brought to a standstill and only resumed after the machine guns had been dealt with by tank attack or artillery bombardment.

Preparations for 1919

Though the war as a military struggle ended on November 11, 1918, it is of some interest briefly to examine the preparations which were then in progress in England for a spring campaign in 1919, for in them lurk the characteristics of future warfare. The Royal Flying Corps which had been divided between the navy and army, in 1918 became a separate service—the Royal Air Force—and extensive preparations were being made to bomb Berlin and other important cities and so attack the nerves of the enemy's civil population. A toxic smoke had been discovered that would penetrate the German respirator, and though it was non-lethal it could totally incapacitate a man. Eight thousand tanks were to be built, and the personnel of the Tank Corps doubled. To mitigate the difficulties of supply, ten thousand cross country tractors were ordered from America. All these preparations in material pointed to the radical nature of the change.

that had taken place in armies since 1914; but none is so dramatic as the change in tactical theory, for the idea underlying the projected 1919 campaign was to be entirely different from that held in 1918.

In place of striking at the enemy's front it was intended to strike at his rear—at his system of command and supply, the foundations of his fighting organization. A force of fast-moving tanks, under cover of smoke, or darkness, was to rush through the German front and attack the enemy's divisional, corps and army headquarters as well as his rail heads and supply centres. Once the hostile rear was in panic, his front was to be smashed by the now normal tank, artillery and infantry assault. As regards this system of attack, it is interesting to note that a somewhat similar operation was carried out before the end of the war. At the battle of Megiddo, which began on September 19, once the British guns had blown a hole in the Turkish line large forces of cavalry were passed through. These, falling on headquarters and communications, created such disorder and demoralisation that the whole Turkish front fell to pieces, and within a fortnight Damascus was occupied.

In spite of Megiddo, in spite of the 1919 project, in spite of four years and more of devastating war, of losses, and cost, and innumerable inventions, directly the war was over all great armies turned a tactical somersault and went back to their 1914 organization with but few innovations. This reversion to type was the most astonishing tactical event of the Great War period.

Relation of War to Peace

At the beginning of this study it was stated that before the outbreak of the Great War both soldier and politician had failed to recognize that the activities of war are closely related to the activities of peace. Because of this separation war was considered as something totally different from peace, as the brutal is different from the human. War was accepted by those who knew anything of it as an instrument of policy. It was understood that peaceful political action should aim at attaining social contentedness and prosperity; it was overlooked, however, that, if war is an instrument of policy, policy in war should aim at those very ends for which we strive by political action during peace time; in short, that in war the aim of a nation is not merely the gaining of victory but the establishment of a better state when peace is restored than the one existing before the outbreak of hostilities. If this state is worse, then the war is morally lost by victor and vanquished alike.

It was because nations looked upon war purely as a physical struggle, a stupendous dog fight, that the Great War

HANDLEY-PAGE IN LEASH FOR AN OFFENSIVE THAT NEVER CAME

Painfully and slowly learnt, the lessons of the war were that with modern methods of defence all frontal attacks were useless without tanks, and that to re-establish mobility it was necessary to strike at the enemy's rear as well. By 1918 preparations were in hand for such an offensive in 1919. One operation contemplated was the intensive bombing of civil centres, for which a huge fleet of Handley-Page machines was ready. Some of them carried a single bomb weighing half a ton.

Photo, 'Flight'

was so destructive, and the peace which followed it so vindictive. They looked upon it as a physical struggle because armies were only organized to destroy, and soldiers were only educated to fight for a physical and not for a moral end. The soldier, surrounded by physical dangers, is bound to think destructively; he wishes to destroy the danger, not because it will influence the future peace but because it is threatening his existence. To change this essentially barbaric outlook on war, we must change the instruments of wars, the destructive weapons, and replace them by others which will render war far less brutal, and simultaneously protect the life of the soldier, and enable him to impose his will on his enemy.

Chemical science introduced not only humanity but efficiency and economy into surgery, and can do the same in war.

The future of Gas Warfare

Gas is a weapon which may conceivably humanise war. It will not end all suffering and destruction, nor will it abolish war any more than chloroform has ended human suffering or abolished surgery. But it may mitigate the horrors of war, because its immense superiority as a weapon over lead and steel is that it can wound without killing, and soon, it is possible, will be able to cause insensibility without wounding. To paralyse an army by chemical action is surely better for humanity than to blow it to pieces. To send a city to sleep is surely preferable to bombarding it or starving it into surrender.

That gas will be used in the next war is all but a certainty, and that it will be used as a brutal lethal instrument is probable. But that it possesses the power of being used as a humane instrument of war is its supreme virtue; for, in spite of human stupidity, little by little will the human brute discover that it is more economical to impose his will on his enemy with the minimum of destruction in place of the maximum. The instrument will change him, if he will only change the instrument, because the instrument will create a new environment, and man is very largely the reflection of his surroundings. Here is presented to us a radical change in the nature of war, a change which must influence all its elements and reform them.

If the moral idea of war replaces the brutal, then the military objectives selected must be such that they offer the lowest possible resistance to attack, for in general the more rapid the war the less suffering and destruction it entails.

There can be no doubt that the most delicate objective in war is the civil population, and the raison d'être of organized armies and navies has always been to protect non-combatants from the enemy's fighting forces. If this is not done, either the war ends disastrously, because the hand which wields the political instrument of war is destroyed, or the people rise, and organized warfare is replaced by guerilla warfare. In the past guerilla warfare was always possible; civil weapons—sporting guns, pitchforks and scythes—differed little from muskets, pikes and swords. But to-day the civil population is all but totally disarmed, for such weapons as they can collect would be useless against artillery, machine guns, gas and tanks. To-day, if the nerves of the civil population can be paralysed by fear the foundations are knocked away from the fighting forces protecting them, and, since the advent of aircraft, armies and navies can no longer directly guarantee their security as they cannot restrict movement in the air.

Civilian nerves the objective

As the Great War advanced, this spectre grew more and more material, and it was for this reason that the British Royal Flying Corps became a separate service. London, Paris and other great cities were bombed, and by throwing the people into panic not only was the national will to win shaken, but war work was slowed down. A raid over a manufacturing district would frequently reduce output to zero for several days at a time, not because of the material damage done, though this was sometimes considerable, but because of the moral shock resulting. During the war high explosive bombs were alone used, but should these in the future be replaced by gas bombs, particularly bombs containing vesicant chemicals, the moral shock to the civil nervous system may well end in a paralytic stroke.

The direct answer to air attack is air counter-attack, and this is so obvious that those to whom the obvious alone is apparent think that air power will totally replace sea and land power. Reflection will show, however, that this is not so, for besides the direct answer there is at least one very formidable indirect one.

Air force is based on ground organization just as armies and fleets are. This being so, the Achilles heel of the air is to be sought not in the clouds, but on the ground, in landing grounds, supply centres and workshops. Without an efficient and secure ground organization an air force is more helpless than a fleet that has lost its port, or an army that has had its communications severed, because aircraft are so potently affected by the force of gravity that all heavier than air machines can only remain in the air for a few hours at a time.

In May, 1918, it was realized that the most sensitive point in an army was its rear, and the result was the 1919 rear-attack project. With an air force it is exactly the same; air power can meet air power 'frontally,' but for air power to destroy the ground organization of air power is most difficult, since aircraft are slaves to gravity from whose clutches they can escape only if they are lightly equipped. Besides, to be certain of hitting a comparatively small target they must fly low and face the anti-aircraft defence of their enemy.

LONDON LYING DEFENCELESS UNDER THE PERIL THAT FLEW BY DAY

The danger in which the great cities of the world will stand in any future war is caught and crystallised in the picture painted by Henry Rushbury from memories of what he saw from the roof of the Royal College of Science, South Kensington, when the German aeroplanes appeared over London in daylight on July 7, 1917. Flying unharmed through a cloud of anti-aircraft bursts they are about to loose their freight of high explosive; what if the bombs had contained poison gas?

Imperial War Museum

SPEED, MOBILITY AND PROTECTION COMBINED: A MEDIUM TANK

Experiments in tank construction did not stand still after the Great War. Even before its end a light, fast-moving tank had been evolved, and since then the main object has been the construction of a weapon combining the protection and obstacle-crossing power of a tank with the speed of an armoured car. This is a British tank of the 'Medium' type (Mark II); weighing about 12 tons with a speed of 20 miles an hour, it is an admirable weapon for outflanking movements

Photo, War Office

If armies could move, let us suppose, a hundred miles a day in place of the present twenty (and remembering that a man in a motor car can easily travel four hundred miles in twenty-four hours, there is nothing impossible in this supposition), then land attack of the ground organization of the enemy's air power should not be a very difficult problem, unless this ground organization is effectively defended. To move at this pace demands a mechanical army, that is an army in which muscle power has been replaced by petrol power. To protect ground organizations similar forces must be used. Thus we see that the general adoption of aircraft as weapons of war will not abolish armies but will recreate them. In fact, the power of mechanical warfare in the air, though it will render obsolete muscular warfare on land, will simultaneously replace the old traditional military forces of to-day by mechanical forces—forces which though armoured can move at a high speed.

The armies of the future must therefore be organized so that they can protect and attack the rear services of an air force with extreme rapidity, in order to lessen the time in which aircraft can strike at the civil nerves. To expect present-day armies to do this is to ask for the impossible, for they are tied to roads and railways, and are as dependent on these as a barge is on a canal. On ground suitable for machines of the tank type infantry are helpless when they meet them; cavalry are equally so, but possess the advantage of more speedy retreat, and horse-drawn artillery, though they can (with increasing difficulty) destroy mechanically propelled weapons when these attack them frontally, are easy prey when attacked in flank or in the rear. During the Great War the terror of the tank became so overwhelming that in September, 1918, the German higher command issued an urgent order that whenever tanks were signalled every gun in the neighbourhood was to fire on them. After the war General von Zwehl wrote: 'It was not the genius of Marshal Foch that defeated us, but General Tank.'

To meet the tank the gunner must mount his gun in a somewhat similar machine. He must be able to hunt the tank as well as fire at it, and if he is to be supported by other arms these too must move forward in mechanically propelled vehicles which, when necessary, can abandon roads and move across country. All supply vehicles must be able to do likewise, or else the mechanical arms will be compelled to waste time in converging or retiring on roads and railways in place of pushing onwards. Here is opened up an entirely new form of war, a war of another dimension, when we compare it to the wars of the past.

We must go back a long way in history in order to paint in a background which will show up clearly the form of war which we have evolved, but which at present we cannot perceive. The Greek phalanx and the Roman legion carried out their assault (for there was little or no attack as we know it to-day) in line. The soldiers linked their shields and virtually pushed their opponents over with their pikes and swords. In such battles the tactical idea was that of the linear attack, and discipline, courage and brute strength won the fight. In the days of Frederick the Great the tactical idea was the same: two lines approached to within thirty

STEPS TOWARDS THE MECHANISATION OF THE BRITISH ARMY

At the top is the latest type of armoured car, intended chiefly for reconnaissance work by cavalry units, but capable of useful employment against the rear and flanks of marching forces; it has Rolls-Royce engines. Below it is a Carden-Loyd Mark VI armoured machine-gun carrier, having a maximum speed of 30 miles an hour. Since its crew consists of two men only, it represents the first step towards the armouring of infantry and a return to the days of the mailed knight.

Photos, War Office

paces of each other and then by volleys of musketry pushed, or rather blew, each other off the face of the battlefield.

Yet the thirty paces between the two lines does constitute a difference, for there is now a small area, a kind of no-man's-land, between the two lines. This area is all important, and one of the great problems of war during the last hundred and fifty years has been to discover methods of taking advantage of it: how to supply the soldier with weapons of greater and greater range, so that he can stand on one side of this no-man's-land in safety, and yet hit his enemy standing on the other side. It was this area and the idea it held which forced the soldier to increase the range of the rifle and the gun, and when the range became so great that it was difficult to hit the target with a single shot, to invent the machine-gun, and to turn solid cannon balls into hollow shells, and to fill these shells with bullets.

Then came the Great War, and still the race went on. Fire power became so terrific that soldiers could no longer fight on the surface of the ground, so they dug trenches, and thus turned the area into a shield. Then others attempted to dig them out with shells, and, as shrapnel is ineffective, shells were filled with high explosives; and as this proved uneconomical the very air above the area was used as a vehicle for poison gas. Thus no-man's-land, the area between the contending armies, expands in all directions—upwards into the sky, and downwards into the earth. From surface warfare we enter what may be called 'cubic' warfare; warfare that is certainly so when aeroplanes appear in their hundreds, and attack from above the rear of the entrenched masses of men.

The expansion of No-Man's-Land

The war began as a linear struggle and it ended as such, but with this difference: tanks could cross bullet-swept areas, and aeroplanes could fly over them, and gas could inundate them. And this difference is daily growing. During the war it was discovered how to contract the area between two lines of men, until armoured tanks could approach the enemy's machine guns as closely as the legionaries of Caesar could approach the Gauls. The could do more than this: they coul destroy the machine guns and pass on wards. In those days they could move a four miles an hour; to-day they can mov at forty. Consequently they need n longer attack the front of an enemy, fo they can move round his front and attac his rear, that is, where he is least prepare to meet an attack. Thus we see the whol art of war changing. Fronts are crumblin away, because the soldier has discovere how to cross no-man's-land between them Areas are becoming more and more the tru battlefields; areas perhaps several hun dreds of miles deep and broad, because th radius of the aeroplane is increasing daily and tanks can now move a hundred mile in twenty-four hours, and armoured car two to three hundred.

It is mainly because of the changes i the element of mobility that we see thes startling changes evolving in methods of protection. In its turn protected mobility must influence offensive power. Gas warfar will wipe out the armies of to-day but how will it influence the mechanica armies of the future? The answer obvi ously is, to a lesser degree; because me will be largely protected from vesican chemicals by the armour of their machine and if necessary these machines can b made gas-tight. As the armoured-cavalr age gave way to the earth-seeking age o infantry, and as the musket ousted th lance, so will the present infantry age giv way to an armoured-artillery age in whic the gun will oust the rifle.

The element of Protected Mobilit

The tank period which we hav examined is in fact but the beginning o this new artillery age in thin disguise for the tank itself is only a mobile gu mounting; and in consequence the lan battles of the future will be pre-eminentl artillery battles, short, sharp and decisive— the destruction will be insignificant, an casualties comparatively few. On thes armoured battles will largely depend th action of aircraft, which will attack th nerves of the enemy's people, and so strik at the foundations of the hostile fightin forces. Such will be some of the futur developments of the offensive element.

he tank first saw action on September 15, 1916. There were two types of this machine: the male, quipped with two 6-pounder guns and a machine gun, and the female, armed with machine guns only. Above is shown a Mark I male tank on the battlefield of the Somme in 1916.

Photo, War Office

British invention, the tank was designed to overcome obstacles which restricted the mobility of fantry, of which the most formidable were bullets, wire entanglements and earthworks. At the ttle of Cambrai, on November 20, 1917, the Mark IV tank, of which one is here shown about to opple' at Wailly, proved its value as a new engine of war; it revolutionised tactics by conquering the spade and wire and reinstating mobility.

ADVENT OF AN INNOVATION IN WARFARE: HEAVY TANKS

Photo, Imperial War Museum

In 1918 the Mark IV tank was replaced by a Mark V model, a faster and more handy machine, whic led the British assault on August 8, 1918, and so decisively defeated the German forces that Gener Ludendorff christened this day 'the Black Day of the German army.'

Besides the heavy tanks, in 1918 a medium machine known as the Medium A, or Whippet, tank wa introduced as a 'cavalry' or pursuit weapon. It could move at from eight to ten miles an hour and its crew consisted of three men. In the above photograph three of these machines are see advancing to attack during one of the great battles of August, 1918.

CHIEF TYPES OF BRITISH TANK IN OPERATION IN 1918

Photos, Mechanical Warfare Supply Dept., and (bottom) War Office

The leader of this line of battleships is the Iron Duke, flagship of Lord Jellicoe while in command of the Grand Fleet, 1914–16. Vessels in this class carry ten 13·5-inch, twelve 6-inch, and four 3-pounder guns; stout armour up to 12 inches thick covers their main gun positions and conning tower.

Badly hit by German shells at the battle of the Dogger Bank on January 24, 1915, Sir David Beatty's flagship, the Lion, was compelled to retire from the line, and was sent to Newcastle for repairs. She was one of the battle cruisers under Beatty's command at the battle of Jutland in 1916, and again had a narrow escape, being badly damaged. This photograph was taken towards the beginning of the war.

ARMOURED SHIPS THAT WERE THE STRENGTH OF THE BRITISH NAVY

Photos, Stephen Cribb, Southsea, and (bottom) Abrahams & Sons, Devonport

aeroplanes and seaplanes co-operated in ever-increasing number. It was, therefore, theoretically possible for one side to command the surface and for the other side simultaneously to hold the zone of water beneath the surface, or the air above it. The change was so far-reaching that no thinker had been able to foresee its full effects, or prepare adequately to meet it.

All the navies, all the staffs, groped in the dark. That the submarine was certain to be formidable they recognized; indeed, they rather exaggerated than under-estimated the danger from it. They had not in peace been able to devise satisfactory methods of fighting it. Depth charges, mines of a type that exploded when a certain depth was reached and shook or shattered the submarine, did not exist in an effective form before 1914; and, if they had done, could not have been dropped in manoeuvres on friendly crews. Nor was it practicable to try such devices as nets for entangling the propellers of submarines, which would probably have involved the loss of these craft and the death of all on board them. In the British manoeuvres of 1913 the hits claimed by submarines were so numerous as to frighten the Admiralty;

U 9, with the enormous death-roll of 1,459 officers and men, proved that without special precautions ships of the pre-Dreadnought type were helpless against submarines. Some 36,000 tons of shipping were sent to the bottom by a craft of only 500 tons. Nothing like this had ever been known in naval war before.

New horrors of Naval War

Added to the peril from the torpedo was the danger from the mine, one of the most insidious and merciless weapons ever invented, and strewn by the Germans on the high seas, in the fairways of ocean traffic and even off remote points on the coasts of the Dominions. Thus the seafarer was never safe when out of port. A crash would be heard; a column of smoke and water would shoot up; and the structure of steel in which he was travelling would collapse and leave him helpless in the water.

At the outbreak of war aircraft co-operation with the fleets at sea did not exist, though the British had one aircraft carrier in service and the Germans had one Zeppelin ready; two others had been destroyed by accidents just before the war. Effective co-operation of the air arm with the fleets was only just coming

This war-time photograph shows an actual discharge of a salvo of 13·5-inch guns from a British battle cruiser. With two exceptions, all British battle cruisers after the Indomitable class carried eight 13·5 guns, a simultaneous discharge of four guns usually constituting a salvo.

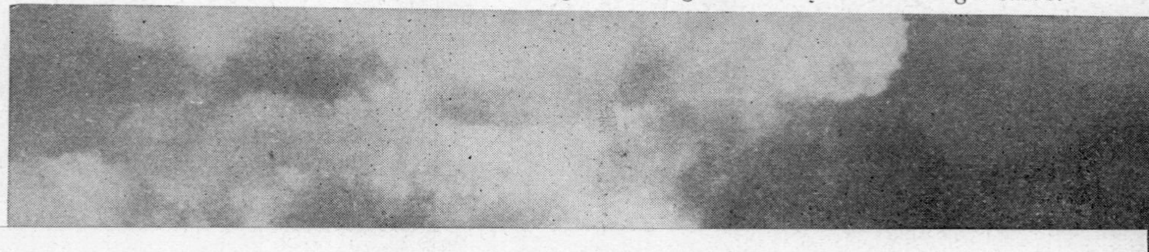

THE FLOATING MINE

Naval tactics were greatly changed by the invention of floating mines with which German destroyers sowed the seas, thus rendering all vessels liable to sudden destruction. This photograph shows a floating mine washed ashore.

Photo, Sport and General

into existence when the war closed, and the world is still uncertain what its future influence will be. The aeroplanes and seaplanes of 1914 were crude and weak machines, and carried no bombs that could hurt a battleship. With one or two unimportant exceptions they were even without any machine-gun armament o satisfactory wireless equipment. Thei climbing power was so limited that the were of little use for reconnoitring. Th Zeppelins which Germany possessed wer far more formidable than the aeroplane of 1914, as they were supplied with re spectable bombs and could rise to 8,00 feet, but they were helpless in storms Though, wisely used, they might hav rendered immense service as scouts in th North Sea, they accomplished little.

In spite of these new weapons and th perplexities which they brought, it was soor proved that the importance of commanding the sea had grown and not diminished When whole nations and not a small per-centage of their able-bodied manhood took the field, even countries which till the war had been self-dependent, or nearly so, were at a grave disadvantage if they could not import raw materials, half-manufactured articles, munitions and food. The collapse of Germany was, in large measure, due to the pressure of economic factors, and that pressure was imposec by the British blockade which strove tc cut off all Germany's foreign sources o

A VICTIM TO SUBMARINE WARFARE : H.M.S. HOGUE

The advent of the submarine provided a new and disturbing element in the naval encounters of the Great War. This was drastically demonstrated on September 22, 1914, when three British cruisers, Cressy, Aboukir and Hogue, on patrol duty off Holland, were torpedoed and sunk by the German submarine U 9. These cruisers, being unaccompanied by their destroyers, were particularly helpless before their unseen assailant. The loss of life on the Hogue was 372 officers and men.

Photo, Sport & General Press Agency

THE GERMAN CRUISER MAINZ GOING DOWN OFF HELIGOLAND

The naval engagement that took place between the British and Germans off Heligoland on August 28, 1914, resulted in a decisive victory for the former. This photograph shows the Mainz, one of the three German light cruisers in the battle, sinking rapidly, while the British destroyer retiring on the left carries on board members of the stricken ship's crew.

Copyright, 'Illustrated London News'

supply. Without control of the surface of the sea by the British navy the blockade would have been out of the question. In any case the blockade was not of the old type in which the blockading squadrons cruised close to the blockaded ports. The British ships operated at a great distance, holding the two entrances to the North Sea. The change was necessitated by the development of the mine and torpedo and the altered conditions of naval war.

The Germans knew that a blockade operates but slowly, and as they were convinced of their capacity to end the war very quickly on land by crushing France, they altogether under-estimated the effect of sea power and the danger of forcing the British Empire into conflict with them. They were prepared for a six months' struggle, so that they were not alarmed at the possibility of having their foreign trade interrupted for that period. The British with the British Allies gained the command of the sea in European waters with startling speed and ease at the very outset of the war, everywhere outside the Baltic. This was largely because fortunately enough the main British fleet was mobilised when war began. Its mobilisation was known to everyone in advance, and had been arranged long

THE BRITISH BLOCKADE IN OPERATION DURING THE GREAT WAR

The German government declared a blockade of the United Kingdom in February, 1915, issuing orders to their submarines to sink all merchant ships at sight. In March the British replied by declaring a blockade of Germany, virtually crushing her overseas export trade. The subject of W. L. Wyllie's drawing is the boarding of a neutral vessel to search for contraband by an armed merchantman of the Tenth Cruiser Squadron. Note the elaborate camouflage (see page 4859).

H.M.S. GOOD HOPE : ADMIRAL CRADOCK'S FLAGSHIP

Commissioned for service as Cradock's flagship in August, 1914, the Good Hope was an old vess which had seen almost continuous service as a flagship of cruiser squadrons from 1902–12. C November 1 Cradock's fleet came into contact with von Spee's squadron off Coronel, and Crado bravely engaged a force vastly superior to his own. In a brief action the Good Hope was struck b repeated salvoes from the Scharnhorst and sank with her admiral and all hands.

Photo, Topical Press Agency

beforehand, in March, 1914, when no shadow of war darkened the political sky.

The early engagements were of no very serious importance. In the battle of Heligoland on August 28, 1914, three German light cruisers and a destroyer were sunk by British cruiser squadrons, including Beatty's battle cruisers; but the British were so overwhelmingly superior in force that nothing else was to be expected. The Germans blundered badly in risking a few weak ships against such tremendous antagonists as the British battle cruisers. On neither side in this engagement did submarines effect anything of importance, though the information obtained by the British submarines was of great he in enabling a severe blow to be struck.

Another valuable means of informatic was provided by tl wireless of both side Each fleet listened c sensitive receiving i struments for the signa of the other. This w one of the new conditio of operations in tl Great War; there ha been nothing even r motely resembling it the past. From tl general superiority of i listening service, tl greater excellence of i instruments, the strict care shown in forbi ding wireless signa when moving again the adversary, and tl fortunate accident th in August, 1914, tl German ciphers ar

ADMIRAL CRADOCK

Sir Christopher Cradock (1862–1914), whose career ended at the battle of Coronel, had earlier served in the Sudan and China. He was placed in command of the Atlantic Fleet in 1911.

Photo, Elliott & Fry

signal books had been captured by the Russians in the wreck of the German cruiser Magdeburg, and transmitted to the British, the British navy had an important advantage over the Germans in this matter. And thus, whenever the Germans made an important move in the North Sea, they found British forces mysteriously on the alert and waiting to engage them. Even when the German ciphers were changed and became more difficult to read, it was possible to ascertain from the character of the signals passing when anything momentous was on foot.

COUNT VON SPEE

Born at Copenhagen in 1861, Maximilian, count von Spee, was one of the creators of the German navy in which he served. He commanded the Far Eastern Squadron in 1914.

Photo, E.N.A.

In the distant seas there was considerable trouble for the British owing to the failure of the Admiralty before the war to build sufficient fast cruisers and to place them in the proper strategic positions. Von Spee, who commanded the formidable German cruiser squadron in the Far East, was a particularly dangerous antagonist from the high quality of the gunnery in his two large armoured cruisers Scharnhorst and Gneisenau, which had won the Kaiser's cup for shooting in two consecutive years before the war. Leaving Kiao-chau when relations became strained, he vanished to a remote island in the northern Pacific and there waited for the outbreak of war. When it came, he crossed the Pacific to the neighbourhood of the west coast of South America and threatened the nitrate traffic, which was extremely important, because nitrates were then indispensable for making munitions and were only manufactured synthetically, by obtaining nitrogen from the air, on a small scale in Germany and Norway in 1914.

The Admiralty sent against Spee's powerful ships Admiral Cradock with a small and weak squadron, the crews of which were for the most part composed of

THE SCHARNHORST IN BRITISH WATERS BEFORE THE WAR

On November 1, 1914, Admiral von Spee's squadron sank Admiral Cradock's cruisers at Coronel. Spee then steamed to the Falkland Islands, where, on December 8, he encountered a British squadron under Admiral Sturdee. The ensuing naval action resulted in a complete triumph for the latter and the destruction of the German squadron. The Scharnhorst, Spee's flagship, here seen near the Victory in Portsmouth harbour, put up a stern fight before sinking with all on board.

Photo, Stephen Cribb

ADMIRAL STURDEE

Sir Frederick Charles Doveton Sturdee, born in 1859, entered the navy in 1871. He was in command at the battle of the Falkland Islands in 1914, and fought at Jutland. He became admiral of the fleet in 1921.

Photo, Elliott & Fry

reservists and most dangerously inferior to the Germans in gunnery. Interpreting a badly worded telegram from London as an order to attack, Cradock steamed up the west coast of Chile with the Good Hope and Monmouth, both old armoured cruisers; the Glasgow, a modern light cruiser but useless against armoured antagonists; and an armed merchantman, the Otranto. Off Coronel he met Spee, whose two armoured cruisers were each in battery markedly superior to any vessel in the British squadron. This material superiority was rendered still more crushing by the superior skill of their gunners.

The engagement that followed on November 1, 1914, was utterly disastrous to the weaker force. The Germans, without themselves receiving a single serious hit, shot the Good Hope and Monmouth into tangles of steel wreckage. Their salvoes beat with appalling rapidity every fifteen seconds on the two doomed British ships which, labouring in a heavy sea, could not work all their guns and so were further handicapped. What happened on board them no man knows, fo all in them perished. But from th German ships it was seen that great fire broke out in them, as all the evidenc suggests from the extreme inflammabilit of the ammunition they carried. Violen explosions were also observed. Fifty-thre minutes after the action had opened, th Good Hope disappeared in the darknes and the tumultuous sea. She must hav foundered with Cradock and all on boar The Monmouth sank a little later, fightin to the very end against hopeless odd The other two British ships escaped. Bu the sacrifice of an admiral, two cruise and 1,653 officers and men, with only few scratches on the German ships t show for it, was a grievous blow, thoug the heroism which the British crew displayed was magnificent. The busine in war is to win, not to be killed; an fearful indeed is the price that has to b paid for mistakes at sea.

Before the result of this battle wa known Lord Fisher had become first se lord; and immediately he learnt of th disaster he took measures to make an en of Spee. He detached from the Gran Fleet in British waters two battle cruisers, vessels overwhelmingly stronger than the German armoured cruisers. He did th in the face of strong remonstrances, an boldly took the risk that in the absence the two all-important ships the Germa main fleet might attempt a blow in th North Sea. He placed them under Admir Sturdee, whom he sent to the Falklan Islands off the south-east coast of Sout America, with instructions to sink ever ship in Spee's force. Spee bore himse gallantly and modestly after his victory but he, too, now committed one of tho mistakes which are so cruelly punished war. Against the advice of one of h most experienced officers, Captain Maerke he determined to steam to the Falkland seize the governor as a hostage for th German governor of Samoa who had bee captured by the British, and destroy th British coaling station in those islands.

Expedition to the Falkland Islan

He carried out his rash plan, having n suspicion of the dreadful surprise th awaited him. Early on December 8 h was off the Falklands, where Sturdee had just arrived with the two overwhelmingly powerful battle cruisers. Dense clouds of smoke rose from the interior of the harbour as the Germans approached. They were really caused by the British raising steam for battle, but they led some of the German officers to imagine that a great success was at hand and that the British were burning their coal and stores as the preliminary to surrender. One or two of the Germans, however, thought they could discern through the smoke tripod masts. These masts at that date were carried only by ships of immense fighting force such as battle cruisers or Dreadnought battleships. But as yet most of the observers in Spee's ships did not make out tripod masts in the harbour. Not till too late did they discover that battle cruisers were actually there, and then at Spee's order they took immediately to flight.

The British battle cruisers could steam 25 knots to the 21 which was Spee's utmost speed, and they were so superior in armament that the issue was never in doubt. The battle that followed was protracted because Sturdee determined to fight at extreme range, so as to avoid any risk of serious damage to his two precious battle cruisers. The day was a brilliant one; the colour of the sea was the deepest blue, and the distance of vision was exceptional when the German ordeal began. About 1.30 in the afternoon the guns opened and with some intervals continued their grim work all that afternoon till about 4 p.m., when the Scharnhorst with only one of her four funnels standing and with great fires blazing in her amidships, slowly turned over and sank, taking with her to the bottom Spee and all who had not been killed in the battle. There could be no attempt at rescue because the engagement

THE LAST OF THE GERMAN BATTLE CRUISER GNEISENAU

In this photograph, taken from the British warship Inflexible after the battle of the Falkland Islands, the survivors of the Gneisenau's crew can be seen struggling in the water. The Gneisenau was a sister ship to the Scharnhorst, and their destruction, together with the rest of Spee's squadron, struck a severe blow at German power on the sea. A number of survivors were taken aboard the British battleship, but many died from exposure to the bitter cold.

continued. The Gneisenau's existence was protracted for another two hours before she, too, went down after fearful losses had been inflicted on her officers and men. So icy was the water, though it was then summer in the Southern hemisphere, that many of the Germans died of exhaustion in the sea or in the boats after the British had reached them. Their total loss was about 1,540.

Two of the three light cruisers with Spee were destroyed the same day by the other British ships, with heavy German loss of life and almost without casualties to the British; but one of his ships, the Dresden, escaped and for many weeks eluded her pursuers. In the battle between the more important armoured ships an enormous quantity of ammunition was expended by the British, but the two battle cruisers did their work and returned with only the most trivial damage. Sturdee coul report that the total loss in both of ther was no more than one man killed. Lik Coronel, this battle shows that in moder conditions a weak surface squadron ha very little chance of inflicting seriou damage or loss on a strong squadron.

The scattered German cruisers wer hunted down one by one, and the sea wa cleared of them, but not until they ha inflicted considerable loss upon the Allie merchant services. The most troublesom of them were the Emden and Karlsruh The Emden was driven ashore an wrecked at the Cocos Islands, where final touch of horror was given to he destruction by the huge land crabs whic attacked her wounded. The Karlsruh was sunk by an explosion on board, prob ably caused by untrustworthy ammuni tion or oil fuel. The Germans would hav

THE EMDEN ENDS HER ADVENTUROUS CAREER ON THE COCOS ISLANDS

The German light cruiser Emden, launched in 1908, inflicted considerable damage upon Britis and allied commerce during the early months of the Great War, and her commander, von Mülle earned a reputation for his humanity towards the crews of the vessels he sank. The Emden wa driven ashore at North Keeling Island on November 9, 1914, after a vigorous action fought wit the Australian cruiser Sydney, to which she finally surrendered. Von Müller was among the save

Photo, Imperial War Museum

been caught much more quickly if the Allied vessels searching for them had been equipped with scouting aircraft, as most light cruisers have been since the war. Time after time they eluded pursuit by a mere hair's breadth.

In all these early weeks of the war the British control of the Channel remained undisputed. At no point then or subsequently were the German surface ships able to interfere with the transport of troops and supplies. Day after day a regular service traversed the Strait of Dover within easy reach of the German torpedo craft, when the Germans on land seized Ostend and Zeebrugge. Division after division of British crossed the great oceans from the Dominions moving to France. Not a single troopship was sunk in this stage of the war, and in the later months of the conflict, even when the German submarine campaign reached its full height, the loss was extraordinarily small, much smaller in proportion than that inflicted on the Japanese by the Russians in the war of 1904–5.

The High Sea Fleet, as the main German fleet was called, to the universal surprise, made no effort to attack the British troopships. Early in the war its leaders were informed by Moltke, the German chief of staff, that the German army was quite capable of settling both with the French army and with the British troops that were being transported to France. This was an error on his part, but unquestionably at the outset the Germans came very near winning the war on land. What offensive movements the High Sea Fleet did make at sea were directed towards bombarding British ports.

British retain Control of the Channel

The Grand Fleet, as the British main fleet was named after the outbreak of war, had many serious difficulties to overcome in its operations in the North Sea. There was no base prepared for it which was reasonably secure against attack by submarines and destroyers and provided with the plant required for keeping a large naval force in good fighting order. The Firth of Forth could not be used till late in the war when enormous booms had been thrown across its entrance so as to enclose a large area of water. In 1914 it offered quite inadequate accommodation for a fleet which numbered at full strength over 200 vessels. The Grand Fleet was therefore compelled to use Scapa Flow, an immense sheet of water in the Orkneys.

PERILS OF THE SCAPA BASE

From this map of the North Sea it will be seen that Heligoland, the German advanced naval base, was almost twice as far from Scapa Flow, where the British Grand Fleet was usually concentrated, as from the mouth of the Thames.

This base had three defects. It was without piers, docks and repair shops. It was nearly twice as far from Heligoland, the advanced base of the German fleet, as Heligoland from the mouth of the Thames. Thus, unless the Grand Fleet started immediately the Germans put to sea, it could not be certain of intercepting them on their return from raids. Scapa Flow was further entirely unprotected against submarines or even destroyers. It had five entrances, all of which had to be guarded. Months passed before it could be made tolerably safe, and there was a period when, after reports (which proved subsequently to be incorrect) that submarines had been seen in the Flow, the Grand Fleet was moved to the west coast of Scotland and to Lough Swilly, to give its officers and men some rest from the excessive nerve strain to which they were exposed in an open harbour.

The failure of the German submarines to attack the Grand Fleet in this period, before Scapa was rendered secure, still remains something of an enigma. But the Flow was remote from observation by spies and its name was never mentioned in British reports or newspapers. The extreme secrecy enforced by the strict censorship on all news probably helped no little to keep the Germans in uncertainty as to where the British main fleet really was. Reconnaissances of the Flow by two U-boats happened to be made when the Grand Fleet was not inside, and doubtless helped to mislead the Germans. Moreover, about the rocks or 'skerries' at the southern entrances to the Flow, which are the most important ones, swirled unusually strong tides and currents. These are the well-known 'roosts' in the Pentland Firth which run not in one well defined stream, but vary constantly and attain speeds of 8 or 9 knots. Such waters were peculiarly treacherous for submarines. Only one determined attempt on the ships in the Flow was essayed by a U-boat, and that was in 1918 by a boat manned with German officers. She made her way through the outer defences, which by that date had been made very formidable but was caught and blown up on the inner line of mines.

In November, 1914, German battle cruisers appeared off the Norfolk coast and fired a few shells at Lowestoft and Yarmouth. In December of that year they loomed up out of the early morning mist and bombarded Hartlepool, Scarborough and Whitby, shelling the residential quarters of the two former places and causing great damage and heavy loss of life. They killed 106 non-combatants and wounded 510. Though squadrons of the British Grand Fleet were moving to cut them off these battle cruisers were not brought to action and destroyed. Indeed, it was lucky for the British that a general engagement did not result—the Germans had almost their entire strength and the British only about half their fleet. Not only were many of the Grand Fleet's battleships unavailable, but it was also weakened by the

IN THE WAKE OF A GERMAN SHELL AT SCARBOROUGH

The bombardment of the English east coast by German battle cruisers in December, 1914, caused considerable damage and mortality in Hartlepool, Scarborough and Whitby. The Grand Hotel a conspicuous building on the sea front at Scarborough, formed an easy target for the raiders, and its restaurant and buffet, shown in the photograph, were wrecked by German shells. Damage such as this was the sum of the injury inflicted by the German surface fleets on the British Isles.

Photo, London News Agency

VICE-ADMIRAL VON HIPPER

Von Hipper, a rear-admiral at the outbreak of the war, carried out the German naval raid on the English east coast in December, 1914. He commanded the cruiser squadron at the Dogger Bank, 1915, and at Jutland, 1916.

Photo, E.N.A.

absence of the two battle cruisers that had been sent off to fight Spee, and a third was guarding the convoys with Canadian troops. This was one of the occasions when the British were misled by their reading of the German wireless signals. The messages which they had intercepted did not reveal that the main force of the German fleet would be at sea.

Some weeks later a fresh raid was attempted by the Germans, but this time without the main strength of the High Sea Fleet following in support of the battle cruisers. On January 24, 1915, the German admiral, Hipper, with three battle cruisers and a ship of weaker type, the Blücher, reached the Dogger Bank only to discover Beatty bearing down on him with five British battle cruisers. The British had detected signs of the German movement and had taken precautions against it. The German ships turned and ran, the Blücher immediately dropping to the rear. Beatty came up in pursuit and a long-range action followed.

Quite early in the engagement it looked as though a decisive victory was to be won. An immense column of flame and smoke was seen to spurt up from Hipper's flagship, the Seydlitz, just after a hit had been made on her by Beatty's flagship, the Lion. A shell pierced the armour of the aftermost turret, setting on fire a large quantity of ammunition inside. The unfortunate men in the turret who were cut off, in an attempt to escape from the fire, must have opened a door in a bulkhead leading to a compartment under a second turret, as in this second turret also the ammunition blazed up. The two turrets and the compartments near them were converted into one great furnace of roaring flame in which 159 of the 165 men in that part of the ship were burnt to death. By Hipper's staff it was thought that the ship was doomed and must blow up, but though six tons of explosive had taken fire and burnt, the magazines were flooded and the Seydlitz was saved. She was however, in a precarious state, with a great deal of water in her and little ammunition available for her other turrets.

By a curious accident the British flagship, the Lion, was also badly hit about this

ADMIRAL BEATTY

The traditional fighting spirit of the British navy was well upheld by Admiral Beatty (born 1871) in the battles of the Dogger Bank and Jutland. In 1919 he was given an earldom and appointed first sea lord.

Photo, Russell

HOW THE GERMAN CRUISER BLUECHER WENT DOWN

This striking photograph, taken from a British cruiser at the battle of the Dogger Bank, shows the German armoured cruiser Blücher turning turtle after her stout resistance to the attacks of the British ships. Abandoned by her sister ships when she caught fire, the Blücher was finally sunk by two torpedoes discharged by the British light cruiser Aurora. Her crew is here seen scrambling down the almost horizontal hull, only 123 out of 885 being rescued.

Photo, 'The Daily Mail'

time, and, like the Seydlitz, was in extreme danger. A shell started a fire in her fore-turret magazine, and those on board her thought the end was at hand until the welcome message came up from the magazine party, working in the stifling heat and smoke far below, that the magazine was flooded and the fire was out. She received another bad hit, however, which gradually reduced her speed, and she fell astern, with the result that she could no longer take part in the action. Meanwhile the Blücher, like the Seydlitz, suffered terribly from a fierce ammunition fire, caused by a British shell. Sheets of flame rose from two of her turrets and she dropped far astern of the other German ships, which abandoned her to her fate. She was destroyed with torpedoes after a gallant resistance. The main battle with Hipper's three battle cruisers was broken off when Beatty fell astern and could no longer direct the attack.

Engagement of the Dogger Bank

Only four hits were made by the British on the German ships which escaped, though the hits on the Blücher were numerous. The German loss in killed and wounded was over a thousand, mostly in the Blücher; the British was only 43. The Germans received a severe blow, but the battle taught them a great deal, as after it they took special and additional precautions against ammunition fires, which, as Jutland was afterwards to show only too clearly, are the surface ship's chief danger in action.

Vast and important as were the services which sea power rendered to the Allies in the war, its strict limitations remained as in the past. Ships were able to accomplish little against forts on land. Repeated bombardments of the Belgian coast by British vessels produced no real impression on the German batteries there, except at the opening of the first battle of Ypres when the fire of the British naval guns secured most important results by preventing the Germans from breaking through the Belgian front.

At the Dardanelles, the attempt to force a passage past the Turkish forts on that long and narrow waterway completely failed. The fleet engaged was composed of old British and French battleships to which two modern Dreadnoughts were attached. It had to deal with mines in the straits as well as heavy guns well mounted ashore. In the main attack of March 18, 1915, two British battleships and one French battleship were sunk, and each of the Allies had another important ship badly damaged. If a joint attack by a strong military force and a powerful fleet had been delivered, the Dardanelles would almost certainly have been penetrated and opened temporarily; but unless the Turkish army, which was mobilised and near at hand, had been thoroughly beaten the result must have been far less decisive than was supposed at the time by the Allied governments.

On the Suez Canal a force of old ships was not able to prevent the Turks from crossing into Egypt, though they were finally repulsed by the greatly superior number of British troops holding the canal. Nor were the British surface ships ever able to penetrate into the Baltic or weaken the German grip on that sea. The pressure which the Allied navies exerted upon Germany was in turn exerted by the German navy upon Russia, where it was beyond doubt one of the causes of the Russian catastrophe.

It was the British desire to give Russia support at sea that led to the battle of Jutland. In the morning of May 30, 1916, the British Admiralty intercepted wireless messages of German origin which told it that some considerable part of the High Sea Fleet was on the move in the North Sea. The Admiralty hoped to force the Germans to fight, to defeat them, and thus to take pressure off the Russians. From noon onwards orders and instructions were sent off to the various British squadrons and commands. When night fell, the Grand Fleet began to steam out from its bases at Scapa Flow, Cromarty and Rosyth towards the coast of Jutland.

By the early afternoon of May 31, invisible to each other, the two large fleets, the British of 150 vessels and the German of 99 vessels, were rapidly nearing one another. In each fleet a force of battle cruisers with light cruisers and destroyers was some fifty miles in advance of the main body and would be the first to engage. The Germans suspected or indeed knew that Beatty with his battle cruisers was at sea. But neither in the reports of their submarines nor in such few wireless signals as they had intercepted was there anything to indicate that Jellicoe with the British battle fleet was also steaming in great strength to Horns Reef, a shoal and lightship off the Danish coast. Nor was there anything to show that with Beatty and his six battle-cruisers were four formidable new battle-ships of the Barham class, each mounting eight 15-inch guns and steaming 25 knots—the most powerful vessels in service in any fleet at that time. The British knew that Hipper with the German battle cruisers was at sea. But they in their turn did

PANORAMIC PLAN OF THE DARDANELLES AS DRAWN BY A GERMAN

Arabic numerals point the various places in the key to this pictorial map of the Dardanelles, showing the dangerous Narrows and the sea of Marmora. It was drawn for the guidance of the Turkish government by a German artist, Zeno Diemer, and lithographed by Franz M. Würbel. This reproduction is made from a copy of the map obtained from the Turkish war office after the war. It can be realized that defeat of the Turkish army would have been essential after any naval success.

ADMIRAL JELLICOE

John Rushworth Jellicoe was born at Southampton in 1859, and entered the Navy in 1872. He was appointed commander-in-chief of the Grand Fleet on the outbreak of the Great War. In 1925 he was created an earl.

Photo, Speaight, Ltd.

not know that Scheer was also out with the German battle fleet. The German wireless signals which had been intercepted suggested that it was still in harbour at Wilhelmshaven. Thus each side was about to experience a surprise.

The Germans sent up five naval Zeppelins to scout, but these airships did not go far or render much service. They reported the weather hazy and the visibility nowhere more than six sea miles or 12,000 yards. The British fleet moved in silence without making wireless signals, which were only to be used if the enemy was sighted, and various British ships were told off to listen on the German wavelengths. The Germans were not so careful; a German wireless signal was taken in just before noon by the British. Its faintness showed that the German force was still at some distance.

At 2 p.m. Beatty's advanced cruisers, far ahead of the British battle fleet, reached the point where contact with the German advance guard was expected to be made. The sea seemed empty, however. There was no sign of any adversary, and only a harmless Danish steamer, the U-Fjord, could be discerned some distance away. The British were preparing to turn north and withdraw, assuming that the Germans had not maintained their movement, when at 2.15 the British light cruiser Galatea saw something suspicious. A long grey vessel with two funnels closed the U-Fjord, apparently to examine her. The suspicious vessel was quickly identified as the large German destroyer, B 109, and at 2.20 the Galatea observed other warships not belonging to the British navy, and made the momentous signal, 'Enemy in sight.' About the same time German wireless signals came in strongly on the British instruments.

The British were quicker by several minutes than the Germans in giving the alarm. Each battle cruiser force, when the signals of contact were received, turned towards the hostile ships and raised its speed to support its light vessels. Already the action had opened; the Galatea was firing at the German light cruiser Elbing. In the other ships the men were at action stations.

GERMAN COMMANDER AT JUTLAND

When the Great War broke out Reinhold von Scheer commanded the battle squadron at Kiel until appointed commander-in-chief of the High Sea Fleet in 1915. His conduct of the Jutland battle was highly praised in Germany.

Photo, Imperial War Museum

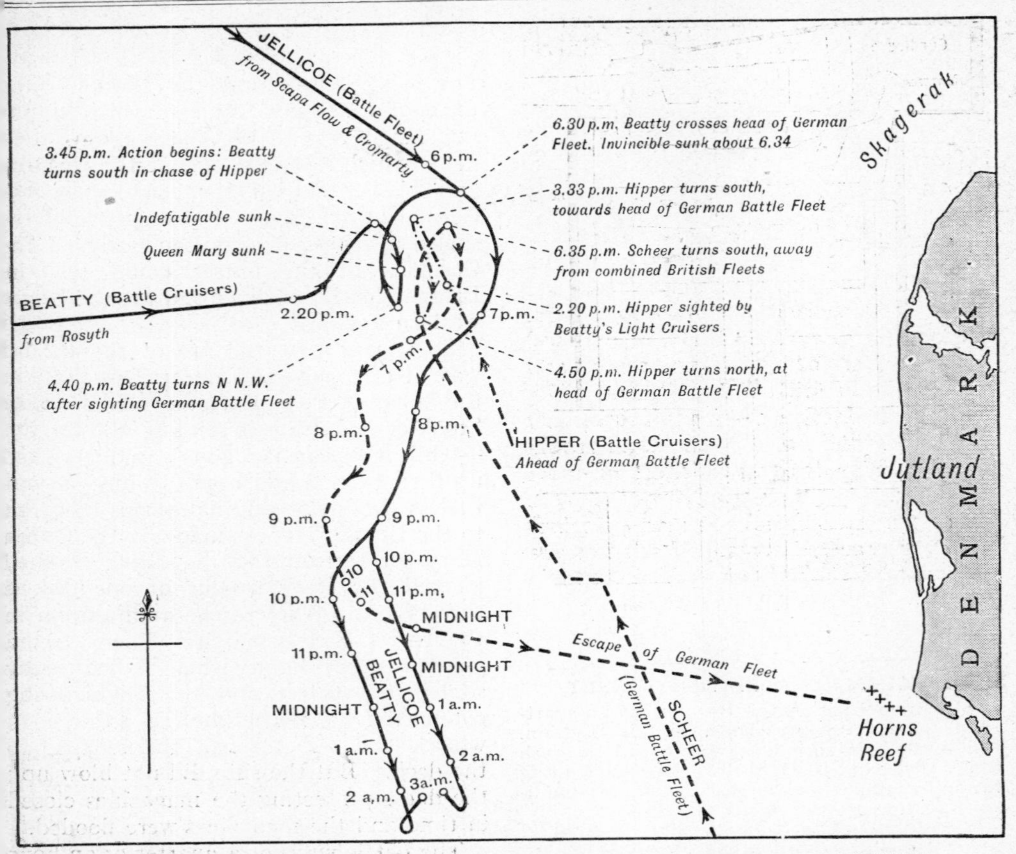

MOVEMENTS OF THE OPPOSED FLEETS DURING THE BATTLE OF JUTLAND

While the over-all scale of this plan is roughly accurate—it can be gauged by reference to the Danish coast in the map in page 4841—the internal scale cannot be guaranteed; in particular, for clarity's sake, the complicated early movements (north) have been slightly expanded at the expense of the rest. Broadly, the course of the battle was this: Hipper drew Beatty's advanced cruiser squadron in pursuit on to the advancing German High Sea Fleet; Beatty, turning, drew the two in pursuit on to the British battle fleet; the Germans turned in flight, and escaped under cover of darkness.

Over the North Sea at the point where these two fleets were about to engage hung patches of mist and haze, especially towards the east—the quarter from which the Germans were approaching. The westward sky in the quarter from which Beatty was moving was clear and free from mist. Beatty so directed his line of movement as to place his ships between the German battle cruisers and their bases, and thus to compel them to fight. At 3 p.m. Commander Paschen, the fire-control officer in the German flagship Lützow, says that he could discern with certainty the massive outlines of Beatty's six battle cruisers and far astern of them the shapes of the four fast British battle-ships of the Fifth Battle Squadron. If he really saw all this his admiral did not report it. On the contrary, Hipper signalled to Scheer twice over that the British force consisted of only six large ships. As for the British, they could only just make out in the mist the dim forms of five German battle cruisers and were not quite certain what these ships were or whether there were any new vessels among them, owing to the poor light to the east.

When the Germans discovered the strength of Beatty's force they turned and steamed as fast as they could towards their own battle fleet, which was far behind them to the south-east. The British increased speed and steadily gained

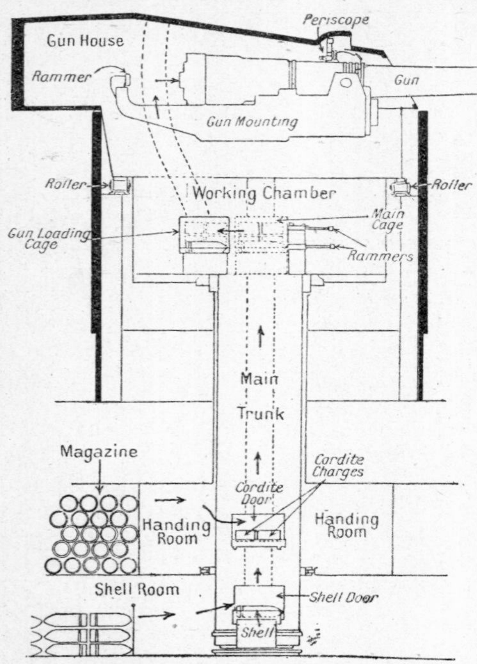

DIAGRAM OF A BRITISH TURRET

The relative positions of the various compartments of a turret are shown in this diagram. Unless the magazine doors were closed the flash from a shell exploding in the turret risked igniting the ammunition down the main trunk. Ammunition fires are the chief danger in action.

From Fawcett & Hooper, 'Jutland,' Macmillan & Co.

on them. At 3.48 the battle between the big ships began. The salvoes beat across the sea and fountains of water rose near the ships, as the fire control officers on both sides felt for their targets.

In battle at sea everything depends on quick hitting, and quick hitting depends on excellent discipline, thorough training, ample target practice, good range finders and instruments, and good conditions of shooting. There was nothing to choose between the men in the two fleets in the matter of discipline and training, but —though this point is still a matter of controversy—the Germans probably had the better range finders. They were also favoured by the light and the mist in a singular degree. This was an entirely new condition in naval war, arising from the enormous increase in the range of naval artillery—that one side should be invisible to the other which it could see quite plainly. Only at rare intervals could the British make out the indistinct shapes of the German battle cruisers For most of the time they had nothing to shoot at and nothing from which to take the range except the flickers of scarlet flame which ran along the eastern horizon and blazed out of the mist when the Germans fired salvoes of four or five heavy shells, discharged simultaneously. The Germans at the outset could see the British clearly, outlined against the brigh western sky.

So it was that the fire of the British was at first slow and uncertain—that, in the words of a German officer, they 'took endless time in finding the target —while the German guns rapidly picked up their targets and began to hit. Nevertheless the first really dangerous hit went to the British. It was made by the Queen Mary on the unlucky Seydlitz; a shell pierced the steel armour of one of the turrets and set fire to the ammunition in the turret and below it. There was a great rush of flame which killed every soul in the turret and the neighbouring compartments, except half a dozen men who leaped out through the escapes to the deck. But the ship did not blow up the doors protecting the magazines closed in time and the magazines were flooded.

Jutland: the Lion in danger

The battle was not a quarter of an hour old when the Lion, Beatty's flagship received from the Lützow a hit which was almost fatal. A shell struck the roof of her centre turret, penetrated it, burst inside the turret, blew half the roof off so that it flew high into the air and fell back on the deck with a terrible clang, and killed or grievously wounded all in the turret. Major F. J. W. Harvey was in command of the Marines, who were working the turret. Mortally wounded, he ordered the magazine below to be closed and flooded and sent the only man who could walk, a sergeant of Marines, blackened and bleeding with torn uniform, to report to the captain what had happened Smoke rose from the turret as fire smouldered there; suddenly the flames blazed up and reached a quantity of ammunition in the hoists and chambers below. A pillar of fire shot up from the ion to a height well above the tops of er masts, but the flash did not reach he magazine and the ship survived hrough the faithfulness of the officers and ien who perished and the strange accident that the destruction of most of the urret roof had provided a ready escape r the rush of gas and flame.

Just after the Lion had received this it, the British battle cruiser, Indefatigble, last in the line, vanished in an upeaval of smoke and flame. She was first it by a salvo of four 11-inch shells from ie Von der Tann, which sent up clouds f smoke and splinters near her mainiast and after turret; her steering seemed ɔ be affected and she sheered out of the ne. She was sinking by the stern when n explosion was observed in her. Another ilvo struck her and there rose from her a rilliant crimson sheet of flame in which ark objects could be discerned flying irough the air. Then the whole hull as shrouded in dense black smoke, and ie vanished, taking with her all but two f her crew of 1,019 officers and men. The flash of the exploding German shells had evidently passed down the ammunition hoists of the after turret to the magazines below. Attention had been drawn to the danger of such a mishap after the battle of the Dogger Bank, but no action had been taken to deal with it. The peril was the greater because the British ammunition was extraordinarily inflammable.

Beatty did not relax his hold on the Germans because of the loss of this precious ship. He resolutely maintained the fight, nor did he hesitate when a second catastrophe befell his force. The Queen Mary was hit by a whole series of salvoes from the Derfflinger and Seydlitz, which both were firing at her, when she 'seemed to open out like a puff ball,' and vanished in the same terrifying fashion as the Indefatigable, with 1,266 officers and men. The evidence of survivors showed that her crew nobly maintained their discipline to the very last when the vessel was manifestly doomed. At most of the battle stations the men died unfaltering

H.M.S. QUEEN MARY BLOWING UP IN THE BATTLE OF JUTLAND

wenty minutes after the Indefatigable had blown up a salvo hit the Queen Mary. Several moments ter a terrific yellow flame burst out, and a heavy and very dense mass of black smoke completely iveloped the ship. The roofs of her turrets were blown 100 feet high, and the whole ship collapsed wards. This photograph, taken from H.M.S. Lydiard, shows the immense size of the smoke-cloud of the explosion, its base being almost exactly the full length of the Queen Mary.

From Fawcett & Hooper, 'The Fighting at Jutland,' Macmillan & Co., Ltd.

because no order to retreat could be given before death was upon them.

Beatty still steadfastly pressed the German battle cruisers and was now receiving support from the four powerful battleships of the Fifth Battle Squadron which were heavily engaged. They startled the Germans by the immense range at which they opened fire, and if they had only been favoured by a good light, and had had shells as powerful as the Germans, they might well have wiped out Hipper's ships with their huge 15-inch guns. But at this moment the British light cruiser Southampton, scouting ahead of Beatty, signalled that a new antagonist had appeared. The German battle fleet was coming up from the south-east. It was supposed to be lying at Wilhelmshaven and this was the first time in the whole war that it had been sighted by a British surface ship at sea. Beatty's position had become critical. He had to turn north in order to fall back on the British battle fleet, just as the grey outlines of the German battleships came into view far away in the mist. They followed him and opened fire on him.

It must have seemed to the Germans that he was at their mercy. But at this juncture the light began to improve for him and to deteriorate for the Germans. The German gun crews were tiring; in several of the battle cruisers they had fired three salvoes a minute from their heavy guns for considerable periods. The British were hitting with effect. The Seydlitz was struck eight times and was badly damaged, and she was also hit by a torpedo, which, however, failed to do serious damage. Through hits or breakdowns in her turrets the Von der Tann had all her heavy guns out of action.

Owing to the distance which parted Jellicoe from Beatty and the practical difficulty of determining the exact position of two sets of ships at sea in battle, where the nerve strain is so great and the instruments are exposed to shock and interference from the enemy's fire, the position of the German ships was not ascertained and reported by Beatty's ships with complete accuracy. Jellicoe thought that Scheer would be farther off than he actually was, and thus did not expect an immediate collision. Meantime,

THE GERMAN BATTLE CRUISER SEYDLITZ ON FIRE AT JUTLAND

The Seydlitz, dimly visible among smoke and flames, was hit many times by the British in the historic sea fight at Jutland. Once a torpedo struck her, but, gravely damaged though she was, she yet survived the ordeal to be numbered among those German vessels surrendered to the British on November 18, 1918. She was sunk at Scapa Flow by her own crew on June 21, 1919.

From Fawcett & Hooper, 'The Fighting at Jutland,' Macmillan & Co., Ltd.

an advance detachment of Jellicoe's fleet, in the shape of three battle cruisers with light cruisers and destroyers under Hood, was steaming fast towards Beatty from the north or north-east, while Jellicoe, with his mass of twenty-four Dreadnoughts, screened by light cruisers and destroyers, came down from the north-west. The culminating moment was at hand when the main British fleet, appearing quite unexpectedly, would engage. As that moment approached the smoke and mist veiling the surface of the North Sea thickened.

Moving in advance of Jellicoe's main force, Arbuthnot, with a squadron of armoured cruisers, struck the advanced German cruisers and attacked them fiercely, almost at the same moment as Hood opened fire upon them. The effect of this double onslaught was to hide from the Germans all indication of Jellicoe's approach. They mistook Hood's battle cruisers for a detachment of British battleships, and turned their entire attention to them. Arbuthnot, in his flagship, the armoured cruiser Defence, drove back the German cruisers and destroyers, when suddenly there emerged from the mist and smoke the forms of five German battle cruisers or battleships, which opened an annihilating fire on the Defence at the short range of 7,000 to 10,000 yards, and in a couple of minutes destroyed her with 903 officers and men on board, leaving not a single survivor. The enormous power of modern naval artillery was illustrated by this incident, and the helplessness of a vessel of inferior class against capital ships. The Warrior, which was with the Defence, was badly damaged and only escaped because of the appearance of the powerful battleship Warspite, which from a steering breakdown circled towards the German fleet, and intervening between her and it drew off the hostile fire.

British disasters at Jutland

At this point of the battle, known as Windy Corner, there was extreme congestion. Jellicoe's ships were coming down and deploying in one long line to the north. Beatty was coming up from the south-west; Hood was approaching from the east; to the south were the light and heavy ships of the German fleet. Nearly 250 vessels of all kinds and sizes were manoeuvring, and no one could clearly see what was happening or make out the exact position and character of antagonists. The light for the Germans grew worse and worse, and mainly because of this they had not discovered that Jellicoe was upon them. The sun was low behind the British, and its rays dazzled the German gunners so that they could not see their foes, while a heavy fire was beating upon them from invisible assailants. For a moment, indeed, a target was disclosed to them. Hood in the Invincible came into view in a clear patch of water. His ship was at once attacked by two German battle cruisers, Lützow and Derfflinger, and blew up as the two other battle cruisers had done from the same cause, flames spouting from two of the turrets before the whole hull opened amidships in a final explosion.

Loss of the Invincible

In the British battle fleet, which was now actually in contact with the Germans, undiscovered by them, little could be seen—only the dim forms of big German ships and the occasional flicker of the German salvoes. Yet the British fire is known from German statements to have been most effective. Just as the British battleships were hitting severely, notwithstanding the difficulty of the light, German destroyers were observed advancing. It was supposed in the British fleet that they were moving out to deliver a torpedo attack, and the battle fleet turned away to elude their onslaught. In reality, the German destroyers had received orders to rescue the crew of the German light cruiser Wiesbaden, which was burning furiously. While approaching the Wiesbaden the German destroyers were ordered to attack in strength, but this order was almost immediately countermanded.

The British turn-away at a critical moment may have saved the Germans, the more so as the British battle fleet did not promptly turn back and endeavour to close. The German system of tactics was more supple, otherwise Scheer's ships, which could only fire some 150,000 lb. weight of heavy projectiles in every broadside, against 300,000 lb. or more in the British fleet, should have been rapidly shot to pieces. Six of his ships were old and quite unfit for an encounter with Dreadnoughts, and though the others had considerably more and thicker armour than the British ships, they had much weaker gun armaments.

From this point onwards the battle resolved itself into a cautious fencing between two fleets of battle ships in the mist and smoke. Twice the Germans approached the British fleet, trying to pass beyond it—for it was interposed between them and their bases—and to secure their retreat, and twice they were driven back by concentrated fire. They only succeeded in damaging one British battleship, the Marlborough, which was hit by a torpedo, and she remained in line until late in the night. Submarines and mines played no part in the battle, and the torpedo had very little material effect on it, though the fear of it strongly influenced the tactics. Owing to grave deficiencies in the British arrangements for night fighting Jellicoe decided not to press the Germans during the hours of darkness, though his fleet was quite close to them and though during the night the noise and flash of a whole series of furious torpedo actions was observed from several of the British battle ships; and in one great explosion the cranes and outline of a German Dreadnought were plainly lighted up.

The British destroyer flotillas attacked as they came into contact with the Germans, but as they had received no definite orders or information as to the position their onslaughts were disconnected. Made with rare bravery and the utmost determination, they inflicted on the Germans only one serious loss, that of the old battleship Pommern, while they suffered severely themselves. But several of the German Dreadnoughts had the narrowest of escapes from British torpedoes.

As that eventful night wore on the German fleet at last managed to get to the east of the British fleet by steaming astern of it, and passed between it and the Danish coast, steering for Horns Reef. It arrived there about daybreak, and was surprised to find no trace of the British. It is still something of a mystery why

NAVAL WAR BY NIGHT AT JUTLAND: THE RAMMING OF THE SPITFIRE

In the night fighting after the battle of Jutland there was great uncertainty as to the character of the German ships encountered. This sketch, based on the reports of British officers, depicts the ramming encounter between the British destroyer Spitfire, of the 4th Destroyer Flotilla, and what is now known to have been the German two-funnelled Dreadnought Nassau. The latter was mistaken by the British for a German cruiser—hence the three funnels in the sketch. Both vessels survived.

From Fawcett & Hooper, 'The Fighting at Jutland,' Macmillan & Co., Ltd.

[ellicoe did not steam to Horns Reef during he night, because it was a point at the unction of the swept passages through the ;erman mine fields, by one of which Scheer must retreat. If the British had concentrated there, they would almost certainly have sunk the Derfflinger and Seydlitz, which were grievously damaged nd hardly capable of fighting; and they night have secured or sunk other less lamaged ships as well. Four of the German battleships, König, Grosser Kurfürst, Posen nd Ostfriesland, and all the older ships vould have found it difficult to escape ad there been an energetic pursuit. But n the naval theories which at that time prevailed in the British fleet, insufficient mportance was attached to decisive victory at sea.

And so the battle of Jutland was an ndecisive engagement in which, for the rst time in recent history, the weaker fleet, with only 21 Dreadnoughts against 37, inflicted upon the stronger fleet just twice ts own loss in tonnage of ships sunk nd in officers and men killed and vounded. Of the German Dreadnoughts nly one, the Lützow, was sunk, as it was ound that she was too much injured to e got back into port, and the Germans orpedoed her.

ndecisive Results at Jutland

Neither side had understood beforehand vhat a naval battle would be like in the nists of the North Sea. The Germans, ecause they had for many years had a cientific staff, came nearer to the reality n their anticipations. The rapidity vith which the largest ships could be estroyed was one of the numerous grim urprises of the engagement. No one an be certain how many German shells it the three British battle cruisers which lew up, but it does not seem that in any ne of them there were more than fifteen eavy hits, and in the Indefatigable there nay only have been five or ten. Long fter the battle and some time after the lose of the war the German battleship aden, serving as a target ship, was sunk y the British fleet with astonishing speed, nough she had much stronger armour nan any vessel that fought at Jutland. imilarly, the new United States battleship Washington, which was used for a target by the American fleet, went to the bottom after only fourteen hits by 14-inch guns, although she was so designed as to be capable of withstanding eight torpedoes without sinking.

Heavy artillery is then still the dominating factor in naval war; the German opinion after Jutland as expressed by Admirals Tirpitz and Von Trotha was that the big, well armoured ship is necessary to any navy which would command the sea.

The battle of Jutland left the High Sea Fleet still in existence with its 40,000 admirably trained officers and men on whom Germany could draw for the manning of the great submarine fleet that she was actively constructing in 1916. A first submarine campaign opened in early 1915, when the German Admiralty proclaimed the blockade of the British Isles. But after the destruction of the Lusitania with 1,198 of her passengers and crew, including more than a hundred United States citizens, the German government reluctantly promised that its U-boats would not sink liners without warning. Though the promise was not kept, it so hampered the German submarine commanders that they reported satisfactory operations against British commerce with it to be impracticable. The Allies' losses from submarine attacks were none the less considerable, if they did not threaten complete disaster.

The German Submarine Campaigns

By the end of 1916, however, the German government determined to carry on what it called a ruthless submarine campaign—by which was meant the sinking at sight of every ship found in the war zone. It resolved to flout neutrals and defy the United States. It intended to transfer the war at sea from the surface to the waters below the surface, so that an extraordinary situation would arise in which the two combatants might simultaneously occupy the same sea, and in which the invisibility of the submarine would be matched against the superior force of the surface ship. The reason for this decision was that the German armies on land had no longer any hope of gaining a decisive victory, while the German naval authorities gave assurances and produced calculations proving that England must infallibly collapse not later than July, 1917, if a ruthless submarine war was waged and if German U-boat commanders were released from all restrictions.

After protracted discussions the emperor William II gave way; he seems to have feared and hesitated up to the last. What Lord Curzon called 'the supreme and terrible climax of the war' was a hand when on January 31, 1917, the fina U-boat campaign began. Had the Ger mans waited only six weeks there would have been no need for them to resort to the methods that sullied the reputation o their navy and forced President Wilsor into action, much against his will. The outbreak of the Russian revolution, quickly followed as it was by the utter collapse of the Russian army and navy, would have freed large German military forces for the western front and have entirely transformed the military problem

The German government had no fear whatever of the United States. As its naval authorities were so positive that England would collapse in six months, it seemed to follow that by no conceivable possibility could American troops in any number be raised and transported to Europe. In January, 1917, the American army was insignificant, and though the American navy was strong it was not at all

GERMAN SUBMARINE PHOTOGRAPHED FROM THE STEAMER IT AFTERWARDS SANK
The methods employed by German submarines in attacking Allied ships were two. Against warships a torpedo was discharged which betrayed its presence by a track through the water, such as is shown in the upper illustration taken from the air. If the object of attack were an unarmed merchantman, the U-boat would rise to the surface, as in the lower photograph, and shell its victim—a procedure less costly than the former method.
Photo, Imperial War Museum

A TRIUMPH OF DISGUISE : ONE OF BRITAIN'S MYSTERY SHIPS

mong the defensive measures introduced by the British naval authorities in face of the intensive erman submarine campaign was the employment of mystery or Q-boats. These vessels, masquerad-ıg as merchantmen, carried concealed guns, and were equipped with lookout posts and wireless erials skilfully hidden. Members of their crews were trained to simulate panic if a submarine ppeared. H.M.S. Gunner, Q 31, seen in the photograph, sank two submarines during the war.

Photo, Abrahams & Sons, Devonport

repared for a struggle with submarine ›es. If the British merchant marine were ıercilessly destroyed by the U-boats, it ould not be able to maintain the steady ow of supplies necessary for the successful esistance of Britain and France, and it ould much less be able to spare any essels to bring over American troops. herefore, defeat of Germany now de-ended on Britain and on Britain's avy and merchant marine alone. If ither failed disaster was certain.

The total available force of U-boats hen this great onslaught from beneath he surface began is now known to have een no more than 111 ; and of these fewer han one-half were at any given moment t sea. The others were refitting or resting heir crews. But even so the total of ıerchant shipping sunk or badly damaged pproached a million tons a month, and here was no visible means of stopping hese frightful ravages. The United States hen it entered the war did not immedi-tely give all the naval aid that it could ave provided. President Wilson per-ıitted the British navy to struggle on, ill upported, and American officers dis-atched to London were instructed by heir authorities to treat the British with uspicion, and not to allow the wool to be ulled over their eyes. France and Italy ad their hands full of the war on land, nd, though they did all that was in their ower, they had to leave the main burden at sea to be borne by the British people. If all the American small craft that were available had been promptly dispatched to Europe, effective protection could have been given to Allied shipping and some millions of tons of vessels would have been preserved from destruction. There would then have been nothing to prevent the transport of large American forces to Europe in the summer and winter of 1917 ; and there is every reason to think that the Germans would have abandoned the war and made peace before the opening of 1918.

Defeat of the U-Boat Menace

If the U-boat onslaught was defeated, it was defeated by the skilful measures which the British navy took and by the patience and determination of the British nation. As the weeks passed the sinkings of British ships did not increase but gradually fell when new methods and greater energy were directed by the British navy to the defeat of the U-boats. Merchant-men no longer sailed isolated, but were dispatched in large convoys under the escort of a few warships or armed trawlers. This had an immediate effect on the U-boat depredations. The British merchant sea-men themselves rose superior to all trials and dangers. They confronted death day after day, firm and unshaken, though by some of the U-boats the crews of sunk ships were treated with extreme ferocity.

All Allied merchantmen were by degrees supplied with armaments; the channels which the U-boats used when putting to sea were persistently mined, and the mines took steady and increasing toll of the U-boats. And thus week in and week out the necessary supplies were carried mainly by British ships to the various fronts. British reinforcements were brought across the ocean; and the utter collapse which the German Admiralty so confidently anticipated did not come. The U-boat losses became so heavy that, though new boats were rapidly constructed, the total number no longer rose. At no time did it exceed 140 effective submarines, and the number actually cruising never exceeded 61. None the less this comparatively small force of underwater craft shook the whole system of the Allies to its foundations. But from August or September, 1917, it grew clearer and clearer to the Allies that the U-boat attack had been defeated, and that, even if the number of the boats were increased, there was no longer any prospect of their gaining a decisive victory.

German losses of Submarines

Yet there were weeks when the balance of fate seemed to oscillate—weeks of almost unimaginable anxiety. There was one black day in April, 1917, when the American admiral, Sims, who was co operating with the Allies, telegraphed 'Allies do not now command the sea Transport of troops and supplies strainec to the uttermost and the maintenance oi the armies in the field is threatened. Everywhere at sea the communications oi the Allies which passed on the surface oi the water were attacked by invisible enemies who vanished into the depths when surface warships appeared. Everywhere on land the German communications were safe and inviolate, maintained by railways at which the Allies had no effective means of striking. Moreover, the mere existence of large sea-going submarines clogged the operations of the Allies anc compelled their ships to adopt devious routes and to zig-zag when steaming on a course, which meant that the length oi voyages was seriously increased at a time when every ton of shipping was urgently needed and all margin on which to draw had disappeared.

The severe restrictions on food consumption imposed in Great Britain and the progress achieved in combating the U-boats made it possible to do in 1918 that which the German staff had dismissed as being quite out of the question—to move American troops by the hundred thousanc to Europe when, after the Bolshevik

AN AMERICAN CONVOY BOUND FOR ENGLAND

America's entry into the Great War was attended by the problem of arranging transport for he thousands of troops to the fighting areas. Although a considerable portion of the Atlantic Ocear was open to German submarine attack, the troop-carrying ships were brought through with ar extremely low rate of casualties by the system of convoy in which the ships were escorted by destroyer or cruisers and by one or more armed merchantmen. The photograph was taken in May, 1918

Photo, Imperial War Museum

ulers of Russia had concluded peace with ;ermany, the German army began its errific offensive in France. The military 'alue of the new American formations at hat date was small; the moral value of heir appearance in Europe was immense.)f the American troops sent to Europe luring the whole war, 51 per cent. were :arried in British and 46 per cent. in United States vessels, the rest being conveyed by [talian and French shipping. But in the supreme crisis between March, 1918, and :he armistice British vessels carried 55 per ent. and American vessels only 41.

It was a stupendous achievement on the part of the British merchant service to provide the large necessary tonnage. But without the protection which the vigilance of the British surface warships afforded, concentrated in the North Sea and paralysing the German surface ships, these vast American movements could never have been executed. The American navy towards the close of the war aided by sending a division of battleships to Scapa. Between April and August, 1918, 1,200,000 American soldiers were transported to France, and by September of that year an average of over 300,000 men a month had been attained. Nothing like this had ever been seen in previous history or indeed thought possible.

Efficiency of the Transport Service

The Allies were puzzled by the complete failure of the Germans to attack the transports. The American troops were moved by sea over waters infested by the submarines with the sacrifice of only three ships sunk and with negligible loss of life. The fact was that all but the boldest U-boat commanders hesitated to face the inevitable risks of attacking vessels which were under the convoy of powerful surface ships. The 'ghostly finger,' as Admiral Sims called the plain white streak which a torpedo on its run leaves upon the surface, pointed to the submarine that had fired the torpedo, and brought on her the terrible visitation of depth charges. Dropped near the U-boat they might sink her, and even where they failed to do this they often so jarred the mechanism of the boat as to render it inadvisable for her to continue on her cruise.

Moreover, the German staff argued that the destruction of merchant shipping which was engaged in bringing supplies would be every whit as effective in defeating the Allies as the sinking of transports with troops. In this calculation they made one grave mistake. Little was heard of the destruction of supply ships, with the stringent censorship which the Allies enforced on news. A great deal would have been heard if transport after transport had been sunk, for such disasters could never have been concealed.

The submarine campaign was watched with growing restlessness and fear by Germany's allies. The emperor Charles of Austria, the last Hapsburg sovereign and perhaps the noblest of his house, had been opposed to it from the first and only allowed himself to be reluctantly overborne when he was assured from Berlin that its success was certain. As the evidence of its failure accumulated, he openly despaired of the German cause and did his best to end the war. But not until August, 1918, did the German government permit any disclosure of the truth in the German press. Then at last a naval officer, Captain Kühlwetter, was put up to confess: 'We have been deceived regarding the enemy's tenacity. We never expected that Great Britain and her allies would be so averse from peace after eighteen months of ruthless submarine war.'

Germany's View of the Situation

Though the loss of life in submarines was not heavy, submarine work was exacting and exhausting. It involved for the beginner the endurance of something resembling slow suffocation. The space in a submarine—even in the large British submarines of the K class, built for work with the fleet and almost as fast on the surface as torpedo boats—was exceedingly limited. The smells and stuffiness are not to be imagined by those who have not experienced them. The motion of the boats in heavy seas, especially in shallow water, was difficult for even seasoned men to endure without sickness. The vessel 'pumped,' or moved like the piston of a pump up and down. At intervals she was compelled to come to the surface, as only on the surface could the motors be worked

EXPLOSION OF A DEPTH CHARGE

Prominent among the weapons with which destroyers fought the U-boat menace was the depth charge. Consisting of a thin-walled cylindrical container, with firing mechanism in the central tube, it detonated a large charge of explosive below the water, being effective within a radius of 75 yards.

Photo, Imperial War Museum

Early submarines were very vulnerable to gun fire—even to the fire of small guns; but the later boats could stand a good deal of punishment. In fighting the U-boats the British employed directional wireless to determine the exact position of the boats, which were in the habit of constantly sending wireless signals and thus disclosing their presence. The boats when located were attacked by surface vessels or Allied submarines. The hotter the pursuit of the U-boats the more difficult was it for them to sink ships with guns or bombs, as was their practice early in the war. They had to use the delicate and expensive torpedo, of which they could carry only a limited supply. According to German submarine experts, the British submarines were the most dangerous antagonists they had to face. The type of vessel most used in fighting the U-boat was, however, the destroyer, which carried a powerful gun armament and a good supply of depth charges.

which charged her storage batteries for running under water. She could remain under water for periods as long as seventy-two hours, and in emergency could go to a depth of 200 feet without disaster.

GERMAN SUBMARINES IN THE MEDITERRANEAN

Diminished hopes of victory on land led Germany, early in 1917, to concentrate upon a ruthless submarine campaign, arousing the ire of neutral countries affected by her unscrupulous methods. In this German photograph the submarines U 42 and U 35 are seen greeting each other during the latter's successful cruise in the Mediterranean. German submarines of this type were especially active in the Mediterranean, where they concentrated on intercepting ships bound for the Dardanelles.

Photo. Imperial War Museum

GERMAN MERCHANTMAN OF THE SUBMARINE VARIETY

he German submarine Deutschland, costing £100,000, was specially constructed for commercial ırposes. Manned by a crew of 29, she successfully voyaged to the United States in 1916 with a .rgo weighing 750 tons, but on that country's entry into the war in 1917 there was no further object r her existence as a mercantile submarine, and she was converted for offensive use. The photograph shows a German U-boat of the mercantile cruiser Deutschland type.

Photo, Imperial War Museum

The submarine merchantman made her ›pearance during the war in the Deutschnd, which twice safely proceeded to the nited States. A sister vessel, the Bremen, ınished at sea, probably sunk by a ritish mine. On either side submarines great size were planned but not cometed. In practice it proved difficult to ındle a submarine so soon as her dimenons approached those of a small cruiser, ıd, perhaps because of these limitations, › power produced a submarine battleship. he nearest approach to one was in the ritish M class, vessels carrying one 12-ch gun which could be fired when the boat, all but the gun, was below the surface. Such large submarines as Germany built were not very successful, and of the large British submarines many were lost during and after the war.

The U-boat crews spied their victims through the periscope, a long tube projected above the surface, down which objects were reflected by a prism. The imperfections of vision in such circumstances led to the introduction of a system of protective colouring for ships, just as animals in their coat or skin adapt their colour to their surroundings. Ships were so painted by a clever system of camouflage

CAMOUFLAGED SHIP THAT PRESENTED A PROBLEM FOR PERISCOPES

ıe submarine danger caused the introduction of camouflage as an important factor in British val operations. An ingenious method of painting and disguising ships made it extremely difficult : the submarine crews to discern through their periscopes the nature and course of vessels so sguised, the distinguishing features of bow and stern being confused. An interesting specimen of the designer's art is H.M.S. London, looking like a harlequin ship in her weird warpaint.

Photo, Abrahams & Sons, Devonport

that at a distance it was surprisingly hard to determine which was the bow and what was the exact distance and course. The first requisite to hit a ship in movement with a torpedo is to know her course and distance accurately. So useful was this form of protective painting found to be that towards the close of the war the Germans copied it from the British for certain of their ships.

New weapons, some of which were not thoroughly tested, made their appearance in the war. One of them was the torpedo-carrying aeroplane, which was first used by the British in the Dardanelles in 1915. It was never tried on a large scale against a battle fleet, but that it has great possibilities is obvious. The Germans only employed it once, for the attack on shipping in the Channel, and then with little success. Another new weapon was the coastal motor boat, a small craft of only a few tons that could defy mines and mine fields by gliding over the surface of the water. One of these little vessels twice torpedoed in the Adriatic the Austrian Dreadnought Szent Istvan, and sank her. No other Dreadnought was sunk by the torpedo in the war, for the two capital ships hit by torpedoes at Jutland, the Marlborough in the British fleet and the Seydlitz in the German, both got safely back to port and were repaired.

New Engines of War

Approaching by stealth, well nigh invisible at night and so small a target that they are practically invulnerable, these boats will have to be reckoned with in the future. The cost is small, not much over £5,000 or £10,000, and they can be built almost anywhere with great speed. Their one disadvantage is that they require calm weather and smooth water, so that they are not particularly suited for such stormy seas as those that surround the British Isles. They were largely used in fine weather by the British against the German submarines, when they carried depth charges instead of torpedoes. In an amazing attack which the British made on Bolshevik battleships in Kronstadt harbour, during 1919, four Bolshevik vessels including one Dreadnought, were torpedoed and sunk in shallow water by seven British coastal motor boats. The British loss was only two boats, though the Bolsheviks had reason to be thoroughly on the alert. This is an indication of the new perils that threaten vessels even when they are lying in harbour. They can be attacked from the air by the bombing and torpedo-carrying aeroplane, and they are also menaced on the surface by the tiny coastal motor boat.

Thus the war confirmed the principles of the past, which can be summed up thus: decisive victory in battle is the most certain method of crushing a hostile navy and if it is not gained then the naval war will be long and costly. The most important factor in the naval battle is the heavily armed and armoured ship which can deal heavy blows and resist them. Blockade, long maintained, is disastrous to the power which has to submit to it, but it does its work with extreme slowness. The submarine and aircraft have not as yet been thoroughly tested, but in the light of war experience it does not seem that they will affect the principles though they will undoubtedly exercise an increasing influence on the tactics of naval warfare.

BRITISH COASTAL MOTOR BOATS STEAMING FULL SPEED AHEAD

The evolution of the light coastal motor boat as a factor in naval warfare was a result of the necessity for meeting new problems with new remedies. Lightly skimming over the surface of the water, this new type of vessel evaded the deep-laid mines that threatened the safety of heavier sea-craft. One of these motor boats sank the only enemy Dreadnought destroyed by torpedo during the war.

Photo, Abrahams & Sons, Devonport

CHAPTER 181

EFFECT OF THE WAR ON FAITH AND PHILOSOPHY

A Study of Current Tendencies in Western Man's Attitude towards Spiritual Matters

By C. E. M. JOAD

Author of Matter, Life and Value, The Future of Life, etc.

THE faith of a community is normally expressed in certain definite tenets or beliefs which are embodied in what is called the religion of the com-unity. Faith which is systematised in is way in a body of religious belief, to hich the bulk of the community sub-ribes, is called orthodox. Now faith this sense is almost always adversely fected by some great national calamity, ch as a war, great wars being usually companied by a diminution in orthodox lief and by a corresponding increase in fferent beliefs of a very varied char-ter. New cults and creeds spring up minister to the needs of those who, ving ceased to subscribe to the tenets orthodox religion, are said to have lost eir faith, with the result that times of tional stress and the periods immedi-ely succeeding them are usually char-terised by a multitudinous diversity of fferent beliefs rather than by a single iform faith. The Great War of 1914–18 fords a good illustration of this ten-ncy; it has been followed both by a cline of faith in orthodox religion and a growth of what we may call for short aith substitutes.'

The difficulties of faith in war time turn ry largely upon the problem of pain and il. Pain and evil exist at all times, and authentic instance of either logically esents the same problem as the omni-esence of both. War, which necessarily volves a mass of visible suffering, merely nders the problem more pressing. When en are themselves in pain and see suffer-g around them, certain questions, which other times they are content to leave answered, insistently force themselves on their attention.

In the first place, God is commonly held to be both omnipotent and benevolent. If He is omnipotent, He must have created pain and evil. But the deliberate creation of pain and evil is not the act of a benevolent being. Therefore God is not benevolent. If, on the other hand, God did not create pain and evil, they must spring from some source other than God, and, assuming Him to be benevolent, continue to exist in despite of His will. But, in this event, there exists in the universe some power or principle other than God and not created or controlled by Him. God, therefore, is not omnipotent.

The problem of human suffering

Secondly, it is sometimes said that pain and evil are the creations not of God but of man, to whom God in His goodness accorded the gift of free will. This gift man has misused, and its misuse has resulted in the introduction of evil and the infliction of pain. But in introducing pain and evil man has either acted contrary to God's expectation, or he has not. If he has, then God cannot have intended that events should follow the course they have. God, therefore, is neither omnipotent nor infallible nor omniscient. If he has not, then God not only knew that pain and evil would be introduced into the world by man, but wittingly consented to their introduction. But wittingly to permit the infliction of pain and the introduction of evil, when one has the power to prevent them and the knowledge that they will appear unless prevented, is not the mark of a good being. Therefore, God is not benevolent.

Thirdly, it is sometimes said that pain and evil are not real, but are illusions which a deeper understanding of the nature of things will reveal to us as such. But either pain is real, or it is not. If it is, then, since on the preceding argument it must emanate from God, God cannot be benevolent. If it is not, then the error we make in thinking pain is real is a real error. There is no doubt that we think that we suffer; and, if this belief is an illusion, then the deception under which we labour is a real one. God, therefore, deceives us about the nature of pain and evil. But an omnipotent being is without the need to deceive; a benevolent being is without the wish.

It is not intended to assert that these problems are incapable of solution. All religions have, indeed, in various ways attempted to solve them.

Disinclination for fixed dogma

But they present real difficulties to suffering men and women, and place a strain upon their faith which it is often unfitted to withstand. The difficulties they raise are increased by the attempt to formulate faith in a creed, and to crystallise belief into dogma. Hence, we shall expect to find that a characteristic of post-war religion is a disinclination to subscribe to definite creeds, with a resultant subordination of the formal element in religion. It is important, therefore, to remember that the number of people who subscribe to the tenets of any particular denomination is no necessary index of the numbers who still retain some form of faith.

Finally, a further special difficulty arises in those cases in which the religious doctrines currently accepted are of such a kind as to express disapproval of the practice of warfare upon which the community is engaged. Many religious beliefs condemn war in common with all forms of violence. That Christianity condemns it more emphatically than most in spirit, even though there may be controversy about the meaning of particular passages, is generally agreed. As a consequence, there arises in wartime an inevitable antagonism between patriotism and faith, between a man's desire to support his country in the struggle in which it is engaged and the doctrines of a religion which bids him offer no resistance to violence and to treat the enemy as his brother.

In this conflict faith suffers in two way First, the strongest impulse of the norma man, who conceives his country to be i danger, is to rally to its defence, a pr ceeding which will almost certainly i volve him in fighting and killing. If th plain intention of his faith is to disappro both of fighting and of killing, he will b driven to seek for some less obviou interpretation which will sanction, or wi at least not explicitly condemn, h present activities. He will be compelle to say, for example, that Christianit although it condemns war in genera does not condemn this particular war or that Christ foresaw this war, prophesie it, and in so doing implicitly approve of it; or that the enemy is antichrist, o if not antichrist, is at least so wicked th to fight him is to fight for Christ and again Satan. Such interpretations were readil supplied to the people of all the belligere countries during the Great War; religio was nationalised for the emergency, an pulpits turned into recruiting offices.

Accepted at the time, these ad h interpretations of doctrines designed t meet a particular need cannot but b regarded with disquietude when viewed in the cold light of later reflection. Minds thus

The revulsion against orthodox

disquieted tend to experience a revulsio of feeling against orthodox belief as whole, allowing their disapproval of th ends that the plain meaning of Chri tian doctrines has been twisted to serv to discredit, somewhat unjustly, the do trines themselves. There is ground f supposing that the attitude of the church during the war, an attitude indistinguis able from that of the ordinary patrio exercised considerable influence on th subsequent decline in orthodox faith.

Secondly, there were in each belligere country a few who, confronted with th conflict between faith and patriotism espoused the cause of faith. Insistin on the literal interpretation of the Ne Testament, the conscientious objectors i England maintained that their religio expressly forbade them to fight, an accordingly refused all participation in th war. Lacking the sanction of the churche these men were subjected to considerab rsecution at the time; subsequently, wever, when the inevitable reaction me, their attitude received a fair easure of general support. It is not to be pected that these men, or those who re later induced to share their beliefs, ll look with favour on a church which, their view, betrayed its beliefs in the ne of crisis. They retain faith, but it not orthodox; and the dissidence of ese ardent spirits has not been without influence in causing a drift away from e churches on the part of others.

It is not easy to obtain precise informan on the extent and intensity of belief nong a people at any given moment. ere is, nevertheless, a general consus of opinion that orthodox belief s declined since the Great War. It is a mmonplace that we live in an irreligious e, and the eyes of believers are anxiously ed on the spiritual horizon in expectan of the rise of a new religious teacher to vive men's beliefs. By some the second ming of Christ is confidently expected.

But, although religious apathy is an doubted fact, it is extremely difficult obtain concrete evidence of its extent.

Did the War use unbelief?

Statistics are of little value here, since they relate mainly to the enrolled numbers of religious ganizations, and these, as pointed out ove, have no necessary relation to the mber of those who have some form of th. Nor can one say with certainty to at extent the decline in faith is really e to the war. It is impossible, not only cause of the difficulty of attributing the neration of a state of mind or belief any concrete event or set of events, t also because of the generally admitted ct that faith was actively on the cline before the war. The English free urches, for example, undertook during e war a prolonged and extensive amination into the state of religious lief in the army, with a view to ascerning what were the spiritual needs of e men serving with the forces. The sults of the survey were published in a oklet under the title of The Army and ligion, the compilers of which declared emselves surprised and pained at the ative ignorance of and indifference to spiritual matters among men of all denominations. In view of these and similar indications of a growth of religious apathy, if not of positive disbelief, before the war, it is difficult to specify precisely the effects of the special causes connected with the war. Did they precipitate a general collapse of faith; did they merely accelerate a process which was already under way and would have proceeded independently of them; or did they have no effect upon this process one way or the other? We cannot hope to answer these questions; all that we can do is to summarise the scanty evidence available.

What indications, then, have we of the state of belief during and immediately after the great war? They are not many.

Absence of a great revival

Hopes were entertained during the war period that the crisis through which the nations were passing might lead to a great spiritual revival. These hopes were not in general fulfilled. In 1916 the Church of England organized a 'National mission of repentance and hope,' which was described as 'a mission of witness by the Church as a whole to the nation as a whole,' and took the form of an endeavour to evoke 'a sincere determination on the part of the nation to seek and deserve divine help.' After various stages of preparation a 'message to the nation' summoning the people to repentance and prayer was delivered in each parish by a large body of 'bishops' messengers' consisting of both clergy and laity. Although the mission was organized on the most elaborate scale, the response was described as 'most disappointing.' It did not succeed in augmenting the dwindling congregations of the churches, nor were there any perceptible signs of its influence in the daily life of the nation. Instead of a general revival of religious enthusiasm, the chief result of the mission was the establishment of a number of committees to consider subjects arising in connexion with it. That the work of these committees was generally regarded as of more importance than the immediate results of the mission itself is a sufficient commentary on the measure of its achievement.

The free churches also made vigorous endeavours to use the national crisis as a means of revivifying the faith of the people; but for them too the war ended in an atmosphere of disappointment and disillusion. So far was either the war or the peace from inaugurating a new moral world, that it was generally recognized that never within living memory had the nation's standard of morals been so lax or the tide of faith sunk to a lower ebb. The various theological colleges, depleted and generally closed during the war years, were only able to reopen very slowly, owing to a lack of recruits; some indeed have not reopened at all. Both the free churches and the Church of England experienced great difficulties in finding a sufficient number of new entrants into their ministries. In the early years of the twentieth century there were some 21,000 clergymen belonging to the Anglican Church at work in England; in 1928 the number was just over 16,000. Although the depreciation of salaries consequent upon the rise in the cost of living may have exercised a considerable influence, at any rate at first, by rendering the ministerial calling less attractive from the economic point of view, the churches would be the last to admit that material considerations of this kind constituted the chief reason for the prevalent lack of enthusiasm.

Decline in congregations

Meanwhile church attendances continued to decline. Detailed statistics of the numbers of congregations are in most cases lacking, but it is significant that a number of churches belonging to the Church of England have been closed through lack of support. The free churches, indeed, with their more precise figures of membership, admit to an actual falling off in their numbers during the decade 1910–20. The decline has been an annual one and is attributed to such causes as the increase of Sunday pleasure, emigration from rural to urban districts and the 'spirit of the age.' There is surely little doubt that in this last consideration is to be found the true reason; the others are symptoms of causes other than themselves, rather than causes in themselves. The figures showing the decline in free church membership are more than borne out by the diminution in the numbers of those attending free church Sunday schools.

Developments in America seem to ha followed much the same lines, althou no actual falling off in the membership religious bodies is reported. Writing These Eventful Years, Volume II, D Shurler Matthews, dean of the Divini School, University of Chicago, say 'During the progress of the war ma hopes were expressed that the ideals f which the soldiers were fighting would gi a great impetus to the spiritual life of t nation. The war, however, brought great spiritual uplift.' No great religio movement seems to have been inaugurat as the result of the war, nor were t methods of appeal found effective amo the soldiers carried over into peace tim

Characteristi of Modernis

The general trend of religious thoug in the United States seems to have fo lowed one or other of two main tendencies: these are Fundamentalism and Modernism. The main characteristics of Modernism are three. First the is a growing interest in life as opposed doctrine, as the result of which the te of faith is found in actual religious e perience rather than in creeds or dogma Secondly, there is an insistence upon t importance of this life for its own sak without reference to its bearing up our prospects in another. And, thirdl there is a feeling that the religious att tude of mind, instead of being confine as it has been in the past, to a particul set of activities springing from an isolat and unique side of our nature vague conceived as spiritual, should embra every aspect of our personality, and e tend into all the avocations of daily lif Hence a new emphasis is laid on the soci side of religion, and the religious point view is defined in relation to the world business and to industrial disputes.

The world, in other words, is out joint. This is a matter of serious concer since life in this world is important in a for itself, but it is only through the appl cation of religion to life that the evils the world can be mitigated. Hence, t aspect of a man's religion, of which it is t business of the church to take cognisanc finds expression in his daily life; h faith is his private concern and shou not, therefore, be confined too close ithin the bounds of any creed. The ay a man lives is, in short, of more nportance than the precise details of hat he believes. These characteristics f the Modernist attitude to religion are early derivable in part from men's recent xperience of war.

The same tendencies are observable in e results of the questionnaire on religious elief which The Nation (London) and The Daily News addressed to their readers in the summer of 1926. The Nation drew up in conıltation with H. G. Wood, J. M. Robertɔn, Augustine Birrell and Bernard Shaw list of questions designed to test the ate of belief among its readers. The aily News, with The Nation's consent, rinted the same list and asked for replies. he questions were of an exceedingly earching character, and, although the eplies were confined to a bare affirmation r negation, the results are sufficiently teresting, both as providing a general ıdication of the state of religious belief ı twentieth-century England and as lustrating the tendencies mentioned bove, to be summarised here (see anexed table). The figures given are ercentages of the total replies returned; ut for comparison it hould be noted that the umber of those who relied to The Nation was ,849 as against 14,043 eplying to The Daily Iews. An examination f the figures reveals the ɔllowing points:

The Nation's questionnaire

The belief in orthodox hristianity is still prevaınt among the great mass f English people. There roughly a 70 per cent. ajority of believers in a ersonal God, personal nmortality, the divinity f Christ and the divine ıspiration of the Bible.

Nevertheless, belief is eadily on the wane. ifty years, thirty years r even twenty years arlier, the majority in favour of these beliefs would have been far greater. One estimate, that of a prominent preacher, maintained that in 1900 the corresponding figure would have been 90 per cent.

There is a great fluidity amounting almost to chaos in current belief.

Free thought, or the absence of faith, is far more prevalent among the literary and intellectual elements of society, as witnessed by the answers of The Nation's readers. If this section can be regarded as in any sense the advance guard of the community in intellectual and spiritual matters—and it is clear that in some sense it can—we may expect future developments to follow the direction in which it points. The decline of faith, in other words, is likely to become more widespread.

The number of active Christian churchgoers is greater (see answers to questions 8 and 9) than the adherents to the doctrine of any particular church.

The number of believers in Christianity as a whole is greater (see answers to questions 6 and 7) than those who are prepared to accept the tenets of any particular creed. Even the fundamental doctrines of the Apostles' Creed are subscribed to by a relatively small number.

QUESTION	THE NATION			DAILY NEWS		
	YES	NO	BLANK	YES	NO	BLANK
1. Do you believe in a personal God?	40·18	55·38	4·43	71·1	26·3	2·6
2. Do you believe in an impersonal, purposive, and creative power of which living beings are the vehicle, corresponding to the Life Force, the 'élan vital,' the Evolutionary Appetite, &c.?	37·75	48·24	13·89	33·5	46·2	20·3
3. Do you believe that the basis of reality is matter?	27·36	57·49	15·14	21·7	59·4	18·9
4. Do you believe in personal immortality?	43·64	47·70	8·65	72·3	22·7	5·0
5. Do you believe that Jesus Christ was divine in a sense in which all living men could not be said to be divine?	35·64	61·43	2·92	68·0	29·8	2·2
6. Do you believe in any form of Christianity?	51·10	43·05	5·83	75·1	20·5	4·4
7, Do you believe in the Apostles' Creed?	21·25	71·01	7·73	53·3	36·1	10·6
8. Do you believe in the formulated tenets of any Church?	24·55	68·41	7·08	52·0	37·7	10·3
9. Are you an active member of any Church?	43·16	55·22	1·62	62·6	34·9	2·5
10. Do you voluntarily attend any religious service regularly? ..	43·15	55·21	1·62	71·40	27·25	1·35
11. Do you accept the first chapter of Genesis as historical?	6·21	91·15	2·64	38·0	53·3	8·7
12. Do you regard the Bible as inspired in a sense in which the literature of your own country could not be said to be inspired? ..	29·36	68·57	3·18	63·8	33·0	3·2
13. Do you believe in transubstantiation?	4·10	93·61	2·32	10·4	86·5	3·1
14 Do you believe that Nature is indifferent to our ideals?	58·46	23·52	18·00	40·7	35·5	23·8

It is these last two points that illustrate more particularly the spread of what I have called Modernism. Commenting upon the answers to the questionnaire in the course of a sermon delivered at Westminster Abbey, Dr. Barnes, bishop of Birmingham, emphasised the widespread drift from the churches, the refusal to subscribe to definite creeds and dogmas ('A generation ago our young people doubted the first Chapter of Genesis; now they are not prepared to accept so simple a statement of belief as the Apostles' Creed'), and the resultant necessity for evolution in religious belief, if religion is to retain any hold upon the people. The tendencies of such an evolution would be a return to the actual teaching of Jesus, a loyalty to truth as conceived by the present rather than to the institutions and traditions of the past, and a growing admission of the relevance of religion in general and the principles of Christ in particular to the daily life of the individual and to his relations with his fellow men. Religion, in short, must become a social force, if it is to maintain its position; it must cease to concern itself with questions of doctrine and dogma, and devote its attention increasingly to the problems of the modern world.

What Modernism seeks to do

Concrete expressions of the Modernist movement include philanthropy of all types, community services, the church support of prohibition in the United States and the intervention of the churches in the mining dispute of 1926 in England. The so-called 'bishops' plan' for the settlement of this dispute, put forward in July, was, though unsuccessful, an admirable illustration of the new conception of the function of religion in social life.

Finally, although there is a majority in favour of the view that the Bible is inspired, the number of those who consider that it is a literal record of actual historical fact is comparatively small (see answers to question 11). Fundamentalism, in other words, has but a small following in England.

Even before the war the success of the Modernist movement had led to active opposition on the part of those who represented what may be called the tradition[al] or conservative position in theolog[y]. These have taken their stand on th[e] verbal infallibility of the scriptures, insis[t]ing upon a literal interpretation of th[e] account of the creation of the world give[n] in the first chapter of Genesis, and of pas[s]ages such as those recording the birth[,] resurrection and ascension of Christ. Th[e] war gave an enormous impulse to th[e] movement. Nor is the reason far to seek.

The war was succeeded by an age of dis[]illusion; it has shattered, at any rate f[or] the time, the Victorian belief in an automatic law of progress, and revealed the weakness of the foundations upon which our civilization rests. There wer[e] times during the war when men doubte[d] whether civilization could be saved[;] there have been times since when the[y] have doubted whether it were wort[h] saving. We have in fact become sceptica[l] not only about the security but eve[n] about the value of our achievement[s]. The tremendous advances of science, th[e] increase of power over nature in whic[h] they have resulted, the spread of educa[]tion, of democracy and of what is know[n] as culture and enlightenment, do not seem to have made men either happier [o]r better. On the contrary, they have n[ot] been able to prevent the greatest socia[l] catastrophe in history.

An Age [of] Disillusi[on]

In face of these developments Chris[]tianity has seemed to have lost somethin[g] of its hold. But may not this loss be du[e] in part to the fact that it has ceased to b[e] Christianity? Scrutinised by the highe[r] criticism, subjected to the study of com[]parative religions, interpreted and re[]interpreted in the light of the spirit of th[e] age, mutilated in order to square with th[e] doctrine of evolution, riddled by rationa[l]ism and diluted by Modernism, the fait[h] of the Fathers has been so whittled awa[y] as to be scarcely recognizable. Geology, fo[r] example, shows that the world took man[y] millions of years in the creating; the firs[t] chapter of Genesis says that the creatio[n] occupied seven days. In order to kee[p] religion up to date and bring it into con[]formity with the requirements of science[,] we are told that the word 'day' must b[e] interpreted symbolically. A 'day' is mean[t] o represent not a lapse of twenty-four hours, but a period of time of indefinite length. But once this method of interpretation is applied to the Bible, it is difficult, if not impossible, to assign to it any limits. There is no recorded event in scripture, from the miracles of Christ to the fall of man, which may not, if this method of approach be legitimate, be interpreted in a symbolic sense or frankly be dismissed as allegorical.

Causes of Fundamentalism

No wonder, it is said, that religion has lost its hold; no wonder it has proved unable to stem the forces of free thought and agnosticism; no wonder that these forces have brought disorder and disillusion in their train. The remedy is clear: to accept the Bible as an actual record of historical fact, to interpret its words in their literal sense, to denounce as wicked all doctrines, such as that of evolution, which conflict with those of the Bible, and to endeavour by a return to the simple faith of the Fathers to rescue the modern world from the waves of materialism and agnosticism which threaten to engulf it. In a world of doubt and confusion men are prone to take refuge in the certainty of the written word. The greater the unhappiness of the age, the greater the disasters that beset it, the more insistent does the need for this remedy become. And so it is to the war more particularly that many have attributed the rapid growth of Fundamentalism.

In America, where it is strongest, Fundamentalism has organized active opposition to the Modernist tendencies described above. It seeks to return to a type of belief as rigid and as narrow as that of seventeenth-century Puritanism. The leaders of Fundamentalism, urging the transcendental importance of salvation and the comparative unimportance of this world, do not hesitate to criticise the activity of the Church in social service, and the attempts of the Modernists to bring the Gospel to bear upon social affairs. They have endeavoured, in some cases with success, to obtain control of the state legislatures in America, and, where they have done so, have forbidden the teaching of evolution in any educational institution supported out of the taxes.

It is, indeed, difficult to assign limits to the spread of Fundamentalism. It may be that it is a late but evanescent development of the war mind which, craving for security in a world that has suddenly become dangerous, finds it and finds it alone in the Scriptures. It is possible on the other hand that it expresses a permanent need of the age, a need which is itself a reaction from the materialism of science and the soullessness of industry. In this event it may conceivably prove to be the first stirring of a real awakening of faith.

Converts gained by Roman Catholicism

Similar causes have contributed to the spread of Roman Catholicism in non-Catholic countries. Roman Catholicism provides a creed in the very fixity and definiteness of which believers find security and comfort. When everything seems doubtful and old beliefs are going by the board, the rigidity and stability of dogma assumes for certain minds a new quality of appeal. Where the dogma is not only definite but detailed, and purports to provide not only a guide to conduct but a 'right attitude of mind' upon all the questions of the day, its attractions for such minds increase in proportion to the difficulty of the times and the complexity of the issues upon which the individual is called upon to adopt a view.

During the war, moreover, the Roman Catholic Church derived considerable advantage from the fact that it was a non-national church. The pope was enabled to adopt an impartial standpoint, and to follow the dictates of humanity and the principles of religion unhindered by the demands of patriotism or the necessity of thinking evil of the enemies of the state. He continued to give signal evidences of the Christian spirit in the repeated notes which he addressed to the belligerent powers, urging them to consider peace by negotiation; in his efforts to mitigate the ferocity of reprisals, and to ameliorate the condition of prisoners in all belligerent countries; and in the arrangements for the transfer of prisoners, for many of which he was responsible. It is to these expressions of the spirit of

Christ, as rare as they were praiseworthy, that some part of the added prestige of the Catholic Church after the war must be ascribed. As to the growth of its influence in non-Catholic countries there can be no doubt. Both in England and in the United States the number of Roman Catholics has been steadily growing ; the number of annual conversions increases from year to year (in England and Wales from 6,511 in 1914 to 12,064 in 1927); there are no complaints of dwindling church congregations, and a movement is on foot for the opening of new churches.

In the sermon by Dr. Barnes quoted above the preacher referred to the growth of superstitious cults and heterodox beliefs consequent upon the general drift away from the churches.

Spiritualism and its appeal

Spiritualism and Christian Science were mentioned as instances of such cults or beliefs, and stigmatised as variants of primitive and obsolete superstitions, symptoms of a religious decay which, in common with unorthodox belief in general, have always flourished when orthodox faith is at a low ebb.

Of the hostility of the churches to what we may call these substitute beliefs, which are recognized as being in some sense the competitors of orthodox religion for the spiritual allegiance of the people, there can be little doubt. The conference of bishops, known as the Sixth Lambeth Conference, which met under the presidency of the archbishop of Canterbury in the summer of 1920, went out of its way to define the attitude of the Church of England to spiritualism and Christian Science as one of declared hostility. The conference saw grave dangers in the tendency to make a religion of spiritualism, 'the practice of which as a cult involves the subordination of the intelligence and the will to unknown forces and personalities,' while the teaching of Christian Science 'cannot be reconciled with the fundamental truths of the Christian faith and the teaching of Scripture.'

Under the heading of psychical research or spiritualism there are grouped together a number of very varied occurrences—table-rapping, automatic writing, water divining, poltergeist phenomena and many others—most of which have no bearir on the question of individual surviv after death, and none of which can l regarded as providing definite eviden of such survival. Before the war th investigation of these phenomena wa viewed with hostility by profession scientists and with indifference by th general public ; nor was there any eviden of a widespread desire to ascertain wheth individual survival could or could not l established. A questionnaire was, in fac sent out in 1904 with the object of testin this desire, and the results, as analysed b Dr. Schiller in the Proceedings of th Psychical Research Society, indicated tha only in a few minds, and in those who interest was quickened by recent bereav ment, was this desire actively present.

The war cut off thousands of youn men in the prime of life and brought sudde bereavement to large numbers of home with the result that public interest in spiritualism suddenly became active, and psychical research, which

Senselessne of Death

had previously occupied the position the Cinderella of the sciences, became a once popular and reputable. The reaso is not far to seek. There is somethin peculiarly pointless about death, especiall when it strikes down men whose powe are still unabated. We cannot bring ou selves to believe that this is really the en that the strength and the laughter, th prowess and the skill, the knowledge an aspirations of the lost one have all com to nothing. Such a conclusion is repelle to our reason and wounding to our conceit it robs human life of dignity and divests of meaning, making of the adventure living, that seems to us so important, mere purposeless incident, devoid alike value and significance. Add to this th craving of those bereaved to see again th face and to hear the voice of the loved or who has gone, and the lively intere in the question of individual surviv which war generates is readily intelligibl

Nor is it an impartial interest ; it predisposed from the beginning by th strongest possible incentive to believ that there *is* survival, and, since th majority of the students of psychic research, including all those who enthusiasm outruns their sense of the value of evidence, are themselves convinced that there is, the post-war popularity of spiritualism as a means not only of establishing the continued existence of the dead, but of communicating with them, needs no further explanation.

The less desirable elements in this change of attitude on the part of the public found expression in the outburst of credulity that was incidentally responsible for the legends of the 'Angels of Mons' and the 'Russians from Archangel,' an outburst to which the ministrations of quack mediums were invoked to give a quasi-scientific countenance. Professional 'psychics' attained an enormous vogue, and assumed the rôle of the modern successors of those astrologists, alchemists, fortune tellers and magicians who in every age have flourished on the fears and hopes bred of times of stress and danger. Even when the mediums were not deliberately fraudulent, they were persons devoid of scientific training and innocent of any suspicion of the tricks which their psychology was capable of playing on them.

A more reputable status, however, was afforded to the whole movement by the publication in 1916 of Sir Oliver Lodge's *Raymond*. The book gives an account of the communications, purporting to come through a medium, Mrs. Leonard, from Sir Oliver's son who had been killed in the war. Neither about the quality nor the quantity of these communications was there anything remarkable. The account of the life of those who had passed over, a life in which ghosts smoked cigars and drank whiskies and sodas, did not differ markedly from the descriptions of the 'summerland,' as it is called, that had been the stock in trade of psychic communications for the preceding fifty years; nor had sceptics any more difficulty in assigning a perfectly natural explanation to the events recorded.

Sir Oliver Lodge and 'Raymond'

Nevertheless the reputation of Sir Oliver Lodge and the state of mind of the public ensured for the book an unprecedented publicity. Scores of similar books written by less distinguished authorities followed in its train. and the stimulus to research provided by this great accession of public interest continued for many years after the war. It is perhaps needless to add that no definite and agreed evidence of survival has rewarded the wave of popular interest, although a great deal of new light has been thrown on this obscure borderland between science and religion.

The tenets of Christian Science

To considerations similar to those which have caused the recent vogue of spiritualism must be attributed the spread of Christian Science. Spiritualism has flourished because men have been unable to tolerate the apparent pointlessness and futility of death; death, they have argued, cannot be really what it seems—it would be too meaningless. Christian Science has spread because of men's refusal to accept the apparent pointlessness and futility of pain. That pain should be just what it seems is no more tolerable than that death should be just what it seems; it must, therefore, be in some sense illusory. And Christian Science, which has asserted that it is illusory, in the sense that a right attitude of mind combined with the proper exercise of will can cause it to disappear, has flourished accordingly. When a generation to which pain has hitherto been an incident is suddenly subjected to gross physical suffering in its most appalling forms, the temptation to adopt this point of view is very strong. To reject it is to imply a doubt on the one hand of the goodness of God, and on the other of the supremacy of mind over matter. That pain is in a sense unreal, that God does not will it, and that it arises because of man's own wickedness has always been the teaching of orthodox Christianity. But suffering men and women may well require a more concrete and sensational application of the doctrine than the Church permits.

Christian Science, which teaches, first, that pain is unreal, and secondly, if somewhat inconsistently, that faith in God combined with prayer and supplication will cause it to disappear, has appealed with peculiar force to the needs of the time. On the positive side there is the fact that drastic ills require a drastic remedy, and that, where the universe appears to be given over to the powers of darkness, and men's traditional beliefs are subjected to an intolerable strain, those who still cling to a faith in the goodness of the scheme of things demand a creed as dramatic as the fears it is designed to allay.

Christian Science is a challenging assertion of the goodness of God, of his direct intervention in the affairs of men, and of the supremacy of the spirit over the flesh. It was, therefore, admirably adapted to the circumstances of the time, which called for a dramatic vindication of beliefs that there seemed only too much ground for doubting.

The following figures provide in this connexion an interesting contrast. A comparison between church and chapel attendances in a typical London area with a population of over 80,000 shows that in 1886–7 the total number of persons attending was 12,996, and the average attendances in 44 services was 295. In 1902–3 the total was 10,370, and the average at 56 services 184. In 1927 the total was only 3,960 and the average in 62 services was 63. In 1906 the Anglican and free churches could claim between them 6,455,719 Sunday-school scholars. In 1918 the number had shrunk to 4,748,872.

Decline in Church attendance

During the same period the number of Christian Science churches increased with great rapidity. Whereas in 1910 there were 1,207, of which 1,077 were in the United States and 58 in England, in 1920 the corresponding figures were 1,804, 1,590 and 98 respectively, and in 1926 the total number of churches had risen to 2,250. In 1914 some 1,500 Christian Science lectures were given to about 1,000,000 people; in 1926, 3,432 lectures were given to approximately 2,669,890 people. Christian Science doctrines have spread since the war to France, Germany, Italy, Denmark, Norway, Sweden, Spain, Russia, Holland and Greece. The spread of faith healing, which was a feature of the years 1923–25, and the beliefs which it implies may be attributed to the same causes.

A few words must be added on psycho-analysis, the growth of which was so marked a characteristic of the post-war years. Between this growth and the decline of orthodox faith already recorde it is not difficult to trace a definite co nexion. The work of Freud and Jur and their respective followers has demo strated beyond the possibility of doul that very little, if any, of our experienc is lost to us. Whenever we say that w forget something that has happene what we do is to repress it into an uncor scious region of our minds. The mind, i fact, has invisible extensions as real an as important as the area which is normall accessible to consciousness. Now whe an idea or experience is forgotten, repressed, that is to say, into this u conscious region, it does not necessaril cease to be active. It exerts an influenc upon our conscious thinking which is non the less potent because unperceived, dete mining alike the colour of our though and the direction of our wishes. This doctrine is developed by many psycho-analysts into the assertion that virtually all our consciou thoughts and desires 'spring,' to adop their phrase, 'from the unconscious.'

The cult of Psycho-analys

It will be readily seen that this doctrin cuts at the basis of human responsibility We are not responsible for the content of our unconscious; we do not know wha is going on in it, and we cannot, therefor control it. Nevertheless, we are told tha what happens in consciousness is th direct outcome of the sum total of the in fluences exercised upon consciousness b the unconscious. It is not here mair tained that this doctrine is true in a that it asserts; nor is its bearing upo the question of free will necessarily suc as is here stated. Some part of it i however, quite certainly true, and all c it is exceedingly popular. A great man people do in one form or another hol the doctrines popularised by the psych analysts, and their view of human person ality and human freedom is unconsciousl affected thereby. In this tendency, whic psycho-analysis undoubtedly encourage to diminish human responsibility th relationship between its spread and th decline of orthodox faith is to be found.

The average human being cannot endur the thought that he is a completely fre agent, the burden of being able to thin and to do precisely what he pleases being for the ordinary man intolerable. That is why the army and the church have always been his two most popular institutions. All codes of morals, and we may add most religions, owe their effectiveness and appeal to their whole-hearted recognition of this fact. They have not hesitated to tell the individual how to act and what to think in any moral or spiritual difficulty with which he may be confronted, and in so doing they have transferred the burden of his freedom to their own shoulders.

The most striking example of the part played by religion in thus lightening the load of human responsibility is afforded by the Christian doctrine of repentance and forgiveness. A man sins—that is to say, he acts in a way repugnant to his conscience or moral sense. As a consequence the moral sense which he has outraged proceeds to make him wretched; he feels, as we say, remorse. This process remains unaffected, whether we regard the moral sense as an unconscious recognition of the fact that something has been done of which society will disapprove, that is, as an unconscious fear of public opinion, as a survival of tribal taboos, or as a direct intimation given to the individual of those actions of which God disapproves. So long as the individual's sense of complete accountability for his wrongful action continues, the remorse persists. The Christian religion provides an avenue of escape from this feeling of remorse by assuring him that, if he confesses his sin and repents of it sincerely, then God will forgive him, and it will be as if he had never sinned at all.

The burden of Freedom

It will be seen that in affording a way of escape from the continuing results of our actions, by putting a term, as it were, to our moral accountability, this aspect of faith abates something of the full rigour of the doctrine of human responsibility, and so lightens the terrible burden of human freedom. But, if he is to find the solace effective, the individual must be quickened by a lively faith in God and His mercy. When this faith is sapped, it becomes necessary for him to find some other method of avoiding, at least in his own eyes, the full measure of moral accountability for his actions. He must find some means of stilling the reproaches of his conscience, and no better method of achieving this end than that offered by psycho-analysis could well be devised.

In assuring him that the springs of his conduct lie in the unconscious, that the desires arising therefrom escape detection and so evade control, it also destroys his accountability for his actions, and so diminishes the full rigour of his sense of freedom. Its appeal, therefore, to those whose faith has suffered as a result of the war is based in part upon that same need of human nature in which the appeal of religion was grounded. The growth of the one is the natural counterpart of the decline of the other.

So far as philosophy in the strict sense is concerned, the war does not seem to have had any discernible effect upon current metaphysics. It is, in any event, too early as yet to affirm with any certitude that such developments as have occurred have been due to or even influenced by the war. Certain tempting theories may be, and have been, advanced; as, for example, that the growth in favour of the theory of the limited deity, a view which finds expression in one or other of the various forms of the modern doctrine of creative evolution, is the outcome of men's recognition of the incompatibility of an all-powerful God who is also benevolent with the phenomena of war; that the acceptance of that interpretation of the universe with which Thomas Hardy's novels have made us familiar, an interpretation which ascribes the occurrence of events to the operations of a blind and indifferent fate, is the product of war psychology; or that the modern insistence upon the importance of instinct as determining man's conduct, and the consequent belittlement of the part played by reason, is due to the same cause.

The War and Metaphysics

But interesting as these speculations are, it is impossible to substantiate them. It is equally certain that there would be no general agreement with regard to any particular connexion which we might seek to establish between these undoubted tendencies of modern thought and the war.

TABLE OF DATES FOR CHRONICLE XXXIII

1918 Nov.: Germany submits to armistice terms dictated by Allies (11th). Yugo-Slav constitutional monarchy and Austrian, Czecho-Slovakian and Hungarian republics proclaimed. William II abdicates. Bulgaria: Ferdinand abd.; acc. Boris.
Great Britain: Lloyd George's coalition ministry.

1919 Jan.: Peace Conference of Paris opened between the 'big five,' attended by the Associated Powers.
Feb.: Ebert elected president of German Republic.
March: Communists seize Hungarian government.
April: Conference adopts League of Nations Covenant.
June: Treaty of Versailles signed.
Aug.: Rumanians occupy Budapest. Anglo-Persian and Anglo-Afghan agreements.
Sept.: D'Annunzio seizes Fiume. Peace treaty of St. Germain-en-Laye with Austria.
Oct.: International Labour Conference for examination of common industrial problems opened at Washington.
Nov.: Peace treaty of Neuilly with Bulgaria.
Dec.: Government of India Act, applying Dyarchy in British India.

1920 Jan.: Mustapha Kemal in Anatolia; 'National Pact' of Angora.
First meeting of League of Nations Council.
Feb.: War between Poland and Soviet Russia; Esthonian treaty of Dorpat with Russia.
March: U.S.A. reject Versailles treaty.
German troops enter the Ruhr to suppress communist disorders.
April: French troops occupy Frankfort and Darmstadt.
Conference of San Remo allots mandates.
June: Greek advance against Turks in Asia Minor.
Peace Treaty of the Trianon with Hungary.
Settlement of Aaland Islands question between Sweden and Finland by reference to the League.
July: Germany at the Spa conference on reparations.
Aug.: Treaty between Czecho-Slovakia and Yugo-Slavia.
Treaty of Sèvres with Turkey (unratified).
Russo-Latvian treaty.
Russians invading Poland defeated on the Vistula.
Oct.: Russo-Polish armistice; Polish troops take Vilna.
Nov.: Treaty of Rapallo (Italy and Yugo-Slavia) to settle Fiume question.
First meeting of League of Nations Assembly.
U.S.A.: Election of President Harding.
Dec.: Irish Government Act becomes law.

1921 Russian treaties with Persia, Afghanistan and Angora. Conferences of Paris and London.
March: Russo-Polish peace of Riga; alliance of Poland and Rumania; Anglo-Russian trade agreement.
Germany declares to incredulous Allies that she cannot pay. Sanctions put in force.
June: Little Entente linked up. British Imperial Conference.
Aug.: Silesian question referred to the League. U.S.A. issues invitations to the Washington Conference on reduction of naval armaments.
Nov.: Washington Conference opened. Albanian republic recognized.
Dec.: Four Powers Treaty takes place of Anglo-Japanese alliance. Treaty of Washington.

1922 Jan.: Cannes conference.
Feb.: Court of International Justice opened.
Great Britain declares Egypt independent, with reservations for security.
April: Genoa conference; German-Soviet treaty of Rapallo; temporary non-aggression pact.
Aug.: Greek rout at Kalahissar.
Sept.: Turks burn Smyrna and march on Straits.
Constantine abd.; acc. George II.
Oct.: Neutrality of Straits preserved; armistice of Mudania. Fascist ministry in Italy under Mussolini. Bonar Law ministry in England. Angora government abolishes Sultanate.
Nov.: Flight of sultan; Abdul Mejid made khalif.
Conference of Lausanne opens for settlement of Turkish question.

1923 Jan.: Germans declared in default with reparations; Ruhr occupied by French and Belgian troops. Germany issues passive resistance order; fall of the mark. Turks reject the draft treaty of Lausanne.
Feb.: China denounces treaties with Japan.
Vilna recognized as Polish territory.
May: German proposals rejected. First Baldwin ministry.
July: Turkey accepts amended Lausanne treaty.
Entente relations strained by Ruhr question.
Aug.: Stresemann ministry takes office.
U.S.A.: Acc. President Coolidge.
Sept.: Cancellation of passive resistance order.
Greek-Italian question of Corfu settled.
Spain: Dictatorship of Primo de Rivera.
Oct.: Mustapha Kemal Turkish president.
Dec.: Two committees of experts appointed to examine German reparation question.
Greek republic proclaimed.

1924 Jan.: Adriatic treaty (Italy and Yugo-Slavia).
Macdonald ministry in England.
Feb.: Turkish government abolishes Khalifate.
March: Adoption of Dawes Reparation Report.
July: London Conference; U.S.A. agree to take part in Reparation Commission.
Aug.: French begin evacuation of Ruhr.
Oct.: England and Turkey accept League settlement of Irak boundary. Publication of Zinoviev letter; second Baldwin ministry. The League adopts Geneva protocol, which is rejected by England in favour of regional pacts (Nov.).
Nov.: President Coolidge re-elected.
England rejects Russian commercial treaties.
Dec.: Sun Yat-sen's government recognized.

1925 Feb.: Germany suggests a security pact relating to the Rhineland.
April: Hindenburg elected German president, but disappoints the hopes of the Junkers.
May: Anti-foreign (especially against British and Japanese) riots in China.
March: Sun Yat-sen d.; constant hostilities between the Kuomintang Nationalist government in the south and Chang Tso-lin's military government at Peking.
July: German proposal receiving favourable consideration, but a supplementary pact relating to the eastern German frontier does not command the adherence of England and Italy.
Oct.: Arising out of this the Locarno Conference meets, with Germany on the same footing as the other powers, in an unprecedented atmosphere of conciliation and good will.
Rhineland pact adopted, with a series of arbitration conventions.
Demirkapu incident; frontier collision of Greek and Bulgar forces; war averted by intervention of the League.
Dec.: Ratification of Locarno treaties; British begin evacuation of Cologne. Deposition of shah of Persia; Rhiza Khan elected shah.

1926 March: Germany's admission to the League suspended by action of Spain and Brazil.
England: Long coal and short general strike.
Rise of Chiang Kai-shek as general of the Kuomintang.
Aug.: French operations against Abd el-Krim.
Sept.: Germany enters the League of Nations.
Nov.: British Imperial conference adumbrates without defining the meaning of 'Dominion status.'

1927 Spring: Kuomintang captures Hankow, Shanghai and Nanking.
Numerous minor arbitration and security treaties; failure of Geneva conference on reduction of naval armaments.

1928 April: Kellogg formula for the outlawry of war submitted to the great powers.
June: Chang Tso-lin d.; Kuomintang established at Peking. Chiang Kai-shek president (Oct.).
Aug.: Acceptance of Kellogg Pact by fifteen 'nations,' followed by others.
Dec.: Albanian republic elects King Ahmed Beg Zogu.
Afghan revolt against Amanullah.

1929 Jan.: U.S.A. ratify Kellogg Pact.
Absolutist revolution in Yugo-Slavia.
Feb.: Vatican treaty with Italy restoring temporal sovereignty to the Papacy.

Chronicle XXXIII

AFTERWARDS: 1918–1929

FOR four years and a hundred days all Europe and much of the world outside Europe had been whirling in the maelstrom of the Great War ithout time or thought to spare for anying but the war in some of its many pects. The war had wrecked the founations of the entire pre-war fabric—ternational, industrial, constitutional, cial, religious. All the greater historic ates and peoples, with the exception only Spain, the Dutch, the Swiss and the :andinavians, had been involved in it as :tive or at least nominal belligerents; nong the active belligerents, determinaon to win at whatever cost had overadowed every other consideration.

When it ended, the Austrian, Russian id Turkish empires had ceased to exist, ough Austria, Russia and Turkey surved; the German empire in Europe was tact save for Alsace, but was no longer cussed in the person of an emperor. alf a dozen nationalities, or groups, had parated themselves from the broken npires and were clamouring for recogtion as independent states, apart from e territorial claims upon one or another them of other already established states. ne territorial chaos was incomparably eater than it had been when Napoleon as interned in St. Helena.

naotic State of the Post-war World

NOT less was the industrial chaos. For the industrial world had been drained its young manhood to fight instead training itself in industry; millions of ese had perished, and millions more ere physically wrecked or at least partially capacitated, and industrial employment uring those years had been restricted the production of the bare necessities life or of munitions of war in some form -not wealth, but the machinery for deroying wealth; machinery which had een appallingly successful in effecting e purpose for which it had been created, hile it perished simultaneously itself. gain, on all sides governments were tottering, if they had not already fallen; the governing capacity of the governing classes, if not of all governments, was in the crucible; they were responsible for the war, the mismanagement of the war, and all the havoc that it had wrought. In the more democratically ruled countries hostility to the old order was less virulent: most virulent in those which had been most despotically ruled in the interests of particular sections of the community. But in all was the virus.

Ethically the disappearance of regulated discipline at home among the young, coupled with the reaction of their elders against the rigid discipline of battle service to which they had willingly or unwillingly submitted themselves, told heavily against moral restraints of every kind; while the fearful devastation and suffering caused men, when they turned their thoughts to religion, to feel as they had felt in the days of the Norman King Stephen when they cried out that 'Christ and His saints slept.' The world, to put the thing in its simplest terms, had to recover balance, and for years after the war was over it was still rocking.

Objects of the Peace Makers

WITH the cessation of hostilities, the first necessity of the moment was to ensure against their present recrudescence, which, from the point of view of the victors, meant to paralyse Germany for hostile action. That was practically effected by the terms of the armistice, which imposed on her immediate disarmament and surrender to the victors of military stores and material. The next step was to formulate such a general settlement as should provide the strongest possible guarantee for the future against the resort to arms for the adjustment of international differences. Theoretically, the Vienna Congress of 1814–15 had the same object in view; but it failed to attain it, though it had prevented international wars for nearly forty years.

Precedent demanded the immediate adjustment of inter-state boundaries, transfers of territory, recognition of new states, indemnities which the victors were entitled to claim from the vanquished in the great conflict. But much more than this was required if the peace was to end not only the war which had just been fought to a finish, but the menace of wars greater and even more destructive in the future. The matter was taken in hand by the 'big five' who had been mainly instrumental in winning the war—France, Great Britain representing the British Empire, the United States of America, Italy and Japan; in consultation with the minor states but clearly with the intention that what the 'big five' agreed upon must prevail; though with the serious difficulty in the background that America might—as she ultimately did—refuse to ratify the decisions of her representative, President Woodrow Wilson.

This however was a point which did not affect the drafting of the peace treaty, in which the American president took a ver leading part, since it was largely base upon the 'fourteen points' which he ha enumerated as essential, and it was he wh most unhesitatingly insisted on the inclu sion of the Covenant of the League c Nations as a fundamental portion of th treaty itself—something vitally differen from the 'Holy Alliance,' not of people but of princes, with which Alexander I having the same object in view, had sough so ineffectually to supplement the Treat of Vienna in 1815.

THE treaty, then, was to be a treaty c peace between the victors and Ge many to which all the signatories woul be pledged; to be supplemented by furthe treaties with Germany's allies. The enor mous task of shaping and drafting i was carried through in the first month of 1919 by the representatives of the bi five—though Japan took active part in i only when it dealt with matte in which she was concerne —with the assistance of th delegates of the other state in relation to matters wit which they were directly co cerned. Germany's share in i was confined to ineffectu protests against terms whic were imposed upon her, havin as the only alternative th advance of the Allied armie into the territories which sh was no longer in a position t defend. On May 7 the Germa delegates met the delegates c the 'Allied and Associated powers, who were already i possession of the treaty term. They were given some si weeks to accept or reject them but it was not till June 28 when they had been threatene with an immediate advanc of the Allied troops, tha the Treaty of Versailles wa actually signed by the as sembled delegates in the sam Hall of Mirrors where, in 1871 William I had been proclaime German emperor.

THE GERMAN FLEET SURRENDERS IN 1918

The terms of the armistice imposed by the Allies included the surrender of all German submarines and the internment of many of their warships. Of the German surface ships which came to Rosyth for internment on November 21, 1918, the majority was sunk by their crews at Scapa on June 21, 1919.

Photo, Royal Air Force, Official Crown copyright

THE SIGNING OF THE PEACE AT VERSAILLES IN 1919

ıe international peace treaty that concluded the Great War was signed in the historic Hall oı irrors at Versailles on June 28, 1919, and its signature is the subject of this fine painting by Sir 'illiam Orpen. Seated, from left to right, are General Tasker Bliss, Colonel House, Henry White, obert Lansing, Wilson, Clemenceau, Lloyd George, Bonar Law, Arthur Balfour, Viscount Milner, G. N. Barnes and Marquis Saionzi ; signing, the German delegate, Dr. Johannes Bell.

Copyright Imperial War Museum

The treaty opened with the Covenant the League of Nations, to which the Iigh Contracting Parties ' declared their reement, and then proceeded to the re-nstruction of the map of Europe in lation to Germany and the conditions, penal or otherwise, to be exacted from her. As a matter of course Alsace-Lorraine—the provinces taken from France in 1871—were restored to France. East Prussia remained attached to Germany, subject to local plébiscites, which proved to be

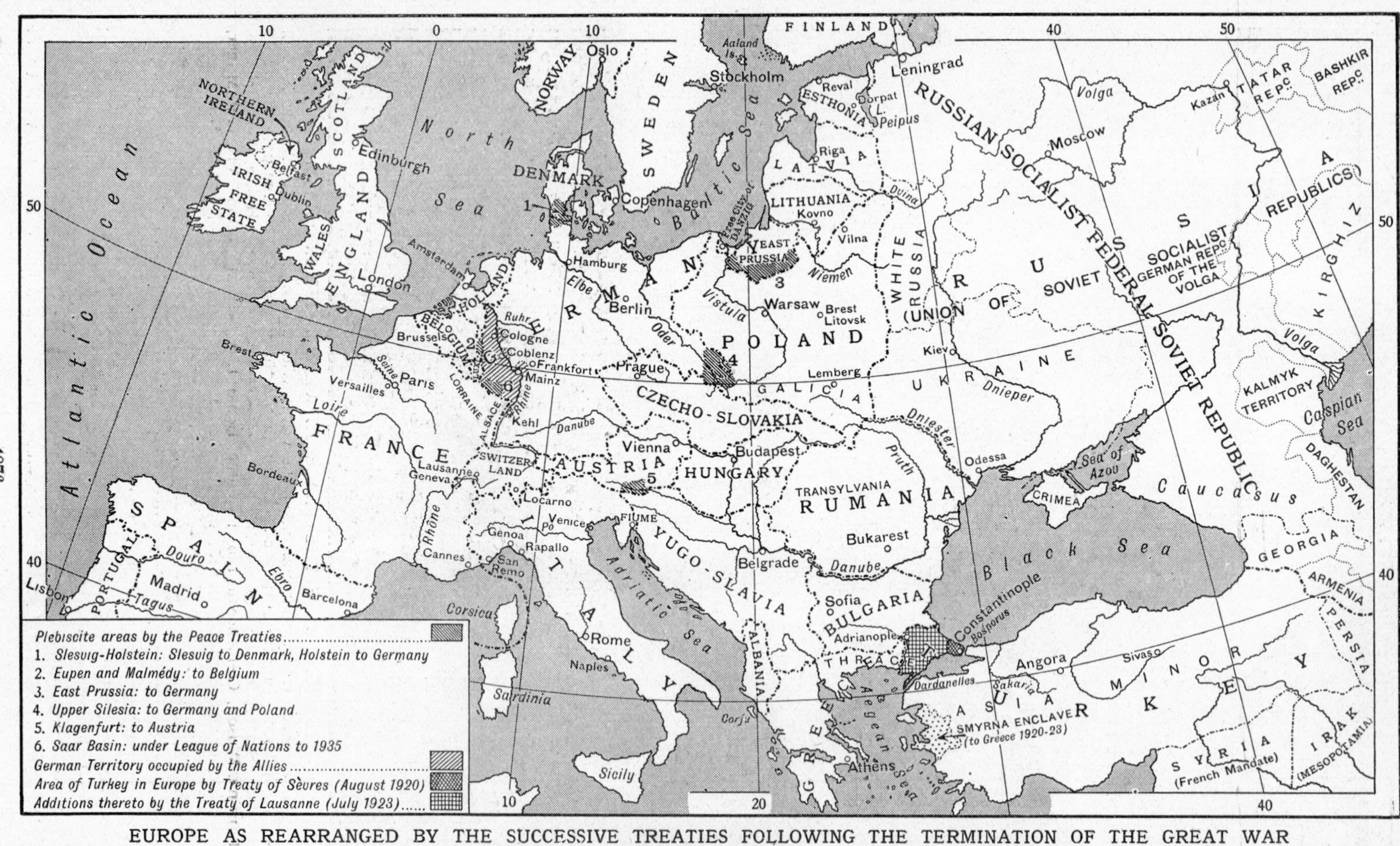

EUROPE AS REARRANGED BY THE SUCCESSIVE TREATIES FOLLOWING THE TERMINATION OF THE GREAT WAR

Whereas after Waterloo the policy on which the redistribution of Europe was effected was governed by dynastic considerations, the basic principle of its redistribution by the Treaty of Versailles in 1919 was the satisfaction of national aspirations and recognition of the right of the smaller nations to self-determination. In this map the main divisions of the new Europe are shown with shaded portions indicating areas where the ultimate settlement was left to lecisively in favour of that course; but she was deprived of the trans-Niemen territory, which was subsequently allotted to the new state of Lithuania. Poland was restored as an independent state, with a corridor to the port of Danzig, which was to be an independent free city under the protection of the League of Nations. Czecho-Slovakia, comprising what had been the northern Slavonic provinces of the Austrian empire, excepting those which were again attached to Poland, was also recognized as an independent state. The question whether certain Germanised portions of these lands should remain German or be included in Poland was left to later settlement, preferably by local plébiscite. Denmark's claim to Slesvig, of which Prussia had deprived her in 1864, was to be decided by plébiscites, which ultimately gave one portion of it to Denmark and another to Prussia. There were adjustments with regard to Belgian territory and a highly complicated arrangement with regard to the German Rhineland on the French frontier, which for ten years to come was to prove a fruitful source of friction.

The territorial arrangements of the Treaty of Versailles were theoretically completed by the supplementary treaties with Germany's former allies. The Austrian treaty of St. Germain-en-Laye opened with the 'Covenant.' It divided what had been the Austrian empire into the separate states of Austria, Hungary and Czecho-Slovakia, while it transferred Galicia to Poland, Bukovina and part of Transylvania to Rumania, and the South Slav districts to Serbia, and gave to Italy not only all the Italian-speaking districts, but also the German-speaking districts of South Tirol. The most serious difficulties here were in the adjustment of the rival claims of Italy and Serbia or Yugo-Slavia. The treaty of the Trianon with Hungary, the other member of the former official Dual Monarchy, of which various portions had been assigned to Czecho-Slovakia, Yugo-Slavia or Rumania, leaving Hungary about half its former size, was not completed until June, 1920. Bulgaria, by the treaty of Neuilly (November), lost her coast line on the Aegean, but was secured 'economic outlets' thereto. The Treaty of Sèvres with Turkey was never signed by the sultan, so that it passed into oblivion. The United States having declined to commit themselves to the League Covenant, that power was not a party to any of the treaties, but made its own separate terms with each of the states with whom it had itself been at war.

Other independent states appeared in the new map of Europe, on the Baltic. Soviet Russia had so far committed itself to doctrines of 'self-determination,' the principle on which the powers had endeavoured to base their treaties, that it could raise no objection when these provinces separated themselves from her.

REPRESENTATIVES OF THE 'BIG FOUR'

Of the 'big five' mainly concerned in arranging the terms of the peace treaty that ended the Great War, Japan only took active part in so far as she was herself affected. Representatives of the other four powers, Britain, Italy, France and America, are (left to right) Lloyd George, Orlando, Clemenceau and Woodrow Wilson.

At the head of the Baltic came Finland, then Esthonia, then Latvia and finally Lithuania, which had been united with Poland under one crown since her Duke Jagellon (see page 3008) acquired the Polish crown, an association which was now terminated.

The rearrangement made by the Treaty of Vienna a century earlier, after the Napoleonic wars, had been based wholly upon monarchist doctrines of dynastic legitimism, entirely ignoring ideas of nationality or affinity, and the claims of peoples—as distinguished from the dynasts—to a voice in their own disposal. Now, 'sceptre and crown had tumbled down' in the defeated states; there was no thought of restoring them; Romanovs, Hapsburgs and Hohenzollerns had fallen, and with them all the lesser dynasties of the German Empire. In the new settlement, dynastic claims counted for nothing; the purpose in view was to give to national affinities the first claim to consideration and, so far as was practicable, to minor groups which did not desire or could not be accorded independence the right of self-determination; that is, of choosing for themselves by plébiscite the recognized state to which they should be attached. But in many areas the populations were compounded of diverse or positively antagonistic elements, so that any attempted solution must fail to be satisfactory to all. That dissatisfaction would rise to angry and even perilous heights was hardly to be doubted; but no settlement could conceivably have been made which would not have involved that risk.

Settlement Outside Europe: the 'Mandate'

GERMANY was the only one among the defeated powers which had possessed dominions over sea. From them she had been completely ejected in the course of the war, and by the peace treaty she resigned all claims to them. They were not annexed to any power, but were dealt with by 'mandate' under the terms of the League Covenant, which entrusted their administration for the most part to Great Britain, to be ruled in the interests of their respective populations. Mandatory powers were to be in effect trustees for the League. Arabia remained under the chief who had been proclaimed sultan of the Hejaz; in 1920 the mandate for the administration of Syria was given to France, and for Mesopotamia and Palestine to Great Britain. For the time the Porte retained almost nothing in Europe except Constantinople, the terms of the armistice with Turkey remaining in force as the Treaty of Sèvres was unsigned.

Difficulties of European Reconstruction

IN the reconstruction of the map of Europe the treaties dealt with a subject bristling with difficulties, conflicting interests and sources of friction not only between victors and vanquished but also among the victors themselves; but by creating the League of Nations (see Chapter 183) it was hoped that they had at the same time provided an instrument by means of which defects in the treaties might be subsequently compensated, since it was morally certain that defects would be found. But besides the territorial arrangements and the creation of the League, they had to deal with another extremely thorny subject—the reparations and indemnities which the victors severally might justly claim from the vanquished for the sufferings and losses inflicted by a war for which in the view of the former the whole responsibility lay upon the latter; who, as they held, had also conducted it with an unprecedented disregard of the recognized ethics of warfare between civilized states. And as against those claims they had to calculate the effective capacity for making them good. And in addition they had to provide security against any attempted repetition of the offence of which in their view those powers had been guilty.

The fear of renewed German military aggression in the future was in the nature of things much more prominent for France and Belgium than for anyone else; on the question of the share of compensation due to itself and to others every state had its own views, and those views were divergent; and on the question of capacity to pay there were not and could not be adequate data, while there was everywhere a strong popular disposition to exact the uttermost farthing rather than to consider the general economic effect of so doing.

The problematic character of the whole situation was further complicated by the fact that Russia was an unknown and incalculable quantity. The powers found themselves quite unable to recognize the Soviet government as one which could be relied upon to keep faith and carry out its engagements; since its agents were notoriously and avowedly employed abroad in a propaganda which aimed at the overthrow of all existing governments, its activities within Russia itself were condemned by all civilized opinion, and it had already repudiated all obligation to carry out engagements undertaken by the Russian government in the past. The powers desired to revive a settled order; Russia desired to destroy settled order; the two aims being obviously incompatible, there was no possibility of arriving at agreement as to the means. The powers wanted security, and Soviet Russia was a standing menace to all security.

On what we have called the third question, then, there were two aspects of the problem for settlement: compensations, and guarantees for Germany's neighbours against future aggression. The latter was concerned with Germany's effective disarmament, the demilitarising of the German frontier territory facing France and the present occupation thereof by the Allies. The indemnities imposed were far short of what was considered adequate compensation, but, on the other hand, according to the Germans far in excess of anything they could possibly pay. If they were compelled to make promises, the promises were accompanied by warnings that it was in fact quite impossible to execute them.

At the same time the withdrawal of the Allied forces from the frontier provinces was made conditional upon their execution; and it continued by no means easy for the Allies, and above all for France, to believe in the honesty either of the German protests or of professions of complete disarmament. Napoleon had disarmed Prussia drastically enough after Jena, but the result had not been what he

BRITISH TANKS ON THE RHINE

The Allied occupation of Cologne and a bridgehead of eighteen square miles on the east bank of the Rhine was provided for in the terms of the Armistice. Cologne became the headquarters of the British army of occupation; its cathedral can be seen in the background above.

Photo, Imperial War Museum

had intended. The Allies were in no mood to rely upon German good faith without the most convincing material guarantees; the Germans were resentful both of the charges brought against them and of the penalties exacted, so that the tone they adopted was not calculated to allay distrust. If the British were disposed to be more lenient than the French, with their devastated lands under their eyes, it was only because it was easier for them to be so. The rival parties to a dispute can hardly be expected to form an unbiassed judgement on the issues, and in the nature of the case one of the parties was here unequivocally the judge as well.

The natural result was that the terms were drastic, and did not tend to early reconciliation. There was a prospect of at least modifying the nervousness of France in the proposal, to which both President Wilson and the British government assented, that America and Great

Britain should jointly guarantee the security of France against German aggression; but it came to nothing, because it was essential that the guarantee should be a joint one, whereas, as with the League of Nations, in the devising of which the president had played so large a part, America refused her ratification. France remained with no more security than she could derive from the Treaty of Versailles. Inevitably therefore she was resolved to let go nothing that she could logically claim under its terms. She would take no risks—and Germany as victor in 1871 had acted strictly upon the same doctrine.

Diplomacy by Conference

THE series of treaties between the 'Allied and Associated Powers' on one side and the defeated powers on the other was left incomplete, inasmuch as the Treaty of Sèvres with the Turks remained unratified. Nor did they cover the agreements which it was necessary for the major and minor powers to arrive at among themselves before a permanent atmosphere of amity could be attained. The powers, however anxious they might be, were by no means ready to submit their rights of private judgement to the control of the new international instrument they had brought into being—the League of Nations—at least until that instrument should be tested and perfected. The League was indeed set in immediate operation; but the method adopted for dealing with the biggest questions was 'diplomacy by conference.'

It was a method, departing from the ordinary practice of diplomacy, initiated in the years immediately following the Napoleonic wars, when congresses had been summoned at short intervals; since then it had been employed on certain notable occasions, such as the Berlin Congress, the Hague Conferences and finally the Conference of Paris which drafted the Versailles treaty; and now during these critical years it was developed and repeatedly brought into full play. Conferences meant not that, as in the ordinary course, each government communicated with each other government through its ambassador at this or that capital, but that the heads of the respective governments or their foreign ministers met together in conclave at San Remo or Lausanne or Locarno or elsewhere for the joint solution of the intricate problems of divergent interests which required to be dealt with; the governments being normally those of the great powers with whom the last word would necessarily lie.

The New States on the Baltic

THE new Baltic states that came into being at this time had been separated from Soviet Russia by the Treaty of Brest Litovsk at a moment when Germany conceived that they would as a matter of course become client states of her own, her troops being in fact in effective occupation. The independence of the Ukraine had been at the same time recognized by the Russians and the Central powers. The authority then acquired by Germany passed to the Allied powers with the Treaty of Versailles, and with it the responsibility not for enforcing but for procuring such a settlement between them—and Poland with them—as should command their common assent, while precluding the association of any of them with Germany. Between Poland and Russia there had been no settlement beyond the tsar's earlier promise of liberation for Poland; and the soviets had announced that they were not bound by any engagements entered upon by the fallen tsardom. Before long, Poland and Russia were at war, and there were also acute differences between Poland and Lithuania.

Finland was prompt to declare herself an independent republic. She had an immediate dispute with Sweden on the question of sovereignty over the Aaland Islands, once in possession of Sweden. The matter was complicated, but the two states were persuaded to submit it to the League of Nations, and both loyally accepted its pronouncements thereon, which were embodied in a Convention signed in October, 1921. Notable in connexion therewith was the League's declaration that the general principle of self-determination did not confer upon every community the right to transfer

-self from one sovereign state to another; he Aaland islanders having expressed a reference for the sovereignty of Sweden. . boundary dispute between Finland nd Russia concerning the title of the ormer to an ice-free port on the White ea was settled in Finland's favour in he peace treaty of Dorpat (October, 1920) etween these two states, which till then ad been technically in a 'state of war,' he Finnish government having much do to repress in Finland the Bolshevik ctivities emanating from Russia.

Esthonia, too, had her initial difficulties, ecause her government, like all governments, was anti-Bolshevik, for the simple eason that everywhere the Bolshevik ropaganda was directed against every overnment not itself Bolshevik. Consequently some of the anti-Bolshevik Russians tried to make Esthonia their own ase for hostilities against the Bolshevik overnment of Russia, which was hardly nore agreeable to Esthonia, because the nti-Bolshevik Russians avowedly did not admit the right of the Baltic provinces to separate themselves from the legitimate Russian Empire. The collapse of the Russian monarchist efforts, however, at the end of 1919 led to the settlement of the Esthonian question to Esthonia's satisfaction by another Treaty of Dorpat in February, 1920, between Esthonia and the Russian Soviet government.

The experiences of Latvia were similar to those of her neighbour. Her independence was in like manner recognized by a Russian treaty in August, 1920; but the relations of these two little states with Russia must remain uneasy so long as she is, and they are not, Bolshevik. Even in conjunction it would be difficult for them to resist aggressive activities on the part of their big neighbour, though for defensive purposes the League of Nations stands behind them.

Between Lithuania, Poland and Russia the relations were complicated. The Russian government had accepted the separation from Russia of Lithuania, as

ZELIGOWSKI'S TROOPS ASSEMBLED IN VILNA AFTER ITS SEIZURE

ıe possession of Vilna, in which the Lithuanian provisional government was originally set up, came a subject of dispute between Lithuania, Poland and Russia. Ignoring the armistice ocured by the League of Nations after its seizure by the Russians in 1920, the Polish general eligowski made his unauthorised march upon the town and effected its recapture. So successful was this coup d'état that Vilna later received European recognition as belonging to Poland.

Courtesy of Polish Press Bureau

distinct from Poland, at the Treaty of Brest Litovsk, with the corollary that Lithuania was intended, in effect, to become a German protectorate. In theory she would be an independent state, as she became when the Versailles treaty washed out the protectorate design. Before the war was over the Lithuanian provisional government was set up at Vilna, but on the German retirement the Russians again took forcible possession of Vilna in January, 1919. Meanwhile, the Poles had established their own provisional government. In their eyes Vilna was Polish, and in April they ejected the Bolsheviks from Vilna.

Settlement of the Vilna Imbroglio

LITHUANIA declined Poland's proposals for the reunion of Poland and Lithuania. The Poles, in spite of Lithuanian resentment, kept their grip on Vilna, which they had won back after Lithuania lost it to the Russians; but in 1920 the Russians renewed the attack and recovered Vilna. They did not stop at Vilna; they marched on Warsaw, the Polish capital, only to meet with very unexpected and altogether decisive defeat on the Vistula. The intervention of the League of Nations brought about an armistice; but a Polish general, on his own responsibility, ignored the armistice, marched on Vilna, seized it, and entirely refused to retire, though, at least officially, he was acting in defiance of his own government. The League, after divers experimental moves which proved ineffectual, left Poland and Lithuania to settle their claims by negotiations between themselves. But the Poles were in effective possession; a majority of the inhabitants of the Vilna district apparently preferred to be attached to Poland, and presently Europe recognized Vilna as being within the Polish sovereignty. Russia withdrew her own claims by the Treaty of Riga (March, 1921) with Poland.

Vilna as part of Poland links up Poland with Latvia, and so with the North Baltic states, but severs Lithuania from Russia. As part of Lithuania, it would be a Lithuanian gateway to Russia and would sever Poland from Latvia. Incidentally, Lithuania is an easier channel of communication between Germany an Russia than Poland provides, since Lithu ania has not the same historic causes a Poland for antipathy to Prussia. It wa perhaps inevitable that western distrus of Germany and of Bolshevik Russi should foster, in France especially, th feeling that Poland must be, so to speal a watch-dog and custodian in the east.

Friction between Italy and Yugo-Slav

OF the big five who had taken part i the war and taken on themselves th peace settlement, America had repudiate responsibility for European affairs, fro which Japan also stood apart. Whatev differences there might be among th others and their fallen antagonists, arme conflict among them was out of the que tion. The public danger lay in the fa that the sense of responsibility weighe less heavily upon the minor states, who it might be difficult to restrain fro appealing to arms for the settlement their disagreements—and bitter exper ence had shown that small fires ma develop into great conflagrations. Th east, therefore, with its great congeries minor states was a constant source anxiety; and between Yugo-Slavia—t new, expanded 'Greater Serbia'—and o of the great powers there were standi sources of friction; the territorial clai of Italy and Serbia on the Easte Adriatic being incompatible.

These last, however, proved themselv capable of adjustment by the good sen of the Italian and Serbian government The most notable instance was the ca of Fiume. France and England had ma engagements with Italy on her entry in the war which they were prepared to kee but they were not prepared to exte them at the expense of the unified Sou Slavs. They would not support h later-asserted claim to the port of Fium which it was extremely difficult to assi to any one nationality. Fiume, li Danzig, was to be an independent fr port. The Italian government reluc antly acquiesced; not so the ferve Italian nationalist and poet d'Annunzi who in Garibaldian fashion raised a tro of his own and seized Fiume. So popul

·wever, was the action of the poet that was not till the end of 1920 that the alian government ventured to conclude th Yugo-Slavia the treaty of Rapallo to force d'Annunzio's withdrawal. Fiume ıs declared independent, but even then e position proved to be so impracticable at finally in 1924 Italy and Yugo-Slavia hieved a pact which gave Fiume itself Italy but secured to Yugo-Slavia privi- ges in connexion with the port which et her most pressing requirements.

ıngary and the Balkan States

ANOTHER of the threatening storm centres in the near eastern lands was ıngary. The Magyars, always resentful subordination to the Teuton in the ıpire under which they were combined, d always been no less insistent on the bordination of the Slav to the Magyar Hungary. Of recent years they had joyed a status of equality with the uton while retaining mination over the Slav. ›w, in the break-up of e empire, Teuton and ıgyar were definitely parated, and so far as sentanglement was pos- ›le the Slavs had broken e from the domination both. But further, the ıvs, while they had no ırs of an Austrian at- mpt to recover ascend- cy over them, felt no h security in regard to Magyars. The same plied to the 'Roumanes' Transylvania, now nsferred to Rumania. ıngary had taken her nd with the Central wers, shared in their miliation, and resented an injustice when ted out to herself the atment in which she d seen no injustice when ted out by herself to bject peoples.

Hungary, moreover, ly became a source of trouble, because in March, 1919, her government was seized by the communist or Bolshevik faction, which presented itself as a menace to Rumania, who in her turn had special grudges against Hungary, born in the recent war. Rumania invaded Hungary; conciliatory missions from the west failed. The communist government fell, but the Rumanian troops did not withdraw till they had exacted severe indemnities from Hungary. There followed some disastrous attempts to restore the Hapsburg monarchy in Hungary, which to Hungary's neighbours was as disturbing as the plunge into communism. It was not surprising, therefore, that Yugo-Slavia, Czecho-Slovakia and Rumania made a treaty of alliance among themselves, which united them in what was known as the 'Little Entente' for the defence of the common interests for which the western powers did not appear to offer

GABRIELE D'ANNUNZIO AT FIUME

Dissatisfied with the attitude of the Peace Conference towards the fate of Fiume, Gabriele d'Annunzio, the Italian poet and patriot, decided to seize the port. He raised a band of enthusiastic troops to assist him in the raid, and annexed Fiume on Italy's behalf in September, 1919. He is here seen addressing his legionaries.

Photo, E.N.A.

them adequate safeguards; interests which appeared to be threatened by Bolshevism on one side, possibly by Italy on the other side, and by Hungary at the centre. Nor is it surprising that from another point of view the safeguarding of those interests meant the depression of Hungary.

It would indeed be a sound general statement to say that conditions gave strong though by no means absolute security against the rekindling of war in the west, but that as regions lay farther and farther from the armies of the western powers the security for peace diminished. The great powers, including Germany, would leave no stone unturned to avoid collision among themselves; but necessarily it was to this end that their attention and energies were most continuously directed, and their control eastwards was comparatively sporadic, and spasmodic, in proportion as their alertness to the course of events waxed and waned. It was in, and in connexion with, what had been the Turkish Empire that the menace of a serious conflagration suddenly made itself most acutely felt.

Troubles of the Turkish Empire

The Turkish Empire had matched the Austrian Empire in the completeness of its collapse. The sultan, for four centuries khalif and official head of the Sunni Mahomedan world, though not so recognized in the Shiah regions, still officially reigned at Constantinople, but his temporal dominion in Europe was reduced to the city itself and outside Europe was woefully shrunken. Egypt had gone, Syria and Palestine had gone, Arabia had gone, Irak (the revived name for Mesopotamia) had gone, Armenia had gone. How those populations, formerly under Turkish sovereignty, wholly without the experience or even the remote tradition of self-government other than the irresistible authority of a local despot, were to be governed now was a sufficiently difficult problem for settlement by the powers who had broken down the military tyranny of the Turk; and how what remained of Turkey was to be made to serve instead of disturbing the welfare of the rest of the world was another; but Turkey's ow revival was the last thing to be expecte

The sultan's government was permitte to remain in Constantinople mainly fc two reasons—the difficulty of placin anyone else in possession (except th Americans, who firmly declined), and th reluctance to inflict on the Khalifate humiliation which might have a disastrou repercussion upon the Mahomedan worl Meanwhile a considerable area abou the straits was demilitarised and Allie troops under British command occupie Constantinople. The responsibility fc Turkey's final collapse had lain with th Young Turks and their leader Enve In his place Mustapha Kemal, who ha displayed marked qualities both c soldiership and statesmanship, was sen to the Turkish headquarters in Anatolia.

Kemal's Reorganization at Ango

While the government at Constant nople was negotiating the Treat of Sèvres, Mustapha Kemal, with ver different views, was organizing a goverr ment in Anatolia, while Enver vanishe into more obscure regions in the east, an Greece, almost unresisted, was by forc of arms making good her classical bu dubious claims to Smyrna and othe coastal districts in Asia Minor. Mustaph called a congress at Sivas and formulate the policy embodied in what came to b called the National Pact, which Constar tinople ignored. Mustapha consequentl ignored Constantinople and set up national government at Angora in 192 The Angora government, repudiating th Sèvres peace terms, failed to extract th concessions it demanded from the Cor ference of London in 1921; while the Gree forces were continuing to advance, ap parently with the intention of sharing th Turkish Black Sea provinces with Armeni till they were checked a long way from the base by Angora troops on the Sakaria.

The Constantinople government was phantom; that of Angora was a realit which commanded the loyalty of th Turks in Asia and was inspired by a lead of genius. It had ignored but not officiall repudiated Constantinople. It struck treaty of its own with the Russian Sovi government. The French and British governments had announced their neutrality in the Graeco-Turkish war, in which the Greeks were conspicuously the aggressors. Without departing from neutrality, but recognizing the facts of the situation, France virtually recognized the Angora government by concluding with it a convention regarding the Turco-Syrian boundaries in October, 1921. Attempted mediation by the powers between the belligerents failed; when the Greeks in the following July proposed to occupy Constantinople the powers, whose troops were in actual occupation, refused to admit them.

Greeks Defeated in Asia Minor

AND then in August Mustapha Kemal, who had bided his time, shattered the Greek army, whose retreat soon became an unequivocal rout, while the Turkish army was engaged partly in keeping them on the run, partly in marching towards the straits, on the way to Thrace. The very considerable Greek population in the districts which the Turks were now overrunning fled headlong to the coast, where it was taken off by neutral as well as by Greek ships. King Constantine, who had been restored, abdicated for the second time, in favour of his son, George II.

If the Angora troops approaching the straits entered the demilitarised zones on the east of the straits, that would be an act of war. Would the Allies resist it? If they did not, their acquiescence might have on the Mahomedan world an effect which Great Britain was not disposed to risk. With or without support from the Allies she was resolved to maintain the freedom of the zones and the straits. France and Italy declined to support her, and withdrew their troops. The strained relations between the Allies were relieved by their agreement on a joint note inviting Greece and Turkey to a peace conference, and the situation was saved by the combined tact and energy of the British commander, General Harington, and Mustapha Kemal's wisdom and controlling influence over forces flushed with victory and far outnumbering the British at the moment. Some Turkish troops actually crossed the boundary, but were withdrawn in time to avoid a collision. There was no act of war. Mustapha held a conference with the British commander, and agreed to open negotiations with the Greeks. The armistice was signed on October 11.

Three weeks later the Angora government proclaimed the abolition of the Sultanate; the sultan, who had never been more than a puppet, fled to security on a British ship, and Turkey became a republic. A new khalif—not sultan—was appointed, but a year later (February, 1924) the government abolished the Khalifate itself—an event which did not have upon Mahomedans at large the disturbing effect anticipated; since it could not be attributed to Christian hostility to Islam. The final peace terms, taking the place of the still-born Treaty of Sèvres, were arranged at the Conference of Lausanne (1922–23), which was followed by the abdication of George II—the

MUSTAPHA KEMAL PASHA

Mustapha Kemal Pasha, born 1882, set up the Angora government in 1920 and became president of the Turkish republic in 1923. His Westernising policy is brought out by this photograph of him dancing with his adopted daughter at the ball given to celebrate her marriage.

Photo, General Photographic Agency

ANGORA: THE ANATOLIAN TOWN THAT REPLACED CONSTANTINOPLE AS CAPITAL OF TURKEY

The rapid growth of Angora since it became the Turkish capital in 1923 was promoted by Mustapha Kemal, who turned a backward country town into a modern city. New buildings and roads replace former unhealthy quarters and narrow streets. The old town, still surrounded by its medieval walls, is seen on the hill at the back, while the new town is spread along the valley below.

Photo, E.N.A.

Greek monarchy could not survive its disastrous failure—and Greece became one more among the new republics.

The Treaty of Lausanne (July, 1923) was the last in the series of treaties, beginning with that of Versailles, establishing peace between the group of victorious powers and the several defeated powers in the Great War, the relations with Turkey having hitherto been controlled by the armistice, not by a definitive peace. It gave to Turkey substantially better terms than she could have obtained under the Treaty of Sèvres, mainly at the expense of Greece, whose aggressive activity had brought that fate upon her. A substantial portion of Thrace was given back to what may be called the new Turkey, as well as Adrianople, the bulwark of Constantinople. The delimitation of the Turkey-Irak boundary was left to the Turks and the British as 'mandatories' for Irak with the League of Nations as referee.

Shortcomings of the Settlement

It will have been clear enough in the course of this Chronicle that the post-war settlement lacked one very vital desideratum. It was not, because it could not be, a settlement by consent in which the interests of all parties concerned were judicially adjusted and all were treated on an equality. It was a case in which one party was in a position to dictate its own terms which the other could only accept, or rather submit to, under protest, nursing its own conviction that they were dictated not by justice, but by vindictiveness, and that it was morally entitled to evade them to the best of its power. Security for the victors against renewed aggression by the vanquished, even in a remote future, was for them the first essential, meaning that renewed aggression must be placed—permanently if possible—out of the power of the vanquished. In the eyes of the victors the vanquished had been guilty of gratuitous and criminal aggression developed by criminal methods which, apart from security, deserved salutary punishment which the victors were entitled to exact. The defeated powers had inflicted damage for which the victors claimed the fullest compensation.

But it was also inevitable that the victors hemselves should not see eye to eye as to he methods by which security should be btained, the extent and the distribution f the compensations available, and the mits beyond which the depression of the anquished would react to the detriment f the victors themselves. The fact that ltimate security against war could only e achieved by the substitution of good vill and mutual confidence for traditional hostility and suspicion was indeed recognized by the creation of the League of Nations; but that was admittedly a tentative experiment which might have incalculably beneficial results but might prove entirely futile. Time alone would show. Meanwhile, an atmosphere of good will was not one of the realities of the situation; and the fundamental necessity was the agreed action of the Allies, whose unanimous will no one else could resist. Hence, the method of 'diplomacy by conference' was substituted for the traditional ambassadorial diplomacy as at once more rapid in action and keeping the Allied governments in closer touch with each other.

The execution of the treaty terms was carried out under the supervision of the Conference of Ambassadors — the accredited agents of the respective governments at Paris. The Versailles treaty itself was the work of the Paris Conference which formally terminated in January, 1920, when the ratifications of the treaty were completed. A fresh conference met in London in February, which dealt less drastically than had been expected with the question of the 'war criminals,' since the chief of them was on neutral Dutch territory where he could not be seized and whence the Dutch government declined imperturbably to eject him. It gave up the attempt to settle the question of Fiume, which it left to Italy and Yugo-Slavia, and it decided that the Turk should be permitted to remain in Constantinople. A third conference met in April at San Remo. It agreed upon the 'internationalisation' of the Dardanelles and the Bosporus, left Armenia to carry on as best it might, and was chiefly occupied with the thorny question of German disarmament.

'DIPLOMACY BY CONFERENCE' AT SAN REMO IN 1920

After the Great War the Allied leaders adopted the conference system as the best method of handling the numerous questions demanding settlement. This photograph shows members of the supreme council assembled at the Villa Devachan, where the San Remo Conference met in April 1920, its main concern being German disarmament. The French premier, Millerand, is seated on the extreme left; Nitti, Italian premier, is in the centre, while Lloyd George and Lord Curzon are on the right.

Photo, Topical Press Agency.

German troops had been marched into the Ruhr district, officially to suppress communistic disturbances there. This looked very much like a move of the German military party; it disclosed the fact that the Germans still had under arms a much larger number of regular troops than should have been the case; and the entry of German troops at all into the demilitarised area was a breach of the peace terms. The French at once took alarm, and replied by occupying Frankfort and Darmstadt. In doing so on her own responsibility France was within her technical rights, though in some quarters her action was felt to be needlessly aggressive, while in others it seemed to be more than warranted, not only by Germany's failure to reduce her army, but by her demands that the period allowed for her disarmament should be extended and the extent of the disarmament itself reduced. A reasonable harmony, however, was restored, and the conference rejected the German demands. The German troops were withdrawn, and the French followed suit. But the Germans were also for the first time invited to meet the Allies in conference for the better execution of the peace terms. Before this conference met at Spa, in July, there were several minor conferences, mainly for the adjustment of French and British points of view, and to consider the financial position in Germany.

Conferences at Spa, London and Genoa

The aim of the Germans at Spa was to obtain very substantial remissions of their treaty indebtedness on the ground that it was not practically possible to make the stipulated payments. They failed to satisfy the Allies of the genuineness of their plea, though the latter repudiated any intention of victimising them. The chasm, however, between the views presented by the Germans and those maintained by the Allies was not appreciably diminished.

Nor did the situation become more promising with the London Conference of February, 1921. The Germans declared that the scheme of reparation payment submitted by the Allies was impossible of fulfilment, and propounded a counter scheme so inadequate (from the Allied point of view) that its uncompromising rejection was accompanied by the threat of the application of 'sanctions' if the Germans maintained what was regarded as a wilful refusal to carry out their treaty obligations. The sanctions were applied; and, by another London conference of the Allies alone, the Germans were give[n] a week to accept somewhat modifie[d] terms. A new but far from stable Germa[n] government submitted. But it soon be[-] came obvious that they would agai[n] default. A Paris conference in Augus[t] failed entirely to agree on the settlemen[t] of another problem, the partition o[f] Upper Silesia between Germany an[d] Poland, which was finally handed over t[o] the League of Nations.

A conference at Cannes early in 192[2] was abortive and was followed by [a] conference at Genoa, in April, which wa[s] productive of more discord than harmony. For so far as France took part in it, i[t] was only to emphasise the fact that he[r] own policy was fixed; Germany was, i[n] effect, declaring herself bankrupt; Bol[-] shevik delegates had been invited t[o] attend, and their contributions to debat[e] only served to intensify the distrust wit[h] which they were regarded, and the genera[l] sense of the utter impracticability of an[y] co-operation with them; and the Germa[n] delegates took the opportunity to strik[e] with them at Rapallo a treaty of 'recog[-] nition and commerce' which the Allie[s] could only interpret as a deliberat[e] defiance, while the French premier—i[n] France, not at Genoa—virtually an[-] nounced the intention of taking suc[h] measures as were necessary to the du[e] fulfilment of the terms of the Treaty o[f] Versailles, preferably with the co-opera[-] tion of the other powers; but, if tha[t] were not forthcoming, without it. I[n] spite of the astonishing attitude of th[e] Russian delegates, Great Britain an[d] Italy endeavoured to procure a conven[-] tion with Russia, which should at leas[t] pave the way for admitting her to th[e] European comity, but failed, since neithe[r] France nor Belgium, nor finally the Sovie[t] government itself, would adopt it.

The Need for Economic Reviva[l]

The reign of good will seemed farther o[ff] than ever, and the conference power[s] even took the precaution of makin[g] a temporary pact of non-aggressio[n] among themselves, Germany and Russia in[-] cluded. But one point of actually hopefu[l] omen was emerging: the powers wer[e] inning to realize that the sickness of ope could not be cured until her nomic conditions were restored on a lthy basis. Economic revival was inning to be recognized not as a minor as a primary necessity.

leanwhile, however, another separate ference had been at work at Washing-, with much more progressive effect; onference called not by the treaty vers, but by the United States of erica, who took at most a watching t in the European conferences. Europe indeed concerning itself with dis-ament, but in the imagination of ope that was mainly visualised as the npulsory disarmament of Germany. To erica, as to the League of Nations, it ant the discovery of a basis for the sistent universal agreed reduction of aments to what might be called a ce level—the standard of controlled e necessary to the guardianship of the lic peace. To a conference with this ect, the limitation of armaments, in v, America invited the four treaty vers, Great Britain, France, Italy and an, to which were added China and three minor European states which e concerned with Pacific and Far tern questions. The conference met Armistice day, 1921, concluding its ions on February 6 following.

hington Conference & 'Four Power Treaty'

HE five great powers dealt with the problem of naval disarmament, since it ame immediately evident that military rmament could not as yet be profitably ussed; the nine with the other group uestions which touched them all. The man navy having ceased to exist, only five were directly touched by the naval stion. America proposed that, subject quivalent action on the part of Britain Japan, she should abandon her existing gramme of capital-ship construction, scrap a number of existing battleships, powers agreeing to limitations on future al construction. Here agreement was nparatively easy; but on the question 'auxiliary' craft it was soon found no common term was possible, the cial needs of the several states being controlled by diverse and divergent conditions. The total abolition of submarines was mooted by Great Britain, but found no favour with those of the powers which regarded them as essential to their own defence, and the conference contented itself with denouncing their use as commerce destroyers, a denunciation which from the British point of view appeared entirely impossible to enforce.

The agreement as to capital ships, however, was a very material advance, as also was the 'Four Power Treaty' between America, France, Great Britain and Japan, which took the place of the standing Anglo-Japanese treaty of alliance, in which America detected a possibility of developments hostile to herself, since there had been considerable friction between her and Japan in the past. With no possibility of German or Russian fleet activities in the Pacific, the continuance of the standing treaty was viewed with suspicion; but when it was translated into the Four Power Treaty it became an instrument of common accord. The new treaty was not technically the work of the Washington conference, but was accessory to it. Similarly the conference conduced to but did not in itself effect a treaty between Japan and China, which was made at the same time, regarding the vexed question of Shantung, from which the Germans had been expelled by the Japanese during the war, while China claimed its reversion to herself. The conciliatory action of Japan in this matter was capped by the British restitution of Weihaiwei to China, and the resignation by other powers of sundry concessions that had been made to them.

Lausanne and the Ruhr Invasion

It was not long after the dispersal of the Genoa conference that Greece suffered her crushing defeat at the hands of Mustapha Kemal. It has already been told how the advance of the Turks led up to the conference of Lausanne, of which the main concern was the settlement of the Turkish question, and the other main feature was the avoidance of the breach which was threatening between the Western powers. It may be noted that at this moment the British coalition ministry fell and Lloyd

George, who was not on the most sympathetic terms with the French premier, was succeeded by the Unionist leader Bonar Law, while the coalition foreign minister, Lord Curzon, remained in office, and almost simultaneously Mussolini became Italian prime minister.

The Lausanne conference was prolong it did not actually conclude until after m summer in 1923, and there were criti moments during its course ; but the m anxious moments of that anxious year w not concerned with the Lausanne neg ations ; for it opened with the declarat by the 'Reparation Commission,' wh was in charge of the matter, that Germa was in wilful default in the discharge the payments due from her, and more p ticularly in the delivery of coal. Two d later, on January 11, French troops concert with Belgium marched into Ruhr district and occupied it ; as, at le in their own view, which it was more th difficult to controvert, they were entit to do in the circumstances under the V sailles treaty. But, with the except of Belgium, the action of France was wi out support from her allies. Their act opposition was out of the question.

The German government did not—pr ably in the state of German pub opinion it dared not—acquiesce. Si active resistance was impossible, th was only one way left—passive resi ance. The coal deliveries ceased, w

MEMBERS OF LLOYD GEORGE'S COALITION MINISTRY

The fine war-time service rendered to the British nation by David Lloyd George (lower left) secu him the premiership in 1916. His coalition ministry was returned in 1918 and held office until resignation in October, 1922. Top : Lord Curzon (1859–1925) succeeded Balfour as foreign secret in 1919, resigning in 1924. Andrew Bonar Law (1858–1923), who for some time shared the coalit leadership with Lloyd George, later helped to destroy it, and succeeded as Unionist premier, 1922–

Photos, Russell, Vandyk and Elliott & Fry

LEADERS OF THE CONSERVATIVE AND LABOUR PARTIES IN BRITAIN

nley Baldwin, born in 1867, succeeded Bonar Law as Conservative premier in May, 1923, and his visit to Poincaré, the French premier, in September of that year, relieved the strained relations n existing between Britain and France. In January, 1924, James Ramsay MacDonald (left) formed inistry and held office until October, when Baldwin again secured a majority. MacDonald, born in 1866, was secretary of the Labour Party 1900–11, and its leader 1911–14.

Photos, Lafayette

sed, all payments were refused. But was on the working population of the hr and in Germany at large that the den of the consequent suffering fell. nce, relatively, was merely inconienced. In Germany the mark dropped a fabulously low level. British public nion generally, but by no means unisally, disapproved if it did not openly ent the French action. The relations ween the two governments, without ose co-operation the restoration of ropean stability was unattainable, were ined almost to breaking-point—but quite.

Iatters in Germany went from bad to se. In May she made proposals that e regarded as too futile to be seriously cussed. The French government would contemplate the evacuation of the hr until the passive resistance ceased. that reason it rejected a second man offer in July. British 'notes' to nce were met by polite but uncomproing replies—including rejection of the gestion, which looked like a reflection n the Reparation Commission, that Germany's capacity to pay should be referred to a commission of impartial experts. It appeared possible that in the impasse which had been reached the British government was contemplating independent action. Germany was only encouraged to maintain the passive resistance by the prospect of a complete breach between France and England—but for that England herself was not prepared. If she had contemplated independent action, she abstained from taking it. The sword remained suspended, even if it was by no more than a hair.

The strain of the fatal passive resistance policy upon Germany was already more than she could bear. She was threatened not only with complete economic ruin, but with political disintegration by a separatist movement in the Rhineland, mainly traceable to the French occupation of the Ruhr and the revolutionary fever born of hunger; a movement not for union with France, but for an independent republic. France remained immovable. But Germany had at last acquired a ministry whose chiefs had the courage to face facts, the insight and the patriotic faith to deal with them unflinchingly. At the end of September the new government withdrew its predecessor's passive-resistance decrees—and the German army instead of breaking into a militarist revolt stood loyally by the government.

Only a few days before, Baldwin, who had succeeded Bonar Law as head of the British government, had a meeting with Poincaré which, without affecting the latter's firmness, did much to relieve the tension. The action of the German government did still more, for France had carried her fundamental point that the cessation of passive resistance must precede any relaxation of the French grip. In November the Reparation Commission itself—with a French chairman—appointed two independent expert commissions of inquiry, the precise point on which the British government had been most urgent, of which the issue was the 'Dawes report' (March, 1924). The French remained in the Ruhr, but with the passing of resistance their activities there became less obtrusive, and the new British premier, MacDonald, approved himself a most judicious diplomatist. Poincaré was succeeded by the conciliatory Herriot.

Recommendations of the Dawes Report

A London conference was opened in July, which was attended by American delegates. The recommendations of the Dawes report were substantially approved, and greatly strengthened by the unexpected discovery that America was ready to cooperate actively by sending delegates to the Reparation Commission, whereby the prospect of raising a loan to help Germany on to her feet would be immensely improved. The vital advance was in the recognition of the economic fact that Germany would continue to default, whether wilfully or not, until she was able as well as willing to make the necessary effort. Till that was recognized she would be neither able nor willing. The hesitation of France to adopt and of Germany to accept the offer which was formulated on the basis of the Dawes report was overcome; and the conference concluded the agreement, which was not in the form of a treaty, under which the Dawes schen was brought into operation. The co ference had taken the first real st towards reconstruction.

The adoption, however, of the Daw report was not merely a material st towards financial reconstruction; it w the first significant omen of an improvi atmosphere, of diminishing hostility a suspicion, of relaxing antagonisms. Refe ences to 'war guilt' had hitherto been unfailing irritant; at the London co ference they had been tactfully dispens with. It was much to the credit of t Allies that they had persuaded themselv —without withdrawing their claims— moderate the form of their demands a to add thereto offers of assistance; it w no less to Germany's credit, and partic larly to that of the small group of state men, headed by the president, Ebe who were piloting her through very diffic waters, that she accepted the offer in corresponding spirit and played up to it

Beginning of German Rehabilitati

The armed occupation of the Rhi districts was due, under the Versail treaty, to be withdrawn by degrees, b ginning with the evacuation of Colog in January, 1925, but only if Germa had duly discharged her obligations that date; she had not done so, and t occupation continued. The French evacu tion of the Ruhr was not completed un after midsummer; but Germany h dropped her attitude of sullen inertia, a was seriously setting about her o economic revival and showing a mark disposition to endeavour at least to car out her treaty obligations instead evading them. Sundry efforts of t League of Nations to evolve a trea giving a real security against the appe to arms in the future had broken dov or were breaking down, when in Februa 1925, Germany herself submitted a tent tive proposal to the French governme the essence of which was a security pa guaranteeing the present territorial stat on the Rhine, the result of her own defe

It was perhaps as well that this notab effort did not attract too much of t public attention, which is apt to produ

ated and recriminating controversy in
 press, while the responsible ministers
 France, Great Britain and other
intries were exchanging views on the
rious knotty points arising from the
ggestion, the practical possibility or
possibility of security pacts not only
 the Rhineland but in other regions
ere boundary questions were inter-
tional sources of friction; matters
on which there were many divergences,
ich did not, however, wreck the keen
sire for concord.

rk of the Conference at Locarno

HE outcome was the momentous Conference of Locarno which met in tober; momentous not so much for what actually accomplished as because it rked and emphasised the attainment of ew plane of discussion in which not anonisms but community of interests held first place. The value of the Locarno t was indeed very great; but it was eeded by that of the new 'Locarno rit.' The past could not be blotted out, t it could be left behind. To revive controversies on the rights and wrongs which men had long made up their nds once for all could benefit no one; subjects of discussion they were dead l buried, and their ghosts must not be owed to walk. The ghosts were not as matter of fact completely laid—they ppear when tempers become provoca-e; but they were quiescent at Locarno. t was the first time that Germany had ne into conference unequivocally on an ial footing with her former foes and as promoter of peace—actually the prime moter of the conference itself, since it s clearly traceable to her initiative in preceding February.

The conference met on October 3; invaluable work was completed in a tnight. The work was done in an atmoere of unprecedented good will, not etrated by controversial comment from sponsible quarters, and facilitated by freedom from formalities in its proure. The agreements arrived at, when ified by the respective governments, re embodied in the Treaties of London, nmonly referred to as the 'Locarno Pact,' in December. All the conference powers guaranteed the French-German-Belgian frontiers and the conditions applied to the demilitarised zone under the Versailles treaty. Germany and France and Germany and Belgium pledged themselves not to resort to war against each other except in defence against an act of flagrant aggression; to refer disputes, where they could not agree between themselves, to some form of judicial decision, and at once to report any violation of the terms to the League of Nations; all the signatory powers pledging immediate support to the aggrieved party if the League confirmed the charge.

Besides accessory guarantees, there were added arbitration conventions between Germany on the one hand and France and Belgium severally on the other. A more elaborate German-Polish and German-Czecho-Slovakian arbitration agreement left open the possibility of future frontier modifications by mutual agreement between those powers. Two complementary treaties were made, mutually guaranteeing frontiers, by France with Poland and Czecho-Slovakia, to which the other powers were not parties, since Great Britain and Italy, while ready to give guarantees in the west, could not extend that readiness to the east. But the vital fact remained. Germany and her former foes had at last persuaded themselves at least to shake hands.

Germany Admitted to League of Nations

THE note of Locarno was the note of reconciliation; confirmed next year by the termination of Germany's semi-outlawry, an outlawry which had been at once an inevitable corollary of her defeat in the war and an insuperable obstacle to European recuperation and reconstruction. It ended with her admission to the League of Nations in 1926, with the status of a great power therein. She had accepted the conditions which could convert her into a colleague instead of an antagonist. We need not here deal with the story and the effects of that change—they belong to Chapter 183, as do the continued abstention of the United States from joining the League, and the persistent hostility of Soviet Russia to everything for which the

League stands. The fundamental point of the change that had taken place was not that reconciliation was complete and suspicion and distrust had vanished, for they still lurked beneath the surface and still occasionally broke loose, but that from this time the note of reconciliation was definitely predominant.

Some reference, however, must here be made to minor episodes illustrative of some of the difficulties of preserving peace and evolving goodwill in a Europe whose nerves had been torn to rags by the strain and the sufferings of the war. Such was the unhappy incident of the murder of some Italian officers upon Greek soil in August, 1923, the consequent high-handed seizure of Corfu by the Italian government, and the compromise under which the League abstained from insistence on its own authority to deal with the matter when Italy chose to acknowledge in its place that of the Council of Ambassadors, whose award probably did not differ substantially from that which would have been made by the League. Such, again, was the sudden menace of armed collision

ALEXANDER OF YUGO-SLAVIA

Alexander, second son of Peter of Serbia, d notable service in the Balkan wars of 1912–1 Proclaimed first king of Yugo-Slavia in 1921, l reply to divisional discord was the establishme in 1929 of a royal dictatorship.

Photo, Vandyk

PRIMO DE RIVERA

Under the leadership of the Spanish soldier and statesman Miguel Primo de Rivera, born in 1870, his country's constitution was suspended in 1923. In 1925 he became premier in the civilian administration which he introduced

Photo, Kaulak, Madrid (E.N.A.)

between Greece and Bulgaria in Octobe 1925, which was stopped by the insta intervention of the League and the se restraint of the two governments concern in the face of intense popular excitemen

THE aim of the statesmen of the Ve sailles treaty was a settlement whi should be in fact a reversal of all that w most dear to the hearts of the statesm of the Vienna settlement of 1815. Th had shaped the map of Europe on t basis of nationalism, regardless of dynast claims; only one monarchy, the Bulgaria survived where the defeated powers h ruled; the new states were all republi save for Yugo-Slavia, which was new on in the sense that the old Serbian kingdo now embraced populations which h before been denied union with it—a Yugo-Slavia was a constitutional mo archy with parliamentary institutio The American president had declared th the peace was to make the world sa for democracy. In short, the settleme s in theory the triumph of at had been known of old 'the Revolution.'

Nevertheless, neither nationst groupings nor democratic litical systems proved to be nple propositions; the first, cause within each of the ger groups were minority oups of diverse nationality ich did not immediately algamate; the second, bease democracy presupposes ertain standard of educated elligence, and of what may called the co-operative spirit. mocracy found its enemy not of yore in hereditary privie, but in communism. In neral, democracy (including

TWO PRESIDENTS OF THE UNITED STATES

Neither of President Wilson's successors, Warren Gamaliel Harding (left), nor Calvin Coolidge (right), carried on his policy of assuming American leadership in European affairs. Harding became the Republican president in 1920, and Coolidge, who was his vice-president, succeeded him on his death in 1923.

Photo, Topical Press Agency

MUSSOLINI IN FASCIST COSTUME

organizing genius of Benito Mussolini, born umble parents in Romagna province in 1883, eloped the Italian Fascist movement as a pon against Bolshevism. Becoming premier 922, he undertook his country's reconstruction.

istry of Foreign Affairs, Rome; photo, Henry Manuel

'constitutionalism') was strong enough to cope with communism; but in Russia communism had democracy by the throat; while it is a somewhat ironic commentary on the whole situation that at the end of 1928 Spain, Italy, Yugo-Slavia and Turkey had in fact passed under the control of unqualified autocrats, and to these may be added Albania.

There was indeed nothing surprising in the fact that the president of the Turkish republic gained such a personal ascendancy that he became an autocrat under republican forms, except that his power arrived without the normal accompaniments of bloodshed, almost as a thing of course. It was equally natural that Albania, which had never in the whole course of her history submitted to any rule save that of some chief endowed with an irresistible personality, such as Skanderbeg, acquiesced in the assumption of the crown by a president who would seem to possess the traditional qualifications. Rivalries and jealousies between the newly united divisions of Yugo-Slavia drove its king to a coup d'état establishing his own autocracy as the only effective means to the enforcement of law and order. For Turks, Serbs and Albanians the 'strong man' had always been necessary to political salvation.

The two Latin kingdoms, however, having very different historic antecedents,

ABD EL-KRIM AFTER HIS SURRENDER

The strife which broke out in 1925 in Morocco between the forces of the rebellious tribal leader Abd el-Krim and the French was brought to a sudden conclusion by the surrender of the former in May, 1926. He is seen (fourth from the left) in this group with his attendants and some French officers.

Photo, Chusseau-Flaviens

present a different development. Spain, for considerably more than a century, had been struggling to build up a strong government on constitutional lines, for the most part under painfully adverse conditions. The reigning king, his mother and his father, had been more successful than their predecessors, but the governing power was still inefficient ; and it was the sense of inefficiency, and perhaps the example that was being set by Italy, that brought about the sudden establishment of a dictatorship still under the crown, in 1923, and the suspension of constitutional rule. This, however, was not a departure from precedent in the theory of government, whatever the developments in store may be ; emergencies have produced dictatorships as their only available immediate solution, from time immemorial—successfully or otherwise according to the abilities of the dictator.

Italy, on the other hand, made a new departure. Parliamentary government had brought her neither political nor economic stability, when at the end of 1922 Signor Mussolini became her prime minister and began to lay the foundations of the Fascist state, hardly veiled by the retention of the hereditary monarchy. The system is one whic would have rejoiced the hea of Machiavelli. It is th negation of what the 'Nordi peoples understand b 'liberty.' The people, bei a congeries of factions, incapable of directing a efficient government ; for i own good it must have a efficient government, and o that is irresistible and h absolutely unlimited pow and right of control ; against the government, th people have no rights. Th state is incorporated in th government, and the gover ment is incarnate in th person of its chief. The la as laid down by the gover ment is supreme ; only th government itself is above th law, and of it no adver criticism may be tolerated. That wou seem to be the theory of Fascism ; and i efficiency in the hands of the Duce is convincing that it is easy to overlook t fact that it is bound up with the personali of the Duce himself.

The League, the economic problems Europe after the war, the story Bolshevik Russia and its influences up Europe, are all essential parts of the histo of the post-war decade, but must find on passing reference in this Chronicle becau they are the subjects of detailed study Chapters 182, 183 and 184. But Europ to which, with Turkey, our attention h hitherto been confined, is not the on field which has to pass under revie While America—in the sense of the Unit States—interested herself actively European and extra-European affairs, s rejected the rôle of leader laid down f her by President Wilson, and under his su cessors, Presidents Harding and Coolidg declined to share the direct responsibilit of the European powers ; an attitu regretted by the latter, and not easily i telligible to the mind of western Europ exciting at times adverse comment whi was not always according to knowledge

In Africa the most obvious product of the war was the elimination of German influences, with the substitution of the influence of one or another European power in the areas where they had predominated. But in relation to Mahomedan Africa, Africa from Egypt to Morocco, it had earlier become evident that German influences could not be established without a sharp conflict with France or Spain or both, if not with Great Britain as well; while on the remaining section of the Mediterranean littoral her 'peaceful penetration' had been checked by Italy's declaration of the Tripoli protectorate. Subject to a reasonable security for her own commercial interests, and a free hand in Egypt, England regarded the expansion of the three Latin powers with a friendly eye, and their relations with each other had shown themselves capable of amicable adjustment.

The African populations, however, were not equally amenable. In Morocco the inland tribes, led by Abd el-Krim, were so successful in their resistance to the Spanish efforts at domination that in 1925 they took occasion to challenge the French also, since the latter were encroaching on what they regarded as their own preserves; and it was only at the cost of severe campaigning that the two European powers were able in combination to compel the submission of the Moroccan champion in 1926. Of the three Latin powers, France was the most successful both in conciliating the tribesmen and in developing the commercial possibilities of the area over which she extended her administrative sway; but the immemorial tribal organization is not of a kind to acquiesce readily in European conceptions of government, or indeed in any alien domination.

In those portions of western Asia where the authority of western 'mandatory powers' took the place of the old Turkish regime, the 'autonomy' which materialised was extremely tenuous. The first king of the Hejaz was displaced by the chief of the puritan Wahabi sect; his son was made 'king' of Irak, but such authority as he had was derived entirely from the British; Syria resented the French regime, which was of a more military character than that of the British in the neighbouring areas. Palestine was judiciously organized largely for the benefit of the Jews, but in such a manner as to develop the prosperity of the non-Jewish populations. In fact, in all these areas the general security was much greater than before, but the new wine of misunderstood Western ideas was fermenting in old bottles. Tact and sympathy were very necessary to insure against disaster.

In fact, the secular problem of the irreconcilable divergences between Orientalism and Occidentalism had come to life again. In Japan the antagonism was least in evidence, because her Orientalism was a thing apart, and she had started on the line of an essentially critical but wholly practical assimilation not of Westernism but of selected Western materials. Something of the kind was being attempted

THE LATIN ALPHABET COMES TO TURKEY

Kemal Pasha's determination to abolish the old Arabic signs in Turkey led to the declaration, on December 1, 1928, that the Latin alphabet should be compulsory. In Constantinople the governor compelled a mobilisation of all between the ages of fourteen and forty to learn the new Latinised Turkish.

RIZA SHAH OF PERSIA

Risen from the ranks of the Persian army, Riza Khan engineered the deposition of Persia's reigning ruler, and, being elected shah, crowned himself at Teheran in April, 1926, with a crown specially made for the occasion.

Photo, Pacific & Atlantic, Ltd.

in Turkey under the inspiration of its president and presiding genius Mustapha Kemal, though the problem had for him the additional complication of Islam, and of resistance to Occidental domination with which Japan was not threatened. Turkey's future was trammelled, as Japan's was not, by her past. But all over Asia—during more than the last half-century, by political and commercial penetration more than by military conquest—the tentacles of European domination had been making themselves increasingly felt, while at the same time Asia was increasingly conscious that it was only by learning from Europe how to do it that she could release herself from the European pressure. Now Asia was much disposed to turn to Bolshevik Russia, still more Oriental than Western at bottom, for the teachers whom Bolshevik Russia was glad to supply. Her own turn would come when the ascendancy of the 'bourgeois' powers had been broken—perhaps.

Turkey had set the example. Persia followed it under the astute leadership of Riza Khan, who successfully engineered the deposition of the dynasty (which had not appropriated Western ideas, but had submitted itself and the country to Western domination) and procured his own recognition as shah. Like Mustapha, he reversed the policy, adopting Western methods while rejecting Western ascendancy. In 1926 Turkey and Persia, the new Turkey and the new Persia, formed an alliance. Some time earlier, a new amir in Afghanistan, Amanullah, had declared that British ascendancy there must end. As the British had no desire to exercise any more control in Afghanistan than would secure her against being used as a cat's-paw by Russia, British acquiescence was readily forthcoming—though the amir's methods had been aggressive enough to enforce a brief but decisive campaign as a preliminary. The subsequent relations were entirely amicable. But it may be noted that the Angora, Persian and Afghan governments all signed treaties with Russia at Moscow in 1921. Amanullah, however, was no less zealous to impose Western practices on his people than to resist Western dictation, so that at the end of 1928 his zeal brought about a revolution and his own expulsion from the kingdom. It is not difficult to see why at that time Bolshevik Russia eagerly propagated and England's enemies eagerly swallowed the curious fiction that the fall of Amanullah was to be attributed to British machinations.

Changes in the British Empire

The relations between the several portions of that 'commonwealth of nations,' the British Empire, had been materially affected by the war, though it had by no means weakened the bonds, whether of sentiment or of interest, which held together that great exemplar of unity in diversity. But it had ceased to be possible to apply the old terminology of 'colonies' and 'possessions' which belonged to a bygone age. The change was marked not so much by legislative acts as by the adoption of unprecedented practices as though they were normal developments from the practices of the past.

The 'Dominions' severally, with India, were admitted to membership of the League of Nations, without actual definition of their status. No formal right was bestowed upon them of sharing in the actual direction of imperial policy, but the sense that they had acquired that right was a pervading one—though not yet absolutely as a matter of course. They did not desire complete independence in the control of their foreign relations, but it was tolerably manifest that they would not hold themselves bound by agreements to which their assent had not been given, though it would be given as a matter of course if they had no strong reasons to the contrary. Apart from foreign affairs their autonomy was unqualified. 'Dominion status' in short was a condition without rigid definition, but as to which misunderstandings in practice were not likely to arise, or likely to prove difficult of adjustment if they did arise.

NOT in the Dominions themselves—though there appeared still to be a few intransigents in South Africa—but in other quarters, demands for separation from the Empire were heard. The scheme for Irish home rule, which had been so much in evidence before the war, broke down as a scheme when the war was over; the old 'Nationalists,' whose loyalty had been so conspicuously displayed in the great crisis, lost control of the movement, which was now guided by the fanatics of separatism, the Sinn Fein party; all the old smouldering passions and hostilities blazed up as fiercely as ever, and Ireland became the unhappy stage of insurrection, outrages and reprisals, until the British government arrived at a compromise with the less fanatical Sinn Fein leaders. They surrendered the demand for an independent Irish republic, the major

AT THE AFGHAN COURT ON THE EVE OF AMANULLAH'S ABDICATION

Although Amanullah, amir of Afghanistan, opposed Western rule in his dominions, he was extremely zealous in introducing Western customs. A revolution broke out among the Afghan people, unappreciative of his reforms, and he fled from his kingdom in January, 1929. Amanullah, wearing morning dress, is seen in the centre of this group of courtiers also dressed in Western fashion at the last meeting of his court before he abdicated. His brother, Inayatullah, in a light summer suit, is on the left.

Photo, Fox Photos

portion of Ulster was allowed to separate itself from the rest and remain attached to Great Britain, and the rest of Ireland became the autonomous Irish Free State with 'Dominion status' within the Empire and membership in the League of Nations. Within the Free State the new Free State government was left with entire responsibility for the preservation of order and the maintenance of law without British interference. The new constitution became law in December, 1923.

Egypt had been formally separated from the Turkish empire and transformed into a British protectorate at an early stage of the war without being actually annexed. From the beginning, however, in 1882, Great Britain had declared her assumption of control to be in intention temporary. When the war was over the old agitation for the complete independence of Egypt revived. Nationalism was so much to the fore in the European settlement that it was difficult to ignore its claims in dealing with Orientals who declined to accept the theory, of which the truth is so obvious to the Western mind, that the arguments for the autonomy of European communities do not apply to other peoples. In 1922 the British government, not without misgiving, made up its mind to end the protectorate and leave Egypt to govern herself—or to find out for herself how to do so. But though she was to be in theory a sovereign state, Great Britain had too many interests of her own, and too many responsibilities at stake, to concede absolutely without qualification this independence, which was granted with reservation of certain subjects. These included the protection of foreigners in Egypt, her defence, and the control of the Sudan, which had never been an effective Egyptian possession and had, as a matter of actual fact, been brought under control not by Egypt but by the British. That control the British were to retain, with due respect for Egyptian interests.

Egypt was presented with a constitutional monarchy under King Fuad, who had figured as sultan during the protectorate. But the agitation, by no means favoured by the king, for the total withdrawal of all British controlling influences, continued;

AN EPISODE IN THE IRISH SINN FEIN MOVEMENT IN 1921

The rebellion, boycott and bloodshed which came to characterise the Sinn Fein movement originated in the strongly nationalist desire of its supporters for Irish independence. The Irish republican army organized under Sinn Fein auspices was responsible for the guerilla warfare which inaugurated the series of mutual outrages and reprisals of 1920–21. In May, 1921, the Customs House at Dublin was fired by Sinn Feiners and street fighting occurred. A Sinn Feiner lies dead in the foreground.

Photo, Central News.

with an accompaniment of occasional assassinations and 'student' outbreaks somewhat embarrassing to a party whose business it should have been to demonstrate its own administrative efficiency. That the limit of concession had been reached was made clear when a sympathetic Labour government in England proved as inflexible as its predecessor.

A GANDHIST PROCESSION IN DELHI

Imprisonment of the Indian nationalist leader, M. K. Gandhi, in March, 1922, did not stop the non-co-operation movement. 'Gandhi Day' was devoted each month in Delhi to anti-British demonstrations; the spinning wheel paraded in this procession proclaims the boycott of foreign cloth.

Photo, Topical Press Agency

THE Asiatic problem—as affected by the war—was no less prominent in India. The loyalty then displayed had given India a right to claim her reward, though whether what her agitators were demanding would be a reward was another matter. A great administrative experiment was at once inaugurated, extending in British India the amount of responsible control to be entrusted to Indians and to Indian elective bodies—the system to which the name of dyarchy was given. It did not touch the autonomous Indian principalities—not under British administration at all—which form approximately one third of the Indian Empire, a very important fact not always realized either in England or elsewhere. To the princes the unity of India meant the union of diverse states, of which they were the chiefs, in an empire by no means homogeneous, focussed in the person of the king-emperor, for which unity the only imaginable guarantee is the British imperial sovereignty. In the nature of the case they do not sympathise with movements in British India which tend to weaken that authority, however anxious they may be, individually or as a group, for an increased influence in the imperial counsels.

It was to British India then that dyarchy was to apply; and dyarchy may be described as provincial autonomy carried as nearly as possible to the safety limit, based on bodies of elected representatives, on the model—mutatis mutandis—of English representative institutions; the supreme government reserving to itself the control of certain specific subjects, a general overriding authority to be brought into play only if necessary, and sundry guarantees. The whole thing was avowedly experimental; it did not and was not intended to convey any promise of full parliamentary institutions, still less of even an ultimate withdrawal of the overriding British authority.

Nevertheless, the British supremacy in India is faced—in certain sections of the community within British India—by that anti-European sentiment which we have noted as prevalent in Asia, and which in India, and elsewhere, is curiously misrepresented, by its most fervent and voiceful propagators, as Indian 'nationalism.' Dyarchy, therefore, is the reverse of satisfactory to the extremists of Indian nationalism, whose desire is nothing less than the extrusion of the European, which it brings no nearer; so that the disaffected faction have directed their energies mainly to the attempt to make the whole reform abortive by withholding co-operation. But in India, as elsewhere, it is to be noted that the anti-Europeans pin their faith, for the defeat of Europe, to methods and theories which are themselves the product not of Orientalism but of Western political and natural science.

China's new Republican Regime

CHINA presented at once the most emphatic and to Western eyes the most chaotic example of this revolt of the East against the West. Very shortly before the war the Manchu dynasty had been abolished, and under the guidance of the idealist Sun Yat-sen the empire had been transformed into what purported to be a democratic republic. Perhaps we may say that the ideal of which the new leaders were in pursuit was that which Japan had so amazingly achieved for herself in her revolution towards the close of the nineteenth century, when she remodelled herself on the basis of a scientific study of Western methods scientifically adapted to her own conditions by the patriotic co-operation of the political thinkers and the military caste, without foreign interference. But in China the political thinkers were befogged quite as much as they were aided by groping among Western ideas; they had no patriotic feudal aristocracy to strengthen their hands; and the Europeans were always in the way. Also from their point of view it might be said that the Japanese counted not as Orientals but as ultra-Europeans. And on the top of this there came the Bolshevik propaganda, fundamentally anti-European—while beneath lay the normally inert masses who were always ready to attribute whatsoever evils befell them to the doings of the foreign devils, more particularly British and Japanese.

CHIANG KAI-SHEK AT HANKOW
The Cantonese nationalist leader Chiang Kai-shek became president of China in October, 1928. He supported the Bolshevik agent at the public demonstration which fomented anti-foreign feeling at Hankow in 1927.
Photo, Topical Press Agency

South China was dominated by the new progressive nationalists, North China by the old reactionaries; agreeing in their hostility to the foreigners and in nothing else; while naturally it was the south, not the north, that was disposed to put its trust in Bolshevik agents.

Though the foreigners had acceded at Washington to many modifications in the treaty rights they had acquired previously, they still retained rights which were galling. Trouble then broke out in 1925 in the form of anti-foreign riots at Shanghai, spreading to Canton, Hankow and elsewhere. The government, whether willing or not, was no more able than it had been in the past to give the foreigners the security for which they had to make provision themselves; and their doing so, as always, inflamed the popular Chinese hostility, while Bolshevik agents poured oil on the flames.

The Chinese republic had never succeeded in establishing a strong central government, even under the leadership of the highly respected begetter of the New Nationalism, Sun Yat-sen, who died in 1925. The Nationalist organization at Canton, whose military head was Chiang Kai-shek, did not recognize the military dictator Chang Tso-lin at Peking; there had already been active hostilities between the two parties, sundry generals intervening, each of them playing for his own hand with a tendency to kaleidoscopic permutations. The Europeans, finding nothing that they could definitely treat as the sovereign authority to deal with, sought to observe a strict neutrality while making such arrangements for security as were possible with any de facto authority which seemed likely to carry out its engagements, and supplementing them by the presence of sufficient naval and military forces for taking action in the last resort.

The civil war seemed in 1926 to be going—with fluctuations—in favour of the Nationalists, whose avowed programme included the demand for the disappearance of all those foreign privileges which, it must be admitted, no European state would have tolerated in its own territories. To those claims Great Britain was much disposed to give full recognition, as soon as there should be a sovereign government in China. But there was no diminution of the anti-British agitation ; though the British went to unprecedented lengths of conciliation in the hope of convincing the Canton or Hankow government of their own good faith ; while the carefully limited strength of their military precautions was denounced as proof to the contrary, and the Kuomintang (the Nationalist government), with which the influence of Bolshevik agents was at its zenith, showed no power of controlling the excesses of its followers.

CHIANG KAI-SHEK'S ARMY MARCHES NORTH

Under the able leadership of General Chiang Kai-shek the Chinese Nationalist army advanced on Peking in 1928. His troops were ejected from Tsinan-fu, where they clashed with the Japanese, but Peking was nevertheless occupied at midsummer. This Southern detachment is seen entering Tsinan-fu.

Photo, Sport and General Press Agency

Its troops captured Nanking (March, 1927), but met with a sharp reverse at the hands of Chang Tso-lin when they advanced on Peking. The Kuomintang was apparently falling to pieces : Chiang Kai-shek tried to absorb its authority into his own hands, and lost his own authority instead in August ; only to be recalled in November as the one man who might succeed in restoring unity. This proved at any rate so far successful that by midsummer the Nationalists were in possession of Peking, the northern resistance was practically broken, and it was reasonably possible to claim that there was once more a supreme government—that of the Kuomintang—in China. Chiang Kai-shek became president in October ; the Kuomintang was shaking itself free from the sinister toils of its Bolshevik advisers ; an efficient government in China was of more value to the Europeans than concessions extorted from one that was thoroughly unstable ; and the year ended with at least a reasonable prospect—though as yet by no means a certainty—of materially improved relations in the near future.

We return then from the Far East to the West. It is to be noted that on the death of the first German president in 1925 the election to the Presidency fell upon the most respected if not the most brilliant of the German war chiefs, Marshal Hindenburg. Some perturbation was caused by the suspicion that this was a victory of the militarist faction, but this was finally removed by his acceptance of the Locarno Pact. When a soldier so distinguished and so loyal had faced the facts and set himself, without shedding a fraction of his patriotism, definitely on the side of European reconciliation, it was easier for Germany both to trust and to be trusted. The entry of Germany into the League followed Locarno in 1926 ; in 1927 began the withdrawal of the military occupation; and in spite of the fact that her claim to have completely fulfilled her obligations to disarmament was in some respects disallowed, the further supervision of her disarmament was transferred to a League commission of control, which replaced the inter-Allied military commission.

Disarmament had now become perhaps the leading international question. The cause was unfortunately little enough furthered by another naval conference, in which France and Italy did not join, while America, Japan and Great Britain failed to arrive at an agreed scheme, and more misunderstandings than understandings were developed. There was a still more curious sequel; for in 1928, with a presidential election pending, it appeared that the security of the United States demanded not reduction but an extended programme of naval construction.

At the same time, however, there came from the same quarter a remarkable proposal not for disarmament but for an international pact renouncing war as an instrument of national policy. This was in reply to a less sweeping proposal from France for a Franco-American pact of perpetual friendship. France suggested that the operation of the pact should be limited to 'wars of aggression.' Nevertheless, a draft declaration was drawn up and submitted for consideration to the greater powers as a basis for discussion. Great Britain led the way in expressing lively interest in the proposal and approving the principle, but urging the elucidation of details—primarily so that it might not be interpreted as an abrogation of the right of self-defence, or as overriding obligations incurred under the Covenant of the League of Nations. From the ensuing discussions it resulted that in July the British Empire generally and its member states severally declared their readiness to sign the pact. In August the Kellogg Pact was actually signed by the representatives of fifteen 'nations' including Germany; while no fewer than fifty declared their adherence to it, though its final ratification by the United States was deferred till January, 1929.

GERMANY SIGNS THE KELLOGG PEACE PACT
There were fifteen signatories, of whom seven represented the British Empire, to the pact renouncing war which was proposed by the U.S. secretary, F. B. Kellogg, in July, 1928, and accepted by the Senate of the United States in January, 1929. Herr Stresemann, the German delegate, was the first to sign.
Photo, Photopress

THE tenth post-war year, then, ended on a note of promise and hope. The world has not succeeded in setting up a machinery which will make war, whether in the military or in the industrial sense, impossible in the future. The millennium has not burst upon the world. The Kellogg Pact for the 'outlawry of war' carries with it no irresistible sanctions. It has not washed out rivalries, jealousies and suspicions; it is perhaps no more than an expression of a world public opinion. But it has manifested the fact that the public opinion is of overwhelming strength, of a strength which even the most recalcitrant and defiant of governments cannot afford to ignore; since it carries with it something approximating to a certainty that the wilful resort to arms for the settlement of differences until every conceivable avenue for peaceable adjustment has been thoroughly explored will result in crushing defeat. The machinery for exploration has itself been provided by the League, and by innumerable arbitration treaties. An extravagant optimism would be fatal, as fatal as extravagant pessimism. But to the eyes of faith at least the clouds are lifting.

CHAPTER 182

THE ECONOMIC CHAOS OF EUROPE

Social Effects of the wide Economic Dislocation wrought by the Great War

By JOHN MAYNARD KEYNES C.B.

Fellow of King's College, Cambridge; Treasury Representative at Paris Peace Conference, 1919; Author of The Economic Consequences of the Peace, etc.

THE direct destruction of material wealth by war is generally exaggerated. Fortunately, the accumulations of man's wealth are not of such a nd that they can be quickly squandered. oads, railways, buildings, machinery, ainage, hedges, fences, ditches and earings embody by far the greater part the accumulated wealth of past generaons. Thus war must be waged in the ain by contemporary effort, and can e up very little more than what is tually produced while it is going on. It nnot destroy knowledge or make an verdraft on the bounty of nature. It nnot even much diminish fixed capital, cept where a countryside is actually vaged; and such devastation, though might be locally overwhelming, affected, en in the Great War, but a small part of e invaded countries and a negligible oportion of the civilized areas of the hole world.

Thus it was possible to make good the aterial destruction, even of the Great 'ar, by a very few years of the comunity's regular savings. All the houses estroyed in France and Belgium were not ore than the normal building programme a year or two in western Europe alone, d the injury to their railways was far ss than a year's new construction in an och of railway development. Within o years the soil of the devastated areas d been already restored by the labour of e peasants. And there is an even more riking illustration. The destruction of ipping was on a far greater scale prortionately than any other type of deruction. The material damage to the ercantile marines of the world was not erely local, but world-wide. Yet by the d of 1921 it had been repaired completely, and the world's mercantile marine had been restored to its former strength.

The severity of the conditions which faced Europe in 1919 were not primarily due, therefore, to those ravages of war which were most evident to the eye. The problem was a problem of disorganization: a problem of the exhaustion of the stocks of food and raw material, and of the breakdown of credit. Owing to the exhaustion of food and raw materials, a vicious circle was set up by which the ordinary productive processes which would have replenished these supplies fell off to an extraordinary degree in their power of productivity. Moreover, normal organization of transport and exchange, by means of which products could be conveyed where they were most wanted, had broken down, while the collapse of credit made it impossible for Europe to purchase its usual supplies from overseas.

Europe in 1919

During the first half of 1919 the vicious circle of acute want leading to acute unemployment was becoming steadily aggravated. Violent and prolonged internal disorder in Russia and Hungary; the creation of new governments and their inexperience in the readjustment of economic relations, as in Poland and Czecho-Slovakia; the loss throughout the Continent of efficient labour through the casualties of war or the continuance of mobilisation; the falling off in efficiency through continued under-feeding; the exhaustion of the soil from lack of the usual applications of artificial manures throughout the course of the war; the unsettlement of the minds of the labouring classes on the fundamental economic issues of their lives; all these things conspired to reduce the actual production of goods to the lowest figure within modern experience, precisely when they were most needed.

There was moreover (to quote Hoover) 'a great relaxation of effort as the reflex of physical exhaustion of large sections of the population from privation and the mental and physical strain of the war.' In July, 1919, fifteen million families were receiving unemployment allowances in one or another European country. The coal production of Europe at that date was estimated to have fallen off by 30 per cent. Whereas before the war Germany produced 85 per cent. of the food consumed by her inhabitants, Professor Starling's report on food conditions i Germany stated that the productivity o the soil in the summer of 1919 wa diminished by 40 per cent., and the effec tive quality of its livestock by 55 per cent

The population of Europe is probabl 100,000,000 greater than can be sup ported without imports. The imports ca only be obtained either from loans or i return for exports. Here again, therefore there was a vicious circle. The credit of large part of Europe had broken dow and loans were unobtainable. Yet it wa necessary that substantial imports shoul take place before exports could be possible

Nor must we overlook in the spirit of oblivio which wipes out ba memories, the physica sufferings of the civilia populations of centra Europe during the late stages of the war, and th aggravation of other diff culties in the first year c the peace resulting fror the appalling condition of health over wide terr tories. In May, 1919, i was reported that ther were in Austria alone a

TEN YEARS AFTER : A TRIBUTE TO BELGIAN ECONOMIC STABILITY

Not only the recuperative power of the soil in war-devastated areas but the existence of a fundament wealth that war cannot destroy are shown in these two landscape views of Mont Kemmel, taken i 1918 (top) and 1928. Kemmel was an important Allied observation post in Belgium and the are was blasted to pieces during its capture and recapture in 1918. Yet ten years later there was nothin to show that this fertile agricultural district had ever known war, except the absence of tall tree

The Times and (top) Daily Telegraph ; photo, Antony d'Ypres

ast 250,000 to 400,000 people ho required treatment for berculosis. As a result of alnutrition a bloodless generation was growing up with ndeveloped muscles, undeveloped joints and undeveloped rain. It is well, too, to record ome of the more horrifying eports of that period. The llowing is by a writer in the ossische Zeitung, June 5, 1919, ho accompanied the Hoover Iission to the Erzgebirge :

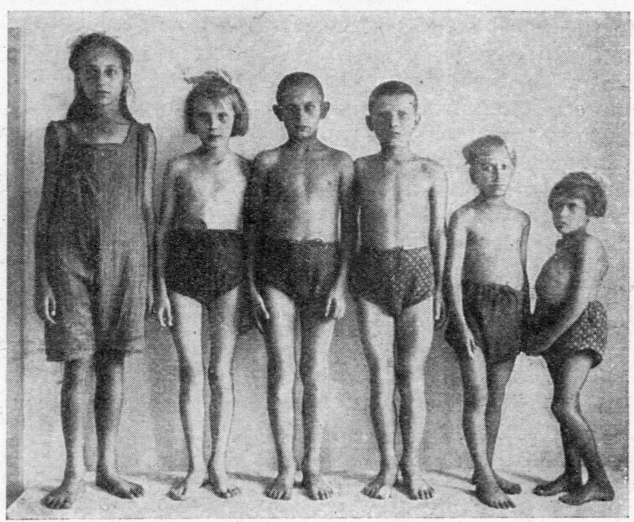

CHILD VICTIMS OF MALNUTRITION

Of these Viennese children, aged 12 years, the girl on the left is normal. The others show the arrested development common in the rickety generation produced by the war-time food scarcity in Austria. Softening of the bones resulting in spinal curvature caused the under-development of the girl on the right.

Courtesy of the 'Save the Children Fund'

I visited large country districts here 90 per cent. of all the chilren were rickety and where hildren of three years are only eginning to walk. . . Accomany me to a school in the Erzgebirge. You think it is a indergarten for the little ones. No, these are children of seven nd eight years. Tiny faces, vith large dull eyes, overshadowed y huge puffed, rickety foreeads, their small arms just skin nd bone, and above the crooked egs with their dislocated joints the swollen, pointed stomachs of the hunger oedema. . . You see this child here,' the physician in charge explained ; 'it consumed an incredible amount of bread, and yet did not get any stronger. I found out that it hid all the bread it received underneath its straw mattress. The fear of hunger was so deeply rooted in the child that it collected stores nstead of eating the food ; a misguided animal instinct made the dread of hunger worse than the actual pangs.'

Nevertheless there were at that time many persons in whose opinion justice required that such beings should pay 'reparations' to the Allies until they were forty or fifty years of age.

When we consider the extraordinary recovery of Europe within so short a period as five years after the war, we may sometimes feel that the anxieties of 1919 were exaggerated. But even in the light of this subsequent happier experience I do not think that they were. It was obvious, even then, that the fundamental sources of the economic life of Europe were in the main untouched. The question was whether Europe could secure breathing space, or whether famine and revolution would destroy organization over increasingly wide areas before the necessary relief could be brought into operation. For the Conference of Paris, which occupied the first six months of 1919 with so many futile discussions, was concerned with almost every problem except the most pressing one. During those months —a point which is apt to be overlooked by most contemporary historians—the blockade of Germany continued. It was still uncertain if Germany would sign the peace treaty. Meanwhile, therefore, nothing could be done which might do even a little towards restoring her strength and courage. The result was that all efforts at reconstruction, not only in Germany but in the whole of central Europe and the Balkans, were necessarily delayed.

Against this sombre background of starvation, unemployment and political disorder, the Treaty of Versailles was signed by the German delegates on June 28, 1919. Fourteen days later the blockade of Germany was at long last raised by the Allies, and Germany was free to knit together again, so far as she was able, the broken threads of her international trade.

Meanwhile, a very different picture was being exhibited by the rest of the world.

In the world at large there was a famine of ready goods, not so acute as that in central Europe, but in a degree quite unprecedented in the annals of nineteenth-century trade. The demobilised armies were returning to work. All governments were reluctant to put any check on the rise of wages. On the contrary, they were only too ready to give every opportunity for the 'good times' which had been promised after the war to be actually realized. Thus the general tendency throughout the world was for money incomes to be in the aggregate unprecedentedly large. Almost every country was off the gold standard, and money was the one commodity to the rapid manufacture of which there was no serious impediment. The restrictions on the rise of price of many of the necessaries of life, which had marked the later phases of the war, were continued. Limitations on the price of bread existed in many countries ; rent-restriction acts were almost universal. Thus the abundant money incomes finding their outlet in daily purchasing were reflected in a rapidly rising price level of all articles whose price was not limited by law.

The Boom and Slump of 1919-21

Furthermore, there is in the modern industrial world a very considerable time lag between the beginning of manufacture and the actual emergence of the finished product, ready for the consumer, out of the other end of the industrial machine. Labour is paid for as soon as it has done its job. But many months must elapse, sometimes more than a year, before there is any corresponding increase of goods available for purchase by the consumers.

A failure to restrict money incomes in 1919 was natural, and perhaps humanly inevitable. But the combination of abundant money incomes with a shortage of ready goods could only have one result. From April, 1919, to February, 1920, the prices of raw materials rose in England by an average amount of 4 per cent. a month, and this was representative of what was going on all over the world. As a consequence, every producer was selling his goods for more than he had anticipated, and at a substantial surplus above his costs of production. Windfalls on this scale to all holders of commodities ha never been experienced before ; while th difficulty of distinguishing between wha might be a more or less permanent increas in price due to the lasting consequences o war finance, and the temporary additiona excess superimposed on this by the trad boom, interfered with accurate forecas even by those who knew very well tha trade booms come and pass away again.

There were two other factors also which multiplied the stream of business transactions. Since many overseas markets had been starved by the war of their usual supplies and were replenishing stocks, it was difficult to know how much current demand represented such replenishment and how much of it was being absorbed by current consumption.

Secondly, the abnormal demand stimulated by all these influences was yet further exaggerated because merchants, experiencing an unusual difficulty in obtaining deliveries, began placing orders on an even larger scale than they really wanted, in order to make sure of obtaining at least a proportion.

Result of Over-ordering

For all these reasons merchants and middlemen in all quarters of the world over-ordered enormously, and this over-ordering engendered, in spite of the poverty of central Europe, a general atmosphere of spurious prosperity and excitement. Employment was excellent, and so long as prices continued to rise profits were enormous. But the apparent prosperity carried within it the seeds of an inevitable reaction. Business men were entering into commitments on a scale greatly in excess of the current rate of consumption and at a price level above that which the currency systems of the world could support, hugely inflated though they were, when once the actual goods were coming into existence and needing finance.

It was not long, therefore, before the money incomes of consumers were inadequate to purchase the gradually increasing volume of goods which were coming forward, at a price level equal to the price which manufacturers had been anticipating or to their actual costs of production. As early as the spring of

920 the tide had already begun to turn, nd by the summer of 1920 prices were alling again almost as rapidly as they ad previously risen. In Great Britain rices reached their maximum in June nd July of 1920, though wages continued o rise till October, 1920. By the beginning f 1922 sterling prices were little more han half what they had been, while ages had fallen to about three-quarters f their maximum figure.

Just as the boom had been generated y active buying overseas and not from he impoverished countries of Europe, o it was the sudden drying-up of the verseas markets—India, China, Australia, outh Africa and South America—which rought about the collapse. Thus at the eriod we are now considering—that is o say, from the spring of 1920 to the ummer of 1921—it was not, as at a slightly later date, the collapse of the European exchanges which caused the trouble, but the collapse of the exchanges between London and New York on the one hand and the leading countries of Asia and South America on the other. Indeed, if we compare February, 1920, when the boom was still in full strength though drawing to an end, with July, 1921, we find that the French and German exchanges on London had actually improved at the latter date; that the dollar value of sterling had also improved slightly; but that the values of the currencies of India, China, Argentina, Brazil and Chile, in terms of British sterling, had fallen by 51 per cent., 60 per cent., 35 per cent., 59 per cent. and 54 per cent. respectively. There were actually short periods when remittance to London, both from South Africa and from Australia, was scarcely obtainable.

DEMONSTRATION OF THE UNEMPLOYED IN LONDON, 1920

he coal strike, which began on October 16, 1920, increased unemployment in some districts, and n October 18 numbers of unemployed marched to Whitehall to demonstrate outside the premier's ouse in Downing Street, where the mayors of the metropolitan boroughs were interviewing him n the out-of-work question. A police charge was necessary to disperse the rioters. This view of the entrance to Downing Street shows a small cordon of police restraining a dense mob.

Photo, Topical Press Agency

Such movements as the above were, of course, catastrophic. The world is inter-related and all quarters play their part. The United States escaped no more than any other country. The manufacturers of Great Britain and of western Europe were now faced not only with the impoverishment of their European customers, but with the cessation of buying from the rest of the world, and found themselves with stocks of goods on hand and in course of manufacture which they could not hope to market at prices by any means equal to the cost of production.

A new misfortune was therefore at hand to aggravate the condition of Europe and the inevitable consequences of the war. The year 1921 was one of the worst ever experienced by traders. The collapse of the boom and of prices throughout the world, calamitous strikes in England, rebellion in Ireland, reparation crises in Europe, famine and the failure of Communism in Russia, bad harvests in Asia broke the general prosperity, and broke it suddenly, to a degree unprecedented. Two isolated facts may be quoted to illustrate the extraordinary degree of the depression: Lancashire's exports of cotton piece goods fell to the lowest figure since the American Civil War; England's output of pig iron was the lowest for seventy years. Perhaps one third of the manufacturing capacity of the world stood idle. Shipping rusted in the ports. But not for lack of goods. Warehouses were full; and there was offered the paradox of universal want apparently caused by the redundancy of goods. While many lacked food and clothing, the misfortunes of trade were attributed to the excessive stocks of commodities.

The History of Reparations

While these violent oscillations were disturbing the trade of the world, the economic consequences of the Treaty of Versailles were very slowly working themselves out in central Europe. The treaty had been ratified on January 10, 1920, and with the exception of Upper Silesia, the partition of which was not settled by the Council of the League of Nations until 1921, the territorial frontiers of Germany were finally fixed by the middle of 1920.

In January, 1920, Holland was called on to surrender the Kaiser; and, to the scarcely concealed relief of the governments concerned, she duly refused. On March 13, 1920, an outbreak by the reactionaries in Berlin (the Kapp 'putsch') resulted in their holding the capital fo

GERMAN REVOLUTIONARY TROOPS PICKETING BERLIN IN 1920

Some 8,000 troops supported the coup d'état which displaced the German government in March 1920, and substituted a new government in Berlin with Dr. Wolfgang Kapp as imperial chancellor and Prussian premier. For five days the revolutionaries were successful in holding the capital but the general strike there hampered their efforts and the outbreak was subdued. The photograph shows a section of the revolutionary forces in occupation of the town.

Photo, Alfieri

REPARATIONS IN KIND: SURRENDER OF THE GERMAN MERCHANT FLEET

ermany's surrender of some three and a half million tons of merchant shipping was a condition
the Armistice, and arrangements were made at the Brussels Armistice Commission in 1919 for
ıe reception of the German ships at various ports. This photograph shows one of the surrendered
essels, the Hamburg-Amerika liner Cleveland, in the Solent, with a large United States destroyer
alongside it. Up to 1921 this was the only sort of reparations of which Germany was capable.

Photo, Central News

ve days and in the flight of the Ebert overnment to Dresden. The defeat of ıis outbreak, largely by means of the eapon of the general strike (the first ıccess of which was, it is curious to note, defence of established order), was llowed by Communist disturbances in 'estphalia and the Ruhr. In dealing ith this second outbreak the German overnment dispatched more troops into e district than was permissible under e treaty, with the result that France ized the opportunity, without the conırrence of her allies, of occupying rankfort (April 6, 1920) and Darmstadt.

Meanwhile, little or nothing was done carry out the reparation clauses of the eaty, which had thrown on Germany ıprecedented and impossible financial ırdens. In the course of 1920 Germany ırried out certain specific deliveries of ods. A vast quantity of identifiable operty removed from France and Belum was duly restored to its owners. ıe mercantile marine was surrendered. ıt it is not surprising that in the midst the political and revolutionary disturbces mentioned above Germany paid no sh, and the real problem of reparation ıs still postponed.

With the conferences of the spring and mmer of 1920 there began the long series of attempts, even after nine years not complete, to modify the impossibilities of the treaty and to make it more workable. It is difficult to keep distinct the series of a dozen discussions between the premiers of the Allied powers which occupied the year from April, 1920, to April, 1921. Each conference was generally abortive, but the total effect was cumulative; and by gradual stages the project of revising the treaty gained ground in every quarter.

The most important results of these conferences were the decisions of Paris early in 1921, by which a revised scheme of reparation payments was proposed to Germany by the Allies very materially less than what was due under the treaty, though still two or three times as great as Germany was likely to be able to pay. At a conference held in London in March, 1921, the Germans offered a counter-proposal, the capital value of which was estimated at about £1,500,000,000, which represented, however, less than a quarter of the demands of the Allies. Two days later Lloyd George read to the German delegation a lecture on the guilt of their country, describing their proposals as 'an offence and an exasperation,' and announced that unless Germany accepted the Paris

BRITISH AND FRENCH TROOPS IN OCCUPATION OF DUESSELDORF

Düsseldorf, the Ruhr capital, was one of the three Rhine towns occupied on March 8, 1921, by the Allied forces in accordance with the ultimatum issued to Germany by the London Conference. General Morland, commander-in-chief of the British troops on the Rhine, is seen at the salute during a tour of inspection. With him is the French commander, General Gaucher.

Photo, Sport & General Press Agency

decisions certain towns on the right bank of the Rhine would be occupied—a threat which was undoubtedly illegal, even under the provisions of the Treaty of Versailles. After various attempts at an accommodation behind the scenes, negotiations broke down. Their rupture, as The Times of March 8, 1921, reported, was received in Paris ' with a sigh of relief,' and orders were telegraphed by Marshal Foch for his troops to march at 7 a.m. next day. This futile phase was not, however, continued for long. The Allies occupie themselves with the preparation of re vised proposals, which were offered t Germany in May, 1921, backed up by th second ultimatum of London, not les illegal than the first, by which the non acceptance of these terms was to b followed by the occupation of the Ruhr i addition to the three towns—an assaul which might be expected to have th result of breaking the economic life c the country. Within the space of a littl

ENTRY OF THE FRENCH TROOPS INTO ESSEN IN 1923

Great Britain played no part in the invasion of the Ruhr district, which was carried out by Frenc and Belgian troops in January, 1923, as a result of the Reparation Commission's declaration th Germany's coal delivery was in default. Essen, home of the famous Krupp Works and one Germany's chief munition centres, was occupied on January 11, and its inhabitants, resentful b curious, are here seen watching the arrival of a battery of artillery.

Photo, Sport & General Press Agency

ore than a year the invasion of Germany yond the Rhine had been threatened e times, and actually carried out twice. this occasion, however, Germany cepted the proposals, and for three years terms of the London settlement minally held the field.

Under this settlement Germany was to y in each year, until her aggregate bility was discharged, a sum of 00,000,000, and a further sum equal to per cent. of the value of her exports, king a total probably in excess of 00,000,000 a year. Progress was unubtedly being made. The gigantic ures of 1919 were rapidly falling, even the imaginations of the Allies. But fortunately it made but little practical ference to Germany so long as the nands, although moderating, were still excess of her capacity to pay.

The acceptance of the London schedule payments was important in that it ured for Germany a brief period of nparative calm. For a short time Germany made certain payments, with the assistance, as we shall shortly see, of foreign purchases of marks by speculors. But it was clear that the respite ild not be a long one. By the summer 1922 it was evident that Germany's erish efforts to collect sufficient reirces to make the required payments ild not possibly be successful. In gust the German government applied the Reparation Commission for a ratorium, and after some haggling rmany was released from further cash yments for the rest of that year. But re was no new settlement, and the yments required from her were merely stponed until the spring of 1923. fore this date was reached, however, rmany was declared by the Reparation mmission (January, 1923) to be in ault in her delivery of coal, whereupon nuary 11, 1923) French and Belgian ops invaded the Ruhr, without, on s occasion, the approval or assistance Great Britain.

arations default

Germany was now paying nothing vards her liabilities for reparation, t her country was invaded by foreign ops and her economic life hopelessly disorganized and impoverished. The very acuteness of the crisis, however, hastened on, perhaps, a radical solution. On November 30, 1923, the Reparation Commission appointed committees of experts to prepare yet one more scheme. Out of this inquiry there emerged the famous Dawes scheme, which was accepted both by the Reparation Commission and by the German government on August 9, 1924. The occupation of the Ruhr was terminated. The normal economic life of Germany was recommenced under conditions by no means intolerable.

Payments under the Dawes scheme

For the Dawes scheme not only made a further cut in the amount of Germany's liabilities, but provided the machinery for curtailing them yet further in the event of the remittance of the required amounts for the exchanges being proved impracticable on the basis of certain predetermined tests. Moreover, Germany's liabilities during 1924 were provided for almost entirely by means of a foreign loan, and not before 1928 were her liabilities to rise to so high a figure as £100,000,000 per annum. Thereafter the figure was to be £125,000,000, with the possibility of a supplementary payment calculated by reference to Germany's degree of prosperity. Up to the end of 1928 Germany was able with some ease to meet her gradually increasing liabilities under the Dawes scheme, though only by borrowing abroad in each year a larger sum than that which she was paying to the Allies; but most expert opinion agreed that the payment of the maximum Dawes annuity without assistance from foreign borrowing would probably be impossible, and that sooner or later yet one more revision would have to be made. Indeed, on December 22, 1928 (the day on which these words were written), the Allies appointed yet one more committee, on which for the first time Germany also was represented, with instructions 'to draw up proposals for a complete and final settlement of the reparation problem.'

It is interesting to tabulate the successive demands and forecasts what Germany would, or should, pay from the date of the British general election in 1918 to 1928.

The figures express annuities of millions of pounds sterling:

1.	Lord Cunliffe and the figure given out in the British general election of 1918	1,440
2.	M. Klotz's forecast in the French Chamber, September 5, 1919 ..	900
3.	The assessment of the Reparation Commission, April, 1921 ..	414
4.	The London settlement, May, 1921	230
5.	The Dawes scheme — normal annuity	125

In The Economic Consequences of the Peace, written in the summer of 1919, the sum of £100,000,000 was put forward by the present writer as the best estimate possible of the maximum annual payments that it would be reasonable to expect; and this is the figure that was received in the year 1927–28.

We have seen earlier how, during the period immediately succeeding the Treaty of Versailles, Germany made virtually no payments in cash in respect of reparations, but how during 1922, after her acceptance of the London schedule of payments and before the occupation of the Ruhr, she was driven to make great efforts to find cash resources. The expedients to which she had recourse in her attempts to meet the demands of the Allies gave rise to one of the most extraordinary episodes in the history of money.

The great Inflations

During the war the exigencies of war finance had brought about a gradual decline in the exchange value of the mark, which was only interrupted at the end of 1917 by Germany's temporary military successes. Up to June, 1918, however, the decline was both moderate and gradual. From June, 1918, onwards the downward movement was more rapid, and with the raising of the blockade in July, 1919, the acute demand for food and raw materials from abroad soon brought the mark to a value between a fifth and a tenth of its nominal parity. One would have expected a collapse of this kind to be so injurious to a country's credit as to be an unmitigated evil, both in its indirect and in its direct consequences. In the case of Germany, however, the initial decline of the mark was paradoxically a means, and probably the sole means available in the circumstances, by which she could secu very substantial financial aid from abroa

After the mark had fallen to such level that more than a hundred marl could be obtained for £1 sterling, mar persons all over the world formed tl opinion that there would be a reactic some day to the pre-war value, and th therefore a purchase of marks or mar bonds would be a profitable speculation. This investment, or speculation, proceeded on so vast a scale that it placed foreign currency at the disposal Germany which at the end of 19 was estimated at from £200,000,000 £250,000,000. When the experts of tl Dawes Committee came to examine tl matter in the spring of 1924 they put tl figure of Germany's receipts through tl sale to foreigners of mark bank balanc and mark banknotes up to December 3 1923, at somewhere about £400,000,00 It was these resources which in the fir instance enabled Germany, partially least, to replenish her food supplies ar to re-stock her industries with ra materials, and subsequently in 1922 meet the financial demands of the Allie at any rate for a few months. In add tion, it even enabled individual Germa to acquire foreign banknotes, or to remo a part of their wealth away from tl risks of German economic life for inves ment in other countries.

Speculatio in the Ma

As matters actually turned out, tl expectations on which these investmen by optimistic foreigners were made we totally disappointed. Apart from inte mittent and short-lived fluctuations, tl exchange value of the mark continued sink, until finally, at the end of 1923, tl whole crazy structure was swept aw and a new currency system introduce By this date the total face value of ma notes which had been issued was estimat at between 400 and 500 trillions (i. million million millions) of marks, and the date when the transition was ma the terms fixed for the liquidation of th incredible mass of paper values declar one billion (i.e. million million) pap marks to be equal in value to one shillin

It follows that the whole of the sum £400,000,000 thus invested by foreigne as totally lost by them, d constituted in fact a esent to the German ople. It provided. in-ed, an extraordinary isode of poetic justice sited on the outside orld as a retribution for e excessive and impos-ble demands which were ing made on the German ople. The alarums and cursions of invasion yond the Rhine, the nferences, the propa-nda and the ultimatums ueezed out of Germany far smaller sum than at with which foreign eculators were simul-neously presenting her.

Let us return, however, the earlier phases of is remarkable story. uring 1920 and the first art of 1921 speculative urchases by foreigners rovided Germany with early enough resources meet her adverse bal-nce of trade. At the beginning of 920, 185 marks were worth £1 sterling, nd twenty months later, in August, 921, £1 sterling was still worth no more han 300 marks. Up to the end of 1920, owever, and even during the first quarter f 1921, Germany had made no cash ayments for reparation, and had even eceived cash (under the Spa agreement) or a considerable part of her coal de-iveries. But after the middle of 1921 the arious influences, which up to that time ad partly balanced one another, began o work all in one direction; that is to ay, adversely to the value of the mark.

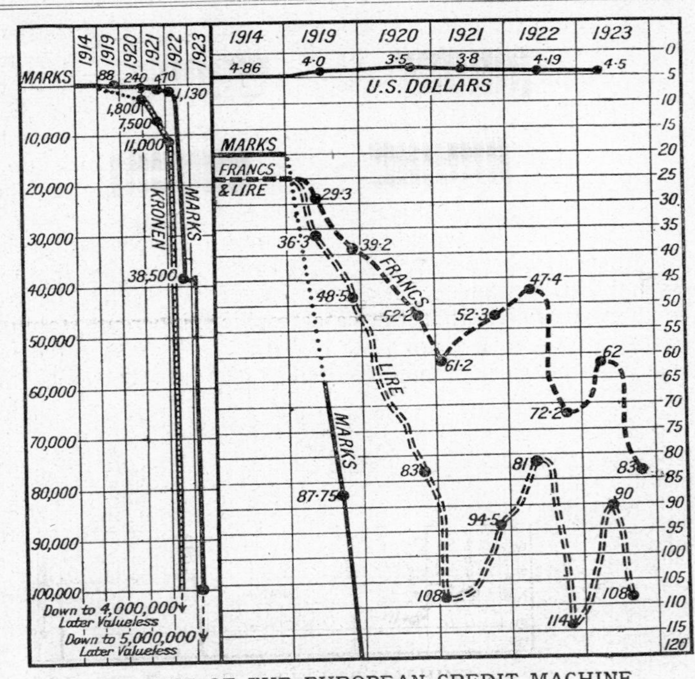

COLLAPSE OF THE EUROPEAN CREDIT MACHINE

The chart on the left shows the fall in the pound-sterling values of German mark and Austrian krone before their stabilisation in 1924; that on the right expands a small fraction of it in order to compare the movements of dollar, franc and lira. Before the blockade was lifted in 1919 the mark had no exchange value.

Currency inflation continued—for the mark banknotes came into existence by the government printing just so many of them as were necessary to meet its expenses—and during 1921 the note circulation of the Reichsbank was nearly trebled. Some foreign investors in marks began to take fright and, so far from in-creasing their holdings, sought to diminish them. And now at last, after the London ultimatum, the German government was called on to make important cash payments on reparation account. By November, 1921, £1 sterling was worth 1,000 marks, and apart from one brief recovery the headlong fall proceeded thereafter at an ever-increasing rate up to the final collapse of 1923.

The precariousness which this extra-ordinary episode introduced, not only into the business life of Germany but into the private affairs of every citizen, was something which had to be experienced to be believed. The value of all money savings was swept away; prices and wages could not move fast enough to keep different values in a suitable relationship to one another. If a man did not spend his wages on the day he received them, they might have halved in value, or worse, before the next morning. The whole of life became an involuntary but hectic gamble. Nevertheless, these experiences may have been necessary to convince the Allies of the futility of their previous methods for extracting reparations, and were perhaps an inevitable prelude to the Dawes scheme and the safeguards, which that scheme incorporated, for the future stabilisation of the German mark.

What happened in Germany was repeated, with minor variations, in Austria and also in Poland, though in Poland the excuse of overwhelming reparation demands was, of course, lacking. There was but little difference in the course of the disease, except that the catastrophic collapse came in Warsaw and in Vienna some months earlier than in Berlin, so that it was these countries that first experienced the full force of a type of speculation opposite to that which had furnished them with foreign resources in the early days of the inflations; namely, that of the bear speculators who, anticipating a further fall, endeavoured much more successfully than the optimistic party to make a profit by selling these currencies in the expectation of being able to buy them back a little later at a much lower value.

It is not part of my task to describe in this place the reconstruction of European economic life on the principles laid down by the Brussels Conference of 192 the Genoa Conference of 1922, and t Dawes Report of 1923. The invasion the Ruhr in January, 1923, was the la act of violence bred out of the war spiri Since that date every important decisi affecting the relations between the peopl of the formerly allied countries and t peoples of the former Central Powers h been, both in intention and in fa of a healing and pacific nature. T inherent stability of the European ec nomic systems has responded with rapidity and completeness which could n have been anticipate Great Britain has troubl of her own due to pri and precipitancy in h financial and curren policies, as in her reversi to the gold standard. B all Europe has stable cu rencies. The devastat areas are entirely restore The standard of life of Ge man working men somewhat higher than was before the war (s page 5071).

RUIN AND RESTORATION IN BELGIUM

Belgium has made a wonderful recovery from her severe w wounds. Nieuport, the 'farthest west' reached by the ener along the coast, was a sorely scarred battle ground. By 19 (top) its market square was shattered almost beyond recognitic The 1928 view shows that it has been reborn.

Courtesy of the 'Daily Telegraph'; photos, Antony d'Ypres

CHAPTER 183

THE NEW EUROPE AND THE LEAGUE

Constitution and Functioning of the new Organization for the Maintenance of Peace

By WICKHAM STEED

Lecturer on Central European History, King's College, London University; Author of The Hapsburg Monarchy, etc.

THE chief distinction between the new Europe and the old lies in the existence of the League of Nations. Without the League, Europe would ave been changed, not renewed. The umber of European states would have een increased, but their relationship to ch other would have remained on the d footing. Europe is new because the ovenant of the League is an insepar- ole part of all the treaties that make up e peace settlement. The terms of the ovenant form the first twenty-six articles all of them, and are as binding upon eir signatories as any of the clauses that late to frontiers or to reparations.

In the conflagration of the Great War e old Europe was consumed. The rrible character of the war, and a belief at it might have been avoided had there isted an international authority strong ough to insist upon discussion and nference between the contending powers, mbined to create in Western countries a nviction that some international organi- tion must be set up to prevent the recur- nce of any similar catastrophe. This nviction, and the movement in favour a League of Nations which it inspired, as strongest in Great Britain and in the nited States, though it was firmly held so in France. In London and New York sociations were formed to promote hemes for a League. The Great War came be regarded as a war to end war, having r its principal object the formation of organization among the principal oples of the world with power to tracise armed force as a means of settling ternational disputes.

Before this idea had gained ground western Europe a plan for positive co-operation between nations on behalf of peace had been drawn up, as early as the autumn of 1914, by an American politician, Colonel House, the friend and confidential adviser of the president of the United States, Woodrow Wilson. Looking upon the outbreak of the Great War as the bankruptcy of European diplomacy, and attributing that bankruptcy chiefly to the lack of any organized system for consultation and agreement, Colonel House suggested that President Wilson should promote such a system between the states of North and South America. He had in mind a League of American states that should safeguard them against aggression and provide a mechanism for the peaceful settlement of disputes.

In its original form his plan fell through, but the idea which inspired it presently found expression in the Covenant of the League of Nations. President Wilson himself certainly entertained the notion of a general association of nations before the end of 1914, but it only took practical shape after he had received reports of conversations between Colonel House and the British foreign secretary, Sir Edward Grey, in London at the beginning of February, 1915. In these conversations Sir Edward Grey insisted that the United States (which was then neutral) should come into some general guarantee of world-wide peace at the end of the war. A similar idea was advocated by Lord Robert Cecil in Great Britain and by Léon Bourgeois in France; and when, on May 27, 1916, some eleven months before the United States entered the war, President Wilson announced in a speech to the American 'League to

Early advocates of the League

Enforce Peace' his acceptance of the principle of a League of Nations, his declarations were based upon material drawn from the conversations and subsequent correspondence between House and Grey.

President Wilson is usually regarded as the real founder of the League of Nations. But for his insistence it is indeed probable that it would never have been effectively established; and it is certain that the embodiment of the League Covenant in the peace treaties was due to his determination that the League should be the basis of the peace. Yet it is true that few, if any, of the ideas in the Covenant of the League were conceived by President Wilson himself. His relation to the Covenant was mainly that of editor or compiler. He had two central convictions—that the League

LORD ROBERT CECIL

Born in 1864, Lord Robert Cecil entered Parliament as Conservative member for East Marylebone in 1906. One of the chief exponents of the League of Nations, he represented Great Britain in its interests at the Paris Peace Conference

Photo, Philip Brain

PRESIDENT WILSON'S ADVISER

Colonel Edward Mandell House, born at Houston, Texas, in 1858, was sent by President Wilson to review the European situation in 1914. In the same year House drew up his plan of international co-operation for peace.

Photo, Keystone View Co.

of Nations was necessary and that it might be brought into existence immediately after the war. But without the thoughtful work of the other advocates of the League his leadership might have little availed.

To President Wilson belongs, in any case, the credit of having been the first responsible statesman to declare that the establishment of a league or association of nations must be one of the main conditions of peace. On January 8, 19[18] (the United States had declared war on Germany in April, 1917), he delivered a presidential address to a joint session of the American Congress, laying down fourteen points, or principles, on which the peace settlement should be based. The last of these 'Fourteen Points' ran: 'A general association of nations must be formed under specific conventions for the purpose of affording mutual guarantees

LEON BOURGEOIS

October, 1919, the French statesman Léon ɛtor Auguste Bourgeois was appointed French ɹresentative of the League of Nations. He s deeply in sympathy with the scheme and ıself the author of a plan for its propagation.

Photo, Henri Manuel

litical independence and territorial in-ɛrity to great and small states alike.' ıereas some of his advisers, and some ders of European opinion, believed at ɑt time that a League of Nations should lude only the 'Allied and Associated wers' which were waging war against rmany and Austria-Hungary and that, any event, the great powers should ssess higher standing and greater in-ence in it than the smaller powers, esident Wilson insisted that the League ıst be 'general,' affording the same ɔtection to small peoples as to big.

Partly as a result of his address to ngress, a British foreign office committee ich had been formed at the instance of rd Robert Cecil in 1916, and had worked der the chairmanship of Sir Walter terwards Lord) Phillimore, made to the itish cabinet on March 28, 1918, a ɔort of which a copy was sent confiden-lly to President Wilson. It was used him in preparing his own draft of a ıgue Covenant. In July, 1918, Colonel use submitted to President Wilson ɔther draft which was likewise based in t on the report of the Phillimore Committee. With the help of it President Wilson wrote out a second draft of his own, which he revised severely after reading a pamphlet, dated December 16, 1918, in which General Smuts had outlined proposals for a League. In January, 1919, when the Peace Conference was about to assemble in Paris, President Wilson began to work upon a third draft so that it might serve as a basis for discussion in the League of Nations Commission at the Peace Conference. But, as he was unable to complete this draft to his own satisfaction, he agreed that the Commission should use instead a joint scheme drawn up by the British and American legal experts, Cecil Hurst and David Hunter Miller, who had at their disposal all the earlier documents as well as a draft convention written by Lord Robert Cecil.

At the first plenary session of the Peace Conference in Paris on January 18, 1919, it was unanimously resolved that the establishment of a League of Nations should be the first point on the agenda of the next session. A League of Nations Commission of the peace delegates was

GENERAL SMUTS

Jan Christian Smuts, born at Bovenplaats, Cape Colony, in 1870, succeeded Botha as premier of South Africa in 1919. His proposals for a League of Nations influenced President Wilson in a draft he was preparing.

Photo, Russell

therefore appointed to draw up the Covenant. All the principal Allied and Associated Powers were represented on the commission, Lord Robert Cecil and General Smuts being the delegates of Great Britain, President Wilson and Colonel House of the U.S.A. and Léon Bourgeois, with a legal expert, of France.

In order that its proceedings might not delay the drafting of the Peace Treaty itself, the Commission sat at night, from February 3 until March 14, in the room of Colonel House at the Hôtel Crillon. It took the Hurst-Miller project and an official French plan as the groundwork of its deliberations. The most serious hitch came on February 11, when President Wilson flatly declined to accept the French demand for the creation of an armed international force that should operate under the executive control of the League. He claimed that the constitution of the United States did not permit of any such limitation of its sovereignty; and Lord Robert Cecil took a similar view in regar to the British Empire. Not without dif culty could the French be persuaded t desist from their demand which, they hel could alone prevent the Covenant fro being a philosophical treatise devoid practical authority. They consente however, to waive it in time for the dra Covenant to be completed on February 1 and to be read to the second plenar session of the Peace Conference on Fel ruary 14. The conference adopted it, an President Wilson left Paris that evenir on a brief visit to the United States.

At that moment it was still undecide whether the Covenant should stand b itself as a separate international conve tion or whether it should be embodied the Peace Treaty. President Wilson's ow views upon this matter had varied fro time to time. He had at first objected the formal constitution of the League, ar had insisted that the League must devel gradually. Yet, on reaching Paris December, 1918, he had wit drawn the American repr sentatives from the vario inter-Allied organizations th might have served as a wor ing nucleus from which a f League could grow. Anoth point of difficulty was that, the Covenant were embodi in the Peace Treaty, neutr states might be unable to si it, though they could sign separate convention. To t actual wording of the dra Covenant President Wilson own contributions were h demand that the new Eur pean states formed as a resu of the war should give equ treatment to all the racial ar religious minorities within th boundaries; and that ea member of the League shou have the 'friendly right' draw the League's attention any circumstances likely disturb international pea or the good understandi between nations upon whi peace depends. He accept the draft Covenant as a wh

PRESIDENT WILSON SAILS FOR AMERICA

The League of Nations Commission appointed at the first plenary session of the Paris Conference in 1919 met a serious obstacle in President Wilson's refusal to agree to an armed international force. The Covenant, without this clause, being adopted, President Wilson departed to visit the U.S.A.

Photo, Underwood & Underwood

and seems not to have imagined, when he sailed for America on February 15, that it would require serious amendment.

But on reaching the United States he found that opposition to him and to the Covenant had become strong in the American Senate, of which the majority was controlled by the Republican party, whereas he and his administration were Democrats. The election of this hostile majority had been due in part to resentment of an appeal which President Wilson had made to the American electorate in October, 1918, to support candidates favourable to the Democratic administration in the elections then impending. This departure from the party truce which had existed since the United States entered the war gave deep offence, and the election resulted in a Republican victory. Further resentment was caused when President Wilson excluded leading Republicans from the American delegation to the Paris Peace Conference.

Consequently the president found the Republican senators inclined to reject the draft Covenant which the Peace Conference had adopted. Instead of appeasing them he defied them and, before returning to Paris in March, 1919, declared in a speech at New York on March 4 that when the Peace Treaty had been completed the Covenant would be so interwoven with it that the one could not be separated from the other 'without destroying the whole vital structure.' He evidently thought it impossible that the American Senate would go so far as to reject the Peace Treaty itself.

Friction with the Republican Senators

This quarrel between the president and the Republican senators was destined profoundly to affect the Covenant, the Peace Treaty and the character of the new Europe which the Paris Conference was creating. On reaching Paris President Wilson insisted not only that the League Covenant should be embodied in the Peace Treaty and be binding upon all its signatories, but that the Covenant itself should be so amended as to make it less distasteful to American opinion. Thus the strong position which he had previously held as arbiter and defender of exalted principles was weakened, and his attitude became that of a petitioner and a bargainer. By asking the other delegations to the Paris Peace Conference to make concessions to his own domestic political requirements, he enabled them to wring concessions from him in their turn; and the Peace Treaty, instead of being a work of justice, became, in many respects, a compromise between conflicting interests and appetites. The Peace Conference complied with his wishes that the Covenant should be incorporated in the treaty; that it should be amended so as to exclude the domestic questions of signatory states from the control of the League; that members should have the right to withdraw from the League on two years' notice; and that the American Monroe Doctrine should be explicitly recognized in the text of the Covenant. But this compliance was purchased at heavy cost to the framework of peace and to the League of Nations itself.

Compromises in the Peace Treaty

President Wilson sought consolation in the thought that, however defective the Peace Treaty might be, the League of Nations would provide means of amending it gradually without recourse to war, and that the influence of the United States in the League could always be brought to bear on behalf of justice. But when the Peace Treaty was completed and signed, he found that the American Senate preferred to reject it altogether rather than accept the Covenant, despite the alterations which had been made in it to placate American feeling. A compromise might have been feasible if President Wilson had been willing to assent to certain reservations which the Republican senators proposed to attach to the Covenant; yet he, who had made so many compromises in Paris, stubbornly refused to enter into an additional minor compromise with his political opponents at home. Therefore the American Senate rejected the Peace Treaty. And when the League of Nations was established, the United States held aloof from it.

Thus an institution that could not have been created without American initiative and support was forsaken by the United

States; and, as a crowning irony and departure from the idealism which President Wilson had entertained and professed, his country proceeded to make with Germany a separate peace treaty from which the League of Nations was eliminated and in which all the concessions which President Wilson had made, against his better judgement, to the governments of the European Allies were retained.

This paradoxical outcome of the peace negotiations has tended to obscure the part played by the United States both in creating the new Europe and in establishing the League of Nations.

American contribution to the Victory

Though the sacrifices of the European Allies were incomparably greater than those of the American people, though they bore the full burden of the war for two and a half years before America entered it, it is obvious that without American assistance the war might not have been won. In any event the victory of the Allies would have been delayed and their losses heavier. If the military contribution of the United States to the Allied triumph was comparatively small, its financial and moral contributions were decisive. President Wilson's answers to the German and Austrian appeals for an armistice and peace in the autumn of 1918 went far to shake the spirit of the German and Austro-Hungarian armies. His firm refusal to treat with Austria-Hungary at the end of October, 1918, shattered the Hapsburg monarchy, and, in shattering it, precipitated the collapse of Germany also. Among the new or re-born states of central and south-eastern Europe, three at least owed to him the full recognition of their right to national unity and independence. No European ally championed so resolutely as he the national causes of Czecho-Slovakia, Jugo-Slavia and Poland.

While it is true that the liberation and independence of these nations had been, in greater or lesser degree, contemplated in the war aims of the European Allies before America became a belligerent, those aims were too vague to ensure a thorough reorganization of Europe. With some reason the Allies thought it more urgent to win the war than to make up their minds beforehand what they would do when the war had been won. With less reason they failed to perceive that a clear statement of their war aims would help them to win the war, because it would encourage all the subject peoples of Germany and Austria-Hungary to strive for liberation. The Allies doubted, indeed, whether their main object should be solely the military defeat of the enemy or the political transformation of Europe so as to ensure peace in future. They only began to define their war aims when President Wilson asked them in December, 1916, to state clearly what they were fighting for.

At that time President Wilson's own ideas were hazy. Neither he nor the Allied governments then understood that the liberation of the races subject to the Hapsburg crown was an indispensable condition of the military and political defeat of Germany.

Liberation of the Little Nations

They hoped vaguely for a restoration of Polish unity, but they felt it impossible to demand Polish independence, inasmuch as Russia, an Allied power, ruled over the greater part of Poland. They imagined and continued to imagine until within a few months of the end of the war, that the dismemberment of Austria-Hungary could be avoided and that it would be enough if it were to detach itself from Germany.

An essential feature of the old Europe had been the subjection of peoples, once free, to the domination of Germany, Russia and Austria-Hungary. Each of these powers possessed a part of Poland and each was interested in preventing the re-birth of a united and independent Polish state. Germany held Alsace and Lorraine, much of which was French at heart, and also some Danish districts whose inhabitants aspired to reunion with Denmark. Austria-Hungary held in bondage the Czechs of Bohemia and the Slovaks of Hungary, the Czechs having enjoyed independent national existence for seven centuries before they were crushed by the Hapsburgs in 1620 and being eager to regain their lost freedom. Austria and Hungary between them kept some 8,000,000 South Slavs in subjection and were determined to prevent their ıion with Serbia. Hungary likewise ›pressed more than 2,500,000 'Rouanes' in Transylvania and was deterined that they should not join their ısmen in the kingdom of Rumania. In liance with Germany, the Hapsburg onarchy formed the main link in the ıain of pan-German ambitions, of which ıe aim was to establish German ascendıcy from Hamburg to the Persian Gulf. nless this link could be snapped Gerany would win the war; and the only ay to snap it was to let loose the explosive rces of the subject peoples.

Tardily, yet earlier than most of the uropean Allies, President Wilson underood this fact. He understood also that ıe association of all these liberated eoples with each other, and with the ɛst of the world, in a general League of ations under a comprehensive Covenant ıight be a means of neutralising to some xtent the drawbacks of 'Balkanising' entral Europe by the creation of a number f small new states. His insistence that the rst act of the Peace Conference should be ɔ establish such a League entitles him to ank foremost among the founders of the ew Europe and of the League itself.

The actual terms of the League Covenınt may be briefly summarised. They re laid down in a preamble and twentysix articles. The preamble states that the signatories of the Covenant agree to promote international co-operation, and to achieve international peace and security, by accepting the obligation not to resort to war; by prescribing just, open and honourable relations between nations; by establishing international law as the rule of conduct among governments; and by maintaining justice and a scrupulous respect for treaty obligations in the dealings of organized peoples with one another.

The first article defines the conditions of membership of the League and of withdrawal from it. The second, third and fourth articles state that the League shall act through an assembly and a council with a permanent secretariat, the Assembly to consist of representatives of the members of the League, and the Council of permanent representatives of the principal Allied and Associated Powers, together with representatives of four other members of the League to be elected by the Assembly. (The number of these elected representatives was later increased to ten.) The fifth article states that the decisions of the Council and the Assembly shall be unanimous except in regard to procedure or to the appointment of committees to investigate particular matters,

TEMPORARY HEADQUARTERS OF THE LEAGUE OF NATIONS AT GENEVA

The covenant of the League of Nations, which was signed by the Allied and German delegates on June 28, 1919, established Geneva as the League's seat of government. Since then many plans have been considered for the construction of a building to serve as the League's permanent headquarters. Meanwhile, it has pursued its operations in this building, formerly the Hôtel National. A tablet in memory of President Wilson can be seen in the foreground.

Photo, Boesch, Geneva

when decisions may be taken by a majority. The sixth and seventh articles authorise the creation of a secretary-general with a permanent staff at the seat of the League, which is fixed at Geneva.

The eighth and ninth articles recognize that the maintenance of peace requires the reduction of national armaments to the lowest point consistent with national safety and with the enforcement of international obligations by common action. The League Council is therefore instructed to formulate plans for the reduction of armaments, taking account of the geographical situation and the circumstances of each state, such plans to be subject to revision every ten years, and a permanent commission to be constituted to advise the Council on military, naval and similar questions. By the tenth article the members of the League undertake to respect and to preserve against external aggression the territorial integrity and the existing political independence of all members of the League, the Council being instructed to advise upon the means of fulfilling this obligation in case of need. The eleventh article declares that any war, or threat of war, whether immediately affecting any of the members of the League or not, is a matter of concern to the whole League, and empowers the secretary-general to summon a meeting of the Council in case of any emergency that is brought to his notice by any member of the League. It also bestows upon each member the friendly right of bringing to the attention of the Assembly or the Council any circumstance whatever that may threaten international peace or the good understanding of nations on which peace depends.

Reduction of armaments

Under the twelfth and thirteenth articles the members of the League agree to submit either to arbitration or to inquiry by the Council any dispute between them that may be likely to lead to a rupture, and they agree further that they will in no case resort to war until three months after an award by the arbiters or a report by the Council, the award having to be made within a reasonable time, and the report not later than six months after the submission of the dispute to the Council. The fourteenth article instruct the council to take steps to set up a per manent court of international justic which shall be competent to hear an decide any dispute of an internationa character that may be submitted to i and also to give an advisory opinio upon any question referred to it by th Council or the Assembly. In default c arbitration, members of the League agre by the fifteenth article to submit an dispute between them to the Counci which shall endeavour to settle it an shall, in any case, make and publish report containing a statement of the fact and recommendations that may be deeme just and proper. The members of th League agree that they will not make wa upon any party which complies with th Council's report ; though they reserve t themselves the right to take whateve action they shall consider necessary i case the Council fails to make a unanimou report, the assent of parties to the disput not being necessary to unanimity.

By the sixteenth and seventeenth articl the members of the League undertake im mediately to sever all trade and financi relations with any member of the Leagu that resorts to war in defiance of the Covenant, and to prohibit all personal or financial intercourse between their nationals an the nationals of the Covenant-breakin state and those of any other stat whether it be a member of the Leagu or not. The members of the Leagu will give each other mutual support i this financial and economic boycott an will take the necessary steps to affor passage through their territory to th forces of any members of the Leagu which, upon the recommendation of th Council, shall co-operate in protecting th Covenant of the League. The eighteent article places upon all members the obl gation to register with the secretar of the League every treaty or inte national engagement into which the may enter, and declares that no suc treaty or engagement shall be bindir until it is so registered. The nineteent twentieth and twenty-first articles er power the League Assembly to advi

Financial and economic sanctio

members of the League to reconsider treaties which have become inapplicable and to give consideration to international conditions likely to endanger the peace of the world. The members of the League agree to abrogate all obligations and understandings inconsistent with the terms of the Covenant, except treaties of arbitration or regional understandings like the Monroe Doctrine, of which the object is to secure the maintenance of world peace.

The twenty-second article places colonies and territories inhabited by backward peoples under the trusteeship of the League, and grants mandates for their protection to those advanced nations which can best undertake the responsibility of protecting such colonies and territories, the mandatory powers being required to render an annual account of their stewardship to the Council. The twenty-third to twenty-fifth articles engage the members of the League to secure and maintain fair and humane conditions of labour for men, women and children, and to treat justly the native inhabitants of territories under their control; empower the League to keep an eye on the traffic in women and children as well as upon the trade in opium and other dangerous drugs, and in arms and munitions; authorise it to foster and maintain freedom of communications and of transit, and to organize the prevention and control of disease in cases of international concern, co-operating to this end with Red Cross organizations. Finally, the twenty-sixth article lays down the procedure to be followed for amending the League Covenant.

Responsibility of mandatory powers

The Covenant was signed by thirty-one Allied powers (of whom three failed to ratify the Peace Treaty and therefore lost their membership of the League) and by thirteen neutrals. Fourteen states were subsequently admitted to membership, including the former enemy states, Austria, Bulgaria, Hungary and Germany. The principal absentees are the United States, Russia and Turkey; and Brazil has given notice of withdrawal.

In accordance with the Covenant and before the rejection of the Peace Treaty by the American Senate, the president of the United States summoned a first meeting of the League Council in Paris on January 16, 1920, and the first Assembly at Geneva in the following November. In view of the disturbed state of Europe these meetings attracted little attention, and the early stages of the League's work passed almost unnoticed. Yet, besides forming its own Permanent Secretariat and organizing the Assembly and the Council, the League convened a financial conference at Brussels—the first really important international gathering after the war—and set about creating a permanent court of international justice. On the basis of principles unanimously laid down by the Brussels financial conference, the League was invited to undertake the financial reconstruction of Austria in 1922 and of Hungary in 1923. The success of its efforts in both these countries encouraged American and European financial experts to seek a solution of the German reparations

GERMANY ENTERS THE LEAGUE

On September 10, 1926, Germany was admitted to membership of the League of Nations. The German foreign minister, Herr Stresemann, here seen speaking at Geneva, was one of the authors of the Locarno Pact.

problem, with the result that the 'Dawes scheme' was worked out and adopted. In addition, the League took in hand matters appertaining to international law and arbitration; and, as soon as it had established the Permanent Court of International Justice at the Hague, it appointed a committee of lawyers to deal with the codification of international law.

In organizing the Permanent Court of International Justice the League was able to overcome a difficulty which had proved insuperable at the first and second peace conferences that were held at the Hague in 1899 and 1907. Then it had been found impossible to agree upon a method of nominating and electing the judges of a permanent court. The existence of the League Council and Assembly provided a means of ensuring that neither the great powers nor the small should be unduly favoured in the selection of candidates for judgeships, and that the eleven judges and four deputy-judges who compose the court should be chosen with every guarantee of impartiality. It was arranged that these candidates—representing fifteen different nations, including the United States—should be balloted for separately in the Council and in the Assembly of the League, and that candidates obtaining an absolute majority of votes in each body should be elected. Thus the great powers, through their position as permanent members of the Council, were able to check unjustified claims on the part of smaller powers; while the smaller powers, by their numerical preponderance in the Assembly, could similarly neutralise any undue influence over the League as a whole on the part of the great powers.

In the first election, which was held in 1921, this system worked well. The judges were elected for nine years, to hold office until 1930. They form a court of law, not a tribunal of arbitration, and are directed to base their decisions on legal principles in the light of treaties and international practices and precedents.

AT THE FIRST SESSION OF THE LEAGUE OF NATIONS AT GENEVA

On November 15, 1920, the first Assembly of the League of Nations met in the Salle de la Réformation at Geneva, proving the truth of the remark made by Paderewski, who was present, that 'the League lives.' Hymans (Belgium), who presided, was elected definite president. A prominent figure was Lord Robert Cecil, who supported the application for membership of Austria, Bulgaria, Albania and Azerbaijan, but declared that he did not wish Germany to be admitted.

Photo, F. H. Jullien, Geneva

All states may bring cases before the court, but no state can be compelled to submit to its jurisdiction unless provision to that effect has been definitely made by treaty, or unless the case concerns two states which have signed what is known as the 'optional clause' of the statutes of the court that binds them to accept its jurisdiction.

SIR ERIC DRUMMOND

The first secretary-general to the League of Nations was Sir James Eric Drummond, appointed in 1919. He had previously served in the Foreign Office and as secretary to H. H. Asquith.

Photo, Russell

Since its foundation the court has been busily engaged and has amply proved its value. The need for some international institution of the kind had long been clear and there was a large measure of agreement upon the functions it would discharge. The chief difficulty lay in establishing it; and without the League it might not have been established. But the worth of the Assembly, the Council and the Permanent Secretariat of the League was more problematic. The Assembly was conceived as the League parliament, and the Council as a sort of cabinet which would sit in public and act as the executive authority. But the Permanent Secretariat was originally looked upon merely as a clerical staff whose members would prepare the work for the Council and the Assembly but would have little authority or influence of their own.

President Wilson never imagined that the Permanent Secretariat would possess any real importance. His only idea was that Venizelos, the prime minister of Greece, should be the first secretary-general. This was found to be impracticable and the appointment was given to Sir Eric Drummond, who had been private secretary to Sir Edward Grey and to Balfour at the British foreign office. But it soon came to be recognized that the Secretariat is as weighty a part of the League as the Council or the Assembly, and that it exercises constant influence. Save when convoked in special session, the Assembly meets only once a year. In ordinary circumstances the Council meets four times—in September, December, March and June—though it may be convened at any moment in case of emergency. The Secretariat, on the other hand, works day in, day out, throughout the year, and really discharges the functions of an international foreign office, with the secretary-general in the position of a permanent under-secretary of state.

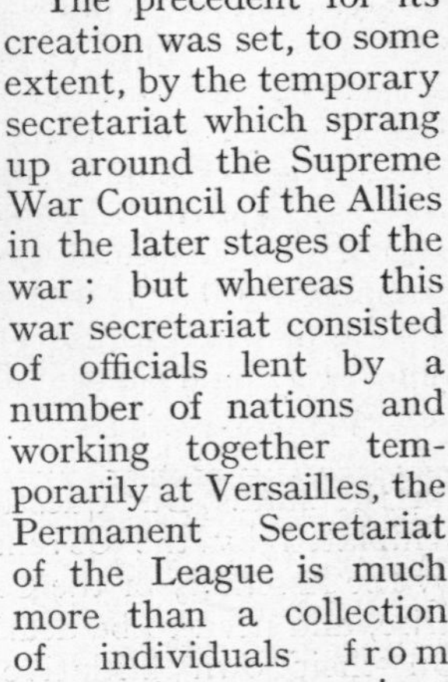

The precedent for its creation was set, to some extent, by the temporary secretariat which sprang up around the Supreme War Council of the Allies in the later stages of the war; but whereas this war secretariat consisted of officials lent by a number of nations and working together temporarily at Versailles, the Permanent Secretariat of the League is much more than a collection of individuals from various countries. It forms a unique international body. From the secretary-general downwards, its members serve the League, not any individual member of the League. They are drawn from nearly every nation belonging to the League—and from the United States, which holds aloof from it. They are appointed and paid by the League and their whole duty is to the League.

The Secretariat is divided into various sections, each of which has its own special sphere of work. One section is political; another deals with technical organizations; a third watches over racial minorities; a fourth supervises colonial mandates; a fifth looks after international health, while others deal with social questions, publicity, legal points and international armaments. The head of a section may be a Frenchman and the principal members of his staff British, Italian or Swiss. Or he may be Japanese with Polish, Dutch, Norwegian, Spanish,

Czecho-Slovak or Greek assistants. The results are a constant interchange of different points of view and the development of a really international outlook inspired by loyalty to the ideal of the League.

The relationship of the Secretariat to the League may be compared broadly to that of the government departments in Whitehall to the British parliament and cabinet—with the important difference that, while the British parliament and cabinet meet frequently, the League Parliament or Assembly, and the League cabinet, or Council, meet only at stated intervals. This circumstance places upon the Secretariat far greater responsibility than usually devolves on British government departments. The routine duties of the Secretariat naturally resemble those of any other official organization. Every decision of the League, and every duty laid upon it by the Covenant, entails correspondence and administrative work for the staff. But questions neither contemplated by the Covenant nor decided by the Assembly or the Council constantly arise, and need to be dealt with promptly. On their own initiative the secretary-general and the heads of sections deal with them, if only for the purpose of obtaining information and of preparing reports for the guidance of the Council.

Functions of the Secretariat

This very process of inquiry may dispose of alleged grievances before they reach the Council. Claimants are invited to lay full information in support of their claims before the League officials at Geneva, so that their respective cases may be prepared for consideration by the Council. In course of this preparation exaggerated or ill-founded arguments are apt to disappear. Sometimes claimants discover at Geneva that their case is not so strong as it seemed to them in the excited atmosphere of their own countries, and that, after being pruned down to what is essential, the difference between them and their opponents is smaller than it appeared at first sight to be. Then the League officials may bring the contending parties together and help them to reach a settlement without troubling the Council.

When serious disputes or difficulties are brought before it, the Council decides upon the procedure to be adopted in dealing with them. One of the earliest of such disputes concerned the Aaland Islands which, in the general readjustment of the Baltic after the war, were claimed both by Sweden and by Finland (see page 4880). Both Sweden and Finland accepted the League's finding; but the efforts of the League to settle the dispute which arose in 1920 between Poland and Lithuania (see page 4882) were less successful.

In the conflict between Poland and Germany in regard to Upper Silesia, on the other hand, the League succeeded where the Supreme Council of the Allies had failed. Feeling ran so high among the contending powers and also among the Allied powers themselves that a complete rupture seemed inevitable. The Supreme Council of the Allies then invited the League Council to recommend a solution which the Allied powers could adopt. After minute investigation the Council put forward proposals which the Allied powers accepted; and in subsequent negotiations between Germany and Poland these proposals were taken as the basis of a German-Polish Convention, which both parties signed. It sanctions the partition of the Upper Silesian coal basin and provides that the Council of the League shall deal with some aspects of future differences and the Permanent Court of International Justice with others.

German-Polish rupture averted

The League contrived also to compose an embittered controversy between Poland and Czecho-Slovakia over the possession of the Javorzhina district in the Carpathians, and to settle a dispute between Lithuania and Memel by arranging that the territory and city of Memel should enjoy a considerable measure of autonomy under a governor to be appointed by the president of the Lithuanian republic.

More difficult and dangerous were the disputes between Italy and Greece over the murder of an Italian general and three other Italians on Greek soil in August, 1923 (see page 4894), and between the British and Turkish governments over the frontier of Irak. In both cases the

THE FLIGHT FROM UPPER SILESIA

The fracas of 1921 between Poland and Germany over Upper Silesia caused many inhabitants of the latter to depart into Germany, for which the photograph shows passes being issued. The opposing parties were reconciled by the League, whose proposals they accepted by signing a German-Polish Convention

Photo, Willi Ruge, Berlin

eague helped to promote eaceful settlements. But its ıtstanding success was gained October, 1925, when fight-ıg had actually begun between reece and Bulgaria. The ulgarian government ap-ealed to the League, under rticles 10 and 11 of the ovenant, on the morning of ctober 23. A few hours ter the secretary-general ımmoned an extraordinary ssion of the Council; and the ıme afternoon the French rime minister, Briand, as ıairman of the Council, tele-aphed to remind the Greek ıd the Bulgarian govern-ents of their obligations as embers of the League and of e serious consequences of ing to war without awaiting s decisions. He urged them to withdraw eir troops within their respective frontiers nding a consideration of the dispute by e Council. On October 26 the Council called upon both parties to inform it within twenty-four hours that they had ordered their troops to ithdraw. Both governments complied, d by October 29 the withdrawal was mpleted. The Council sent immediately special military commission to the spot, d afterwards a commission of inquiry, hich reported within three weeks, found at Greece had been to blame and commended that the Greek government ould pay £45,000 as reparation to ulgaria. This was done and the dispute ttled. In co-operation with the Pan-merican Conference the League succeeded so at the end of 1928 in preventing war tween two of its members, Bolivia and araguay, whose forces had already come blows.

raeco-Bulgarian quarrel settled

While the prevention of strife and the omotion of agreement between con-nding parties has been and is likely to main a principal task of the League, it s also engaged in constructive financial rk. As already mentioned, it took in nd the financial reconstruction both Austria and of Hungary, appointing in both cases a commissioner-general to supervise the application of the schemes it had recommended and inducing various powers to join in floating a reconstruction loan of some £30,000,000 for Austria and another of £10,000,000 for Hungary. The work of reconstruction was successful and two central European countries were saved from financial collapse. Hardly less striking was the contribution of the League to the establishment in Greek Macedonia of 1,500,000 destitute Greek refugees from Asia Minor. A loan of £10,000,000 was floated for this purpose. Other loans have been granted for the settlement of refugees in Bulgaria, for the consolidation of the currency in Esthonia, and for the development of the free city of Danzig which is under the League's jurisdiction.

In addition to these financial achievements the League has created an advisory technical organization to watch over communications and transit between one country and another and to supervise inland waterways of international importance. This technical organization held a first conference at Barcelona in March, 1921, to which forty states sent transit experts. The conference framed an international convention that stipulates complete freedom of transit and equality in conditions of transit, and contains a provision that disputes shall be submitted to the Permanent Court of International Justice should the technical organization of the League be unable to settle them. A second general conference held at Geneva in November, 1922, established conventions in regard to international railway traffic, the equality of shipping in seaports, the international transmission of electric power, and the development of hydraulic basins situated in territory belonging to two or more states.

Alongside of the League, though independent of it except that its budget forms part of the general budget of the League, an international labour organization has been established at Geneva. Once a year it holds a general conference which is attended not only by delegates of the governments which belong to the organization, but also by representatives of the organized workers and employers in each country. These delegates are divided into groups, the workers' delegates from every country acting together in a 'workers' group' and the employers' delegates forming an 'employers' group.' The government delegates form the strongest group and, to some extent, hold the balance even between the conflicting claims of employers and employees.

League's Labour Organization

This general conference corresponds to the Assembly of the League, while its Governing Body corresponds to the League Council. It has drawn up a number of conventions dealing with hours of labour, night work by women and children, labour conditions at sea, the compensation due to shipwrecked sailors, statutory precautions against industrial accidents and many other aspects of industrial welfare. Though none of these conventions has yet been made legally binding through formal ratification by all the countries of the world, nearly every convention has been ratified by some, and many have passed the laws which the various conventions recommend.

These subsidiary activities of the League have gone on independently of the discharge of its main task—to build up guarantees against the recurrence of war and to ensure that civilized nations shall no longer look to armed force as th principal means of safeguarding the security or promoting their interests. Th Covenant places upon the League th duty of reducing armaments. Its sign tories recognize that the maintenance c peace requires that armaments should b decreased to the lowest point consister with national safety. But since th foundation of the League it has bee realized clearly that nations will nc disarm unless they feel secure agains attack. The armaments problem ha been seen to involve a larger problem c security which, in its turn, involves th whole problem of international relations.

As soon as the League had complete its own organization it began to see means of providing for its membe stronger guarantees of security tha those defined by the Covenant. special committee, appointed for th purpose, put forward the first concrete proposals in 1923. They took the form of a 'draft treaty of mutual assistance' unde which signatory states would agree tha aggressive war was unlawful, and woul bind themselves to come to the help of an other state in the same continent whic might be unlawfully attacked. In retur for this pledge, all signatory states woul accept proportional disarmament. If the failed thus to disarm, they would forfe the protection of the treaty.

Draft treaty of Mutual Assistan

This draft treaty of mutual assistanc was submitted to the members of th League, but failed to secure their fu approval. At the annual Assembly c 1924, when the objections of the variou governments to the draft treaty had bee made known, the problem was recor sidered; and, on the basis of a joir resolution which was moved by th British and French prime minister Ramsay MacDonald and Edouard Herrio and adopted by the Assembly, a 'pr tocol for the pacific settlement of inte national disputes' was framed and unan mously recommended by the Assembl to the earnest attention of all the goverr ments represented. This protocol, usuall called the Geneva Protocol, was founde upon a formula put forward by th

·ench prime minister, 'arbitration, se-.rity, disarmament.' It provided that e signatory states should recognize the risdiction of the Permanent Court of ternational Justice as compulsory in all sticiable questions; that they should ree to a system of compulsory arbitra-)n in cases not susceptible of legal treat-ent and in which mediation had failed effect a settlement; and that any ate resorting to war in violation of its gagements should be automatically signated as the aggressor.

The Council of the League was em-wered to declare that such a state had en the aggressor; and, pursuant to ch a declaration, the other states signa-ry of the protocol would be under an ligation to co-operate—in the degree ich their geographical positions and the condition of their arma-ments might allow—in supporting the Covenant and in resisting the gressor. The validity of the protocol as to depend upon the adoption of a an for the reduction of armaments a special disarmament conference ich was to be summoned as soon as given number of states should have tified the protocol.

'ailure of the eneva Protocol

Like the 'draft treaty of mutual sistance' before it, the Geneva Protocol iled to secure the necessary support. score of states signed it, but only one tified it. Had the British government gned and ratified it, it would probably ve been adopted. But it had been awn up with the help of British delegates pointed by the Labour government; d the Conservative government, which ok office a few months later, declined to cept the obligations which the protocol ould have involved. At the meeting of e League Council in March, 1925, Sir isten Chamberlain, the British foreign cretary, stated that while sympathising th the objects of the protocol, the itish government could not accept the otocol itself, since it thought that a more tisfactory method would be to avoid neral commitments and to supplement e Covenant of the League by making ecial international arrangements to meet ecial needs. Such arrangements, he thought, should be framed in the spirit of the Covenant and be in harmony with the purposes of the League.

This British declaration gave the death blow to the Geneva Protocol. A solution of the problems of security and disarma-ment seemed farther off than ever. The protocol had, however, had the effect of eliciting from Germany a statement that she would be prepared to enter into an international arrangement of the kind it had contemplated. Conse-quently negotiations began between Great Britain, France and Germany for a 'western security pact.' In October, 1925, they led to the conclusion of agreements at Locarno (see page 4893) between Germany, France, Belgium, Great Britain and Italy for the security of the Rhineland, and between Germany and Czecho-Slovakia and Germany and Poland for the settlement of disputes by arbitration. Before these agreements were made, the League Assembly adopted, in September, 1925, a resolu-tion sanctioning efforts to restore mutual confidence by special treaties and conven-tions in harmony with the principles of arbitration, security and disarmament on which the Geneva Protocol had been based. Thus the Locarno negotiations were brought under the auspices of the League; and, after the conclusion of the agreements, they were formally registered with the League Secretariat.

The Locarno agreements

Meanwhile the endeavour to promote international disarmament was continued. At the suggestion of the League Assembly a preparatory committee for a disarma-ment conference was set up, and in the light of its work a general disarmament conference was held at Geneva in May, 1927. Though its positive results were few, some progress was made in the direction of defining the difficulties to be overcome. Its attention was restricted to land armaments, since the limitation of naval armaments had been dealt with by the Washington Conference of 1921–22 and was to be further examined by another naval conference at Geneva in June, 1927. This conference ended in failure; and, in the hope of providing a basis for future agreement, an Anglo-

French naval compromise was concluded in the summer of 1928. The United States, however, rejected the compromise. Negotiations then began for a wider settlement in accordance with the Kellogg Pact (see page 4904), which was signed by fifteen nations at Paris in August 27, 1928, and has since been accepted by thirty-five other governments.

It is by its ultimate success or failure in solving the problems of security and disarmament that the League will be judged. Its general utility is beyond doubt, for its work in settling disputes, in promoting international health and sanitation, in checking the traffic in women and children, in regulating the opium trade, in repatriating more than 400,000 prisoners of war belonging to twenty-six different nationalities, and in establishing an international slavery convention to which thirty different states have adhered, could scarcely have been performed by any other agency. It exercises also supervision over the mandates granted by the Peace Treaty to Great Britain, the British Dominions, France and Belgium over the former German colonies and over parts of Asia Minor; and it holds measure of control over the treatment racial minorities in countries which belor to the League. Yet all these functions a subsidiary to the main purpose for whic the League was founded — promotir international co-operation for the mai tenance of peace and the outlawry of wa

It is fair to ask whether the prospec that the League will be able to discharg this main function are now more favou able than they were when it was estal lished; but the question is not easy t answer. In and by itself the Leagu possesses little authority. Its pow resides in the will of its members activel to fulfil their engagements under th Covenant. The Covenant forms part the peace treaties; and, like the peac treaties themselves, it can be amended b general consent. Article 19 of the Covenar empowers the League Assembly to advis members of the League to reconsid treaty engagements which have becom inapplicable and to take account of inte national conditions of which the co tinuance might endanger the peace of th world. What is to happen if some memb

RATIFICATION OF THE LOCARNO TREATIES IN LONDON

The Locarno Conference of 1925, whereby various agreements were reached between the seve subscribing powers to the pact there formulated, was held with the sanction and under the auspic of the League of Nations. The ceremony of ratification took place at the Foreign Office, London, i the December of the same year. At the head of the table sits Baldwin with Sir Austen Chamberla beside him. Others present represent Germany, France, Belgium, Italy, Poland and Czecho-Slovaki

f the League thinks its treaty engage-
ients inapplicable and draws the atten-
on of the Assembly to them, only to
nd the Assembly unwilling or unable
) consider a revision of them ?

The defeated states, Germany, Hun-
ary, Austria and Bulgaria, look upon
ome of the provisions of the peace treaties
s unduly harsh, and are likely, in course
f time, to bring their grievances before
ie League and appeal to it for redress.
f they fail to secure redress, they may give notice of withdrawal from the League, deny its authority and prepare to enforce their wishes by arms.

**efects of
e League**

gainst them the countries interested in
aintaining the treaties would arm in
ieir turn. A new era of competition in
rmaments would begin, and the pros-
ect, not to say the certainty, of another
onflagration would threaten the very
xistence of the new Europe and of
uropean civilization itself.

When the idea of establishing a League
f Nations was first put forward, two
endencies became apparent. The first
as to make of the League an inter-
ational authority possessing the right
nd the power to enforce its decisions
pon all states belonging to it. The
eague, thus conceived, was to be a
uper-state endowed with super-sover-
ignty, overriding the sovereignties of
idividual states and commanding armed
orces of its own that could be used to
oerce the disobedient. This conception
ound favour in France and was upheld
y the French representatives on the
eague of Nations Commission at the
aris Peace Conference. The other tend-
ncy was to regard the League as a
oluntary association of nations, each of
hich would retain absolute sovereignty
ver its own domestic concerns and also
n relation to foreign affairs, except in
) far as its international action might
e circumscribed by agreed limitations.

It was the second tendency that pre-
ailed in the drafting of the Covenant.
etween the view that the League
hould be administered chiefly by the
reat powers and the principle that
ll its members should possess equal
tatus and rights, a working compromise
was adopted. The principle of absolute
equality involved the danger that great
and powerful states might refuse to be
out-voted by a number of small states,
or to run the risk of seeing their vital
interests misunderstood or ignored by
countries unaware of the responsibilities
of a great power. Therefore the greater
Allies were given permanent representation on the Council of the League, and
it was understood that if and when other
great nations, like Germany and Russia,
should join the League, they too would
be entitled to permanent seats on its
Council and would not be subject to
periodical re-election by the Assembly like
the representatives of the smaller states.
At the same time a safeguard against
arbitrary decisions was created by the
provision that, in all its principal acts,
the Council must be unanimous.

Against the danger that the require-
ment of unanimity might paralyse its
action the League has developed a technique of its own. Questions are rarely
submitted to a vote of the Council unless it is certain that the vote will be unanimous. Every

**Development of
League technique**

resource of mediation and conciliation,
discussion and argument is employed in
private to promote agreement between
contending parties before the Council is
asked to decide upon a controversial issue.
For instance, there might not be unanimity if the Council were asked to decide
which of two combatant states was the
aggressor; but there would probably be
unanimity in calling upon both to cease
hostilities, and to withdraw into their
own territories, pending an inquiry into
their dispute. The state which should
refuse to comply would designate itself
the aggressor.

At Geneva the League spirit is strong;
and when representatives of governments
assemble there under its influence they are
apt to take a more conciliatory view of a
given question than they might have taken
in their own capitals. It is this local
tendency towards conciliation that is
sometimes called the 'Geneva atmosphere.'
It is a reality, not a fiction; one of those
realities, indeed, which the framers of
the League Covenant hardly foresaw.

The meeting of many of the foreign ministers, and sometimes the prime ministers, four times a year to transact the business of the Council at Geneva enables them informally to exchange their views, to gain personal knowledge of each other and to discuss delicate matters which, in the old Europe, they could scarcely have discussed at all. Whenever leading statesmen met before the war, they were suspected of meeting for some definite and selfish purpose—that of making an alliance against other states or of engaging in some intrigue dangerous to peace. Now they are able to meet at regular intervals, not only on the neutral soil of Switzerland, but under the auspices of an organization which is itself neutral save in so far as it exists for the purpose of promoting international co-operation and good will.

Yet another subtle influence has entered into the life of nations since the establishment of the League. Every government belonging to it feels that in the last resort it may be obliged publicly to defend its policy before the League Assembly, where it can be publicly answered and compelled to face the judgement of its peers. This feeling makes for prudence in diplomatic action and tends to refine international manners. Almost unconsciously, statesmen are made aware that it may be more important to have a good case for presentation to the League than a powerful army to uphold a bad case. Mere insistence upon national susceptibilities or ambitions carries little weight at Geneva. In the League atmosphere the international aspect of things stands in the foreground.

The fundamental problem of peace is whether the spirit of international co-operation will prevail over selfish national aims and international jealousies. It is often asserted that the new Europe is worse than the old because it has been split up into a larger number of independent national states, each with its own ambitions, each eager to protect its separate political and economic existence and each having an exaggerated idea of its own importance. The tendency of modern civilization, it is sometimes argued, is towards the formation of large, comprehensive units in politics as in trade and industry; the policy of setting up of a number of small new nations was contrary to this tendency and was therefore unsound. The 'Balkanisation' of Europe by the creation of countries like Finland, Esthonia, Lithuania, Latvia, Poland, Czecho-Slovakia, Yugo-Slavia and Albania, not to mention the enlargement of Rumania by the inclusion within her frontiers of a notable portion of the former territory of Hungary is alleged to be a less favourable and

THE LEAGUE OF NATIONS HOLD THEIR FIRST COUNCIL MEETING IN ENGLAND

On February 11, 1920, the second Council Meeting of the League of Nations—the first held in England—took place in the Picture Gallery at St. James's Palace. The eight delegates who attended and Sir Eric Drummond, Secretary-General of the League, are, left to right: Caclamanos (Greece), da Cunha (Brazil), Matsui (Japan), Léon Bourgeois (France), Balfour (Great Britain), Sir Eric Drummond, Ferraris (Italy), Paul Hymans (Belgium) and Quiñones de Leon (Spain).

Photo, Graphic Photograph Union

.tural order of things than was the ntrol formerly exercised over most of ose territories and their peoples by the ıssian and German empires and by e Austro-Hungarian monarchy. For this ason the new Europe fashioned by the ır is often looked upon as less permanent d workable than the old Europe out of ıose rivalries and appetites the war ose; and it is maintained that if the ague of Nations attempts to protect e existence of all these new small states will essay an impossible task.

The answer to these criticisms of the w Europe is to be found in the history of the old Europe.

ge-long movement vards emancipation

It is too often forgotten that the old Europe formed in 70–71 was by no means stable, for it ted less than fifty years. The war and effects cannot be understood apart m the movements which had marked course of European affairs since the formation in the fifteenth and sixteenth ıturies. Out of the philosophy of the formation and its assertion of individual edom of conscience came, in course of ıe, the philosophy of the French volution with its assertion of the rights man. Out of the French Revolution, ich stimulated the spirit of nationality, ne the movements that culminated in unification of Germany and Italy, in progressive emancipation of Balkan oples from Turkish rule and in the ival of Czech and Polish aspirations independent national existence. The ond half of the nineteenth century was rked by the resurgence of one submerged nationality after another, until problem for Europe was whether this ocess of emancipation should go forward fulfilment, or whether it should be bed by the desire of the great empires maintain their sway irrespective of the hes of subject peoples.

This was the issue really at stake in Great War. It began and was symbo- d by the attempt of Austria-Hungary subjugate a small nation, Serbia, lest kindred South Slav provinces under psburg rule be irresistibly attracted it. Characteristically, too, the war was rked in western Europe by the German attack upon another small people, the Belgians, despite solemn international guarantees of their independence and neutrality. Great Britain fought to uphold the sanctity of these guarantees, to which she, like Germany, had subscribed; and all the Allies proclaimed the rights of small nations as one of the main principles they were resolved to vindicate. In these circumstances they could not oppose but were rather bound to favour the demands of the Czecho-Slovaks, of the Poles and of other races for national independence, and those of the South Slavs and Rumanians for national unification. The watchwords of 'self-determination' or of 'government with the consent of the governed' to which President Wilson gave currency were accepted as expressions of the democratic idea of individual freedom as against the idea of imperial organization and domination represented by Austria-Hungary and Germany.

Of these democratic ideas the League of Nations was intended to be an embodiment. The recognition it gave to small nations as well as to great was a denial of the right to rule over and constrain a people in defiance of its wishes. A remedy was sought for the multiplication of national individualities by the establishment of a system of international co-operation for peace that should tend to assuage the strife of incompatible national ambitions and should seek to co-ordinate them in the service of a common ideal. Co-ordination was felt to be indispensable among nations which the growing rapidity and facility of communications were rendering more and more interdependent, and it was hoped to attain this co-ordination by voluntary agreement.

Embodiment of Democratic ideas

When the League of Nations was conceived, it was generally assumed that Western civilization would be democratic and that the conduct of foreign relations by democracies would be as pacific as their control by dynasties had, in the past, been warlike. But before the League was founded the Russian Empire had crumbled, and its autocratic tsardom had given place to a communist Soviet system based ostensibly on the 'dictatorship of the proletariat,' yet thoroughly hostile to the liberal democracy of the West. Within a few years more than one member of the League forsook the democratic ideal and adopted systems of dictatorship. In Spain a military directorate overthrew the constitution and set up a dictatorial regime. In Italy the head of an armed Fascist militia gained control of the state, destroyed the constitution on which the unity of Italy had been founded, rescinded the liberty of the press, abolished freedom of opinion and proclaimed an extreme nationalist military policy. The example of Fascism and the influence of the nationalist spirit it fostered affected other countries and stimulated an anti-democratic reaction throughout Europe. The prospects of the League of Nations cannot be gauged until it is seen whether this reaction—which is inimical to the idea of international co-operation for peace upon a democratic basis—will be lasting or temporary. They could hardly fail to be affected by a definite triumph of forces incompatible with the League ideal.

The chief hope for the League lies in the general recognition that another great war might utterly destroy European civilization, and that, however defective the peace treaties may be, it is better to tolerate their imperfections until they can be removed by friendly agreement than to seek to correct them by force. Broadly considered, the new Europe is more justly framed than was the old Europe. It is better that the Polish people should be united and independent than that they should be split into three sections under Prussian, Russian and Austrian rule. It is better that the Czechs should have regained their freedom after three centuries of servitude than that they should remain unwilling subjects of the Hapsburg crown. It is better that the 2,500,000 Roumanes of Transylvania should have been enabled to join their kindred in the kingdom of Rumania than that they should continue to be oppressed by the Magyars. It is better, also, that the Serbs, Croats and Slovenes of Hungary and Austria should have been linked with Serbia to form a united Southern Sla state than that their unsatisfied aspir tions to freedom and unity should be permanent danger to peace.

General fear of another war

If, in the establishment of the Polis Czecho-Slovak, Greater Rumanian ar Yugo-Slav states minorities of other rac were inevitably transferred in their tu to alien rule, this evil of the peace treaties is less than the evils of which those treaties made an end. Before the war the were 100,000,000 members of raci minorities in Europe subject to alien ru and no means existed to improve the lot. To-day there are only 20,000,00 such members, and the League is enabl to deal with their grievances. Taken t gether there are probably 160,000,000 sou in Europe—excluding the people of Gre Britain—who are determined not to perm any return of the old order, as again some 80,000,000 who might wish to retu to it. Yet even these 80,000,000—wh may be taken to include the populatio of Germany, Austria and Hungary—a by no means unanimous in desiring restoration of the former political syste A section of the German people is strong Republican and another influential secti believes the republic more conducive to i interests than a monarchy or an emp would be. The prospect that Germa will engage in aggressive war see almost as faint as the prospect that a neighbouring people will attack German

Majority in favo of the New Syste

There exists, moreover, a network protective alliances among the new stat and between some of them and Fran with the express object of upholding t peace treaties. Of these alliances the mo important are the agreements which bi Czecho-Slovakia, Rumania and Yug Slavia together in what is known as t Little Entente. There are also allian between France and Poland, Fran and Czecho-Slovakia, and Rumania a Poland. All of these alliances have be registered with the Permanent Secretari of the League of Nations. On the oth hand, there exists a 'treaty of mutu friendship' between Germany and Sovi Russia, and an agreement between Hu gary and Fascist Italy. More import han any is the main Locarno Treaty, by which Great Britain, France, Belgium, Germany and Italy undertake to uphold he peace settlement in western Europe against attack from any quarter.

Nevertheless, there remain enough elements of discord to justify doubt whether the peace of Europe is entirely assured, and whether some incident may not inflame national passions to a point at which the consequences of armed strife would be overlooked. The Germans are not reconciled to the existence of the corridor of territory which links Poland with the free city of Danzig and gives her an outlet to the sea, since that corridor separates the province of East Prussia from the rest of Germany. Nor do they believe that the division of the Upper Silesian coalfields between Germany and Poland is just or can be lasting. The Poles, for their part, regard both the Danzig corridor and the Upper Silesian settlement as vital interests to be defended by every means in their power. Many Germans and not a few Austrians desire also the union of Germany with Austria. This desire is opposed by Czecho-Slovakia, Yugo-Slavia and Italy, whose security an Austro-German union might menace. Soviet Russia claims a right to the —mainly Rumanian—province of Bessarabia which was returned to Rumania at the peace after having been held by Russia, in whole or in part, for a century. Hungary demands the restoration to her of sundry districts, partly peopled by Magyars, which were allotted to Czecho-Slovakia, Rumania and Yugo-Slavia; while the German inhabitants of what is now the Italian Tirol yearn to escape from the Italian Fascist yoke.

Surviving elements of discord

In addition to these local causes of unrest, the question of German reparations to the Allies awaits a final solution; and with the reparations question are linked the continued Allied occupation of portions of the Rhineland, and the secret armaments of Germany in defiance of the Peace Treaty.

Thus, even without the disturbing influence of Russian Soviet propaganda for a world revolution, there exist enough points of friction to warrant caution in assuming that the future of Europe will be marked by untroubled peace. Had the League of Nations not been established, and had it not justified its existence by actually preventing armed strife, as well as in a dozen minor respects, the outbreak of another European conflagration would be but a question of time. At worst, the existence of the League, and the habit of informal consultation between European statesmen which it has fostered, should be safeguards against any sudden catastrophe. Though not all the antecedents of the Great War have yet been revealed, sufficient is known of them to substantiate the view that the war would not have broken out when it did and as it did had there existed any international agency with enough authority to summon the contending parties to a conference and to gain time for calm consideration of the issues at stake.

The League of Nations is such an agency, armed with the requisite authority. Any power which should ignore a call to state its case before the Council or the Assembly of the League would put itself in the wrong and would be likely to turn the opinion of the civilized world against it. During the war most of the belligerent nations spent huge sums on propaganda, that is to say, in attempting to influence the opinion of the world. In future, no propaganda would be likely to avail a government which had either declined to inform the League of its demands or had flouted the deliberate judgement of the League. The moral power of the League remains immense and, rightly exercised, probably decisive.

Justification for the League

This probability has been enhanced by the conclusion of the Kellogg Pact. Without binding the United States to support the League, the pact diminished the risk that American policy would be opposed to that of the League in regard to an international conflict, since any aggressor would violate the pact and the League Covenant simultaneously. Thus the prospects of peace have been increased by the tacit association of the United States with the main purpose for which the League was founded.

SOVIET OF SOLDIERS', WORKERS' AND PEASANTS' DEPUTIES IN SESSION

This remarkable photograph shows a session of the Soviet of Soldiers', Workers' and Peasant Deputies which was called by Lenin to Petrograd in the summer of 1917, and was the advance age of the Bolshevik revolution in the autumn of that year. While these large congresses gave semblance of democracy to the new regime they were composed mainly of illiterate men ignorant the art of government, with the result that executive control was held by Lenin and his colleagu

Keystone View Co.

CHAPTER 184

THE RUSSIA OF THE BOLSHEVIKS

Swift Change from Autocracy to Communist Despotism and its Military Success combined with Economic Failure

By F. A. MACKENZIE

Author of Russia Before Dawn, etc.

The Russian Revolution, judged by the extent of territory and the number of people affected, is the most tremendous upheaval the world has ever known. The empire of the tsars covered one seventh of the earth's surface and included one twelfth of the world's population. It was an established autocracy, supported by the largest army in the world, and it had behind it an elaborate, numerous and powerful bureaucracy. Within a few days tsarism and the whole machinery of tsarism were destroyed, and a few months later the entire basis of society as it had existed for centuries was overturned.

No such change could have been attempted, much less carried through, had not the conditions of national life prepared the way. Those who seek to find the real explanation of the Communist revolution must first examine the conditions of the Russian people at the time the revolution began. Autocracy, useful and effective at one stage of the national existence, had been outgrown, but the mass of the Russian people, illiterate and inexperienced in affairs, had not been prepared for constitutional self-government. Even in the days of Peter the Great, as Kluchevsky, Russia's greatest historian, has pointed out, the autocratic imposition of the will of one strong man on the mass of the nation had failed to effect permanence. But now tsarism had taken the form not of one strong man imposing his will on a backward people, but of one notoriously weak man acting through an oppressive bureaucracy.

For a hundred years the movement for freedom had been growing. Alexander I, at the beginning of the nineteenth century, was not altogether unsympathetic to constitutional reform. In 1822 officers of the guard, most of them personal associates of the new tsar, Nicholas, made an attempt to secure constitutional government by force. December was the month when they revolted, and they are therefore known as the Decabrists. Their effort failed; five of them were hanged and many others sent to life-long exile in Chita, in eastern Siberia. Alexander II carried out many great reforms, culminating in the abolition of serfdom; but he hesitated to go as far as many wanted, and hesitated all the more because reckless revolutionary parties were rising, especially in the universities. The Nihilist movement aimed to accomplish reform by dynamite. Anarchist groups planned violence. The Liberal party strove for moderation, and was at one time dominated by Hertzen, whose demands, however extravagant they seemed then, would not be counted unreasonable now, including as they did a free press, independent justice, trial by jury and a constitutional government. Youthful revolutionists, impatient at the slow progress of reform, took extreme courses. In 1866 a young nihilist made an attempt to shoot Alexander; a few years later, in 1881, the tsar was blown to pieces by revolutionary bombs in the very heart of St. Petersburg. He had already signed but had not yet issued a decree granting the desired constitutional government. After his death that decree was destroyed.

Alexander II, the 'Tsar Liberator'

The murder of the Tsar Liberator was to put back reform for a generation. Alexander III, his successor, was defiantly reactionary and strengthened absolute autocracy in every way within his power. Reformers were sent wholesale to prison, exile or the scaffold. But still, despite all,

FACTORY WOMEN OF ST. PETERSBURG
In Tsarist days factory workers of Russia laboured for the most part under very bad conditions. Frequently housed on the factory premises, they were subjected to strict discipline. This is a drawing made in 1905 of female factory hands in their sleeping room at St. Petersburg.

the leaven was working. After Alexander's death it was thought that his successor, Nicholas II, would take a more liberal line. That expectation was disappointed. When the men of Tver presented him with an address congratulating him on his marriage, and expressed a hope that at the beginning of his reign the voices of the people and their desires would be heard, and that law would stand supreme 'above the changing views of the individual instruments of the extreme power,' Nicholas rebuked the men for their 'senseless dreams' and declared himself the champion of an unswerving adherence to the principle of autocracy.

So long as the revolutionary parties in Russia were drawn from the student, professional and aristocratic classes there was little danger from them. But the situation was changed towards the end of the nineteenth century by the rapid advance of Russian urban industry. Large factories were opened in the great cities, and these attracted hundreds of thousands of peasants to the towns. The government laid down an elaborate and beneficent system of regulations for the protection of the factory workers; but these were little more than a dead letter in most districts, because of the wholesale and general bribery of police and inspectors. There were model factories and model industrial centres as at Vladimir, but in general the condition of th hands was very bad. Thei housing in particular wa almost incredibly wretched 'Let us go to our coffins was a common saying amon them when returning home.

These large bodies of work ing people, drawn closel together and resentful at th conditions under which the were living, proved fuel fo the fire of revolutionar teaching, and all the more s because of the refusal of th authorities to permit organize labour to form free trad unions. The town worker went back in due time to th villages and spread the ne doctrines there.

Groups of revolutionis

The revolutionists were divided int several groups. The strongest moderat section was the Cadets, the Constitutiona Democrats ('Cadet' being formed of th initial letters of their Russian name), who were largely composed of Liberals of the educated classes and who relied upon political reform. The came more extreme bodies—the S.R. (Social Revolutionists), the Social Demo crats and the Anarchists. The S.R. sprang from a revolutionary party c peasants and were terrorists, believin in an active campaign of violence again the autocracy. They organized man dynamite and other outrages and as sassinated with bomb or pistol man leaders of the autocracy. The Soci Democrats relied mainly upon educatio and organization of the town workers, s that they might be able to bring abou revolution by armed revolt at the rig moment. Their leader for many yea was Plekhanov, one of the fathers of th Russian Social Democratic movement i the 'eighties. But he became too modera for many of his party.

Early in the twentieth century a ne leader appeared, a young exile, Nikol Lenin by name. The party, as a resu of Lenin's campaign against Plekhano split into two groups, the Bolshevik who advocated strict adherence to th

Communist doctrines of Karl Marx (see page 4985), and the Mensheviks, willing to co-operate with some moderate sections and to adjust Marxian doctrines to actual conditions. In addition, there were numerous smaller bodies. The Anarchists could not have the compact centralised organization of the other revolutionists, but were represented by numerous separate organizations in Russia and abroad, their membership varying from idealistic philosophers like Prince Kropotkin to men in such savage revolt against society that they were prepared to kill, rob and destroy at random.

In the early years of the present century the position of Russia was one of unique interest. In area, in wealth and in population the empire of the tsars stood in the foremost rank of the nations. The Russian army was the strongest numerically and believed to be one of the two most powerful in the world. The building of the trans-Siberian railway had opened up a vast and wealthy new land for development. The growth of industry had been phenomenal. The developments of mining and of agriculture had been more rapid than ever before. But the obverse showed a very different picture. The state Church, gorged with wealth, had become notoriously venal and most monasteries were centres of licentiousness. The bureaucracy throttled thought and official corruption was taken almost as a matter of course. There was no freedom of speech, no free press, no independent justice. The mass of the peasantry, nine tenths of the nation, could not read or write. Among the educated classes there had been a general discarding of the old standards of religion and morality. The younger intellectuals, charged with revolt against the autocracy and tsarism, had spread their propaganda among workers and peasants.

Russia, land of contradictions

The first great chance of the revolutionists came during the Russo-Japanese War in 1904–5. The Japanese government, as a legitimate method of war, secretly financed and encouraged some of the revolutionary groups. When the tsarist armies and fleet were defeated in battle after battle, tremendous discontent manifested itself throughout Russia. Father Gapon, a democratic priest, led a group of workers and peasants one Sunday in January, 1905, known henceforth as Bloody Sunday, through the streets of St. Petersburg to the Winter Palace, the home of the tsar, to present a petition to him. The processionists were stopped by lines of troops, and suddenly the order was given for the troops to fire. Very large numbers were killed and wounded. Within a few days revolt had broken out in many parts of the country. There were months of upheavals, street fighting, cruel assassinations and vindictive reprisals. The attempt at revolution ended in the autumn of 1905 by a prolonged battle in Moscow, when, after hard fighting, the revolutionists were completely defeated and most of their leaders captured.

In the midst of the struggle Nicholas made some concessions to the popular demands. Up to 1905 there had been little religious liberty. For a Russian to leave the Orthodox Greek Church was in itself a crime, rendering him liable to severe punishment. The Old Believers, a strictly orthodox sect, had been sent into exile generations before (see page 3932). It was a great step forward when the tsar,

PRINCE KROPOTKIN

Prince Peter Alexeivitch Kropotkin (1842–1921) propagated his revolutionary doctrines among the Russian working classes, his followers forming an anarchist group; his Memoirs of a Revolutionist appeared in 1899.

On February 1 the tsar granted a belated interview at Tsarskoye Selo to representatives of the strikers. The workmen's delegates are seen in this drawing leaving the Alexander Palace placated by vague promises.

In January, 1905, the first serious movement of the impending Russian revolution began, with a strike at the Putilov Ironworks in Petrograd. The campaign was organized by a priest, Father Gapon, and on January 22 he led the strikers towards the Winter Palace to present a petition to the tsar. The approaches to the Palace Square were barred by troops, who turned a murderous fire upon the crowd. Father Gapon was badly wounded at the Narva Triumphal Arch (inset).

SCENES OF SLAUGHTER AND UNREST IN RUSSIA IN THE REVOLT OF 1905

Lower photos, E.N.A.

FOE OF THE REVOLUTIONISTS

Piotr Arkadievitch Stolypin (1862–1911) had already achieved a reputation for statesmanship when he became prime minister of Russia. His relentless campaign against the revolutionists made his name a byword for cruelty.

Photo, E.N.A.

at Easter, 1905, issued a decree permitting Russians to withdraw from the state Church and join another communion. But even then the person who had persuaded the Russian to change his faith was liable to heavy penalties, and the convert himself could be thrown into prison to be held as a witness against him. As late as 1916 every Baptist church in Russia was closed and the pastors sent to Siberia.

On October 3, 1905, the tsar signed a further decree, hailed by the press of the world as a 'charter of liberty to one tenth of the human race.' In it he promised the nation civic liberty, based on inviolability of the person and freedom of conscience, speech, union and association. A duma (parliament) really representative of the Russian people was to meet, and no law was to be made without its sanction. The first Russian parliament was opened at the Winter Palace in May, 1906.

But it was clear that the tsar was weakening in his zeal for reform. Having summoned the Duma, he set about thwarting it and depriving it of power. A merciless campaign was opened against all suspected of sympathising with the revolutionary uprising. Hangings, torture, exile and life imprisonment became common. It was estimated that during this wave of reaction a hundred thousand people were sent to Siberia. The revolutionary organizers were hunted down. The revolutionists, or the remnants that were left of them, replied by a succession of murders of statesmen and generals. At the head of this regime of oppression was the premier, Stolypin. To this day the carriages on the railways where prisoners are shut in barred cages are known as 'Stolypins,' and hanging as 'Stolypin's neck tie.' Stolypin was shot and killed at a theatre in Kiev in 1911.

Nicholas was no man to ride a storm or to control a great people. Feeble, superficial, impatient, easily led, his closest advisers soon came to regard him as one who did not know his own mind and who could be trusted in nothing. Behind him stood his wife, the empress Alexandra Feodorovna, descended from the grand-ducal house of Hesse-Darmstadt, who was always urging him to resist reform and to keep power and might in his own hands.

RIGID BELIEVER IN AUTOCRACY

Princess Alix of Hesse married Tsar Nicholas II in 1894 and took the name of Alexandra Feodorovna. She was assassinated with her husband and other members of the imperial family in 1918. She is here seen in 1914.

Photo, E.N.A.

The outbreak of the Great War in 1914 produced a reaction in favour of Nicholas. A wave of patriotism swept the Russian people, old differences were forgotten and the tsar had once more a united Russia in his hands. Even revolutionary leaders who for years had fought hard against tsarism came voluntarily and surrendered themselves, offering to serve their emperor as he pleased. But as the war went on a slow change came over the Russian people. Corruption, extortion and bribery did their work. The traders and merchants earned universal hatred by their greedy exploitation of the nation, and in particular by their manipulation of food prices. The army, thanks to the corruption of some of its leaders, went into the field with many of its men unarmed. Hundreds o thousands were ruthlessly slaughtere through bad staff work. Prisoners i German camps were left to starve. Th people felt that their self-sacrifice and th heroism of their sons were being throw away by the incompetence of their rulers

The popular reverence for the imperia throne had already been destroyed by th folly of the empress in her worship of a extraordinary fakir, Grigory Rasputin, character difficult to imagine in any othe country than Russia. A rough, uncouth Siberian peasant, after a wild youth h had taken to religion and proved himse a magnetic preacher and teacher.

Reports of his miracle-working qualitie spread abroad. He could heal the sic of body as well as of min In time he reached St. Peter burg, where he had an entré to some of the greatest house The empress, who had bee greatly disappointed becaus she had no son, sent for Ras putin. He spoke to her as seer or prophet, and is allege to have said: 'Go to Saro little mother, pray over th sacred relics of S. Seraphi and that which you wish sha come to you.' While the trut of this prophecy may be ques tioned, it is a fact that i the following year a son wa born.

Rasputin was now high i favour with the empress an the court, and nothing wa too good for him. He was man of double life, and whi on this one side he preache and worked as a saint, h was also amazingly licentiou Idolised by the most excl sive Russian society, he sti retained his peasant way bullied his myriad wome worshippers, ate out of dish with his fingers and spok roughly to the highest. The were many women 'disciples in his house, his harem. H made many women of th greatest families his willin

EVIL GENIUS OF AN EMPRESS

By his mystical and hypnotic gifts Grigory Rasputin (1873–1916), the illiterate son of a Siberian fisherman, obtained a profound influence over the Russian tsaritsa. His consequent political power proved so dangerous a force that his assassination was encompassed by Russian nobles in 1916.

From Youssoupoff, 'Rasputin,' Jonathan Cape, Ltd.

THE TSARITSA'S BEDROOM: A KEY TO ONE ASPECT OF HER CHARACTER

Rasputin's uncanny influence over the many women who fell under his powerful spell is reflected in the religious obsessions that afflicted his most highly placed victim—the tsaritsa Alexandra Feodorovna herself. The walls of her bedchamber in the summer palace at Tsarskoye Selo were almost covered with religious pictures, crucifixes and images. The Soviet maintains it in this condition.

Photo, Topical Press Agency

victims. He preached that you must sin to obtain forgiveness. 'How can we repent if we have not sinned?' was his doctrine, and he would show his victims how to sin.

The tsar's ministers were alarmed about the influence Rasputin had over the empress and, through her, over the emperor. During the Great War the scandal of his influence became more and more marked. He was now the power behind the throne, dictating political appointments, even of ministers and generals. Grand dukes, statesmen, close relatives begged the emperor to rid the court of him. It was suggested, although probably falsely, that he was in German pay.

The emperor struck a fatal blow at his own prestige by dismissing, on the advice of Rasputin, the grand duke Nicholas from the post of commander-in-chief of the army and assuming that office himself. In the autumn of 1917 there was great distress in the cities of Russia. The whole country was suspicious of the empress and of Rasputin. A prominent conservative

GRAND DUKE NICHOLAS

The grand duke Nicholas, created commander-in-chief of the Russian armies by Nicholas II upon the outbreak of the Great War, conducted operations against the Austro-Germans until 1915. Rasputin's influence secured his dismissal, and the tsar took over the high command.

politician, Purishkevitch, rose in the Duma and caused a great sensation by eloquently pleading with the ministers to go to the tsar and beg him to rid the country of this curse. Next day, among the visitors who congratulated Purishkevitch was one who pleaded for action. 'Why not let us kill this foul thing?' asked Prince Felix Yusupov. Within a few days a plan was arranged. The plotters were not revolutionists but extreme imperialists and conservatives who believed that Rasputin's power threatened tsardom itself. Chief in rank among them was the grand duke Dmitri, cousin to the tsar.

Prince Yusupov invited Rasputin to come late at night to his family palace on the Moika Canal, telling him that there would be a feast and that he would meet a lady, a countess, whom he had often desired. Here he drank wine heavily charged with cyanide of potassium, but it scarce seemed to injure him. He ate cakes packed with enough poison to kill a score of men, with little apparent result. After a long and anxious time of waiting,

PRINCE FELIX YUSUPOV

A foremost participator in the conspiracy which rid Russia of Rasputin's evil influence was Prince Felix Yusupov. It was to his house that the malign favourite of the empress was invited for the specific purpose of being done to death.

Photo, Hay Wrightson

AT THE LAST RUSSIAN DUMA

Created in 1905, the Russian Duma (see page 4442) or representative state council of the empire was swept away by the revolution of November, 1917. This photograph shows a sitting shortly before its final dissolution. In the chair is president Rodzyanko, beneath a portrait of Nicholas II.

Photo, Illustrations Bureau

Prince Yusupov shot him, and he and his friends left him for dead, only to see him a little later crawl across the room and try to escape into the street. Purishkevitch, following him, shot again, and he finally killed him. His body was taken to a bridge outside the city and thrown under the ice. When the news became known, the empress was torn with grief, but the nation rejoiced.

The killing of Rasputin was the final spark that lit the flames of revolution.

The overthrow of tsardom was the result not so much of a deliberate plot as a spontaneous uprising of the people against a feeble, inept and intolerable tyranny. In December, 1916, the grand duke Paul begged the tsar to grant Russia a constitutional government. The prime minister, Rodzyanko, himself moderate reformer, repeatedly dared he tsar's rebuffs to place before him the rgent necessity for action. But Nicholas vas adamant. He seemed in these vital ays more like a drugged man, incapable f listening to anything but the empty, nsistent demands of the empress that he hould be strong and unyielding.

The Duma, which during the preceding ear had been the scene of many open rotests, reassembled on February 27, 1917, and its members met with a de-termination not to allow their assembly to be broken up until something real was lone. In Petrograd (to give the city the name bestowed on it when the Great War began) the food situation was growing daily more serious, and long queues of people waited outside the bakers' shops for bread. There was a disturbance in one of these waiting crowds and the police fired on the people. Within a few hours a general strike was declared in all factories, and all schools in the city. The police tried to put the people down, but soldiers began to take the side of the people and Cossacks fought mounted police. Big processions marched defiantly through the main thoroughfares. Policemen posted in houses and at critical points with machine guns fired on the crowds; but the moment had gone by when the people could be further terrorised.

On Monday, March 12, nearly the whole of the Petrograd troops, led by the Volhynian Guards regiment, came out on the side of the Revolution. The crowds now were beyond all control. They hunted down the police, and shot them, wherever they were found, like dogs. They opened prison doors and set the prisoners free. They captured arsenals and distributed arms. They burnt the headquarters of the political police, and when a few troops, loyal to the emperor, tried to resist them they were overwhelmed.

REVOLUTIONARIES ASSEMBLED BEFORE THE WINTER PALACE

A crisis was reached in Russian affairs early in 1917. The gravity of the food situation gave rise to a series of strikes and outbreaks of violence, while the defection of large numbers of the soldiery to the side of the people further complicated the problem facing the government, who vainly sought a solution by terrorism. Many military uniforms can be seen in this section of a vast mob outside the Winter Palace, Petrograd. Within a week a provisional government was proclaimed and with scarcely a protest the tsar acquiesced in the demand for his abdication.

Photo, E.N.A.

A. F. KERENSKY
On the outbreak of the Revolution Alexander Feodorovitch Kerensky became minister of justice in Prince Lvov's provisional government and in July premier of the coalition government. He fled after Lenin's coup d'état in November, 1917.

That same afternoon, the Duma, whose members had remained despite an order postponing their assembly, formed a provisional government with Rodzyanko the premier as temporary president. A great council of delegates from councils of workers' and peasants' deputies, formed in the different barracks and factories, met in the palace of the Duma that evening and resolved to support the new government. The tsar's own regiment, the Preobrazhenski, threw its cause in with the people, and the grand duke Cyril and the officers of the regiment placed themselves at the service of the new government.

The Social Democrats had been at first unwilling to join the government, thinking that it was too middle-class and aristocratic, but when, two days later, the names of the members of the new provisional government were announced, it was seen that Kerensky, a young and brilliant Social Revolutionist leader, had received permission of the workers to take the post of minister of justice in it. The same evening the councils of the workers gave it their conditional allegiance.

The main programme of the ne government was simple, its vital propos being the calling of a constituent assembl based on universal suffrage, soldiers ha ing civil rights. The new government depended on the army, and it was a sign of its weakness that the soldiers of th Petrograd garrison had secured as a retur for their adherence a promise that the should not be moved from the city Another step was taken with the army a a whole that in the end destroyed it a an effective military force. The council of the workers secured an order for th formation in every regiment of a com mittee composed of delegates of the rank and file which should be the real govern ing body of that regiment. To rule a regiment in war by a committee is as ma as it would be to seek to control a grea ship in a storm by singing hymns. The Bolsheviks, already watching their oppor tunity, knew this, and when later on the obtained power one of the first thing that they did was to abolish the committees and re-establish strict military control.

Main programme of Kerensky's governme

The emperor was at the front when news came to him of what was happening. He sought to send some troops under General Ivanov to Petrograd to suppress the revolution, but they were unable to reach the city. On March 15 two delegates of the provisional government met him at Pskov and demanded his abdication. He signed the decree dethroning himself with scarce a protest and named as his successor, not the tsarevitch, whose health was such that he could not live till manhood, but his brother, the grand duke Michael. The grand duke, however, said that he would not accept the throne until invited by the Constituent Assembly. The invitation never came and the Romanov dynasty joined the ranks of the rulers who have passed. The ex-tsar was sent to his palace at Tsarskoye Selo, outside Petrograd, as a prisoner at large.

The scenes that followed in Petrograd, in other Russian cities and throughout the country were amazing. The people felt that the shackles of generations had fallen off and that for the first time they were

:ee to speak as they pleased, write what hey pleased, do almost as they pleased. Public vengeance wreaked itself on some f the police, and from the country there ame news of peasant risings and of the laying of unpopular landowners. But the mount of internal violence was comparaively small. There was general rejoicing and freedom was the word of the hour. Subject states were set free. Poland was given its long-desired independence. New neasures were initiated for Finland, and even the Ukraine was granted a large neasure of autonomy. The provisional government was determined to keep on with the war against Germany and her associates and to remain true to its allies. But it was already clear that the Russian army had had enough of fighting.

Vital questions of social reform awaited solution. Theorists rejoiced when the death penalty was abolished even for traitors. A few months later the commander-in-chief began to enforce it in the army against deserters, despite the reformers, and the government had to sanction it. The peasants clamoured for complete ownership of the land. Prince Lvov, who became prime minister, tried to decentralise administration as much as possible. He resigned office in July and was succeeded by Kerensky, the Social Revolutionist. Much was expected from Kerensky, whose youth and eloquence had made him a popular figure. Of Kerensky's sincerity there can be no question, but he proved wholly inadequate to rule a great nation in such a time as this. The soldiers left their games to listen to him, cheered him to the echo as he spoke, and then, when he had gone, returned to their games. It needed a Cromwell to control new Russia drunk with the new wine of liberty, and Kerensky was no Cromwell.

The real enemies of the provisional government were not the tsarist forces, which already had almost disappeared, but the extreme revolutionists. The Bolsheviks, at that time a comparatively small group, were not satisfied with what was happening. They were not popular even among the workers, and were suspected on all sides of being German agents, working for German pay. But they set to work deliberately and systematically to undermine the provisional government. Their hands were immensely strengthened in March by the arrival of the Communist leader, Lenin, from Switzerland.

NICHOLAS II IN CAPTIVITY

Shortly after his abdication on March 15, 1917, the tsar was arrested, and with his family confined in the Imperial Palace at Tsarskoye Selo. A military escort kept observation upon his every movement indoors and about the grounds.

The return of Lenin and other extremists was made possible by the liberal policy of the new government. The exile system was swept away immediately tsardom was broken and old political offences wiped out. Men and women who had languished for years in the living tombs of Schlüsselburg or in the prison of Peter and Paul, in solitary confinement in cells where they were not allowed to raise their voices beyond a whisper, found their prison doors open and sunshine and freedom ahead. The revolutionists who had escaped to the capitals of Europe or to America could return to the streets of Petrograd in safety once more. Many of the exiles came back feeling no gratitude to the men who had set them free, but resolved to overthrow the whole basis of modern society. Lenin was their leader.

Lenin, the leader of the Bolsheviks, had lived during the Great War in Geneva, whence he had conducted a vigorous pacifist campaign, advocating the immediate laying down of arms by the workers of all nations and the ending of the war. The German secret service had already made use of his activities. When the Revolution broke out, it offered him and his friends a safe passage in a special train through Germany to Russia, and further offered to provide funds for conducting an anti-war campaign among the Russian people. These funds were actually sent into Russia through a Swedish banker. Lenin had no preference for Germany over the Allies and was opposed to the war on general principles; but he saw a chance here of using the resources of one capitalist country to help to destroy capitalism in another country, and he took advantage of it. He arrived in Petrograd in April, was given a big reception on his arrival, and at once started an active campaign against the provisional government.

Lenin returns to Russia

Nikolai Lenin, whose real name was Vladimir Ilyitch Ulianov (Lenin being a 'nom de révolution'), stands out without rival as the supreme figure of the Communist party. He was born in 1870 at Simbirsk, and was the son of a school inspector, being brought up in the ordinary surroundings of a middle-class family. As a schoolboy he was noted as bei studious, reliable and somewhat inclin to religion. His brother was hanged 1887 for participation in an attempt the life of Alexander III, and Lenin soo showed revolutionary tendencies. At th university of Kazan, where he studied, was suspended at the end of a month fo participating in a students' revolutionar movement. He succeeded, however, taking his law degree four years later, bu made no real effort to practise at the ba

He went to what was then still S Petersburg. Already a convinced Marxis and revolutionist, he came in contact wit some of the older revolutionary group there and plunged into secret illega propaganda, writing pamphlets, speakin at secret meetings and the like. He wa arrested, spent some time in prison an then went abroad to escape re-arrest.

He lived in London in poor lodgings in Bloomsbury, passing a large par of his time studying in the British Museum. Although able to read English, he never acquired a fluent speaking knowledge of the language. He wrot an important book, The Development o Capitalism in Russia, which won him a foremost place among Marxist economists. According to his disciple, Zinoviev, he spent fifteen hours a day in libraries and at books. He and some others published a paper, Iskra (The Spark), which became the real organ of Russian revolution. He developed under a quiet exterior a dominating and imperious personality. This element of his character caused him and his followers to revolt from the older leaders and to set up the Bolshevik party in London in 1903, with Lenin as its chief. He lived before the Great War mainly in London and in Paris, and after the war broke out, as already said, made Geneva his headquarters.

Lenin's lif in Londo

Shortly after Lenin reached Petrograd the second great figure of Communism arrived. Leon Trotsky (real name, Leiba Bronstein), son of a Jewish merchant in S. Russia, who had been exiled to the Arctic under tsarism, had made a spectacular escape and had more recently been working in Paris and New York as a journalist on a small Russian Jewish paper.

When Nicholas was dethroned, Trotsky orrowed money from his friends and set ut for Russia. At Halifax, Nova Scotia, he British authorities arrested him on hipboard as a firebrand and shut him up a camp at Amherst. He was released little later at the request of the provi-ional government and allowed to pro-eed to Europe. Trotsky had not up to his time been a Bolshevik, but had been ttempting to reconcile the two groups, he Bolsheviks and Mensheviks. At once, owever, he threw himself in with Lenin. 3old, picturesque, eloquent, he imme-liately made his power felt. He feared nothing and nobody. The story is told hat when the provisional government, orced by his attacks upon it, ordered his rrest, Trotsky waited for the soldiers to ome and take him, and then spoke to them n such a way that they cheered him, arried him around on their shoulders and afterwards—took him off to prison.

Members of the Lenin group

The immediate group around Lenin included a number of experienced revo-lutionary workers. His personal assistant was a young Russian Jew, Apfelbaum, formerly a bank clerk, who had taken the revolutionary name of Zinoviev, and who was to prove himself in the years ahead the cruellest and most extreme of all the Com-munist leaders. Then came Dzherzhinsky, a Pole, who had long been one of the secret organizers of revolution and who had been often imprisoned, only being set free when tsardom ended. Leon Kamenev, whose real name was Rosenfeld, was the son of an engineer in the Caucasus, and seemed more like a quiet, successful professional man than a maker of discords. Another equally strange figure was Leon Krassin, for long a prosperous engineer and chief manager in Russia for the great house of Siemens Schukert. There was a young, pale-faced, student-like figure, who might have been an artist, by name Lunacharsky, fresh from Paris. The most aristocratic member of all the group was Georges Chicherin, formerly a member of the tsarist diplomatic corps, who had thrown over family tradition and settled first in Berlin and then in London as a revolutionary organizer.

It will be noticed that all the revolu-tionary leaders so far mentioned were men of noble, professional or prosperous busi-ness families. The Russian Revolution, like the French, was planned not so much by the workers themselves as by men of the better educated classes who dominated the workers. Some working men, how-ever, stood out, such as Kalinin, the son of a peasant, who had spent many years in the Putilov engineering works in St. Petersburg. Later Kalinin was given office equivalent to that of president of the Republic, and he was regarded as one of the most kindly and sympathetic figures in his party. Schmidt, the leader of the trade unions, and Zverdlov, fresh from the aggressive unionism of the Ural workers, were two other noted men from the ranks of labour.

Programme of the Bolshevik leaders

The Bolsheviks organized committees in every factory, every regiment and almost every village to overthrow the govern-ment. They captured the Petrograd Soviet. A number of active revolutionary plotters arrived in Petrograd during the summer from America by way of the Trans-Siberian railway, and were given strategic posts. Every man had his rifle. In July, 1917, the Bolshevik leaders formu-lated their programme—immediate peace, the land for the peasants and the fac-tories for the workers. They preached class war, and by midsummer felt them-selves sufficiently strong to plan an armed demonstration at the capital. On July 16 they provoked an uprising, which for the moment seemed to threaten the existence of the government. But picked troops arriving from the front saved the situa-tion, and when the Volhynian regiment of the Guards, which had led the earlier revolutionary movement, came out against the Bolsheviks, it was clear that they had lost. Wholesale arrests followed. Trotsky was thrown into prison, and Lenin escaped into Finland. The prisons were full, and Kerensky threatened in an eloquent speech to institute a regime of 'blood and iron' against the traitors. But his severity ended in words.

The Bolshevik agitation continued in secret, and grew greater all the time on account of the discontent of the peasantry, the increasing weariness of the nation with the war and the weakness of the provisional government. General Kornilov, the commander-in-chief, was reported to be planning a coup d'état against the Republic itself, and the restoration of the imperial family. He and Kerensky were alleged to be plotting to betray the people. In October the Bolsheviks, who had grown greatly in strength, resolved to strike again. Lenin returned secretly to Petrograd; Trotsky and other leaders had been set at liberty by Kerensky. Their plan of campaign was most carefully drawn, so carefully that many people imagined at the time that the German general staff must have been responsible for it. Vital points were to be seized. The adheren of a large body of troops and sailors ha already been won. An All Russian Co gress of Soviets, the working class revol tionary organization, had been called i Petrograd for November 7.

It was expected that Kerensky, by th use of his troops, would try to scatter th gathering. Therefore, the Bolshevik centred themselves first on winning ove the garrison, particularly the machin gunners. The decision t attempt an armed rising wa made by the central com mittee of the Bolsheviks o October 28. A military re volutionary committee, at tached to the Petrogra Soviet, acted as the genera staff of revolt. It appointe commissars to all section of the Petrograd garrison

SOWING SEEDS OF REVOLUTION IN THE RUSSIAN ARMY

Control of the army was essential to the establishment of Bolshevism, and very early in their proceedings the Bolsheviks organized committees in every regiment to detach the troops from their loyalty. This photograph shows a revolutionary captain addressing the 56th regiment in Petrograd, where most of the garrison were won over by the beginning of November, 1917. Bolshevik troops were supplied with the badge shown above—a star with the design of a hammer and a plough.

Photo, Central News

nd secured the control of the distribution of all arms. When the men in ontrol of arsenals or the owners of rivate stocks of arms objected, the soldier ommittees controlling the regiments made heir authority felt. An extraordinary ituation existed. Kerensky's government was responsible for the country as whole, but the Petrograd Soviet, led by he Bolsheviks, really controlled, through ts commissars, a large part of the Petrograd garrison.

Throughout the city meetings were held mong the people urging revolution in the nost violent language, and the government was not strong enough to prevent hem. The Smolny Institute, formerly a chool for the daughters of nobles, had een taken over as the headquarters of he Petrograd Soviet and became the evolutionary centre. The regular staff of he army tried to retain control of the roops, but with many of the regiments t could do nothing. The very Volhynian egiment which had played a leading part n suppressing the revolt in July was now vith the Bolsheviks. On November 4 he Bolsheviks openly paraded the streets nd called for the downfall of Kerensky, none daring to stop them.

Fall and flight of Kerensky

By November 6 the revolutionists had nost of the garrison with them and had established a network of agencies spreading far beyond Petrograd. Their military revolutionary committee at the Smolny was now in permanent session. That evening Kerensky demanded the approval of the Provisional Assembly for suppressive measures against the Bolsheviks, but he had delayed too long.

On the morning of November 7 the cruiser Aurora, ordered by the Ministry of Marine to get under way and leave Petrograd, refused to obey. That same morning the Kerensky government seized the offices of the Soviet newspapers. The Revolutionary Committee sent the Volhynian regiment to re-open them, which it did. The cruiser Aurora came up the river and shelled the Winter Palace, the headquarters of Kerensky and the Admiralty. She was joined by the guns in the fortress of Peter and Paul across the Neva. Kerensky fled and in a few hours Petrograd was in the hands of the Bolsheviks.

The only people apparently who put up any fight were groups of military cadets, the Junkers, little more than schoolboys, and the regiment of women, one of the Battalions of Death formed in the last desperate struggle of free Russia. What happened to the women's battalion in the end is not quite clear. According to the Bolshevik account, the men just rushed the women, took away their arms and hustled them off. But, if some eyewitnesses are to be believed, the square in front of the Winter Palace ran blood, and the bodies of many of the women, shot in the fighting, lay around.

Fight for the Winter Palace

There came two dramatic moments. The All Russia Congress of Soviets was meeting that day, and in it were not only Bolsheviks but many Mensheviks and Socialists of other schools. Lenin and Trotsky made their appearance in the great Assembly while the sailors and Red guards were fighting in the streets. Then came the sound of guns, the guns of the Aurora firing into the Winter Palace. At once a protest was raised. 'You are political hypocrites,' cried one man, facing Lenin and his group. 'You have called us here to settle the question of power, and while we are debating it you are settling the question with your guns.'

Another man arose and declared that if their comrades in the Winter Palace were to die, they would die with them, and so a procession of politicians was formed, Mensheviks, Socialists, Anarchists and the like, and formed fours to march through the streets and die. A line of armed sailors stopped them. 'We have orders to allow no one to pass,' they said. 'We will go by! Shoot us if you like!' the men and women shouted back. The sailors hustled and threatened them. 'Let us go back,' said one of the delegates at last. 'Let us return to the Duma and discuss how to save the country.' And so the politicians marched back.

A few hours later there came another move. A group of Junkers, boy cadets, swept down in the morning on the Central Telephone Exchange and seized it. They had been ordered to do so by some of their adult leaders who were not themselves over eager to risk their skins. They were attacked by a furious crowd of the Reds, backed by armoured cars, and many were killed. This was the only real fighting in the capture of Petrograd.

In Moscow there was a fiercer conflict. Here the Junkers got together and put up a battle lasting for days. Some regular regiments held the Kremlin, the fortified palace castle of the tsars, and prolonged fighting followed. The Bolsheviks had big guns and, it was said, German gunners behind them. Some of these guns were placed in strategic posts and their shells made the position of Kerensky's followers impossible. They had to yield, and officers and Junkers were butchered ruthlessly.

Kerensky escaped from the Winter Palace and got in touch with forces, outside Petrograd, still loyal to the provisional government.

End of the Provisional Government

The 'Savage Division' of Cossacks, General Kornilov's finest fighting men, rallied to him. They advanced from the south and captured place after place, including Tsarskoye Selo and Gatchina. The revolutionists called on the Petrograd troops to proceed against them. Three regiments refused point blank. 'Let us try peaceful methods first,' their committees declared. The Bolshevik Revolutionary Committee hurried up all its forces, sailors from the fleet, Red Guards and volunteers. Large numbers of guns and machine guns were moved forward and for two days the Reds made ready. Then they opened their attack with a tremendous artillery barrage. Armoured cars advanced and the sailors and workers moved forward to the attack. The order was given for the Savage Division to retreat, and the retreat soon degenerated into a rout. Some of Kerensky's troops at Gatchina laid down their arms and surrendered. The provisional government was over.

The Reds had captured the government by a coup d'état, but their position was one of extraordinary difficulty. They had actually only taken by force two cities, Petrograd and Moscow. Lenin himself did not expect to be able to hold power for long. He thought that at the best he and his followers would repeat the experience of the Communards in Paris in 1871 and would be wiped out after a few weeks of daring experiment.

Russia was still at war with Germany and her allies; the Russian army lacked both the means and the will to resist a vigorous German advance, and it was anticipated in most quarters that Germany would force an offensive, occupy Petrograd and end Communism. Even should the Germans not do this, there were other military dangers. The general staff of the army was against the Reds and still had the command of considerable forces. The Petrograd garrison had gone with Lenin in the critical hours, but a few days hence it might equally turn against him. The Constituent Assembly, chosen from the whole nation, was soon to meet, and it was certain that the Bolsheviks would be in a minority in it. The Bolsheviks were only a small section of the revolutionists and the others could combine against them and overthrow them. The various trade unions and popular organizations, which had sprung to life immediately after the March uprising, were carefully united, had a central administration and controlled the means of production and of transit. They were none too friendly to Lenin. Hunger still prevailed in Petrograd, for the change of government had not brought more food.

Lenin set about his work coldly and deliberately, like a master chess player making his moves. The commander-in-chief of the army, General Duhokin, was summoned for a conference with a young lawyer officer, Lieutenant Krylenko, sent as representative of the Revolutionary Committee.

Lenin assumes control

Duhokin and Krylenko met at a side railway station, and one of Krylenko's followers shot and killed Duhokin, so that the general staff was robbed of its head. Krylenko was appointed the new leader of the army. It was necessary to maintain the old military machinery, but as quickly as possible one or two Communists were placed over each army commander, under the title of Red Commissars. The officer saw to military action; the comissars watched him day and night to ake sure that he did not play traitor. t the first sign of treachery they shot m. The soldier committees were olished as quickly as possible and placed by Communist military groups.

Lenin made no secret of the fact that he as establishing not a democratic governent but a revolutionary dictatorship. e and his chief followers formed themlves into an executive and administrative mmittee, with all power. For name ey chose, on the suggestion of Trotsky, Council of People's Commissars.' One of e first acts of the council, carried through hen Lenin was temporarily away, was abolish the death penalty for military serters. When Lenin returned and und what had been done, he was furious. otsky has described the scene. 'That madness,' Lenin repeated. 'How can e accomplish a revolution without shootg? Do you think you can settle with ur enemies if you disarm? What pressive measures have you then? nprisonment? Who pays any attention that in a time of bourgeois war, when ery party hopes for victory?'

The Constituent Assembly met on nuary 18, 1918. It was preceded by her popular congresses, where there ere many evidences of opposition to the Bolsheviks. The peasants were especially offended because the Bolshevik party as essentially composed of town workers d not of peasants. The Constituent ssembly was equally hostile; out of 703 embers, there were only 168 Bolsheviks. e Assembly met at eight in the morng and chose as its chairman a prominnt non-Bolshevik revolutionist, Victor hernov.. There was tremendous exciteent, for it was recognized that here as the great testing point between nin and the men of the other revoluonary groups. The Tauride Palace, the ene of the gathering, was packed. The lshevik leader Sverdlov presented a claration which the Soviet government manded should be adopted by the ssembly as its working basis. In this claration the Assembly was called upon pledge itself to 'support the Soviet rule and accept orders of the Council of People's Commissars.' It was evident from the first that the Assembly was fiercely hostile. After nearly sixteen hours' discussion, the Assembly rejected the declaration. Thereupon Sverdlov and the Bolsheviks withdrew and sailor guards soon after cleared out the Assembly by force. It never met again.

Meeting of the nstituent Assembly

Realizing their weakness, the Bolshevik leaders were anxious to reach some temporary compromise with their enemies. While the negotiations were in the air for peace with Germany, Trotsky saw British and American representatives and offered to continue on the side of the Allies in return for the recognition of the Soviet government, and for Allied assistance in renewing and reconstructing the railroads and communications of Russia. The Allies rejected the proposals, largely on the advice of the French general staff officers, who did not consider that the Bolsheviks could be of any possible service. Judged to-day, this seems an amazingly foolish decision. But it must be remembered that when it was made almost everyone on the spot believed that the Bolsheviks could not last at the most more than a few weeks.

Bolsheviks make peace with Germany

Bolshevik and German delegates met at Brest Litovsk to discuss terms of peace. Lenin had determined to end the war at any price. If necessary, he declared to his followers, he and they would retreat to the east to the Ural-Kuznesty basin, form a fresh republic there, and gradually recover the great cities of Russia. Trotsky, now foreign minister under the title of People's Commissar for Foreign Affairs, was in favour of renewing the war, or at any rate of threatening to renew it, in order to obtain better terms from the Germans. If this could not be done he wanted to end the war without making a formal peace. Lenin did not regard this as practical politics. 'What are we to do if General Hoffmann marches his troops against us?' he asked.

General Hoffmann, the German delegate, was haughty and contemptuous. The terms when presented were such that even Lenin recoiled. Most of Russia that had been gained since the days of Peter the

Great, including the Baltic provinces and Poland, was to go, and Germany was to be given all privileges for the economic exploitation of the country.

While the Bolshevik leaders were hesitating, a message was received from General Hoffmann's representative that the truce was over and war would begin again at once. There was nothing to do but to yield. Trotsky, still protesting that they should let the Germans attack them first before they yielded, was overborne and resigned his post as foreign minister. The Central powers had concluded a separate peace with the Ukraine and occupied large parts of the south with their troops.

The People's Commissars issued a number of remarkable political and economic decrees, changing the basis of Russian society. All newspapers criticising the Bolsheviks were suppressed although it was declared that this decree was of a temporary nature and would be revoked when normal conditions of public life were re-established. The free right of public meeting was ended. All local soviets were ordered to form a workers' militia, and this became the basis of the Red army, the future fighting revolutionary force. All unoccupied houses were taken over to be used for the homeless. One decree promised complete social insurance of wage workers and of the town and village poor. Another, issued by Lunacharsky, who had been appointed commissar for educa-

SCENE OF AN ABORTIVE DIPLOMATIC TRIUMPH FOR GERMANY

Brest Litovsk, in Russian Poland, was captured by the Germans in August, 1915, and here, in this house, the Germans received the Bolshevik delegates in December, 1917, to negotiate the treaty, signed March 3, 1918, which terminated hostilities. Representatives of the Central powers shown in the upper photograph included, from left to right, General Hoffman, Count Czernin, Talaat Pasha and Herr von Kuhlmann. The treaty was annulled by a proviso of the armistice of November 11, 1918.

Photo, Topical Press Agency

on, forecast a great :heme for popular instruc-on. The prohibition of :rong drink was con-nued. All classes and lass divisions, all class rivileges and limitations, ll titles and all denomina-ions of every rank were bolished, the one general itle being 'citizen of the Russian Republic.' All lass institutions of any ort with their property vere to be handed over to he local authorities, and he property and institu-ions of all nobles and of nerchant and middle-class organizations were to be aken also. The Com-nunists set out to fight eligion by every means in heir power.

UNIVERSAL LABOUR IN SOVIET RUSSIA

Compulsory work for all was a principle of communism to which the Bolsheviks gave early effect, gratifying their class prejudices by employing members of the fallen aristocracy in the hardest and most unsavoury tasks. In Petrograd, for example, delicately nurtured women could be seen helping in the scavenging of the streets.

Photo, Dr. L. Haden Guest

The economic policy of he Bolsheviks advanced rapidly. At irst Lenin seemed inclined to permit old business methods to continue under stricter state control. But it was soon letermined to seize every form of wealth and every means of production.

Appropriation of all property

All property of every kind, including the possessions not only of the Church and of the state but of private individuals, was, by a series of decrees, declared the property of the state. All business of every form was taken over. The system of private credit and banking was destroyed. At first people who had accounts at banks were permitted to withdraw small quantities of money. Soon this privilege was abolished. Insurance organizations came to an end. All private ownership of land was abolished and the use of the land was given to the peasants. All factories and workshops were placed under the administration of the committees of workers.

Shops of every kind were closed and their stocks expropriated. It was forbidden, under the heaviest penalties, for any person to own private reserves of food, and a system of universal rationing was established in the cities. People were divided into three groups, the first, including all the Communist officials and administrators, receiving an adequate supply; the second, the workers, a smaller share; and the third, the old intelligentsia and upper and middle classes, a starvation diet. Even this last was not fully issued, and soon there were wholesale deaths from hunger and disease.

Class war and the dictation of the working classes were made the foundation principles of the state. Only working men and women were given the right to vote, and the aristocracy, business men and members of religious orders were specifically excluded. The old courts of law were abolished, and 'people's tribunals' were established, which were to decide and sentence, where there were no specific decrees to guide them, 'according to the proletarian conscience.' The Communists became an inner group, guiding and controlling all private and public activities. Communist 'nests' were gradually formed in every factory, organization and regiment. 'Red guards,' the Communist militia from the factories, dragooned the people. They searched apartments wholesale for concealed stocks of food, and arrested or shot the owners when food was found. They 'expropriated' (that is, seized nominally for the state) everything they wanted.

One principle of Communism was the universal obligation to work. Gentlefolk were set to manual labour. Clever people got into government offices, where they idled royally. Harsh officials made the work of the old aristocracy as hard and disagreeable as possible. It was considered a rare joke to make an ex-countess clean lavatories or sweep the streets. Housing was rationed, and the family of a doctor or professor might find half a dozen factory workers sent to share their home. Universal labour did not increase production. It seemed rather to diminish it.

The capital of Russia was moved back from Petrograd to Moscow, the city that, by historic interest and geographical position, is the real heart of Muscovy. Moscow had been greatly damaged during the revolutionary fighting. After this was over the people had poured out from the slums and had occupied the palaces of the one-time rich, transforming them in turn into slums. The winter of 1917 and the spring and summer of 1918 was a time of much suffering and of great uncertainty. The Treaty of Brest Litovsk, however inevitable it had been, did much to damage the prestige of the People's Commissars. They knew that the mass of the members of other socialist organizations were watching a chance to overthrow them.

Then came a step which hardened, strengthened and revived the Bolshevik cause. Social Revolutionists made attempts on the lives of some of the leaders. Uritski and Volodarski, who had earned an evil name by their cruelty to their opponents in Petrograd, were shot and killed. A young Jewish woman, a Social Revolutionist, Dora Kaplan, shot and seriously wounded Lenin in the same city. The result of this was an outburst of popular indignation. Trotsky has described the result. 'In these tragic days the Revolution suffered an inward change. Its good nature gave way. The party steel received its last tempering. Firmness and, when necessary, ruthlessness grew out of it. At the front the political divisions struggled hand in hand with the shock troops and the tribunals to develop the power of the young army.'

An organization had been formed, soon after the revolution, well suited to be an instrument of terror, the Cheka, a picked force of Communist political police. It was built up on the lines of the old tsarist police. At the head was a very remarkable Polish revolutionist, Dzherzhinsky, a tall, blue-eyed fanatic, disinterested, wholly sincere, humane in his personal life, but relentless and remorseless

NIKOLAI LENIN, 'THE RED TSAR'

Vladimir Ilyitch Ulianov (1870–1924)—world-famous under his assumed name Nikolai Lenin—secured control of the government of Russia in November, 1917. In 1918 he transferred the government to Moscow and lived in the Kremlin closely guarded by Chinese mercenaries.

From Valeriu Marcu, 'Lenin,' Paul List Verlag, Leipzig

n his official capacity. Among his chief ssistants was a Lett, Jacob Peters, ormerly a tailor's presser in the East End f London, who had been placed on trial here for participation in the notorious Houndsditch Anarchist murders some ears before, but had been found not uilty. A number of Letts were enlisted n the new service, and Chinese who had een brought over to Russia during the reat War were used as its special troops. fter a time, however, these Chinese were isbanded and sent home again.

At the beginning the Che-ka was not xceptionally cruel. It carried out a ertain number of executions and imrisoned a number of suspects, but the otal of these was not excessive, considerg the vast area of disturbance. There ere signs that the rank and file of e revolutionary fighters regarded their aders as too hesitating over this matter killing. They were not to have reason complain much longer.

A MAN OF BLOOD

Felix Dzherzhinsky (1877–1926), a fanatical Polish revolutionary, was identified with the worst atrocities of the Red Terror inaugurated in 1918. As head of the Che-ka he was responsible for innumerable executions.

Photo, E.N.A.

Following the attempt on Lenin large ands of Reds marched through the reets of Moscow, Petrograd and elsehere, dragged prominent men of the old gime from their beds and butchered em or hanged them. The Soviet government deliberately resolved to strike terror to the hearts of its opponents. Thousands prominent men and women were rested as hostages, and numbers were ain. A campaign to incite the people to slaughter and violence was deliberately begun.

Jacob Peters, on behalf of the Che-ka, issued a proclamation that the crime against Lenin would be answered by a mass terror. 'All representatives of capital will be sent to forced labour and their property confiscated. Counter-revolutionaries will be exterminated.' 'Thousands of our enemies must pay for Uritski's death,' declared the Red Gazette. 'We

REVIEW OF THE MILITARY BRANCH OF THE CHE-KA IN MOSCOW

ranny has always forged a potent weapon for itself in a highly organized system of reliable secret lice, but seldom if ever has that weapon been used with more savage ruthlessness than in Russia the Soviet government, when in 1918 they inaugurated the Red Terror to exterminate the last unter-revolutionary. Their political police, the Che-ka, comprised both a civil and a military branch. This photograph shows a review of the latter in the Square, Moscow, early in 1928.

Photo, Planet News, Ltd.

In September, 1917, the imperial family was removed to Tobolsk and imprisoned in the Governo general's house, on the roof of which they are seen in the upper photograph. From left to rig the figures are, the grand duchesses Olga and Anastasia, the tsar, tsarevitch and grand duche Tatiana, with the grand duchess Marie standing behind. In April, 1918, they were transferred Ekaterinburg where, in the cellar shown below, they were all shot on the night of July 16–17.

LAST STATIONS ON THE IMPERIAL FAMILY'S JOURNEY TO THE GRAVE

must teach the bourgeoisie a bloody lesson.' The same paper, the organ of the Red army, on the day following the attempt, published an article, Blood for Blood, in which it said :

We will turn our hearts into steel, which we will temper in the fire of suffering and the blood of fighters for freedom. We will make our hearts cruel, hard and immovable, so that no mercy will enter them, and so that they will not quiver at the sight of a sea of enemy blood. We will let loose the floodgates of that sea. Without mercy, without sparing, we will kill our enemies in scores of hundreds. Let them be thousands, let them drown themselves in their own blood. For the blood of Lenin and Uritski, Zinoviev, and Volodarski, let there be floods of the blood of the bourgeois—more blood, as much as possible.

What happened all over the country during the next few months was terrible beyond words. In many cities big office buildings were taken in a convenient central position, were surrounded by special guards and were turned into houses of confinement and death. People who did not belong to the working classes were arrested by the tens of thousands. Often men and women, girls and young men, were packed in the same room, where they were left, some of them for weeks or months, till they were shot or died of disease. They were given no open trial, save in exceptional cases. Revolutionary tribunals, composed sometimes of soldiers, sometimes of groups of working men, sometimes of members of the Che-ka, decided their fate in secret. During the night guards would come to the door of each room, call out a certain number of the people by name and lead them away. The usual fashion was for the victims to be led down a passage way and suddenly to be shot behind the left ear with a heavy army revolver.

Horrors of the Red Terror

Sometimes a district would be surrounded and all the people in it arrested and left in prison for as long as the authorities pleased. Some visitors to the old prison in Kharkov in 1922 saw an old peasant woman crouched in the corner of a cell, looking a picture of such unutterable misery that they inquired about her. Investigation showed that two years before she had come into Kharkov from the country to sell some goods. While going through the streets she had passed some people who were marked down by the police for arrest. They seized her along with them, flung her into prison and forgot her.

The insanitary condition of these prisons, where, as a rule, there was little or no provision for the most primitive needs, caused outbreaks of epidemics among the prisoners. Far more died from disease and starvation than died from bullets. Some prisons earned a grim notoriety—Odessa, where the commandant loved to play with and kill his victims like a cat with a mouse, and Kharkov, where, when a rescuing army arrived, they found victims crucified on the floor, and the skins of men who had 'had their gloves taken off,' that is, had had their hands skinned while they were alive. In many of the prisons torture was freely employed to extract evidence. At the slightest suspicion of anti-revolutionary activity groups of prisoners, the higher the better, would be taken out to be shot.

The Red Terror horrified the world, but it succeeded in its main purpose. It stopped the campaign of assassination which had been planned by one group of the Social Revolutionists. It struck such fear into the hearts of the masses of the anti-Bolsheviks that they did not dare so much as whisper a word against the government. Trotsky said frankly that in war, military or civil, the one thing they must do was to destroy 'the will to resist' of their enemies. It is impossible to give exact figures of the number of deaths under the Red Terror, for no exact figures were kept. The authorities themselves did not trouble to retain the names of many of their victims. The total was certainly enormous.

Counter-revolution overwhelmed

Before the second revolution, Kerensky had sent the ex-tsar and his family to Tobolsk in Siberia. In the spring of 1918 Nicholas, the ex-empress and the grand duchess Marie were being moved to Ufa when, as their train was passing through Ekaterinburg, the heads of the local council of soldiers', workers' and peasants' deputies seized them and imprisoned them in a house in their city. A few weeks later the ex-tsar's other three daughters and the invalid tsarevitch joined them. They were kept close captives until July, when the local authorities, having failed to secure the permission of Moscow, shot the whole family in the cellar of the house where they were confined, and afterwards sought to destroy the bodies by burning and soaking the remnants in sulphuric acid.

The opponents of Communism were at first overwhelmed by the entire collapse of the fabric of society, but soon they began to revive. They found themselves hampered by differences that in the end were to destroy them. The Communists were united, while the anti-Communists were divided into many groups. Even those groups that were willing to work together for a time were torn by fundamental differences. Many of the old generals, who now came to the front as White (i.e. anti-Bolshevik) military leaders were at heart monarchists, who desired the restoration of the old economic and social system. There was a gulf between them and the Cadets, the constitutional reformers; there was a still greater gulf between the Cadets and the moderate Socialists. In Siberia the White military leaders were busy at the same time fighting the Communists and eliminating the anti-Communist reformers by the simple process of shooting their leaders and shoving their bodies through holes in the ice.

GENERAL DENIKIN

After the revolution of 1917 Denikin, here seen inspecting a tank corps, became chief-of-staff to General Alexeiev, on whose death in 1918 he succeeded to the command. Denikin's armies collapsed by the beginning of 1920.

Photo, J. Preston

Anti-Bolshevik Campaigns

The Allied powers maintained a loose connexion with the Bolsheviks for some months, to see what would happen. They felt that the Bolsheviks had betrayed them by declaring peace with Germany, and felt justified in working against them. The situation with the British was made immensely worse by the murder of a British official, Captain Cromie, in Moscow. Britain withdrew her nationals, maintained a blockade of the Russian ports, and gave men, money and munitions in abundance to aid the anti-Bolshevik cause.

The first definite fighting moves against the Bolsheviks came from the Cossacks of south-east Russia and from the Czecho-Slovak corps. The large numbers of Czecho-Slovak prisoners of war in Russia at the time of the first revolution made common cause with the Kerensky government and were armed and equipped by it as an independent unit. When the Bolsheviks took power, their relations with the Czecho-Slovaks grew strained, and in the end the Czechs moved against them, seized parts of the Trans-Siberian railway and drove the ill-trained Red guards off.

The Cossacks, under the leadership first of General Alexeiev and General Krasnov, and then of General Denikin, took control of much of the country to the south-east and south. The Germans, who had been sweeping over large parts of the southern country, tried to come to terms with them, but they would have nothing to do with their enemies. Under General Denikin, backed by Britain, a very considerable volunteer army was raised, which, between June and October, 1919, captured a number of cities, including Kharkov and Poltava, and expected to reach Moscow by November. Denikin, however, made the fatal mistake of attempting to restore the old regime of the nobles behind his lines. This alienated the peasantry, and in addition to the Bolsheviks on his front he had to fight the people in his rear. In the autumn of 1919 the Bolsheviks advanced against him, his men were defeated in fight after fight, and he was forced to retreat.

In the spring of 1920 General Wrangel took over control of Denikin's remnants and established himself in the Crimea, where the Whites thought their position secure, the approach from the mainland being covered by the supposed impregnable defences of Perekop. In the autumn of that year, however, the Reds attacked the fortress and after prolonged fighting captured it. They then advanced through the Crimea. Most of the wreck of Wrangel's army and large numbers of civilian refugees, 143,000 in all, escaped on Allied ships. Many could not escape. On these the Communists wreaked summary vengeance. Bela Kun, a well-known Hungarian revolutionist, who had been defeated in his own country, was sent down as commissar and had thousands of Russian officers shot.

From the west, General Judenich advanced in the spring of 1918 from Esthonia with 30,000 men known as the north-western volunteer army. He advanced so far that the capture of Petrograd seemed probable. Zinoviev, the Red leader, prepared to escape, but Trotsky, who had hurried up to the front from Moscow, took charge and ordered the Red army to advance, leading the way in person. They advanced with such strength that Judenich's forces were eliminated.

A serious effort, under British leadership, was made to start a counter-Bolshevik movement from Archangel. Large British, American, Canadian and other forces were landed along the northern coasts and occupied the country as far down as Breznik, being aided by considerable remnants of the old Russian army. In the end the Russian troops, won by Bolshevik propaganda, turned in many cases on their foreign allies, and the Allies had to withdraw to save themselves from being overwhelmed. There

Abortive results of Allies' intervention

GENERAL WRANGEL

Born at St. Petersburg in 1879, Baron Peter Wrangel served in the Russo-Japanese War and in the Great War. He succeeded Denikin in command of the anti-Bolshevik force in the Crimea, but was defeated in 1920.

was a tragic sequel. Some thousands of young Russians who had aided the British were arrested and massed on one of the islands close to Archangel. Here the Bolshevik guards turned machine guns on them and slew them to a man.

The greatest anti-Bolshevik military campaign was made from the east, where Admiral Kolchak, with the assistance of the five Allied powers, captured the whole of Siberia and carried his forces right into European Russia. There seemed a time when victory was certain. But here, too, the people turned against Kolchak. He found it impossible to hold the long line of the Trans-Siberian railway. After defeat at various points, his armies started a tragic retreat, one of the most terrible military disasters of modern times. The Czechs, who were with him, made the situation worse by the way in which they pushed their own forces through at the cost of many others. Thousands of refugees, civilian and military, froze to death. Tens of thousands perished of typhus. Admiral Kolchak took refuge with the Czechs. The Reds demanded his surrender, and the Czechs handed him over. Kolchak and his chief supporters were shot, and the expedition was completely broken. This remnant fell back upon Eastern Siberia, where, with the assistance of the Japanese, they held Vladivostok. In the end Vladivostok, too, had to be evacuated, and the Bolsheviks had secured all of old Russia.

The Bolshevik campaigns abroad had, however, not been so successful. There had been violent attempts at revolution in Finland and in the Baltic states, which were overcome after heavy fighting, and these countries secured their independence. There came war between Poland and Russia, and the Red guards advanced so far that the sound of their guns was heard in Warsaw itself. But the Polish staff, under French military leadership, drove back the attack, and Communist Russia had to make peace with the sacrifice of a considerable section of White Russia. The British boycott terminated, and a trade agreement was arrived at between Britain and Russia, from which at the time much was hoped. The German forces had withdrawn from South Russia, and Moscow ruled from the Pacific coast to Poland.

The civil war had been accompanied by hideous cruelties on both sides. It had devastated and ruined a large part of the country, and had checked every kind of moral, social and political progress. Large numbers of Russians who had no sympathy with Communism felt themselves bound to help their country when foreign troops invaded it to help the Whites. It was generally admitted afterwards that the Allied intervention to help the Whites was a mistake, not merely in that it meant the waste of hundreds of millions of money and of many lives, but also in that it strengthened the hands of the worst elements of Communism and tended to make the Communist leaders more extreme, merciless and unbending than before.

One acute problem facing the Bolshevik leaders was their relation to non-Communist revolutionary groups. Should they make themselves dictators of Russia alone or

MEN WHO HELD THE CONFIDENCE OF THE ARCH-BOLSHEVIK LENIN

Comrade Kamenev (right) joined the Communists in 1901, presently incurring exile to Siberia as one of the leaders of the Bolshevik movement. After the Revolution he became Lenin's right-hand man, although an advocate of more moderate methods in the official policy. Zinoviev (left) was also a leading member of the Bolshevik Central Committee ten years before the war and shared exile with Lenin. As president of the Third International he directed the Soviet's unofficial foreign policy.

Photos, General Photographic Agency and Central News

ead a constitutional movement in co-operation with others? Several of the leaders, including Kamenev, then editor of the Communist paper, Pravda, and Zinoviev, favoured co-operation, declaring that a constituent assembly must be called, or else they would have to 'form a purely Bolshevik government by means of political terror.' They attempted to force Lenin to follow their lead by resigning their places on the Central Committee of the Communist party. Lenin overwhelmed them, and in a few days they yielded, returning to work.

Henceforth the only road to office or power in Russia was by strict adherence to Communism. The whole machinery of state fell into the hands of the Communist party. The other groups that had helped to make the revolution protested and struggled, but in vain, for Lenin had the power. From protest, the rival groups turned to struggle. Before a year was over multitudes of the old allies of the Bolsheviks had been sent to prison or had already been shot. 'I was twenty years a captive of the tsar because I sought liberty,' one Socialist leader said from his cell. 'Am I now beginning another twenty years in prison, held by the Communists, because I still seek liberty?'

A MASTER BUILDER OF THE REVOLUTION

Formerly a journalist by profession, Lev Davidovitch Trotsky formed the Bolshevik Revolutionary Committee that overthrew Kerensky in 1917. In the government that he established he became commissar for foreign affairs with Lenin as president. Coming into conflict with Stalin, after Lenin's death, he was disciplined and exiled. Later, he found refuge in Constantinople.

This war against all other political groups led logically to the revival of the methods of oppression employed by tsarism. The exile system was, in the end, restored, and the political police were given power to arrest, imprison and send into exile—without open trial—any person objectionable to them. Great concentration camps were established, in Solovetzky Island and elsewhere, where tens of thousands of men and women supposed to be unsympathetic to the government were kept under penal conditions. Old Social Revolutionists and Anarchists, as a rule, were granted some of the usual privileges of political prisoners, but the mass of exiles were treated as convicts.

Lenin began to build up his machine of government. The first stage was military dictatorship. Russia was divided into four federal republics, each with its groups of soviets (committees) which administered all local matters. The affairs of Russia generally were controlled by the Central Executive Committee of the Communist party sitting in Moscow, which ruled through the Council of People's Commissars, themselves members of the Executive Committee. The commissars divided the work of the state into departments. Lenin was president and leader; Trotsky had taken over the work of national defence, Lunacharsky education and Chicherin foreign affairs. The commissars were assisted by two bodies, the Che-ka and the Red army.

The old army had crumpled up after the peace of Brest Litovsk. The Red guards had then been developed into a revolutionary army, the remnants of the old army being amalgamated with them. Old army officers were compelled to serve, under threat of death, and were kept faithful by the intimation that their families would be regarded as hostages for their good behaviour. Service in the army was made compulsory for the working classes. The Red army was at first poorly clad, badly equipped and ill disciplined ; gradually the military genius of Trotsky built up a great and powerful military organization.

It must not be imagined that this orderly planning of the administration of the state into well defined departments bore any close relation to actual conditions. The departments existed, but on paper. In practice there was the wildest confusion. Each section overlapped the others. The leaders would spend half their days and nights in committees, furiously debating fundamental principles. Attempts to introduce rules of procedure produced such complications that the simplest orders often took weeks to receive necessary signatures. Every commissar had to do a thousand things himself that subordinates should have done, because there was no efficient staff organization. Routine, delay, confusion were universal.

Later on, a much more elaborate constitution was adopted, under which Russia became a part of the Union of Socialist Soviet Republics, a world-state organization. This union is divided into four main groups of republics, Russia, White Russia, Ukrainia and Transcaucasia, which in turn are divided into united smaller states. Each state has its series of local administrative bodies, soviets, which may be compared to village councils, borough and rural district councils and county councils, and a state gathering chosen from the urban and county councils. These are elected by workers only, the workers' vote being taken in the mass, delegates being chosen in open assembly. Non-workers,

COMMANDER TROTSKY REVIEWS A LETTISH REGIMENT AT MOSCOW

At the beginning of the Great War many Letts were serving in the Russian army and in June, 1915, they were made into a separate force under Lettish officers. Although after the armistice of 1918 Latvia became an independent republic, a large number of Lettish troops remained in the Russian service. This photograph shows Trotsky reviewing one such regiment at Moscow in 1919. A number of Letts were employed in the Communist political police force known as the Che-ka.

erchants, traders, people living on nearned incomes and ministers of religion nd old police officials are not allowed) vote. The votes of peasants count or less than those of town workers, to ompensate for the overwhelming voice easants would otherwise have.

A monster congress—it cannot be called parliament—numbering many thousands, neets each year and agrees to the choice f the All Russia Central Executive Committee of between three and four undred, which meets three times a year, nd can be described as the Russian parliament. This congress elects administrative committees and the Council of People's Commissars, who carry on the outine administration of the state and have very extensive powers of legislating by decree.

The Council of People's Commissars consists of leaders of the Communist party. The ultimate control of the state rests not with the elected bodies, but with the Communist party. Numbering about 600,000 members, it has its committee, one small central group in Moscow, which says the final word on all affairs of state, and local committees in every district. It stands as a firmly established unit behind every organization, and nothing can be done without its consent and co-operation.

Communists in Supreme Control

The plan of the open election of delegates to the soviets meant at first that no man dared to propose any other candidate but those of the Communist party. Gradually, however, it has been found that, both at the elections and at the congress, people are beginning to recover their courage and to be more free in criticism and denunciation. The Communist government has created an electoral machine which, under future developments, may prove a real organ of the national will.

The Communists had won great military and political success. They had kept Russia and most of Siberia united. The Baltic states, Finland and Poland had, it is true, gone, as they were bound to go. But they were in no sense part of Russia, except by former conquest. Bessarabia had also been occupied and was held by the Rumanians, who claimed that this was part of their land. The Japanese and the Whites still occupied parts of Eastern Siberia, but it was already clear that they could not remain there long. For the rest, from the Polish frontier to far beyond Lake Baikal, and from the Arctic Circle to central Asia and to the Caucasus and Crimea, the Communists had established absolute rule. Their enemies had been not merely defeated, but crushed, demoralised and disheartened. The leaders of the opposition Socialist groups were nearly all dead or in prison. The Red Terror was nominally over and military communism at an end, although the real terror exercised by the Che-ka still continued.

But economically and socially their rule had been an equally complete failure. The country was a ruin. Industry was paralysed and agriculture had declined amazingly. The cities were most of them more like mortuaries than the homes of living men. The streets of great capitals like Moscow and Petrograd, four years before bright and cheerful, with throngs of well-dressed and prosperous people, with gay restaurants and bright shops, were now sombre centres of gloom, the shops and restaurants closed—save for an occasional hairdresser or government store—many houses in ruins, the factories operating feebly, the people ill-dressed, cold and hungry. The main centres of activity were the government offices. These abounded, and hundreds of thousands of men and women were occupied in doing work that might have been done by hundreds. The clerks were so cold, for there was little or no fuel, that they could scarcely fumble over the papers that they held; they were so weak from lack of food that they could not think what they were doing; and bureaucratic details had been developed to such an extent that the most ordinary decisions often took months to make.

Economic and Social Disaster

The prisons were full, so full that in many cases the gaolers had forgotten the names or the crimes of many of the people who packed their cells. Starvation was taking its heavy toll inside the gaols. Official returns showed that in the prison of Ufa, in three months and a half, out of a thousand prisoners 414 had died, 169 from hunger and 245 from other causes.

Typhus was making its appearance everywhere, and there were many signs of coming famine. The typhus was due to the conditions of dirt, neglect and hunger throughout the land. Soap was a rarity; cleanliness was impossible. Vermin multiplied because there was no way of killing them. In Moscow almost every house, including the office of Trotsky himself, was overrun by great rats. Walking down the streets at night time, one would see monster processions of rats crossing the road, rats that were breeding unchecked in the warehouses where the Communist authorities had closed and sealed the goods that they had expropriated. The doctors had no medicines, no dainty foods, not even the simplest appliances. The hospitals lacked anaesthetics, bandages, surgical instruments and medicines of all kinds. The official drug stores were open, but their shelves usually empty.

The ruin of industry was complete. Thi ruin had been encouraged by the blockad of Russia, but its real cause went deeper The working men had shot or driven ou their foremen, their technicians and thei managers, but they were not capable o administering their own concerns, even i they had abundant supplies of raw materia available. There was little or no discipline In great engineering shops, equipped wit the finest plant, men would take at wil whatever parts they wanted from any machine they could find to re-equip their own machine, with the result that the most modern plants soon became wrecks. In some cases the workmen for sheer devilry burnt and destroyed their own factories.

UNDER BOLSHEVIK RULE IN PETROGRAD

The distress prevalent in many Russian cities strikingly testified to the economic failure of the Bolshevik government. In Petrograd many cafés fell, like this one (top), into dilapidation. Provisions made for the population's food supply proved inadequate. Below: a bread queue.

Photos, Dr. L. Haden Guest

The Communist leaders were trying to check this by establishing a system of state control over the factories, but this was being fought bitterly by the men. Even when a factory was being run by a conscientious group of workers they found themselves hampered in every way by inept and impossible regulations. In four years the number of factories through Soviet Russia had declined two-fifths; the number of workmen had fallen by over 75 per cent. and the quantity of goods produced had fallen

) a contemptible total. In agriculture ie decline was equally marked. The rea of cultivated land was only one alf in 1921 what it was before the war. he number of horses had declined from 5,000,000 to 10,000,000.

Not only were private individuals :arving, but the state could not obtain ifficient funds to carry on public affairs. ommunism had deliberately destroyed :ate credit; but it found that a working :ate cannot dispense with credit any more ian a working peasant can. Since all rdinary forms of wealth had been bolished, there was nothing left for the :ate to tax, and so it lacked funds to ay the most necessary expenses. State nterprises, in nearly every case, resulted ot in gain but in heavy loss. The state rinting presses could turn out paper ioney to any extent, but the more they irned out, the less became its value. The ominal value of the rouble was 2s., or en to the £ sterling; in the autumn of 921 the rate of exchange was 300,000) the £; fifteen months later it had become 50,000,000 to the £.

Still more significant, some of the lasses that had led in creating the evolution were now the fiercest critics of the new regime. The peasants, who had been won to Communism by the promise of the land, vere seething with discontent, and there vere serious uprisings in various provinces. The sailors of the Baltic fleet, vho had ensured the defeat of the provincial government when the Aurora helled the Winter Palace, were now beginning to ally themselves with the other ide. They had imagined themselves to e the liberators of Russia, and so long s they could be kept apart from the masses f the people they continued to think so. 3ut with the conclusion of the actual ghting they had been given leave to visit heir homes in different country parts, nd there, to their amazement, they found hat they were considered not the liberators ut the enslavers of their land.

ronstadt sailors' discontent

In February, 1921, there were great trikes in Petrograd factories due to the old and hunger of the people. The ironstadt sailors, when they heard this, expressed their loud sympathy with the strikers. They sent a deputation to Petrograd to investigate conditions. Their committee drew up a report of the most appalling character, showing that corruption, starvation and oppression prevailed throughout the city. They drew up a series of demands and presented them to the Petrograd Soviet. The main points were:

1. Elections by secret ballot after free electioneering.
2. Freedom of speech and press for other revolutionary groups, for workers and peasants and for labour and peasant organizations.
3. Liberation of all working class political prisoners, and the investigation by a commission of the cases of those held in prisons and concentration camps.
4. Equal rations for all.
5. The abolition of separate Communist fighting units and 'nests.'
6. Freedom of action for peasants so long as they did not employ hired labour, and freedom for the individual to produce by his own efforts.

The Communist authorities at once denounced these Kronstadt sailors as the victims of White agitators. Prominent Communist leaders came to a meeting of the Petrograd Soviet and vilified the sailors as traitors, and the Soviet passed a resolution that the sailors should surrender or be wiped out. Trotsky had been expected to speak at this meeting, but he was otherwise engaged, preparing his ships and artillery for action. The sailors refused to submit, and orders were given to attack them. There was much unrest among the Red troops at Petrograd over this order and a number of soldiers refused to obey. They were at once shot. All the sailors of the port were disarmed and sent to distant stations. Fighting was begun on March 10, and on March 17, 1921, Kronstadt was captured by assault and its garrison slaughtered in wholesale fashion. Those who were killed were happy, for those who were spared were sent to living death in prison camps in the Arctic.

The final blow was the refusal of the peasants to cultivate their lands. The state took all the crops that the peasants grew away from them, allowing them sufficient for their own needs and giving

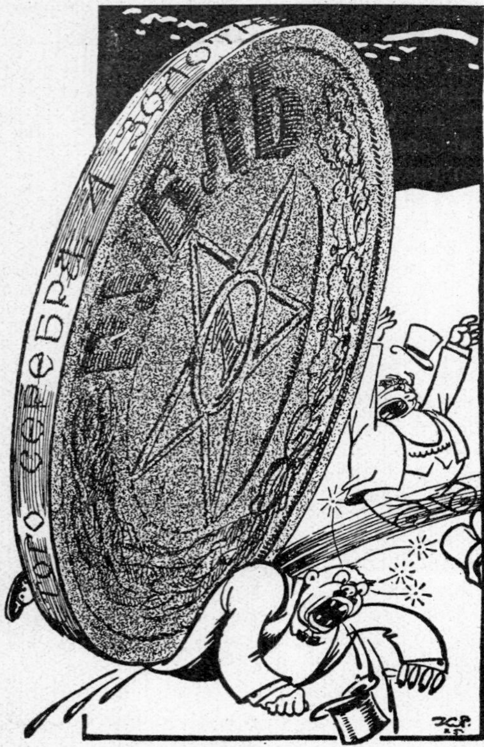

'NEP ECONOMICS'

The right to resume private trade was restored to Communist Russia by the New Economic Policy, commonly called Nep, which Lenin instituted in 1921. Its triumphant progress is the subject of this Russian caricature.

From Fülöp-Miller, 'The Mind and Face of Bolshevism,' G. P. Putnam's Sons

them in theory supplies of manufactured goods from the towns. In practice the peasants were having everything taken from them and receiving nothing. They responded by growing just sufficient for their own needs, and no more. Starvation threatened the whole country.

At this stage Lenin called a halt. The menace of famine was coming daily closer. The regime of relentless oppression could not go much farther. In the summer of 1921 Lenin compelled the Communist party to modify its policy and to abandon strict Communism. The New Economic Policy (popularly known as Nep) was instituted. Under this policy farmers and peasants were given the right to deal in their own products; private trade was re-permitted; the system of universal rationing was abandoned; payment by results was restored in factories; and the former owners of small factories were encouraged to take back their old enterprises and to manage them independently. The state proposed still to keep all public enterprises and great industries in its hands.

Lenin sent out a twofold invitation to the world, for foreign capitalists to co-operate in developing the latent resources of Russia, and for foreign nations to help to relieve the coming famine. The first invitation received a meagre response. Britain, the United States, France and Germany had invested hundreds of millions of pounds in Russian enterprises and loans in the years before the revolution. Britain had led the way in the industrial expansion of Russia, largely through old firms of English merchants who extended wide credit to Russian traders. The British had also promoted many great mining and textile enterprises. French peasants had sunk their savings in Russian loans. America, through the National City Bank of New York and various insurance companies, had sunk much money in Russia. All these investments and enterprises had been confiscated by the Soviet government. It had ignored and repudiated the old imperial and municipal foreign loans. It had seized mines, factories and warehouses owned by foreigners and repudiated private as well as public debts.

Problems raised by debt repudiation

The immediate demand of the great powers, backed by the international financiers, was that the Soviet government should recognize the old debts of Russia before seeking fresh credits. They did not ask that these debts should be paid immediately, well knowing that that was impossible. The Communist leaders could not, without betraying their Marxist creed, formally recognize old debts, but they suggested arrangements by which the foreign countries would obtain returns compensating them to some extent for their old losses. Krassin, who had now become the commissar for foreign trade, was especially active in seeking such a middle course. The Communist authorities declared that, while repudiating the old debts, they would meet all liabilities they incurred; and this they did. A few foreign firms e-entered the Russian market, but enerally their experiences were not satis-actory either to themselves or to the ommunist government.

The appeal for humanitarian relief truck a more responsive chord. Dr. Jansen headed one great scheme, backed y the League of Nations. The British reated their organization, and the Ameri-ans responded in wholesale fashion. The merican Relief Administration, a semi-ublic body, was organized by Hoover on he scale and with the resources of a lepartment of state. The administration n Russia was placed under the direction of a prominent officer in the United States rmy, Colonel Haskall. A large staff of icked men, mostly army officers and ngineers, was brought in. The A.R.A., vith its own fleet of ships, with scores of nillions of dollars behind it, and with an rganization military in its discipline and cientific in its arrangements, set to work rom Odessa and the Crimea in the south o away beyond Petrograd in the north, nd from the Urals to the Polish border.

Difficulties of Famine Relief

The relief agents found themselves con-ronted by an appalling task. The railroads of the country had almost completely broken down. The famine had already reached a stage where large communities, especially around the Volga, were confronted with absolute starvation. The economic system of Communism elped to make the famine much more evere than it otherwise would have been. In ordinary times, most peasants in the famine-stricken areas would have had reserves of grain and fodder to carry them over many months, for the Russian peasant stores his grain as others keep their money in a bank. But all reserves of food which had not been destroyed by civil war had been expropriated by the Communist government. Much of the grain from the peasants had been wasted by official mismanagement. When the first American relief agents reached Odessa they found people lying dying in the streets, scarce able to move, dying of hunger. When they traversed the villages of the steppes, they found a land like iron, with the very grass dead, and with even the camels—which are supposed to be able to get a living from nothing—dying. Cities like Samara and Buzuluk were overwhelmed by armies of refugees from the villages, starving to death by the many hundreds. An epidemic of typhus accompanied the famine.

In most other countries an experience such as this, fostered, as everyone knew that it was fostered, by the incapacity of the government, would have meant the overthrow of the ruling power. But Russia had had enough of revolution. All the old leaders capable of stirring up revolution had been killed or were in prison or exile. There was no alternative to the Communist government, and the Communist government survived.

Beginnings of economic revival

Meanwhile, the New Economic Policy was beginning to make its effects felt. Dzherzhinsky brought his great executive ability to the task of re-organizing and re-equipping the railroads. Shops re-opened in the great cities; restaurants, some of them of a sumptuous character, revived, and life became more normal. The Soviet government wisely reorganized its internal finances, and in place of the rouble, which had now sunk too low even for contempt, it established a new currency, the 'chervonitz,' based on a gold reserve. This reform was carried out very successfully. The value of the chervonitz was maintained in foreign markets at or near par.

The struggle over famine relief afforded the authorities an excuse to intensify the war upon organized religion. They demanded that the churches should surrender their selfish treasures, supposed to be of incalculable value, for famine relief. Patriarch Tikhon and the leaders of the Church, while declaring that they were willing to make sacrifices and help all that they could, maintained that church treasures were not theirs to surrender. A large number of church folk, including the patriarch, were arrested. Benjamin, the archbishop of Petrograd, a kindly and sincere prelate, was brought to trial for refusing to obey the government's order, and was sentenced to death and shot. All over the country men and women, priests and church workers, were sent to death or to long terms of imprisonment. Parties of soldiers raided the churches. It was soon found, however, that the treasures were worth a mere fraction of what had been expected, and actual money obtained was comparatively little. But the issue served its purpose in stirring up a campaign among the working classes against the Church.

The Russian Church was also being attacked in two other ways. A group of reforming churchmen, including Archbishop Antonin, the archbishop of Nijni-Novgorod and Vvedensky, an eloquent and ambitious Petrograd incumbent, promoted a new movement, the 'Living Church,' which was to displace the patriarch and the older prelates. The Living Church was strongly supported by the Communist leaders, who saw here a chance to disrupt the religious life of the country. Its leaders summoned a council of the Church, and by all manner of political manipulation excluded the majority. They forced the deposition of the patriarch Tikhon, and made themselves the new governing body. With the support of Communist administration, they seized great cathedrals and churches all over the land.

PATRIARCH TIKHON

The Soviet government's demand for a surrender of the Church's treasures was met by an implacable refusal from Tikhon, the patriarch of Moscow and all Russia, who was thereupon arrested. His deposition was enforced by the 'Living Church.'

Photo, E.N.A.

With much of the theory of the Living Church it is impossible not to feel sympathy. But in practice the leaders proved themselves the tools of the Communists for attacking and weakening religion. Their campaign failed to influence the mass of the people, who would have nothing to do with them. To them the old patriarch was still their father in God. The few churches left to the followers of the patriarch were crowded with worshippers, while the new were mostly empty. When Tikhon was released from imprisonment, having agreed to submit in temporal matters to the Soviet government, he was received everywhere as saint and hero.

Coupled with the movement of the Living Church to disrupt religion, came the violent attack of working-class and Communist organizations upon all religion.

Organized attack upon all religion

A cleverly illustrated paper, Besbozhnik ('Without God') was widely circulated under official auspices. It contained the bitterest attacks upon all that Christians hold most sacred. The decrees against religion were being more strictly administered. It was now illegal to give class teaching in religion to young people under the age of eighteen. The Salvation Army, which had established itself on a small scale immediately after the first revolution, was suppressed. A group of leaders of the great Catholic Church, including Archbishop Zepliak and Archdeacon Budkevitch, were brought to trial in Moscow for offences against the religious laws of the state. Zepliak and Budkevitch were sentenced to death and the others to long terms of imprisonment. It was at first the intention of the Moscow authorities not to execute the death sentence, but their anger was aroused by strongly worded protests from abroad, particularly by an injudiciously violent protest from Poland. Budkevitch was shot, and the archbishop sent to solitary confinement. The judicial murder of Budkevitch did Communism great harm in the eyes of the rest of the world.

The campaign against the opposition Socialist groups, which had terminated in ieir complete oppression, had its after-ath in the open trial of thirty-six Social evolutionist leaders, who had been kept r years in prison. Everything was done give the affair the air of a state remony, and to convict the Social evolutionists of having conspired against e Russian people. Among the leaders ought to trial were Gotz, who had spent n years in prison under tsarism, the volutionist Domskoy, and others equally mous. A few of the prisoners sub-itted before the trial and turned against eir comrades. The main body assumed a attitude of defiance, refusing to admit e right of the Bolsheviks to try them the possibility of their obtaining justice efore a Bolshevik court.

The Socialists of Europe had sent andervelde, the Belgian Socialist leader, help to defend them. Vandervelde und his position impossible, and after few days retired. The prisoners took very possible opportunity to interrupt e court and to defy it. 'I am com-letely indifferent about the sentence ou will pass on me,' said one of them, erusov by name. 'It has already ctually been fixed by the Central Com-ittee of your party. I despise it.' 'You an kill men,' said Gerstin, 'but you are owerless to annihilate ideas with bullets nd bayonets.' The Communist authorities organized working-class demonstrations in the streets against the prisoners, nd one night a crowd of Communists urst into the court, stormed the plat-orm where the trial was taking place, nd seemed likely to lynch the prisoners. welve were sentenced to death, but heir sentences were modified to imprison-ment in strict isolation, subject to the ood behaviour of other Social Revolu-ionists, who were warned that if they enewed their activities the sentence of eath on their leaders would be executed.

ocial Revolutionists efy the Communists

Lenin, who had forced his party into nore moderate courses, was stricken early n 1923 with serious illness and had o loosen his grip on the machinery of tate. The opportunity was seized by the nore extreme elements in the party to ring about a return to more active and aggressive Communism. In this, Zinoviev, Lenin's old personal assistant, played a leading part and was assisted very largely by another rapidly emerging figure, Stalin, the secretary of the Russian Communist party. Stalin, a young, forceful Georgian, had by skilled political organization grasped the whole machinery of the party. He appointed his delegates as heads of the different groups of Communists in the country, forcing the local authorities to accept them. He maintained rigid discipline, so rigid that many murmurs were heard. A group of Communists, headed by Trotsky, demanded that the party government should be more really representative, and that peasants should have their interests more carefully studied. During the summer of 1923 the underground movements of the struggle could be heard, but for a time outward signs of it were suppressed so far as possible, largely because of respect for Lenin, who was then evidently nearing his end.

A SOVIET DICTATOR

Josef Vissarionovitch Stalin, born of peasant stock in 1879, became secretary of the executive committee of the Communists. As a Bolshevik leader he ousted Trotsky's party from power in 1927 and made himself virtual dictator.

Photo, E.N.A.

Nothing that skill or care could do was spared to prolong Lenin's life. The greatest physicians of Europe were summoned to his bedside. He was kept as far as possible from every trouble and anxiety. But overwork and the fierce struggles of his earlier life were now exacting their penalty. Paralysis had come. On January 21, 1924, Lenin passed away at his country home about thirty miles from Moscow. His body was brought amid wide-spread signs of national grief to Moscow and was given a public burial in the Red Square a few days later.

The scenes that accompanied the lying-in-state and the funeral were remarkable evidences of the hold this man had secured on the soul of the Russian people. The weather in Moscow was appallingly cold, 20° F. below zero. The body lay in sta for days in the House of the Unions, fine public building formerly the Noble Club. Hundreds of thousands of peop poured in from all parts, standing in tl streets for hours, waiting their turn to fi past the corpse. On the day of the funer half a million men and women paraded tl streets for hours. The cold had no become still more intense, and thousanc of victims of frostbite had to be admitte to the hospitals. But no cold coul restrain the wave of emotion. It was funeral such as few emperors have had.

RUSSIA'S GRIEF FOR HER LOST LEADER

Remarkable proof of Lenin's great power over the Russian people was shown by the surging crowds who waited for hours in the intense cold that they might have one last glimpse of their hero lying in state in Moscow, seen in this excellent wood-cut. His great mausoleum stands in front of the Kremlin.

From Fülöp-Miller, 'The Mind and Face of Bolshevism,' Putnam's Sons

The name of Petrograd was altered t Leningrad. Leninism became semi-religious cult. The bod of the leader was preserve and later on placed in a hal underground pantheon in th Red Square. This was visite daily by processions of peopl like the shrines of the grea saints of old.

Trotsky's friends claime that Lenin, in his last illness wrote a letter to the party t be read at their annual con ference, a letter suppressed b Stalin and his friends, in whicl he declared that Trotsky, i spite of his too great self-con fidence, was a devoted revolu tionist and the outstandin member of the Central Com mittee. He further, they said criticised Stalin as concentrat ing too much power in hi own hands and being to brutal, and dismissed Zinovie and Kamenev contemptuously

One figure was conspicuou for its absence at the cere monies, Lenin's greatest col league, Trotsky. During th past few weeks he had flung himself in revolt against th men who were controlling th Communist machine. Bu the machine was stronger than even this man. He had broken down in health at the most critical hour, and had been ordered to the Crimea by his medical advisers. He had

:en forced to resign his control of the my, and a campaign of vilification had :en started against him by the party aders. All day long during the funeral :ople had expected Trotsky, the man who d borne with Lenin the supreme task of aking the revolution, to return, but no rotsky arrived. Instead came a message grief and sorrow from a railroad station 1 his way south.

With Lenin dead, the reactionaries ithin the Communist party had all their vn way. A large number of members of 1e party who had set themselves to ppose the supremacy of Stalin were xiled or turned out of the ranks of the arty. A series of decrees was passed odifying the New Economic Policy. rivate trade was once more to be wiped ut, this time by high taxes, and strict ommunism was to come in again.

The attempt which was made during 1e summer and autumn of 1924 was a omplete failure. Private traders, it is :ue, were largely compelled to close their oors, and private enterprise was once 1ore heavily penalised. In many cities o per cent. of the private shops had to close. But the Communist machine was incapable of taking the place of the private rader. From all parts of the country here arose bitter complaints from the easants that they could not buy manuactured goods that they required. The easants, who had revived their activiies under the New Economic Policy, egan to slow down again, and in the utumn of 1924 the government found tself faced by a serious economic situation.)nce more the sporadic and spasmodic trike of the peasants all over the country 1ad defeated the plans of the politicians.

Gravity of the :onomic situation

Trotsky returned to Moscow in the ummer of 1924, still under the deep dis)leasure of the authorities. That autumn 1e had once more to go south for his 1ealth, and during the winter of 1924–25)ne group of extreme Communists would ave had him shot as a disturber of party peace. Meanwhile economic events had been moving rapidly. Stalin, who a year before had seemed to incline towards rigid Communism, now changed his tactics, after the fashion of Lenin, and became the champion of more moderate courses. In this he was supported by many of the old leaders. Trotsky, on the other hand, allied himself with his old enemy Zinoviev as a champion of stricter Communism. They tried to organize the anti-Stalin forces; but their plans were exposed, they were brought to trial within the ranks of the party, and Zinoviev was deprived of his position as head of the international Communist party and of the Leningrad Soviet. Trotsky was also disciplined.

Stalin was now endeavouring to place Russia on a sounder economic foundation. Greater facilities were again extended to all private traders, and everything was done to encourage foreign capitalists to enter the country. The machinery of state had been greatly improved since the early days of the Revolution. Officials had learnt the routine business, and many mistaken methods had been rectified. But any attempt by Stalin to encourage the peasant to increase his holdings and his output was at once regarded by the extremists as playing into the hands of the rich against the poor. Every effort to control the workers so as to place them under greater discipline and make them produce more met with very real opposition. The masses of the people had been systematically taught to hate the merchant and the bourgeoisie, and so when they found the government to some extent encouraging the merchants, real uneasiness was manifest, uneasiness which Trotsky, Zinoviev and their friends were quick to turn to advantage. They went so far during the summer of 1926 that they were brought to public trial within the party and still further disgraced, Zinoviev being deprived of place and power and removed from the leadership of the Communist International.

Extremists resist moderate measures

The malcontents refused to be put down. Repression was met by underground propaganda. On the tenth anniversary of the revolution, which was celebrated throughout the republic with great state, the reformers tried to stage an open demonstration in Moscow. This was suppressed not by troops, but by large numbers of other workers. Trotsky was sent into exile in Turkistan, and in the early days of 1929 was expelled from Russia. Thousands of his followers were removed under administrative decree to the Arctic and Siberia. Some of the exiles recanted. Zinoviev was restored to a minor post, but an abler man, Bukharin, editor of Pravda (' Truth ') and one of the stoutest leaders of Communism, expressed his discontent with existing conditions and was temporarily removed from office.

The Bolshevik government found itself hampered at every turn by lack of resources. Russia needed re-equipping with machinery of all kinds. Plants were exhausted and there was no money to buy fresh. Factories with broken and poor machinery were costly to operate ; labour was inefficient, and consequently every kind of manufactured goods that people required was exceedingly dear. The break-up of many homes, due to the laxity of the Bolshevik marriage laws, helped to make large numbers of children homeless and ill-disciplined. There were many beggars in the cities and many unemployed.

The government tried to divert the wrath of the town workers against the peasants, by announcing that they were responsible for food shortage by hoarding stocks of grain. A punitive campaign against the peasantry in several regions began, but this defeated itself, for it still further reduced sources of grain supply. In the autumn of 1928 the food situation became markedly worse, owing to a parti failure of the crops.

The government programme has mor recently been marked by two main feature industrial expansion and centralised farm ing. Hundreds of millions of roubles wer raised by heavy taxation and intern loans to advance the construction of bi water-power, irrigation, electricity an manufacturing plants. Here the govern ment was faced by two difficulties, th excessive interest that had to be paid o loans and the high cost of constructio which far exceeded what had been anti cipated. The plans for centralised farmin aim at the ultimate transformation of th peasantry into an industrial class, workin on great state farms, as wage earners. Thi plan is regarded by the peasantry generall with suspicion and distrust.

The revolution divides itself roughl into two parts—the uprising, which wa inevitable owing to the shortcomings o the autocracy, and the Communist dic tatorship, which, by attempting to confin the administration of the country to a comparatively small political party an to wipe out all freedom of thought o action, produced a tyranny rivalling th one it had helped to destroy. Communism has succeeded politically and militarily and has kept Russia together. Bu economically it has been a failure. It ha shown that men cannot by decrees o resolutions prevent the operation o economic laws.

PATHETIC PLIGHT OF BOLSHEVIK RUSSIA'S DESTITUTE CHILDREN

One of Communism's most tragic products is the number of homeless children to be found in Russian cities under the Bolshevik yoke. Dirty and demoralised, these wretched urchins prowl the streets by night, sleeping in fitful snatches during the day. This huddled heap of sleeping humanity gives a representative idea of child life in the slums of many cities.

Photo, Topical Press Agency

CHAPTER 185

SOCIALISM, COMMUNISM AND WORLD REVOLUTION

Theories and Policies which attack the Economic Order based on Private Property and their Failure in Practice

By ARTHUR SHADWELL M.D. LL.D.

Author of Industrial Efficiency, The Socialist Movement, The Breakdown of Socialism, etc.

It is difficult to say clearly and satisfactorily what socialism is, because few terms, if any, are used so loosely in so many senses. Socialists have themselves produced hundreds of definitions, and are constantly engaged in controversy about the true meaning of the term. Yet for that very reason an attempt should be made to define it.

The ground may be partly cleared by recognizing in the first place that socialism has to do primarily with economic conditions; and in the second place that it presents itself in three aspects: as an economic theory, an economic system based on the theory, and a political movement or agitation for securing power to set up the system. The three are mixed up by having the same label indiscriminately affixed to them. When, for instance, it is said that socialism has spread all over the world, the theory is meant; but when the only cure for various ills is said to be socialism, the system is meant; and when, again, the advance of socialism in this or that country is spoken of, the political movement is meant.

The idea comes logically and historically first, and it is the most difficult part of the subject, because of the interminable differences among socialists, and the confusion between economic and ethical aims to which those differences are largely due. For this reason it is most important to bear in mind what has already been said, namely, that the problem which socialists have set out to solve is primarily an economic one; it has to do in the first instance with material conditions, with the production and division of wealth. Such abstract principles as justice, equality, freedom are contingent on the economic problem and depend for their realization on its solution. But many socialists put them first and make an emotional appeal to them. In reaching out after the ideal they overlook the real.

The resulting confusion is further increased by the practice of extending the idea of socialism, as a universal panacea, to many other large fields of thought and action, moral, social and philosophical. It is brought to bear upon such questions as religion, moral law, free will, crime and punishment, vice, war, patriotism, sex, marriage, the family, evolution, the state, revolution, the philosophy of history. The relations of socialism to these and other matters outside the proper sphere of economics are the subject of incessant controversy, not only between its advocates and its opponents but still more between the several sects or schools of thought bearing the same label. The result is an unparalleled confusion of ideas swirling round the subject; for sometimes one and sometimes another of its multitudinous aspects is put forward as its central or most important feature.

Definition of Terms Required

In order to escape from this maze and lay hold of something definite, at least as a starting point, the best plan is to disregard all differences and extraneous matters and fix attention on what is common to all the schools of socialism, for if there is anything on which they agree, that must be the heart of the matter. And there is something: it is condemnation of the existing economic order called capitalism. Strictly, complete agreement does not extend beyond this, for some socialists content themselves with denouncing capitalism and predicting its collapse, without going any farther.

That was, in fact, the position assumed by Marx as economist. But his followers have never adhered to it; they have striven actively to assist and hasten the process, and the aim of abolishing the existing order must be added to its condemnation as common to socialists in general. That is, however, a purely negative attitude. Its positive counterpart and the logical sequel to abolishing the existing order is the substitution of some alternative, since economic life must be carried on; and though socialists in the past have paid much less attention to the problem of creating a new order than to doing away with the old, they have always assumed that there will be a new one fashioned by themselves. It will be socialism realized as an economic system.

Common Ground for all Socialists

There has never been agreement about the precise form of this hypothetical system or about the manner of effecting the change, and it is here that the chief difference between socialism and communism, in its modern sense, comes in. Socialism stands for peaceful, more or less gradual, change by constitutional means, that is, through the standing political machinery; communism for complete, sudden and violent change by revolutionary, non-political action. But the essential character of the change has always been thought of broadly in the same sense by all the schools of socialism. It turns on the legal principle of ownership. The present economic order rests on the principle of private or individual ownership. All socialists would change it for some form of public or common ownership, and their agreement, which does not extend any farther, warrants the conclusion that this is the central idea of socialism.

The idea is very much older than socialism as an organized movement. The latter dates only from the period following the conclusion of the great European wars in 1815, when the term was coined as a name for the movement then inaugurated; whereas the idea is a legacy from remote antiquity. It is the lineal descendant of the ancient idea of communism, in its true and original sense, not in that current to-day and explained above. It meant having all property in common, as stated of the members of the Christian Church, founded by S. Peter: 'And all that believed were together and had all things common' (Acts 2, 44). In adopting this system, which was purely voluntary and did not last long, they were following precedents which reach back to the remotest antiquity.

It is indeed generally assumed that common ownership preceded the institution of private property in the evolution of human society, and the hypothesis is reasonable; for private ownership, which consists in a right recognized by law, implies a considerable degree of civilization. Consequently 'primitive communism' is commonly spoken of as an economic system antecedent to any based on private ownership. There is not much direct evidence for it, but some is furnished by the practices of primitive peoples in our own time, though doubt has been thrown by modern research on the earlier conclusions of anthropologists on the subject which have been too readily accepted. Professor Malinowski, whose thorough studies of the Pacific islanders have quite superseded the older authorities, says that their conclusions are based on hasty generalisation from superficial observation.

Aristotle on Ownership

However this may be, it seems certain from the nature of things that some limited measure of common use, starting with the family and extending to the tribe or clan, must have preceded the general introduction of private ownership and use in a more advanced stage of civilization. In that case the various examples of partial communism in the ancient world may be regarded as relics of an obsolete system. The whole subject was discussed by Aristotle with his usual comprehensive grasp and sagacity; and his conclusions are so pertinent to the question that they are worth recalling. He pronounced in favour of private ownership in general on the ground of its superior economic efficiency, because things are better looked after by men who have a personal interest them, and for the sake of social peace, ecause men quarrel more when they have nings in common. But he thought that ne use of property should be freely shared y its owners with non-owners in a spirit f benevolence, which legislators should ndeavour to cultivate. It must, however, be voluntary. Compulsory sharing y state regulation was condemned.

The judgement of Aristotle was enorsed and repeated in the thirteenth entury in its application to Christian eaching by S. Thomas Aquinas; and its alidity has been proved by the results of he principle of common ownership. The urvival of the idea was largely due in he ancient world to the myth of the Golden Age, when men had all things in ommon and evil did not exist, and to the arly Christian vision of the millennium, which represented a return to the Golden Age. Many of the experiments have been nade under religious influences, and they nave lasted longer than the secular ones; out whether religious or secular they have all consistently failed through economic nefficiency or internal dissensions or both. Nevertheless the idea persisted. Sir Thomas More adopted it for his Utopia (1516), and its revival in the eighteenth century was the forerunner of socialism.

In France Jean Meslier (d. 1733—his Testament was published in 1764), Morelly (Code de la nature, 1755), Mably (De la législation, 1778), all advocated communism. In England Thomas Spence (The Mode of Administering the Landed Estate of the Nation, 1775) and William Ogilvie (The Right of Property in Land, 1782) advocated land nationalisation; William Godwin (Enquiry concerning Political Justice, 1793) condemned private property altogether and advocated pure communism on an individualistic, that is anarchical, basis without the state. These were all theorists; but Morelly's sketch of an ideal society inspired, after the French Revolution, a movement for establishing state communism in France. This movement, carried on by Gracchus Babeuf and the 'Society of Equals' (see page 4143), was the first project and concerted attempt to institute a planned system of national

Eighteenth-century Propagandists

ANARCHY'S ADVOCATE

William Godwin (1756–1836) made an influential contribution to contemporary political thought in his Enquiry concerning Political Justice, published 1793, in which anarchic doctrines, incorporating intensive communism, are preached.
National Portrait Gallery, London

economy on communist lines, thirty years before the rise of socialism. Nor was any second attempt made for more than fifty years. To these eighteenth-century forerunners should be added the name of Hugo, the German jurist, who attacked the institution of private property from the juridical standpoint in 1799.

Among the writers named Mably and Godwin deserve particular mention, because they discussed the underlying ethical principles of equality and justice, to which socialism makes an emotional appeal, much more thoroughly than any modern socialists, who indeed have not discussed them at all, but merely claim them as attributes of their proposed system, without any attempt to show how or why it would realize them.

The ground was further prepared on the theoretical side for the advent of socialism by other writers early in the nineteenth century. The most outstanding names in France are Claude de Saint-Simon (1760–1825) and François Fourier (1772–1837), whose disciples eventually formed rival schools of socialism. Saint-Simon's earliest work was a pamphlet, called Letters from a Resident in Geneva to his Contemporaries, published in 1802. It contains in embryo the principles of his proposed reorganization of society, afterwards developed in other works published at intervals until his death. He was a man of essentially constructive mind and more occupied with projects for promoting material progress than with existing defects, on which he wasted no time; but he was the very reverse of a systematic thinker, though full of ideas, which stimulated other minds.

The letters from Geneva were a plea for the endowment of men of genius with a view to the organization of national economy and the administration of affairs by the ablest men in science, art and industry. This was always his leading thought. He was the only man in the whole range of socialist literature who fully realized the practical importance of intelligence in the direction of economic activities in order to secure production, wherein he anticipated one of the latest discoveries of Continental socialists, who have shown a tendency to resuscitate him. He laid particular stress on science, in

FRANCOIS CHARLES FOURIER
Born at Besançon in 1772, François Charl Fourier devised a new social system which described in his works, of which the Theory the Four Movements (1808), and The New I dustrial World (1829) are the most notable.

CLAUDE DE SAINT-SIMON
The French reformer Claude de Saint-Simon advocated a new order of society embodying an aristocracy of intellect. His theories, which were widely read, are chiefly expounded by him in The Industrial System, 1821.

which he had been educated, and pr jected the conception of the state tran formed from an organ of authority ov men in the hands of politicians in one for the administration of affairs b the ablest men of science. This ide was taken up by Marx in the form of th theory of the 'withering away' of th state, and it is much in favour to-da with some socialists. Saint-Simon pr posed that the supreme intellectual spiritual authority should be wielded b savants and artists and the tempor authority by industrialists, including work men; and that the first aim should be t 'ameliorate as quickly as possible the l of the poorest and most numerous sectio of the people.'

In his last work, published posthun ously in 1825 under the title of The Ne Christianity, he urged that the conduct the new order should be guided by th Christian moral law. He relied entirel on persuasion for its introduction an expressly repudiated the use of forc The notion that he was a dangerou revolutionary and the catspaw of secr conspirators is absurd; the early socialis were none of them such.

François Fourier was nearly contem porary with Saint-Simon. In 1808 h published his first work, the Théorie des quatre mouvements, in which the need for an economic reconstruction of society was urged in connexion with a general philosophical theory of harmony in the universe and a special psychological theory, curiously anticipatory of psycho-analysis, that vice and crime are due to repressed passions. He called for co-operation in industry and social harmony, and drew up an elaborate scheme of organization, which did not, however, include the abolition of private property or capital. He recognized, though less fully than Saint-Simon, the importance of intelligence or 'talent' in industry, and laid down a division of the product in fixed proportions—five-twelfths to labour, four-twelfths to capital and three-twelfths to talent. Like Saint-Simon and unlike most socialists he had some knowledge of business; but his plan for putting his system into operation was the impracticable one of setting up small model communities after the manner of those established by religious bodies and mentioned above.

In England other ideas were brought forward about the same time. In 1805 Charles Hall, a medical man, struck a new note with his Effects of Civilisation on the People in European States, and laid the foundation of the economic indictment of capitalism, which became and still is the main preoccupation of socialists, by pointing out not only the contrast between rich and poor, which had been done by Tom Paine in his Agrarian Justice (1797), but also the exploitation of the wage earners, who produce the existing wealth but enjoy only a fraction of it, because the greater part is taken by the owners in the form of rent and interest. All later economic arguments are merely elaborations and variations of this theme.

Economic indictment of Capitalism

His chief remedy was less original. Like the writers just mentioned he advocated nationalisation of the land, and for its cultivation partition among individual holders, as in the Russian Mir system. He founded no school at the time, perhaps because the war with France absorbed public attention. It was not, in fact, until after the war that socialism took shape as a concerted movement by the formation of societies for the propagation of the various theories brought forward under that name, which was then coined. And when this took place attention in England was monopolised by Robert Owen; but the school he founded was greatly influenced by the ideas of Hall on the exploitation of wage earners.

Robert Owen (1771–1858; see page 4280) began as a benevolent employer and social reformer. The starting point of his socialism was the theory first put forward in 1813, that character is determined by environment, that there is no free will and that belief in the moral law inculcated by religion is the cause of all social evils. Put men in the right surroundings, make them comfortable and they will do right. This theory, implied or expressed, is at the bottom of all forms of sentimental socialism, although it is in flat contradiction with the character assigned by the same socialists to the comfortable classes, who are habitually accused of greed, selfishness, hard-heartedness and tyrannical conduct. Owen was more original and better inspired in advocating the constructive principle of co-operation, as opposed to competition, in industry. It is a fundamental idea, very much alive to-day; but, like other fundamental ideas, susceptible of various interpretations. Owen's plan for realizing it was the old one of establishing limited communistic societies on a voluntary basis. He brought this forward in a memorandum presented to a parliamentary committee on the poor law in 1817, and it attracted much favourable attention.

Theories of Robert Owen

Like Saint-Simon, Owen had an essentially constructive mind and an unshakable confidence in his own ideas. Both men were full of projects—entirely different projects—which they pressed on rulers, statesmen and the world at large in the certain belief that they had only to be understood in order to be taken up and realized at once. Both impressed their personality on younger men, who formed societies for the propagation of their teaching. It was in these societies that socialism first became a cult or concerted movement, marked by the appearance of the term.

This happened about the same time, but quite independently, in England and in France. The earliest appearance in print of the word socialist that has yet been discovered (by Max Beer) was in the Co-operative Magazine for November, 1827. This monthly periodical was issued by the London Co-operative Society, founded in 1824 for the discussion and propagation of Owen's theories; and the meaning of the word is explained. It turned on the question of the ownership of capital, whether this should be individual or common. The orthodox economist thought it should be individual; 'those who thought it should be common were the Communists and Socialists.' At this time, when communism still retained its old meaning of community of goods, the two were used indifferently as equivalents. In France, the word socialisme was coined about 1830 by Pierre Leroux, a member of the Saint-Simonian school; it occurs in Le Globe of February 13, 1832, the official daily paper of the school presented to it by Pierre Leroux.

First use of the word 'Socialist'

The speculative ideas formulated by forerunners and leading up to this development have been explained. But other influences contributed to it and must be taken into account. In the first place the conclusion of the war of 1815 and the transition to peace caused a general economic collapse similar to that following the war of 1914–18. The resulting widespread unemployment and suffering heightened the contrast between the haves and the have-nots and brought out into strong relief, especially in England, the ill effects of the Industrial Revolution which had been developed during the preceding four or five decades. The prosperity it had brought disappeared with a sudden rush and left only the seamy side exposed. The inevitable consequence was general discontent, breaking out into occasional disorder.

This state of things, so contrary to the humanitarian spirit then rising, naturally stimulated the tendency to question the existing economic order and the principles on which it was based, with a view to finding an ideal alternative; and a further stimulus was furnished by the rising interest in political economy, which invited speculation on the subject of wealth, its production and distribution. The current theory of the day was, on the one hand, all in favour of free enterprise and free competition, but on the other appeared to assert the proposition that all exchangeable value was created by 'labour.' Since, however, labour, in the sense of the wage earners, received only a fraction of the value created, and competition tended constantly to depress even that fraction to the lowest level compatible with existence, there was something manifestly wrong with the system and the economic theory that supported it.

All these influences ran together to form a broad stream by which the new movement was floated on and up. The wretched condition of the wage earners appealed to humanitarian sentiment, and the depression of trade that caused or accompanied it gave point to the attack on the principles of private enterprise and free competition ('laissez faire') upheld by orthodox economists, while the labour theory of value called in the sense of justice to strengthen the case. That theory had found its most complete expression in David Ricardo's Principles of Political Economy, published in 1817. In 1819 Sismondi, the Swiss economist, published his New Principles of Political Economy, in which he made the first formal attack on 'laissez faire' economics and, basing his argument on the labour theory of value, maintained that rent, interest and profit represented the 'surplus value' created by labour and appropriated by others. He was not a socialist; but his theory, which gave a technical form to Charles Hall's earlier criticisms, was too well suited to the cause to be neglected by socialists. It was taken up in England by Owen's disciples, and notably by William Thompson, who published his Inquiry into the Principles of Distribution of Wealth in 1824.

First Attack on 'Laissez faire'

The theory of surplus value, on which Karl Marx's Das Kapital is built, was taken from him and from Sismondi. Thompson postulated the juster distribuion or, rather, division of wealth as the great economic problem to be solved, taking production for granted; and all but the most modern theories of socialism have ever since put the problem of distribution in the forefront. He attributed the existing disparity to the fact that capital was possessed by one set of individuals and labour by another, and held that they should be in the same hands, to which end all productive labourers should become capitalists. This was to be accomplished in the Owenite co-operative communities.

Meanwhile, in France, the Saint-Simonian school, founded about the same time, was growing, and became very active about 1830. They also started from the same fact of disparity and stressed the distinction between earned and unearned income, which is the problem of surplus value regarded from a slightly different point of view. But their remedy was different. They sought no artificial equality and repudiated community of property. The principle they adopted was 'from each according to his capacity, to each according to his works,' which implies inequality. Their remedy for unearned income was the abolition of inheritance, whereby land, capital and the means of production would be gradually transferred to the state, but the state as conceived by Saint-Simon and explained above, not the ordinary state.

Saint-Simonian Socialism

This school soon developed internal dissensions and began to split up. As an organization it fell to pieces in 1832, but propagation of socialism by individuals and groups proceeded apace and developed innumerable sub-varieties.

Up to 1830 the movement was wholly intellectual in both countries, but after that date it was reinforced by the entry of wage earners on the scene. In England, where trade unions had been legalised in 1824 and had grown rapidly, the National Union of Working Classes and Others was formed in 1831. It was a mixed body, with headquarters in London, where weekly meetings were held; and it was first occupied mainly with political and social reforms. But it gradually developed a socialistic tone under the influence of the theory taught by Thompson, Hodgskin and other Owenite writers, that labour produces everything and ought to enjoy the whole product, but is exploited by capitalists. (See further in page 4671.)

In France, where trade unions were prohibited and the general atmosphere was different, the same elements were present, but asserted themselves in a more explosive manner. In 1831 the weavers of Lyons demanded a minimum living wage, and on its being refused rose in arms, descended on the town and put the authorities to flight. Other disturbances followed, and in 1834 a more serious rising occurred at Lyons, where the insurgent workmen in their desperation fought the military for five days. It was in connexion with these troubles that Pierre Leroux, a Saint-Simonian socialist, formulated the division of society into two classes—namely employers and employed—and called them 'bourgeoisie' and 'proletariat.' The stirring events of the time stimulated theoretical socialism to great activity and elicited a flood of ideas from the younger men.

Labour trouble in France

From 1835 onwards the teaching of Fourier was taken up and developed into a rival school to the Saint-Simonians. In 1840 Louis Blanc, who had belonged to the latter, published his celebrated Organization of Labour, in which he adopted the motto 'to each according to his needs, from each according to his capacity,' laid down the principle of work or maintenance and advocated a sort of guild socialism. Industries were to be run by the workmen engaged in them, who would be started and provided at first with the necessary means by the state. In the same year Etienne Cabet published a Utopian romance called Travels in Icaria and revived the idea of the communistic settlement; while Pierre Proudhon startled the world with his first work entitled What is Property? to which the answer was 'property is theft.' Two years later, in 1842, Constantin Pecqueur published his New Theory of Social and Political Economy, in which he advocated the suppression of individual ownership, the socialisation of all forms of capital and the conduct of industry by the state.

In this period Paris was a factory for the production of socialist theories and schemes, while Chartism was agitating England and a revolutionary ferment was rising in central Europe. As it advanced it became associated, through the formation of secret revolutionary societies, with the idea of communism, and that term then acquired the meaning, which it has to-day, of violent revolutionary action as distinguished from the peaceful voluntary transition advocated by all schools of socialism. Exiled Germans were particularly active in this sort of communistic agitation. They took refuge in Switzerland, England and Belgium, but above all in Paris, then regarded as the Mecca of freedom. In 1843 Karl Marx came there from Germany, where he had edited an advanced Radical journal.

He was twenty-five years old and at that time knew very little about socialism; but in Paris he met prominent French socialists and imbibed their ideas. In 1845 he was expelled and went to Brussels, where he joined a secret German society called the League of the Just, which in 1847 was transformed into the Communist League with headquarters in London. For this body he wrote, in conjunction with Engels, whom he had met in Paris and Brussels, the Communist Manifesto which contained an outline of his theories and in particular preached the class war. In 1848 the storm that had long been brewing burst with the revolution of March in Paris, followed by revolutionary risings in Belgium, Germany and Austria. Their failure, the breakdown of socialist experiments in Paris and the collapse of Chartism in England, brought the first period of socialism to an end.

PIERRE JOSEPH PROUDHON

The French political philosopher Pierre Joseph Proudhon (1809–65) launched his fierce attack on property in an essay which appeared in 1840. He takes an important place in socialist thought as the supposed originator of anarchism.

We have treated it fully because the whole evolution of socialism as theory belongs to this period. All the original and creative ideas covered by the term were brought forward then; everything since in the field of ideas has been only repetition and elaboration or revival.

Socialism in its Political Aspect

When socialism reappeared after the eclipse that followed 1848, it did so as a political movement based on the earlier ideas, and so it continued down to the Great War; there was nothing fresh about it. We know it, in fact mainly as an organized political movement carried on in each country by a party striving for power, like other political parties, but with ends of its own handed down from the period with which we have been dealing. It will, therefore, be convenient to follow the historical sequence and take the political aspect now.

In this respect also the earlier period furnishes a precedent in Chartism (see also page 4435), which was an organized campaign for securing political reform and a more democratic constitution in the United Kingdom; originally with a view to promoting the economic changes demanded by socialism, though these rather fell out of sight in the ardour of the conflict. Chartism differed, however, from the political socialism of more modern times in that it made no attempt to form a parliamentary party, but sought only to influence Parliament by agitation in the country, popular demonstration, petitions to Parliament and similar means, which were in themselves constitutional but not easily restrained within constitutional bounds. There inevitably developed a revolutionary left wing, which advocated 'physical force,' split the movement, liscredited it and caused its collapse. The political socialism that came later was of a different character, more systematic and regular, less excited, though its purpose was fundamentally the same. It originated in Germany and had no connexion with Chartism.

The German movement, which was destined to spread throughout the world, had a double origin in two schools of thought, of which the founders were Ferdinand Lassalle (1825–64) and Karl Marx (1818–83), both members of well-to-do middle-class Jewish families. Lassalle led the way with an address to Berlin workmen in 1862 and a pamphlet written for a labour congress at Leipzig in 1863, and known as the Open Reply. He drew his inspiration chiefly from Louis Blanc, aimed at the organization of labour with state aid for the self-control of industry and advocated the formation of a political Labour party. This took shape as the General German Workers' Union founded in the same year. He died from the results of a duel in 1864, but his disciples carried on the organization so begun. In 1869 a rival organization, called the Social Democratic Workmen's Party, was started by the disciples of Marx; and for several years the two competed for support among the working classes, but came together in 1875, when they adopted a joint programme.

Ferdinand Lassalle and Karl Marx

Marx himself was all this time living in London, whither he had retreated after the failure of the attempted revolution of 1848 in Germany, in which he had taken part. In 1859 he published his Critique of Political Economy, which contained an outline of the arguments afterwards elaborated in his principal work, Das Kapital (Vol. I published in 1867); in 1864 he played a leading part in founding the International Association of Working Men (afterwards known as the First International). It was nominally an organization of British trade unionists, but was inspired by Marx and used by him to propagate his theories. In England, where it was born, it met with very little response; but it helped to plant the seed of Marxian socialism on the Continent in the years before the Franco-German War of 1870–1, after which it was moribund, lingering till 1876, when it was formally buried.

FERDINAND LASSALLE

Ferdinand Lassalle (1825–64) assisted in the organization of the General German Working Men's Association in 1863. Unlike Marx, whose ideas were international, Lassalle confined his activities to the workers of Germany.

Such was the origin of political socialism, as we know it; but it did not become effective, even in Germany, until 1871, when two socialists were elected to the Reichstag, and not until many years later in other countries. Its subsequent advance down to 1914 can be summarily stated in terms of election results.

Germany takes first place as the country of origin, which gave a lead to the rest of the world and furnished the predominant formula. The following table gives the results of successive Reichstag elections:

Year	Votes Cast for Socialists	Socialists elected
1871	124,655	2
1874	351,952	10
1877	493,288	13
1878	437,158	9
1881	311,961	13
1884	549,990	24
1887	763,128	11
1890	1,427,298	35
1893	1,786,738	44
1898	2,107,076	56
1903	3,010,771	81
1907	3,259,020	43
1912	4,250,329	110

A GERMAN LEADER

From 1864 August Bebel (1840–1913) was identified with the German working-class movement. In 1871 he became a member of the Reichstag, where he was the recognized leader of the Social Democrats until his death in 1913.

In the forty-one years covered by the table the votes cast for Socialist candidates increased from 3·2 per cent. to 34·8 per cent. of the total, and the Social Democratic party had grown from the smallest to the largest group in the Reichstag, with 110 out of 397 members. Between 1878 and 1890 their advance was to some extent checked by a repressive law; but the great progress subsequently made was coincident with the period of Germany's most rapid industrial expansion and economic prosperity.

The rise of political socialism in Germany epitomises the whole movement, in which the Germans led the way, in time, in numerical strength and in doctrine. One reason for their success was the fact that after the fusion of the Lassalleans and Marxians in 1875, noted above, they remained a united body. There were internal differences, but no secessions or rival organizations, as in most other countries. This unity was due mainly to the German sense of discipline, but it also owed much to the political sagacity of August Bebel (1840–1913), who had been active in founding the Marxian movement in 1869, was elected to the Reichstag in 1871 and remained the parliamentary leader of the party until his death in 1913. He was originally a workman, a wood turner by trade, but in 1864 he set up for himself and became a successful manufacturer. Another reason for the advance of the party shown above was the hold it obtained on the largest of the several trade-union groups, namely, the free or social-democratic unions, which were originally started about 1865, but only attained large proportions after 1890.

The German Social Democratic Party

Before proceeding to the rise of political socialism in other countries it will be convenient here to explain the policy of the German Social-Democratic party whose principles and programme served as a model for the rest, were adopted by most socialist organizations and influenced all. It has already been stated that the rival schools of Lassalle and Marx came together and formed a united party in 1875. The name adopted was Socialist Workmen's (or Labour) party, but the term Social Democratic or simply Socialist party was more commonly used. The programme declared the aim to be the emancipation of the working class by conversion of the means of work into common property and proposed the establishment with state assistance of socialist productive co-operatives under democratic control—that is, Louis Blanc's system.

In 1891 this was completely altered and a purely Marxian programme adopted in the famous Erfurt programme, proclaiming the class war and the inevitable failure of capitalism through increasing misery, for which the only remedy was the conversion of private ownership of the means of production into social ownership. This contains all the essential elements of Marxian socialism, which was made up of ideas derived from various sources and worked together into a connected whole. The philosophical basis was Hegel's interpretation of history as a process of evolution carried on by the resolution of two opposed ideas into a new one, but for opposed ideas Marx substituted two opposed economic classes, namely the bourgeoisie and proletariat, into which eroux had suggested that society is vided, as explained above.

Hegel and Leroux together provided ıe formula of the class war, which ust inevitably end in the break-up of ıe present economic (capitalist) order ırough the working of its own internal ws that involve the progressive op-ression of the many, who grow more ımerous, by the few, who grow fewer ırough the concentration of capital, and ve by the appropriation, in the form of rofit, interest and rent, of the surplus alue created by labour, as Sismondi, hompson and other English Socialists ıd argued. The remedy is the system of ate ownership advocated by Pecqueur.

Such is the 'scientific socialism' which ıspired the German Social Democratic arty and all its imitators for so many ears. The 'science' in it was the law f evolution by economic class conflict he materialist interpretation of history) nd the law of capitalist production by ırplus value. It has not stood the test of me and criticism, but it nominally held ıe field up to the Great War and is still ıught by the revolutionary left wing, ho call themselves Communists. The nmediate object of the Social Democrats as to conquer political power through ıe electorate and then establish socialism.

ival Sects n France

In France this doctrine first gained a old in 1879, when it was adopted under ıe influence of Jules Guesde at a labour congress held at Marseilles, to which intellectuals were admitted. A long period of confused strife followed, in hich different socialist sects contended or control of the trade unions. The latter ere very weak before 1884, when they ere legalised, but after that they grew apidly and in 1886 formed a federation, hich adopted Marxian socialism. This ed to the rival trade-union movement f syndicalism in opposition to state ocialism, initiated in 1892 by the rades councils or 'bourses du travail' nd established on a firm basis by fusion vith the other federation in 1902.

Thenceforward the weight of trade nionism in France was against political ocialism. To this cause of weakness was dded the division of socialists into several groups, which, together with frequent changes, make a simple numerical statement of parliamentary strength difficult or misleading. They first tried to enter the Chamber of Deputies in 1885, but without success; in 1889 seven were returned; in 1893 they numbered 43, and in 1898 about 50. In 1905 the two principal parties coalesced and the subsequent result of elections can be stated thus:

Year	Votes cast for Socialists	Socialists elected
1906	877,999	54
1910	1,106,047	76
1914	1,391,373	102

The Chamber consisted of 597 deputies, so that the socialists were relatively weak. The policy of the unified party was based on the German Erfurt programme—class war, increasing misery, socialisation.

Socialist revival in England

The revival of socialism in England occurred nearly ten years later than in France and twenty years later than in Germany, whence it was imported. From the first the movement was divided into groups and it did not assume political importance until 1900. The earliest organizations were the Social Democratic Federation, which took that title in 1884, but had been originally started without it in 1881; and the Fabian Society, founded in 1884. The Independent Labour party followed in 1893. These were—and are—the most important societies, though not the only ones. They all represent the constitutional type of socialism, and differ rather in the degree of definiteness and the stress laid on particular points than in aims or principles. The S.D.F. is frankly Marxian, and emphasises the class war; but all were inspired by the Continental idea of state ownership of land and industrial capital—otherwise collectivism.

From time to time other more revolutionary organizations have been formed by the secession of left-wing members, such as the Socialist League, which broke off from the S.D.F. in 1884. Socialism began to penetrate the trade unions about 1887, and this led to the foundation of the Independent Labour party for the purpose of carrying on their conversion more systematically. In 1892 two Socialists were elected to Parliament, but there was no Socialist party before 1900, when the Labour party was founded under the name of Labour Representation Committee. It was formed of socialist societies and trade unions, and its progress before the Great War was as follows:

Year	Votes cast for Socialists	Members elected
1900	62,698	2
1906	323,196	29
1910	505,690 (Jan.)	42 (Dec.)

In 1914 the Labour party officially adopted the formula of collective socialism. It had previously refused to make a confession of socialism a condition of affiliation, in order to avoid alarming the trade unions, but its policy had always been determined by the socialists.

Other European countries are less important and can be briefly dismissed:

AUSTRIA: Organized socialism dates from 1888; members elected to the Reichsrath (membership, 516) were: 1897, 17; 1901, 10; 1907, 87; 1911, 82. Principles and policy the same as those of German Social Democrats, but the party much weaker in the trade unions, being opposed by the Christian unions, who were relatively stronger than in Germany.

BELGIUM: Organized socialism dates from 1885, when a Labour party was formed; members elected to the Chamber (membership, 166): 1894, 28; 1911, 35; 1912, 39. Programme modified German—class war and nationalisation of land, etc., but national services to be administered by autonomous corporations, not by the state. Co-operative societies highly developed by socialists.

DENMARK: A Social Democratic party formed in 1878; members elected to Folketing or House of Commons (membership, 114): 1844, 2; 1900, 12; 1906, 24; 1913, 32. Policy based on Erfurt programme.

FINLAND: Labour party formed in 1899. Constitution secured in 1906, women given the vote and seats in National Assembly. Socialist members elected: 1907, 80; 1911, 87 (9 women) out of 200; they polled 40·1 per cent. of the votes. Policy based on Erfurt programme.

HOLLAND: Social Democratic Labour party formed in 1894, in opposition to a communist movement started in 1888. Members elected to lower Chamber (membership, 100): 1897, 3; 1901, 7; 1905, 7; 1910, 7. Policy moderate German; oppose by a small revolutionary party.

ITALY: Socialist party formed in 189 Members elected to Chamber of Deputie (membership, 508): 1892, 6; 1897, 16 1900, 32; 1904, 23; 1910, 40. Policy base on German. Movement weakened by dis sensions and revolutionary elements.

NORWAY: In 1885 a Social Democrati Federation was founded, and two years late a Labour party. Members elected to th Storthing or National Assembly (member ship, 123): 1903, 3; 1906, 10; 1909, 11 1912, 23. Policy German.

SPAIN: The political movement in Spai is more revolutionary anarchism thai socialism, but there is a small Socialist Labour party, which in 1910 had on member elected to the Cortes.

SWEDEN: In 1887 a Social Democrati Labour party was formed. Members electe to Lower Chamber (membership, 230) 1896, 1; 1903, 4; 1906, 13; 1909, 33 1911, 64; 1914, 87. Programme based on German.

SWITZERLAND: A Social Democratic party formed in 1870, an off-shoot from Germany. In 1888 a unified party formed after various dissensions. Members elected to National Council (membership, 167): 1905, 2; 1908, 7; 1911, 15. Policy mainly German.

RUSSIA: Socialism was illegal and severely repressed before 1917, but revolutionary agitation on the lines of the Communist Manifesto and of anarchism had been carried on by intellectuals since 1863. The German type of Socialism began to spread surreptitiously in the 'nineties after suppression of anarchists; meetings were held and papers published abroad; split into Social Democrats (Marxian) and Social Revolutionaries (Non-Marxian); in 1903 former split into Bolsheviks (majority) and Mensheviks (minority); Bolsheviks for extreme concentration and violence, Mensheviks for more moderate and constitutional action; in revolutionary risings of 1905 a workers' council (soviet) formed in St. Petersburg. In 1910 there were 16 socialists in the Duma (432).

Of the remaining European countries it need only be said that political socialism gained a footing and spread everywhere in this period, largely through the influence of the Second International, founded in 1889 partly at the instigation of the British Trades Union Congress. Two rival congresses were held that year in Paris, but the next one, held in Brussels in 1891, was a joint affair. In 1893 the anarchist section was expelled. The organization grew rapidly, and in 1900 was placed on a permanent footing; at the congress held at Copenhagen in 1910 thirty-three nations were represented, including Persia, Japan, South American states and British Dominions. It had spread over the world. The policy was Marxian of a moderate kind, and the German Social Democrats held the lead; but except as an agency for propagating socialism the International exercised no influence, and it especially failed in the prevention of war, which was one of its chief objects.

Of non-European countries two have a particular interest, though for different reasons, and deserve separate mention. They are Australia and the United States.

The socialist movement in Australia was started about 1885 by William Lane, an Englishman and a journalist, with the aid of some emigrant members of the English Socialist League, mentioned above.

Socialism in Australia

Leading events and dates are: 1890, Australian Labour Federation formed, and great strike of sheep-shearers in Queensland; 1891, general shipping strike, 37 socialists returned to state legislature of New South Wales; 1893, 80 socialists in state legislatures, while Lane went to Paraguay to found New Australia; 1901, Commonwealth established; 1904, Labour party assumed office as largest party in Commonwealth Parliament; 1908, Labour party again takes office, after being turned out in 1904; 1910, Labour party secures majority in both Chambers; policy: nationalisation of monopolies, government steamships and sugar refinery, rejected on referendum. In the course of twenty years political socialism had achieved more success in Australia than in any other country. Before the Great War it held the reins of power in the Commonwealth and in three of the six provincial legislatures.

To turn to the United States, in 1871 the First International was nominally transferred to New York, and from that time onward several socialist societies were founded; in 1877 three of these combined to form the Socialist Labour party, a strictly Marxian organization. It never attained much strength and on the appearance of a rival twenty years later it wasted away; on several occasions it ran a candidate for the Presidency with insignificant results. The rival was the Social Democratic party, formed in 1898; in 1901 it absorbed some other societies and changed its name to the Socialist party. It was more successful than the older body and in 1912 its candidate for the Presidency polled 800,000 votes (out of 17 millions), showing a great advance on its first attempt in 1900, which yielded 97,000 votes (out of 14 millions). Its policy was also Marxian, but of a moderate kind.

Political Socialism in the United States

Political socialism has had a moderate amount of local success, but in no industrialised country is it so weak. The chief reason is the steady and uncompromising opposition of the principal trade-union organization, the American Federation of Labour. It may be laid down as a general proposition that political socialism is weak or strong in every country in proportion to the support secured from trade unionism.

It has been shown in the preceding pages that the primary aim of modern socialism, which is the conquest of political power in order to establish a new economic system in place of the existing one called capitalism, had been achieved before the war in one country only, namely Australia. In others it had made a progressive advance in that direction; in some cases more, in others less. As a whole the movement was going forward, both intensively and extensively, but gradually; confident of eventual success, but not anticipating it in the near future.

That situation was dramatically changed by the war. The first effect was to suppress the International and stop the political movement, completely in belligerent countries, less so but still sufficiently in others. The great bulk of the socialists everywhere rallied to the patriotic call and supported their governments. But that very action had another side, which was not perceived at the time. It put the socialist parties in a new light and raised them in general estimation. They not only supported the national cause, but in some countries, of which Great Britain was one, individual members joined with other parties and shared in the administration. By so doing they really served their own cause far better than the few exceptions, who held aloof or actively opposed the government. They won favour in previously hostile quarters by showing that they could put national interests before dogma, and they prepared the world for the possibility of socialist administration.

They reaped their reward after the war in a great accession of strength and a new status in the political world. If they later lost ground again, as they did in certain countries, it was due to their own failure and the excesses of the left wing. But the immediate sequel of the war was in several instances to place in their hands, partly or wholly, the political power for which they had been striving ever since the movement began, and to furnish the opportunity of realizing their economic aims. So for the first time in history we have been enabled to see modern socialism in being, as distinguished from the old, isolated communistic settlements, and to study it as an economic system.

Modern Socialism in Practice

The great example is Russia, which receives full treatment on the historical side in Chapter 184. The leading principles of the Bolshevik organization were community or state ownership and workers' control. The whole economic apparatus was taken over and nominally communalised. The market, buying and selling were abolished and replaced by a system of exchange between rural and urban producers conducted through official agencies, and of distribution of necessaries in kind on a certificate of work done.

No attempt to establish a systematic economy with elimination of private ownership on a small scale was ever a more complete failure. The peasantry refused to practise communal production, the town workmen proved totally incapable of carrying on industry; neither had their elementary needs satisfied. So far from adjusting production to consumption the system reduced it below the level of subsistence. Nor was the attempt to 'militarise' labour by enrolling all individuals in industrial battalions under the most rigid discipline any more successful. After a three-and-a-half years' trial it had to be given up. That was freely admitted by Lenin when he introduced the 'new economic policy' (see page 4957) in 1921, by which capitalist econom[y] was to a certain extent restored. Leni[n] called it State Capitalism.

Improvement followed at once in spit[e] of the famine that year, and continue[d] until the authorities became alarmed a[t] the success of private enterprise, whic[h] threatened completely to falsify th[e] theories on which their system had bee[n] built and to destroy it. The result was [a] partial reversal of policy and repression o[f] private trading, coupled with an attemp[t] to improve public enterprise. This wen[t] on in 1924 with such disastrous effects tha[t] it had to be abandoned in 1925 and mor[e] favourable treatment of private enterpris[e] again adopted. So the experiment ha[s] gone on, alternating between Marxia[n] theory and economic necessity. Just s[o] far as capitalism has been re-introduced improvement has taken place; when it i[s] allowed to function the situation is eased when it is again repressed, decline at onc[e] sets in. This makes the experiment a fa[r] more instructive object lesson in socialism as an economic system than if it had bee[n] wholly abandoned.

The story is not finished yet, but so fa[r] as it has gone the lesson is unmistakable Nor has it been ignored. Every excuse i[s] offered for the failure of the Russian experiment, but no one denies that it occurred.

Failure of the Russian experiment

Socialists and even communists, wh[o] try to persuade the world that all i[s] now well and Russia prosperous, say tha[t] they would avoid the mistakes that hav[e] been made. But how they would avoi[d] them is not stated. The main criticism urged, at least by socialists, is that th[e] great mistake was trying to establish socialism all at once; the process should be gradual. But this hardly meets th[e] case; the causes of failure appear to b[e] more fundamental. The Russians, wh[o] are as well versed in the theory of socialism as anyone else, have tried every expedient but each effort makes it more clear that the root cause of failure lies in the principle of centralised public control to th[e] exclusion of personal responsibility and initiative. If the assumptions on which the theory of socialism is built were at al[l]

.lid, the system could not have been such complete failure, even though it was tablished too suddenly.

No such object lesson as the Russian periment has been furnished by other untries, because no other has ventured to ıt theory to the test of practice; but me have been faced by the problem of ing so, and their experience is hardly ss instructive. The most important of ese is Germany, where the revolution of ovember, 1918, placed the reins of power mpletely in the hands of the Social emocrats, who formed the first prosional government by general consent d without opposition. They were excted by their supporters to fulfil their omises and realize the theories of cialism at once, or at least to make a ginning; but they found themselves tally unprepared to deal with the oblem, having all their lives confined emselves to the purely negative teaching Marx, and having paid no attention to e constructive side of socialism.

Being Germans they were not minded to llow the Russian example; for Germans not plunge into action without thorough nsideration and preparation. And, oreover, they did not approve of the Bolshevik reading of Marxism, which had split the socialist movement in Russia, and was already splitting it in Germany. ıey required time for deliberation, and erefore appointed a commission of quiry into 'socialisation,' which had en accepted as the aim of their policy hile still remote, but had never been amined at close quarters with a view realization. The whole situation was anged by the sudden transition from olitical agitation to the responsibility of tion, and they dared not risk a false step.

ıution in Germany

The commission, which consisted of ading socialists and sympathetic econnists, reported on December 10 to the amorous democracy that no immediate eps could be taken and the existing stem must be retained for the present, in der to restore production and trade; ıt they recommended a gradual and utious advance towards socialisation, ginning with coal and iron as the dustries most 'ripe' for conversion. Two months later a formal report on socialisation of the coal mines was presented. It unanimously condemned both the private and the state mines, the former on account of their monopolistic character, the latter on account of their inefficiency; and it recommended state ownership of the whole industry, but under the control of a joint statutory body, in which management, miners, consumers and the state would be equally represented. On the treatment of private capital in the mines the commissioners were divided; the majority were for its total exclusion; the minority held, on practical grounds, that this could not be done at once.

A general socialisation act of a purely permissive character was passed by the National Assembly in March, 1919, and by virtue of it a coal mines act, providing for the control of the private mines by a joint National Coal Council, but not for their appropriation. This was disappointing to the nationalisers, and in 1920 the commission of inquiry was reconstituted. Various schemes were laid before it and discussed, but agreement was not reached and eventually nationalisation was abandoned. The only result of all the agitation about socialising the private coal mines was their consolidation and the setting up of a joint council of control, representing owners, miners and consumers. The potash industry was similarly treated.

Socialism or Joint Control?

The idea, which has now become widespread, is that the consumers' representatives will exercise control over prices, but experience has shown that they are powerless against the owners and miners, and that the latter simply follow the lead of the former in this respect. The system of joint control of monopolistic large-scale industry, which is the principal feature of the new economic order, has been accompanied by another change, namely the commercialisation of publicly owned undertakings by their conversion from state departments into autonomous companies, for the avoidance of bureaucracy. This has been done on an extensive scale in Germany in regard to coal mines, railways, war factories and also municipal undertakings. The movement has become general, and it appears to give satisfaction, but it is not in any sense an instalment of socialism. In sum the experience of Germany corroborates that of Russia so far as to prove that the realization of socialism presents unforeseen economic difficulties and demands a much more thorough investigation before it can be undertaken with any assurance of success.

The experience of Austria teaches the same lesson. The circumstances were different in many respects, and the Social Democratic party never secured such complete power as in Germany immediately after the revolution; but they were sufficiently dominant to inaugurate their own policy, and they held power longer than their colleagues in Germany, who lost ground and political influence under the new democratic constitution. In Vienna, indeed, which is a self-governing city state, the socialists have enjoyed complete power ever since the revolution, but their administration has made no attempt to convert private into public ownership.

Object Lesson of Austria

In the republic of Austria the Social Democrats dominated the coalition government in 1919, and Dr. Otto Bauer, who also conducted an inquiry into socialisation, tentatively introduced a system of economy which he hoped would develop into a form of socialism. He took some of the war factories belonging to the state and instituted a joint organization in which the state, the co-operative societies, the works councils and trade unions took part. A number of undertakings were organized on these lines, but with much variety in detail, and for a time some, at least, did well. But they did not develop as he expected and later were either dropped or gradually reverted to the ordinary commercial type. This is in keeping with the tendency shown by other economic enterprises planned in accordance with theory, such as productive industries, run by workmen on a real co-operative basis. If they succeed and carry on, they gradually change their character and become indistinguishable from ordinary concerns. Otherwise they fail and come to an end.

The lesson is the same as that taught by the Russian experience, and it is that the prevailing system of economy is n an arbitrary creation but a natural grow corresponding to the actual conditio and forces of life—in short, the survival the fittest.

In other countries also, in which the has been no revolution as there has be in Russia, Germany and Austria, politic socialism has advanced since the war far as to assume the responsibility government and consequently to face t practical problem of realizing econom socialism. That is the case with Swed and Denmark, particularly the forme which was the first European country instal a socialist administration throu the ordinary political procedure. T Social Democratic party had already, 1914, become the largest party in t Lower Chamber of the Riksdag, and 1917 they joined the coalition gover ment; in 1920, having increased the strength, they formed a government their own. It did not last long; b they returned to office in 1921, held it f eighteen months, and again for ninete months in 1924–26, when they were t largest party in both Chambers.

They have therefore had considerab experience of administrative respons bility and ample opportunity to attem some measure of socialism, but they have attempted none. In 1920 Branting, leader of the party and prime minister, followed the German example and set u a commission of inquiry into socialisatio It was scientific or technical rather tha political, and has since carried on i researches continuously and publish volumes of reports at intervals. The pri cipal object was to discover the best form industrial organization, and reports we issued dealing with different industries. T first dealt with railways, and it is the o that has come nearest to a practical ou come, though not yet carried out. I Sweden the railways are partly owned a operated by the state, partly by priva companies; the report recommended t reorganization of the state railways c commercial lines, with representation all interests in the controlling body. I June, 1926, the socialist government w defeated and resigned. No proposal h

Sweden a Denmar

een made for socialising the privately wned railways or other enterprises.

In Denmark the socialist party assumed ffice in 1924, after a general election which nade them the largest party in the Folieting. It has attempted no measure of ocialism. In Great Britain the Labour arty took office in January, 1924, though ot the largest party, and retained it until November, but attempted no measure of ocialism. In Belgium the Labour party rew level with the Centre at the general lection and formed a coalition ministry vith them in equal proportions. In 926, 3,000 miles of state railways were ommercialised by transference from state dministration to a 'national company,' n autonomous composite body formed n the principle of joint representation of ll interests on the controlling authority.

There remains Australia, which is preminently the land of state enterprises. They have been dispassionately reviewed y Professor J. B. Brigden, of the Uniersity of Tasmania, in a special article written for the International Labour Review (July, 1927). He says that the growth of state usiness enterprise in Australia is not lue to 'any deliberate intention to levelop some kind of socialism, for lthough this idea has been vaguely nfluential with the Labour party, by far he greater part has been promoted by vowed anti-socialists, who sought nothing nore than to provide facilities for the xpansion of private enterprise.' He attriutes it to the habit of relying upon the overnment, to the ease with which overnments can be moved to act, the till greater ease with which they can raise apital in Great Britain, and the temptaions of a new country to develop its esources at the cost of posterity.

tate Enterprise in Australia

He divides the state enterprises into even classes, of which the 'intentionally ocialistic' ones form the last class, and e says of them that they 'have been are in fact, although much has been dvocated and much alleged.' Queensand is 'the only state that has had a onsistent policy avowedly directed tovards socialism.' The Labour party there ecured a majority in 1915 and has been in power ever since. Political socialism has therefore had a longer trial in Queensland than anywhere else. The story of the twelve years, Professor Brigden says, is 'largely one of disillusionment so far as the original ambitions are concerned.'

Yet those ambitions represent a very modified form of socialism. In 1918 the premier, Ryan, declared that 'the object has not been to secure monopoly or to squeeze out of business legitimate private traders, but to protect the public by competing with the latter on fair and efficient lines.' A state trading department was set up, to manage a number of experiments, including cattle stations, butchers' shops, produce agencies, fish supply, fruit canneries, hotels and railway catering. Of these, the trading concerns—butchers' shops, produce agencies, hotels and catering—have been successful, which means have made profits; but the profits have been overwhelmed by the heavier losses made in the other (productive) undertakings, particularly the cattle stations—'an industry that is peculiarly dependent upon individual initiative and resource.' The fish supply was given up; and it is to be observed that a state fish-trawling enterprise, started in 1915 in New South Wales, was sold in 1923 with a total loss of £317,850. The failure was attributed to incompetent management. Other experiments in Queensland that have resulted in continuous losses are coal mines, iron and steel works (abandoned), oil bore (abandoned), ore batteries, smelters, ore-treatment works.

Experiments in Queensland

Next to Queensland, New South Wales has been most active in state enterprises. An industrial undertakings act was passed in 1912, for the administration of trading concerns. Some have been successful, others not. The following have been abandoned with accumulated losses: fish trawlers, timber yards, saw mills, power station. The successful concerns are all connected with the building industry. They are brickworks, metal quarries and construction, pipe and concrete works. There is also a large land settlement scheme, which does not pay its way; but the conditions are exceptional. As in

Queensland, it is the trading concerns that succeed. But the Commonwealth line of steamships, started in 1916 and successful during the war, made such heavy losses afterwards that in 1923 the capital was written down from £12,766,588 to £4,718,500 and the management transferred to a board. In 1925 the government decided, on the advice of the board, to dispose of the fleet, the total loss then amounting to over £4,000,000.

Altogether the Australian experience is very chequered. Advocates of socialism claim 'indirect benefits,' but that implies a complete change of objective and of principle—public enterprise for the regulation, not the displacement, of private.

The position in 1928 was this. The after-war advance of political socialism has in several countries brought the movement face to face with the problem of translating theory into practice and establishing economic socialism. In Russia the attempt was boldly and confidently made to banish capitalism and install full socialism, with such disastrous results as to compel a reluctant return to some degree of capitalism. The aim was not abandoned, only postponed; but subsequent experience has furnished a further proof of its impracticability within any predictable period of time. Elsewhere in Europe the difficulties were found to be so great that no attempt has been made to solve the problem, though many solutions have been proposed.

Acid Test of Responsibility

This experience has reacted on the theory of socialism, which has everywhere undergone revision. It is perceived that the old simple conception of private ownership of capital, etc., replaced by public ownership—vaguely embodied in the term 'nationalisation' or 'socialisation'—does not correspond with the realities of economic life and is quite inadequate. The most thoughtful socialists recognize that the practical problem has never been understood or even seriously studied. The result is that the whole movement is in a state of confusion and uncertainty on the theoretical side, split in two on the political side and paralyse for practical purposes. Only the mor fanatical or the more ignorant cling to th old formulas and expect to see 'socialism in our time.' The more fanatical are th communists, who follow the lead of Russi and adopt the Bolshevik creed.

Hence the great split in the politica movement, signalised by the establish ment of two rival Internationals, the Re or Communist International, founded i 1919 with its seat in Moscow and run by the Bolshevik leaders; and the Labour and Socialist International, which is the old Second Internationa revived at Hamburg in 1923. Th latter represents the more intellectua and rational elements in the move ment, with the German and German Austrian Social Democrats in the fore ground. But their standpoint has bee shifted. The prevalent views on bot the old and the new economic orde —that is capitalism and socialism—hav changed, and the change is reflected in th general revision of programmes. Bu nothing is settled; there is no agree ment; the whole thing is in a stat of flux.

The two riva Internationa

For practical purposes, howeve socialism, apart from communism, ha come to mean social reform of a radica type, and particularly a policy of equalisin material conditions by financial measure within the framework of the capitalis system, which is itself undergoing con tinuous change. Communism has com to mean world revolution, with no definit economic aim and no economic prospec except universal ruin. This is the chie object of Bolshevism, and the instrumen is the Communist International wit branches in every country. Its influenc fluctuates with circumstances, of whic the most important is the amount o money spent in propaganda. It has no the remotest chance of success, but it persistence in abusing hospitality an exciting disturbances is exhausting th patience of one country after another, no of governments only, but still more of th people, including the trade unions.

CHAPTER 186

THE ECONOMICS OF CAPITALISM

How the System works on which the modern Social and Industrial State is built up

By J. A. HOBSON

uthor of The Evolution of Modern Capitalism, Incentives in the New Industrial Order, etc.

L IKE many other 'isms,' capitalism eludes all attempts at close definition. But it is for common convenience taken to mean the modern usiness system, conducted by the owners f the capital employed, or their repre-ntatives, for the sake of private profit. his description, however, does not get s out of the wood; for both 'capital' nd 'profit' are shifty terms. Capital as two faces, according as it is regarded rom its monetary or its material aspect.

For all book-keeping purposes capital is eckoned in terms of money, the capital of company in shares. The 'saving' which orms capital is the saving of money. In ities a 'capitalist' means a man who ossesses, or can procure, money, or credit, or purposes of investment or speculation. But this money is only an index of what ve may call the 'real' capital in the usiness system. That consists of all sorts of marketable matter embodying labour, ools and machinery, buildings and 'improvements,' fuel and power, raw materials and manufactured goods in various processes towards completion, together with stocks of goods in the hands of merchants before they pass by purchase to consumers, thus ceasing to be capital.

It will be observed that land, with its mineral and other resources, so far as it does not represent 'improvements,' is not here classed as capital. But monetary investments and estimates of the capital in a concern include any land values which may have been acquired, and some economists have proposed to merge land in capital, instead of treating it as a separate factor in production. But on the whole it is more convenient to treat land separately, and confine capital to the embodiments of human labour. So also with the proposal to include in capital the acquired strength, skill, knowledge of workers, what is sometimes called 'human capital'; it is too wide a departure from the ordinary way of looking at the business system to be accepted.

But, before proceeding further, certain popular conceptions of capitalism and capitalist deserve attention. What of the 'conflict between capital and labour,' and the capitalist as he figures in the imagination of the class-conscious worker? Though there is sometimes a real conflict of interests between those who seek profit from investing their capital in a business and the wage earners in that business, the immediate conflict of the workers is always with the directors and the management. Under ordinary conditions of free competition it could not rightly be said that any conflict of interests existed between worker and capitalist, whether the latter were owner, manager or shareholder. For under such conditions profits or dividends would be kept at a subsistence level, as well as wages, by competition in the market. Conflict could only arise when competition was restricted, or when a general boom in trade, or some special advantages in methods of production or in markets, put a business, or a whole industry, in a position to earn high profits. Labour would then seek to divert some of this surplus profit into higher wages. In a word, there is harmony between capital and labour when competitive conditions keep prices and dividends low, conflict where some 'surplus' exists.

Popular ideas of Capitalism

The worker, not following these conditions of the market, and visualising a 'bloated capitalist' driving to his office in his Rolls Royce, often falsely dramatises the real issue. Most 'capitalists' are not rich men, but small share or debenture holders in businesses where they have virtually no control, and the dividends they get (unless they have been lucky in their purchase) are usually 'the market rate.' There are large unearned fortunes made under the capitalist system, but they are mostly taken by specially favoured groups of financiers and entrepreneurs, not by the rank and file of the owners of industrial capital, except in cases of inherited wealth.

In any community that did not deliberately seek the simpler life of medieval poverty, whether socialist, communist or any other, capital in large quantities would be still required, and upon its adequate provision the progress of industry and the enlarged comforts of the people would depend. In that sense the permanence of capitalism is a necessity of progress, however the control of capital may be shifted. A socialistic nation would require quite as much capital as a nation working under private enterprise—or even more, if capital were used wastefully.

Power-driven machinery has been the chief instrument of modern capitalism. Amid a multitude of inventions and variations, modern machinery consists of three parts, which, though mechanically connected, are essentially distinct: the motor mechanism, the transmitting mechanism and the tool or working machine. Increased automatism has constantly been added in the modern factory or works, pushing a larger proportion of the employees on to the care and control of machinery, a smaller proportion to mere machine feeding. Thus, though in its earlier stages modern capitalism narrowed and subdivided labour into small monotonous routine, its later stages often call for some skill, responsibility and judgement in the performance of operations which, by reason of some irregularity in material or process, require the human intelligence to intervene.

Chief instrument of Capitalism

Modern capitalism, no doubt, means for the ordinary worker less interesting, less varied, and less skilful labour than prevailed in an era of agriculture and handicraft; but for all that its net effe at any rate in its later development, humanising rather than the reverse. F on the whole, the large town life is m interesting, and literally 'civilizing,' th country life pursued under the old even modern conditions, and the town i product of capitalism. Society, educati recreation, with a higher standard of co sumption and some shortening of the wo day, are compensations for the routi workers and machine tenders. Moreov as statistics show, the volume of emplo ment in purely mechanical processes is n increasing but diminishing in the advanc industries, and an increasing proporti of the occupied population finds emplo ment in transport and distributive wo where there is some variety and some rel from mechanical routine.

The second distinctive feature capitalism is the expansion of mark which large-scale production and improved facilities of transport brought about. Before the days of modern capitalism most articles of food, clothin furniture and other necessaries a conveniences of life were made at hon or within a few miles of home; on a few raw materials, such as cott and metals, together with some forei luxuries like tea, silk and tobacco, car from distant parts. Now home pr duction, save in remote rural plac has almost disappeared, and every town man, or villager, supplies his wants fro distant countries whose very name often does not know.

Expansi of Mark

Two other necessary features of t new industrial order need mention. the beginning of the eighteenth centu joint-stock capital was very narrow confined in its operations. The Fund Debt, the Bank of England and a fe chartered companies for foreign trad such as the East India and Hudson's Ba companies, were almost the only reliab investments on a large scale open to t saving public. Joint-stock enterprise manufacture was virtually non-existe in the mid-century, one of the earlie instances being a company formed 1764 with a capital of £100,000, f manufacturing fine cambrics. Adam Smi ıdicates the limits of joint-stock enterrise in the later eighteenth century in he following passage:

> The only trades which it seems possible or a joint-stock company to carry on uccessfully, without an exclusive privilege, re those of which all the operations are apable of being reduced to what is called routine, or to such a uniformity of method s admits of little or no variation. Of this ind is, first, the banking trade; secondly, he trade of insurance from fire and from seaisks and capture in time of war; thirdly, he trade of making and maintaining a avigable cut or canal; and fourthly, the imilar trade of bringing water for the supply of a great city.

These limits were slow in breaking down before the demands of co-operative capital for manufacture and commerce. In the first half of the nineteenth century the law of unlimited liability, by which a shareholder became responsible for the whole debts or losses of the company, restrained the more cautious investors. Not until limited liability was established in 1855 was the full stream of capitalistic finance free to do its fertilising work, first in railroads, shipping, mining, banking and insurance, next in the supply of municipally or privately owned local services, and finally in the rapid growth of industrial and trading companies. The development of banking, investment and insurance companies is important, however, not merely as an example of joint-stock enterprise, but as the necessary financial instrument of the new capitalism gathering from ever wider areas and strata of population investable savings, and distributing them in accordance with the needs of the various industries and countries as indicated by their comparative values in stock-exchange securities.

The unit of Capitalism

These investments differ also in the conditions attached to them. The familiar distinction of ordinary and preference shares and debentures expresses different degrees of risk and of control, while bank credits play in many instances an important part in assisting joint-stock businesses with short-time loans for running expenses. In some countries, especially in Germany, banks have played a much more important part in the initiation of and participation in industrial and commercial enterprises. In Great Britain banks have played a smaller part, occasionally in underwriting issues of stocks, and normally in making advances for specified periods.

The joint-stock business, the true unit of capitalism, thus constituted, is in its formal government a limited democracy; it is controlled by the vote of shareholders at a general meeting, each share carrying a vote. Virtually, however, the government is vested in the board of directors, the personnel of which was in most cases largely self-appointed at the formation of the company, and can only be displaced with extreme difficulty as a result of conspicuous incompetence. In a large proportion of cases a managing director has autocratic power over the ordinary conduct of the business. The ordinary body of shareholders has neither the knowledge nor the desire to take any real part in the running of the business, or businesses, in which they have put their savings, while in many cases the ownership of shares is merely temporary and for speculative purposes. The speculation of stock exchanges has introduced a fluidity in ownership which greatly enhances the power of the few directors and large owners whose interests are permanent.

The transformation of private businesses into companies has become very rapid in Great Britain and the United States. It serves several conveniences. If financial assistance is needed from banks or other outside sources, share capital is a better security; and for purposes of inheritance and taxation the company form is more convenient. The number of registered companies in Great Britain trebled itself in the first quarter of the twentieth century. The only great branch of production lying almost entirely in individual hands is agriculture. Mining, transport by land and sea, electric power, the staple manufactures, finance, wholesale distribution and an ever growing proportion of retail shopkeeping are joint-stock enterprises. Small employers and individual workers are, however, still found in large numbers in the building and

Joint-stock enterprise

furniture trades, in some branches of the clothing trade and in subsidiary metal trades, as well as in certain luxury and personal services and in repair work.

In America census figures show that in manufactures the proportion of the product turned out by 'corporations' amounts to some 90 per cent. of the total, while the proportion of wage earners thus employed stands at about the same figure. In other industrialised countries, especially in Germany, Japan, France, North Italy, Holland and Switzerland, the same tidal movement towards joint-stock capitalism is clearly discernible.

Constant demand for new Capital

A vast network of financial institutions, banks, investment, trust and insurance companies gathers in the savings of individuals throughout the civilized world and supplies the fresh capital continually needed to start new trades, enlarge or improve old trades, develop backward areas of the earth and equip them with docks, harbours, railroads and the fabric of civilized cities. As modern science speeds up invention in the technique of industry, there is a constant demand for new adventuresome capital, and rapid fortunes often await those who are first in the field. Huge tracts of the world, in particular Russia, China and South America, are ripe for capitalist development upon a scale that would absorb all the spare resources of the more developed West for the next generation. Certain essential raw materials, such as oil, rubber, copper, cotton, are in such urgently growing demand that the whole earth is being ransacked to find increased supplies, and to this task great sums of new capital are consecrated.

This growing mobility of capital has had important reactions on the structure of businesses and industries. When most businesses were in the hands of individuals who worked them with their own resources, or with some occasional bank aid, their size and quality of equipment depended upon this limited finance, and one found in the same trade and the same locality a great variety of businesses of different magnitudes, some employing up-to-date machinery, others clinging to obsolete methods, because they could not afford to change. Under the new conditions, in most staple trades, the capital and labour tend to flow into business units of a more or less uniform size and technical equipment.

Thus, it is possible to talk of 'the representative business,' and though there will be some businesses varying from this type (perhaps working some special patent or supplying some particular market) most of the capital employed in the trade will take this uniform shape. Among the spinning and weaving mills of Lancashire there is a representative mill, in respect of numbers of spindles and looms. This type is larger to-day than in 1900, but definitely, not indefinitely, larger. In each branch of work there is a size or type which is most favourable and economical in working. What applies to textile mills will apply more or less to other trades, in proportion as they are standardised in methods of production and outside capital is freely available. It is more difficult to find a fixed type in engineering, and businesses which supply the changing tastes of consumers, or where new methods of working are in process of discovery cannot easily be brought under this rule.

Size limit of Business Units

But it is right to realize that most manufacturing plants have some limit of size and capital expenditure, beyond which, or below which, it is not economical to work. The rough idea that a large business can be conducted more profitably than a small one because the overhead expenses are reduced per unit of the output, is only true up to a point, and that point stands differently in every sort of trade. This has an important bearing upon the tendency towards 'concentration of capital.' If it were generally true that the bigger a business, the lower are its costs of production, it would seem to follow that bigger businesses would drive smaller ones out of the field and that every industry would gravitate towards a monster trust which would wield the power of a monopoly.

Since this is held to be the chief menace that capitalism presents to the world, it is worth while inquiring how much truth it ontains. The fact that in most trades here is a limit to the size of a productive plant, due partly to economy in distribution of power, partly to conditions of efficient management, does not settle the problem of the tendency towards monopoly. For, though it may not pay o put up a plant of more than a certain size, it may pay a company to own and work a large number of these representative plants, and so it might come to pass that a big concern could monopolise a trade by reason of its financial strength. A big concern, with large capital and greater facilities for obtaining more if required, is in a stronger position for meeting trade emergencies and fluctuations than a small one-mill concern, however well equipped for production. The big concern can often organize its purchases of materials and its market more advantageously; it can employ expert scientists and scrap its out-of-date machinery more easily. In a word, the financial is usually much larger than the technical limit of efficiency.

It will, however, generally be agreed that there is some limit even to this larger type of business. Certain wastes are engendered in a very big business, due chiefly to the human limitations of the managing personnel. A single brain cannot function with full efficiency when the number and intricacy of the business issues are too great. How far does this consideration supply an adequate safeguard against monopoly? The loose way in which the term monopolist, like the term millionaire, is flung about to express the envy and distrust of small traders towards their more successful rivals does not relieve us from the task of ascertaining how far capitalism does run towards monopoly, and of inquiring what the dangers of monopoly are and how they can be met.

Size limit of Monopolies

In his work, Trusts in British Industry, Morgan Rees distinguishes four monopolies—natural, legal, social and artificial:

Thus a natural monopoly would be one in some natural product such as oil or salt; a legal one that granted by law, such as a patent for a machine, or process, or a copyright; a social monopoly would be of the kind that provides public services such as the post office or a water company; while, lastly, artificial monopolies are those which are due to industrial organization and financial power.

The economic problem of capitalism is chiefly concerned with the last order. It is, however, right to add that few monopolies are purely 'artificial' Most of the strong American trusts, for example, are rooted partly in strong finance and organization, partly also in preferential access to raw materials or to transport facilities or to tariff protection. The Standard Oil, the United States Steel Corporation, the Sugar Trust are cases of this mixed origin. Mere size of plant or of capital seldom, if ever, suffices to explain the origin and success of a trust. In America access to the best available raw materials, coupled with some 'pull' upon the railroads, enabled the earlier trust makers to grow until they obtained so large a share of the market that other smaller independent businesses found it safer to follow their lead in price fixing, instead of attempting to compete.

Trusts & Monopolies in America

The trust, an American invention, was a device whereby hitherto competing companies agreed to accept from a body of 'trustees' certificates in lieu of shares in their several concerns, and to receive dividends from a common pool representing the united profits of all the businesses. This device was declared illegal, but the name 'trust' stuck to the various sorts of combine, 'holding company' or other method of substituting combination for competition. Until the close of the nineteenth century successful trusts were very few, but since that time a very large proportion of manufacturing, mining, transport and communications in America has been brought under some strong single financial control.

But the term trust is still loosely used, and though in most cases there is a strong price-fixing power and some control of markets, in very few instances is there anything like complete monopoly. Trusts are sometimes classified as horizontal and vertical, the former consisting of combinations of businesses performing the same productive operation, for instance shoe-machinery making; the latter linking up the various processes by which raw materials, for instance iron and steel, are converted into finished goods, tools, machines, furniture, etc. There is nothing contradictory in the processes, but convenience sometimes decides for one, sometimes for the other, and the modern tendency favours the simpler process of combining firms specialised to a particular line of work, though in some trades, such as metals and machine making, there remains a disposition to control some good supply of raw materials or power.

Besides the American trust, the German 'cartel' has sprung into quick prominence.

The German Cartel system

Long before the war many branches of German production had formed themselves into selling syndicates for fixing prices and common marketing arrangements, both domestic and foreign. In certain scientific products, especially synthetic dyes, chemicals, photographic apparatus and scientific instruments, this trade organization became so efficient as to secure something approaching a world monopoly. Since the war the cartel system has been both extended and intensified. Combination has for practical purposes superseded competition in most staple industries, and the five comprehensive trusts of coal, electricity, potash, textiles and steel dominate the industries of the country.

In Great Britain the art of combination has pursued no single path. The Committee on Trusts, which reported in 1917, described various methods by which the members of a trade got together to regulate prices and maintain 'a reasonable profit.' Some of them were loose and informal, 'gentlemen's alliances,' trade associations for stopping price cutting and preventing over-production. But many of these associations had fixed meetings and committees for the regulation of their local or national trades. Some of them fixed output, leaving prices to take care of themselves ; others fixed prices only. But the tendency even before the war was towards a form of combination that regulated both output and prices and established selling agencies, while a more complete consolidation, approaching to the American trust, was formed in certain textile, metal, chemical and builder furnishing trades.

The war, of course, did much to faci itate and accelerate this movemen Advisory committees and trade associa tions were organized to control prices an regulate production. War finance mad it impossible to get capital for new ente prises, and the large profits made by man firms were put into an extension of the works and an acquisition of weaker com peting businesses. Conferences of manu facturers led to concerted plans, and th after-result was a series of amalgamation

The same movements towards combina tion and association are plainly visible i the distributing trades. Here the store and the multiple shop are taking an in creasing share of retail business, while th chemist, stationer, oilman, draper, chin store display an increasingly miscella neous lot of wares. Only in the highe grades of quality and fashion does the nicely differentiated shopman still survive. Shops in an ever increasing number are tied to som manufacturing firm, as in the boot an shoe trade, or are virtually the agent of some wholesale manufacturer c furnisher, who supplies the packet good they sell and regulates the prices. Organ izations of food vendors are rife in a towns and are stated to restrict supplie (sometimes by destroying surpluses) i order to maintain high prices, especiall in the perishable commodities of fish fruit and vegetables.

Combination of Middleme

Much of this concentration of busines is obviously waste-saving, and when suffi cient competition survives is serviceabl to consumers. But the temptation t maintain high profits and prices is irre sistible when the vendors of any par ticular commodity can easily get together and the passing of a large proportion of local trade into the hands of a few bi firms tends towards more or less regula price arrangements as the sole alternativ to cut-throat competition.

As might have been anticipated, bankin and insurance are two economic activitie which have lent themselves to a hig degree of concentration. The grip o bankers and financiers over the credi machine, and thus over industry in every advanced country, is growing stronger. In 1890 the number of joint-stock banks in England and Wales was 104; in 1900 it had fallen to 77; in 1914 to 38; in 1924 to 18, and, of these, five held 84 per cent. of the aggregate deposit and current accounts. In the insurance world, while competition for business is kept up, the terms on which the business shall be done, and the distribution and pooling of risks, impose a measure of monopoly greater than that prevailing in any other market.

But the concentration of banking and insurance has a much farther-reaching influence than the similar structural change in any other department of economic life. For money and credit are the life blood of the whole system. It is on this account that, not in socialistic circles only, but among sober-minded, practical business men, a grave feeling of uneasiness attaches to the growth of a 'money power' which, through the ramifications of investments and the manipulation of credit, wields a power of life and death over whole industries and provinces of the earth.

Not once, but in a score of instances, bankers have forcibly intervened, for good or evil, in matters of high political as well as economic moment. The collapse and recovery of national monetary systems, the supply or refusal of necessary capital to broken countries, the liquidation of international indebtedness, the general work of restoration after the war have turned mainly on the action of a few great financial magnates in London, Paris, Berlin and New York. Though the British banks have never taken the directly active part in promoting and financing industrial enterprises which Continental banks have done, their control of credit gives them an immense power over the conduct of business.

Danger of a 'Money Power'

It is, therefore, not unnatural that in periods of trade depression many critics should find the fundamental defect of capitalism in the 'money power.' We have, it is contended, no proper security in a monetary system conducted by private financiers for profit that the volume of purchasing power shall expand or contract in accordance with the needs of trade and the consuming public. Bankers' policy, it is claimed, is not directed by a clear sense of the monetary needs of the community. Especially are they charged with curbing and contracting the activity and productivity of industry in order to maintain high prices and high profits in the businesses which they control or finance. This criticism receives a plausible support from evidence which indicates that, while the general industry of Great Britain suffered from depression and unemployment in the post-war years, the banking business throve.

Many authoritative economists have associated themselves with some aspect of this attack upon financial capitalism, urging that the supply of bank money and the direction of the flow of capital shall be brought under public supervision and control. If capitalism were a purely national concern, this demand for the control of money might appear a tolerably simple matter, having regard to the concentration of the banking business in so few hands. But capitalism and the investment market are world phenomena. Countless thousands of citizens in Great Britain and America are part-owners of lands, railroads, minerals, factories, municipal plants and public revenues in all parts of the world.

Attacks on Financial Capitalism

In 1914 the total amount of British capital invested abroad was estimated at about £4,000,000,000, French foreign capital at £1,800,000,000, German at £1,200,000,000. The financing of the Great War, however, materially affected these sums, reducing the British sum by perhaps £1,000,000,000 and almost wiping out the French and German investments. British losses have already been made good to a large extent, though annual receipts from investments abroad are less than before the war. Germany, of course, is becoming a debtor nation on a constantly increasing scale, since her reparation payments are effected, not out of her balance in foreign trade, but by loans and advances from abroad, principally from America. Similarly, France finds great difficulty in paying even the reduced interest on her foreign debts out of her own resources.

The United States stands out as the greatest representative of triumphant capitalism. During and since the war she has not only paid off the bulk of her indebtedness to Europe in respect of the large sums advanced for the making of her railways and the early development of her manufactures, but she has assumed the first place as a foreign investor. Most of the money for the re-establishment of central Europe was found in America, whose high tariff policy compels her to re-invest in Europe, or elsewhere, the large sums due to her for war loans, and any surpluses from her large and growing export trade. Thus the United States' boasted political isolation is countered by enlarged economic stakes in Europe, South America and the Far East.

International Co-operation

But international capitalism is taking a more formal shape in the growing co-operation of capitalist groups in the advanced industrial countries. Banking and finance for a very long time past have had a strongly international character. Money being the most fluid form of capital, it has been convenient for the great financiers to place branches and agencies in foreign countries, and to co-operate with foreign financial groups in large undertakings. A striking example has been the Chinese Consortium, by which banking groups in Europe and America have agreed to pursue a common policy in loans to China, acting with the consent and aid of their national governments.

But the biggest new step in international capitalism is the extension of the cartel. For some time before the war agreements were made in branches of the metal trades between groups of manufacturers in different countries, and a few trusts, ranging from explosives to cotton thread, were successfully established. The Committee on Commercial and Industrial Policy after the war thus reports the pre-war situation :

> British combinations and firms have in a number of instances been parties to international agreements for the delimitation of markets and the regulation of prices. A well-known case is that of the International Rail Syndicate, and other examples relate to such diverse commodities as wire-netting, aniline oil and sulphur black and some other chemical products, glass bottles, tobacco and certain non-ferrous metals.

After the temporary interruption of the war this international capitalism is taking clearer shape. The deliberate policy pursued in Germany, with governmental backing, for the organization of all leading industries into national cartels has had considerable effect as an example to other countries, called upon either to fight these cartels in the world market or to come to terms with them by forming similar national organizations, and linking up with one another. The revival of the steel cartel on the Continent is the first-fruit of the movement, and the coal situation is for many a lesson in the necessity of national co-ordination, in order to come to some agreement which shall enable the industry in the different producing countries to mobilise its output and regulate its prices. Cut-throat competition, violently fluctuating prices, unreliable employment are relics of economic barbarism which capitalism must eliminate if it is to survive.

Attempts to subvert Capitalism

The attack upon capitalism, as business organized for private profit, has taken several shapes. Whole-hog socialism is discussed in Chapter 185, but wherever the experiment has been seriously undertaken it has hitherto proved a failure. Indeed, the general tendency throughout Europe is in the direction of more public regulation, but the limitation of publicly conducted enterprises to a few fundamental industries and other services, either of national or local extent. On the other hand, the Consumers' Co-operative Movement, with its organization of wholesale and retail trade, supplemented by a limited amount of co-operative production, has bitten sharply into capitalism at certain points, controlling a large and growing volume of business, the profits of which are returned to the consumers. In Denmark, Holland, Switzerland, Ireland and parts of Russia much agriculture has taken on a co-operative shape, especially for purchase of materials and machinery and for marketing.

Enthusiastic co-operators have sometimes envisaged co-operation as replacing capitalism over the general body of industrial operations. But there is little solid support for such a vision. Producers' co-operation has taken but shallow root in Great Britain, or any great industrial country. In few cases do workers on a farm, in a factory or mine or in any other capitalist business seem able or willing to save enough to buy any substantial holding in the business, or to launch out for themselves in a new enterprise. Their earnings as a rule leave little margin out of which the considerable capital needed to ensure success can be provided, and these small savings are generally needed for acute family emergencies. Moreover, the wage-earning life seldom gives a sufficient insight into the conduct of a successful modern business to fit the manual worker for effective participation in the management.

Others seek to remove the barriers between the capitalist and the wage earner by schemes of profit sharing and co-partnership, which are intended to enlist the interests of the workers in the high productivity and the monetary success of the business. It is, however, doubtful whether either of these methods is suitable for general application.

Scheme of Profit Sharing

Profit sharing has been successful in certain monopolistic industries, such as gasworks, and in special cases where the personal enthusiasm and generosity of the employers have been inspiring elements. But recurrent periods of bad trade, in which there was no 'profit' to divide, have proved fatal to many experiments, and the suspicion of trade unions at attempts to break the 'solidarity of labour' is a deterrent influence. Co-partnership, if it is to harmonise the interests of capital and labour, implies that large sections of the employees become shareholders to such an extent that they can influence policy. Bonus shares not endowed with voting power do not fulfil this test, and there is very little opportunity for British workers to effect enough savings to become substantial ordinary shareholders in the business where they work.

In America, where wages and possible savings are much higher, successful attempts have been made to induce employees to invest in the telephone, telegraph and other quasi-public co-operations, and the steel trust and other large businesses advertise the wide distribution of their shares among their employees. But there is no general disposition of workers to invest their savings in this way, and such savings as they make go largely into houses or pass through labour banks, insurance or investment companies into the general body of invested capital. If the cleavage between the owning and the working classes is to disappear by any wide and considerable diffusion of property among the workers, the possible margin for saving of wages must be a good deal larger than it is now in any European country.

In Britain and throughout Europe capitalism seems likely in the near future to undergo considerable modifications. State and municipal ownership will continue to gain ground in such fundamental industries as transport, mining, electric power, banking and insurance, while in the operation of these public industries central bureaucracy may to some considerable extent be replaced by local managing bodies upon which labour will be represented. If, as is likely, the improved organization of big business in general passes into the form of cartels or other combinations, some effective public supervision and control, both in the interest of consumers and of other industries, must be devised, so as to prevent the price control exercised by these cartels being abused. In other industries, less developed in structure and competitive in character, private capitalism will continue to have a wide field for initiative and enterprise.

Municipal and State Ownership

If, as some hold, the political state is congenitally unfit for performing the difficult and delicate work of this control, the world will have to reconcile itself to the control of economic life by big financial and industrial groups organizing production for profit, with such consideration for the interests of workers and the consuming public as humanity, fear or some dim sense of social service may evoke.

Sir Joseph John Thomson (left), born near Manchester in 1856, was educated at Cambridge, where he became a lecturer and professor. To his brilliant researches are due the epoch-making discovery of the electron and the present state of knowledge concerning matter. It is to Max Planck (right) that we mainly owe the quantum theory and investigations into the propagation of energy.

Modern conceptions of cosmogony and stellar physics have been largely achieved as a result of the investigations of Sir James Jeans (left), who was awarded the Royal Astronomical Society's Gold Medal in 1922. Arthur Stanley Eddington (right), appointed Plumian professor of astronomy at Cambridge in 1913, is celebrated as the enunciator of the so-called principle of indeterminacy which bears on the geometrical properties of space.

CONTRIBUTORS TO MODERN KNOWLEDGE OF THE MATERIAL UNIVERSE

Photos, E. O. Hoppé, Topical Press Agency and (bottom) Russell

CHAPTER 187

THE NEW PHILOSOPHY OF SCIENCE

A Sketch of modern Progress in clarifying fundamental Problems of Physics with a Discussion of Relativity and Physical Symbolism

By HUGH ELLIOT

Author of Modern Science and Materialism, etc.

The outstanding characteristic of the twentieth century has been the vast expansion of philosophical physics. From the wide morasses of metaphysics a great extent of territory has been reclaimed and added to the province of physics. The result is that the philosophy of this century has become, more than ever before, associated with science. Independent systems of philosophy have arisen from time to time; the most notable is that of Bergson, which for a brief period even acquired popularity. Bergson's system professed to be founded on science, but it never succeeded in attracting the support of scientific workers. It was highly speculative and metaphysical and owed its success more to the literary and oratorical powers of the author than to any firm scientific foundation.

There has indeed been no room for transcendental philosophy of the old-fashioned kind. The discoveries of science have in two decades taught us more about the nature of the universe than we had learned in two millennia of metaphysical speculation. Those interested in the ultimate problems of the universe find more to satisfy them in the conclusions of modern science than they could ever find in philosophy; and, although 'ultimate' questions remain as heretofore unanswered and unanswerable, so much real progress has been made towards allaying curiosity that speculative metaphysics has gone entirely out of favour.

The progress made has been along several lines. First, much has been discovered concerning the nature of the universe, as disclosed by powerful telescopes, and the position of the Earth in the universe. Secondly, the constitution of matter has been explored, and conclusions reached of profound philosophic import. Thirdly, there is the principle of relativity, which must rank up to date as the greatest philosophical discovery of the century. Problems of life and mind have undergone no corresponding advance. Of the true causes of evolution (see page 4529) we are still as ignorant as before. The nature of mind has not been further illuminated, though the relation of mind and body is better understood.

Limitation of the stellar universe

The extent and nature of the universe are subjects that have already been treated incidentally in Chapter I on the Birth of the World, so that only a summary of the most significant facts need be given here. The ancient question was whether the stars occupy a limited portion of space, or whether they continue ad infinitum, so that if there are no limits to space there is no limit either to the number of stars. This question has now received a very definite answer. It is found that the more deeply we probe into the remoter portions of space the scarcer do the stars become. This conclusion has no relation to the greater difficulty of seeing them, but represents the actual fact that the stars at very great distances thin out, until at still greater distances there are probably none left at all. The universe of stars thus represents an island poised in the midst of space. The island is conceived as being of the shape of a bun; that is to say, the stars range for much greater distances in one plane than they do in other directions. It is not possible to fix a definite boundary, for the stars thin out gradually; but they extend about five times as far in one plane as they do in directions at right angles to this plane.

The absolute distances are fabulously great. One way of stating distances is in terms of the time taken by light to traverse space. Light travels at about 186,000 miles a second ; travelling at this velocity, the distance which it covers in one year is called a light-year. The most remote stars of our island universe are about 27,000 light-years away ; in the direction of the shorter axis of the system, the most remote stars are about 5,400 light-years away.

If the stellar universe is limited, it follows that the number of stars must also be finite. The most powerful telescope in the world is at Mount Wilson in California (see page 58) ; and it is estimated that this telescope can detect about 1,000 million stars. Naturally there is a far greater number, too faint for detection, and it is believed that the total number is of the order of 30,000 million.

These stars all belong to one gigantic system or universe, the boundary of which is marked by the Milky Way, and which is therefore called the Galactic System. This system is not merely a random collection of stars, but a connected whole, probably having a common origin. The stars are thickest near the middle, and most sparsely scattered near the edge ; but even where they are packed closest they are still four or five light-years distant from each other. Their movements within the system also indicate a common origin, with a general tendency to rotation about the axis of the Galaxy. The age of the stars is considered to be of the order of from five to ten million million years.

Nature of the Galactic System

The stellar universe does not comprise all the objects visible through large telescopes. At far greater distances than any yet dealt with other bodies are discernible of the most gigantic proportions. These objects, whose nature is investigated in Chapter I, are the spiral nebulae. Their mass is of the order of a thousand million suns ; their volume is of the order of the Galactic System itself. The nearest of them is distant nearly a million light-years, and the farthest that can be seen about 140 million light-years. Within that range there are believed to lie about two million nebulae at more or less uniform distances from each other. The Earth is but one of many planets, going round the Sun ; the Sun is one of thirty thousand million stars, comprising the stellar universe ; the stellar universe is one of two million other universes ; and what there may be beyond is outside the range even of speculation.

Modern theory suggests that all the nebulae are of about the same age, and that they also may have had a common origin. That origin may have been an excessively attenuated gas spreading through the whole of space, as we know it ; for calculations show that such a gas would break up into masses of about the sizes and distances apart actually found in the nebulae. The nebulae in their turn would break up into other masses of about the sizes and distances of the stars. The origin of the solar system, however, is conceived of somewhat differently, as set forth in pages 66–76 of Chapter I, where the ' tidal theory ' is enunciated.

One circumstance of profound philosophic interest—also a cardinal conclusion of Chapter I—is that the whole process of stellar evolution involves the disintegration of matter. The material substance of the universe is uniformly wasting. The processes which we witness cannot therefore have been going on for ever. They are but a phase, which must some time have had a beginning and will some time have an end. But of what are they a phase ? If matter is perpetually vanishing out of existence, and if no contrary process has ever either been observed or imagined, how was it originally created ? To that problem modern science gives not the slightest clue, nor should we be surprised thereby. Unimaginable as are the magnitudes and distances which we have described, they may be but a speck by comparison with some other order of existences, far beyond the range of our possible knowledge. And in this other order of existences there may occur the complement of the processes which we now witness. Man is usually surprised to find that his new discoveries do not explain everything. All that we can ascertain is the kind of process now occurring in our particular corner of space ; and all we can infer is that in some other part

Disintegration of matter

f space or in some other period of time ther processes must be occurring, or ave occurred, radically different from nything of which we have cognizance.

Increasing knowledge of the size and ature of the universe is not the only in- uence in determining the tendencies of odern thought. Researches into the ltimate constitution of matter have been profound and fruitful of discovery that hey have given a new direction and npetus to philosophy. Philosophy is eing dragged in the wake of physics ; and cience has begun to incorporate new onceptions, which were formerly held to e the subject matter of metaphysics.

verthrow of the Atomic Theory

At the end of the nineteenth century he atomic theory (see page 4525) was stablished as a fact. Matter was shown to consist of an inconceivable quantity of molecules ; the molecules again were composed of still smaller units, called toms. Ninety-two kinds of atom, and inety-two alone, were recognized as xisting on the earth. From the various ombinations of these atoms all molecules ere formed ; and matter as we know it as merely a vast collection of molecules.

The atoms themselves were imagined as ard, spherical, incredibly minute balls of atter. Any object, such as a table, was hus conceived as consisting of an infinity f tiny billiard balls flying about in empty pace. If it were possible to magnify the tructure of matter sufficiently, it was supposed, these little balls would actually be een. The theory certainly seemed odd, ut was perfectly intelligible. It amounted this, that matter is really discontinuous. t consisted of an incredible multitude of mall particles ; but these small particles ere still composed of 'matter.'

The twentieth century has completely verthrown this simple scheme. Research as been concentrated on the composition f the atom ; and it has been found that, o far from being merely a speck of plain atter, it has a constitution so remarkable s to upset some of the firmest conclusions f science, philosophy and common sense. he science of the nineteenth century nded with the atom ; the science of the wentieth century begins with the atom.

All atoms are found to consist of two essential parts : a central nucleus, called the 'proton,' and one or more 'electrons' revolving round it. An electron has only about the two-thousandth part of the weight of the atom. It is the seat of an enormously powerful charge of negative electricity. The proton is far smaller, but has a mass comparable to that of an atom. It is the seat of a correspondingly immense charge of positive electricity.

The electron not material

In the previous century mass was defined as 'quantity of matter.' But another astonishing discovery of physics was that mass was conferred also by electric charge ; and, on reckoning up the size of an electron and the electric charge upon it, it was found that the electric charge alone was sufficient, or almost sufficient, to account for the whole mass of the electron. In other words, an electron is not in the ordinary sense a particle of matter at all : it is a particle of electricity, and matter appears to have vanished altogether. It is merely a gross appearance based upon electrical energy.

The Victorian doctrine of the indestructibility of matter likewise fell. Electrons can and do vanish out of existence, giving rise to radiation which travels away into the depths of space. The substance of the stars, as we have seen, is gradually disappearing. In its place waves spread out through space, some of which are in the form which we know as light. The old distinction between matter and energy has broken down ; for energy also has properties formerly attributed to matter alone. Rays of light are deflected by gravitation ; and an estimate can be formed of how many tons of sunlight fall upon the Earth in the course of a day.

For a brief period it was supposed that electrons represented the final stage in the analysis of matter, but their preeminence has turned out to be shortlived. Hitherto we have dealt purely with particles, always smaller and smaller, but still imaginable in our mind's eye. It is now suggested that electrons are 'disturbed areas' in space caused by the convergence and coalescence of waves in an imaginary 'sub-aether.' Another point must be mentioned on account of its profound philosophic interest; namely, that they seem in a peculiar way to be outside the laws of science altogether.

The principle involved is called by Eddington 'the principle of indeterminacy.' If an electron is a moving particle, it would appear that at any given instant it must have a definite position and a definite velocity, both of which might be defined if the measuring appliances of science were sufficiently refined. They are sufficiently refined, but they give an apparently unintelligible conclusion. The position can be ascertained with great exactness, but the measurement of velocity immediately becomes vague. So also the velocity can be measured with great exactness, but only at the expense of vagueness in position. The discrepancy is not due to any imperfection of scientific appliances; it is in the nature of the object itself. To affirm that a particle has at a given moment a certain position and a certain velocity, both precisely defined, corresponds to a very clear idea in the human mind, but to nothing in the objective universe.

Principle of Indeterminacy

We here impinge upon the principle of relativity, and before embarking on that theory a word of caution may be useful. In the older science we might not be able actually to see the objects described, but we could always form an imaginary model of them. Models indeed were constructed showing the atoms within the molecule, and the electrons within the atom. All that we had to do was to reduce them in imagination to infinitesimal dimensions; and we had then a real idea of what they were supposed to represent. But, in the light of relativity, no models are possible. Models are replaced by symbols; and from a world of concrete images we pass into a world of symbolism. Models can be constructed, but they are lame and inept. The difficulty found in grasping relativity is due to our inherent tendency to work in visual images; it is not due to any real difficulty in the subject itself.

Imagine that there existed in the universe only one body, poised in the midst of universal emptiness. Suppose it was desired to ascertain whether thi body was in motion or not, how shoul we set about it? Every physical proces occurring on the body would be the same whether it was in a state of motion or c rest. The Earth, for instance, is movin round the Sun, and is also moving at hig velocity through space with the rest of th solar system, but neither of these motion can be detected by anything occurring o the Earth's surface. On a solitary bod in the universe there would be a complet absence of any internal evidence of motion Neither would there be any externa evidence. It would not be getting neare to anything nor farther from anything since we have assumed that there i nothing else in the universe. In shor the conception of motion would b spurious. We might with equal propriet affirm that it was at rest, or that it wa moving a thousand miles a second Neither statement would mean anything nor correspond to any objective fact.

But now suppose that there are tw bodies; the conception of motion imme diately arises. For they may be gettin nearer to one another, or farther off. And if there are a number of bodies, their relative motion can be perceived. Motion is relation between separate bodies. Thi is expressed by saying that all motion i relative. Absolute motion is an abstrac tion in words, with no real meaning.

Motion and siz mere abstractior

Size is also an abstraction. If ther were just one body in the universe, ther would be no meaning in saying that it i large or small. Size only takes a meanin when two things are compared. On thing may be larger or smaller tha another, but there is no such thing a absolute size.

Conception of time is in the same cas If no change ever occurred in our singl body in the universe, it is clear that t specify a second or an hour or a year woul have no kind of meaning. Time onl begins to arise when events occur whos duration can be compared. Even then can only be said that one event last longer or shorter than another. Absolut time is another verbal abstraction whic has no counterpart in reality.

For our own personal con-
nience we have set up
andards of distance and of
ne. We have yards and
iles, and we have seconds
d hours. But these are no
ore absolute than the space
d time which they set forth
measure. In different cir-
mstances they may measure
iite different things.

Suppose that a balloon is
iling in the wind and a
one is dropped from it to
e surface of the earth, an
server in the balloon, look-
g downwards, will see it fall
umb beneath him. It will
pear to follow a straight
ne downwards. But to an
server standing on the earth
will appear to describe a
rabola. For while falling to
e earth it still possesses the
otion which it had in the
lloon; and, though the point
which it strikes the earth is
ill directly under the balloon,
at point is a considerable
stance from the point at
hich it would have landed
d it fallen 'in a straight
ne' downwards. The path
scribed by the stone appears
one observer as a straight
ne and to the other as a curve.
hich is right?

INTERPRETER OF SPACE, TIME AND MATTER

Einstein, whose photograph appears in page 4704—this is a portrait done in 1920 by Hermann Struck—was the first to resolve the problem raised by the famous Michelson-Morley experiment on the propagation of light; his solution (1905) is called the special theory of relativity. The general theory (1915) embraces all natural phenomena, especially gravitation.

From Einstein, Das Relativitätstheorie, F. Vieweg & Sohn, Verlag

Both of them are right from
eir own point of view: neither is
ght in any absolute sense. To observers
fferently situated, the stone may appear
describe any kind of peculiar curve.
o point of view is more fundamental than
ny other. But we live upon the surface
the earth, under certain conditions,
d it is convenient for us to take the
int of view of an observer on the
rth. Convenience is the sole criterion.
here is nothing absolute about a straight
ne. From the absolute point of view,
is just as much curved as straight;
the same way that a single body
oised in the universe may be regarded
being at rest or in motion, with equal
opriety and equal futility.

The standards of space and time which we adopt for our own convenience work exceedingly well, so long as we do not attempt to apply them under conditions very different from those in which we live. But as soon as we pass this limitation peculiar things appear to happen. It is found that a body travelling through space at very high velocity (relative to ourselves) becomes shortened in the direction of motion. A book flying through space sideways would become thinner; if it was travelling lengthways it would become shorter. But, viewed by an observer on that other body, it is we who are flying through space, and it is we who are becoming flattened in the direction of our motion. Which is right? Both are right from their own point of view: neither is right in any absolute sense. Length is purely relative; except as a standard of comparison, it has no real meaning.

The same discrepancies arise with time. At two bodies, remote in space, two events take place. Which happened first? If we observe under particular conditions from one point of space, we may form a different verdict from that which we should have formed under other conditions elsewhere. But which really happened first? The question is futile—like asking whether a given trajectory is a curve or a straight line. It is either, according to the point of view. There is no absolute answer to be given.

The principle of Relativity

The fact is that, to suit our own convenience, we have chopped up nature into a system of space, time, stresses, etc., which are valid enough for our personal standpoint. But as soon as we get on to problems remote from the conditions of human life, the framework into which we parcel out nature becomes inadequate. Space and time are not absolute properties of nature; they are put into nature by the human mind, for ease of reference and measurement. But after a certain point they no longer serve that purpose. They are for ever leading to contrary results, according to the point of view. Is it not possible, then, to supply a new framework which will not lead to a paradox at every turn? It is; and that is just what the relativists have done. They do not measure space in three dimensions, height, width and thickness, and time in another dimension. They weld space and time into one framework of four dimensions. They add at will other dimensions derived from mechanical concepts; and they thus obtain an altogether new framework, which gives the same results for any point of view of the observer.

The principle of relativity has given a new conception to the law of gravitation. Newton imagined gravitation as a force; and a force is an independent sort of existence that has nothing particular to do with either space or time. But by welding space and time into a singl[e] framework there appears to be no furthe[r] need for the idea of force. If a fly were t[o] walk in as straight a course as it coul[d] over a sheet of paper that was crumpled its path would be highly tortuous. Tha[t] is the effect of crumpling in space. Bu[t] the new continuum of space-time i[s] also susceptible of being crumpled. Th[e] proximity of matter does in fact introduc[e] kinks into it; and the path of a plane[t] travelling round the sun is merely the nor- mal path of a body negotiating the kink in space-time set up by the proximit[y] of the sun. There is no need for the ide[a] of gravitational force. The ordinary geo- metry of space-time accounts adequatel[y] for the observed phenomena. The ten- dency is for geometry to swallow u[p] mechanics, and, instead of conceiving th[e] universe as the seat of the interplay o[f] physical forces, it suffices to assume [a] highly complex geometrical structure.

Quantum theor[y] of Energy

Closely connected with relativity is th[e] famous quantum theory. Long ago speculation on the nature of light hovere[d] between two rival doctrines: one, that it consisted of small corpuscles moving at enormous velocity; the other, that it con- sisted of waves in an imaginary aethe[r]. Not till the present century was it dis- covered that light presents some sort o[f] analogy to an atomic structure. It i[s] emitted as an enormous aggregation o[f] units, which are called 'quanta.' [A] quantum is not a material corpuscle, no[r] is it a fixed quantity of energy. Cor- puscles and energy are conceptions o[f] the ordinary three-dimensional world and the quantum resides in the highe[r] sphere of four dimensions. It is obtaine[d] by multiplying energy by time. This give[s] a new kind of existence, to which ha[s] been given the name of 'action.' [A] quantum is merely an atom of actio[n]. The quantum theory of light combines therefore, both the corpuscular and th[e] undulatory theories of the past. It over- steps the limits of thought, which can b[e] comprised within three dimensions, an[d] introduces us to a four-dimensional actio[n] which is cut up into universally equa[l] atoms or quanta.

Passing now from the more strictly ientific aspects, we have to examine the :neral effect of these revelations on odern thought, and how they fit in with 'e-existing philosophic systems. As yet ey are all too new to have been woven to any general system of thought, and e progress of discovery is so rapid that) such attempt is likely to be made. The ost revolutionary philosophic fact is at, as the light of science penetrates ore deeply into the unknown, we pass ıt of the world of concrete entities into a :w world consisting of symbols alone. atter is gradually analysed down to ırticles smaller and still smaller, till in e end we reach something which is not particle at all, but merely a symbol, mething which however greatly it may : magnified remains radically different om what we imagine in a crude particle matter. Not only a change of size, but change of nature has occurred.

To many minds such a conclusion pears self-destructive. But to philophic minds there is nothing particularly surprising about it. One large school of philosophy has always regarded matter as a symbol. Such a view is always been entertained by idealism. ong ago in the history of thought it was ointed out that subjective feelings are e sole experience of man. Here, for stance, is what we call a table. We ıow it chiefly by the senses of sight and uch. But what really happens is that e alleged table creates impressions on e nerve endings in the retina and skin. ıese impressions start nervous currents hich set up a commotion in the brain, ıd that commotion is accompanied by a eling, or mode of consciousness, which e designate by the name of table. All at we have experience of is the conscious eling. What has a conscious feeling to) with external reality? The objective ble is but a symbol; it is not the thing which we have immediate experience, ıt an inference or generalisation; and, there were no such thing as a sense of sion, the inference would assume a totally fferent form. A nervous process in the ain cannot possibly resemble a table, d the nervous process (or its psychical accompaniment) is all that we have cognizance of when we speak of a table. Modern physics has not, as sometimes imagined, whittled away reality to symbols. It has merely replaced the old symbolism by a new symbolism which works better.

ymbolism of odern physics

Like space and time, matter is relative to ourselves. It is not an absolute reality, but a construction of our minds, woven out of the raw material provided by multitudinous sense impressions. These constructions work well enough, as long as we do not wander too far from home, but they break down as soon as we take an extensive journey into the unknown.

Causation and Determinism

While modern discovery is entirely in accordance with philosophic idealism, it is equally illustrative of scientific materialism, as distinct, of course, from the crude materialism of past times. The relation of cause and effect is nowhere obscured; nor is there any relaxation from the rigid determinism underlying the workings of nature. This last statement has been denied, and that too by a very high authority; but the denial appears to be based on a misunderstanding. It has been alleged that the principle of indeterminacy, mentioned above, indicates an aberrant or lawless factor at the root of natural phenomena. But statistical law presents a similar indeterminacy. Out of a million people of a certain age it is possible to forecast with a high degree of accuracy what percentage will die within a year; but it is not possible to forecast the duration of life of the actual individuals. Indeterminacy does not mean a denial of causation. The confusion arises from remnants of old metaphysical conceptions clinging to the idea of causation. It used to be supposed that cause produced effect by some sort of compulsory action. The very word 'law' carries with it a suggestion of compulsion. It is entirely contrary to modern thought to imagine scientific law as a kind of supernatural force compelling the obedience of natural phenomena. It is now looked upon rather as the expression of an identity, such as that two and two make four. Cause and effect are no more than the statement of an identity; they are two different sides of the same thing, joined by a time-relation. The terms themselves are metaphysical, because the whole of language has a metaphysical basis. It is not the theory of causation that is at fault, but the words in which the theory has to be stated.

In one respect progress in the twentieth century follows uninterruptedly the progress of the nineteenth. The centrality and supremacy of man become more and more discredited. In the Victorian age man learned that he was but one kind of animal, among innumerable others, inhabiting a small planet attached to a small star. He now learns that his perception of space and time, and his measurements of matter, are but one way of looking at things, out of an infinity of other possible ways. The larger trend of philosophy has always been away from human centrality; and it is realized that one of the main obstacles to knowledge is in the inveterate habit of mankind of looking at everything from the point of view of their own centrality, and to assume that everything is by nature exactly what it appears to them to be.

Physics and Psychology

The problems of physics seem to be approaching those of psychology. External nature, as ordinary people see it, consists so largely of what is unwittingly put into it by the human mind. Relativity gets rid of much of this intrusive element; but most people still find an almost insuperable difficulty in disentangling the physical and the psychological.

In the sphere of psychology itself the same difficulty arises, and gives birth to such hoary metaphysical controversies as that of determinism versus free will. The position left over at the end of the nineteenth century was that all human activities were due to physico-chemical processes, and that a human being might be regarded as an extremely elaborate machine. On the other hand, there was the immediate verdict of consciousness that various activities could be initiated by an act of will, and were therefore psychical. Continued research has associated ever more closely the physical with the psychical; and now the belief has arisen that they are in fact not two different things in close correspondence, but an actual identity. According to this theory, a process of mind is no more nor less than a material process in the brain. The identification of two things which appear to be so widely dissimilar need not disconcert us. Physics has already established identities no less surprising. Light, for instance, is an oscillation. Mass is a curvature in space-time. In these instances two phenomena which at first sight seem wholly incommensurable, are perceived to be the same thing looked at in different ways. So, too the ultimate identification of physical with mental processes may not be far distant. Such a theory is neither materialistic nor idealistic; it is both. Determinism and free will are merely a puzzle of words which dissolves away as the meanings of the words are more clearly defined. Like so many metaphysical controversies of the past, the antagonism is a verbal one. It is due, as the physicists would say, to the use of two different frames of reference.

Ultimate Solution still unattainable

While modern thought succeeds in untying various metaphysical knots of the past, it must not be supposed that we are in any way approaching a solution of final problems. The more we learn about nature, the more do we become aware of our own ignorance. Every problem that is solved opens up a fresh series of problems not hitherto thought of. The sphere of the Unknown is infinite: the sphere of the Known may be expanding but is always finite. We are no nearer to ultimate solutions than Thales or Pythagoras; the quest for ultimate solutions is merely the symptom of a disordered mind.

What has already been accomplished should satisfy the aspirations of the most exacting seeker after truth. If the past affords any index of the future, the progress of knowledge will continue at ever-increasing speed; and the present century is likely to witness revolutions in thought greater than any which we have here attempted to describe.

CHAPTER 188

MODERNISM IN LITERATURE AND ART

New aesthetic Standards raised in Revolt against Romanticism and the tendency to subordinate Feeling to Form

By OSBERT BURDETT

Author of The Beardsley Period, Critical Essays, The Brownings, etc.

VERY decade has its modernist movement; but for our purposes we mean by modernism in England the movements, which are varied, at have arisen since the end of the ictorian age (see Chapter 171). Equally ery country has its modernist movement; but in dealing with such a wide ıbject it will be found necessary to conntrate on a few representative examples. Who, in England, were thought to be odernist between 1900 and 1914, and hat were the qualities by which their ork was welcomed or attacked as such? efore attempting to answer these quesons, we must remember this. Though e year 1914 will be regarded by hisrians as the formal end of the Victorian a, the ideals on which its social and litical fabric rested had shown definite gns of decay more than twenty years efore (see page 4535). Beardsley, Ibsen, ietzsche and Butler had startled attention y holding the Victorian conventions up ridicule. With the end of the century e old pattern had been broken in pieces, ut nothing had appeared to take its place. ore people can tell you the things that ey disbelieve than the things that they ave faith in, and in an atmosphere of ental confusion the human imagination oes not create so freely or harmoniously in a mood in which fundamental beliefs e taken, by most people, for granted.

The years from 1900 to 1914, then, show particular direction or movement in terature. They show, at most, the estructive criticism of the preceding ecade, less shrill in tone, persisting, and ying here and there to be constructive, o. The realists and 'ninety men' had eed writers from several restrictive taboos; no one was now abused for saying in a novel that two lovers kissed each other on the mouth; no one any longer believed that unions without the sanction of the church were relations impossible to mention in a book. George Eliot had lived and dared. It was no longer supposed that the whole duty of a parent was to break the will of his child, or the whole duty of a man to be respectable and to make money. Girls were leaving their homes, and finding openings of all kinds in shops and offices, as a matter of course. Young men were presented with latchkeys; and writers had won a similar freedom for their pens. In this more sociable world young women on their own were as common as blackberries, and, if they were that way inclined, made friends and had affairs much like their brothers.

Reaction against Victorianism

The doors had been opened. It was all very pleasant—but what was literature to do? There was no driving motive, unless description was one, and no further influence from France arrived to replace the one that Zola and the realists, Flaubert and the passion for beautiful writing, had given to the outmoded Yellow Book school. In this relatively happy but rather rudderless decade all we can do is to follow the course of literature up to the Great War.

Like a bomb set to explode some time after the fuse had been lighted, The Way of All Flesh was published in 1903, a year after Samuel Butler's death. Its wonderful fidelity to the life of one type of mid-Victorian home was not fully recognized for a year or two. Young people had already reacted violently from the Victorian age, and the adjective Victorian had degenerated into a word of uncritical contempt. They were now forcibly reminded of the atmosphere from which they had escaped, though they did not always remember that they had escaped because their parents had interfered with them much less than their grandparents had with father and mother.

The Way of All Flesh had been written of such a parent, though Butler himself remained a bachelor to the last. His book showed how the parents of his hero had tried to break the will of their son, and had been defeated; how religion had been made an excuse for punishing him, education for deceiving him (as it always is more or less), and duty for making him do everything he loathed, and for forbidding him everything his healthy instincts craved for. The bad side of domestic life in the Victorian age had been put into a book at last, a book faithful and detailed, and the more impressive because the author did not

THOMAS HARDY

Already a dominant figure in Victorian literature by virtue of his gifts as poet and novelist Thomas Hardy (1840–1927) produced his masterpiece in the epic drama of The Dynasts, published when its author was nearing seventy.

Photo, Walter Thomas

SAMUEL BUTLER

In his posthumously published novel, The Way of All Flesh, Samuel Butler (1835–1902) presented the early twentieth century with a faithful picture of the conventions and restraints that typified life in the Victorian Age.

Painted by C. Gogin; National Portrait Gallery, London

attack the parents but showed them behaving, with the best intentions, according to the convention of what was then thought respectable and appropriate. Its dusty, gritty style suited the dreary domesticity of the scene. Young people who have no nerves, stomached this bitter dish without difficulty, and awoke to the discovery that, if the Victorian age was at once romantic and material, it was also interesting and worth study, like any other period. Reaction was virtually over: study and criticism about to begin.

The virtues of the book were proclaimed by Bernard Shaw, who became himself a figure of controversial interest to the younger generation in the following year 1904, when with John Galsworthy and a few other playwrights he began to present play after play for two years at the Court Theatre. He told his audience that idealism was the devil; that the behaviour of the parents in Butler's novels had been inspired by romantic ideals; that a person had a duty to himself, and that if he would only follow his own instincts, as Butler's

›y had done in resisting his parents, he ould discover that he had restraining ıpulses as well. Shaw also said that all tablished religions were incredible but here being fashions in human beliefs) ıat the theory of evolution was not. He ıen wrote a play called Man and ıperman (followed twenty years later by ack to Methuselah) to show that a ligion might be made of this way of oking at life. He was also a socialist ıd filled his plays with discussions of dustrial society from a point of view so ›tached that it was often very witty; and scussed marriage, doctors, the Salvation rmy, the suffragettes, from the point of ew of one with the latest information ›out all these things and with no other ea than to bring the searching light of mmon sense to bear on them.

In a word, he made the theatre do all ıose things which the newspapers are ıpposed to do, and do not; and he was good-humoured about it all that he was resistible to any youngster with a scrap curiosity about life. Though Shaw had een hammering away at all these matters r twenty years, he seemed very modern those who had never heard them dis- ıssed until his wit surprised them into tention at the Court Theatre. Galsworthy ıd Granville Barker were doing similar work in their own way at the same time and place, and the English theatre, still deaf to the enthralling plays of Ibsen, woke up to the fact that discussions could be made interesting on the stage.

In 1904–8 the veteran novelist Thomas Hardy, who had returned to poetry late in life, published The Dynasts, a huge epic drama of the Napoleonic wars, in which the conception of the whole human destiny also arose from the evolutionist's stand-point. The theory was inspiring poetry at last. In the novel H. G. Wells's vivid imagination and lively creation of character and atmosphere were inventing romances of the future of man, as he might be conceived evolving, and descriptions of poor shopkeepers and clerks suddenly turning their backs on the counter and finding their own souls in a free, if desperate, struggle with life. Galsworthy described the home life of the well-to-do, Arnold Bennett the provincials of the Midlands. Theirs was a much more sober affair than Wells's dashes for freedom, but no less true to life.

Almost at the same moment a genuine tramp, who happened to be a genuine poet too, told his personal experiences of people who live without a stiver and without work, and reminded his hearers that the possibilities of life, and even of fellowship

WRITERS WHO ACHIEVED EMINENCE IN THE EARLY TWENTIETH CENTURY

ıe original genius of the Irish playwright George Bernard Shaw (left), born in 1856, has produced series of witty, unconventional plays which intrigue and stimulate modern audiences. Brilliant ›wers of imagination and expression have raised Herbert George Wells (centre), born in 1866, to oremost position among contemporary novelists, while it was the great gift of Arnold Bennett (right), in his forceful novels, to bestow vitality upon the humdrum lives of ordinary people.

Photos, Vandyk, Gainsborough Studios and E. O. Hoppé

and travel, are by no means stifled under these conditions. The class that W. H. Davies described in his Autobiography of a Super-Tramp, which first appeared in 1908, was new to modern literature, though the type is as eternal as the stars. Human nature in the raw, when a man has enough simplicity or imagination to describe it vividly, is always modern, and his book was a welcome reminder that a life of disreputable adventure is as possible as ever, even in a rigidly policed modern city, without necessarily getting on the wrong side of the law. Novelists like Arnold Bennett, whose Old Wives' Tale made his success in 1908, and a little later Rose Macaulay and Compton Mackenzie, were busy describing contemporary society in the more respectable, but now innumerable, walks of life.

Human nature always modern

All these authors held, in effect, the modernist outlook, implicitly at any rate. Bennett revelled, as illiterate folk with comfortable bank balances would revel if they had his capacity, in modern de luxe hotels, commercial swank and display, big tips and heavy dinners, garish lights and the whole machinery by which expensive life is organized on a paying basis by cosmopolitan big businesses. He found the spectacle of lavish spending amusing after his provincial studies of the drab Five Towns. To read some of his novels was like entering a huge restaurant, and attempting to be intimate with one's guest above the blare of the band. The Grand Babylon hotel, jazz music, dance clubs for everybody! What could be more true to the day, what more free from the earnest ideals that the benighted Victorians had held dear? How could anyone have taken them seriously?

In this whirligig a very amusing book of criticisms was published under the title Heretics. Written by Gilbert Keith Chesterton, it appeared in 1905. The word 'heretics' had gone out of fashion with the beliefs that had given it meaning, and the heretics whom Chesterton had in mind were precisely such modernist writers as we have glanced at. He was as lively as the liveliest of them, and more paradoxical in his manner than most. The fun was this: he used his gusto and flashed his epigrams in defence of th old-fashioned things, of romance, of religion, even, if you please, of Christianity It is the merit of Chesterton's Orthodoxy published in 1908, that it forestalls revival which is stronger to-day than i was then. His defence of tradition fron the romantic quarter is now enforced b T. S. Eliot's from the classical.

The last sauce to jaded palates was t see the advanced guard sharpshot by on of themselves; and Chesterton's reader were reminded, as a fact worth notice that Shaw, Wells, George Moore, and s forth, were not orthodox Christians. Tha the reader was not one either, very likely made him sit up the more if he, too, ha lazily admired, without intelligent scrutiny these critics of the old order. The boo had a deserved success, and Hilair Belloc's volumes of poetry, history fantastic romance or political criticism written by a Roman Catholic and a demo crat, soon followed, to proclaim tradi tional beliefs and opinions once more The pair laughed at sceptics, reminded us that many sweeping scientific assertions were unproved, mocked socialists, attacked teetotalers and did this with such spirit and humou that the books were jolly to reac Indeed, Belloc showed a gift for recall ing our ties with the remote past as rea at least, as Wells' gift of successiv guesses at the future. Once read Belloc' Europe and the Faith, James the Secon or How the Reformation Happened, an you begin to realize how one-sided wa the history taught at school. His sens of historical perspective gives you a unforgettable vision of our creator, the pas

Chesterton an Hilaire Bello

The two, Chesterton and Belloc, als showed a talent for invective that onl comes from sincerity of feeling. They we the first to attack the secrecy of the politic party funds, the sale of honours and th wire-pulling by finance that seem in separable from politics. They warned u that 'social reform' might lead us to th 'servile state.' Their claim to give voic to the normal, uncorrupted English in stincts for beer and skittles, religion an romance, was not affectation, becaus there is French blood in both of them

What we take for a matter of course, or have forgotten, is vivid to an observer with a more detached and critical view.

The chief new poet of the time was Walter de la Mare, whose magic, recalling Poe and Coleridge but exquisitely his own, was generally revealed to the world by The Listeners, published in 1911. A group of younger poets, collectively coming to be known as the Georgians, was also producing volumes of verse. If none created a sensation, they attracted attention to contemporary

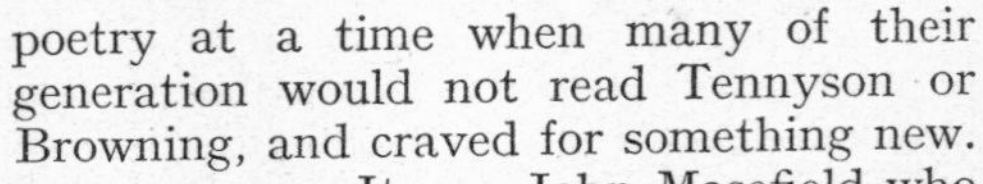

poetry at a time when many of their generation would not read Tennyson or Browning, and craved for something new.

It was John Masefield who supplied the need with his galloping narrative poems, sometimes spattered with the language of ruffians. These began to appear, also in 1911, with The Everlasting Mercy. Nothing could have been more up-to-date than the matter or the manner of these exciting novels in verse. The first was written with great vigour, and added the abuse of the gutter to the

George Moore

W. H. Davies

G. K. Chesterton

Hilaire Belloc

John Masefield

Walter de la Mare

Joseph Conrad

POETS AND PROSE WRITERS WHO REPRESENT THE MODERN AGE

In Walter de la Mare and John Masefield the poetic spirit found modern interpreters, and W. H. Davies, tramp and poet, struck a new note in literature with his Autobiography of a Super-Tramp, published in 1908. G. K. Chesterton and Hilaire Belloc produced works of outstanding merit in widely divergent fields, with a prevailing note of fantasy. Great imaginative power characterises the writings of Joseph Conrad, while the stories of George Moore may be classed as realism.

Photos, Elliott & Fry, Swaine, E. O. Hoppé, Foulsham & Banfield, Elliott & Fry, and Annan freedom recently not won, but recovered, for print.

Another aspect of the mild impatience with the respectable routine of middle-class life was a revival of interest in the gipsy volumes of George Borrow, who had found a poet's pleasure in the society of the people of the roads, with their scorn of appearances, of settled habits and the regular smug comfort of our town and suburban life. The gypsy's tent (see Augustus John's earlier pictures) became as fascinating as the artistic Bohemia which du Maurier had made popular in Trilby some twenty years before.

It was now a century since England had been engaged in any war in the west of Europe. The machinery of settled society seemed to be running with the repetitive movement of an engine. Where was youth to escape boredom except in the free and easy life of the studios, or in the open air among villages whose traditional remoteness was already being invaded by the inquisitive motor? There was a mild restlessness in the air; the book of ideas and the life and literature of Bohemianism, in wild Wales or Whistlerian Chelsea, were the only recognized escapes. Both of these were too tame to be long satisfying, for did not the new garden cities take a respectable delight in them?

Growing impatience with Convention

All this created little lasting literature, but it was the atmosphere in which any original genius that might be forthcoming had to grow. The impulse, as the bare description shows, was too thin; there was neither the impetus of some personal example, nor the excitement of a new artistic theory, to quicken the imagination. For ideas about things, that is, the realm of opinion (always changing as circumstances change), produce the best journalism; they rarely produce fine literature. The reason is that the realm of opinion is superficial, and the aim of the journalist to produce an immediate effect by the straightest road. Now both such subjects and such treatment address the fringe of the mind rather than the imagination, while the influence of poetry and art is always indirect: by casting a persuasive spell upon the feelings, and touching us in letters by unforgettable combinations of sound and sense which we cannot, and do not desire to, analyse.

Shaw and Wells were journalists of genius: Aristophanes, Swift and Voltaire, with whom they have been compared, were beautiful writers as well, and are now read for the literary art of which they were masters. The prose of the two moderns is rotten with journalistic catchwords, with the hasty and dusty phrases that lie like waste paper or yesterday's posters on the pavements of Fleet Street. There are finer passages, of course, but in the main, to use an image of W. B. Yeats, both prefer 'plain water to every vintage, so much metropolitan lead and solder to any tendril of the vine.'

The consequence was that, except for the village well of W. H. Davies' poetry and the magic spring divined by the rod of de la Mare, the most imaginative work of this decade was being done by an older generation whose autumn seemed to release new powers, as the leaves in the fall of the year flame with more than the summer's colour. Hardy gave himself to poetry, and, crabbed in style as it may be, and monotonous in its note of tragic disillusion, it was original, highly personal to the author, and often beautiful. Joseph Conrad, too, was beginning to come into his own, with the brooding mystery with which at his best he endows his characters, in a style looming with shadow and shot with light. Against the enormous background of the open sea or sky Conrad's creatures, like Hardy's peasants, are vested with an imaginative dignity that mere fidelity to present-day circumstances can rarely give. Conrad's brooding imagination had made his novels moving, for there was no overt departure from tradition here. With the short stories of Irish character, collected under the beautiful title of The Untilled Field, in 1903, and with his novel The Lake, of 1908, George Moore first created the last and most beautiful of his three styles. He composed tales as human and lovely as the old Greek legends, and, in the plenitude of his powers, entered on the path that was to lead him to his finest short

Indian Summer of the older age

stories, A Storyteller's Holiday, and to the purest of his very personal criticism, Avowals. Nor was the Irish school dead; Yeats, now more austere in manner, continued to compose in verse and prose; James Stephens gave us in 1912 his fantastic fairy tale The Crock of Gold; Lord Dunsany was inventing his imaginative plays and stories, half Oriental, half grotesque, sensitively and delicately written.

The long afternoon into which Victorianism and its overflow seemed to have settled was ended when war was declared in August, 1914. As we now see, the shock of this, though (as usual) the war itself inspired little good literature, released the new talents that were preparing. Its immediate effect was to fix on Rupert Brooke as the poet typical of all the others that went down with him in the conflict. His poetry became accepted when the demand arose for sonnets as well as shells, and his five, in spite of obvious weaknesses, show a talent true if slight. His name, moreover, was a beacon to the group of Georgians of which he was already the best known.

It is invidious to single out names among the war poets, for war poetry rarely endures. Its ardours seem unreal when the inevitable reaction has chilled them, and its bitterness becomes alien to our sympathy once the horror is a hateful memory which we wish to forget. Siegfried Sassoon was more cruel in truthfulness than most; but what imagination can survive such suffering unscathed? The war apart, some of James Elroy Flecker (d. 1915) is worth remembering, and the relative artistic success of his Oriental play Hassan, which was better to read than to see acted, proved that he could write prose and dialogue with some of the opulence of De Quincey. He might yet have given to us that poetic drama for which we still have to wait. Ralph Hodgson, in Eve and in The Bull, to take his best known poems, has added to English lyrics, both modern in the sense that the modulation was his own.

After eighteen months of war the craving for literature, which nothing can still, began to assert itself insistently. A still younger group, including Aldous Huxley, Sherard Vines, Edith Sitwell and her two brothers, produced an anthology of 'new poetry' called Wheels, and about

DISCIPLES AND DEMONSTRATORS OF 'THE NEW POETRY'

With the verses of Edith Sitwell, whose annual anthology of modern poetry, Wheels, was first published in 1916, there came a new, at first anomalous, reaction in literature. Among the contributors to this 'new poetry' were Sherard Vines (centre) and Aldous Huxley (left), whose brilliant wit and satire have earned him his high reputation as a novelist. Right: P. Wyndham Lewis, member of another poetical group who experimented forcefully with new forms and subjects.

Photos, Elliott & Fry, and Press Portrait Bureau

the same time the artist Wyndham Lewis and another group united in Blast, the title of which was an apt summary of the manner. To the man in the street the only quality that distinguished much of this new work from prose was that it was printed differently; but there was far more than mannerism in the best of it. Put summarily, the idea is to break the fixed regularity of ordinary verse much as Blake and the Lake Poets broke through the strings of the couplet; to write entirely by ear, to shun logical repetitions of beat and to bring new subjects into poetry—because all that could be said of the rose or the moon, the spring or one's mistress, had been said already to weariness, at least in the familiar forms of verse.

EUROPEAN AUTHORS OF DISTINCTION

The Sicilian playwright Luigi Pirandello, born in 1867, is famous for his powerful dramas Henri IV and Six Characters in Search of an Author. The French Marcel Proust (1871–1922) used a Freudian method in his A la Recherche du temps perdu, a brooding analysis of his life's experience.

Photos, E.N.A. and Otto

New subjects and new forms were wanted, and the new poets made a gallant experiment to find them, which inevitable ridicule did not kill. When Dr. Ernest Jones issued at the close of the war his Studies in Psycho-analysis the new clue to our human make-up fell on fertile soil. Its apparent contempt for the convention of human dignity gave a zest to those who had seen human dignity amid the slaughter, and had no illusions to be dispelled. Psycho-analysis promised a field as fertile to the novelist as the now familiar theory of heredity; but these special clues to character appeal, in literature, to a curiosity that, soon satisfied, is short-lived.

With the admission that all new truth and all new forms in art seem ugly on their appearance, for the unfamiliar is suspect at first, we have to use our intelligence to discover who is genuine and original, who imitative or absurd. It is now apparent why D. H. Lawrence should be preoccupied with sex; he wishes us to share his explorations, to grow in wisdom and sorrow, in the old phrase, and to compensate us, if he can, with discovery of beauty in the old mystery he would unravel. Of the same generation is James Joyce, who published The Dubliners in 1914, A Portrait of the Artist as a Young Man in 1918, and his gigantic study of all that passes, unconscious or conscious, through the mind in a bare twenty-four hours, in Ulysses in 1922. A single day was described in a thousand pages. The new poets, too, sometimes make abstract

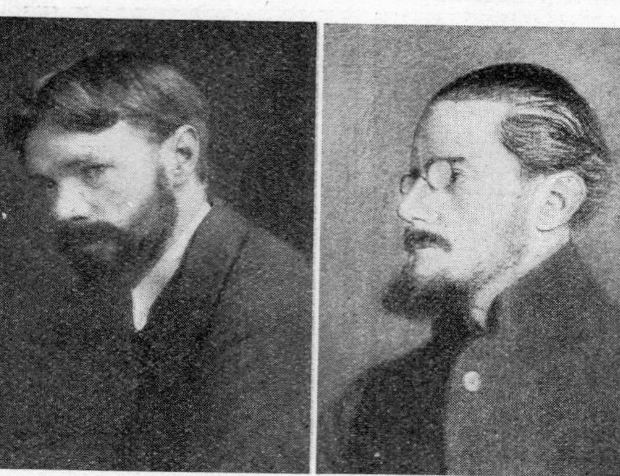

WRITERS OF THE PSYCHO-ANALYTIC SCHOOL

James Joyce (right), born in Dublin in 1882, is best known for his Ulysses, published in 1922. Among his other works are The Dubliners and A Portrait of the Artist as a Young Man. David Herbert Lawrence (b. 1885) has written novels, stories, plays and poems which express the reactions of sex conflict.

Photos, Elliott & Fry and from H. S. Gorman, 'James Joyce,' Geoffrey Bles

atterns with words, intended to please y their rhythm, perhaps by their incongruity, rather in the manner of nonsense hymes, though deliberately without hyme or regular verses.

Without any war, as we shall be seeing ı the studios, this would have been ttempted, for a live tradition implies xperiment, but the war probably gave n impulse to the desire. For example, he Victorian age was now seemingly emote, and people began to study it rom a standpoint that was called cynical, artly because the standards had moved. 'he satire of one generation may become he common sense of the next. Lytton trachey's Eminent Victorians, which xamined famous personages off their edestals by the light of a critical intelligence, and his later study of the character of Queen Victoria, displayed a welcome detachment that would hardly have been possible to men of the old time, simply because they were too close to one another. It is still too early to see existing modernists in perspective; Cardinal Manning and Gladstone were similarly handicapped in respect to one another. Modernism is anti-romantic, experimental, critical and possibly too detached and disillusioned to create great poetry, though the sincerity of its attempt to reflect and illuminate the groping currents of the time is sincere. In The Constant Nymph, 1924, Margaret Kennedy recovered the pre-war atmosphere beautifully.

About the same time Pirandello's plays reached the English theatre. He has added nothing to philosophy, but he has made Berkeley's two-hundred-year old

NATURE AS EXPRESSED BY THE DELICATE ART OF COROT

'rominent among members of the Barbizon School was Jean-Baptiste Camille Corot (1796–1875), hose Flood is reproduced above. This painting is a typical example in the artist's later manner, nd reveals the atmospheric qualities and softness of handling which are the dominating features of is work. In such simple subjects as this did Corot and the impressionists who followed him find full and lasting expression of their conceptions of nature.

National Gallery of British Art, Millbank; photo, W. F. Mansell philosophy the basis of fascinating and, at first, bewildering plays. From France has come the influence of Proust, whose vast novel in eight volumes, Remembrance of Things Past, had explored the recesses of memory with a marvellous skill. His involved style becomes the very skein of memory, beginning at the point where workaday memory fails.

The plastic arts, modernist painting and sculpture, being more independent of ideas, and tied to stiffer material, may strike the eye more oddly but are easier to understand. The Romantic movement in painting culminated towards the end of the nineteenth century in the impressionists. These had turned aside from the servile copying of nature, which everyone could recognize at once, because they did not want to go on doing what had been done to perfection ever since the discovery of perspective over four hundred years before. On a flat surface perspective had been able to represent a square house, a whole valley, a range of mountains, so that a landscape hanging on the wall gave the effect of looking through a window into the country. The impressionists saw also that objects appeared to different people differently, and severally determined to paint what they saw; not merely what they knew to be there.

To the eyes of Corot, the leaves on a branch in the twilight were as indefinite and as lovely as a puff of fading smoke, and no landscapes give one man's response to the poetry of nature more exquisitely than Corot's. The impressionists also

DEGAS' BRILLIANT EXPOSITION OF HIS FAVOURITE THEME

This picture, Répétition d'un ballet sur la scène, is representative of the subjects that inspired the French artist H. G. E. Degas (1834–1917) to produce much of his best work in painting, pastel, etching and aquatint. A stern realist, he always looked behind the scenes, preferring to surprise the faults and strivings of a rehearsal rather than the glittering perfection of final performance; a washerwoman at work, a fat person drying herself, an odd movement of the body, rather than a 'beauty' or fine clothes. He was a superb draughtsman.

The Louvre; photo, Giraudon

RIVER SCENE BY THE FOUNDER OF THE IMPRESSIONIST SCHOOL

aude Monet (1840–1926) is accepted as the founder of the impressionist school of painting and a aster of 'luminism.' His knowledge of the resolution of white light into the seven colours of the ectrum resulted in his adopting colour schemes of surprising brilliance, and a novelty in his techque was the use of broken colours, producing a shimmering effect which was especially happy in his representations of moving water or a flood of sunshine.

Photo, Drouet

w that the colour of everything changed th the play of light, and that perhaps a nsitive eye would never twice see grass identical tones. So they studied the fects of light, whether the shimmer in e blaze of sunshine or the subtlest of nes under a cloudy sky. In this way ey tried to teach the rest of the world see the complex colours really before instead of the crude colours crude en expected to find.

The art of their pictures—at their orst, smudges of colour and mist—chnically lay in the combined truth and rmony of the innumerable gradations of licate tones that they assembled. It as an individual and truthful way of oking at the world: individual because e artist gave the impression that he had ceived, truthful because he gave it in ery range of tone, without heed to the ay in which it might impress a cruder eye. What more was left for the painters who came after to do? Had not naturalistic painting been carried to its limits by impressionism?

The post-impressionists, as they called themselves, reached the general public of London about ten years after they had won recognition in Paris. An exhibition of their works was held at the Grafton Galleries in 1910, though the work of Manet and Gauguin and Van Gogh was becoming known to a few English artists already. The post-impressionists declared that painting had become too complex and too naturalistic. The impressionists, they said, had sacrificed too much to representing nature with scientific subtlety, and were doing, if more truthfully, what their predecessors had done. Art, said the newcomers, is not truth; it is not nature; it is a pattern or rhythm of design that we impose on nature.

Impressionism was a development of the ' plein air ' method of painting whereby subjects are pr sented realistically in full daylight. Edouard Manet was the originator of the plein air school, an in his works realism and impressionism are blended with the happiest results. A notable exampl is this Bar des Folies Bergère, first exhibited in 1882, a triumph of composition and colour an extraordinarily clever use of reflections.

Courtesy of Mr. Samuel Courtauld

Paul Gauguin (1848–1903) began as an impressionist under the tuition of Camille Pissarro, but d veloped on independent lines. His work, of which this Nevermore is admirably representative, essentially decorative, broad outlines constituting the principal feature of the construction of t pattern and enclosing large areas of rich colour applied in masses. In 1891 he went to Tahiti a specialised on painting the primitive people of the Pacific Islands in a primitive style.

REPRESENTATIVE WORKS OF POST-IMPRESSIONIST MASTERS

Copyright, Syndicat de la Propriété Artistique

SUNFLOWERS BY A NEO-IMPRESSIONIST
issarro, Gauguin and Seurat chiefly influenced ie technique of Van Gogh, who in his brief areer developed into one of the foremost neo-npressionists. The feature of his work is broad design with masses of splendid colour.
State Gallery Munich; photo, Hanfstaengl

it satisfies that sense alone? Let us unload all this knowledge, and set our imagination free! Why copy? Why not invent? Is not a beautiful invention a richer expression of your own imagination than a literal rendering, however subtle or exquisite, of any subject external to you? The impressionists had shown to normal eyes aspects of nature which they had missed. The post-impressionists went beyond the impression in search of the quality by which an object stirs the soul.

For example, everyone knows Blake's poem called The Tyger. It has not a word of description. It does not show a tiger as its stripes divide in the glare of the desert sun or fade in the shadow of a passing cloud; but it gives with extraordinary

SELF PORTRAIT OF VAN GOGH
Vincent Van Gogh (1853–90), a Dutchman, began to paint in Paris in 1886. A landscape is given in the plate facing page 5027. Always a highly temperamental man, his mind became unhinged toward the end of his short life.
Courtesy of Mr. Samuel Courtauld (copyright Syndicat de la Propriété Artistique)

One of the first English artists to react gainst impressionism was Augustus John, hose pictures, often figures placed as art of a decorative design in a landscape, end towards simplification. All are ecorations, and the same is true of the est of the portraits that came from him fter his reputation was made.

The beauty of art resides in the arrangement, though why such and such a elation of line and colour should be eautiful no philosopher has explained, nd no artist needs to know. Beauty is ie name we give to a form which happens have significance to our imaginations. he imagination satisfied, the sense of eauty satisfied, who cares whether the attern itself is like anything else? Is not Persian mat as beautiful as any landcape? Indeed is not the appeal purer, iore imaginative, precisely because

A FOREMOST BRITISH MODERNIST

Fine draughtsmanship, simplification of form and decorative use of large masses of colour are notes of the work of Augustus John (b. 1878), who, in his earlier work particularly, shows a predilection for gypsy types. The Orange Jacket, charged with intensity and personality, is typical of John's method.

National Gallery of British Art, Millbank; courtesy of the Artist

It may appeal to the im- agination to a degree that a 'good likeness' or a recogniz- ably drawn horse can neve reach.

Curiously enough, a grea impressionist painter, Mane himself, was also the bridg to post-impressionism. By painting his objects with th light full upon them he had to simplify the planes int which all pictures of soli objects in the flat necessaril fall. This simplification wa not only true to nature, bu sometimes had the effect o an abstract pattern. He ha ceased to be interested in th gradual play of light and shade; he put plain colour side by side. He converte his subjects into a simplifie pattern of lines and oppose colours. The black and whit squares of a chess-board ar a simple abstract pattern; in deed, the check is a patter that is never long out of favou in clothes and hangings. Such abstract patterns as were sug gested by the interior of a room, with its shapes of chai and table-legs for instance began to be painted.

They were received wit ridicule because the public could onl see that the painter had bothered littl with exact perspective and had ap parently arranged his lines and contraste his colours as a clever child might us his paint box before he had been 'taugh to draw.' People were blind to the forma pattern, because they were looking fo what they expected to find—that is literalness of rendering, the very objec that the artist was determined not t give. As useless, then, to tell these foll that the design was beautiful and th chair and table used to form a desig chosen by the imagination, as to giv Blake's poem to a scientist who wa curious to study tigers.

It was Cézanne who carried the leas impressionistic side of Manet's work to it

beauty and vividness the mental sugges- tions that the word 'tiger' arouses in the mind: the strength, the terror, the splendid animal ferocity of the beast. So with the paintings of the post-impression- ists. A scientist who had never visited the Zoo or seen a photograph or picture would be puzzled and indignant if pre- sented, for his purposes, with the lines of Blake's poem. The verses do two things: they give us the tigerishness of the tiger, and they make a beautiful abstract pattern in words. They simplify the animal to the sensation, none the less beautiful for its terror and strangeness, that it evokes. Thus, too, a rocking horse, or a child's drawing of a person (which is hardly more 'like' any human being than an extrava- gant caricature), may be a work of art.

THE SMILING WOMAN

In respect of no other quality is the portraiture of Augustus John so entirely individual and distinctive as in its almost uncanny penetration into the enigma of personality. His Smiling Woman, a representative canvas, is further remarkable among his works for the completeness of its finish.

National Gallery of British Art, courtesy of the artist

To face page 5026

As a post-impressionist, Vincent Van Gogh showed indifference to naturalism in colour, concerning himself chiefly with pattern. In this Landscape with Cypress Trees something is reflected of the unrest which affected his always sensitive mind.
National Gallery of British Art, Millbank

Subtle modulation of colour and delicate sensitiveness to atmospheric vibrations are distinguishing characteristics of Paul Cézanne's landscape work, in which also particular care is devoted to structure and design. Although, under the influence of Pissarro, he gradually enlarged his palette, he ever had a preference for subdued, almost sombre, tones, as exhibited in this charming study, Les Grands Arbres.

REPRESENTATIVE LANDSCAPES BY TWO FRENCH MODERNISTS

full independence. The result was to remind people of primitive work, work done long before the trick of perspective was discovered, in the childhood of mankind. Now all design, all pattern, as the chess-board reminds us, is at root geometrical, an arrangement of straight lines, squares and curves. It was this return to simplification to which Cézanne led the way. He made pictures like patterns, for the pleasure a pattern can give. Gauguin and Van Gogh used the same method to express visions and feelings, as if Blake's poem represented, as the words indeed imply, not so much the first tiger as the idea burning in the mind of God before He called this wild creature into existence. From the complexity of appearances that art had learned to render to perfection, and had thus left painting

SELF-PORTRAIT AND EASEL PICTURE BY A POST-IMPRESSIONIST

During his life Paul Cézanne (1839–1906) was rated with the impressionists, but as a realist much more interested in the solidity, density and geometrical form of objects than in the fugitive effects of light upon them, he was rather the first of the post-impressionists. Power of characterisation distinguishes his portraiture, of which the self-portrait (top) is typical. The Card Players, one of several versions of the subject, shows his appreciation of the dramatic value of contrasting light and shade.

The Louvre; photos, Archives Photographiques and (top) Mansell

nothing more to do except repeat, the simplicity of form and structure was disentangled. The resulting pattern, in the hands of an artist with a sense of design, produced a new beauty; refreshing because it was abstract, a type, as it were, eternal because free from the minor differences of individual and perishing substances.

Now abstract form and colour have a mysterious and grand appeal to the imagination. There is much of mathematics in music and architecture, and the higher mathematics have been called the poetry of pure reason, as anyone can understand who notices how, to take a simple example, the problems of Euclid are 'beautifully' worked out. Thus from one point of view the post-impressionists returned to primitive, even to barbaric, simplicity. They brought negro sculpture into fashion. From another point of view they sought in art to give the abstract pleasure of pure symmetrical forms. Weary of copying nature, they returned to the simplicity of the child—or of the savage—artist in one direction, and aspired to the contemplation of abstract design in another.

This endeavour was carried farther by Matisse, whose search for abstract pattern often went so far as to deprive his subjects of almost any resemblance to nature. It was natural that the public should ridicule such work at first, because the whole progress of art, hitherto, had appealed to the public by ever closer resemblance to the appearances of things which were apparent to everybody. As this resemblance was further departed from, and the appeal was increasingly made to the sense of pure design, it was inevitably found that this sense is cultivated by few, and that the public's delight in art should be revealed to be mainly the pleasure of applauding imitation. It was very easy to caricature and to imitate the new convention. Nothing more seemed to be required than helpless ignorance of drawing, the putting of the crudest colours side by side, with no aim but to irritate and startle.

VASE OF FLOWERS BY MATISSE

The barbaric simplicity which the post-impressionists reintroduced into art was carried to extremes in the designs of Henri Matisse, born in 1869, whose pursuit of the abstract inclined to produce the unnatural. Characteristic features of his style are restraint and delicacy of colouring.

Copyright, Syndicat de la Propriété Artistique

This modernist painting, however, is not an extravagance bequeathed by the war, but was a movement already on its way before the war started. It spread to the applied and decorative arts when Roger Fry opened his Omega workshop, the 'last word' in decorative design. You could see there a rug or a carpet with a fringe at one end only, and apparently composed of unrelated fragments of different patterns. The idea was this. Every pattern, from the pip of an ace of hearts upon a playing card, is the

CUBIST PORTRAITURE

. Spaniard born at Madrid, Juan Griz (1888–927) settled in Paris in 1905, and with Picasso, f whom he painted this portrait in 1912—rangely unlike the self-portrait below—was ne of the founders of the Cubist movement.

Courtesy of 'Artwork' (Flechthein Collection)

epetition of two halves, the second eversed. An old Persian mat, any geoietrical pattern, if cut in two and eparated will suggest its other half withut difficulty. The missing half is a ogical repetition of the first half turned ver. When, however, the mind knows xactly what to expect, the imagination ıay be bored rather than satisfied, for here is always something strange and eyond explanation in every beautiful hing. How could this wonder, that the kilful achievement of the completed attern had originally excited, be reovered? Could it indeed be recovered vithout disappointing the eye of the epose that formal repetition gives?

Roger Fry showed that the imagination ould be satisfied if it replaced the logical epetition of the first half with an quivalent, but not an imitation, of the econd. The effect of repetition was given without the repetition itself. A block of formal design at one corner of his rug would be balanced by a corresponding mass of plain colour at the other, and so on. In his best rugs the eye took as great a pleasure in imagining, say, the expected fringe at the other end as in finding it there. Once you looked for harmony and no longer confused harmony with exact repetition, these rugs ceased to seem unfinished or absurd. After all, poetry ever suggests more than it says; and one of the joys of music is that it cannot be tied down to a precise meaning. It may suggest different things in different moods.

The next development was cubism, which originated in 1908 at Paris. As the name implies, it sought exclusively abstract pattern. Roger Fry defined its aim to be 'a purely abstract

PABLO PICASSO BY HIMSELF

Pablo Picasso, a most versatile painter, was born at Malaga in 1881. For many years he was a foremost figure in the Cubist school, but later he developed a realism much more conformable to the natural appearance of things.

Photo, W. F. Mansell (copyright, Syndicat artistique)

language of form—a visual music.' The imitation of nature was desired no longer. The new motto was: do not copy what you see but paint what you feel, for the feeling is what excites the imagination of the onlooker. This theory had its obvious dangers. A man's feelings are his own and, left to themselves, without the discipline given by respect for the object that excites them, may run riot into absurdity. An abstract theory may be as enslaving to the imagination as the concrete theory that art should copy things. The cube or crystal was supposed to be the abstract primitive form, and circles to be cubes that had lost their edges! Thus the 'primitive form' of a man, on this theory, is six cubes; four for his limbs, and two for his trunk and his head. Each cube, too, is a pattern in itself, and there is no denying that a beautiful pattern may be made on this convention, once the desire to imitate nature takes second place.

Pablo Picasso was the leader of the new school, and the most puzzling things in the new pictures were their titles. Instead of explaining, they puzzled you to find out where the subject was conceale in the apparent tangle of planes and cube in front of you. The subject had cease to be important in order that it might b suggested (in the abstract) instead o rendered. Picasso, as Frank Rutter ha explained, also presented his subjects i fragments, put together from differen points of view. Early Egyptian reliefs d the same when they show us the face i profile, the eye full face, the shoulder square to the spectator and the legs, onc more, seen from the side (see pages 501–2)

Obviously, such work lent itself to wil extravagance, but since our concern i with the real and not the vagary, w will pass over expressionism, futurism attempts to paint the passage of time b drawing ten arms to represent a single arm in motion, which the Italian Marinetti, a excitable journalist, proclaimed in nois articles and lectures about the world. Le us be content to note the increasing interes in machinery, the tone of violence, whic were affecting the arts before the war.

The best, perhaps, of these weir compositions is Giacomo Balla's pictur

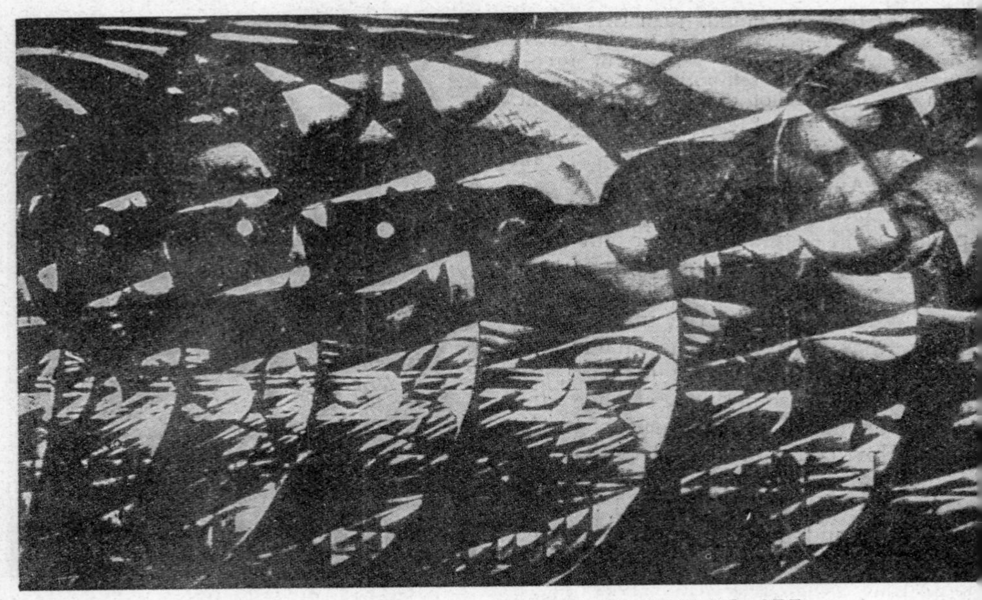

FUTURISM IN ITALY: SPECIMEN OF BALLA'S ART

Signor Giacomo Balla, with the ambitious aim of giving concrete expression to an abstract subjec selected for this picture the theme of Centrifugal Force. A striking effect is produced by the rangir of gold and silver spheres, shooting off sparks in apparently rapid revolution against a background sapphire blue. Unlike some futurist creations, this study is less likely to amuse than to impres

From Frank Rutter, 'Evolution in Modern Art,' Geo. Harrap & Co., Ltd.

ernard Meninsky was born in 1891 and studied in London at the Slade School and in Paris. Sim-icity is the keynote of his water colours, and in his landscapes, of which this Landscape in Hamp-ire is a characteristic example, he exhibits the modern tendency to eliminate irrelevant details and concentrate on the main essentials of composition and the production of brilliance of tone and light, employing flat washes of colour strengthened by heavier pen and brush work.

Courtesy of the Artist

he art of wood engraving has revived considerably during the twentieth century, and since the Great Var has become increasingly important. Leading figures of this revival are the brothers Paul and John ash, born respectively in 1889 and 1893. The dramatic quality of John Nash's work is exemplified this Interior of a Wood, in which he has created an extraordinary impression of depth by his clever use of light and shade and skilful balance of masses.

MODERN TENDENCIES IN PAINTING AND WOOD ENGRAVING

Courtesy of the Artist and 'The Studio'

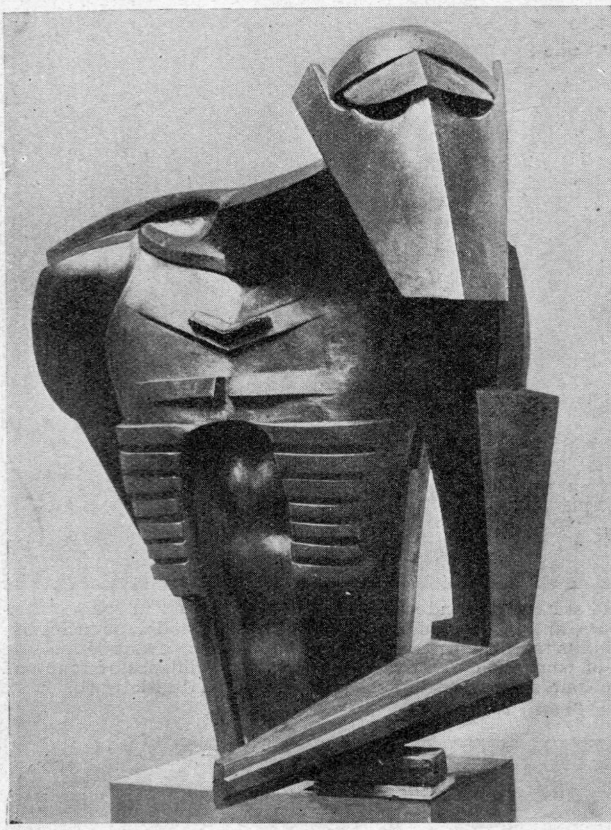

MACHINERY AS THE MASTER OF MAN

Violent controversy has raged round the work of Jacob Epstein (born 1880), but that it is the expression of a genius peculiarly sensitive to current ideas is conceded. The Rock Drill, executed in 1913, is a highly imaginative representation in the vorticist manner of the relentless mechanical spirit in modern life.

Photo, Paul Laib; courtesy of the Artist

of Centrifugal Force, and note the prophecy of Wyndham Lewis' composition of planes and wedges entitled Plan of Campaign. This was exhibited in the June of 1914 in London. Painting was the plaything of ideas, and yet there was an (as yet) undefined aspect of modern life for which the best artists were seeking an expression. The vorticism of Wyndham Lewis, a variation on cubism and futurism, was more than a reaction, as was clear when it found its appropriate subject in the mechanism of modern weapons and in vast armies of human automata at drill or on the march. Now this mechanism, this discipline, is also prominent in industrial life. We have the mass production of useful things and the mas production of ideas in news papers, which manufacture th opinions that they profess t represent. This is not th whole of modern life, but it i its most prominent and per haps, for the individual, it most oppressive trait.

The modern principle c private judgement in th course of time produces a rio of private opinion, counter balanced by mass suggestio from above, and it was onl natural that art, in one of it phases, should mirror thi The symbol for a mechanica crowded, struggling, and there fore regimented age was pro duced by Jacob Epstein in hi monster called the Rock Dril It might have been called th War God, the Spirit of Machin ery, the Human Brute, th Voice of the Crowd, the Frenz of a Mob or the Hysteria c a Newspaper, Moloch, Brut Wealth, or Brute Poverty. I was an idol, representin any or all of these blind an callous forces: the tyranny c materialism and its product

It was the same force tha G. F. Watts had tried to sym bolise in his painting of th Minotaur. But Watts had ac cepted the form and name c a dead Greek monster, and thus did nc probe our consciences half so keenly a Epstein's image, which any modern blas furnace might have spawned. Idols, whe works of art, are hideous without bein ugly. The ugliness is in the evil spirit tha they represent. The beauty is in th definition which controls the design, in th imaginative truthfulness of the line tha circumscribes it. The Rock Drill fascir ates but appals. Yet, since the imagina tion is happier in its loves than in it hatreds, great art is usually most cor cerned with the Vision of Good, and turning aside from its main path when concentrates, as at times it must, upo the Vision of Evil.

ARCHITECTURE'S ADAPTATION TO MODERN BUSINESS NEEDS

Revolutionary changes are being effected in modern architecture by the use of concrete and steel in construction and the exactitude with which these materials can be adapted to calculation and theory. A first result has been the American skyscraper, with façades so developed that all the windows admit the maximum of air and sunlight. A superb example is the Telephone Building in New York, notable for the zoning principle of construction in the upper half.

Photo, Central News

Modernist interpretation of Gothic principles in ecclesiastical architecture has found masterly expression in Liverpool Cathedral, designed by Sir G. G. Scott, the foundation stone of which was laid in 1894. Situated on S. James's Mount, the red sandstone mass of the eastward portion already built dominates the city, and, when completed, the vast church, with the majestic central tower that is a principal feature of the structure, will be a landmark visible for many miles.

In England the American type of skyscraper has not yet found acceptance, but concrete and steel are being used ever more freely in construction, especially for commercial buildings. In its combination of strength and lightness, Adelaide House, at the city end of London Bridge, has an aesthetic aim of its own, the slight vertical fining of the pylons at the four corners of its rectangular mass being a particularly happy concession, derived from Greek models.

THE NEW SPIRIT IN ECCLESIASTICAL AND COMMERCIAL BUILDINGS

Photos, Donald McLeish and (top) Stewart Bale

Large scale experiments by Le Corbusier at Bordeaux and elsewhere have proved the utility, economy and aesthetic value of blocks of maisonettes built on the 'honeycomb' principle. Each of these two-storeyed dwellings has its terrace garden.

odernist architecture starts from the proposition that new conditions require the discarding of l methods and old styles, and for industrial and domestic purposes alike advocates mass production ilding, of standardised materials, adapted to new requirements of hygiene, and with a beauty to be rived from utility and from uniformity subordinated to the general effect of the whole. Examples the two types are the business offices (left) of a firm of publishers in Berlin and (right) a private residence at Stuttgart by Le Corbusier.

MASS PRODUCTION BUILDINGS FOR THE OFFICE AND THE HOME

Photos (left) E. O. Hoppé; (right and top) courtesy of Fredk. Etchells

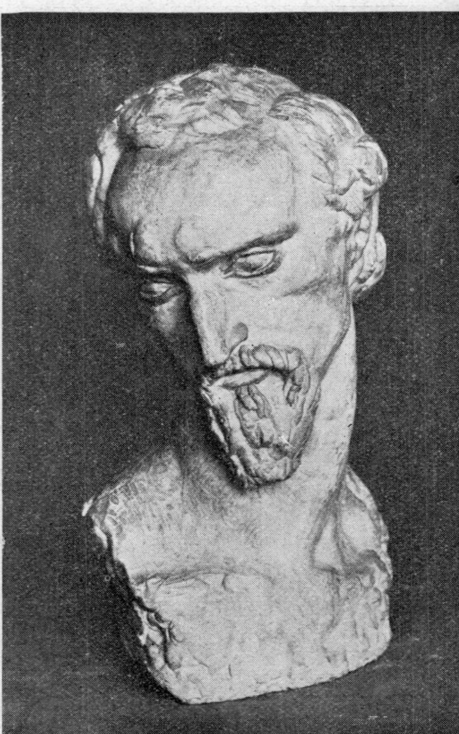

In his second period, beginning about 1917 with his bronze 'Christ,' Jacob Epstein produced a serie
of bronze portraits remarkable for their power of design and intensity of characterisation, as seen i
this bust of Paul Robeson, the negro singer, done in 1928. Ivan Meštrović's self-portrait (right) i
equally interesting in its strength of modelling and interpretation of the sombre Slav temperament

Left, courtesy of the Artist (photo, Paul Laib); right, National Gallery, Millbank

Abyssinian, Egyptian and archaic Greek art greatly influenced Jacob Epstein in his symbolic sculptur
of which this Rima panel—suggested by, not a portrait of, Rima—on the memorial to W. H. Hudso
in Hyde Park is the example that aroused the widest and most animated discussion. By gener
consent it demonstrates the sculptor's exceptional skill in direct stone cutting and his feeling f
form, and it is admirably representative of his entire originality of thought and design.

PORTRAITURE AND SYMBOLISM OF TWO MODERNIST SCULPTORS

Photo, Topical Press Agency

Another sculptor much discussed was Meštrović, in whose work both abstract design and dramatic treatment are conspicuous. No one who visited the exhibition of his sculptures at South Kensington can forget his bust of Rodin, with its mighty hand at rest, or the dramatic relief in which a winged head whispered the awful word of Annunciation to Mary.

In the Great War machinery, masses in movement, human beings reduced to the level of obedient automata, provided abundant subjects for painters like Lewis and Nevinson. The German excuse that 'war is war' was the counterpart of that 'peaceful' motto, 'business is business.' Whether on the battlefields, or in the Black Country at home, painted by Edward Wadsworth, the new technique and manner of painting were suited to its theme. Luckily four years do not last for ever, but the legacy of the experiments that had gone before remains with the artists of to-day.

Ideas and theories are not the main inspiration of the present. The respect for simplification remains: the flat manner, the definite vision, the contempt alike for sentimental or vague treatment in paint. The water colour and the wood-cut have returned to favour, to lend their separate means to express the same attitude in art. It is grave, flat, decorative, simplified, though one modernist, Charles Ginner, loves detail, and rejoices, much more than photographically, in the separate bricks of a house or cogs in a machine. The general effect, however, is clean, clear, proportioned. All this may seem a restriction to the prose of life; but only the few who study prose know how rich prose may be in beauty. There are few more satisfying architectural sights than the ancient brick masonry of Rome. Truth of view and simplification of design can touch, also, the heights of grandeur and of pathos. Is not a peasant a simple and moving figure? Pathetic in his loneliness, fine in his humility, he is an eternal type of human strength and human weakness. To look at modern life with something of his tragic share and personal understanding of nature is the aim of many artists.

If the modernism of to-day can be summed up in a sentence, we may call it the end of the romantic movement, the return of classicism. Form, once more, is being set above feeling, but we are still in the transition: a tendency rather than a movement is to be observed.

IVAN MESTROVIC'S 'ANNUNCIATION'

Ivan Meštrović, Yugo-Slav sculptor of international reputation, was born in 1883 and studied in Vienna, where a collected exhibition of his work was held in 1907. Imagination and religious feeling are expressed in much of his work, of which this dramatic and individual 'Annunciation' is representative.

Courtesy of the Artist; photo, E. O. Hoppé

Fresh air, sunlight, good food, rest and carefully regulated exercise are the methods of treatment for consumption in sanatoria, of which King Edward VII Sanatorium at Midhurst is a notably good example. Exercise includes graded outdoor labour and outdoor recreation, of which putting and croquet are particularly suitable forms.

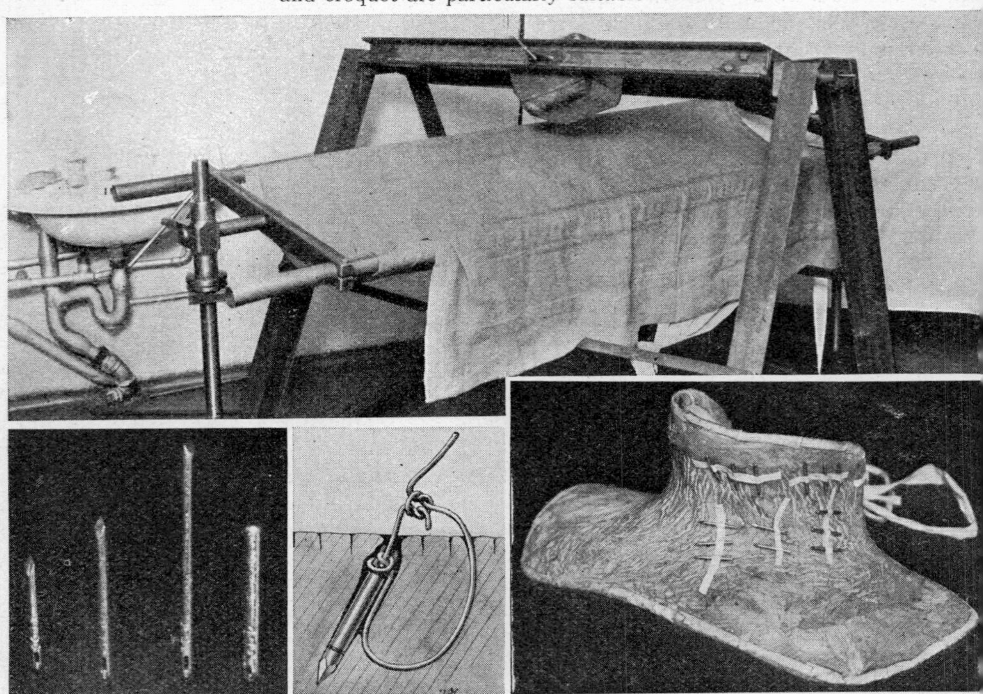

For distance irradiation a so-called 'bomb' of lead containing a gramme of radium is used at Westminster Hospital. The lead box can be tilted in any direction. The stretcher can be inclined or moved up or down or horizontally, so that the cone of gamma rays can be brought to bear on any part of the body. Platinum needles (left—actual size) containing radium are used for insertion in cancerous growths, being secured in place by the stitch shown in the diagram, centre. For surface irradiation of the lymphatic glands in the neck when invaded by cancer a 'collar' (bottom right) is used.

MODERN TREATMENT OF TWO COMMON DISEASES

Courtesy of E. Rock Carling, F.R.C.S., and Stanford Cade, F.R.C.S.

CHAPTER 189

PUBLIC HEALTH: A RECORD OF MEDICAL PROGRESS

How the Development of Scientific Method and the Sanitary Idea produced the New Hygiene of the Twentieth Century

By SIR GEORGE NEWMAN K.C.B., M.D.
Chief Medical Officer to the Ministry of Health; Author of An Outline of the Practice of Preventive Medicine

THE progress made by the science and art of medicine since the dawn of civilization, especially as it concerns the community, is one of the great stories of mankind. It is a romance connected with adventure, war and love; it is interwoven inseparably with social life and the evolution of human custom; and it is intimately associated with man's moral aspirations. Frazer would trace its origin to 'primitive instinct' and the impulse to magic; Wordsworth would follow it back to 'primal sympathy.' Both would be right. The instinct of self-preservation, the natural prompting of the maternal passion and the sympathetic longing to save one's friends from suffering or premature death have played a predominant part in the growth of both preventive and curative medicine.

There has been one other factor always at work—observation. To stem the advance of disease, whether of the individual or the community, men have tried first one thing and then another, observing their effects, and thus have arrived empirically at certain tentative conclusions, and it is upon these practical tests that they have built up an immense superstructure of experience. Magic, the intervention of the gods, astrology, trial by ordeal, the king's touch, and an innumerable series of drugs and simples, of blood letting, potions and plasters, make up the art of medicine over 6,000 years. Dark ages, if you will, but always with a ray of light from which sprang hope in the human breast.

We know that surgery was practised in Egypt in the Middle Kingdom (see page 562) and that domestic medicine chests existed even earlier. Indeed, the first physician of whom we have record (Imhotep or Iemhetep) flourished in the Old Kingdom. In Assyria there was the Hammurabi Code (see page 575), some of whose enactments deal in detail with the medical treatment of wounds, abscesses, fractures, and diseases of the eye.

Historicity of Greek Medicine

Greek medicine seems almost modern compared with the more distant history of medical art in Egypt and Assyria. Yet it also recorded the growth of this art for periods much earlier than its own. The practice of hygiene, baths, life in the open air, the therapeutic value of sunlight, physical exercise and dietary were all matters of daily routine to the Greek of the fifth century before Christ. The sun temples of Cos and Epidaurus and the health principles of Hippocrates (see page 1475) and Diocles belong to well recorded Greek history as much as the epidemics of the Peloponnesian War described by Thucydides.

It is evident, therefore, that the art of medicine was neither primitive nor rude in the golden age of ancient Greece, but advanced and constructive. What happened to it all? The answer to this question is twofold. First, it became fixed as a doctrine not only in the Hippocratic writings but also in the Galenical books (see page 2079). Not until the Renaissance in the sixteenth century did anyone arise to question the infallibility of Galen, or wish to alter or add to his voluminous records. And, secondly, Greek medicine became disseminated over the world partly in the form of the Hippocratic writings, and partly as Galen's interpretation of them.

One channel of propagation was directed from Greece to its great colony Magna Graecia in Sicily and southern Italy, and thus to Salerno and Padua and Leyden and Edinburgh; a second stream flowed through the Byzantine Empire and ended in wider distribution when Constantinople fell in 1453; the third and much the largest current was carried in the wake of the heretical Nestorian church first to Edessa in Mesopotamia, and then with the evicted Nestorians to Jundeshapur (see page 2313) in Persia. The Nestorian centre at Edessa became also a hospital and medical centre, a city of monasteries and learning, and Jundeshapur became the famous school of Mahomedan medicine.

When Edessa was captured in 638 by the Arabs, they became acquainted for the first time with Greek medicine, and in due course set to work to translate Hippocrates and Galen into Arabic. But in the meantime the Arabs had conquered the Orient. It was this mighty invasion which proved the means of introducing Greek medicine in Arabic guise to western Europe. Thus came Hippocrates and Galen to Córdova, to Montpellier, to Paris (see Chapter 97 and page 3291).

Arab dissemination of Greek learning

Whether Galen's writings reached Britain during the last half of the 400 years of Roman occupation we do not know. But we know that his doctrines spread through western Europe, and in the Middle Ages we can find the beginnings of a practice, though not a science, of medicine in Europe and certainly in Britain. Two influences were at work. First, there was the effect of pestilence, and, secondly, the social efforts to stem it.

In Chapter 122 it is shown how the establishment of leper hospitals was the beginning of the present hospital system and of our method of notification and isolation; and how the prevalence of plague in the hovels of the poor demonstrated the necessity of sanitation. The first sanitary Act was passed by the English parliament at Cambridge in 1388; it was followed by quarantine laws, by the appointment of scavengers, by sanitary watchmen (now called sanitary inspectors) and by a system of penalties for the concealment of infected persons.

It was not, however, until the Restoration, after the Commonwealth, that practical sanitation and hygiene began to take its modern form, and not until 1720 did the science of the public health begin.

Among the obvious results of leprosy and plague in western Europe were their social effects. It is strange how readily men forget that epidemic disease changes the destiny of nations. Now as social changes have often been the result of disease, so they have provided the basis, sometimes even the directive influence, of the ways by which men have endeavoured to control disease. Looking back in the history of England, we can see the social origins of some of the chief means of the modern treatment of disease. Domesday Book was a statistical survey of the whole country in 1085–1086, its villages, its acres and their usage, its industries, its population and their social standing; it thus proved the forerunner of the census returns, the primary data on which the whole of the vital and mortal statistics are founded. The monasteries and the guilds were institutions out of which grew dispensaries and the insurance system. They sprang out of the social aspirations of the people.

Nor was it the doctors who alone led the way. Nothing is more instructive in the evolution of medicine than the contributions made to it by non-medical men. Plato and Aristotle gave the trend to the medicine of the Greeks; Roger Bacon, the Franciscan monk, introduced the methods of science into England in the thirteenth century; the botanists who wrote the old herbals classified and illustrated the plants used in the manufacture of drugs; Galileo led the Paduan physiologists to study the part which physics and mechanics play in man's body; some of the great painters, Albrecht Dürer and Leonardo da Vinci, advanced human anatomy by their drawings of the nude; John Graunt, the Cornhill linen draper, had a hobby to collect the records of death, and thus initiated the bills of mortality; Bentham, a philosopher, Chadwick, a poor law

Medicine's debt to lay thinkers

inspector, Robert Owen, a 'socialist,' Lord Shaftesbury, a peer, Florence Nightingale, a nurse, Röntgen, a physicist, and Pasteur, a chemist, are illustrious examples of non-medical workers who in the nineteenth century took an eminent part in the advance of medicine.

The Great Divide between the old medicine and the new, the event which seemed almost to close the Arabic epoch, was the publication in 1543 of the famous book of anatomy by Andreas Vesalius (see pages 3338 and 3828). Vesalius ended Galenical doctrine by going back not to authority or the written word, but to nature herself. He dissected the human body, he observed its form and function and recorded what he found in his wonderful volume, the Fabrica Humani Corporis. 'This book,' said Sir Michael Foster, 'is the beginning not only of modern anatomy, but of modern physiology.' Its publication at Basel in 1543 ended the long reign of fourteen centuries of precedent and authority. It introduced a new method of medical science and engendered a new spirit.

It also brought students of all nations to the old university at Padua. Professors and students stimulated each other, and Padua had its glorious century from 1543 to 1643. Vesalius was followed by Fracastoro (see page 3114), Fabricius and Galileo, and these four men—an anatomist, a practitioner, a physiologist and a physicist—spread its doctrines and its spirit all through Europe. Among its students was William Harvey (see page 3829), the Englishman, the discoverer of the circulation of the blood, and a group of men who, though not as famous as Harvey, are of historical interest because they carried the torch from Padua to Leyden, where, in due course, Boerhaave lighted the torches of his disciples, and thus spread the light in Europe and America.

Harvey's discovery of the circulation of the blood was announced by him at the College of Physicians in London in 1616, and published in his book De Motu Cordis at Frankfort in 1628. This event was so important that we must understand it. When Harvey went to Padua and sat at the feet of old Fabricius in 1600 much was known about the heart and the blood. He listened to Fabricius, he then studied the matter for himself in man and animals ; he considered the structure of the circulatory system and its purpose, and he 'weighed' (to use his own term) the physical factors affecting it. Briefly, this is what he found.

EXERCITATIO
ANATOMICA DE
MOTV CORDIS ET SANGVINIS IN ANIMALIBVS,
GVILIELMI HARVEI ANGLI,
Medici Regii, & Professoris Anatomiæ in Collegio Medicorum Londinensi.
FRANCOFVRTI,
Sumptibus GVILIELMI FITZERI.
ANNO M. DC. XXVIII.

TITLE PAGE TO HARVEY'S TREATISE

The discoveries of William Harvey (1578–1657), who studied at Padua under Fabricius, constitute a landmark in medical history. His views on the movements of the heart and blood were first put forward in 1616 and his Treatise on the Circulation of the Blood was published in 1628.

British Museum

He first showed the nature and purpose of the heart beat, that the heart undergoes a contraction and a constriction, and forces all its contained blood into the arteries, the right ventricle into the pulmonary artery to the lungs and the left into the great artery (aorta) to the body, and no blood passes through the intervening wall. Secondly, he found that the blood coursing through the body was passing from the heart in the arteries and 'climbing back' to the heart in the veins by the support of their valves, 'a motion, as it were, in a circle.' Thirdly, he saw that though the blood undergoes changes in the lung (the lesser circulation) and in the body tissues (the great circulation), it is one and the same blood. That is Harvey's threefold discovery.

Its effect was amazing. For his mode of procedure vindicated for ever the experimental method. Here was an end of 'spirits' and 'vapours'; here was the beginning of a new science of physiology. Its influence on the whole of medicine grew slowly. The great practitioners of the seventeenth century, led by Sydenham, excelled their predecessors in the observation of disease, and there was immense growth in general science and understanding. Yet the progress of Harveian physiology halted. It was the eighteenth century that applied the new knowledge and began the modern epoch.

DR. RICHARD MEAD

In 1714 the English physician Richard Mead (1673–1754) succeeded John Radcliffe as recognized head of the medical profession. He played an important rôle in the prevention of disease, his Discourse on plague appearing in 1720.

From Pettigrew, 'Medical Portrait Gallery'

For in the eighteenth century there was an astounding expansion of man's mind and a readier application of existing knowledge to the betterment of man's estate. Everywhere things were happening. Men were thinking, and the needs of the time made them think socially. All this led to a critical spirit of inquiry of rationalism and of systematic classification, and this spirit permeated medicine and created a new incentive to the application of the science and art of medicine to the problems of the time.

Advances in the Eighteenth Century

There were three kinds of medical advance in the eighteenth century, and the first was due principally to a remarkable group of medical practitioners in England. They were restricted in their sphere by the limitations of medical education and by the sanitary circumstances of the time but by their individual labours they achieved great things for the progress of medical observation and treatment. One of the most prosperous of the eminent London physicians of the day was Dr. Richard Mead. He was not only a fashionable doctor who succeeded to the practices of Lower and Radcliffe, but he was one of the first medical men called by the government to advise the nation on the prevention of disease.

The subject was plague, which had appeared at Marseilles, and which it was feared would spread to England. He wrote therefore a Short Discourse concerning Pestilential Contagion (1720), which passed through seven editions in twelve months. He discussed the origin and nature of plague, as then understood the causes of its spread (alleged to be diseased persons, infected goods and a corrupt state of the atmosphere) and the steps to be taken against it. Mead recommended the appointment of a Council of Health, of 'searchers' for those dead of plague, and of special physicians to attend the sick. He advocated certification of

A MEDICAL RECORDER

The direct observations and notes made by William Heberden (1710–1801), distinguished London physician and classical scholar, were incorporated in his valuable History and Cure of Disease, which was published in 1802.

From Pettigrew, 'Medical Portrait Gallery'

affected persons, prompt isolation of the sick and the disinfection of persons and houses. The expenditure incurred ought, he thought, to be borne by the public.

The diseases which tested the skill of medical practice at the time were small-pox, influenza, puerperal sepsis, scarlet fever, typhus and plague, and Mead's suggestions were accepted as applicable in a general way to them all. These conditions, it was urged, must first be diagnosed and differentiated, and then treated or prevented.

Mead's Discourse may be accounted one of the first elementary publications of the new preventive medicine, and there soon followed in his train a substantial group of English medical men who introduced scientific methods of inquiry for the first time into their ordinary medical practice. One of the earlier of them was Heberden, an accomplished and scholarly man. He was a prolific note-taker who left behind valuable commentaries on the History and Cure of Disease, which owed little to books and nothing to authority, but consisted of his own close observations of disease in the living patient, and this without any of the modern instruments of precision or diagnostic tests. Heberden agreed with Dr. Cullen of Edinburgh that there are more false facts in medicine than false theories, and he set himself to check and record facts regarding chicken-pox, measles, night blindness, epidemical cold (probably influenza), the pulse in disease, and so on.

The famous Quaker doctor, John Fothergill, was of the same type though more austere and ascetic. His practice, like his circle of friends, was large, and out of both was born his remarkable influence in England and America. Like Heberden he published his clinical records of practice. He was a botanist, a meteorologist and a philanthropist, and related these subjects to his study of disease. Diet, fresh air and exercise were leading features in his treatment. He gave only a second place to blood letting, purging and blistering, and relied mainly on stimulation of vital processes and the resistance of nature. One of his chief contributions to medicine was his study of epidemic sore throat in 1747, a form of malignant scarlet fever.

Many medical practitioners living in the provinces were not behind their

DR. JOHN HUXHAM

Of great importance in eighteenth-century medical progress were the researches into epidemic diseases made by John Huxham (1694–1768), the seasonal colic and palsy so common in Devon receiving his special attention.

From Pettigrew, 'Medical Portrait Gallery'

London colleagues in investigational clinical medicine. Dr. Huxham of Totnes, a pupil of Boerhaave, kept clinical notes on epidemic disorders for thirty years. One of the subjects which arrested his attention was the seasonal colic and palsy which was suffered by his patients who drank the Devonshire cider. In the winter of 1724–1725 Huxham found it so common 'that there was scarce a family amongst the lower rank of people that had it not,' and he sometimes saw five or six persons lying ill of it in one house. He was the first to describe this condition in 1739, though he did not know the cause of it. A similar malady was observed by Cadwaladr in 1745 in the West Indies in drinkers of rum distilled through leaden pipes, and in 1757 by Tronchin, the talented physician of Geneva, in drinkers of lead-sweetened wine.

Ten years later this mystery was cleared up by Dr. (afterwards Sir) George Baker, a near neighbour of Huxham in Devonshire, though he did not practise there, who rose to become president of the College of Physicians. His Essay concerning the Cause of the Endemical Colic of Devonshire showed that the disease was connected with large pieces of lead used in the vats and cider presses, and he extracted lead from the cider itself. His work, though it concerned a small and circumscribed problem, was so logical, accurate and inductive that it afforded a new method of investigation into the contamination of food supplies, which has been pursued by innumerable workers ever since. It opened a new chapter in the book of preventive medicine.

There was practising in Chester from 1767 to 1793 a highly observant medical man named John Haygarth. Several years after starting practice he began his epidemiological inquiries into smallpox and typhus, and an enumeration of the inhabitants of Chester in order to check the incidence and progress of disease, and to introduce a system of notification. His description of typhus fever was one of the first and most reliable, and this led him to formulate the nature and condi-

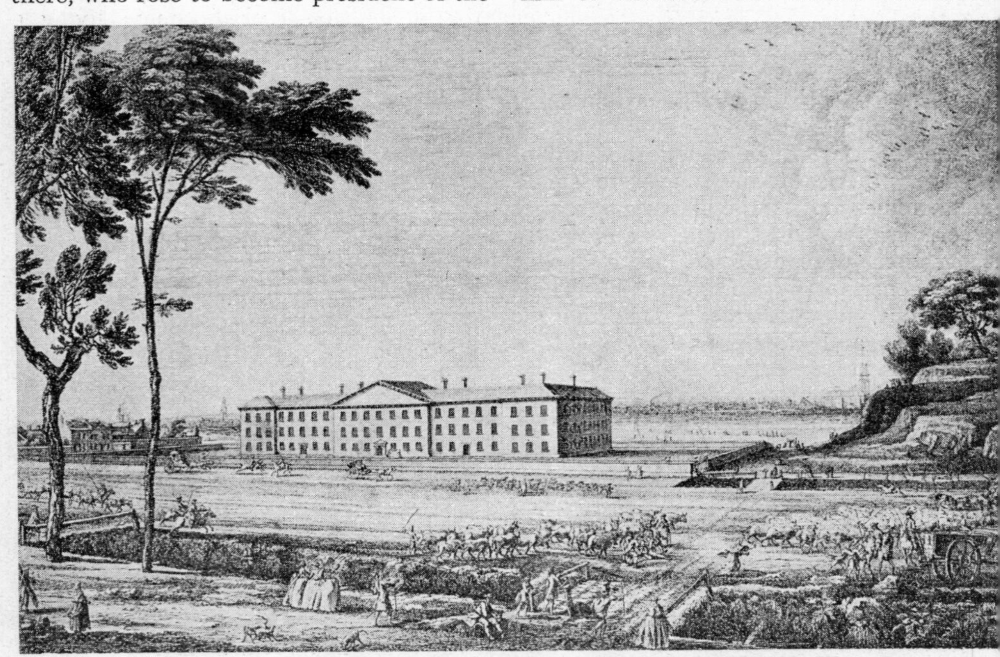

EVIDENCE OF A NEW HUMANITY: THE LONDON HOSPITAL IN 1753

Advancing medical knowledge throughout the first half of the eighteenth century was accompanied by a philanthropic spirit which showed itself in the foundation of hospitals and infirmaries. A small infirmary established in Featherstone Street, Whitechapel, in 1740, was the beginning of the London Hospital, later transferred to Prescott Street, Goodman's Fields, where it can be seen in this painting by William Bellers. It was again moved in 1757.

tions of febrile infections. He took two villages for comparative purposes and made observations upon differential symptoms, proportions of population infected and insusceptible, the channels, the dosage and conditions of infection, the effect of ventilation and uncleanliness, distance over which infection is carried, and, above all, the length of the 'latent,' or, as we now call it, incubation period. Upon these data he established the necessity for isolation (1775) and drafted rules for the institution of fever hospitals.

Thus Haygarth was one of the first to distinguish different kinds of fever by their periods of incubation and to suggest their notification, and he was the first to insist on isolation, a practice begun at Chester in 1783 and followed at Manchester in 1796, and subsequently at Liverpool, Edinburgh, Newcastle, Dublin and other towns, in the institution of what were then described as 'houses of recovery.' Haygarth also made a valuable study of acute rheumatism, and described rheumatic nodules in 1780.

First of the Factory Laws

A third example was Thomas Percival, of Manchester. He was physician to the infirmary, and had a large practice. He wrote on hospital regulation, medical ethics, smallpox, measles and bills of mortality. As a mathematician, he devised methods for taking the census and for accurate death and sickness returns. He was one of the pioneers in the reform of the factory system as concerned with sickness and accidents, excessive hours of labour, unwholesome conditions and insanitation. Sir Robert Peel acknowledged his indebtedness to Percival and his medical associates in the preparation of the Health and Morals of Apprentices Act of 1802, the first of that great stream of factory laws which revolutionised industry.

A second feature in the progress of medicine in the eighteenth century was the communal attack on the medical disabilities of the time. It is true to say that the period was an unhealthy one. The death rate in England was as high as 28 per 1,000 in 1701–10; from 1720-1740 it rose to 35, and it was not until 1788–90 that it had fallen again to 28. A hundred years later it had fallen to 18, and in 1926 it was less than 12. In London from 1720–40 the death rate reached the figure of 37 per 1,000. These high death rates were due to influenza, smallpox and typhus, to alcoholic excess, to maternal and infant mortality, and to the immigration into overcrowded London. Typhus was localised and epidemic, but influenza and smallpox were almost endemic. 'The real grand destroyer' was gin drinking. Smollett said that:

> Such a shameful degree of profligacy prevailed that the retailers of this poisonous compound [gin] set up painted boards in public inviting people to be drunk for the small expense of one penny, assuring them that they might be dead drunk for twopence, and have straw for nothing; they accordingly provided cellars and places strewn with straw, to which they conveyed those wretches who were overwhelmed with intoxication; in these dismal caverns they lay until they had recovered some use of their faculties, and then they had recourse to the same mischievous potion.

The mortality of women in childbirth and of the newly born infants was also excessive in the years 1720–40. Childbirth was indeed a risky adventure for mother and child. The maternal death rate before the establishment of maternity institutions in 1740 was extremely high, and though it was much improved thereafter it often reached 20 in the 1,000. It is now rarely above 5 per 1,000. Fifty per cent. of all the children born died before they were five, and from 1730–49 in London 74 per cent. died under five years of age.

These serious national problems, the prevalence of disease in epidemic form, the excessive drinking and the high mortality among mothers and children, led to the organization of public relief. It did not come suddenly, but it grew in volume and wisdom. It grew also in response to demands from the people and as a result of the religious movement of Methodism and what came to be called the 'new humanity.' A spirit of sympathy and compassion spread through England, and associated as it was with the advance of medical knowledge it proved the means of introducing important sanitary measures.

Hospitals and dispensaries were established. The Westminster, Guy's, St.

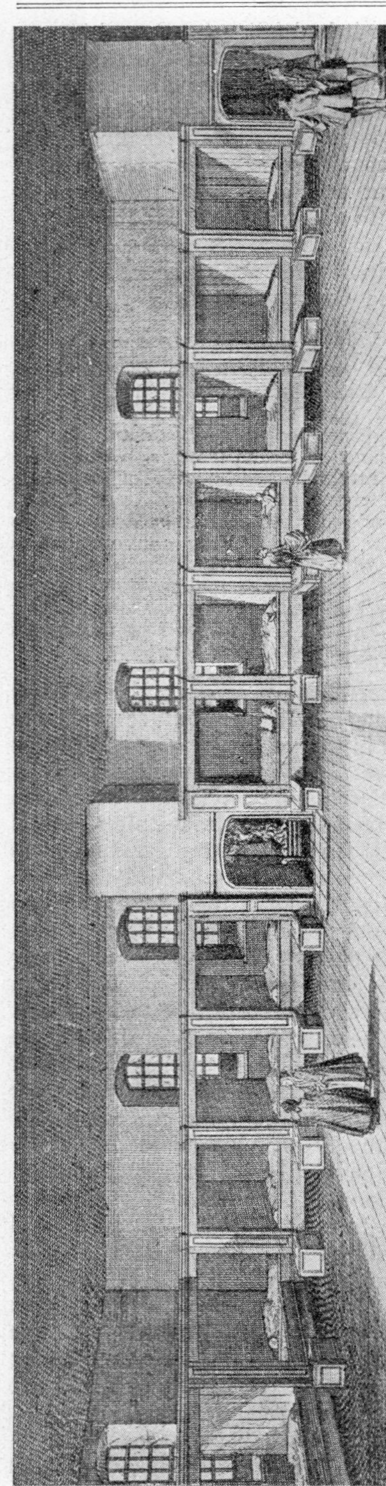

VIEW OF A WARD IN GUY'S HOSPITAL IN THE YEAR OF ITS OPENING

On January 6, 1725, Guy's Hospital was first opened 'for the relief by physick or surgery of sick persons whose illnesses were of so severe a nature as to lead them to be deemed incurable.' This view of one of the wards in 1725 affords an instructive contrast to the Lister surgical ward shown in page 5054. Besides building and endowing the hospital named after himself, Guy was a generous benefactor of S. Thomas's.

British Museum

George's, the London and the Middlese Hospitals were all founded in the firs half of the century ; maternity homes an lying-in hospitals were started, followe by dispensaries for the 'infant poor for general sickness and for inoculatio against smallpox. 'In the nurture an management of infants as well as in th treatment of lying-in women,' wrote D Lettsom, 'the reformation hath equalle that of the smallpox ; by these two ci cumstances alone incredible numbers hav been rescued from the grave.' The reduc tion in maternal mortality was largel due to improved methods in midwifer introduced by Smellie, William Hunte and Charles White, of Manchester.

Reform of th medical schoo

Another far-reaching reform was tha of medical education. Edinburgh, th principal medical school of that day inaugurated its medical faculty in 1726, and during the century the medical schools in London were greatly improved. Their evolution pro ceeded by four steps. First, there wa from ancient times a system of apprentice ship, by which the medical practitione had a pupil or apprentice to whom h taught the art and mystery of his craft Then, when hospitals were established th physician or surgeon took his apprentic to 'walk the wards.' This began at St Bartholomew's in the seventeenth cen tury, and the practice was adopted at th London Hospital in 1741, and at Edin burgh even before that. The Londo hospitals made informal arrangement with their medical staffs that thei private apprentices should take a cours of hospital work under their supervision Thus the private apprenticeship syster became something of a communal appren ticeship system in the hospitals. Th medical staff became a medical faculty and the apprentices became clerks an dressers in the wards.

The third step was the holding o private classes in chemistry, anatomy an pathology, and of clinical classes at th hospital. Before John Hunter, surgery wa well taught only in Paris, and before th Monros began at Edinburgh anatom flourished only on the Continent. Privat instruction, such as that of Cheselde nd Pott in surgery, Smellie's school of bstetrics, the Hunters' school of anatomy nd surgery, Baillie's classes in morbid natomy and Harrison and Blizard's linical class at the London Hospital, was he beginning of modern ways.

The fourth stage, which overlapped with hese proprietary classes, was the establishment of chairs in the universities. At he opening of the century, chairs of natomy were founded at Edinburgh, Cambridge, Glasgow and Oxford, and hairs in clinical medicine at Edinburgh nd Oxford. The London medical schools rew up in the eighteenth century alongside the great new hospitals that had just een built.

Lastly, there was medical reform in the rmy and navy, owing to the work of Sir John Pringle and Dr. James Lind.

Medical reforms in the Army and Navy

Pringle was 'physician general' to the forces during the campaigns of 1742–48 in Flanders, Germany and elsewhere, and gave the irst impetus to the study of this subject by the publication in 1752 of his classic book on Diseases in the Army. At the beginning of the century fleet after leet had been decimated by scurvy, for he treatment of which Huxham had recommended vegetable diet and cider. In 1751 Dr. Lind investigated and described the disease, and advised the use of lemon juice and the adoption of personal hygiene, which was followed by Captain Cook in his voyage round the world and by Sir Gilbert Blane in Lord Rodney's fleet. Their methods abolished this immemorial disease from the mercantile marine and the British navy. The advance in hygiene in the army and navy reacted favourably on the civil population; never before or since have they learned so much essential hygiene from the services.

The eighteenth century was thus a time of improved medical practice and of its wider extension to solve the problems of communal ill health. But there was a third kind of advance. Alongside this expansion in the art of medicine there went a concurrent development of its science. A hundred years after the death of Harvey (1657) a great book on the Elements of Physiology was written by Albrecht von Haller, of Berne, an old pupil of Boerhaave at Leyden. It was the beginning of the systematic and integrative study of physiology from a modern standpoint. It was a summary, a review and a forecast, so masterly as to make famous the year of its publication.

SIR JOHN PRINGLE

Valuable reforms in military medicine were accomplished by Sir John Pringle (1707–1782) whose book on Diseases in the Army is classic. He became president of the Royal Society in 1772. Portrait by Sir Joshua Reynolds.

By permission of the Royal Society

But Haller was not alone. Four years later came the founder of modern pathology, Morgagni; six years after him came Buffon and his great compilation on natural history; and there followed Cullen's Classification of Diseases, Rutherford's discovery of nitrogen, Priestley and Lavoisier on oxygen, and the zenith of the all-pervading influence of John Hunter. It was Hunter whose genius enlightened all departments of medicine and surgery, for he taught men to see that the foundations of preventive medicine are an understanding of and a reliance upon the laws of nature, as they concern all forms and conditions of life; an appreciation of the capacity of the physiological functioning of the human body and its inherent powers of repair; and a knowledge of the cause and circumstance of disease.

JOHN HUNTER : PATHOLOGIST AND SURGEON
The creation and development of English pathology was the work of John Hunter (1728–1793), whose investigations and observations influenced all branches of medicine, surgery and anatomy. He began private practice in Golden Square, London, in 1763. This portrait is by Sir Joshua Reynolds.
By permission of the Royal College of Surgeons

Not as an anatomist nor yet as a surgeon, but as a naturalist, who was a co-ordinator and explorer of the unity of the human body, John Hunter must rank as one of the fathers and founders of modern preventive medicine.

At the beginning of the nineteenth century came the dawn of the modern renaissance, and we pass into a golden age of medicine. Probably it is true to say that no period of human history shows anything comparable to the advance of medicine since 1798. Yet all that had gone before had been a preparation for it and had led up to it. This modern period was an age of inquiry, both individual and collective. The workers of the eighteenth century had stimulated inquiry, those of the nineteenth joined the chase and prosecuted it with a vigour, a persistence and an inquisitiveness which had never been excelled. No branch (knowledge seemed to escap this passion for research– biology, chemistry, physic: social conditions. The futur was evidently going to be ver different from the past an men desired to find their wa about the new world whic was arising around them. The must henceforth find the fact: Adam Smith, Jeremy Benthar and Malthus had directe their attention to the socia life of the people as it wa affected by industry, by form of government and by in crease of population. Mean while, immense possibilitie seemed to be emerging fror the discoveries of science, an political emancipation wa certain.

Out of the astonishing co lection of new facts wreste from nature, verified or ap plied in practice, we hav space here only to refer t six generalisations. The firs is vaccination. Somewher about 1768 Edward Jenne a country practitioner i Gloucestershire, heard a youn woman say that she coul not have smallpox ' for I have had cow pox.' Jenner talked to his fellow prac titioners and neighbours, and in 1780 h told one of them of the idea growing i his mind that cowpox might prove th antidote to smallpox. Early in 1788 h married, and in 1789 he made the grea venture and inoculated his own chilc a few months old, with swinepox matte and subsequently on three occasions wit smallpox virus. None of these smallpo infections gave the child the disease Seven years later (1796) he inoculate James Phipps, aged eight and a ha years, with cowpox matter from the han of a dairy woman who had contracte cowpox from her master's cows, an three months later he inoculated th child with matter from a smallpox case Phipps did not get the disease. Jenne continued his observations, and two year ıter published his immortal Inquiry into ıe Causes and Effects of the Variolae 'accinae, a Disease discovered in some f the Western Counties of England, articularly Gloucestershire, and known s the Cowpox (1798). Jenner was now famous man with a unique repute preading all through the world, and his 'accination was a universal method for preventing smallpox.

Then, as now, there were critics and pponents. In 1811 he wrote to Lettsom hat 'the chief impediments to its general ıdoption are our newspapers and some of ɔur magazines. Whenever a case of what s called failure starts up, in it goes to ı newspaper, with all the exaggeration with which envy and malice can garnish it.' Even educated people, he complained, 'decide upon the merits of vaccine inoculation unaided by a competent knowledge of the matter.'

Jenner described cowpox as he saw it in nature, and he contributed to its differentiation from other similar outbreaks among animals. He showed that cowpox was inoculable upon man, and could be transferred from man to man. Above all, he proved that vaccinia in man protected against smallpox. One may say that none of these three discoveries was new, and, speaking generally, that is true. Different persons, medical, veterinary or lay, had made observations on these points. What Jenner did was to bring them together and prove their validity. It has been thus in all the great discoveries. But, in point of fact, Jenner did much more than introduce vaccination for smallpox. He opened the gates of immunity. We now have many forms of vaccination for various diseases. We now see that immunity is one of the great high roads to the conquest of disease. There are many gaps in knowledge and practice to fill in, but the method is proved.

In the same year that Jenner published his Inquiry an apothecary at Penzance parted with his apprentice, a youth named Humphry Davy, because the lad went to be assistant to Dr. Beddoes who had established a 'pneumatic institute' at Clifton for the treatment of disease by medicated gases. In experimenting with various gases Davy discovered the comforting effect of breathing nitrous oxide. More than forty years afterwards Jackson and Morton of Massachusetts used ether as an anaesthetic in dentistry, and Warren tried it in a surgical operation in October, 1846, and Simpson of Edinburgh in midwifery in January, 1847. Recognizing the shortcomings of ether for this purpose,

FOUNDER OF VACCINATION

The efforts of Dr. Edward Jenner (1749–1823) to discover a preventive of smallpox were rewarded by the success of his first inoculation with cowpox in 1796. Further successful experiments followed and, despite some inevitable opposition, made rapid headway. This portrait is by James Northcote, R.A.

National Portrait Gallery, London

VACCINATION ATTACKED IN A CRUIKSHANK CARTOON

Furious controversy long raged between the supporters and opponents of vaccination regardi the wisdom of its practice, and arguments were forthcoming to prove that inoculation with cowp did not always secure its object of rendering a person immune from smallpox, and might even infe him with other diseases. Reaction against the process is indicated in a cartoon by George Crui shank, of which the central scene representing the funeral of 'Vaccina' is shown here.

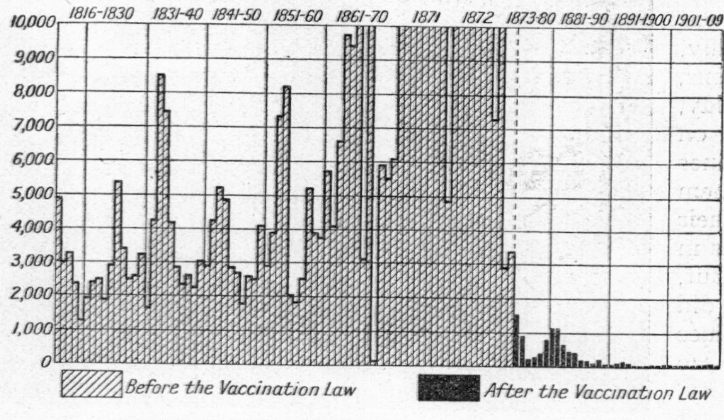

VACCINATION JUSTIFIED BY STATISTICS

Convincing proof of the efficacy of vaccination in reducing smallpox mortality is supplied by this chart of the results in the German Empire. Whereas in 1871 and 1872 the mortality exceeded 10,000, it dropped to about 1,500 in 1875 when compulsory inoculation was introduced, and later fell almost to zero.

After Osler, 'The Evolution of Modern Medicine'

Simpson experimented himself with chlorofor and in November, 184 he established i anaesthetic power. T discovery of anaesthes ended the terrible orde of agony hitherto asso ated with surgical ope ations and made possib an enormous expansion surgical treatment. made surgery 'safe,' abolished pain, and provided for long a careful operations on parts of the body.

The third of the gre medical 'discoveries' whi marked the nineteen century, was that of the cause of infective disease, the new science of bacteriology. Its founders were Louis Pasteur and Robert Koch. The former was the son of a country tanner in Jura, who became professor at the Sorbonne and director of the Institut Pasteur in Paris, and the latter was a young German doctor in Wollstein who spent his leisure with his microscope and became a director in the Imperial Health Department in Berlin and professor of bacteriology in the university. Pasteur showed that fermentation was due not to chemical changes but to bacteria, that spontaneous generation did not occur, that each infective disease had a specific organism as its cause, and that many such diseases were curable by antitoxins and preventable by inoculation of their vaccines. Koch introduced the method of staining bacterial films with aniline dyes and of cultivating bacteria on solid media. He discovered the causal organisms of tuberculosis (1882) and cholera (1883).

SIR JAMES SIMPSON

While professor of medicine and midwifery at Edinburgh University Sir James Young Simpson (1811–70) experimented with chloroform in obstetrical practice and surgical operations, and introduced the art of practical anaesthesia.

From 1870 to 1905 there followed that wonderful succession of discoveries which have distinguished for all time the age in which we live, and which gave us the bacillus of leprosy (Hansen), the gonococcus (Neisser), the typhoid bacillus (Eberth-Gaffky), the micrococci of suppuration (Ogston), the bacilli of tuberculosis (Koch), of cholera (Koch), of diphtheria (Klebs-Löffler), of tetanus (Nicolaier) and of plague (Kitasato and Yersin), all between 1871 and 1894. In 1880 Laveran announced the discovery of the plasmodium malariae, and eighteen years later Ross demonstrated its transmission by the mosquito, which had been suggested by Manson. In 1878 came the trypanosoma of Lewis, to be followed by various members of its genus; in 1883 Friedlander described the pneumococcus, and four years later Weichselbaum the meningococcus and Bruce the micrococcus of

PASTEUR, FOUNDER OF BACTERIOLOGY

Louis Pasteur (1822–95) was France's most brilliant biological chemist. His researches into isomerism led him to study the processes of fermentation, and resulted in the discovery of the bacterial origin of various diseases and his preparation of vaccines for their prevention and antitoxins for their cure.

Malta fever. The last to be named in this brief review is Schaudinn's spirochaeta of syphilis, discovered in 1905. These then were the principal authentic representatives of that unseen world the existence of which had been long foretold, even from the days of Fracastoro of Padua.

But the discovery of the disease-producing bacillus was only the first step in establishing a trinity of knowledge. What did the bacillus do? And what could restrain, prevent or control its activity? In 1888 came the brilliant work of Roux and Yersin, in which they demonstrated by filtration the existence of the toxins of the bacillus of diphtheria and thus opened a new chapter in pathology. Only the year before Mechnikov had shown the bactericidal powers of the leucocytic cells of the healthy body and had introduced his famous theory of phagocytosis, and two years later (1890) Behring and Kitasato completed the case by producing the antitoxin of diphtheria —the final step in the establishment of

A GREAT RUSSIAN BIOLOGIST

By his study of the white blood corpuscles Iliy Mechnikov (1845–1916) established the theory phagocytosis. He became widely known by h advocacy of sour milk as a preventive of inte tinal putrefaction, to which he attributed senilit

Photo, E.N.A.

GERMANY'S GREATEST BACTERIOLOGIST

Robert Koch (1843–1910) ranks with Pasteur as the founder of bacteriology. His new contribution to science was the growth of micro-organisms in a pure culture outside the body and inoculation with the cultures. Koch isolated the comma bacillus of cholera and the tubercle bacillus, and was the discoverer of tuberculin. This drawing is from life.

the far-reaching conceptio that though the healthy bod of man may be subject to th bacillus and suffer its toxi effect, it is able of its ow cells and fluids to provid defence, in the form of th destruction and assimilatio of the invading bacillus. Thu was built our modern cor ception of the bacillus a agent, of the toxin as produc of the bacillus, of the antitoxi as the body's defence agains the effects of the toxin.

Further research by man workers has added knowledg in regard to the antitoxin of tetanus, of cholera, c typhoid; has detected th filterable viruses; has give us the beginning of an under standing of the place c opsonins, agglutinins and pre cipitins in the body defences and has provided us wit autogenous and other vaccine Lastly, in 1910, Paul Ehrlic announced his discovery c

606,' the arsenical compound salvarsan, which is able to destroy in the living body the parasite of syphilis. Thus was the illuminating chapter in the new learning respecting the agents of infection and the body's natural defences begun in 1857 by one chemist and so far completed in 1910 by another—a significant illustration of the interdependence of the sciences in the pursuit of truth.

It was these discoveries which put into our hands for the first time a new power over disease. It is true that certain diseases such as tuberculosis and smallpox were being controlled before their bacterial cause was known, but it was the work of the bacteriologists that gave mankind a fuller understanding of the ways and means of combating infective disease. Until the actual cause of anthrax, of typhoid fever, of cholera, of lockjaw, of malaria or of syphilis was proved, we were working in the dark. We did not know the exact point to attack. Most of all was this true of the septic diseases which carried off such a large percentage of surgical cases. It was in 1865 that the discoveries of Pasteur were first applied by Lister, then a surgeon in Glasgow, to the treatment of surgical wounds, and in 1867 he was able to announce the first principles and methods of the antiseptic system of surgery which ended the long reign of hospital blood poisoning. This is what he said in August of that year:

The two large wards in which most of my cases of accidents and of operation are treated were amongst the unhealthiest in the whole surgical division of the Glasgow Royal Infirmary. Since the antiseptic system has been brought into full operation, and wounds and abscesses no longer poison the atmosphere with putrid exhalations, my wards, though in other respects under precisely the same circumstances as before, have completely changed their character, so that during the past nine months not a single instance of pyaemia, hospital gangrene or erysipelas has occurred.

Subsequently in Edinburgh and in London Lord Lister perfected his technique and proved the soundness of his views, so that his method of preventing the contamination of the wound with septic germs, or of destroying such germs as had gained access to the wound, became applicable in all surgical work and in all parts of the body. 'The investigations of Pasteur,' Lister wrote in 1875, 'long since made me a convert to the Germ Theory, and it was on the basis of that theory that I founded the antiseptic treatment of wounds in surgery.' It is impossible to measure the beneficent results of the antiseptic principle in surgery; it revolutionised, of course, the whole art of surgery, but it did more than

PIONEER OF ANTISEPTIC SURGERY

Joseph Lister (1827–1912), created Baron Lister in 1897, was professor of surgery at Glasgow, Edinburgh and King's College, London. Following Pasteur's discoveries he revolutionised surgery by developing his antiseptic technique, relying chiefly on carbolic acid. Portrait taken at Glasgow in 1868.

Courtesy of Wellcome Historical Medical Museum

that; it revolutionised the attitude of men's minds to all forms of infection. After Lister it was clear that man could control infection by other means than escaping it. Neither Hunter nor Lister would have claimed as surgeons to be fathers of preventive medicine, but such, in fact, they proved to be.

The nineteenth century was thus a period of extraordinary advance in the true apprehension of the fundamentals of public health and preventive medicine. Here are four great generalisations the validity of which was then established, vaccination, anaesthesia, the cause of infective diseases, and antiseptic surgery. It is the communal application of these advances that has characterised recent times. Out of them was born what Chadwick called 'the sanitary idea.' In a word, men saw that the answer to the problems of communal disease was an attack, directed by the growing knowledge of medical science, upon the origins and circumstances of such disease, and this meant sanitation. The alarm caused by pestilence, the advance of medical knowledge and the demands of an enfranchised people moved Parliament to appoint various commissions of inquiry and to pass a series of sanitary acts which have led to the improvement of the external environment of the people.

Two royal commissions, one in 1843 and the second in 1869, produced reports which constitute a sort of Domesday Book of the conditions of life in England at that time and resulted in the appointment of medical officers of health and the imposition of health duties upon the local

WHERE LISTER ELABORATED HIS ANTISEPTIC TECHNIQUE

Before Pasteur's elucidation of the germ theory of putrefaction an appalling number of surgical operations were followed by pyaemia due to contamination of wounds by virulent bacteria. Lister's supreme service to mankind was the perfecting of the antiseptic technique, entailing sterilisation of all instruments and dressings and everything brought into contact with actual wounds. This photograph shows a section of a reconstruction of the ward in Glasgow Royal Infirmary where Lister, between 1861 and 1869, did much of his more important work.

Courtesy of Wellcome Historical Medical Museum

authorities established in 1835. The need for co-ordination of such officers and duties led to the establishment of a central board of health, now called the Ministry of Health. Anyone who reads the preamble of the report of the commission of 1869 on the history of the sanitary laws will find that they are concerned with nuisances and their removal, sewerage and drains, sewage treatment, the paving, lighting and cleansing of streets, artisans' dwellings, smoke abatement, local government and the burial of the dead. The great Public Health Act of 1875 brought together and extended these enactments. That act and the Elementary Education Act of 1870 were forms of germinative legislation which bore fruit in a single generation and have impressed all subsequent health enactments.

The Public Health Act dealt, broadly, with the environment, but it is significant to observe that the succeeding acts have become steadily more personal in objective. With the twentieth century came a series of laws dealing with mothers and children; with midwives and nursing; with notification of birth, employment of children, school meals; with the medical inspection and treatment of school children, physically and mentally defective children and the Children Act itself; with the protection of food; with pensions for the aged, for widows and orphans, and the insurance of the adolescent and adult against sickness, accident and unemployment; with dentistry; with infectious diseases and fever hospitals; with tuberculosis, mental deficiency, lunacy, blindness and venereal disease; with factories and workshops and the industrial welfare of the workers.

Enlarged scope of preventive medicine

What does this change in the centre of gravity really mean? It means that there is a larger understanding of the purpose of preventive medicine, both in the object and the methods of securing the health of the people. It is no longer a question of stamping out pestilence or of providing a sanitary environment. The purpose of preventive medicine is how to develop and fortify the physique of the individual and thus increase the capacity and powers of resistance of the individual and the community; to prevent or remove the causes and conditions of disease or its propagation; to postpone the event of death and thus prolong the span of man's life.

The basis of the public health must always be a sanitary environment; but the new hygiene seeks to develop the innate capacities of man, physical, mental and moral; it aims at the avoidance of disharmony and disease in its early stages, in order to escape its later results in the body. Let us see what its modern programme is.

First, wise human nurture, an effective maternity service, infant welfare and child hygiene are designed to build a healthy race. Secondly, good housing, a pure and abundant water supply, drainage and sewerage, the reduction of nuisances and the abatement of smoke, a wholesome and sufficient food supply and industrial hygiene are to create a sanitary environment. Thirdly, the provision of sound nutrition, life in the open air, exercise and rest, vaccines and antitoxic sera are to establish immunity and a resistant body. Fourthly, the control of epidemics, the destruction of infective agents, the isolation and treatment of infectious persons, disinfection, quarantine, avoidance of cough-spray or expectoration are methods of reducing mass infection. Lastly, adequate and sufficient medical practice for the sick and disabled of all ages and classes, clinics, dispensaries, hospitals, sanatoria and a health insurance system are medical services for the early diagnosis and treatment of disease.

Programme of the new Hygiene

Modern physiology has laid emphasis upon the body itself as the key to the position. The essential contributor to disease was formerly believed to be an unhealthy environment; then came the period of the dominance of the infecting germ, and later the susceptibility of the non-resistant body. Hence the modern ideal is a resistant body, the maintenance of its harmonious functioning in relation to nature and to human society. Progress would thus seem to depend more upon social and moral evolution than upon the advance of sanitary science, more upon wisdom than knowledge, more upon public opinion than legislative enactment, more upon sociology and biology than medical intervention. Yet all are necessary, for the art of preventive medicine is social in structure and medical in inspiration.

These general principles have found remarkable illustration in the concentrated attack in modern times upon certain strongholds of disease. The disappearance of plague after 1666 is still something of a mystery, but that of typhus fever two hundred years later was probably due to the better housing of the people, higher wages, cheaper and more nutritious food and a more adequate medical service. 'The disappearance of typhus and relapsing fevers,' says Creighton, 'is one of the most certain and most striking facts in our epidemiology.' But it is not alone. Cholera has vanished and typhoid fever shown an astonishing decline. Both improvements followed on a pure water supply and segregation of infected persons.

Tuberculosis has also been steadily falling during the last eighty years, and its mortality is now but a quarter of what it was in 1849. Formerly believed to be hereditary, it is now known to be mainly conveyed by infection, and the system of notification, attendance at clinics (or dispensaries), sojourn in a sanatorium, appropriate social after-care, is steadily winning its victory. Much of its decline is indirectly due to improved social conditions, better nutrition and public education, and the sanatorium principle (rest and nourishment under open-air conditions) is of wider application than the sanatorium system. The treatment of tuberculosis of bones, joints, glands and skin has been greatly advanced by the application of direct sunlight (ultra-violet rays) or the use of arc lamps. Indeed, it

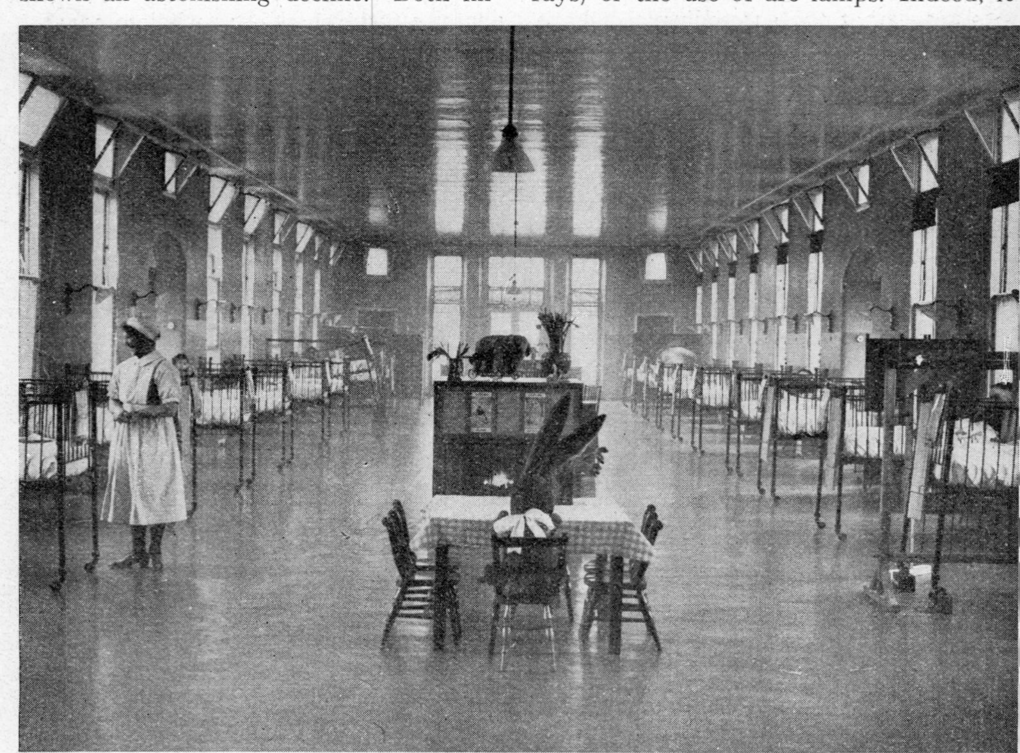

VIEW OF THE CHILDREN'S WARD IN A MODERN LONDON HOSPITAL

The foundation of King's College Hospital on its present site at Denmark Hill was laid in 1909, and the building was opened in 1913. Some idea of its splendid construction and equipment can be gained from this view of the children's ward, affording a striking contrast to the old-fashioned type of ward illustrated in the eighteenth-century picture of Guy's Hospital shown in page 5046.

Photo, Central Press

SUNLIGHT TREATMENT : 'THE BABIES' CIRCUS' AT THE LONDON CLINIC

A beneficent and important part of the medical services now organized under the Ministry of Health is the provision of clinics where people of any age, sex, or class can obtain advice and treatment to prevent or arrest disease. Thus at the London Clinic in Pimlico there is perfect equipment for the application of the ultra-violet rays to patients in the early stages of tuberculosis and other diseases for which actino-therapy is an effective preventive or curative instrument.

Photo, courtesy of London Clinic

is not unlikely that actino-therapy will prove in this and other diseases to be one of the great instruments of preventive and curative medicine.

The incidence of venereal disease increased during the Great War and necessitated active prophylaxis and treatment. In 1916 a scheme of special clinics was established in Great Britain and the use of salvarsan was widely and successfully introduced. The effect of this drug is to diminish infectivity. As in the campaign against tuberculosis, so in that against venereal disease, public education on the avoidance of infection has been invaluable.

Cancer and acute rheumatic fever remain as yet undefeated. The widening sphere of modern surgery has made early removal of cancerous growths practicable, and early removal has been proved to be ameliorative in exceptional degree. We are still, however, without exact knowledge of the causation of cancer or acute rheumatic fever, for which indeed there is at present no treatment other than prolonged rest.

In general, the prevalence of disease, apart from such maladies as influenza, appears in recent times and in civilized countries to respond chiefly to personal hygiene, direct surgical treatment and good social conditions. It is the amazing advance in these three spheres that has given us the prolongation and enlargement of life which we enjoy.

TOWERING EDIFICES THAT BREAK THE SKY-LINE OVER NEW YORK CITY'S BOROUGH OF MANHATTAN

The western type of civilization has reached its most intensive development in America. All over the United States the urban population is expanding largely and rapidly, while the rural population is either expanding slowly or actually declining. Of the ten million people inhabiting the State of New York eight million live in cities, five and a half million of them in New York City. More than half of this number occupy the island borough of Manhattan, where accommodation has had to increase vertically since it cannot further expand laterally. This has resulted in the development of the skyscraper style of architecture (see page 5033), which is a marvel of constructive genius and gives New York a beauty distinctively and peculiarly its own.

Photo, Aerofilms

CHAPTER 190

SOCIAL SURVEY OF THE WORLD TO-DAY

Lines of Weakness revealed in Western Civilization by the Shock of War and the Reactions of Democracy to Responsibility

By IAN D. COLVIN

Author of the Safety of the Nation, Life of General Dyer, etc.

THOSE who browse among library catalogues may have been struck by the rapid growth of a new branch of study, proudly called by its adepts sociology. Every year, and chiefly from the United States of America, come more and more books upon this subject, so that the shelves of our libraries groan under their number and bulk. Every State University in America appears to have its Professor of Sociology, and every professor has written a text book. All these text books differ from one another in their methods and in their conclusions; but they are alike in the use of an imposing and apparently scientific vocabulary, and they unite in describing their study not as a mere philosophy but as a science.

Thus, if we take Benjamin Kidd as the most illustrious modern representative of the sociologists, we find him advancing the claim that sociology is not merely a 'true science' and a 'real science,' but a 'master science,' and the 'first of the theoretical sciences.' 'It is,' he says, 'the social process which is constructing the human mind in evolution. This is the ultimate fact which raises sociology to its true position as a master science.'

Impressed by these imposing claims, we set out hopefully to find the guiding principles, the established conclusions, which may help us to a social survey of the world; but we are discouraged at the outset by the discovery that our latest sociologists not merely throw down the structures but dig up the foundations of their predecessors. There is, for example, little or nothing left of the imposing system of Auguste Comte, who founded a 'methodical and positive philosophy' of society on the hypothesis that 'reason is the superior and preponderant human element which settles the direction in which all the other faculties shall expand.' This 'true and conclusive system,' as its founder proudly described it, was pulled to pieces by the 'social psychologists' who pointed out that man is moved not by reason merely or chiefly, but by a whole complex of instincts and passions.

Herbert Spencer (see page 4533) took up the study no less systematically and almost as positively as Comte. Warned, no doubt, by Comte's example, he did not attempt to reform society upon any preconceived plan. On the contrary, he pointed out, in a famous passage in his Study of Sociology, that to try to correct the irregularities of society was like hammering on a cockled iron plate to get it flat—a difficult and expert business which could only be done, if at all, by little taps here and there and not by heavy blows. Spencer, however, like Comte, embarked on the study hampered by certain preconceptions, notably that the individual was of greater importance than the society of which he formed a part. 'No one doubts,' says a later sociologist, W. G. Summer, 'that the personal experiences and complexes of men like Herbert Spencer had an overwhelming importance in the development of their social and political thinking.'

Doctrines of the Sociologists

Benjamin Kidd went further, and asserted that Herbert Spencer had begun at the wrong end: instead of arguing from the individual to society, he should have argued from society to the individual; his individualist principles, in fact, his doctrine of a 'beneficent private war,' in which the personal unit works out the good of society by following his own advantage, was an offence to the nostrils of the next generation of sociologists. Kidd, starting at the other end, attempted to explain the individual upon a social hypothesis. Unfortunately, he also had his preconceptions. His Social Evolution, and Principles of Western Civilization, which were both written before the Great War, were inspired, or perhaps we might say inflated, by certain political ideals. He held that society was gradually rising to a 'more organic type' in which 'social freedom' was displacing the 'closed absolutisms' of the past. Or again, in even more imposing terms: 'The principle of efficiency in modern civilization is the enfranchisement of the future.'

This evolutionary process had already gone so far 'that it is almost impossible that one nation should attempt to conquer and subdue another after the manner of the ancient world.'

It might seem odd that Kidd, who began by founding his science of society upon the Darwinian hypothesis of the struggle for survival, should end in the

GRAHAM WALLAS

In his Human Nature in Politics (1908) Grahai Wallas advocates an international science eugenics wherein each race should improve it own type. He was a lecturer at the Londo School of Economics, 1895–1923.

comfortable belief that war had becom 'almost impossible'; but it appears tha the natural struggle is somehow sublimate and rendered innocuous when it enter into society. 'The social process i primarily evolving in the individual,' h says, 'not the qualities which contribut to his own efficiency in conflict with hi fellows; but the qualities which contribut to society's efficiency in the conflic through which it is gradually rising to more organic type.' We are not tol against whom this 'social conflict' is bein waged; but it is evident that, despit Darwin, nature, at least when she ente into society, puts on kid gloves and is n longer 'red in tooth and claw.'

Another sociologist of this moder school, Graham Wallas, in his Huma Nature in Politics, goes so far as t explain how the doctrine of the surviv of the fittest may be applied witho blood and tears to human society. 'A international science of eugenics,' say Wallas, 'might . . . indicate that th various races should aim, not at exte minating each other, but at encouragin the improvement by each of its own raci

PRE-WAR SOCIOLOGIST

The sociological theories of Benjamin Kidd (1858–1916) are set forth in his Social Evolution, published in 1894, and his Principles of Western Civilization, which appeared in 1902. His system was shattered by the advent of the Great War.

Photo, Elliott & Fry

type.' In this happy compromise between 'racialism' and 'internationalism' the world would march into the dawn of a perfectly amiable but apparently indeterminate ideal.

If sociology were, as is claimed, a 'true science,' we should expect such leading conclusions to stand the test of at least ten years of experience. But the Great War, coming close upon the heels of Benjamin Kidd, left his system in more complete ruin than that to which he and his brother sociologists had reduced the systems of Spencer and Comte. And we are almost driven to the sad conclusion that sociology, so far from being a master science, is something less than a philosophy, since it is based on nothing more substantial than the prejudices and preconceptions of those who engage in it.

Sociology not a Science

Nor is this surprising when we consider the difficulty of steering a course through the shoals and deeps, the million islands and uncharted intricacies of the sea of humanity. How, for example, are we to define and how divide society? Man himself is almost infinitely various; that equality, which is the basis of so many political systems, is found to be, upon the most cursory examination, merely a convenient fiction. In a single race there are some who fall below the beasts and others who approach divinity.

And races are no less diverse than individuals. How are we to look for like results from the Bengali, who may be said to pride himself upon his timidity, and the Prussian, described by Napoleon as hatched from a cannon ball? We have living on the earth to-day, and sometimes within a mile or so of one another, races who belong in their habits, customs and equipment to the Stone Age, and races in the highest state of civilization.

Even in those institutions which we regard as common to humanity there are radical differences. Take the family: there are monogamists, polygamists and polyandrists; among some races inheritance is through the mother, because paternity is thought impossible to discover; in parts of Asia and Polynesia there are whole tribes that share a common house. In some societies woman is a chattel; in others she is almost a goddess. In some family systems the father rules, in others the mother; in still others the mother-in-law. The typical Chinaman, says J. E. Baker, in his book Explaining China, 'lives in the same enclosure not only with his own wives and children, but also with his father's wives and their children; a great company of parents, grandparents, uncles, aunts, cousins, concubines and more distant kin.' We are accustomed to look upon family responsibility as the beginning of citizenship; but 'for thousands of years there has been no definite location of responsibility in the Chinese family.' The women preside over the inner courtyards; the men find tranquillity nearest the street.

Whether, then, the individual creates his society, as Herbert Spencer suggests, or is a social product, as Benjamin Kidd supposes, the result is no less perplexingly varied. And if we look at the larger divisions of mankind we still find dissimilarity. A great part of mankind comprehends no allegiance beyond the village; another great part obeys the will of the tribe or clan; a considerable part is rigidly divided into castes. In Europe men are divided into classes and nations; but both divisions, as we shall presently see, are difficult to define, and over a great part of the world national division is unknown.

Heterogeneity of Mankind

And the motives, the beliefs and the customs of man are equally the reflection of his almost infinite variety. One religion consists of rules for this life; another concentrates optimistically on the next; one is preoccupied with divine, another with sexual love; there are religions devoted to the sword and the law; ritualism, the delight of one part of mankind, is the abomination of another. If we say that self-interest is the ruling motive of mankind, how shall we explain a creed whose fundamental tenet is renunciation? With such heights and depths, such contradictions and contrarieties, it is a tribute rather to the courage than to the discretion of mankind that so many answers to its own riddle have been so confidently given.

If, however, we admit, what we can hardly deny, that man is part of nature, and that society is a human and therefore a natural composite, we might surely go farther and expect to find some guidance in those principles which are found in the rest of animate nature. It may be that the sociologist errs in aiming too high; he has possibly forgotten the humility with which Darwin treated the species of which he was a member: 'We must acknowledge that man with all his noble qualities . . with all these exalted powers —man still bears in his bodily frame the indelible stamp of his lowly origin.'

If man is an animal, as we are not disposed to deny, he takes his part, now as always, in the struggle for existence. Where he has organized himself into societies and nations, it is in the course of this struggle; the larger unit, like the individual, develops and progresses by selection and survival. So much is clear, but these generalities do not help us very far. With whom and with what is this struggle waged? Is it between man and man or between man and nature; between nations and nature or between nation and nation? Is the struggle, perhaps, for the survival of one racial or national type? Or is mankind expected to mix with increasing friendship until all national and racial divisions are obliterated? In both events mankind would have a very long way to go since racial and national divisions are usually ancient, deep and obdurate.

The Struggle for Existence

Mazzini, most ardent of nationalists, looked on the nation as God's work marred by man. God, he said, divided humanity into distinct groups or nuclei upon the face of the earth . . . foolish governments had disfigured the divine destiny. But here we are faced with the difficulty of definitions. How are we to describe a nation? Under the overlaid national boundaries the older racial divisions of mankind still exist, although sometimes invisible to the casual eye, like a palimpsest upon which the later writing conceals the earlier (see Chapter 7). These make lines of weakness which are apt to show in times of stress, like the racial division between southern Ireland and the rest of Great Britain, or the manifold divisions of the Austrian Empire—in both cases fatal to national unity. What are we to say of the claim of the Indian nationalists, covering a geographical area never united save by the British Empire which they desire to displace? British India comprises no fewer than 150 distinct languages. It is divided not only between races which despise, fear or hate one another, but between the two great religions of Mahomedanism and Hinduism —a division more deep and bitter than any difference which divides the nations of western Europe.

Again, in the United States we have a nation speaking one language but drawn from all the nationalities of Europe, with a contingent from Asia and twelve million negroes besides. That problem we shall have to consider separately; in the meantime we cite it to illustrate the pitfalls which lurk in the path of those who confuse race and nationality. There is, besides, the miraculous case of the British Empire, which unites in a loose confederation under one crown all manner of peoples and many forms of government. All we need say of these national divisions for the moment is that they are units for livelihood in peace and defence in war, that they usually have a racial basis, that they strongly adhere, and that they play their parts in the struggle for existence. National divisions are deep and national patriotisms strong.

The meaning of Nationhood

The League of Nations is founded on the theory that they are permanent, yet some of our 'forward-looking' idealists ask us to believe that all national divisions are a barbarous survival and that mankind should be divided not perpendicularly between races or nations, but horizontally between class and class. The disastrous results of this theory we shall presently see. In the meantime we need only note that a class can hardly be a unit in the struggle for existence, since all the classes frequently live by co-operation in the same industry, and all owe their hope of continuance to combination of effort.

Let us, however, turn from these large questions of theory, and look at facts as they are. If the future will still be dark to us we shall nevertheless in the past and in the present see processes of evolution actually at work in mankind, and we shall find that they surround and concern the immediate end of the struggle for existence—the means of livelihood.

If we look back a century or so, we find that Europe, with a population of about 150 millions, lived in the main by agriculture. Her industries generally were small and primitive, but Great Britain had been making certain surprising and important discoveries (see Chapter 163) which so far enlarged her power of production as to make her supreme in the world. The German economist, List, writing in the second quarter of the nineteenth century, speaks of England as 'a world's metropolis which supplies all nations with manufactured goods. . . . a treasure house of all great capital—a banking establishment for all nations, which controls the circulating medium of the whole world, and by loans and the receipt of interest on them makes all the people of the earth her tributary.' Germany—and Prussia in particular—was a mere market for British goods, a producer of raw material.

This progress of Great Britain then was due to an intensification of her industrial power, and in a struggle for survival the other nations of Europe were forced to follow her example or sink to the position of permanent economic serfdom. We gradually see the several great powers developing round their own industrial and commercial systems. France found her new power in the coal field of the Pas de Calais and the iron ore of Lorraine. Germany between 1815 and 1879 consolidated three industrial systems, the Silesian, the Saxon and the Westphalian, and by war took over the cotton and woollen manufactures of Alsace-Lorraine and the Minette iron fields, the largest of their type in the world; Belgium, small but favourably placed on sea and land, also developed an independent industry and commerce, which, however, she had not the power to protect. In general we see each nation striving to develop its own economic system of basic and secondary industries, commerce and banking, and all these systems gaining in speed and power, in continual struggle and friction one against another.

Industrial progress in Europe

The population of Europe grew with the power to support it, so that by 1914 it numbered 460 millions, concentrated chiefly in the industrial and commercial centres. In addition, it spread and overflowed. Between 1820 and 1921 thirty-four and a half million emigrants entered the United States, the British and Dutch leading the way and being followed first by the Scandinavian and German peoples, and then by the swarming races of the Mediterranean, so that at the present time the United States themselves, with a population of 110 millions, possess the most powerful industrial system in the world, while Canada with nine million people tends to follow in the same direction. There was, besides, a great migration chiefly from Spain, Portugal and Italy to Central and South America, of Dutch and British to South Africa, and of British to Australia and New Zealand.

Here we have the framework of what is called progressive or Western civilization. It is not one system but several. It is divided into national organizations, and these in their turn rest on agricultural, industrial and commercial systems. The industries are in constant and active motion, but expand or contract by the pressure of the others, and according to their relative power and speed the nations which exist by them rise and fall in relation to the rest.

Western type of Civilization

Speed and mobility are its chief characteristics. Little more than a century ago the whole world was on much the same level of speed and power. On land the horse and the ox, on sea the sail and the oar, were man's chief aids in the conflict with time and space, and whether on land or sea eight miles an hour was the limit of his mobility. Not only so, but at this slow pace he could move, in a coach, a mere handful of eight or twelve passengers or in a ship a few hundred tons of merchandise. He can now transport by the thousand at a time and at the rate of sixty miles an hour on land and twenty knots at sea. As one invention gathers ideas from another even these rates are being exceeded. In 1929 Major Segrave in a racing motor of British manufacture reached a speed of 231·36 miles an hour, and in 1927 in a British seaplane Webster made a record of 281·49 miles an hour, to be beaten later by the Italian, de Bernardi, with 318·6 miles an hour (March 30, 1928).

These extraordinary achievements in speed were attained not by one but by many lines of progress. For example, in the steam engine weight was thought necessary to stability; the sole pre-occupation was the development of power; coal being cheap there was no over-mastering necessity to economise in fuel; iron being cheap there was no great need to economise in material. But the invention of flight set the human mind working on hitherto neglected problems, with the result that the engine which enabled Webster to win the Schneider Cup was a masterpiece in these new economies, yielding 1 horse-power per pound of weight. Mechanical progress is produced by the interplay of one invention with another, and goes forward in a continual race between the various sources of power to the improvement or displacement of one by another.

Thus, for example, man began his inventive career by using water power, as we see in the hammer ponds of Sussex, and in the application of water wheels to the first power looms and spinning jennies. Steam for a while displaced water, and then, with the discovery of electricity and the use of the water turbine, water power returned to its own. By the aid of what the French call 'l'houille blanche' new industrial systems were created in areas altogether unsuitable to the older industrial systems, as in the mountainous regions of Norway, Switzerland and northern Italy, where weight of water and the force of gravity can be most advantageously utilised.

One master invention leads to another. The liberation of gas from coal came into practical use about the same time as the steam engine and was long used for lighting purposes only; but

EMBODIMENTS OF SPEED: MAJOR SEGRAVE AND THE GOLDEN ARROW

All previous records of human mobility on land were broken on March 11, 1929, when Major H.O.D. Segrave attained a speed of 231·36 miles per hour over a measured mile on Daytona Beach, Florida. The car, Golden Arrow, in which this feat was accomplished, had a 12-cylinder, 1,000 h.p. Napier-Lion engine, and was designed by Captain J. S. Irving, after whom it is officially named the Irving Special. In recognition of his achievement the King conferred a knighthood upon Major Segrave.

Photo, Central News

later, power as well as light was derived from gas, and for stationary purposes the gas engine has become a strong rival of the steam engine. Not only so, but the decomposition of coal into all its constituents produced a whole series of utilities, synthetic dyes and the most powerful explosives among them, and the by-products utilised for road surfaces seconded the invention of the motor car, which in its turn for mobile traffic became a formidable rival of the steam engine. The road, at one time superseded by the rail, took again its old importance, and the railways, threatened in their stronghold, are now taking measures to restore the economic balance by returning to the roads. So in other lines of invention, what is called the electric current was first carried along wires as a means of communication and later as a means of power. The invention of wireless communication and its economic development in the beam system of signalling threatened the cable companies, and have induced them to seek an alliance or amalgamation with their younger rival.

SEAPLANE'S RECORD SPEED IN 1927

International competition for the Schneider trophy has resulted in astonishing development of marine flying machines. On September 26, 1927, Flight-Lieut. S. N. Webster covered the Lido course of 218 miles at the then record average speed of 281·49 m.p.h. in a Super-marine Napier S 5 monoplane.

Photo, Daily Mirror

An invention in one industrial system may lead to victory in another. The Thomas process of treating low-grade and refractory ores was developed to deal with the sulphurous and hitherto useless ironstones of the Continent, and gave Germany an advantage promptly utilised.

Thus the silent economic warfare of these mechanical processes balanced or subjugated one another, and also made conquest of vast areas in distant parts of the world. The abbé Dubois, who travelled in India in the early part of the nineteenth century, gave a pathetic account of the havoc wrought among the hand-loom weavers of Madras and Bengal by the power looms of Lancashire. Busy centres of industry were reduced to idleness and famine, or sought refuge in agriculture. Towards the end of the nineteenth century, India began to import cotton machinery from Manchester and to drive out the products of Lancashire, so that the north of England was threatened with the fate with which its inventive genius had once overwhelmed the people of India. But the superior ingenuity of the Western mind found a mechanical means of producing the exquisite filaments of the silk-worm, and partially restored Europe's position in the markets of India with fabrics that combine the sheen of silk

LONDON TELEPHONING TO NEW YORK

Contact with America by wireless telegraphy was first effected in 1902, and on October 7, 1907, wireless telegraphic stations for trans-Atlantic communications were established. Wireless telephony presented greater difficulties, but on January 7, 1927, a trans-Atlantic wireless telephone service was opened to the public.

Photo, Sport & General

with the cheapness of cotton. Thus, in the realms of mechanical invention we are able to trace the struggle for existence and the survival of the fittest which Darwin saw in the realm of nature.

The idealists see in this mechanical progression the promise of an age of universal peace; but those who consider events must admit that so far it has not altered the fundamental fact of an eternal struggle for existence. For, as we have already pointed out, not one but several great industrial, commercial and economic systems are in continual rivalry one with another, have their conflicts and form alliances for attack or defence, but have their own centres of intense but natural egotism and self-interest.

Those who contend that the interaction of industry and commerce is reducing the separate entities which have been rivals to a co-operative commonwealth with a common interest ignore certain rather stubborn facts in the situation. There are, it is true, delimitations of areas and exchanges of patents between the various industrial systems, but these systems themselves still firmly rest upon a national basis. The great Steel Corporation of the United States is American in control and interest. The German Stahlwerksverband is a cartel of German steel producers, and although it has made arrangements with similar steel cartels in other Continental countries it has in no way modified its characteristically German composition and uses the power of its combinations for a fundamentally national attack on the British steel industry as well as for competition with the American steel industry in the markets of the world. The lending of capital by one economic system to another may exploit, but does not unite; nor, as we saw in the Great War does it prevent a conflict.

League of Nations not international

The League of Nations itself is not a real international organization, since the powers which compose it jealously preserve their independence. It rests indeed, upon a franchise of present military and naval power, ignoring both the growth and decay of nations and that eternal struggle between separate national and economic systems which is the root of war. In sum, it permits the cause while forbidding the effect, and as the cause seems to be nothing less than a struggle for survival, which is held to be a law of nature, any prohibition would appear to be futile. Even if nations should not think it worth while to resort to the more violent forms of warfare the economic and industrial warfare would still proceed, and would enslave and exploit and might even destroy those races and nations least fitted for survival. Man cannot contract out of nature or the struggle for existence.

If, however, the eternal struggle is for the means of livelihood, it might be argued that the mechanical power, which increases the means, should abate or odify the struggle. And so it appears t first sight ; but we have to remember hat the increase in production is to some xtent balanced by the increase in demand and the increase in population. Not only are there more people but these eople have greater needs than the old opulation in its more primitive form of fe. Yet the statistician finds comfort in emonstrating that the growth of production does draw a little yet sensibly head of the growth of demand, so that here is a rise in the level of living. The tandard of life and the level of real ages have both risen since the age of echanical expansion began, and that at east we may call progress.

Civilization, in its growth, not only eeps pace with the increase of its people ut raises their lot. Its mobility, as we ave seen, has enormously increased. It an bring its requirements in bulk from the nds of the earth ; it can feed itself from he pastures of Argentine, Australia and ew Zealand. As it can control temperature it can bring its provisions not merely salted down or canned, as of old, but chilled and esh to its table. It has, besides, ultiplied the productive power of griculture. It has invented harrows wenty-five feet wide ; multiple ploughs hich turn several furrows at once at ouble the pace of the horse ; harvesters hich cut a swathe of fifty-two feet, and ot only harvest but thrash the corn in he field. It has so modified the character f wheat by selection that it defies the osts of Canada and is vastly extending he wheat belt of the world. For clothing brings the wool of the Antipodes to he looms of Bradford. It has, if we take ivilization as a whole, 165 million pindles for the spinning of its cotton ; it an turn a forest into silk or into paper ; brings up gold, oil and coal from depths f thousands of feet.

ow Civilization betters Life

By all these means civilization conrives to keep a little ahead of the growth f its population, and this fact, which we ave dared to call progress, gives buoyancy nd hope to Western thought. 'The ving organism,' says Wyatt Tilby in his uest of Reality (1927), 'has to maintain itself against the external world as a first charge on its resources.' 'The balance of unspent energy' is, therefore, 'the source of our free will.' If humanity has increased its balance of unspent energy by all these inventions its free will is correspondingly enlarged.

True, the margin of free will is as yet small. It is, for example, salutary to remember the ratio between man's top speed of a little over 300 miles an hour, and the speed of light. It is well, also, to keep in mind that this progress is local and relative, and may be temporary. The standard rises with the progress and expansion of a particular industrial system, but when that system sustains a severe shock, as in the Great War, or falls behind in the race, the scale of living becomes stationary or goes down. Sir Josiah Stamp has calculated that the average level of real wages to-day in Great Britain is four times as high as it was in the beginning of the nineteenth century ; in other words the average wage earner at the present time can command four times as much of the necessities and luxuries of life as his forefathers of a century ago, and this although the population has increased fivefold. But since the war, owing to the disorganization of the industrial system, there has been no such progress.

Progress may be temporary

Experts, like Professor Bowley, Sir Josiah Stamp and the Colwyn Committee, compute that the national income in 1924 was the same in real value as before the war. It has to be allowed, however, that the population increased in that time by nearly 7 per cent., so that, there being more people to share it, the income per head is lower. 'It seems likely,' says the report of the Liberal Industrial Inquiry (1928), 'that in spite of unemployment, short time, etc., the real income per head of the country is only a little lower than before the War. It must be counted a poor achievement that after fifteen years of startling scientific advance we have scarcely maintained the real income per head of 1911.'

In the United States, on the other hand, where the profits of the Great War were larger than the losses, the upward

MAN POWER IN CHINA

Even where railways exist steam power has not completely ousted man power for goods transport in China, where the two can sometimes be seen side by side. A Chinese coolie can carry logs weighing 200 lb. ten miles a day.

Photo, Camera Craft, Peking

progress in well-being has been continuous, and the ratio of wages to commodity prices has steadily increased. This is clearly shown by a Report of the Federal Reserve Board of the United States, which examined the figures in thirty-four representative industries for the year September, 1924, to October, 1925. The board found that whereas employment had increased 6·4 per cent., the wages bill had gone up by 12·6 per cent., or nearly double. Nor was the increase extorted from the employers by trade union action, since the industries in which the greatest increases took place followed a system of payments by results. The rise in wages coincided with abundant prosperity and expanding markets, as is shown by the fact that the production of the industries examined in the period under review increased by 28·8 per cent., more than double the rise in wages.

Furthermore, the United States Depart ment of Labour in its table of wages an prices, using the 1913 level as the unit c 100, calculates the 1920 wage rate at 19 and the 1924 wage rate at 228 ; the pric level in 1920 stood at 226, but by 1924 i had fallen back to 150.

These results are made possible by a industrial system of enormously and con stantly expanding power. Thus, a singl American motor company employs n fewer than 200,000 workmen, at a mini mum wage of 29s. 6d. a day, and sell 2,000,000 motor-cars a year.

Here then we have the leading physica characteristic of what is called Western o progressive civilization. It springs fror the application of gigantic natural forces– steam, water power, electricity—to th tasks and burdens formerly laid on th hands and backs of men and beasts There is an obvious and interesting com parison to be made with what might b called static or stationary civilizatio which still exists in a great part of th world and notably in Asia, and we ar given materials for this comparison in book called Explaining China, by Joh Earl Baker, from 1916 to 1926 adviser t the Chinese Ministry of Communications.

Standards in China & U.S.A

In mere man power, China, with a popu lation of more than 400 millions, is enor mously superior to the United States which, according to the census of 1920, had a population of under 106 millions ; but whereas in China work and transport are still in th main primitive, in the United State they are done largely by machinery. Sc according to the census of 1923, th United States in their manufacturin establishments had a mechanical hors power of over 33 millions, which give an equivalent man power of somethin like 400 millions. There was besides th mechanical power used in agriculture, i mining, in forests and in transportation In 1923 the railways of the United State hauled freight equivalent to 416 thousan million tons the distance of one mile. O the generous assumption that a man ca carry 100 pounds on his back 20 mile every day in the year, this railway powe of transportation added over a thousan million man power to the industrial strength of the United States.

Thus, whereas in China there was an adult working male population of, say, 100 millions, in the United States there was added to the 25 million working males something like two thousand million man power in machinery. And the result is that whereas in China consumers outnumber producers by 4 to 1, in the United States producers outnumber consumers by 20 to 1. Accordingly, the consumption per head in America might be 60 or 80 times as great as in China without depleting accumulated wealth. Of course, we must allow for the fact that there are some railways, a certain amount of machinery and a very considerable amount of water transport in China; but it remains true that human carriers still compete for its transport. The general result is that famine is never far from the door of a very large proportion of the Chinese people, and millions of Chinese have not the wherewithal to satisfy their bare animal needs, or to protect themselves against hunger, cold, wet, injury and death, even in the prime of life (see further in Chapter 173).

Material power of the West

When we remember that James Watt applied steam power to rotatory movement only 150 years ago, and that before that time Europe was much on a level with Asia, and America infinitely behind, we arrive at some conception of the superiority of Western civilization in mere material well-being, in power of production and provision of those necessities and luxuries that go to the life of man. Before the shock of the Great War weakened and partially paralysed civilization, this superior power of transport and production had given to the West an easy supremacy in the world, had penetrated South America, Africa and Asia, had made them the base of its supplies and was forcing them to choose between following in its wake, as in the case of Japan, or accepting a position of economic inferiority.

We have already hinted that there is a danger in describing this impressive phenomenon as progress. We are chastened by the knowledge that other civilizations, hardly less imposing, have risen like waves from the surface of the sea to fall again in ruinous chaos, and 'throw that faint thin line upon the shore'; that history shows no continuous and steady advance upwards, but that successive civilizations, like a series of waves, arise only to fall again, and leave hardly a trace behind them. Before the Great War, Western civilization seemed to rest on so strong and world-wide a foundation that there were hardly any who questioned its permanence; but even then there were bitter or despondent spirits who turned with chagrin from the imposing structure of the Occident; some sought to reform, others to destroy civilized life.

Reactions against Civilization

In considering these lines of criticism and attack, which have developed so formidably since the war, we must allow something for the fatigue which comes from the increased pace of civilization, and we must allow also for the satiety which is apt to follow the increased gratifications of modern society. The critic of life often lays bare only his own soul to the pathologist. That 'Weltschmerz,' or weariness of life, which has inspired so many attacks on Western civilization, may spring from some subjective weakness or weariness following excess, which turns with disgust from what it has eaten of too greedily.

If we want a clue, for example, to Count Tolstoy's bitterness against society, we find it in that depressing masterpiece, The Kreutzer Sonata, a study of the loathing which comes from loving too much. The superhuman vanity which springs from a disordered mind may have been the hidden spring of Nietzsche's doctrine of the 'super-man'; his demand that everyone should live his own life, free from every social restraint, in a species of anarchy. A weakness of physical equipment may have led John Ruskin to denounce all modern life as ugliness, and seek refuge in an ideal period before Raphael, or may have prompted Thomas Carlyle to invoke some fist strong enough to shatter the sorry scheme of things as he saw them. So, possibly, in the later case of Oswald Spengler, the author of Der Untergang des Abendländes (The Decline of the West), who described civilization as a sickness or senility, who likened the modern spirit to Faust, consuming himself with feverish unrest and longing, selling for enjoyment his soul to the devil.

Such enmities, whatever their motive, are formidable because they appeal to a considerable body of the disaffected. The increasing speed of civilization ; the jolts it gives to settled life ; the scars of the new roads it cuts across the world ; the friction and heating of bearings ; the changes, resettlements and readjustments ; the thousand and one strains and stresses, as it impinges on this side or the other of its line of advance—all lead to reactions and resistances dangerous to its stability.

We shall best see the substance of these complaints and attacks by looking a little more closely into the results on society of the developments which we have just described. Although in the course of a century the population of Europe has increased fourfold, and that of the United States nearly a hundredfold, and although wealth has increased in an even greater ratio, the expansion has not been uniform or constant. There has rather been concentration in the towns and a change from a predominantly rural to a chiefly urban form of life. In 1790, for example, Philadelphia was the largest American city and contained 42,000 people. The four million people who then lived in the United States were chiefly farmers, planters, seamen, lumbermen and trappers. Now, in the state of New York, of a total of ten million people eight million are urban ; and more than half the population of the United States lives in cities. 'In whole states and in hundreds of counties,' says A. P. Brigham, in his United States of America, 'the rural population is either declining actually, or increasing more slowly than the urban groups.'

LEO TOLSTOY

The Russian writer, Leo Tolstoy (1828–1910) won fame as a novelist, an advocate of international peace and a preacher of social equality. In his greatest work, War and Peace, he vividly describes the horrors of war in Napoleonic times.

DR. OSWALD SPENGLER

Oswald Spengler (b. May 29, 1880) combined scientific study with the study of history and art and wrote much on cultural and political problems. His most important work, Der Untergang des Abendländes, was published in 1918.

Photo, E.N.A.

And so in Europe. In England, London has increased sevenfold, and while Lancashire, the West Riding of Yorkshire, Glasgow and other industrial areas have grown enormously, the rural population has in many cases been either stationary or in a state of decline. France has contrived to maintain a better balance between agriculture and rural industry ; but has fallen behind in the race for population as compared with Germany, whose owerful industries support an enormous rban population. Even in new countries hich support themselves chiefly by razing and agriculture, we note the same endency. About two-fifths of the entire opulation of Australia is contained in e two cities of Sydney and Melbourne.

In some cases the rural population has ared the benefit of the general advance well-being. The Prussian peasantry ere described by William Jacob, who was nt by the British government to report n the state of Germany in 1819 and 1826, s in a condition of poverty more abject an we see in China at the present day. he implements of their usbandry were as poor as eir working cattle; their loughs were made chiefly of ood and very little iron; the se of rollers was unknown, nd the clods were broken ith wooden mallets. They ved in miserable dwellings n the lowest and coarsest od, many of them eating nly potatoes and rye. An arthen pot was the most aluable article of their furniure, and they wore coarse omespun wool or linen as long as their garments could hold together. Prussia was then almost without industries and lived precariously by war, and the sale of her surplus corn.

The great development of railways, of machinery and of electrical power, however, has transformed northern Germany into one of the most prosperous countries of Europe. The scientific culture of the sugar beet has introduced deep tillage and supplied with manure the sandy soil of Prussia. Every rural sugar factory is a wealth-distributing centre; a network of transmission lines supplies the farms and villages with electric power and light; the

PLEASANT HOMES AND PROSPEROUS PEASANTS IN EAST PRUSSIA

Vhereas in the early nineteenth century the East Prussian peasantry were apathetic, indolent, l-nourished and ill-housed, they are now an industrious, prosperous people owing to the development of the beet sugar industry. More than a million acres are under sugar beet, providing work for omen as well as men. Housing conditions are admirable, as in the post-war village of Gross Sobrost top), where the peasants' cottages have all been built from designs by a prominent German architect.

Photos, E.N.A.

ALEXANDER STAMBOLISKY

Himself of peasant origin, Alexander Stambolisky (1879–1923) became the leader of the agrarian party in Bulgaria. In 1918 he headed the insurgents who deposed Tsar Ferdinand and became premier in 1919. He was shot in 1923.
Photo, E.N.A.

cattle are maintained through the winter by the help of feeding stuffs imported from a distance, and the peasantry, instead of being idle and listless as they were described by Jacob, are now energetic, well clad and well housed.

Yet it remains true that over a large part of the rural area of Europe the country population has not kept pace with the town, and in Great Britain especially, and in other countries as well, the town came to rule the country without much regard to the rural interests.

In England, owing to its insular position, the crisis was never so severe, but on the Continent where war disorganized the whole system of European commerce the industrial centres could no longer feed themselves with imported food, and the country again reasserted its ancient power. The farmers once more controlled the food supplies, and when the 'proletariat' turned hungry eyes on the land a shrewd peasantry was not slow to realize that its turn had come again.

And so it came about that the revolutions immediately after the War were largely, although by no means altogether conflicts between country and town. The towns attempted to force the country to provide them with food, offering a debased paper currency in exchange. When the peasantry resisted, there were attempts to 'socialise' the land; thus, in Hungary where the Reds divided the country into 'communal' estates, the peasantry attacked and destroyed the Communist republic. In Finland a White Army recruited from the peasantry overthrew the Communist government; in Bavaria the revolutionaries of Munich and elsewhere were starved out by food blockades; the Bauernbund, or Peasants' League, of Switzerland was organized to blockade the industrial centres and suppress industrial revolution.

A shrewd American observer, Lothrop Stoddard, in his study of Social Classes in Post-War Europe (1925), describes this widespread but unrealized war between town and country that succeeded the Great War between nations. Its most dramatic manifestation was in Bulgaria, where Stambolisky led the peasants in an anti-urban crusade, and was elected prime minister in 1919 by an overwhelming majority. This rural dictator proclaimed to the assembled peasants in Sofia shortly afterwards that not the town but the village should henceforth rule Bulgaria. The towns were centres of wickedness and corruption; the country must reform society. 'We are now able to do what we will,' he exclaimed; 'Sofia is another Sodom and Gomorrah, inhabited by speculators and producers of nothing. Let the townsfolk take warning lest their town be turned into a village.'

War between Town & Country

The failure of this experiment is no less significant. After ruling four years, corruptly and ignorantly, Stambolisky fell as a victim of a conspiracy organized in the capital. The town reasserted its higher intelligence and concentrated power. The country showed itself strong in a crisis but weak in sustained effort and organized administration. The town, after all, is a social necessity.

Nevertheless, the war had the effect, at least temporarily and in eastern Europe of strengthening the country and weakening the town. The Green International, as it was called, in 1925, after an existence of five years, claimed to be several millions strong, and to have given one prime minister to Czecho-Slovakia and another to Poland. An organization of farmers and peasant proprietors, it opposed its quiet power to the violence of the Red International, and the Communists recognized in it a formidable and irreconcilable opponent.

It was, however, in Russia (see Chapter 184 for fuller details) that this conflict between the Red and the Green, the town and the country, was fought out on the largest scale and with the most notable consequences. At the beginning of the revolution, the peasantry, tempted by the prospect of taking over the land of the great landowners, joined in the orgy of massacre and robbery; but having possessed itself of this land, its interest in revolution ended, and when the hungry and disorganized urban mob turned to the country for food, offering nothing in exchange, the peasantry became for some time actively, and always passively, hostile. The 'dictatorship of the proletariat' decreed the confiscation of the surplus of grain; the farmers replied by ceasing to produce a surplus; the weapon of terror was met by the weapon of famine.

This conflict between town and country suggests one weakness in modern civilization; but it is overshadowed by another and more threatening fissure which began as a mere crack about the middle of the nineteenth century, had grown deeper in the years that followed, and, suddenly widened by the strain of the Great War

MEETING OF AN INTERNATIONAL CLASS-WAR ORGANIZATION IN TRAFALGAR SQUARE

Carrying the Marxian arguments about capital and labour to their extreme logical conclusion, an international party of Communists advocated war between the employing classes and the proletariat the whole world over. In London, where this photograph was taken in January, 1929, these fanatical propagandists were treated with characteristically British tolerance by the authorities. The placards denounce 'capitalist terrorism' in China, Poland and Italy, as well as in Great Britain.

Photo, Photopress

threatened to engulf the whole fabric of modern civilization.

We must beware in approaching this social struggle of accepting the terms commonly used to describe it, since they are apt to lead to false conclusions. To call it, for example, a struggle between capital and labour is to beg the question, for both of these abstract terms may be made to mean anything or nothing. To call it a struggle between employers and employed is also misleading, since in many industries and most countries the great majority both of employers and employed refused to accept such a division.

The Marxian case (see page 4986) is that, all wealth being created by labour, the employing class, by its monopoly of capital, contrives to exploit the worker and possess itself of the surplus wealth it has created. As this process is continuous and progressive it follows that the employing class is destined to become richer and the working class poorer until there remains to the latter 'nothing but their chains.' Hence, the 'class war' and 'revolution,' so that the 'employing class,' the 'industrial system,' 'capitalism,' and in fact society, may be swept away, and the 'proletariat'—the many without property—may possess the world in common.

Breakdown of Marxian case

Now, if the Marxian argument were well founded, we should have had to trace in our survey of industrial expansion a continuous lowering of real wages, whereas, as we have seen, it was actually accompanied by a continuous growth in real wages, and this despite the great growth in the population to be supported. We have seen also that where industrial expansion is checked by such a cataclysm as the Great War, there is a check also to the growth in well-being or real wages. Still further, we have seen that where industrial organization is highest and mechanical transportation most developed there also are to be found the highest real wages and most prosperous conditions; and that where mechanical power and transport are least developed there we find the greatest poverty and the hardest forms of existence.

If Karl Marx were right the opposite would be the case; we should have the greatest prosperity in China and the greatest misery in the United States; we should have a continuous degradation from the agricultural Germany of Jacob's survey a century ago to the industrial Germany of the present time. Moreover, we should expect to find the fiercest 'class war' where industrial development is high and the contrary where it is low; yet the opposite is true. In the United States at the present time there is general industrial peace, whereas in the Russia of the Revolution there was the fiercest industrial war. So also in England; before the War, when its industrial system was expanding, both the number and the extent of industrial conflicts were much less than after the war when industries were losing ground.

Facts of the industrial situation

Let us look at these industrial and social questions a little more closely. Two English engineers, Bertram Austin and W. Francis Lloyd, in their book, The Secret of High Wages, give an account of an industrial tour in the United States, undertaken not for any political purpose but to examine methods of factory organization. They show that, at least in engineering, the employers and workmen in America have come to a modus vivendi on the basis that the interests which divide them, namely, the division of the profits of their production, are very much less important than the interests which unite them, that is to say, the progress and health of the industry by which they both must live.

A system of payment by results encourages initiative and promotes efficiency; high wages are given only for good work; the lower the cost of the article produced and the greater the production the higher the reward of the producer. So far from the worker having 'nothing to lose but his chains,' he owns commonly his own house and his own motor car. So far from the 'class war' increasing in intensity, the statistics of industrial disputes in the United States show a decrease from 4,450 in 1917 to 1,227 in 1924.

If we turn to the industrial conditions in Great Britain we have to note a series of great strikes culminating in the general

SCENES OF DAILY LIFE IN THE BRITISH GENERAL STRIKE OF 1926

Prolonged industrial depression in Great Britain, especially in the coal industry, where partial unemployment was accompanied by reduction in wage rates, led in 1926 to a general strike which threatened to paralyse every public service and deprive the community of vitally necessary supplies. The Government dealt energetically with the situation, in London organizing a depot in Hyde Park for the collection and distribution of milk, and guaranteeing protection for volunteers who carried on the train and omnibus services from molestation by pickets and strikers.

Photos, Topical Press Agency and (bottom) The Times

strike and coal strike of 1926, when a great part of the workmen were reduced to organized idleness, and we find that this increase in strife coincides with a long depression in the staple industries of the country. The British steel industry, capable of producing 12 million tons a year, was producing only 7 or 8 million tons; in the woollen industry no fewer than 200 mills went out of business in four years, and the export of woollens fell from 186 million square yards in 1922 to 163 million square yards in 1926; in the cotton industry the industrial crisis was hardly less severe; but it was most devastating in the coal industry, where, moreover, the proportion of labour to production is higher. In that industry, profits had altogether disappeared, and as his wages are based on results, the miner was faced not only with partial unemployment but a reduction in wage rates. Thus, a period of fierce industrial conflict roughly coincided with the severe industrial depression, and the conflict was fiercest where the depression bore most directly on the position of the workmen.

It is obvious that we cannot press these parallels too far, since in some of the industries most depressed there was no industrial struggle, employers and workmen realizing equally the plain truth that to fight over the sharing of their diminished profits would merely lessen the profits to be divided. Yet, looking at the position broadly, we see that in this case also the Marxian doctrine bears no sort of relation to the facts.

We come to an even clearer demonstration of these simple truths when we consider the case of the country from which what is called 'capitalism,' or the machinery of modern civilization, has been swept away in order to provide a clear field for the alternative 'system.' Russia never had a very high economic organization, although she possessed considerable industries. She lived before the War chiefly on her own produce and by the business of selling to western Europe a great part of the food and raw material by which it lives. Wheat, flax, eggs, timber, furs, oil were supplied to the west in enormous quantities, and Germany and the north of Europe generally, where cattle have to be housed and fed in winter, looked to Russia to supply them with those coarse kinds of grain which are most suitable for that purpose, and in return Russia bought those manufactured goods and clothing that she was unable to manufacture herself. The exchange of food and raw material for manufactures is not the most profitable sort of livelihood, but it served to maintain the people of Russia beyond the reach of famine.

A Communist experiment

This way of life, brought to a stand by the war, was altogether destroyed by the Revolution of 1917. The Bolsheviks made a clean sweep of the whole system—government, banks, commerce and organized industry—in order that they might have a tabula rasa for their experiments. In the course of the struggle and the famine which immediately succeeded it there was a loss of life estimated at 16 millions, or greater than was caused by the Great War. There was in the end no resistance, but economic facts eventually forced the Soviet to its New Economic Policy (see page 4970).

Such small concerns, however, as were permitted thereby were so jealously watched and so frequently interfered with that, for the most part, people refused to take the risks involved. In 1925–26 only five per cent. of the industrial concerns—and these usually employing not more than twenty men—were in private hands. The state had therefore a monopoly of large industry, and it commanded besides not only the factories and plants which it took over from the old system, but the labour trained under that system, with the power to requisition such experts and works managers as were left alive in Russia.

Anton Karlgren, Professor of Slavonic at the University of Copenhagen, in his book on Bolshevik Russia (1927), makes a careful comparison between the progress claimed and the actual position. He points out that the Soviet's statistics are usually based on comparisons with positions in 1921, when as a fact there was almost no production. In that year, for example, the yield of iron had fallen to two per cent. of what was produced before the Revolution. It was by this comparison with virtual zero that Kalanin, in 1924, was able to claim 'quicker progress than any of the Western European bourgeois countries whatever.' If, however, comparison is made with the pre-revolutionary Russia the truth begins to emerge. In the report, October, 1924, to September, 1925, the Soviet government states that the total of its industrial production amounts to about 70 per cent. of that under the old regime.

Actual state of Russia

Moreover, although the goods were assumed to be weight for weight the same, they were, in fact, 'immeasurably inferior in quality.' And further, while the old industrial system paid its way, the new was heavily subsidised. This expedient was forced upon the Soviet by the very curious economic crisis of 1923. Although the manufactures were only 30 per cent. of the yield before 1917, there was a glut of goods in the stores and no possibility of sale. The Russian people could not afford to buy its own manufactures. 'It became clear to us,' wrote Dzherzhinsky, 'that the prices of our goods must be lowered, and we followed this up by the principle that the cost of production must not always be the determining factor in the price.'

What in private enterprise would be regarded as ruinous was hailed by the Communists as a 'lever that will lift our industry to an unforeseen height.' It was this system of selling under cost that brought production to 70 per cent. of the old standard. Besides direct subsidies these losing industries obtained increasing advances from the state banks. Whereas in October, 1924, they owed the banks 466 million roubles, 12 months later the debt was 926 million roubles.

With this economic bankruptcy there was no improvement in the lot of the workers. The Soviet, as Stalin confessed, was almost overwhelmed by 'the wave of strikes and unrest which in August, 1923, rolled over parts of the Republic in regard to wages.' The Soviet tried to mend matters by appointing Dzherzhinsky, who had been head of the Terror, to preside over the Supreme Economic Council. He was a man of daemonic energy; but the indiscipline of the workers proved too much for him. In a speech made in December, 1924, he drew a remarkable comparison between labour then and in 1913. Taking the production of 100 men in 1913 as a comparison, coal required 214 men, naphtha 213 men, shoe-making 234 men, chemicals 292 men, tobacco 218 men to produce the same result. Whereas in 1913 the value of a year's work of one man in the South Russia metal industry was valued at 3,227 roubles, in 1923–4 it was estimated at 988 roubles. And he concluded his comparison with this devastating summary: 'The number of workers is nearly the same as before the war; but the production is only one third of what it was then.'

Decline in the quality of work

It is not altogether surprising that his failure so wrought upon his fanatical brain that he broke out into wild abuse of the dishonesty of the whole system and died with suspicious suddenness.

The disastrous failure of this extraordinary experiment was indeed inevitable. What the socialists call the 'capitalist system' is in fact no system at all, but rather the living and intricate growth, intensified and enlarged by mechanical inventions, of the means by which man has always lived since he emerged from barbarism. The savage, if he lives in a kindly climate, may satisfy his daily needs as they arise, from the shore and the sea. He starves when nature fails him, and when he begins to lay by and exchange the surplus of his daily toil he takes the first step towards both capitalism and civilization. The accumulation and free currency of these surpluses makes civilization possible, nor is there any alternative but starvation.

Capitalism a fact of Nature

It would be misleading to leave the reader under the impression that the state of Russia is due to a mistaken theory of economics, carried out by amiable theorists who have gone wrong. The 'terrible sect,' as Mr. Winston Churchill called the Communist party, was a small minority, at the beginning probably only a few thousand strong, composed largely of alien criminals and fanatics, and using hatred, ignorance and the passions produced by the Great War as a means to power. Lenin, in one of his bursts of frankness, told his brother Communists that 'among a hundred so-called Bolsheviki there is one real Bolshevik with thirty-nine criminals and sixty fools.' The medical professors of the University of Kiev found an opportunity of examining the leaders of the Red Terror, with the most startling and significant results. The professors found degeneracy, alcoholism and syphilis in nearly every case.

We are too apt to think of civilization as an even process permeating every individual and all society in equal degree, and leaving nothing of the barbarism it has displaced. The truth is otherwise. Civilization is a recent growth of a few thousand years, behind which lies age upon age of the mere brute, the unrestrained savage, whose primordial nature is strong in the make-up of humanity. 'The most civilized empires,' says Rivarol, 'are as close to barbarism as the most polished steel is to rust; nations, like metals, shine only on the surface.'

Modern investigations suggest that the 'advance' of man is probably the work of a superior minority which has dragged the neutral masses unwillingly or passively in its wake. When the United States entered the Great War, the army authorities, faced by the task of rapidly sorting out a mass of 1,700,000 young men, applied a series of intelligence tests, carefully devised so as not to depend upon literacy or language, and the result showed that less than 1 in 20, or 4½ per cent., possessed high intelligence. Major Yerks and Major Yoakum in their Army Mental Tests (1920) describe this most elaborate examination ever made of the mental powers of a nation. Nor does it stand alone, for similar tests have been made upon large numbers of American school children.

Mankind's low mental average

An American writer in some alarm says:

> If those examined are representative, it means that the average mental age of Americans is only about 14; that 45 millions, or nearly one half of the population, will never develop a capacity beyond the stage represented by a normal 12 year child; that only 13½ millions will ever show superior intelligence, and that only 4½ millions can be considered talented.

These tests, moreover, suggest a permanent inequality due to family, race, or physical equipment, and not removable by education. Two American authorities, Messrs. Popenoe and Johnson, express the following opinion:

> No matter what trait of the individual be chosen, results are analogous. Whether it be speed in marking off all the A's in a printed sheet of capitals, or in putting together the pieces of a puzzle, or in giving a reaction to some certain stimulus, or in making associations between ideas, or drawing figures, or memory for various things . . . or success in any one of the hundreds of other mental tests, the conclusion is the same. There are wide differences in the abilities of individuals, no two being alike, either mentally or physically, at birth or any time thereafter.

These results, which have suggested the most disturbing and uncomfortable doubts in the minds of thinking Americans about the validity of those principles of equality on which all their institutions are founded, may also help to explain how vast crowds may be led to their own destruction by a few designing and fanatical agitators. Lothrop Stoddard in his book Revolt against Civilization (1922) goes so far as to formulate 'an iron law of inequality.' 'Nature herself,' he says, 'having decreed him incivilizable, the Under-Man declares war on civilization.'

If these American reports may be allowed as representative there is probably a vast stratum of people in every nation which is either passive or resents what is to it the overstrain of civilization. But there are, besides, the actual enemies of civilization who know how to work upon this mass. Boris Brasol in his scientific study of the Elements of Crime (1927) explores these 'delinquent strata of society,' inspired by a common hatred of civilization. He argues:

> The professional criminal cannot stand alone amidst a society which he hates, and which in turn is hostile to him. Verily, isolation is a dangerous state for a person who ventures to challenge the social order. He is therefore compelled to co-operate with those who, by reason of their own morbid propensions and immoral conduct, are dwelling in discord with society.

Revolutionary doctrine, according to Brasol, makes a definite appeal to this delinquent class, and the bloodthirstiness of a good deal of Communist and Socialist propaganda goes to support this position. 'Le couteau entre les dents!'—'With your knife in your teeth!'—is the cry of the French Communist, Henri Barbusse, and we find this strain of ferocity through revolutionary literature. Thus Babeuf (see page 4143) planned the assassination of 'all civil and military employees, all government agents and magistrates.' Says Brasol:

> Proudhon, Kropotkin, Reclu and Babeuf may not have contemplated the unfortunate consequences which their writings have caused in the minds of their undeveloped, underaged, and often half-illiterate pupils. These theoreticians might have earnestly believed that dynamite and murder are capable of

bringing about social equality and universal happiness. Be that as it may . . . the inflammatory demagogy of these apostles of anarchy appeals to the egocentric emotions slumbering in all men, nourishing the lowest bestial instincts which, at times, reach the degree of a psycho-pathological obsession . . . Once acquired, the feeling of anti-social irritation steadily grows in its intensity and ultimately generates a species of anthropoids who aim at the complete destruction of civilization, and thus become the vanguards of international criminality.

In normal times, when life is settled and employment good, society is commonly too strong for these rebels, who show their presence only by some sporadic act of assassination ; but the strains of war, the sufferings and passions which it lets loose upon the world, expose the weaker side of civilization to attack. The great mass of the neutral and the ignorant, driven almost to despair by poverty and unemployment, are easily affected by crowd impulses of rage and hate, and if the government is, as we frequently find it, weak, vacillating and cowardly, all the disciplines and restraint of civilization may give way, the organized system of livelihood by which all live together may break down, hunger and panic may add force to the convulsion which rocks society, until the whole structure is brought crashing to the ground.

When civilization itself fell in Russia, it is not surprising that it was shaken in western Europe. We have seen that Benjamin Kidd looked upon democracy, and what he grandiloquently called 'the enfranchisement of the future,' as the most permanent, valuable and characteristic part of modern civilization. The Great War was fought, or so we were told by the politicians, 'to make the world safe for democracy.' Yet, second only to the abandonment of civilization itself in Russia, the destruction of the democratic system of government over a large part of western Europe is one of the most impressive features of the post-war period.

Departures from Democracy

The truth would seem to be that systems of government, which to the few assume almost the sanctity of religion, to the many are tested merely by their power to govern. In the easy times before the war the flattering fiction of 'government of the people by the people for the people' had been generally adopted in various forms, and under different constitutions, throughout Western civilization. It had led in practice to governments composed of men apt in the demagogic arts, fluent and skilful in the use of words ; but ill equipped for the stern business of defending the nations they governed in a life and death struggle, whether against national enemies or the forces of disorder and anarchy.

Thus in Italy a weak and corrupt government of professional politicians brought themselves into hatred and contempt by their mismanagement of the war, and looked on helplessly at the disorder sloping down into chaos which followed. The enemies of civilization, grown bold like wolves in a hard winter and hunting no longer alone, but in packs, terrorised the population of northern Italy. Anarchist outrages grew more frequent and more terrible until the crisis came in Milan on March 12, 1921, when a bomb thrown in the Diana Theatre during the last act of a musical comedy killed seventeen people and wounded a great multitude. Strike followed strike, culminating in a general strike which was in fact an attempt at revolution ; factories were seized ; shops were looted ; trade was disorganized, and the ordered life of the community brought to a stand.

The Italian revolution

The revolt led by Benito Mussolini (see page 4896) was in every way in notable contrast to the revolt led by Lenin in Russia. By a strange coincidence the two men both belonged to what is called the 'revolutionary intelligentsia,' and both had sought refuge in Switzerland from a social order which they found oppressive in their own countries. But there the analogy ends. Lenin governed 'against the hair'; Mussolini expressed and embodied the national will. Neither the doctrines of Karl Marx nor the philosophy of Rousseau had ever appealed to the Italian people. Mussolini expressed the Italian sense of order inherited from Rome ; he believed in power, which the Italians respected ; he disbelieved in democracy, which the Italians despised ; but above all he delivered Italy from a system of government which the Italians well knew to be corrupt and effete. Events in Spain followed a somewhat similar course, and teach a similar lesson.

Thus in Italy and Spain that constitutional system of government which had been hailed before the war as a universal principle destined to govern the whole world was swept away not merely with the acquiescence but the gratitude of the nations concerned. It went not by an act of tyranny, but because in practice it failed to secure the order and discipline, the law, justice and good administration, necessary to national well-being. And when we go farther afield we find these warnings reinforced in various directions.

In Russia the attempt to create an elective duma was a disastrous failure; Greece, which once boasted of its constitutionalism, lives by a series of bloody revolutions. And that boasted work of Allied statesmanship, the democratic constitution of Jugo-Slavia, was brought to an end at the beginning of January, 1929, by King Alexander after an ignominious life of barely ten years. Asia takes even less kindly to the principle of popular government. In Turkey hardly the pretence of popular government remains. The well meant efforts to impose it upon India in moderate doses have led to such convulsions as should make one dread its wider application. In Afghanistan the liberal reforms of Amanullah brought his throne tumbling about his ears. In China, whose constitution was hailed as the dawn of a new era in the East, it speedily degenerated into mere misrule and civil war, and it is too early to make any calculations on the unstable equilibrium of the Nanking government. Even in Japan, according to a disillusioned Japanese (the poet Gonnoské Komai) 'the masses are led to believe that there is scarcely any difference between the

'IL DUCE': BENITO MUSSOLINI WITH HIS CHIEFS OF STAFF

Benito Mussolini began his political career as a socialist, but modified his views as a result of the Great War, in which he fought in the Bersaglieri. In 1919 he organized the Italian nationalists into a society known as the Fascisti, popularly known as Blackshirts, with the purpose of stamping Bolshevism and extreme Socialism out of the country. After 1922, when he was appointed premier (see page 4896), he rose to supreme power as the recognized exponent of the national will and spirit

Photo, E.N.A.

governments formed by Conservatives, Liberals, Coalition or Labour. They all seem bent on squandering people's money in spite of cessation of war-time excitements and necessities.' Egypt also does not appear to have profited by those essays in the popular system which were hailed with so much hope and eloquence. The Great War, which was to make the world safe for democracy, has led to its downfall in so many places as to leave all but its most enthusiastic exponents somewhat shaken in their belief in its efficacy.

The position in Great Britain

In Great Britain, either because the fabric was stronger or the people more phlegmatic, the social and political results were less violent in appearance, yet here also the storm of war started many seams, economic and political, so that despite every effort to pump the hold and stop the leaks, the ship of state lies visibly lower in the water.

Fortunately for Great Britain her system of food supply did not so far break down as to produce the breach between town and country which we saw on the Continent; but there were other fissures hardly less disastrous. In most countries ancient racial divisions show themselves under more recent national unions. Thus in the unified group of the British Isles the politically overlaid racial division between Ireland and Great Britain widened until hardly a ligament remains between the two.

With this perpendicular fissure there went many lateral strains hardly less threatening and disastrous. In Ireland itself the national appeal covered an anti-social movement directed against law and property. In Great Britain fierce and continual agitation culminated in the great coal strike and general strike of 1926, directed not so much against industry as against the state and society itself. These disorders were not suppressed by force as in Italy and Spain, but were soothed and diverted by measures of palliation and compromise. From the beginning of the Great War until the present time, a long series of expedients—the shortening of hours, the raising of wages, state subsidies, unemployment allowance and poor relief—averted immediate trouble by some change in the economic or social balance, and these measures were accompanied by two enormous extensions of the franchise.

As the working expenses of a country must in the end be borne by the industries which produce its wealth, these measures increased the cost of production, and, as the cost of production determines the struggle for survival among nations, intensified the troubles they were designed to cure.

A Treasury return issued in November, 1927, showed that the expenditure on social services had increased from £22,644,334 in 1891 to £351,515,957 in 1926. But this is only part of the sum, since besides the contribution of the state, which is met by taxation, there is the direct cost to industry itself. A parliamentary committee under the chairmanship of Sir Arthur Balfour gave the following estimate of the cost per head of five social services in the various industrial countries of Europe. Thus:

	£	s.	d.	Per cent.
Great Britain	3	18	6	100
Germany	1	17	6	48
France	0	13	0	17
Czecho-Slovakia ..	0	11	0	14
Belgium	0	5	6	7
Italy	0	3	6	4

It is not surprising that industries thus overburdened were disabled in their power of employment. In 1925—seven years after the War—the average weekly figure of unemployment for Great Britain still stood at more than 1¼ millions, and on January 28, 1929, the total number of persons on the registers of the unemployment exchanges in Great Britain was 1,394,190.

As the beneficiaries of the various social services (including free education) constitute the great bulk of the nation, a great part of the people are interested in maintaining a system which is draining the national resources. The extension of the franchise has thus a close bearing on the economic position, since it places in the hands of those partially or wholly maintained by the state the power to increase the benefits which they enjoy and the costs of which are borne on the shoulders of others. And the politicians who impose these measures of relief are tempted to extend the franchise in order to reap the precarious harvest of political gratitude. Thus the increase of the national expenditure and the extension of the electorate are apt to go together.

The Reform Act of 1918 added nearly 13 million voters, including nine million women, to the parliamentary register. The Reform Act of 1928 was designed to add 3,650,000 women over the age of 25, and about 1,590,000 under that age, or about 5,240,000 new women voters. The total electorate in 1924 was 21,731,320 and with the latter addition substantially exceeds 27 million.

The future of Democracy

Can democracy bear the strain of its own extension? J. J. Rousseau, arch-priest and prophet of the system, conceived of a state small enough for the people to know the representatives and for the representatives to know the people. But the great modern growth of population makes this mutual knowledge more and more difficult. And not only is there this difficulty of mere numbers. The theory of democracy postulates a more or less static population, all knowing and all more or less concerned in one another's affairs; but modern life tends both to mobility and specialisation. A large part of the electorate may not even do its business in the constituency in which it resides, and one part of the electorate may be entirely ignorant of the interests of the other. Democracy may have been easy in the small and simple state of Athens, but becomes increasingly difficult in the complex and multitudinous life of the modern nation.

It is, indeed, difficult to compare one democratic system with another, since in most cases not only is the franchise different, but there are wide differences in the powers conferred upon the popular assemblies. In Germany and the United States, for example, there are federal systems by which the powers of the central government are limited by the powers of the states; in Great Britain and France the governing power is unified, so that there are no state rights to act as a check on central authority. Even in the British Empire, while there is a unified system in the mother country, there are federal systems in Australia, Canada and South Africa, and in each of these federal systems the allocation of powers is different, to say nothing of the various checks and restraints of the different bicameral systems and the powers of referendum and dissolution.

All these varieties of system make comparison difficult; but it may be said generally that with the growing complexity of political life power tends to pass into the arcana of the political machine. The party organization encroaches upon the province both of the electorate and the member; it may even assume the powers of government, and may influence and corrupt administration. So far from the people freely electing their own representatives, they have frequently no alternative but the nominees of the political organizations, and the struggle resolves itself into a contest in which the power of the rival machines plays a decisive part.

Man's inherent inequalities

There are other difficulties in the way of those who regard the enfranchisement of the future as the goal of humanity. Whereas Rousseau laid it down that men were born free and equal but are everywhere in chains, the modern ethnologist arrives at a contrary conclusion. So far from man having been born free, slavery was an institution almost universal in the early stages of civilization, and was perpetuated until supplanted by the wage system. Neither are men naturally equal. Not only have individuals of the same race widely different equipments of character and mind, but there are differences even wider between one race and another.

The relations between Europeans and Africans, both in the United States and in Africa itself, make a case in point. Starting with the coast as a base, the white man has spread over large regions of South and East Africa, especially in the high interior plateau where the climate is temperate and suitable. In the Union of South Africa alone there are now close on $1\frac{3}{4}$ million Europeans. This population governs itself on democratic lines; but the native population of five millions upon which it is superimposed it governs, so to speak, patriarchally. Only in the Cape Province is the native admitted to a limited franchise, and members of both houses of the Union legislature must be British subjects of European descent. The principle of equality is denied both in life and in government. 'We are to be lords over them,' said Cecil Rhodes when he was prime minister of Cape Colony. 'Treat the natives as a subject people as long as they are in a state of barbarism and communal tenure; be the lords over them, let them be a subject race, and keep the liquor from them.'

This will always be the point of view of a higher race when it feels itself threatened by a lower. When, after the Civil War in America, the political theorists of the North, who had then no negro problem, tried to impose upon the South an electoral equality which would have put the negro in power in some states, the white minority applied the unconstitutional remedy of the Ku Klux Klan; the stronger race in its instinct to dominate and to rule terrorised the weaker and drove it from the polls (see page 4493). However the political moralist may condemn this attitude, it is in vain to quarrel with that racial instinct which is one of the strongest impulses in man. The negro has been liberated and educated; but the natural and inherited difference of equipment remains.

Negro problem in America

We may say in passing that nature appears to be settling, in her own quiet way, this negro question in the United States. Although the actual growth of the negro population in America is from three-quarters of a million in 1790 to 10½ millions in 1920, the percentage of negroes to whites goes on steadily declining; whereas in 1790 it was 19·3, in 1920 it was 9·9, and whereas in the ten years following the first census of 1790 the increase was at the rate of 32·2, in the decade up to 1920 it was only 6·5, and even in the South, where there is little immigration from Europe, the whites have been increasing faster than the blacks. Although there has been a considerable migration of blacks from the South to the North, it does not affect the main problem. A. P. Brigham, from a careful examination of the figures, concludes that the black is nowhere swamping the white population, and Professor Wilcox holds that the negro population, which was one-fifth of the whole in 1790 and one-tenth in 1920, will decline to one-twentieth by the end of the century.

Is there a Law of Progress?

It has been suggested that there may be a lurking error in the view that the extension of democracy is part of an inevitable and universal march of progress. It might even be dangerous to assert that there is any general line of progress at all. Rudyard Kipling claims as one of the virtues of classical education that it restrains us from the illusion that the world is progressing 'when it is only repeating itself.' The theory of evolution itself contains no such assurance, since evolution is not a progress in any straight line but a process of adaptation to environment. We know too well that many civilizations have fallen to be assured of the permanence of our own.

We have seen that Western civilization has certain lines of weakness, some of which we have examined—the growth of population, the concentration in cities, the 'ugliness' of industrial life which offended John Ruskin and William Morris, the contrasts between poverty and wealth which gave point to the Marxian attack on society, the conflicts of class, race and nation in the eternal struggle for existence—all these and others contain elements of danger to the stability of civilization.

Yet it has been comforting to note also that the problems which appal one generation are found to be soluble by the next. Take, for example, the chief of all human problems, the growth of population. Unchecked, according to the Malthusian 'law,' man increases in a geometrical ratio, whereas his power to produce the means of life grows only in arithmetical proportion. If this be nature's iron rule, then indeed mankind is doomed to eternal or ultimate famine, pestilence and war as the only ways out.

On the other hand, the race or nation which seeks to limit itself by methods of birth control finds itself threatened by less restrained neighbours. Thus France, which has long maintained a population approximately equal to her limited means of subsistence, found when attacked by the swarming invaders of Germany that she had an insufficient margin to supply her losses in the field. In consequence she was fain to open her doors to other European nations which greedily filled the places of her unborn and her dead. In 1925 the foreigners in France numbered two and a half millions, or 6·4 of the total population. The Italian immigration into France increased from an average of 48,428 for the years 1920–21 to 80,845 per annum from 1922 to 1925. And Italy is inclined to press the advantage, if we may judge from Mussolini's declaration that she must raise the birth-rate, lower the death-rate and restrict emigration so as to attain a population of sixty millions. Thus the nation or class which limits its natural increase lays itself open to attack and supersession.

VICTIMS OF UNEMPLOYMENT

Even in districts where mines were kept open distress was acute owing to reduction of wages. Elsewhere unemployment reduced thousands to penury, relieved by the national system of Poor Relief and Unemployment Insurance.

Photo, Special Press

Here then would seem to be an insoluble problem; but, as we have already seen, there are other factors, unknown to Malthus, which are opening a way out. The progress of invention also proceeds in geometrical ratio, and one discovery may increase man's means of livelihood a thousandfold. Take, for example, the progress made in perfecting early and frost-resisting wheat which opens out the vast prairie lands of the north for the production of food; or the spineless cactus grown by Luther Burbank to provide a succulent pasture for cattle in the arid regions of the south; or the new methods of dry-farming and extension of irrigation which are making the desert blossom as the rose.

Solutions for the population problem

So in other fields. The manufacture of artificial silk makes it possible to turn the waste products of the jungle into fine raiment; the study of tropical diseases offers hope that vast regions now dangerous to mankind and his domestic animals may one day become his most fruitful farms.

It is true that the United States have seen reason to limit the invitation inscribed at the base of the Statue of Liberty, 'Send us your huddled masses yearning to be free'; but there are great areas of the earth's surface, in Canada in South America and in Africa, which still remain undeveloped. The inventiveness of man and the prodigality of nature make a marriage so fruitful that it seems cowardly to set limits to the expansion of humanity.

Its concentration in cities and the ugliness of its industrialism may also be passing evils, bogeys of the feeble and faint-hearted. The development of the motor car, the transmission of electric power, such inventions as wireless and the gramophone, are forming a new balance of town and country before our eyes. The class hatred which was nurtured by these passing conditions may be mollified, as we have noted in the case of America, by improved industrial relations. Despite the agitators, 'capital and 'labour,' which are the component parts of one interest, are arriving at their own modus vivendi.

CHAPTER 191

THE PHILOSOPHY OF HISTORY

A Discussion of the Belief in a Law of Progress and its Value as a Factor in Human Development

By L. P. JACKS

Professor of Philosophy and Principal of Manchester College, Oxford; Author of The Alchemy of Thought, etc.

THE word 'progress,' like most words that have come to play a prominent part in philosophy, is obviously a figure of speech, or metaphor, based on the idea of walking or marching. 'Progredior,' the Latin word from which it is derived, means to step forth, and the frequent use of the phrase 'steps of progress' in the modern literature of the subject shows that the idea of stepping or marching towards an objective has not been lost. The idea of an objective towards which the stepping or marching is directed is indicated, of course, by the prefix 'pro.' Whoever speaks of 'progress' shows that he has drawn the distinction between forward and backward, and knows, or thinks that he knows, which is which.

'The march of progress,' another phrase in common use, reveals the image in a somewhat fuller form. It implies not only that each of the marchers has drawn the distinction between forward and backward, and knows in which of the two directions he is moving, but also that the marchers have come to an agreement on the point; a march being a concerted movement and obviously impossible if the 'forward' of one marcher is the 'backward' of another, or if forward and backward can interchange their meanings. Unless the distinction between forward and backward can be drawn it is therefore idle to speak of *pro*gress in any connexion whatsoever. We shall find that all the difficulties which the philosophy of history finds in the idea of progress turn on the drawing of this distinction.

How great the difficulty is may be seen in a remark of the historian Freeman: 'In history every step in advance has also been a step backwards.' This seems to indicate that whether a given movement in history is to be regarded as progress or the reverse depends on the point of view of the observer. Examples of progress are apt to become examples of regress when they are estimated in terms of what they cost to achieve. Thus, when a higher civilization rises on the ruins of a lower, it is always possible to argue that the lower would have done better in the long run than the higher which has crushed it out, if only time enough had been given it to develop its possibilities.

The End of All Things

Moreover, the end of all things must be kept in mind. And if the end of all things human, in a future no matter how distant, be the extinction of the race, as astronomers and geologists predict, it would follow that what we called progress while we were actually engaged in it would have to be otherwise estimated when the final catastrophe had taken place. Strictly, a movement which begins in nothing and ends in nothing can be called neither progress nor regress, however interesting the historical transactions may be which occur in the interval between the two 'nothings.'

If, for example, we had two worlds, one beginning at the point of highest perfection and then passing through a slow and gradual decline to the lowest point of imperfection, and the other beginning at the lowest point of imperfection and rising by slow and gradual advance to the highest point of perfection, it would be the same history in either case, with the order of the chapters reversed; any being who had lived continuously through the history of the one world would have encountered the same series of events as if he had lived in the other.

But this we are apt to disguise from ourselves by crediting our Golden Age, Utopia or Kingdom of Heaven with an infinite 'staying power.' We take it too readily for granted that the consummation we desire, once established as an achievement of 'progress,' will maintain itself automatically as long as we choose to imagine. But the Golden Age cannot be defined in any terms which do not leave it a precarious age for man to live in. The Greek poet Hesiod showed his perception of this by placing the Golden Age at the beginning, and in reading history as a lesson in the tendency of human nature to decline from its best.

Tendency to degenerate

Certain it is that the conditions which make perfection hard to win make it hard also to keep. The believers in progress have not sufficiently considered that the tendency of human nature to advance towards the best has its counterpart in a tendency to decline from the best when it has been attained. After all, it makes little difference whether we put the Golden Age at the beginning or the end of any historical process; for if we place it at the end it is still only the beginning of what is to come next. And what is that ?

In estimating the value of the belief in progress as a factor in human history, it seems an obvious remark that such a belief helps to accelerate the progress believed in; in other words, that an age or society which has the belief, as our own appears to have, will progress more rapidly than an age which has it not. Even if the idea be an illusion, or a superstition, it may yet be valuable as a kind of tonic for keeping up the courage and vitality of social effort, especially in times when without it men would be inclined to despair. In that sense we may say that no effort would ever be consciously or deliberately made by man unless the belief in progress was at the back of it. Every such effort implies the postulate, in the mind of the man who makes it, that he himself or somebody else will be better off after the effort has been made than he was before.

The belief in progress, so understood, is in fact a psychological necessity for all action that is consciously directed t an end. It may even be said to sustai the suicide in putting an end to his lif It will be better for him, he argues, nc to be than to be; or, society will b better off, he may think, when he is n longer here to trouble it, and will 'prc gress' to the extent represented by h removal. In the same sense the belief i progress must have been present at th moment when the human will, emergin from the instincts of the ape, made i first conscious selection of any line c action whatsoever, though the idea c progress had not yet detached itself an received a name. Since then all th has happened to the belief in progre has been a fuller articulation of i meaning through conscious reflection.

Value of a belief in Progre

Whether this fuller articulation of th idea has actually increased the power c the belief as a motive of human condu is a question not easily resolved. Th well known saying, 'the healthy know not of their health but only the sick,' is not altogether untrue, and may possibly hav its parallel in this connexion—'the prc gressive know not of their progress bu only the unprogressive'; a consideratio that has prompted more than one cyn to remark that whenever an age or party calls itself progressive, hypocris is at work.

The study of history does not confir the belief that the ages when most progre has been made were always the ages i which progress was most talked abou Man was a progressive being long befo the idea of progress received a name, whic happened, according to Dean Inge, whe Lucretius wrote his poem De Reru Natura. It may be reasonably co tended that the most important steps c man's progress took place not when th printing press or the steam engine wa invented, but when the use of fire wa discovered, or even earlier, when me began to guide themselves by intelligenc instead of instinct.

In general, it can hardly be doubte that the invention of man's simpl tools presupposes a degree of intelligenc in the early ages which invented the not less striking than is revealed by the invention of complicated modern machines; while the early forms of law and order, as we find them in Egypt, Babylon or China, are fully as significant in view of their after-effects, and betoken as high an intellectual and moral endowment in their authors as any that later ages can claim.

On the other hand, the habit of reflecting upon progress and discussing it has unquestionably served to spread the conviction that progress is a duty imposed upon individuals and societies, and that it ought to be continually attempted. It has greatly stimulated the desire for conditions better than those in which the human race finds itself immersed at the moment, and has aroused wide-spread inquiry about the final end to which progress should be directed; a point still unsettled in any common agreement, but needing to be settled before concerted action can be organized.

Most important of all, among the effects produced by reflection on this idea, is the growing perception that without concerted action, organized on a world-wide scale and under a definite conception of the end to be aimed at, progress cannot be achieved in the modern world. The empty paeans on the mere fact of progress, which were characteristic of mid-Victorian times, have thus changed into a more serious search for some principle of unity among classes and nations, the belief being that when this is attained mankind will be able to progress to what heights it will.

Search for a common Principle

Along with this belief there generally goes, in the writings of those who represent it, a warning note that without a common principle or ideal the outlook for the future is extremely dark; and from this attitude we may gather that the conception of progress as a law of human history, fulfilling itself automatically no matter what men may do to promote its action, has been largely abandoned. Indeed, the very fervour with which believers in progress throw themselves into their propaganda shows conclusively that they look on progress as something which needs all their efforts to sustain it.

It might be contended, of course, that progress is a movement that must go on in any case, but will go on all the faster if human beings put their backs into promoting it; the forward movement being guaranteed by the constitution of the universe but the rate of advance depending on human effort. This, however, as we shall see, is not a philosophical view. Whoever controls the rate controls the movement altogether.

The conception of progress as a law of nature, or an inevitable process, was expressed by Turgot in a famous saying uttered some years before the French Revolution: 'The total mass of the human race marches continually, though sometimes slowly, towards an ever increasing perfection.' Equally confident are the statements of Herbert Spencer: 'Progress is not an accident, but a necessity'; 'it is certain that man must become perfect'; 'the ultimate development of the ideal man is certain.'

Progress as a Law of Nature

If we believe this, what is likely to be the effect on the course of history? The answer is not easy. When the mid-Victorian paeans about the 'progress of the species,' on which Carlyle used to pour out his scorn, were at their height, John Grote, in his Examination of Utilitarian Philosophy, put forth an extensive argument which has now become a commonplace of philosophy, to show that the logical effect would be to induce a blind and sterile confidence that the universe might be safely left to look after its own evolution.

But this, though it is unquestionably the logical conclusion, is not the whole truth of the matter, nor is it safe to assume that the logical conclusion is the one that men have drawn or are likely to draw from premises so cheerful. There is a certain exuberance about the doctrine which is infectious. It brings vitality and cheerfulness into the general atmosphere, and gives one the feeling of being in a universe that is really worth while. The total effect of that is probably much more in the direction of increased activity, increased enterprise, increased desire to do good, than in the direction of indolence.

Oddly enough, however, the same seems to be true of the opposite doctrine, as set forth by Huxley in his Romanes Lecture. According to this thinker the course of nature is in opposition to everything that can be called progress from the point of view of our moral ideals. This, again, will be found exhilarating or depressing according to the temperament of those who receive it. The brave will be stung by it to a greater heroism, while the cowardly will show themselves the better logicians by promptly running away. For, if it comes to a stand-up fight between man and the universe, there can be no question which side is going to lose. Yet on the whole there is an emotional stimulus about Huxley's doctrine, like that of a drum beating for battle, to which many would respond even while their intellects told them that they were fools.

Rival doctrines result in nothing

From all this it seems a reasonable conclusion that the effect on human conduct of Turgot's and Spencer's optimism and of Huxley's pessimism would be much the same in the long run. In neither case, however, does the effect appear to have been very great, either in speeding up or in slowing down the energies of the human race. Turgot's comfortable and soporific doctrine was almost immediately followed by the immense upheaval of the French Revolution, and by the desperate social struggles of the nineteenth century, in all of which there was nothing to indicate that the nations of Europe were at all disposed to sit still with folded hands and trust the 'law of progress' to remove the causes of their discontent; while the years that intervened between Huxley's heroic defiance of nature and the outbreak of the Great War were as unheroic as any in European history.

This, however, is not surprising. For a deeper examination of the two positions—the one affirming progress as a law of nature, the other denying it—shows that they are not so far apart as their outward contradiction suggests. Both doctrines, in fact, are prompted by the desire for progress and rest upon the belief in its possibility. Huxley is as much concerned as Spencer that man should improve his lot by the realization of his moral ideals, and in giving us the advice he deems necessary for that purpose—to oppose the pro cess of cosmic evolution rather tha to follow it—he shows his belief that huma progress is possible, at least up to a poin provided that we rouse the heroic energie needed to achieve it.

On the other hand, Spencer and th optimists in general, when they urge u to fall in with the law of evolution an model our own actions upon it, are vir tually making human progress depend no on an inevitable law of nature but o our willingness to act as they advise u to act. 'Accept our views about evolu tion and act upon them,' they say in effect 'and the gradual progress of society wi follow. Reject them and act upon th rejection and we cannot promise that th desired progress will take place.' S much we may fairly say is implied by th immense pains these thinkers take t convert us to their point of view. A law of progress whose working thu depends on our willingness to fall i with it cannot in strictness be calle an invariable or necessary law, at leas so far as human affairs are concerned

Meaning of 'the Rate of Progress'

It may be said, of course, that whil the general fact of progress is assured b the law of evolution the rate of it in human history depends on the degree of assistance which men are willing to lend to its operations But this, as we have said above, is a contradiction. If a traveller is goin from London to Edinburgh, by goin slowly enough he can prolong the journe to eternity, and never reach Edinburg at all; while, on the other hand, there i no fraction of a second so short but that by a sufficient acceleration of his pace, h could reach his destination in a shorter.

This may serve to remind us ho futile all interpretations of progress becom which read the meaning of it solely i terms of the goal arrived at—Kingdom o Heaven, 'far off divine event,' and s on—but take no account of the tim occupied in getting there, and of th transactions that take place betwee departure and arrival. If the pace b infinitely retarded, the goal is neve reached; if infinitely accelerated, th interval between goal and starting poin vanishes, and the idea of progress from one to the other becomes meaningless.

Unless this point be borne in mind our judgements on the course of human history are apt to suffer gross perversion. By assuming that progress is compatible with any degree of slowness that we choose to assign to it, the difference vanishes between the causes that further and the causes that hinder the interests of mankind. Make your conception of progress sufficiently slow and the greatest crimes of history can be accommodated to it as easily as anything else, Judas as easily as Christ. Nothing, in fact, could impugn the idea of progress when so conceived. If the whole world were to break out into cruelty and violence and every civilized nation fall back into barbarism we should only have to say that progress was 'slower' than we previously thought, and that we should have to wait so much longer for the promised millennium.

The factor of Responsibility

After all, the only kind of progress in which the human race can take an interest, or which can properly be called human progress, is the progress which men themselves are responsible for achieving. Were some power not our own perpetually engaged in turning us into better men, whether we willed it ourselves or not, the phrase 'better *men*' would cease to have any meaning, the word 'man' connoting just that element of responsibility for his own condition which on this hypothesis would not exist. Goodness, beauty and truth are values for us only so far as we are engaged in winning them by our own efforts and at our own risk.

A process of evolution which is automatically turning us all into angels is morally indistinguishable from one which is turning us all into devils, since the angels who emerge from the one process deserve no more credit for their angelic nature than the devils who emerge from the other deserve blame for their fiendishness. 'Poor devil' would be the proper phrase to apply to both of them, since neither could help being what they are. Our condition would then be like that of a block of marble which the sculptor is working up according to his fancy, with the addition that in our case we are conscious of what the sculptor is doing; but it is hard to say what difference it would make to us whether he was turning us into statues of gods or into statues of beasts.

Progress and Environment

The same may be said, mutatis mutandis, of all evolutionary doctrines of human progress which represent it not as an affair of sudden leaps from bad to good, but as a slow and gradual improvement brought about by the slow and gradual action of improving 'conditions' or environment. Wide-spread as the belief now is that the causes of progress lie in the environment, and fond as we are of saying that the improvement of mankind depends on the improvement of conditions, it may be seriously questioned if any of us would accept that doctrine as defining the terms on which he himself would wish to become a better, or even a happier, man. To tell a man that he cannot become a 'better' man unless the forces of his environment conspire to make him so, is almost to insult his self-respect.

This aspect of the idea of progress, as a change for the better brought about by the action of environment, is commonly overlooked, owing to the habit people have of applying the doctrine to others and forgetting to apply it to themselves. They apply it to the poor, to the uneducated and to those in general who are less fortunately placed than they. It seems an act of charity to attribute the shortcomings of these unfortunates to their 'conditions' or to their environment. But if the dependence of character on conditions be true at all, it applies equally to those who stand in the vanguard of progress as to the remotest straggler in the race, to those who win in the battle of life as to those who lose, and would require the fortunate ones to say that their own victories, like the defeats of those whom they pity, have been won not by them but for them, by a favourable environment.

Putting all these considerations together we shall find that little difference is made whether we assert a law of progress in the sense of Spencer and other evolutionists, or whether we deny it in the sense of Huxley or of Bertrand Russell or of Dean Inge. It is clear that the law of progress can be counted on to work only on the condition that men in general believe in it and fall in with it, which, as the arguments of Huxley, Bertrand Russell and Dean Inge clearly show, all men are not disposed to do. That such a refusal to believe is a possibility with which to reckon, and which, if realized, will give the law of progress a serious set-back, is clearly shown by the vehemence with which the school of Spencer argues for the existence of that law.

Both groups of thinkers end, therefore, on the same note and leave us at the same point, namely, this: that progress is possible if we prove teachable and act wisely, but not possible if we prove unteachable and play the fool. They differ, of course, in their conception of what wisdom consists in, and of what playing the fool consists in, Dean Inge's conception being no more identical with Bertrand Russell's than it is with Herbert Spencer's. They differ also by the fact that whereas in Huxley, Russell and Inge the inevitability of progress is formally disavowed and its contingency avowed, in the Spencerian group it is the other way about. But these differences do not amount to very much in view of the common agreement of both groups that progress, so far as we may hope for it at all, depends on our believing what they have to tell us and acting accordingly.

Progress only a contingency

At this point several difficult questions present themselves. Though both the groups mentioned above seem to be agreed that human progress will not take place unless people generally believe in it and act accordingly (and no guarantee can be given that they will), it does not follow from this that progress will take place if they do so believe and act. Indeed, both Huxley and Dean Inge remind us fairly often that in spite of our heroic defiance of the evolutionary process (Huxley), and in spite of our pursuit of the eternal values (Dean Inge), the race, if wise enough to take either line, will be completely beaten in the long run, so far as its temporal fortunes are concerned, by the cooling down of the planet.

Here the question arises whether the name progress can be given to any process merely on the strength of victories won at intermediate stages, if the final stage, in which all these victories come to their issue, is to be total overthrow and extinction. Might we not say that the increasing splendour of the intermediate victories only deepens the tragedy of the subsequent defeats and of the final overthrow? Is not the evolution of humanity so regarded only another name for the road to ruin, the true nature of which we disguise for ourselves by restricting our vision to short views, and by over-concentration on our passing achievements? Ought not the 'triumphs of civilization' to be interpreted in much the same way as the victories won by the Germans in the early stages of the Great War—not as proving their 'progress' but as heralding their downfall and making it more terrible when it came?

Implications of a Final Catastrophe

A 'millennium' which is to last for that definite number of years inevitably provokes the question, 'What next?'; and not until that question is answered can the philosophy of history say whether the attainment of the millennium is or is not a conclusive proof of human progress. A thousand years of perfect happiness (or of any other perfection) is certainly worth having when regarded per se, but its value will be greatly diminished if it contains the seeds of its own death, so that in the next thousand years the race will see itself gradually deprived of the happiness enjoyed in the first. In such case the question might reasonably be asked whether the first thousand was worth having at all, whether that 'sorrow's crown of sorrow,' which consists 'in remembering happier things,' would not be more than an offset for the past joys so painfully remembered.

The rule of 'living for posterity' is not well fulfilled if these things are overlooked; if, that is, the rule takes the form of endowing intermediate posterities with happiness or with privileges which have no self-maintaining quality, and which a later posterity is destined to have the agony of losing. May we not say, in fine, that the value of the millennium is strictly dependent on its staying power—that a millennium which is not to be followed by other millenniums as good as itself is somewhat of a cheat ? The author of the Book of Revelation saw this very clearly when, after predicting the reign of the saints, he added that they were to reign for ' ever and ever.'

John Fiske, the American exponent of Spencer, sees the same difficulty. He overcomes it in the only way possible, by defending the thesis that the moral and spiritual values achieved by the race in the course of its evolutionary progress on earth will be preserved and continued in another life. This point Spencer himself does not make, though some have believed that they could extract it from his writings. His picture of the final goal of evolution, when human intelligence will be raised to the highest pitch of wisdom and an automatic altruism will have established itself as the rule of human conduct, leaves the mind with grave doubts as to its staying power and therefore as to its value. His assumption is that when moral equilibrium, which is the final goal, has been once attained it will naturally and inevitably maintain itself, the moral forces which have been engaged in winning it being sufficiently developed, by that exercise, to keep it in being when won.

Ultimate goal of Evolution

But in view of Spencer's main doctrine, that human well-being depends on adjustment to the environment, it is hard to see how moral equilibrium could be maintained without a stable environment to correspond. But this is not to be. In course of time the solar system will run down and the race will have to face the task of adjusting itself to an environment continually changing to forms less favourable to human life, and each new adjustment will involve a new disturbance of whatever moral equilibrium may exist at the moment. What the staying power of Spencer's ' millennium ' would be in these circumstances it is impossible to say, but one can hardly think that it could be self-maintaining.

In any case, what Spencer presents as the final goal of evolution is obviously not final. In view of what is said to await mankind in the closing chapters of its history on this planet the attainment of moral equilibrium, whatever that may mean, would have to be regarded as the prelude to moral difficulties more severe than any encountered at an earlier stage, and not as the end of all moral difficulties whatever. It is possible, of course, that the human race will have learnt the lesson of ' dying like gentlemen ' by the time these major difficulties present themselves. But can we count upon it ?

Short of that heroic temper the word progress will not be applicable to the final stages of man's history. The philosophers of that age will describe the idea of progress as an illusion in which men indulged before they knew to what they were coming. Arguments which are now used for proving the existence of a benevolent control of history will then be used for proving the existence of a malevolent one.

History to those despairing philosophers of the future will seem to tell an ugly tale. It will tell how man was led on through a series of resounding victories, triumphs of civilization and so on, to believe himself the heir of everlasting perfection, and how it turned out later on that he had been brought to these giddy heights only that his subsequent humiliation might be the more bitter and disastrous. ' What further proof do you want,' they will ask, ' that the devil created the world ? '

Philosophy of the distant future

But, perhaps men will have learnt the lesson of ' dying like gentlemen.' The opinion may even be ventured that since the time of Plato, who taught that philosophy is a meditation on death, the only philosophers who have been able to throw a clear light on the evolutionary process are those who have taught mankind how to ' die like gentlemen.' A fine example of that manner of dying is to be found in Plato's account of the death of Socrates ; a still finer in the New Testament.

Such a death involves much more than a melodramatic gesture. Those who die like gentlemen in the Platonic or the New Testament sense are those who represent human nature at the summit of its development, so far as any summit is conceivable by us; compared with them the endlessly 'happy' are contemptible. If it be possible for one man to reach that level it should be possible for all men; and that being so, there is nothing to prevent us hoping that the last stages of man's temporal history, in spite of increasing hardships and the visible approach of racial extinction, will be more splendid than any that have gone before.

We cannot indeed assure ourselves that this will be so; man may perish as the beast-like creature he was when he made his first appearance, the doctrine of human progress having become an exploded fiction long before that stage is reached. But we can assure ourselves that a time must come when the race will have to face the problem of impending extinction, and adjust itself thereto, either by dying like beasts or by dying like gentlemen.

'Dying like Gentlemen'

Putting together all that can be learnt from the two tendencies in modern philosophy, the one apparently affirming progress, the other apparently denying it, as a law of human life, we come to the following conclusions.

There is no law in nature which compels mankind, irrespective of its own behaviour, to progress towards any particular end that may be considered desirable, such as perfect happiness, or moral perfection; and, since mankind's behaviour is an uncertain quantity, no guarantee can be given that any such end will ever be realized in the secular history of the race. There is nothing in the constitution of the universe to enforce upon anybody the belief in certain progress, or the disbelief in it, the proof being that some philosophers believe in it while others disbelieve. All that evolution has accomplished up to date, which is certainly most impressive, is offset by the possibility of a corresponding decline in the future, when the moral gains of man, which have been evolved along with all the other gains, will be by no means exempt from the danger of perishing.

But while there is nothing in the constitution of the universe upon which the philosophy of history can pitch as guaranteeing progress in any of the forms in which we happen to desire it, we nevertheless find that the nature of the universe is admirably adapted to the purpose of beings who desire to possess themselves more and more of certain qualities named goodness, beauty and truth, or wisdom, power and love. The means are there if we choose to make use of them; our choosing to use them being an indispensable condition of their becoming efficacious. On the other hand, if the end is catastrophe the fault will be our own.

Whether the progress achieved up to date means that we are so much nearer the consummation, or so much nearer the catastrophe, cannot be determined, unless the human race is prepared to pledge itself to a certain line of action. That the human race has progressed in the acquisition of 'eternal values' may be conceded, but there is no guarantee that it will continue to do so indefinitely. Looking to the past, we get the impression that while man has made a considerable use of the opportunities for progress which nature afforded him, he might have made a much greater use of them. However far he may be said to have advanced, he might have advanced much farther. It is by no means clear that he has done the best he could. Whether he will do better in the future remains to be seen.

Acquisition of 'Eternal Values'

It would thus appear that philosophy cannot apply the name 'progress' to the movement of human history save on the condition that it knows definitely how, when, where and in what the movement is going to end. Short of such knowledge of the end, which clearly does not exist, all that philosophy can say is that change takes place, that movement is going on; but it cannot affirm that the movement is forward, onward, upward or the reverse. Such adjectives are indeed freely used, even taken for granted, but they imply an act of faith, which is entitled to respect, but is not philosophical.

Even if it were possible to show (and it is not) that, up to date, progress has been made towards all the ends which man considers desirable, it would not be egitimate to infer that the progress is lestined to go on indefinitely to a perfect form of the ends in question. In the absence of precise knowledge of the end, it may be that the gorgeous flowers which the plant has produced up to date are the prelude to poisonous berries later on, that the hard-won happiness of mankind contains the seeds of coming misery, that the pleasant places at which we have arrived after so much toil are only stations on the road towards disaster.

Even if we define progress as 'the gradual change of a thing towards a completer form of itself,' and assert that every living being in the universe shows that tendency, we should still be very far from having identified the progress of man with the 'improvement' of man. For what kind of a being is man? Unless he is fundamentally a good being his gradual change to a completer form of himself offers nothing in which we could rejoice. And how can we know that he is fundamentally good unless we know that he is destined to be finally good also?—which is the very point to be proved.

The Change to completer forms

The devils also—and if there are such beings we can hardly deny that the law of evolution applies to them—are changing into completer forms of themselves; but the process can hardly be called an improvement. Or, to take a more familiar case, why should we assume that the evolution of a 'bad' man necessarily means his transformation into a good one, rather than his transformation into a worse man than he was before—that is, into a completer form of his original bad self? We assume it because, neglecting the evidence which his badness affords, we have already the faith which asserts that, despite his 'badness,' he is potentially 'good' to begin with.

If finally the question be raised whether a real advance has been achieved in the value of human life during the period covered by history—whether, as one might say, human progress is a fact or not—it will be found that the phenomena to be taken into account are too multitudinous, too confusing and too susceptible of diverse interpretation to admit of an unqualified answer. That an immense number of interesting changes has taken place cannot be questioned; but there is always a danger, in estimates of progress, of getting confused between the interest we take in the changes and the real value of the changes themselves. A change which has a high value to those who inherit its fruits may have a low value, or none at all, to those who achieve it.

Difference in the point of view

To the student of history, for example, industrial civilization will seem to reveal an immense advance upon the conditions of the Stone Age, and all doubts on the subject may seem absurd; but, if this same student of history were to find himself suddenly transformed into a slum dweller or a process worker in a modern industrial city, it is not clear that he would find himself better off than the men who fought against the mammoth. There is a great difference between the outside and the inside view of such things.

That there has been an immense increase in the mass, volume or quantity of human life maintained on the planet, as well as in the complexity of its inner relations, is beyond question, and if that is all that is meant by progress there need be no hesitation in saying that progress is a fact, at least up to date. But the real question turns not upon the quantity of this life, nor upon its complexity, but upon the quality. Whether men are happier than they were depends on what we mean by happiness, and it is notorious that no term is more difficult to define. Whether they are better than they were depends on what we mean by goodness. Whether they are wiser than they were depends on what we mean by wisdom.

A surer criterion may seem to be afforded by the growth of man's power over nature as this has been brought about by scientific discovery. Here again the array of facts is most impressive, not to say astounding. But the interpretation to be placed on the facts is by no means clear. In discussing them the assumption is commonly made that nature is somehow inferior to man, so that any transference of power from the natural to the human side is a change for the better; in other words, that it is better for man to rule nature than for nature to rule man.

This at first sight seems obvious enough. But there are philosophies that contradict it, those, namely, that teach us to order our life according to nature and to show our wisdom by submitting to her laws—notably to her law of evolution. In this way of thinking we acknowledge nature as supreme, and our definition of progress will have to be made not in terms of the power we win over her, but in terms of the power she has over us and of our willingness to submit to her. To think of progress as consisting in our growing power over nature, and at the same time as consisting in our growing submission to nature's laws, is to show that we have self-contradictory notions both of nature and of ourselves. A good deal of sophistry will have to be employed before the two positions can be brought into apparent harmony with one another.

Man has yet to prove his fitness to have power over nature, even in the degree in which he now possesses it. He certainly must prove it before claiming, as is now so commonly done, that the acquisition of such power constitutes a real advance. And the only proof he could give would be by producing evidence that the growth of his control over nature is accompanied by a parallel growth of control over himself. Short of some such assurance it is quite conceivable that the power which man has won over nature may ultimately be used for his own undoing. Philosophers, like Bertrand Russell, who are unable to help themselves out by an act of faith are sometimes inclined to think that this undoing is actually in process.

Danger in Power over Nature

Those who are content with the assurance that mankind is improving at the present moment, and likely to improve for some time to come, will find in existing conditions a good deal on the one hand to support them, and about as much on the other to damp their hopes. The spread of education and the improvement of its methods unquestionably promise a vast improvement of the human individual, and therefore of society as a whole. As against this we have to set the certainty that, as the human individual learns through education to realize his own value he will be less and less inclined to do the monotonous work on which industrial civilization reposes, no matter what wages be given him for doing it ; from this refusal, when it becomes wide-spread, there may result a collapse of the whole industrial fabric.

Another sinister fact remains to be noted. An industrial civilization is a civilization that lives by work ; whence it would seem to follow that no real advance of its fortunes can take place unless there is a real advance in the quality of its work, the advance being measured by the degree of human interest which the worker takes in doing it. This interest under present conditions appears to be on the decline. While the work of industrial civilization, in the form of mass production, goes on under tremendous external pressure, it is losing inner vitality and significance for the human individual, and becoming more and more of a burden to be endured for the sake of the money wages which compensate for it. And since no exact method of compensation can ever be found for work in which the worker takes no interest, it is probable that the restlessness of those who have to do it will continually increase.

Decline in the quality of work

This loss of vitality in work, which results from its transformation into a mechanical process, threatens to arrest the entire process to which the alleged progress of the last century and a half is commonly attributed. It is not inconceivable, therefore, that an interlude of great and protracted misery is in store for the more civilized portions of the human race. Against all this must be set the unlimited capacity of man to deal with difficult situations as they arise, a factor in the case not uncommonly forgotten by those whose outlook for the future dwells on these gloomy possibilities. Man is a being made for the overcoming of great difficulties ; and in that lies the chief hope of wise men for the progress of the human race.

C

D

E

F

G

H

I

L

M

N

S

U

V

W

List of Errata

Vol. 1, page x. Folding Colour Chart, Rise and Fall of Empires—for ' page 420 ' read ' 402.'

Page 149, 1st line under illustration—*for* ' on ' *read* ' near.'

Page 407, under illustration—*for* ' B.C.' *read* ' A.D.'

Page 417, date of First Olympiad—*for* ' 766 ' *read* ' 776.'

Page 442, first line under illustration—*for* ' page 346 ' *read* ' page 436.'

Plate facing page 528. Last line under illustration—*for* ' Nebuchadrezzar II ' *read* ' Nabonidus.'

Plate facing page 529, third line—*for* ' tin ' *read* ' silver.'

Plate facing page 609, top-right inscription—*for* ' M. III ' *read* ' M.M. III.'

Page 614, col. 2, 14 lines from bottom—for ' Chapter 21 ' read ' Chapter 20.'

Page 699, last line—*for* ' Taurt—childbirth ' *read* ' lions.'

Page 1184, col. 1, 13th line from bottom—*for* ' Chapter 55 ' *read* ' Chapter 52.'

Page 1394, 15th line from top—*for* ' page 1562 ' *read* ' page 1550.'

Page 1499, first line under illustration—*for* ' A.D. 78 ' *read* ' A.D. 120.'

Page 1560, last line under illustration—*for* ' altitudes ' *read* ' attitudes.'

Page 1599, 3rd line under illustration—*for* ' page 1614 ' *read* ' page 1596.'

Page 2128, col. 1, 19th line from bottom—*for* ' A.D. 224 ' *read* ' A.D. 324.'

Page 2269, first line—*for* ' 467 ' *read* ' 567.'

Page 2384, col. 2, 27th line—*for* ' former ' *read* ' latter.'

Page 2505, col. 2, last line before heading—*for* ' 953 ' *read* ' 1053.'

Page 2505, col. 2, 10th line from bottom—*for* ' 954 ' *read* ' 1054.'

Page 2513, last line—*for* ' 1300 ' *read* ' 1030.'

Page 2876, 2nd line, *for* ' 473 ' *read* ' 404.'

Page 2883, heading under illustration—*for* ' Upward-soaring Piers that Support ' *read* ' Aspiring Verticality of the Piers In.'

Page 3117, 4th line from bottom—*for* ' Chapter 190 ' *read* ' Chapter 189.'

Page 3263, 6th line from bottom—*for* ' Lord Coke's definition ' *read* ' Sir Edward Coke's definition.'

Page 3561, last line under illustration—*for* ' long since demolished ' *read* ' demolished after the fire at Westminster in 1834.'

Page 3762, col. 1, 10th line from bottom—*for* ' Patkal ' *read* ' Patkul.'

Page 3787 ; though the point is disputed, most modern authorities now place the Peacock Throne in the Diwan-i-Khas.

Page 3962, 3rd line under illustration—*for* ' 1855 ' *read* '1835.'

Page 3966, 1st line under upper illustration—*for* ' 1720 ' *read* ' 1790.'

Page 4276, 3rd line under illustration—*for* ' Italy ' *read* ' Chile.'

Page 4299, last line—*for* ' London ' *read* ' Loudon.'

Page 4301, col. 1, 17th line and 3rd line under upper illustration—*for* ' London ' *read*, ' Loudon.'

Page 4586, third line under illustration—*for* ' eighty ' *read* ' eight."

CLASSIFIED LIST OF MAPS

Arranged by Continents, Countries, Nations and Cultures in Order of Time